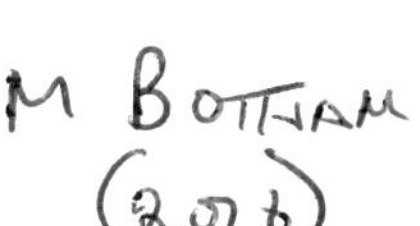

Restrictive Covenants under Common and Competition Law

AUSTRALIA
Law Book Co.
Sydney

CANADA and USA
Carswell
Toronto

HONG KONG
Sweet & Maxwell Asia

NEW ZEALAND
Brookers
Wellington

SINGAPORE and MALAYSIA
Sweet and Maxwell Asia
Singapore and Kuala Lumpur

Restrictive Covenants under Common and Competition Law

Fifth edition

Alexandra Kamerling
and
Christopher Osman

London
Sweet & Maxwell
2007

Fifth Edition 2007

Published in 2007 by
Sweet & Maxwell Ltd of
100 Avenue Road, Swiss Cottage
London NW3 3PF

Computerset by Servis Filmsetting Ltd, Manchester
Printed in Great Britain by T.J. International

No natural forests were destroyed to make this product;
only farmed timber was used and replanted.

A CIP catalogue record for this book is available from the British Library

ISBN 978 1847 030269

Contents

Appendices

Preface to the Fifth Edition

While this book aims to provide a good overview of key case law relating to the law of restrictive covenants and business secrets, its also seeks to provide a more practical guide to the drafting and litigation problems associated with this area of the law. With this in mind, the authors hope that in particular the appendices will provide such easily accessible and practical assistance, with the Quick Reference Guides on all main cases in this area, precedent clauses and, what is new to this edition, some checklists.

The previous edition (4th) resulted in a major redrafting to provide more comprehensive discussion on the approach of EU and UK law to common law restraint of trade clauses that may also restrict competition (e.g. exclusive agreements, tying arrangements and non-compete clauses). This was done in recognition of the fact that with the introduction of a prohibition regime in the UK similar to that under Articles 81 and 82 of the EC Treaty, and the modernisation of EU competition law (allowing national competition authorities and national courts to apply Article 81(3)) has meant that local business agreements which contained restrictive covenants may now also be subject to scrutiny under competition law. Given the supremacy of EU competition law over inconsistent national law and the framework of Regulation 1/2003, UK Judges are precluded from applying the common law restraint of trade doctrine to prohibit an agreement that is acceptable under EU competition law, unless it can be shown that the UK law pursues predominantly an objective different from that of protecting competition on the market. The distinction as to whether the restraint is in a commercial agreement (i.e. between "undertakings") or not has therefore become even more crucial.

In relation to commercial agreements, restraint of trade clauses will now almost inevitably be scrutinised under competition law and require a detailed assessment as to the effect of an agreement on the market. This brings with it public policy considerations and moves away from what may have been the intention of the parties at the time of entering into the contract. Arguing that a restraint of trade clause is void has therefore become a considerably more complex matter, and both parties are likely to incur additional costs in trying to determine what the effect of a restrictive clause is on the market, as has been amply illustrated by the *Crehan* saga through the various courts, and the House of Lords' decision that while an EC decision on the same market (UK beer) but between different parties is persuasive, a national judge must reach his own decision on the evidence. Nevertheless, since the 4th Edition there has been growing momentum as parties are increasingly using competition law arguments in relation to restraint of trade clauses in commercial agreements. See, for example, *Adidas Saloma v Roger Draper & Others* [2006] EWHC 318. This is being fully supported by the EC Commission and the OFT who have both published discussion papers to see how private enforcement of competition law can be further facilitated. In this Fifth Edition we have therefore expanded the litigation section to cover this more specifically. Two new checklists in the appendices will hopefully further assist the readers.

The period since the publication of the 4th Edition has seen further, if not necessarily ground breaking, additions to the body of case law relating to restrictive covenants in the employment context. The mantra that each case depends upon its own facts continues to apply when it comes to the enforceability of the various forms of restrictive covenant used by employers, but some recent cases have picked up and applied the three stage process for determining the reasonableness of restrictive covenants suggested by Mrs Justice Cox in *TFS Derivatives Ltd. v Morgan* [2005] I.R.L.R. 246, and this case, together with others such as *Dyson Technology Ltd. v Strutt* [2005] All E.R. (D) 355 and *Intercall Conferencing Services Ltd. v Steer* [2007] EWHC 519, suggests that the most draconian form of restrictive covenant, i.e. a non-competition covenant (moreover in those cases without geographical limitation) can still be appropriate and enforceable in certain circumstances, notwithstanding that most professional advisers will talk down the merits of such provisions when considering the scope and extent of restrictive covenants with clients. Although the sample (based as it is on a relatively small number of reported cases) is too small to say that they are indicative of any general change in sentiment on the part of the Courts, plainly this type of provision is far from being down and out. *TFS* is interesting for another reason in that the Court also considered the alternative of a garden leave provision. The judgment contains some comments about why, despite their popularity, such provisions are not necessarily suitable alternatives to the more traditional restrictive covenants and is a reminder that their imposition (even on the basis of an express provision) may breach the implied trust and confidence term in the contract of the employment, and that the duty of fidelity and good faith may not survive during garden leave. *Allan Janes LLP v Johal* [2006] I.R.L.R. 599, is also a timely reminder that the reasonableness of covenants will be judged by reference to the circumstances at the time they were entered into (often separated by some years from the time when it becomes necessary to consider their enforcement) and that these circumstances may lead to quite widely drafted restrictions (in this case non-dealing/non-solicitation) being upheld because, at the relevant time the covenants were agreed, the circumstances warranted this. As always, the reverse can equally be the case.

When it comes to the enforcement of restrictive covenants (and for that matter notice periods and garden leave provisions) the professional advisers' thoughts will always turn to the issue of whether there is scope to bring proceedings against a third party (generally the new or perspective new employer) on the grounds of inducement of the employee to breach the contract of employment. In this regard, the latest of the *Douglas v Hello!* judgments (*Douglas & Others v Hello! Ltd. & Others* [2007] UKHL 21) provides a welcome analysis and re-assessment of the economic torts of inducement to breach of contract and causing loss by unlawful means, and the restoration of these as two distinct and separate torts against the background of their having become, in the words of Lord Hoffman, "muddled" since the early part of the 20 century. The key in relation to inducement to breach a contract (the most relevant tort in relation to restrictive covenants) is that the party responsible must know they are inducing a breach of contract and intend this as is well illustrated by the case of *Mainstream Properties Ltd. v Young* [2007] UKHL 21, one of the three combined appeals to the House of Lords that included the *Douglas* case.

These and other developments together with recent case law are reflected in this updated 5th Edition and the main employment cases are also included in the Quick Reference Guides; additionally the appendices include summaries of considerations relevant to the incorporation of restrictive covenants, garden leave and confidentiality provisions and the recruitment of employees who may be the subject of restrictions in their contracts of employment.

The authors would like to acknowledge and thank their colleagues Alistair Woodland (Clifford Chance) and Kate Vernon (DLA Piper) for their valuable assistance in relation to the litigation chapters for this Fifth Edition.

The law is as stated at July 31, 2007.

Alexandra Kamerling
Partner
DLA Piper (UK) LLP
3 Noble Street
London
EC2V 7EE

Christopher Osman
Consultant
Clifford Chance LLP
10 Upper Bank Street
London
E14 5JJ

Table of Cases

D v M [1996] I.R.L.R. 192, QBD 3.5, 6.2, 9.3
D v National Society for the Prevention of Cruelty to Children (NSPCC) [1978] A.C. 171; [1977] 2 W.L.R. 201; [1977] 1 All E.R. 589; 76 L.G.R. 5; (1977) 121 S.J. 119, HL 5.5.4
DC Thomson & Co Ltd v Deakin [1952] Ch. 646; [1952] 2 All E.R. 361; [1952] 2 T.L.R. 105, CA 8.8.2
Dairy Crest v Pigott [1989] I.C.R. 92, CA (Civ Div) 3.6, 8.5.3
David and Matthews, Re [1899] 1 Ch.378 ....11.3
Davies v Davies (1887) L.R. 36 Ch. D. 359, CA 2.4.3, 3.3
Davies, Turner and Co v Lowen (1891) 64 L.T. 655 ....8.5.4
Dawnay Day & Co Ltd v de Braconier d'Alphen [1998] I.C.R. 1068; [1997] I.R.L.R. 442; (1997) 94(26) L.S.G. 30; (1997) 141 S.J.L.B. 129, CA (Civ Div) 8.4, 8.4.3, 10.2, 13.5.2, 14.1, 16.4
Days Medical Aids Ltd v Pihsiang Machinery Manufacturing Co Ltd [2004] EWHC 44; [2004] 1 All E.R. (Comm) 991; [2004] 2 C.L.C. 489; [2004] U.K.C.L.R. 384; [2004] E.C.C. 21; [2004] Eu. L.R. 477, QBD (Comm) 2.1, 2.4.3, 3.5, 12.2.3, 17.2, 21.1, 21.8, 21.9.1, 22.1
De Francesco v Barnum (1890) 63 L.T. 514 ....8.8.2
De Maudsley v Palumbo [1996] E.M.L.R. 460; [1996] F.S.R. 447, Ch D 5.1.2
Decro-Wall International SA v Practitioners in Marketing [1971] 1 W.L.R. 361; [1971] 2 All E.R. 216; (1970) 115 S.J. 171, CA (Civ Div) 23.8
Delimiters v Henniger Brau [1991] E.C.R. I-935 ....21.10
Den Norske Bank ASA v Antonatos [1999] Q.B. 271; [1998] 3 W.L.R. 711; [1998] 3 All E.R. 74; [1998] Lloyd's Rep. Bank. 253, CA (Civ Div) 24.6
Denilauler v SNC Couchet Freres (125/79) [1980] E.C.R. 1553; [1981] 1 C.M.L.R. 62, ECJ 23.12.3
Denmark Productions v Boscobel Productions [1969] 1 Q.B. 699; [1968] 3 W.L.R. 841; [1968] 3 All E.R. 513; (1968) 112 S.J. 761, CA (Civ Div) 23.8
Derby & Co Ltd v Weldon (No.8) [1991] 1 W.L.R. 73; [1990] 3 All E.R. 762; (1991) 88(2) L.S.G. 33; (1991) 135 S.J. 84, CA (Civ Div) 5.2.2
Diamond Stylus Co Ltd v Bauden Precision Diamonds Ltd [1972] F.S.R. 177; [1973] R.P.C. 675, Ch D 8.2.1, 25.3.3
Dickson v Pharmaceutical Society of Great Britain. *See* Pharmaceutical Society of Great Britain v Dickson
Dietmann v Brent LBC; sub nom. Dietman v Brent LBC [1988] I.C.R. 842; [1988] I.R.L.R. 299, CA (Civ Div) 8.1.3.2
Distillers Co (Biochemicals) Ltd v Times Newspapers Ltd [1975] Q.B. 613; [1974] 3 W.L.R. 728; [1975] 1 All E.R. 41; (1974) 118 S.J. 864, QBD 5.2.3.4
Dixon v Stenor [1973] I.C.R. 157; [1973] I.R.L.R. 28; (1973) 8 I.T.R. 141, NIRC 8.1.4.4
Dockray & Laddie (1990) 106 L.Q.R. 601-620 ....24.6
Doherty v Allman (1877-78) L.R. 3 App. Cas. 709, HL 23.8
Doherty v British Midland Airways Ltd [2006] I.R.L.R. 90, EAT 8.1.4.6
Douglas v Hello! Ltd (No.1) [2001] Q.B. 967; [2001] 2 W.L.R. 992; [2001] 2 All E.R. 289; [2001] E.M.L.R. 9; [2001] 1 F.L.R. 982; [2002] 1 F.C.R. 289; [2001] H.R.L.R. 26; [2001] U.K.H.R.R. 223; 9 B.H.R.C. 543; [2001] F.S.R. 40, CA (Civ Div) 5.2.1, 5.2.2
Douglas v Hello! Ltd (No.3); [2003] 3 All E.R. 996 ....26.3
Douglas v Hello! Ltd (No.6); sub nom. Douglas v Hello! Ltd (Trial Action: Breach of Confidence) (No.3) [2005] EWCA Civ 595; [2006] Q.B. 125; [2005] 3 W.L.R. 881; [2005] 4 All E.R. 128; [2005] E.M.L.R. 28; [2005] 2 F.C.R. 487; [2005] H.R.L.R. 27; (2005) 28(8) I.P.D. 28057; (2005) 155 N.L.J. 828, CA (Civ Div) 5.9
Douglas v Hello! Ltd (No.6); sub nom. Douglas v Hello! Ltd (Trial Action: Breach of Confidence) (No.3) [2005] EWCA Civ 595; [2006] Q.B. 125; [2005] 3 W.L.R. 881; [2005] 4 All E.R. 128; [2005] E.M.L.R. 28; [2005] 2 F.C.R. 487; [2005] H.R.L.R. 27; (2005) 28(8) I.P.D. 28057; (2005) 155 N.L.J. 828, CA (Civ Div) 5.1.2, 5.2.2
Douglas v Hello! Ltd (No.8) [2003] EWHC 2629; [2004] E.M.L.R. 2, Ch D 26.3.1
Dowden & Pook Ltd v Pook [1904] 1 K.B. 45, CA 8.5.1
Dowson & Mason v Potter [1986] 1 W.L.R. 1419; [1986] 2 All E.R. 418; (1986) 83 L.S.G. 3429; (1986) 130 S.J. 841, CA (Civ Div) 26.3.1
Dranez Anstalt v Hayek [2002] EWCA Civ 1729; [2003] 1 B.C.L.C. 278; [2003] F.S.R. 32; (2002) 146 S.J.L.B. 273, CA (Civ Div) 5.10.1, 18.3
Dryden v Greater Glasgow Health Board [1992] I.R.L.R. 469, EAT 8.1.4.6

Table of Statutes

Table of Statutory Instruments

2001	Competition Act 1998 (Public Transport Ticketing Schemes Block Exemption) Order (SI 2001/319) 22.5.2
	Financial Services and Markets Act 2000 (Confidential Information) (Bank of England) (Consequential Provisions) Order (SI 2001/3648) 5.2.3.2
2004	Competition Act 1998 (Land Agreements Exclusion and Revocation) Order (SI 2004/1260) 22.4.8
	Art.6 ....22.4.8
	Competition Act 1998 and Other Enactments (Amendment) Regulations (SI 2004/1261) 22.4.4
2005	Competition Act 1995 (Public Transport Ticketing Schemes Block Exemption) (Amendment) Order (SI 2005/3347) 22.5.2
2006	Transfer of Undertakings (Protection of Employment) Regulations (SI 2006/246)
	reg.4(2) 3.6

Table of European Legislation

Chapter 1

Introduction

1.1 The restraint of trade doctrine

The essence of the restraint of trade doctrine is still contained in the famous speech of Lord MacNaghten in *Nordenfelt v Maxim Nordenfelt Guns and Ammunition Co Ltd* [1894] A.C. 535:

> The public have an interest in every person's carrying on his trade freely: so has the individual. All interference with individual liberty of action in trading, and all restraints of trade of themselves, if there is nothing more, are contrary to public policy . . . .

A slightly more recent re-statement is given in the judgment of Lord Morris of Borth-y-gest in *Esso Petroleum Co Ltd v Harper's Garage (Stourport) Ltd* [1968] A.C. 269:

> In general, the law recognises that there is freedom to enter into any contract that can lawfully be made. The law lends its weight to uphold and enforce contracts freely entered into. The law does not allow a man to derogate from his grant. If someone has sold the goodwill of his business, some restraint to enable the purchaser to have that which he has bought may be recognised as reasonable. Some restraints to ensure the protection of confidential information may be similarly regarded. The law recognises that if business contracts are fairly made by parties who are on equal terms such parties should know their business best. If there has been no irregularity, the law does not mend or amend contracts merely for the relief of those for whom things have not turned out well. But when all this is fully recognised yet the law, in some circumstances, reserves a right to say that a contract is in restraint of trade and that to be enforceable it must pass a test of reasonableness. In the competition between varying possible principles applicable, that which makes certain covenants and in restraint of trade unenforceable will in some circumstances be strong enough to prevail. Public policy will give it priority.

The restraint of trade doctrine is, therefore, an aspect of public policy and before relying on older authorities it must be remembered that the perception of what constitutes public policy may change, as it has in the context of the application of some of the principles with the advent of the UK Competition Act 1998.

1.2 Purpose of restraint of trade clauses

The usual purpose of most restraint of trade clauses is to limit competition. But public policy leans against the achievement of such an aim. In *Herbert Morris Ltd v Saxelby* [1916] 1 A.C. 688, Lord Atkinson said ". . . no person has an abstract right to be protected against competition *per se* in his trade or business". The most important words there are "*per se*": for a person can legitimately prevent competition indirectly if the restraint is reasonable and is attached to a proper interest which merits protection. Usually the restraint must protect either business goodwill or business secrets or help promote the provision of goods or services. These considerations have now also been embodied in EU and UK competition legislation which will apply where the restraint in question is part of an agreement between two businesses.

It has also been held that an employer has a legitimate interest in protecting his business from poaching of staff by a former employee.

The law insists that a former employee cannot be prevented from turning to his own account his professional skill and knowledge even though it may have been acquired while in employment and at the employer's expense. On the other hand, where circumstances are such that the employee has been put in a position of acquiring special intimate knowledge of the clients of his employer or the means of influence over them there exists subject matter which is entitled to the court's protection. Otherwise, as Evershed J. said in *Routh v Jones* [1947] 1 All E.R. 179:

> . . . the master would be exposed to unfair competition on the part of his former servant—competition flowing not so much from the personal skill of the assistant as from the intimacies and knowledge of the master's business acquired by the servant from the circumstances of his employment.

Part I

Restraint of Trade Doctrine

Chapter 2

The Issues

First one needs to carefully consider the relationship and differences between competition law and the common law restraint of trade. Then, more specifically, under the restraint of trade law one needs to consider four issues. These are, in logical order of application:

(a) Does a restraint of trade exist in this case/does the restraint of trade doctrine apply to this class of case?

(b) Is there an interest meriting protection?

(c) Is the restraint reasonable as between the parties?

(d) Is the restraint reasonable in the public interest?

Each question is now examined in turn.

2.1 The relationship between the restraint of trade doctrine and EU/UK competition law

In relation to employment contracts, the restraint of trade doctrine clearly needs to be considered, and only this doctrine. However, where there is a restraint of trade in a commercial agreement, one will now also need to consider the possibility of the clause being void under competition law. The restraint of law doctrine was developed well before UK practitioners had to consider validity under competition law, particularly if the agreement merely related to UK parties and arguably EU law did not apply. With the introduction of a prohibitive regime in the UK, where a defendant wants to argue that a restrictive clause is void, he will now have significant additional arsenal.

Equally, if a clause is allowed under EU competition law, the supremacy of EU law (as per *Walt Wilhelm*, ECJ Case 14/68 [1968] ECR 1) means that a national judge will be precluded from ruling a clause is void under the national restraint of trade doctrine. This is explicitly covered by Art.3(3) of Reg.1/2003 which provides that national law may not prohibit an agreement which does not restrict competition, i.e. is not caught by Art.81(1) or fulfills the exemption conditions of Art.81(3) (i.e. individual exemption or a block exemption regulation)—unless the national law "predominantly" pursues a different objective than Arts 81 and 82 of the EC Treaty.

Cases such as *WWF v World Wrestling Federation Entertainment Inc* [2002] EWCA Civ 196 (Carnwath L.J. at paras 64–66) and *Apple Corps Limited v Apple Computer Inc* (No Challenge Interlocutory) [1992] R.P.C. 70, Ch D (judgment of Nicholls L.J. at paras 109–113) have considered the close relationship between the common law restraint of trade doctrine and EU competition law—despite the differences in characterisation. The qualification in Art.3(3) of Reg.1/2003 is more likely to be aimed at consumer protection laws relating to unfair contract terms and such like, and less likely to allow a difference of outcome under the common law doctrine of restraint of trade, which after all was developed as the result of a public policy need not to unduly restrict trade—in other words to protect competition. See Langley J. paras 254–266 in *Days Medical Aids v Pihsiang Machinery Manufacturing* [2004] EWHC 44 where a five year renewable exclusive distribution agreement was considered under both the restraint of trade doctine and EU competition law.

While some of the terminology used in relation to the two approaches is similar, as one considers the scope and duration of a restriction, whether the restriction is protecting a legitimate interest and it is reasonable (or under competition law, not unduly restrictive), nevertheless the analysis that needs to be carried out is significantly different.

In relation to commercial agreements, under the common law doctrine of restraint of trade, the courts are increasingly prepared to decline to interfere with the terms negotiated and agreed between the parties, particularly on the sale of a business where consideration is received. On the other hand the competition authorities, while recognising that a buyer will want to protect the goodwill and value of the business acquired, are more concerned that actual and potential competition continues to exist in the market place. Under neither approaches can a purchaser of a business expect to get an unlimited protection from possible competition in the future, although the two approaches could result in differences as to the scope or duration.

Furthermore under the common law doctrine the courts are focused on the effect of the clause between the parties, while under competition law the focus is on the effect of the clause on the market place in which the parties operate. Hence a non-compete between two small local UK businesses may well not have an appreciable effect on competition and be acceptable under competition law, but its application may be unreasonable on one of the parties under common law. Equally a seven-year post-sale non-compete may be reasonable under common law, and yet raise concern under competition law.

Finally, one of the key differences between the common law doctrine and competition law is the timeframe within which one considers whether the clause is valid. Under the common doctrine the relevant moment is what was reasonable when the parties entered into the agreement (see *Gledhow Autoparts v Delaney* [1965] 1 W.L.R. 1366). In contrast, under competition law the question is whether the agreement affects competition in an anti-competitive way at the time one is seeking to enforce it—as agreements can move in and out of validity depending on market conditions and the parties' share of the market (see *Passmore v Morland Plc* [1999] 3 All E.R. 1005—discussed in Chapter 21).

As to whether one should argue one or the other, tactically each analysis has its pros and cons. In negotiations, both common law and competition law can be raised as the consequences are the same, the potential invalidity of the clause. The main difference between the two in the case of a sale of a business is that competition authorities have issued guidelines as to what type of clauses will be *prima facie* valid as being ancillary to the merger.

In terms of subsequent litigation to enforce a commercial restriction or escape its effect, it is likely to be easier for a UK judge to consider a restrictive clause under the restraint of trade doctrine and analyse the scope and effect of the clause on the individual parties. In most cases this can be done in interlocutory proceedings. On the other hand, under competition law, the issue could be brought before a judge or a complaint could be made to a competition authority (in which case there would be no litigation costs involved—although typically the agreement would need to raise sufficient interest for the authority to want to pursue it). Also, depending on the circumstances of the case, it may be that in addition to invalidity of the clause, damages for breach of competition law can also be claimed. See for example *Crehan v Inntrepreneur Pub Co* [2003] EWHC 1510 (Ch D) where the publican was claiming damages for breach of competition law regarding a tied beer tenancy (see further Chapter 21 below); whereas the older petrol tie cases were pursued under the restraint of trade doctrine, e.g. *Esso Petroleum v Harper's Garage* (see para.2.2.1). In both cases at issue was the fact that cheaper products were available outside the tie. However, to rule whether a clause is in breach of competition law will require a substantial analysis of the economic effects of the restriction on competition on the relevant product and geographic markets. Under competition law the relative strength (both in terms of bargaining position and market share) of the respective parties will also be relevant, the stronger the party is in whose favour the restriction applies, the more likely the restriction may be caught by competition law, and if the stronger party bore signifficant responsibility for the distortion of competition, the *in pari delicto* rule may not apply (see *Courage v Crehan*, Case C-453/99 [2001] ECR I-6297, discussed in Chapter 21).

Appendix 6(B) provides a checklist comparison between the restraint of trade doctrine and competition law.

2.2 Does a restraint of trade exist in this case/does the restraint of trade doctrine apply to this class of case?

It is necessary before undertaking an analysis of whether a restraint in a particular case is reasonable to decide whether in the first place the doctrine has any part to play. If it does not, then quite clearly questions of reasonableness are irrelevant. First, in many cases the doctrine will, on a common sense view, be irrelevant and no court will permit a defendant to raise it. For example, if there is a simple contract for the sale of a chattel it would be impractical to say that the restraint of trade doctrine applied. On the other hand the doctrine clearly applies to contractual terms by which the covenantee, an employer or a purchaser of a business, seeks to forbid the covenantor (the employee or seller) from carrying on his trade or restricts the way in which he may carry it on *after* the purchase and sale of labour or the business has been completed.

Over the years there have been several judicial attempts to define the scope of the common law doctrine.

2.2.1 Modern judicial views on the ambit of the common law doctrine

In *Petrofina (Great Britain) Ltd v Martin* [1966] Ch. 146 two members of the Court of Appeal attempted to define what amounts to a restraint of trade. Lord Denning M.R. said:

> Every member of the community is entitled to carry on any trade or business he chooses and in such manner as he thinks most desirable in his own interests, so long as he does nothing unlawful: with the consequence that any contract which interferes with the free exercise of his trade or business, by restricting him in the work he may do for others, or the arrangements which he may make with others, is a contract in restraint of trade. It is invalid unless it is reasonable as between the parties and not injurious to the public interest.

Diplock L.J. said "A contract in restraint of trade is one in which a party (the covenantor) agrees with any other party (the covenantee) to restrict his liberty in the future to carry on trade with other persons not parties to the contract in such manner as he chooses".

As Lord Morris said in the *Esso* case these are helpful expositions provided that they are not used too literally. Two years after *Petrofina* the House of Lords laid down guidelines as to what did and what did not fall within the doctrine in *Esso Petroleum Co Ltd v Harper's Garage (Stourport) Ltd* [1968] A.C. 269.

The appellants, suppliers of petrol to garage owners, entered into two agreements with the respondents in relation to two garages, M and C. The agreements were on the appellants' standard forms. In respect of garage M the appellants agreed to sell and the respondents agreed to buy from the appellants for a period of four years and five months their total requirements of petrol for resale. The respondents agreed, inter alia, to keep the garage open at all reasonable hours and if they sold the garage, to ensure that the buyer entered into a similar agreement with the appellants. In respect of garage C the agreement was identical except that the period was 21 years. In addition, garage C was subject to a mortgage whereby the appellants advanced, under a loan agreement, £7,000 to the respondents who covenanted to repay it by instalments over a period of 21 years. In the mortgage deed the respondents further covenanted that they would purchase all their requirements from the appellants exclusively. Each agreement also contained a resale price maintenance clause. Subsequently, because low priced petrol came on to the market the appellants wrote to all of their dealers, including the respondents saying that they would not insist on the implementation of the resale price maintenance clause. In answer to this the respondents who were in favour of this clause and its enforcement said that they now deemed that the sale agreements were null and void and they began to sell another brand of petrol at both garages. They also announced their intention of redeeming the mortgage. The appellants considered the mortgage could not be redeemed without their consent unless in accordance with the covenant for repayment over a period of 21 years. The appellants sought injunctions restraining the respondents from buying or selling petrol other than that supplied by them at the two garages during the subsistence of the agreements and in respect of garage C during the period of the mortgage.

It was argued on behalf of the appellants that two distinct categories of restraint might exist in any particular case. First, there were contracts restraining a person from carrying on some trade or business; these were clearly subject to the doctrine. Secondly, there were restrictive covenants affecting land and so imposing a burden on the land rather than on any person. It was argued that such covenants are often contained in conveyances, leases and mortgages, and that these had never been subject to the doctrine of restraint of trade and consequently the test of reasonableness. The present case fell into the second category and not the first as far as garage C was concerned. It was argued on behalf of the respondents that the doctrine applied to a covenant which was imposed for the benefit of the trade of the covenantee and which either forbids the covenantor to carry on his trade or restricts the way in which he may carry it on. Further, when a covenant is taken for the benefit of property, the doctrine does not apply, but when it is taken to protect both property and a business, or solely a business, the doctrine applies and therefore the question of reasonableness arises.

The members of the House of Lords did not express a unified view as to when the doctrine would be relevant. Lord Reid said:

> Restraint of trade appears to me to imply that a man contracts to give up some freedom which otherwise he would have had. A person buying or leasing land had no previous right to be there at all, let alone to trade there, and when he takes possession of that land subject to a negative restrictive covenant he gives up no right or freedom which he previously had.

As the respondents were already in possession when they entered into the solus agreements, he concluded that the agreements were within the doctrine of restraint of trade, Lord Reid's view that the restraint of trade doctrine only applies if the covenantor has given up a freeedom which he previously possessed was supported by Lords Morris and Hodson. An attempt was made in *Alec Lobb Garages Ltd v Total Oil (Great Britain) Ltd* [1985] 1 All E.R. 303, to take advantage of this view. The oil company granted a lease-back with a tie to the individual shareholders of a company; the company itself having granted the lease. It was argued that the doctrine could not apply as the shareholders had given up nothing, only the company had. However this was described by the Court of Appeal as a device and the doctrine was applied. See also *Amoco Australian Pty Ltd v Rocca Bros Motor Engineering Co Pty Ltd* [1975] A.C. 561, *Sadler v Imperial Life Assurance Co of Canada Ltd* [1988] I.R.L.R. 388 and the discussion at para.16.3 below.

A second test is also contained in Lord Reid's judgment. He concluded that not only had the respondents agreed negatively not to sell other petrol but that they had agreed positively to keep their garage open for the sale of the appellant's petrol at all reasonable hours throughout the period of the tie. It had been argued that this merely regulated the respondent's trading and tended towards the promotion rather than the restraint of his trade. To this Lord Reid said that to regulate a person's existing trade may be a greater restraint than prohibiting him from engaging in a new trade. He seemed to imply in this that even if the covenantor had *not* previously enjoyed a certain freedom then the restraint of trade doctrine might still apply if he is, as a result of the restraint, under a *positive* duty to do something which restricts his current freedom.

A third test appears frst in Lord Pearce's judgment, but is most clearly stated by Lord Wilberforce:

> No exhaustive test can be stated—probably no precise non-exhaustive test. But the development of the law does seem to show that judges have been able to dispense from the necessity of justification under a public policy test of reasonableness such contracts or provisions of contracts as, under contemporary conditions, may be found to have passed into the accepted and normal currency of commercial or contractual or conveyancing relations. That such contracts have done so may be taken to show with at least strong *prima facie* force that, moulded under the pressures of negotiation, competition and public opinion, they have assumed a form which satisfies the test of public policy as understood by the courts at the time, or, regarding the matter from the point of view of the trade, that the trade in question has assumed such a form that for its health or expansion it requires a degree of regulation. Absolute exemption from restriction or regulation is never obtained: circumstances, social or economic, may have altered, since they obtained acceptance, in such a way as to call for a fresh examination; there may be some exorbitance or special feature in the individual contract which takes it out of the accepted category: but the court however must be persuaded of this before it calls upon the relevant party to justify a contract of this kind.

He expanded this view by referring to a number of authorities, which could only be truly explained by saying that certain contracts have become part of "the accepted machinery of a type of transaction which is generally found acceptable and necessary; so that instead of being regarded as restrictive they are accepted as part of the structure of a trading society". Thus sole agency contracts had become part of the accepted pattern or structure of trade. They therefore encouraged or strengthened the trade rather than limited it. Applying these notions to the particular contracts in question he decided that the solus system was both too recent and too variable for it to have become part of the "accepted machinery". Part of Lord Wilberforce's test is extremely difficult for the practitioners to apply. It would have been tempting for an adviser to have thought in 1968 that a solus agreement involving the exclusive purchase of petrol was of sufficiently established commercial importance to fall within that class of cases to which Lord Wilberforce said the restraint of trade doctrine would not apply. Indeed, it was found as a fact in the case that out of 36,000 petrol stations in the United Kingdom nearly 35,000 were subject to solus agreements. Of the 35,000 over 6,600 were solus agreements with Esso. Moreover, the provisos and developments which Lord Wilberforce admitted might make an accepted commercial agreement subject to the doctrine in any event make this test difficult to apply. This test was considered in *A. Schroeder Music Publishing Co Ltd v Macaulay* [1974] 1 W.L.R. 1308 where Lord Reid, by way of answer to the argument that a standard form of publishing agreement which had stood the test of time was the very same agreement about which the defendant was then complaining, said that this test could only be satisfied when the contracts were "made freely by parties bargaining on equal terms" or "moulded under the pressures of negotiation, competition and public opinion". These requirements were not satisfied in *Schroeder* because the contract was imposed on the plaintiff by a defendant who had greater bargaining power which he had used oppressively. In *Watson v Prager* [1991] I.C.R. 603 an agreement between a boxer and manager on terms prescribed by the British Boxing Board of Control was subject to the doctrine as it was not a commonplace commercial contract (Scott J.).

A more recent development is the fact that the competition authorities (both the EC Commission and the Office of Fair Trading) have published Regulations and Guidelines applicable to restrictions that are considered ancillary to mergers, and typical restrictions in various vertical and horizontal agreements (e.g. petrol and tied-beer tenancies). As such one can only assume that these types of commercial restrictions (as opposed to employment ones) have now become "accepted machinery of a type of transaction which is generally found acceptable and necessary".

A fourth test proposed in *Esso Petroleum Co Ltd v Harper's Garage (Stourport) Ltd* [1968] A.C. 269 was also stated by Lord Wilberforce. In concluding his judgment, he examined the claim that the designation of the transaction as a mortgage in itself protected the entire contents of the mortgage deed from the strutiny of the restraint of trade doctrine. He said, referring to the contents of a mortgage deed: "If their purpose and nature is found not to be ancillary to the lending of money upon security, as, for example, to make the lending more profitable or safer, but some quite independent purpose, they may and should be independently scrutinised" (i.e. subject to the restraint of trade doctrine). What Lord Wilberforce was saying was that one examines the content and not the form of a restraint and if there appears "some quite independent purpose" behind the restraint, i.e. a purpose outside the essence of the agreement, then the doctrine applies. This test appeared to have the support of Lords Morris and Pearce.

There may be some merit in the argument put forward on behalf of the respondents in the *Esso* case that all contracts are subject to the doctrine but that most contracts are quite clearly reasonable. All contracts could be described quite properly as being in restraint of trade, but this was not a term of abuse, and only those contracts which were in unreasonable restraint of trade would be struck down by the courts. This is an attractive argument which seems to provide an easy answer to the problem by disregarding it entirely. It is supported by Lord Hodson in *Esso* and in *Pharmaceutical Society of Great Britain v Dickson* [1970] A.C. 403. The difficulty with the argument is that it may provide a rogue's charter. In practice, because of the powers which the court has to deal with unmeritorious points, we think it is a reasonable approach, although its application is bound to create a degree of uncertainty which may be unacceptable, especially in commercial cases.

An important aspect of the *Esso* case is that it illustrates that the restraint of trade doctrine is applicable to those restraints which exist during the primary contractual period, and not only to those which continue after the end of that period. Indeed, there is earlier authority for the application of the doctrine during the main period of contract though as these cases are very much in the minority, they are sometimes forgotten. In *McEllistrim v The Ballymacelligott Co-op Agricultural & Dairy Society* [1919] A.C. 548 a co-operative society had changed its rules so as to prevent any member from selling milk other than to the society. If a member did so there was a heavy penalty. Moreover there could be no termination of membership without the society's permission. The House of Lords applied the restraint of trade doctrine. Nowadays one can assume that such a case would also be considered under EU and/or UK competition law, as to the extent to which the exclusivity provision restricts competition, and whether its benefits outweigh its restrictive effect. In *English Hop Growers Ltd v Dering* [1928] 2 K.B. 174 the Court of Appeal had to consider an agreement under which the defendant contracted to sell his crop to the plaintiffs for a period of five years. The Court of Appeal applied the restraint of trade doctrine and found that the agreement was reasonable.

In *R. v General Medical Council, Ex p. Colman* [1990] 1 All E.R. 489 the Court of Appeal on one view appear to have refused to apply the restraint of trade doctrine when asked to do so by a doctor who complained that the General Medical Council (GMC) had refused to allow him to advertise. It was found that the decision of the GMC to prevent advertising in the press was a lawful exercise of the statutory powers conferred on it by s.35 of the Medical Act 1983, and that if a statutory power was exercised *intra vires*, reasonably and in accordance with the purpose of the Act conferring the power (even though it restricted the plaintiff's freedom to trade or practise his profession), the court could not review the exercise of the power on the basis that it caused a restraint of trade, since the exercise of the power in accordance with the policy and the purpose of the Act could not be contrary to public policy and any review by the court would be unconstitutional. An alternative view might be that as the court had been prepared to consider whether the GMC had exercised its power in accordance with the Act it had in fact embarked on an exercise which involved making a finding of reasonableness (or the lack of it) in a fashion analogous to an application of the restraint of trade doctrine.

2.2.2 Extension of the principles

In recent years there has been an extension of the principles behind the restraint of trade doctrine so as to embrace:

(a) restraints in contracts which do not fit neatly into what was hitherto regarded as amounting to a restraint of trade;

(b) situations where the contract in question was not between the plaintiff and defendant and to which the plaintiff was not privy although he was affected by the working of the contract; and

(c) situations when no contract existed at all but the plaintiff could claim that a set of rules or certain conduct affected him prejudicially.

See *A. Schroeder Music Publishing Co Ltd v Macaulay* [1974] 1 W.L.R. 1308; *Eastham v Newcastle United Football Club Ltd* [1964] Ch. 413, *Nagle v Feilden* [1966] 2 Q.B. 633, *McInnes v Onslow-Fane* [1978] 3 All E.R. 211 and *Leeds Rugby Ltd v Harris* [2005] EWHC 1591 (QB).

These cases are referred to as "restraint of trade" cases and indeed that phrase was used in them. They can rightly be described as such because in each case the plaintiff's freedom and ability to earn a living was affected. It was that which gave him *locus standi*. The *Schroeder* case concerned an agreement between a young songwriter and a music publisher. There came a stage when the songwriter no longer wanted to be bound by the agreement so he sought a declaration that it was contrary to public policy and therefore unenforceable. The case reached the House of Lords and at every hearing the plaintiff succeeded. Lord Reid identified why the agreement was in restraint of trade. He said that the agreement was on its face unduly restrictive having regard to:

(a) its likely duration;

(b) the publishers' right to assign copyright in songs which they had acquired in full under the agreement, so that it could not be argued that they would be unlikely to act oppressively and so damage their goodwill;

(c) the fact that the publishers were not bound to publish or promote the songwriter's work if they chose not to do so, so that he might earn nothing, and his talents be sterilised, contrary to the public interest; and

(d) the absence of any provision entitling the songwriter to terminate the agreement.

Lord Reid went on to point out that this case was not of the type which would usually have been described as in restraint of trade; there was for example no provision which prevented the plaintiff from working once the contract had run its course. He said:

> Any contract by which a person engages to give his exclusive services to another for a period necessarily involves extensive restriction during that period of the common law right to exercise any lawful activity he chooses in such manner as he thinks best. Normally, the doctrine of restraint of trade has no application to such restrictions: they require no justifcation.

However he went on in an important passage to say that if contractual restrictions appear to be unnecessary or to be reasonably capable of enforcement in an oppressive manner then they must be justified before they can be enforced. By "justified" he meant "proved to be reasonable". Therefore, there seem to be two bases on which a contractual term can be attacked even though it does not attempt to restrain a party after the contractual period had ended. These are:

(a) The restriction is unnecessary.

(b) The restriction is reasonably capable of enforcement in an oppressive manner. (There appears to be some foundation for this approach in Lord Pearce's judgment in *Esso*.)

Note that it does not have to be shown that there has actually been oppressive enforcement simply that such is "reasonably capable". What is clear is that the word oppressive does not necessarily mean that the defendant has been induced to enter the restriction by fraud, misrepresentation, deceit or forced to enter it by duress. The question of oppression or unconscionable conduct was further considered in *Alec Lobb Garages Ltd v Total Oil (Great Britain) Ltd* [1985] 1 All E.R. 303. There it was pointed out by Dillon L.J. that inequality of bargaining power was not sufficient on its own to enable a court to strike down a contract. It was also necessary to show unconscionable conduct. Moreover, as was pointed out in *Multiservice Bookbinding Ltd v Marden* [1979] Ch. 84 unreasonableness is not sufficient to amount to unconscionable conduct. This is the traditional view. It is generally accepted that in order to succeed on a plea of unreasonableness it is not necessary for the covenantor to show that the covenantee had acted oppressively. Indeed in *Watson v Prager* [1991] I.C.R. 603 Scott J. specifically stated that the reasonableness of the contract was to be tested by its terms and not by how it has been performed. *Schroeder* however does appear to equate unreasonableness with oppression but it is suggested that it was not laying down any principle to that effect: it so happened that on the facts in that case unreasonableness and oppression both existed.

The *Schroeder* case was applied in *Clifford Davis Management Ltd v W.E.A. Records Ltd* [1975] 1 W.L.R. 61, in which Lord Denning M.R. pointed out that the agreement was not in restraint of trade in the traditional sense because:

> It does not preclude a man from exercising his trade at all. But it is an agreement which is 'restrictive of trade' in this sense, that it requires a man to give his services and wares to one person only for a long term of years to the exclusion of all others.

See also *Lloyds Bank Ltd v Bundy* [1975] Q.B. 326 and *Elton John v Richard Leon James* [1991] F.S.R. 397.

A further example of the wide application of the restraint of trade doctrine is found in *Eastham v Newcastle United Football Club Ltd* [1963] 3 All E.R. 139. In that case, the plaintiff was a professional footballer registered with a league club, Newcastle United. He had asked to be transferred, but his club had given him notice of retention and refused to release him. He refused to sign again with his club and sought, *inter alia*, declarations that the rules of the Football Association relating to the retention and transfer of football players, including the plaintiff, and the regulations of the Football League relating to retention and transfer were not binding on him, because they operated in unreasonable restraint of trade. He also claimed a declaration that the refusal of the directors of Newcastle United to release him from its retention list or alternatively to put him on its transfer list was unreasonable. Wilberforce J. held, among other things, first, that the retention provisions, which operated after the end of the employee's employment, substantially interfered with his right to seek employment and therefore operated in restraint of trade; secondly, that the transfer system and the retention system, when combined, were in restraint of trade and that, since the defendants had not discharged the onus of showing that the restraints were no more than what was reasonable to protect their interests, they were in unjustifiable restraint of trade and *ultra vires*; thirdly, that the court could examine a contract between employers only and declare it void on grounds on which such a contract would be declared void if it had been a contract between an employer and employee, and that it was open to an employee to bring an action for a declaration that such a contract was in restraint of trade, inasmuch as it threatened his liberty of action in seeking employment, which was a matter of public interest; and, fourthly, that it was a case in which the court could and should grant the plaintiff the declarations sought. *Leeds Rugby Ltd v Harris* [2005] EWHC 1591 (QB) is another sporting example where an option to re-employ a player transferring from a Rugby League club to play Rugby Union for Wales was held, notwithstanding the highly unusual features of the contractual arrangements surrounding this, to be an appropriate provision in relation to which to adopt the conventional analysis in restraint of trade cases. In that case, the option was held to be enforceable. See also Chapter 19 below for discussion of other similar cases.

In *Balston Ltd v Headline Filters Ltd* [1987] F.S.R. 330 it appears that an express confidential information clause which sought to protect secrets other than "business secrets" (in the narrow sense that that phrase is used in *Faccenda Chicken v Fowler* [1987] Ch.117, CA, see para.8.2.2 below) was subjected by Scott J. to the restraint of trade doctrine (see also Harman J. in *Systems Reliability Holdings plc v Smith* [1990] I.R.L.R. 377). This is consistent with the principles enunciated by Lord Morris in *Esso* (see para.1.1 above) and although it is unusual to find a specific reference to the doctrine in this context, it appears that the doctrine is the basis for the refusal of the courts to prevent an employee from using his skill, knowledge and experience once his employment has ceased, even though he may have gained it whilst working for his former employer. The usual approach of the courts is to examine whether any confidential information exists, whether it is protected by an express or implied term and, subject to arguments as to the balance of convenience, grant or refuse the injunction sought.

2.2.3 Conclusion

One can conclude that:

(1) The following classes of case are usually subject to the common law doctrine:

  (a) employment contracts regarding the period after the contract has ended;
  (b) contracts analogous to (a) such as some agency agreements and partnership agreements;
  (c) business sales contracts which preclude the vendor from competing with his former business;
  (d) solus agreements; and
  (e) any situation, not necessarily involving a contract, in which it appears a party has acted unreasonably, unfairly or oppressively so as to restrict another party, usually the plaintiff in the action, in the exercise of his trade, profession or employment.

(2) The following classes of case are usually not subject to the common law-doctrine:

  (a) those which include a restraint which does not involve the covenantor in giving up a freedom which he would otherwise have enjoyed unless the restraint creates a positive duty to do something which restricts his freedom during the period of its operation;

(b) those which, under contemporary conditions, may be found to have passed into the accepted and normal currency of commercial or contractual or conveyancing relations;

(c) those in which the purpose and nature of the restraint is coterminous with the purpose of the contract; and

(d) those in which powers conferred by statute have been exercised *intra vires*.

2.3 An interest meriting protection

In order to succeed, the party arguing for the validity of the restrictive covenant must first persuade the tribunal that the facts demonstrate the existence of a legitimate interest meriting protection. The nature of the interest meriting protection will differ according to the type of restraint under consideration. In employment contracts the interests are usually business secrets, trade connections or goodwill and protection of the workforce. In solus agreements efficiency of distribution, and in cases concerning sporting organisations the proper promotion of the sport, have been held to be interests meriting protection.

"Goodwill" is made up of two components: trade connections and reputation. The latter is usually only relevant when considering business sales, however the former is important in all types of situation.

The application of these principles is well illustrated in *Stenhouse Australia Ltd v Phillips* [1974] A.C. 391. Lord Wilberforce examined the interests which an insurance-broking business might have in preventing an employee canvassing its clients once he had left. He said that in the business of insurance and insurance broking, a successful enterprise depends upon a number of factors which vary according to the nature of the customer, or client, with whom business is done. The more varied or diversified the business of the client, and the larger the amount of insurance to be placed, the more likely it is that he will look around the market for himself in order to obtain the best terms. With a less diversified business, the likelihood grows that, while he is satisfied with the service he gets, he will keep his business, at least for a period, with the same insurer, and place it through the same broker. The advice and guidance, based on collation of information, by the broker, will be more valuable in such a case, to both broker and customer. In either case, in order to obtain and to retain business it is necessary to cultivate and accumulate knowledge of the client's requirements and of his record, so as to be able to offer him attractive terms. To develop this may be a fairly long-term affair: even if it has been developed there is always the risk that the client may decide to go elsewhere if better prospects offer. It is clear from this, he said, that the connection between an insurer or insurance broker and his client is not nearly as firm as, for example, that between a solicitor and his client. On the other hand its comparative fragility makes the risk of solicitation of clients by a former employee more serious. A client is not easily detached from a solicitor who has been handling his affairs over a period of years, but a comparatively mild solicitation may deprive an insurance broker of valuable business which otherwise might safely be reckoned on for a period. He concluded that the facts demonstrated the existence of a protectable interest.

Regarding business secrets, a problem which arises in practice is the necessity in employment cases to make a distinction between what is a business secret and what is simply the general skill of the employee. That distinction is dealt with in Chapter 8 at paras 8.2.2 *et seq*. However the courts have consistently recognised the interest that the employer or any other covenantee has in protecting business secrets. For example, in *Littlewoods Organisation Ltd v Harris* [1978] 1 All E.R. 1026 Megaw L.J. said:

> . . . it is appropriate that a covenant, restricting an employee from full freedom of taking other employment when he leaves his existing employment, should be included in the contract of employment where there is a real danger that the employee will in the course of that employment have access to and gain information about matters which could fairly be regarded as trade secrets; and that applies even though the information may be carried in his head and even though (perhaps, particularly though) it may be extremely difficult for the employee himself, being an honest and scrupulous man, to realise that what he is passing on to his new employers is matter which ought to be treated as confidential to his old employers.

Once the party seeking to enforce the restraint has established that there is an interest meriting protection the next question is whether the restraint is reasonable between the parties.

2.4 Reasonableness between the parties

The question whether a particular restraint is reasonable in the interests of both parties generally divides into three parts:

(a) Is the scope of the activities which the clause restrains reasonable?

(b) Is the geographical extent of the restraint reasonable?

(c) Is the duration of the restraint reasonable?

In all three parts "reasonable" means providing no more than relevant and necessary protection for the legitimate interest of the covenantee. Before relying on any case as a precedent for what is reasonable between the parties the important observations made in the case of *Esso Petroleum Co Ltd v Harper's Garage (Stourport) Ltd* [1968] A.C. 269 must be noted. Lord Reid said that where a party, who is in no way at a disadvantage in bargaining, chooses to take a calculated risk, then he could see no reason why the court should say that he had acted against his own interests. Lord Hodson said that in the case of agreements between commercial companies for regulating their trade relations the parties are usually the best judges of what is reasonable. In such a case, as Lord Haldane said in *North Western Salt Co Ltd v Electrolytic Alkali Co Ltd* [1914] A.C. 461, the law "still looks carefully to the interests of the public, but it regards the parties as the best judges of what is reasonable as between themselves". Although the matter has not been argued in any reported case it is only a matter of time before an employer argues that the stern scrutiny to which covenants in employment contracts have traditionally been subjected should not apply where the parties were possessed of equal bargaining power. Is it really correct that a managing director cannot manage to have his interests looked after by his managers?

Certainly in the context of a restriction in a commercial agreement, the relative bargaining powers of the contracting parties has been taken into account in the application of competition law to determine whether damages were available to the weaker party for an illegal restriction (see *Courage v Crehan* [2001] E.C.R. I-6297 and Section 21.10 below).

2.4.1 Scope: activities restrained

In order to demonstrate that a particular provision is reasonable between the parties it is necessary to demonstrate that the scope of those activities is reasonably referable to a legitimate interest, although it is not necessary to have absolute consistency between the restraint and the relevant interest. In *M & S Drapers v Reynolds* [1957] 1 W.L.R. 9, Morris L.J. said "I do not consider that a restriction . . . would necessarily be held to be unreasonable merely because it could be shown possibly to extend to one or two cases beyond the range of contemplated protection". It is submitted that this is sensible: if the party seeking to enforce the restraint were required to match the restraint exactly to the interest very few restraints, if any at all, would be found to be reasonable.

2.4.2 Geographical extent

Important factors to be considered when examining a geographical area are not simply the distance involved (usually a radial measurement from a given place) but the character of the area, the ease of travel/communication and the character of the business in question. Certainly the geographic scope should not extend beyond the area/country/region in which the business is actually carried out. It is generally true to say that if the area is predominantly rural then the geographical extent of the restriction can sometimes be greater than if an urban area is under consideration. For example, in *Routh v Jones* [1947] 1 All E.R. 179, Evershed J. paid especial regard to the rural nature of an area in deciding that a restriction which extended to ten miles from a certain place was not unreasonable (see also *Hollis v Stocks* [2000] I.R.L.R. 712, CA, where a covenant preventing an assistant solicitor working as a solicitor within a 10-mile radius of his former employer's office in Sutton in Ashfield was held reasonable by a Judge who knew the area well). In *Office Angels Ltd v Rainer-Thomas* [1991] I.R.L.R. 214, however, the Court of Appeal pointed out that an area restriction was an inappropriate form of covenant because it would do little to protect the plaintiff's connections with their clients; the clients' orders were placed over the telephone and it was of no concern to them precisely where the office was located.

In a world where many companies profess to operate on a global basis, the question will arise whether it is therefore reasonable to extend the restriction across the globe. Where the restriction is being placed on an individual, e.g. a regional manager or director, it may well be that his knowledge gained while working for the company is limited to a country/region. On the other hand, on the scale of a business it would usually be considered reasonable to extend the restriction to all existing areas of operations, and even those areas where detailed business plans exist (see *Commission's Notice on Ancillary Restrictions*, para.23 OJ 2005 C56/24, see further Chapter 21.14.2).

Assuming that even large multinationals do not necessarily operate in every corner of the globe, one way to circumvent a finding that a world-wide restriction is unreasonable would be to draft the covenant on the sale of a business as providing that "X" (the vendor and former owner) will not engage in the production of the relevant products, or the supply of the restricted services in competition with any [Group company of the sold business] in any part of the world. This prohibition is against competition; it is not a blanket ban as Mr X could carry on these activities in any country of the world in which, in all the circumstances, he is not trading in competition with the covenantees. (See *Emersub XXXVI Inc and Control Techniques plc v Wheatley*, unreported, July 14, 1998, Wright J.) In the employment context, as *Office Angels* demonstrates (see also *Allan Janes LLP v Johal* [2006] I.R.L.R. 599), getting the geographical extent of a non-compete covenant right is difficult and so non-dealing and non-solicitation covenants focused upon customers/clients the individual has had dealings with might well be preferable in many instances.

2.4.3 Time restrictions

If there is no mention of a time restriction in a covenant then the courts will normally infer that it is intended that the restriction should last forever. No general rules can be laid down as to the reasonableness of a time period because these obviously depend on the facts of each case, however as Lord Shaw said in the *Herbert Morris* case "as the time of the restriction lengthens and the space of its operation extends, the weight of the onus on the covenantee grows". It is important to remember that a classic type of restraint of trade clause frequently mentions two quite separate time periods. The first and obvious one is the period to which the covenant relates once the contract is at an end. The second occurs in those clauses which seek to circumscribe contact with those who were, for a given period, clients of the covenantee. An example of such a clause is one which says the employee is not to canvass or solicit during a period of 12 months from the date of the determination of the agreement any person, company or firm who were customers of the employer with whom he dealt during the last 12 months of his employment (see, e.g. *Wincanton Ltd v Cranny* [2000] I.R.L.R. 716, CA). There is no reason why both periods should not be scrutinised under the restraint of trade doctrine.

Under competition law the duration is certainly a factor in the analysis and may be determinative as to whether the clause can be assumed, prima facie not to be caught by the Art.81(1) or Chapter 1 prohibition (see both the EC and the OFT's Guidelines on Ancillary Restrictions Chapters 21 and 22). The duration of a non-compete restriction in a vertical agreement may well determine whether the agreement can benefit from the Reg.2790/1999 (Art.5).

In drafting agreements, there have been various attempts to circumvent the problem of a longer duration being found to be void by either including a renewal mechanism or including a clause whereby, if the longer duration is found to be void, the parties will agree to a shorter period that is valid (given that under the "blue pencil" rule a court can strike out an offending duration, but cannot modify it to make the clause reasonable).

With respect to a renewal mechanism—if it is by way of an automatic rollover, it is likely to be interpreted as having been entered into for an indefinite period. Under EU competition law an indefinite exclusivity restriction would mean the agreement would not benefit from the Vertical Agreements Block Exemption, Reg.2790/1999 (see Art.5(a)). Equally such clauses may be ineffective as being too vague to enforce or unlawful.

In *Davies v Davies* (1887) L.R. 36 Ch. D. 359 the Court of Appeal held that a restriction on a retiring partner which stated "to retire from the partnership; and so far as the law allows, from the business . . ." was too vague to be enforced (see Bowen L.J. at p.392). One member of the Court (Cotton L.J.) also held that the covenant was void on the ground that it was an unlawful restraint of trade because it prevented the retiring partner during his lifetime from earning his livelihood by carrying on his trade (at p.386).

In *Days Medical Aids v Pihsiang Machinery Manufacturing Co Ltd* [2004] EWHC 44 (QBD (Comm)) one of the issues under consideration was the duration of an exclusive distribution agreement which was expressed to be for "the initial period" of a "five-year term commencing on the date of signing" but subject to a right of renewal as follows:

DMA [the distributor] will endeavour to increase sales year on year. On the expiry of the first five-year term of this agreement provided that [the distributor] has discharged its obligations under the agreement and is maintaining a sales level of not less than 5000 units per annum, [the distributor] shall have a *right to renew the agreement for another five years on the same basis as herein*, except that the amount payable each year under Clause 2 shall be US $20,000.

This right of renewal shall extend to all subsequent five-year periods on the same basis *for as long as permitted by law*. (emphasis added) para.2 of the Judgment.

Langley J. considered there were two possible outcomes:

(i) that the whole of the last sentence had to be treated as ineffective, with the consequence that the Court dealt with the issues as if the Agreement were for 10 years; or

(ii) that only the offending seven words were ignored (in italics above), with the consequence that the agreement was renewable every five years indefinitely.

Both parties supported the second of these alternatives for different reasons. Langley J. held that the clause should be read as providing for one five-year renewal and no more (para.82 of the Judgment).

2.5 Reasonableness in the public interest

It has been common in the past to underestimate the importance of public policy or the public interest in the restraint of trade doctrine. See *A-G of the Commonwealth of Australia v Adelaide Steamship Co* [1913] A.C. 781. Although it is usually true that if the interests of the covenantee and the covenantor are satisfied then so is the public interest, it is important to realise that in some cases the courts have chosen to examine the restraint primarily from the point of view of the public interest rather than from that of the parties.

In the *Esso* case Lord Reid said "as the whole doctrine of restraint of trade is based on public policy its application ought to depend less on legal niceties or theoretical possibilities than on the practical effect of a restraint in hampering that freedom which it is the policy of the law to protect". Lord Reid went on to say that the reason that the court will not enforce a restraint which goes further than affording protection to the legitimate interests of a party is because too wide a restraint is against the public interest.

What is public policy? Although, as Lord MacMillan said in *Vancouver Malt & Sake Brewing Co Ltd v Vancouver Breweries Ltd* [1934] A.C. 181, it is important to realise that "public policy is not a constant" it appears to have some easily recognisable and immutable general characteristics. For example, the two competing public interests in employment cases are:

(a) a person should be held to his promise; and

(b) every person should be free to exercise his skill and experience to the best advantage of himself and of those who may want to employ him (see Lord Atkinson in *Herbert Morris v Saxelby* [1916] 1 A.C. 688).

In business sales cases the conflicting public interests are that a man is not at liberty to deprive himself or the community of his labour and expertise unreasonably and yet he must have a freedom to sell his business for the best price; which may be only obtainable if he precludes himself from entering into competition with the purchaser (see James V.C. in *Leather Cloth Co v Lorsont* (1869) L.R. 9 Eq. 345).

However, judicial opinion has varied in its view of what is the dominant ingredient of public policy. For example, in *English Hop Growers Ltd v Dering* [1928] 2 K.B. 174 Scrutton L.J. said "I have always for myself regarded it as in the public interest that parties who, being in an equal position of bargaining, make contracts, should be compelled to perform them, and not to escape from their liabilities by saying that they had agreed to something which was unreasonable". However, it should be noted that Scrutton L.J.'s words were said in a case involving a contract between commercial parties and it now seems that the insistence that public policy is primarily concerned with holding people to their agreements is out of favour. Likewise, it is submitted that no modern court would say as Sir George Jessell M.R. did in *Printing and Numerical Registering Co v Sampson* (1875) L.R. 19 Eq. 462:

> . . . if there is one thing which more than another public policy requires it is that men of full age and competent understanding shall have the utmost liberty of contracting, and that their contracts when entered into freely and voluntarily shall be held sacred and shall be enforced by courts of justice. Therefore, you have this paramount public policy to consider—that you are not lightly to interfere with this freedom of contract.

If one sets that quotation against the context of modern cases such as *A. Schroeder Music Publishing Co v Macaulay* [1974] 1 W.L.R. 1308 one is left in no doubt that the courts nowadays, whilst paying tribute to the sanctity of contract, will vigorously refuse to uphold contracts which in their view are oppressive or unreasonable. Indeed, it is submitted that the reasoning in *Schroeder's* case was based on public policy; Lord Diplock explained what was meant by public policy. He said that the public policy which the court was implementing was not some nineteenth-century economic theory about the benefit to the general public of freedom of trade, but the protection of those whose bargaining power is weak against being forced by those whose bargaining power is stronger to enter into bargains that are unconscionable. It is submitted that this is not a complete modern definition of what amounts to public policy but is one facet of that definition.

Important cases in which public policy has been the paramount or only reason for striking down a provision as an unreasonable restraint of trade include *Herbert Morris v Saxelby* and *WC Leng & Co Ltd v Andrews* [1909] 1 Ch. 763. Moreover, in *Strange (SW) Ltd v Mann* [1965] 1 W.L.R. 629 Stamp J. said that an employee's skill and knowledge "is in no sense the employer's property and it is contrary to public policy to restrain its use in any degree". In the *Esso* case both Lords Hodson and Pearce specifically based their judgments in striking down a solus agreement which extended to 21 years on public policy grounds.

Finally, it can be said that the public interest and public policy have played an especially important part as a vehicle for providing a reason for giving redress in those cases in which the parties are not contractually bound. For example, Slade J. in *Greig v Insole* [1978] 3 All E.R. 449 charmingly described the public interest in that case as the "public pleasure" in watching cricket played by talented cricketers, and described the Football Association and the Football League in *Eastham v Newcastle United Football Club Ltd* [1964] Ch. 413 as being "custodians of the public interest". It may well be that certain judges see themselves as such custodians. They would no doubt argue that in that role they are entitled to advance arguments which may not have been relied upon by the parties. Nowadays moreover, it is generally recognised as part of public policy that competition must not be unduly restricted, in the interests of consumers generally—not just the party seeking to deny the restrictions applies to him. This has led judges to consider the application of competition law to a restrictive clause, even when the parties no longer sought to argue the point (see *Bim Kemi AB v Blackburn Chemicals Ltd* [2004] All E.R. (D) 96 (Feb)).

Chapter 3

Restraint of Trade

3.1 The form of the agreement

The form of a restraint is irrelevant. Only its contents are important. It may be a direct or an indirect restraint or it may be contained in an agreement outside the primary contract between the parties.

3.1.1 Direct and indirect restraints

Most cases quite obviously involve a direct restraint which prevents the covenantor from doing a certain thing or things. However, some cases do involve indirect restraints. In *Wyatt v Kreglinger and Fernau* [1933] 1 K.B. 793 the restraint was contained in a letter dealing with the plaintiff's retirement rather than in his contract of employment and it effectively said that the defendants would pay him a pension if he refrained from working in the wool trade. This restraint was held by the court to be an indirect one and on the facts of the case it was found to be unreasonable and therefore the plaintiff was not entitled to his pension.

A further example of an indirect restraint is found in the case of *Mineral Water Bottle Exchange and Trade Protection Society v Booth* (1887) L.R. 36 Ch.D. 465 where a trade association had a rule that no member should employ an employee who had left the service of another member without the consent in writing of his late employer until a period of two years had elapsed from the time of the end of his employment. This was quite clearly not an agreement between the employer and the employee but had the effect of being an indirect restraint on any employee who wanted to work for another member of the trade association within the two year period. The rule was struck down as being an unreasonable restraint of trade when the Society attempted to prevent the defendants from employing an employee who had recently left another member of the association.

A more recent example of an indirect restraint is found in *Kores Manufacturing Co Ltd v Kolok Manufacturing Co Ltd* [1957] 3 All E.R. 158.

In that case the plaintiffs and the defendants were two companies which manufactured similar goods. They entered into an agreement by correspondence, each company writing in substantially the same terms to the other that they would not, without the written consent of the other, at any time, employ any person who during the past five years had been an employee of the other. The covenant was held to be an unreasonable restraint of trade. See also *Bull v Pitney-Bowes Ltd* [1967] 1 W.L.R. 273.

In *Sadler v Imperial Life Assurance Co of Canada Ltd* [1988] I.R.L.R. 388 the question of whether an indirect restraint of trade existed was considered. The defendants, a life assurance company, employed the plaintiff as an insurance agent. He was in fact an employee rather than an independent agent and had worked for the defendants for 17 years. He then resigned from his employment in accordance with the terms of his employment contract and brought an action against his former employers relating to commission payments. The plaintiff was remunerated by a commission calculated by reference to the premium paid by the insured persons introduced by him. The purchaser of a life assurance contract does not make one payment at the beginning of the contract but pays a premium in instalments over a number of years. This fact was reflected in the commission structure that the defendants agreed to pay the plaintiff. Commission was payable to the plaintiff on premiums paid during the first ten years of any policy. The commission was paid on a reducing basis so a substantial amount of commission was calculated in respect of the premium paid in the first policy year and a lower commission paid in subsequent years up to the tenth year. It was recognised by the defendants that when the employment of an agent came to an end it was likely that there would be in existence a number of policies which would have been effected during the period of the plaintiff's employment in respect of which commission would normally have been paid in future years if the employment had continued. The employment contract between the parties dealt with this eventuality by the continuance of such payments to the employee after he had ceased to be employed "provided that the agent's entitlement to such commission will immediately cease if the agent enters into a contract of service or for services directly or indirectly with any limited company, mutual society, partnership or brokerage operation involved in the selling of insurance or would be in breach of any part of clause 9A hereof were this contract still subsisting". Clause 9A of the contract incorporated a restraint on competing activities during employment. It effectively prevented him from working for another insurance company during that period.

In his statement of claim the plaintiff admitted that since termination of the contract he had by reason of continuing to work within the insurance industry acted in such a way that, if the contract were still subsisting, he would have been in breach of clause 9A. It was in the light of that breach that the defendants had refused to pay the plaintiff any post-determination commission.

It was argued on behalf of the plaintiff that:

(a) the proviso quoted above constituted an unlawful restraint of trade;

(b) the proviso was severable and might be struck out of the contract without affecting the remainder;

(c) the plaintiff's entitlement to post-determination commission accordingly continued notwithstanding his admitted breach of clause 9A.

The defendants argued that:

(a) The proviso quoted above came within the first test enunciated by Lord Reid in the *Esso* case (see para.2.2.1 above) i.e. that it did not deprive the plaintiff of any freedom which he would otherwise have had; accordingly that it did not operate as a restraint of trade and therefore that it was effective on the admitted facts to terminate the plaintiff's entitlement to commission.

(b) That if the effect of the proviso were to impose a restraint of trade then the consequence was that not only the proviso but also the whole of the paragraph to which the proviso related and which contained the stipulation that post-termination commission would be paid was void. Therefore, the plaintiff would have no entitlement to post-termination commission at all.

It was agreed by the parties that if the proviso on its true construction operated as a restraint of trade it could not be justified on the ground of reasonableness. The judge found that the substance of the post-termination commission clause was that in the event of termination following a prescribed period of service, commission would be paid to the plaintiff in respect of premiums actually paid under the relevant policies issued during his appointment but that it was subject to the proviso that the agent's entitlement to such commission would cease if he entered into competing activities. The judge concluded that there was thus a direct financial inducement for the agent not to enter into such activities but to restrict his post-termination employment to non-competing activities. The effect of the proviso was that if the plaintiff were to recover post-termination commission he would be required to give up some freedom which he would otherwise have had, namely the freedom to take employment in whichever field he wished. He therefore found that the facts of the case were indistinguishable from those of *Wyatt* and *Bull*. The proviso was found to be an unreasonable restraint of trade but was severed and the plaintiff was entitled to be paid the commission. But *cf. Peninsular Business Services Ltd v Sweeney* [2004] I.R.L.R. 49, EAT, where it was held a commission agreement under which entitlement ceased on leaving employment was not a restraint of trade. See also *Marshall v NM Financial Management Ltd* [1997] I.R.L.R. 449, CA.

3.1.2 Object or effect

Both Art.81(1) EC and s.2(1) Competition Act 1998 prohibit agreements which have as their object or effect the prevention, restriction or distortion of competition. From the EU case law, such as *Société Technique Minière v Maschinenbau Ulm*, Case 56/65 [1966] E.C.R. 235 p.249, these words are to be read disjunctively and not cumulatively. Thus, first it is necessary to consider what the object of the agreement is and secondly, only if it is not clear whether the object of an agreement is to harm competition is it necessary to consider whether it might have the effect of doing so.

Some types of agreement clearly have an anti-competitive object. By "object" is meant the objective meaning and purpose of the agreement considered in the economic context in which it is to be applied, rather than the subjective intention of the parties entering into the agreement. As a matter of law, where an agreement has as its object the restriction of competition, the EC Commission/OFT (or any other party opposing the agreement) does not have to prove that that kind of agreement has an anti-competitive effect, although other requirements like appreciability and effect on trade between Member States still has to be proven. If the object of an agreement is anti-competitive the onus is then on the parties to show that it satisfies the criteria under Art.81(3) which would entitle it to an exemption. Agreements that have as their object the restriction of competition involve an obvious infringement of Art.81(1) and are the agreements that are particularly likely to attract fines (e.g. price-fixing, market-sharing or the control of outlets).

In most cases however it is necessary to demonstrate that an agreement will have an anti-competitive effect (see CFT's judgment in *European Night Services v Commission of the European Communities*, Cases T–374/94 etc. [1998] ECR II–3141). Beer ties, non-compete restrictions or restrictions relating to business secrets are likely to be analysed in terms of their effect on competition particularly where they were intended to protect what would be considered a legitimate interest under common law.

3.1.3 Proximity of the restraint to the main contract

A covenant in restraint of trade is usually contained in a contract. For example, an employee will have a written contract of employment in which clauses will provide for the restraint of trade and for the protection of business secrets. However, it is not necessary for the restraint of trade clause to be part of the main contract so long as it is possible to argue that it is referable to it or that it otherwise has contractual force. In *Commercial Plastics Ltd v Vincent* [1965] 1 Q.B. 623 the contract of employment was concluded on December 20, 1959 and yet the restraint of trade clause was contained in a letter of November 27, 1959. It was accepted by the Court of Appeal that the letter had to be construed as part of the written contract. In *Stenhouse Australia Ltd v Phillips* [1974] A.C. 391 the restraint of trade clause was part of an agreement made between the parties after employment had ceased as it had been in *Wyatt's* case. In the *Esso* case, the restraint in a supply and purchase contract was reinforced in a mortgage deed. The court refused to accede to the appellant's argument that the fact that the restraint was contained in a mortgage deed excluded the application of the restraint of trade doctrine. Lord Morris said that a consideration of the facts and documents led him to the view that the solus agreement, the loan agreement and the mortgage could be linked together as an instance of one transaction and that the intention was that in providing that the mortgage should be irredeemable for the period of the tie it should become a support for the solus agreement. See also *Marley Tile Co Ltd v Johnson* [1982] I.R.L.R. 75 in which the Court of Appeal found that restrictive covenants which formed part of the employee's original terms of employment applied to his subsequent appointment on promotion notwithstanding that a memorandum and a letter of appointment to the new post did not expressly contain the restrictive covenants. Most examples concern restraints entered into at the start of employment or during employment, although some form part of severance agreements which are entered into on termination. Even if there was no covenant in the original contract it is usually entirely legitimate for, say, an employer to seek to protect himself in a severance agreement by a covenant of reasonable bounds against the risk that the employee might otherwise disclose or use its confidential information or damage its legitimate trade connections (see Simon Brown L.J. in *J A Mont v Mills* [1993] I.R.L.R. 172 at para.52 and Glidewell L.J. at para.57). The question of incorporation was considered by the Court of Appeal in *Credit Suisse Asset Management Ltd v Armstrong* [1996] I.R.L.R. 450 with the result frequently arrived at in interlocutary proceedings *viz* the employer succeeded in showing that the restraint had been incorporated.

3.2 The time at which reasonableness is considered

This is one aspect where there is significant divergence of approach between the common law doctrine and competition law.

3.2.1 Under common law

It is generally accepted under the common law doctrine that the relevant time at which reasonableness is to be considered is the time of entering the contract which contains the restraint. Therefore a court will ask the question was the restraint reasonable when it was entered into by the parties? The matter was discussed extensively in *Commercial Plastics Ltd v Vincent* [1965] 1 Q.B. 623. Pearson L.J. said when construing the restraint "although the time for ascertaining the competitors is the time of termination of a contract of employment, the time for ascertaining the reasonableness of a restrictive covenant or provision is the time of the making of the contract". This highlights one of the problems of the approach that the time at which reasonableness should be considered is the time of entering into the contract. Many restraints, as in *Commercial Plastics*, refer to the fact that a party may not solicit or compete with the other party in relation to those who were customers at the date of the determination of the contract. One therefore has the dichotomy of examining what is reasonable at one time (i.e. the start of the contract), whilst also examining the ultimate purpose of the restraint at another (i.e. the end of the contractual period). However, there is no doubt that the majority of authorities do favour an examination of reasonableness at the time of contracting. The practical effect of this is illustrated by the case of *Strange (SW) Ltd v Mann* [1965] 1 W.L.R. 629 where at the time of entering the contract the business was exclusively a credit-betting business and it was accepted by all parties that the validity of the covenant fell to be tested without regard to the fact that subsequently betting shops became legal and that a betting shop had been set up by the plaintiff. Stamp J. therefore considered the reasonableness of the restraint purely in the context of a credit-betting business. Indeed, it was this fact which principally led him to describe the restraint as unreasonable.

An important consequence of this approach is that generally the courts have refused to accept that supervening events (i.e. events subsequent to the start of the contract) can render an initially reasonable covenant unenforceable. It seems that the reason for this is that to hold otherwise would be to give rise to an unacceptable degree of uncertainty. In *Gledhow Autoparts Ltd v Delaney* [1965] 1 W.L.R. 1366 Diplock L.J. said:

> It is natural . . . to tend to look at what in fact happened under the agreement; but the question of the validity of a covenant in restraint of trade has to be determined at the date at which the agreement was entered into and has to be determined in the light of what may happen under the agreement, although what may happen may be and always is different in some respects from what did happen. A covenant of this kind is invalid *ab initio* or valid *ab initio*. There cannot be a moment from which it passes from the class of invalid into that of valid covenants.

Moreover, in *A. Schroeder Music Publishing Co Ltd v Macaulay* [1974] 1 W.L.R. 1308 Lord Reid said that a consequence of examining validity at the time when the contract was signed made it unnecessary to deal with the reasons why the respondent (originally the plaintiff) now wished to be freed from it. This must mean that cross-examination about these reasons is irrelevant to the issue of reasonableness.

Although one looks at reasonableness at the time the agreement is entered into, it is only practical also to take into account the legitimate expectations of the parties at that time regarding the future, and what is reasonably foreseeable. See *Putsman v Taylor* [1927] 1 K.B. 741 and *Lyne-Pirkis v Jones* [1969]

1 W.L.R. 1293, *per* Edmund Davies L.J. So, by way of illustration, in *Allan Janes LLP v Johal* [2006] I.R.L.R. 599, (Ch D), a non-dealing provision in an assistant solicitor's contract which related to all the clients of the firm (whereas the solicitor in practice only acted for some 10% directly and a further 5% indirectly) was held to be reasonable because, at the time of the solicitor's employment, she was employed in a senior position with the parties anticipating that she would progress to become a partner with the result that it was within the parties' contemplation that, in this capacity, she would eventually be working for all the firm's actual and proposed clients. However it may be that expansion of the business goes beyond the reasonable expectation of the parties; in which case it may be necessary for the covenantor to renegotiate the ambit of the restraint. In order to attempt to provide for this possibility there should be a contractual provision which permits renegotiation. See also *RS Components Ltd v Irwin* [1974] 1 All E.R. 41.

In *Shell UK v Lostock Garage Ltd* [1976] 1 W.L.R. 1187 Lord Denning M.R. explained what he thought was meant by the proposition that reasonableness is to be considered at the time when the contract is made:

> If the terms impose a restraint which is unreasonable in the sense that it may work unfairly in circumstances which may reasonably be anticipated, the courts will refuse to enforce the restraint: but it will not hold it to be unenforceable simply because it might work unfairly in certain exceptional circumstances outside the reasonable expectation of the parties at the time of making the agreement.

He found that the circumstances which had arisen were not foreseeable at the time of the start of the contract but he still decided to take into account supervening events: this made the contract unenforceable and unreasonable. He specifically disagreed with Diplock L.J.'s judgment in *Gledhow* quoted above and he particularly said that there was no such thing in this area of law as a contract which was void or invalid *ab initio* because an unreasonable restraint was only unenforceable if a party attempted to enforce it. He said that there were two situations in which the court would not enforce a clause:

(a) if at the time of making the contract it is seen that it may in the future operate unfairly or unreasonably; or

(b) if after the time of making the contract it is found to operate unreasonably or unfairly even if those circumstances were not envisaged beforehand.

Therefore it was possible to have supervening unenforceability. It seems that Kerr J. at first instance had come to the same conclusion as Lord Denning via a public policy route. However, Lord Denning was in the minority in the Court of Appeal for both Ormrod L.J. and Bridge L.J. disagreed with him. Furthermore as authority for his departure from Diplock L.J.'s judgment, Lord Denning relied on dicta of their Lordships in *Esso Petroleum Co Ltd v*

Harper's Garage (Stourport) Ltd [1968] A.C. 269 which are of doubtful support. However, whilst Lord Denning's view does not represent the law on this topic, it is submitted that his lack of faith in the traditional approach because the question of reasonableness is bound to be viewed with hindsight, is a valid criticism. It is rare for counsel to be stopped from cross-examining on what actually did happen during the currency of an agreement, or addressing the court on this, even if such events were not reasonably foreseeable. Moreover in the area of business secrets a different approach is almost inevitable. If what was a secret at the time that the contract was entered into subsequently becomes public knowledge (other than through the actions of the defendant) then it would be unrealistic if the court were simply to examine the question of reasonableness at the time when the contract was entered. On the other hand, it could be said that this type of objection does not relate to reasonableness but is concerned with breach or with the willingness of the courts on public policy grounds to refuse to enforce a contractual provision which seeks to protect a piece of information which is in the public domain.

3.2.2 Transient voidness under competition law

While the reasonableness, and therefore the validity, of a restraint is determined at the time of entering the contract under common law, the prohibition in Art.81(2) EC is "temporaneous (or transient) rather than absolute" and validity may therefore be "turned on or off" depending on the surrounding facts.

In *Passmore v Morland plc* [1999] 3 All E.R. 1005 the Court of Appeal held that an agreement could move from voidness to validity, and back again, depending on the actual effect the restrictive agreement may have on the market. Chadwick specifically considered the argument made on behalf of Passmore as to the principle of legal certainty which should lead to the conclusion that the beer tie in question was void at the time it was entered into and remained unenforceable. Nevertheless Chadwick maintained that what was relevant were the circumstances prevailing the relevant market at the time and that therefore agreements can, over a period of time, float into and out of voidness depending on market conditions (see also para.22.2).

Section 2(4) of the Competition Act 1998 provides that "any agreement or decision which is prohibited by sub-section (1) is void". This mirrors Art.81(2) EC and therefore the Court of Appeal's ruling in *Passmore v Morland plc* as to the transient nature of the invalidity under EU law is presumably also true of s.2(4).

3.3 Construction

The problem of construction only arises if ambiguity exists. Throughout the cases it is possible to discern two distinct approaches to construction. The first, which is currently out of favour, although it made a brief reappearance in *Commercial Plastics Ltd v Vincent*, is the literal approach. The second, which received heavy support in *Littlewoods Organisation Ltd v Harris* [1978] 1 All E.R. 1026, holds that the object and intent of the whole contract should be found and that the specific restraint should be construed in its light. The problem with a literal approach is that it has frequently been used to persuade a court that wholly unlikely consequences might arise and that the court should, in the light of those consequences conclude that the restraint is unreasonable. On the whole, the champions of the literal approach have been the party attempting to strike down a particular clause whilst the object and intent approach tends to favour parties who are attempting to uphold the restraint. In our view, particularly because of the extravagant results that have arisen in some cases by applying the literal rule, there can be no doubt that in the modern context the object and intent rule is much fairer. The object and intent approach really has its basis in the reaction of the courts against the *reductio ad absurdum* type of argument put forward by counsel on behalf of defendants. In *Rannie v Irvine* (1844) 7 Man. & G. 969 Tindal C.J. said "if the contract is reasonable at the time it is entered into, we are not bound to look out for improbable and extravagant contingencies in order to make it void". In *S. Nevanas & Co Ltd v Walker & Foreman* [1914] 1 Ch. 413 Sargant J. said "The covenant has not been held bad because it might work unreasonably in certain exceptional circumstances not within its main and principal purpose and meaning".

Other cases which have consistently championed the object and intent approach are *Mills v Dunham* [1891] 1 Ch. 576, *Moenich v Fenestre* (1892) 61 L.J. Ch. 737, *Underwood (E) & Son Ltd v Barker* [1899] 1 Ch. 300, *Haynes v Doman* [1899] 2 Ch. 13, and *Caribonum Co Ltd v Le Couch* (1913) 109 L.T. 385 in which Eve J. used the object and intent approach in order to construe a business secrets clause.

More recent cases such as *Home Counties Dairies Ltd v Skilton* [1970] 1 W.L.R. 526 and *GW Plowman & Son Ltd v Ash* [1964] 1 W.L.R. 568 show the sense of the approach. In *Plowman's* case it was argued that on its true construction the restrictive covenant was too wide as it applied to goods of all kinds and would prevent canvassing by the employee in articles of trade of any kind. Harman L.J. agreed that no specification had been expressed but in applying the object and intent test he said:

> . . . one must regard the contract as a whole, and this is a contract where a sales representative in South Lincolnshire serving a firm which, as appears from the very clause in question . . . is a corn and agricultural merchant and animal feeding stuffs manufacturer. In my opinion it is no wider than that: the articles in which he may not canvass are the very articles in respect of which his employer employed him.

See also *Marion White Ltd v Francis* [1972] 1 W.L.R. 1423; *Business Seating (Renovations) Ltd v Broad* [1989] I.C.R. 729 in which Millett J. followed *Plowman* and *Arbuthnot Fund Managers Ltd v Rawlings* [2003] EWCA Civ

518, Chadwick L.J., setting out the approach to be adopted in construing the restrictions at the interlocutory stage of the proceedings. The court must steer a course between giving to the clause a meaning which is extravagantly wide; and giving to the clause a meaning which is artificially limited. The task of the court, in constructing the contractual term is simply to ask itself: "What did these parties intend by the bargain which they made in the circumstances in which they made it?" (*per* Chadwick L. J.). Also, in terms of the intention on the terms of the parties, *per* Cox L. J. in *TFS Derivatives Ltd. v Morgan* [2005] I.R.L.R. 246, QBD,

> If, having examined the restrictive covenant in the context of the relevant factual matrix, the court concludes that there is an element of ambiguity and that there are two possible constructions of the covenant, one of which would lead to a conclusion that it was in unreasonable restraint of trade and unlawful, but the other would lead to the opposite result, then the court should adopt the latter construction on the basis that the parties are to be deemed to have intended their bargain to be lawful and not to offend against the public interest.

In *Hanover Insurance Brokers Ltd v Shapiro* [1994] I.R.L.R. 92 it was properly conceded by the defendants' counsel that the business in that phrase "canvas, solicit or endeavour to take away the business" must refer to the business of insurance brokereage i.e. that business in which the defendants were employed and did not encompass any other business which a subsidiary of the plaintiff might carry on.

In *Littlewoods Organisation Ltd v Harris* Lord Denning M.R. said that by construing a restriction according to the object and intent rule the courts refuse to hold a convenant bad merely because of unskilful drafting and will cut it down so as to reveal its essential reasonableness. However he said that the courts will only do so if the covenant is "intrinsically just and reasonable". Therefore it would seem on this approach that the court first has to decide whether the covenant is intrinsically just and reasonable before it applies the object and intent test. In practice this may be a very difficult exercise to undertake because in order to decide what is intrinsically just and reasonable the court will surely have to apply some rule of construction. However Lord Denning M.R. also put forward an alternative test. This applies when the words are so wide that on a strict construction they cover improbable and unlikely events. In such cases the court should not apply the strict construction so far as to make the whole clause void or invalid or unenforceable. All that should be done is that, if that improbable and unlikely event ever takes place, the courts should decline to enforce the clause. He then construed the words in a restrictive covenant which prevented the defendant from working for Great Universal Stores (GUS) or any of its subsidiaries. The clause read:

> In the event of the determination of this Agreement for any reason whatsoever [Harris] shall not at any time within 12 months after such determination: (i) enter into a Contract of Service or other Agreement of a like nature with GUS Ltd or any

> company subsidiary thereto or be directly or indirectly engaged concerned or interested in the trading or business of the said GUS Ltd or any such company aforesaid . . .

The defendant was proposing to work for the mail order subsidiary of GUS Ltd. Did the inclusion of "subsidiary" invalidate the restrictive covenant as it was accepted that many subsidiaries did not deal in the mail order business (one was a restaurant in Alice Springs)? He concluded that it was proper to look at the GUS group as a single entity. Therefore it was fair for the provision to cover subsidiaries as well. As the group was under one unified control it was possible for an employee to be moved around within the group or at least have "his information and knowledge" so transferred making it important that Littlewoods should have protection regarding the whole GUS group. If they did not and Harris had been free to work for a GUS company which was not in the mail order business he could still have passed Littlewoods' business secrets back to the mail order companies because of the structure of the GUS group. *Beckett Investment Management Group Ltd. v Glyn Hall* [2007] EWCA Civ 613 is a recent example of the Court of Appeal adopting a similar object and intent approach but construing a covenant expressed to be only in favour of the employment parent company (that did not undertake the business activities to which the covenant related) as extending to include subsidiaries (that did).

The next point which posed a problem in *Littlewoods* was that the clause was unlimited in geographical area; the business of Littlewoods being solely within the UK whereas the businesses of the GUS group were worldwide. Lord Denning decided that if the clause was limited by its perceived object it applied only to such part of the GUS group as operated within the UK. It was therefore reasonable on this basis. The final point was that the only business of Littlewoods which could reasonably require protection was their mail order business and not their retail chain store business. However, the clause did not make this clear. Lord Denning said that it should be limited to the mail order business only because Harris' contract was at all relevant times with the mail order part of Littlewoods' business. The problem with this reasoning is that it comes very close to construing a clause to the extent that the plaintiffs seek to enforce it rather than as it stands. This approach was specifically rejected in *Gledhow* by Sellers L.J. and it is submitted that he was right to do so.

Megaw L.J. agreed with Denning M.R. but Browne L.J. dissented: he said that the majority were effectively remaking the contract which was something which the court was not entitled to do. It is respectfully submitted that there is a great deal to be said for Browne L.J.'s view. On the majority view the defendant was actually left free to work for a subsidiary of GUS which was not involved in the mail order business in the United Kingdom even though that would have been in clear breach of the restriction. The approach of the majority seems to have been that even if such a breach had occurred the courts would have refused to acknowledge that it existed. It is respectfully submitted that the views of Browne L.J. in *Littlewoods* case are to be preferred and that the approach of the majority is an extreme example of the object and intent approach which should not be followed but see *Beckett*.

In his judgment Lord Denning M.R. was highly critical of the decision in *Commercial Plastics Ltd v Vincent* because the agreement there was just and made in good faith and, as both he and Megaw L.J. pointed out, a number of important authorities which supported the object and intent approach had not been cited to the court. In that case the Court of Appeal was very much attracted by a *reductio* argument put forward on behalf of the defendant. However they decided the case on another basis and Pearson L.J. said:

> it may be said in answer to the possibility of such a *reductio ad absurdum*, though no doubt, it has to be taken into account, is far from conclusive, because it may involve unlikely hypotheses, which would be outside the reasonable expectations of the parties at the time of the making of the contract of employment.

This is correct though we doubt if a *reductio* has to be taken into account and prefer the approach of non-fanciful construction which has been reaffirmed in *Home Counties Dairies v Skilton* (see above p.33). This seems to chart a safe course between the extremes of *Littlewoods* on the one hand, and *Commercial Plastics* on the other. It is submitted that a number of cases which in the past applied the literal rule would now be decided in the opposite way. However in *J A Mont (UK) Ltd v Mills* [1993] I.R.L.R. 172, CA Laws J. at first instance went too far in adopting an approach to construction which even Lord Denning would have rejected. His approach was rejected by the Court of Appeal.

The literal appoach to construction has been most consistently and, it is submitted, most erroneously applied in a line of cases concerning general medical practitioners. In *Routh v Jones* [1947] 1 All E.R. 758 the Court of Appeal held that a restraint on a medical assistant to a partnership which prevented him from practising "in any department of medicine, surgery or midwifery (or accepting) any professional appointment" was unreasonable because it covered, inter alia, practice as a consultant or medical officer of health. There were other good reasons for not enforcing the covenant—length of time and its geographical scope, instead of resorting to an unconvincing analysis of the contrast between the legitimate interest of the plaintiffs and the width of the restraint as construed on a literal basis.

Routh v Jones was followed by Romer J. in *Jenkins v Reid* [1948] 1 All E.R. 471 in which a restraint on a medical assistant to an ordinary country general medical practice was struck down because, as it prevented practice as "a physician, surgeon or apothecary", the plaintiff would be unable to practice as a consultant in the geographical area covered by the restraint. Once again there were other reasons for not enforcing the covenant which did not involve taking an unrealistic and literal approach to the activities restrained. A similar approach was taken in *Lyne-Pirkis v Jones* [1969] 1 W.L.R. 1293 and in *Peyton v Mindham* [1972] 1 W.L.R. 8.

Since then the Court of Appeal has changed its approach to construction in cases involving general medical practitioners: see *Clarke v Newland* [1991] 1 All E.R. 397. The case is important because the Court of Appeal considered in some detail the way in which a restraint of trade clause should be construed. The parties were partners in a general medical practice in central London. The plaintiff was the senior partner and the defendant the junior partner. Clause 15 of the partnership agreement stated: "in the event of a partnership being [so determined] the salaried partner undertakes not to practice within the practice area . . .", the practice area being defined. At first instance the judge, in refusing the injunction, decided that he was bound by the decision in *Lyne-Pirkis v Jones* and the plaintiff appealed. The case for the plaintiff was argued on four bases:

(a) The verb "practice" in the relevant clause had to be construed in the context of the agreement as a whole and in the proper factual matrix. In particular the attention of the court was drawn to clause 1 of the agreement which referred to the practice carried on by the parties as a "practice of general medical practitioners".

(b) The agreement had to be given a purposive construction.

(c) If so construed the word "practice" plainly meant practice as a general medical practitioner. It was not a question of implying a term but giving the proper construction to the relevant word.

(d) The decision in *Lyne-Pirkis v Jones* and the decision of the Court of Appeal in *Routh v Jones* were clearly distinguishable. In both those cases the express words used and the relevant clause could be compared with other express words used elsewhere.

On behalf of the defendant it was argued that some limitation had to be placed on the word "practice" and the natural and proper limitation was to imply the words "as medical practitioners". There was no warrant for implying the more restrictive limitation "as general medical practitioners". Both the plaintiff and defendant were free to practice either as doctors in a hospital or as medical consultants. In approaching this case the court first stated that there were many cases where a court has to construe a standard clause in, for example, a charter party, and there may be some earlier decisions on the same clause or on a clause which is in terms which are indistinguishable. In some of these cases the earlier decision would be a binding authority and it would have to be followed. In other cases in this category the earlier case, though not formally binding, was often followed in order to provide certainty and consistency in an area where commercial relations may depend on an accepted construction. In the present case however the court was not concerned with a standard clause and therefore it decided its approach should be different. The court was satisfied that the right approach was to try to reach a conclusion on a proper construction of the relevant clause before turning to any other cases where similar clauses had been used. Having reviewed the authorities which dealt with the construction of restraint of trade clauses, the court applied the following rules:

(a) The question of construction should be approached in the first instance without regard to the question of legality or illegality.

(b) The clause should be construed with reference to the object sought to be obtained.

(c) In restraint of trade cases the object is the protection of one of the partners against rivalry in trade.

(d) That the clause should be construed in context in the light of the factual matrix at the time when the agreement was made.

Applying those rules to the facts of this case the Court of Appeal decided that the word "practice" in the partnership agreement clearly meant practice as a general medical practitioner and did not mean anything wider. *Lyne-Pirkis v Jones* was distinguished on the basis that in that case there was an express antithesis between the phrase "as general medical practitioners" in a recital and "as a medical practitioner" in the relevant clause. What this case clearly shows is that one has to be very careful in assuming that in restraint of trade cases a phrase ascribed a meaning in one case will also be given the same meaning in another.

In *Business Seating (Renovations) Ltd v Broad* [1989] I.C.R. 729 it was claimed by the defendant that a non-solicitation covenant was void because the business not to be solicited was not defined. Millett J. had to deal with the argument that it would be a breach of the covenant if the defendant were, during the remainder of the period of restraint, to solicit any business of any kind from any company which happened to have been a customer of the plaintiff company during the relevant period. It was said that if the defendant took employment as a milk roundsman he would not be able to solicit orders for milk from any of the customers who had had their chairs renovated by the plaintiff company. The judge pointed out that another clause in the contract of employment expressly described the prohibited business: it was clearly restricted to repairing or renovation of office furniture and commercial seating. The evidence before the judge also showed that that was the nature of the plaintiff's business. The defendant was employed as a sales representative who sold the service of renovating and repairing office furniture and commercial seating and the judge correctly decided that that must be the business which was referred to by the restraint of trade clause.

In *Rex Stewart etc. v Parker* [1988] I.R.L.R. 483 the court was asked to consider a non-solicitation clause which related to any person ". . . who to your knowledge is or has been during the period of your employment a customer of the company . . .". It was successfully argued that the phrase "is or" could only relate to a customer when the soliciting is taking place. Accordingly it would catch persons who may not have been customers of the plaintiff at the time when the defendant left his employment but who had become customers subsequently. This is a clear example of inept drafting. The phrase should simply have said "was". The crucial topic of construction has been examined recently in *J A Mont (UK) Ltd v Mills* [1993] I.R.L.R. 172 in which the Court of Appeal had to consider a restrictive covenant in a severance agreement. Under that agreement the defendant's employment was terminated and he was paid the equivalent of a year's emoluments without discount for accelerated receipt, was released from any obligation to work for the plaintiff during that year but was, inter alia, required to abide by a restriction which stated:

> This total payment is made on condition that you do not join another company in the tissue industry within one year of leaving our employment.

The judge at first instance (Laws J.) had approached the clause in what can only be described as an extraordinary manner. Basically he was prepared to "cut down" the clause so as to make it reasonable. Such an approach is contrary to all authority and was inevitably rejected by the Court of Appeal. On appeal the defendant argued that the clause was too wide as it operated without geographical limit and because it prevented him from working in any capacity in any sector of the tissue industry (in which he had been employed for all his working life). The plaintiff sensibly did not seek to support the judge's approach to the case but did argue that the clause was reasonable on three bases. The first basis was that of purposive construction. This was rejected by the Court of Appeal which pointed out that in the authorities on which the plaintiff relied (*Haynes*, *Plowman*, *Home Counties Dairies* and *Littlewoods*) there was an attempt to formulate the covenant so as to focus upon the particular restraint necessary to guard against the defendant's possible misuse of confidential information. However, no such attempt had been made here. Moreover, it was pointed out by Simon Brown L.J. that if the plaintiff's approach were correct there would be no incentive for employers ever to impose restraints in appropriate and limited terms with the effect that the employee would be put in an impossible position of uncertainty. The second basis (which concerned "whittling down" the covenant) was founded on four arguments:

(1) In "garden leave" cases (cases, that is, where employers do not require their employee to attend for work but remunerate him fully to a given date provided that he does not work for anyone else), the courts recognise a continuing obligation of good faith on the employee and are prepared to grant injunctive relief to prevent him working for a trade rival, if necessary narrowing the scope of a contractual embargo to do so.

(2) Whilst in "garden leave" cases the employer/employee relationship is continuing, following a severance agreement the question of whether or not the employment contract has actually been terminated may be a

highly technical one, and in any event should not, as a matter of principle, govern whether the employee (or ex-employee) continues to owe an implied duty of good faith.

(3) Here the defendant has at his own request been paid in advance for the full year of his notice and yet, subject only to the covenant, been given his freedom. The plaintiffs should not be in a worse position than if they had kept the contract alive and insisted upon the defendant honouring his obligations not merely of confidentiality, but of good faith and loyalty too.

(4) The object of restraint of trade law has been to strike a balance between the employers' legitimate interest in safeguarding their secrets and the employee's need to earn a living. Where, as here, the employee's financial interests have been secured over the period of restraint, the balance shifts and the law should be the readier to underpin the continuing duty of confidentiality by enforcing restraint of trade covenants, albeit only to the extent necessary to prevent the employee working for trade rivals.

The court rejected each argument. It said that the primary basis for the first two points was a misunderstanding of the judgment in *Provident Financial Group plc v Hayward* [1989] I.R.L.R. 84, a leading case on "garden leave" (see para.23.10), and that it is crucial to that decision that the court there was concerned with the duty of good faith owed by an employee *during* employment and not with the more limited duties owed by him once employment had terminated.

The third point was based on a factual mistake: if the employers had chosen to seek to put the defendant on garden leave or provided him with inadequate work he could have treated that as constructive dismissal and brought the contract to an end. In any event the employers had chosen not to take that course. The fourth point was rejected on the ground that public policy demands not merely that an employee receives a financial benefit but also that he is able to make proper use of his skills and that competition exists. If the plaintiffs were correct an employer would always be able to purchase the right to stifle competition.

Finally, there are five general points. The first is that in cases of doubt the courts will construe the restriction *contra proferentes*. Secondly, it seems that the courts construe business sale covenants more liberally than restraints of trade in employment contracts and do so in an effort to make business sale covenants more easily enforceable: *Ronbar Enterprises Ltd v Green* [1954] 1 W.L.R. 815. Thirdly, it is of fundamental importance in a few cases to consider whether the covenant is too vague to be enforced or void for uncertainty. This is a general ground for striking down a covenant. See *Davies v Davies* (1887) 36 Ch. D. 359 where a covenant which sought to restrain trade "so far as the law allows" was found to be too uncertain to be enforced. Vagueness was resorted to by the judge in *Jenkins v Reid* in order to explain why a reformulation of a clause was unacceptable and in *Gledhow Autoparts Ltd v Delaney* [1965] 1 W.L.R. 1366 Danckwerts L.J. criticised the phrase "districts in which the traveller had operated" as being too vague especially as instructions given as to where he should work were purely oral. Fourthly, it was pointed out sensibly in *Littlewoods* by both Lord Denning M.R. and Megaw L.J. that a clause made *inter rusticos* (i.e. without legal help on either side) can be properly construed in the light of the way in which both parties thought it would be likely to be interpreted. See also *Normalec Ltd v Britton* [1983] F.S.R. 318. A similar approach is permissible where the covenant suffers "a mere hint of accuracy of expression" (*per* Sir Nathaniel Lindty M.R. in *Haynes v Doman* [1899] 2 Ch. 13, CA). Fifthly, amongst practitioners and indeed judges, there persists a fallacious view that a clause can be cut down by the court in order to render it reasonable. Quite simply this is not the case. Conceptual confusion has been caused by a misreading of the judgments in *Provident Financial Group plc v Hayward* [1989] I.R.L.R. 84. There, Dillon L.J. said:

> But counsel for the defendant persists that the negative term that is actually enforced must be expressed in the agreement; it is not possible to have a wide term in the agreement which the court will whittle down so as to enforce as much of it as the court thinks right. Of course that is correct when you have in the service agreement a contract restraining the employee after termination of his agreement from operating in a particular line of activity within a specified geographical area or over a prohibited period of restriction. If it is held that the area that has been chosen by the employer or the period of restriction are too wide or too long, the court will reject the whole clause as void and will not enforce whatever maximum shorter or smaller field of restriction the court thinks would have been permissible if the parties had made such an agreement.
>
> But that, as I see it, is not the case. The negative clause here not to work for anyone else during the term of the contract of service is a common form clause which has often been held to be valid. The question is whether it should be enforced in particular circumstances by injunction. The lesser form of relief suggested, not to work during the continuance of the service agreement for specified rivals or rivals generally, if there were no express contract not to do so in the service agreement, could still be restrained as a breach of the employee's obligation of good faith, as appears from the decision of this Court in *Hivac Ltd v Park Royal Scientific Instruments Ltd* [1946] Ch. 169 . . .

Taylor L.J. put it thus:

> In my view, the Court has power to grant an injunction and, if necessary, to narrow the scope of the contractual embargo. It would be undesirable to hedge the Court's power in this field by imposing the highly technical drafting requirements contended for by [counsel for the defendant].

It is important to remember that that case was discussing a clause which sought to restrain the employee from working for anyone else *during the period of employment*. Even if such a clause had not existed the law would have implied a restraint in recognition of the employee's general duty of fidelity to his employer; similarly if the clause had been drafted too widely. Subject to two qualifications it can be stated that *Provident* is the authority for the proposition that if, in a contract of employment, there is an express covenant by the employee not to work for anybody else during the continuance of his employment which is so worded as to be unreasonably wide, an injunction in restricted and therefore reasonable terms may nevertheless be granted to enforce the employee's implied obligation of fidelity during the duration of his employment (see *J A Mont (UK) Ltd v Mills* [1993] I.R.L.R. 172, *per* Glidewell L.J.).

Those two qualifications come in the form of the decisions in *William Hill v Tucker* [1998] I.R.L.R. 313, CA, and *Symbian Ltd v Christensen* [2001] I.R.L.R. 77, CA.

William Hill concerned a senior dealer who managed the spread betting business conducted by his employer. He was subject to a six month notice period. There was no express garden leave provision in the contract of employment. When the employee gave one month's notice of termination of employment, the employer sought to retain him for the duration of his notice period on the basis that he would not be required to work during the notice period and would continue to be paid in full. Morritt L.J., giving the judgment of the Court of Appeal was of the view that there was no inherent "right to work" but whether there was an implied right to impose garden leave depended upon the terms of the contract and, in this particular case, based upon its facts, there was no such right, with the consequence that an injunction would not be granted restraining Mr Tucker from joining a competitor until the end of his notice period. The factors which were taken into account were (a) the post of senior dealer which he held was specific and unique, (b) the skills necessary for the performance of his duties required frequent exercise and (c) his contract contained an express right of suspension in certain circumstances which was unnecessary if there were an implied right to place him on garden leave. Accordingly, unless there is an express garden leave provision in a contract of employment, there is no certainty that one would be imposed in any particular case.

In *Symbian*, Scott V.C., at first instance, was of the view that imposing garden leave destroyed the employment relationship (although not the contract) and that the implied duty of good faith did not survive during the garden leave period as a consequence with the result that a garden leave injunction could not be based on the implied duty of good faith. In that particular case, however, there was a provision commonly found in contracts of employment to the effect that, during the term of the contract of employment, Mr Christensen would not "be directly or indirectly engaged or concerned or interested in any capacity in any trade, business or occupation whatsoever other than the business of the group whether or not competing in any material respect with the business" and, on this basis, an injunction was granted restraining him from joining his new employer during the garden leave period. On appeal, the Court of Appeal did not deal with Scott V.C.'s statements concerning garden leave and the duty of good faith, although counsel for

Mr Christensen "confessed to some difficulty" in seeking to justify that part of Scott V.C.'s judgment in his client's favour. There seems to be considerable tension between Scott V.C.'s dicta and the Court of Appeal's decision in *Provident*, and it is submitted that the latter is to preferred.

Interestingly, Cox L. J. in *TFS Derivatives Ltd. v Morgan* [2005] I.R.L.R. 246, QBD, in the context of responding to a suggestion that a non-compete covenant should not be upheld because it was contended that it was more appropriate for the employer in that case to employ a garden leave provision, expressed the view that it might constitute a breach of the implied term of trust and confidence if the employee were to be placed (on the facts of that case) on six months' garden leave, irrespective that this would be on the basis of an express contractual right on the part of the employer to do so. In practice, it is submitted, it will depend on the facts of each particular case and, in particular, the employer's reasons (and therefore justification) in seeking to impose a particular period of garden leave; essentially, is the employer protecting a legitimate interest?

3.4 Words and phrases

Common words and phrases found in restrictive covenants include the following.

3.4.1 "Soliciting or canvassing"

These words are synonymous and involve an approach from the covenantee to a customer/potential customer of the covenantor with a view to appropriate his custom for himself. The approach can be a meeting or a letter etc. It must involve some direct or targeted behaviour. To advertise generally would probably not be an act of solicitation although to advertise to a small specific audience which includes the customer of the covenantor could well be, see further the judgment of Lord Herschell in *Trego v Hunt* [1896] A.C. 7 which is quoted on this topic at para.11.1 below. It is submitted that his approach is a sensible one and although stated in a case concerning a business sale it is also applicable to employees.

It is clear that it is not solicitation for the covenantee to react favourably to an approach from the customer. If business is done between them that amounts to "dealing" and must be specifically referred to in the covenant if the covenantor is to prevent its continuance or obtain damages for it. "If they do not themselves or by their agents make the approach they are not canvassing or soliciting the person in question" (Dillon L.J. in *Hanover Insurance Brokers Ltd v Shapiro* [1994] I.R.L.R. 82, CA). See also the approach of Vinelott J. in *Austin Knight (UK) Ltd v Hinds* [1994] F.S.R. 52 and additionally *Ward Evans Financial Services Ltd v Fox* [2002] I.R.L.R. 120, CA.

In *Allied Dunbar (Frank Weisinger) Ltd v Frank Weisinger* [1988] I.R.L.R. 60 Millett J. when discussing a clause which prevented soliciting (but not dealing) appeared to give judicial approval to the defendant's understanding that the clause prevented him approaching a client on a secret or confidential basis and telling him that "he can still advise him but only if the client makes the approach".

3.4.2 "Deal with/do business with"

These phrases are clearly of wider ambit than "canvass/solicit". They would prevent the covenantor from responding to any approach to him by a client.

3.4.3 "Endeavour to take or entice away"

It is perhaps difficult to see how this phrase can have a wider meaning than "canvass/solicit" especially as the latter words are usually prefaced by the words "directly or indirectly". In *Hanover Insurance Brokers Ltd v Shapiro* [1994] I.R.L.R. 82, CA the defendants argued that the words "or endeavour to take away" were too uncertain to have any meaning or that they equated to the words which preceded them, viz "canvass/solicit". At first instance Latham J. said that "endeavouring to take away" connotes positive action which may not constitute direct persuasion of the client but nonetheless constitutes a positive act to produce that result, which might otherwise, in the hands of a clever lawyer, be capable of being described as something other than soliciting or canvassing. Dillon L.J. disagreed with that approach. He asked whether the defendants would be endeavouring to take away the plaintiff's business if the client made the approach to them and they responded favourably or even enthusiastically and business was then done on terms which undercut the plaintiff. Our answer to that question would be unequivocal; if the plaintiff had desired to achieve that result it could have done so by using "dealt with" or any similar common phrase. The matter was resolved by the plaintiff's counsel stating that the words were only intended to prevent active seeking out of its clients. That seems to us to mean "canvassing" (a word which was already part of the order) but curiously both Court of Appeal judges accepted what was said and allowed the phrase to stand, Nolan L.J. stating that the words might cover an advertisement, depending on its content and nature.

In *Austin Knight (UK) Ltd v Hind* [1994] F.S.R. 52, the court had to examine a clause which sought to restrain the defendant from soliciting, interfering with or endeavouring to entice away certain customers of the plaintiff. It was argued on behalf of the plaintiff that by submitting an offer or making a presentation to a former customer, even one who had approached the defendant or her new employers, or who had put out work for tender, this amounted to soliciting or endeavouring to entice away that customer. Vinelott J. rejected that submission. He stated:

> That is not I think, comprehended in the usual meaning of soliciting, and as regards endeavouring to entice a customer away, if [the plaintiff's] submission were well founded the covenant would amount to a covenant not to deal with customers of [the plaintiff], even customers with whom [the defendant] had never dealt while an employee of [the plaintiff] and with whose relationship with [the plaintiff] she was wholly unaware. On that construction the covenant would amount in substance to a contract without territorial limit not to take employment in the field in which she had been previously employed and would plainly be an unreasonable restraint.

In *Hydra plc v Anastasi* [2005] EWHC 1559, the court, in the context of considering an obligation not to solicit or entice away any employee of the company, after considering *Hanover* and *Austin Knight* accepted that the appropriate synonyms for "entice" were "tempt, lure, persuade, inveigle" again connoting positive action.

See also Chapter 9.

3.5 Severance

There are two different uses of the word severance.

The first concerns whether the offending covenant can be cut out altogether from the contract—leaving an entire contract behind: see *Alec Lobb Garages Ltd v Total Oil (Great Britain) Ltd* [1985] 1 All E.R. 303 and *Stenhouse Australia Ltd v Phillips* [1974] A.C. 391. Thus, in some cases where the covenant is all, or substantially all, the consideration, a consequence of a finding of unreasonableness is to strike down the whole contract. However, even if the covenantee would not have entered the agreement without the covenant, the contract may not be invalidated as a whole if there is consideration independent of the covenant: see *Vancouver Malt & Sake Brewing Co Ltd v Vancouver Breweries Ltd* [1934] A.C. 181 and *Amoco Australia Pty Ltd v Rocca Bros Motor Engineering Co Pty Ltd* [1975] A.C. 561. The ultimate question for the court is whether the absence of the covenant changes the contract in character from the original.

The second approach is to consider whether an objectionable part of a covenant can be severed so as to leave an enforceable obligation. This is the approach most commonly discussed in restraint of trade cases.

Severance of the constituent parts of a restraint, if more than one part exists, can often be critical. The availability of severance frequently has a direct effect on whether the court considers the clause to be reasonable. A party seeking to enforce the clause which has been attacked as being an unreasonable restraint of trade will usually argue in the first place that the restriction as a whole is reasonable and secondly that any part which is unreasonable can be severed (by applying that "blue pencil") thereby leaving only the reasonable part which should be enforced. It is therefore important to know when severance is available. There appear to be two distinct approaches. The first, which is much more liberal, is most frequently found in business sales cases. This strains to make severance available in order to enforce the restraint. The second approach is much more strict and applies predominantly in employment cases.

In *Attwood v Lamont* [1920] 3 K.B. 571 it was said by Lord Sterndale M.R. ". . . a contract can be severed if the severed parts are independent from one another and can be severed without the severance affecting the meaning of the part remaining". Younger L.J. said that severance was only permissible where the covenant is not really a single covenant but is in effect a combination of several distinct covenants. It is submitted that this is the strict and correct approach to severance. Earlier authority for it is found in *Mills v Dunham* [1891] 1 Ch. 576. It was applied in *Commercial Plastics Ltd v Vincent* [1965] 1 Q.B. 623 where it was said that as the provision was a single one and could not correctly be divisible into two or more parts severance could not take place. However, in *Ronbar Enterprises Ltd v Green* [1954] 1 W.L.R. 815, Jenkins L.J., having reviewed some earlier business sale cases in which severance had taken place viz *Goldsoll v Goldman* [1914] 2 Ch. 603 and *British Reinforced Concrete Engineering Co Ltd v Schelff* [1921] 2 Ch. 563, said that *Attwood v Lamont* could be distinguished because it concerned an employment contract. This distinction has been criticised subsequently in *T Lucas and Co Ltd v Mitchell* [1974] Ch. 129. The court struck down an area restraint on dealing by an employee but severed that from a restraint on soliciting and supplying. The court held that there were two relevant questions: is there in reality more than one restraint? If so, is the excision of the unenforceable part capable of being achieved without other addition or modification? It rejected the majority view in *Attwood* that, in employment cases, there existed a third consideration viz: it is for the court to decide in its discretion whether or not to treat the two restraints as separate or not. It may have been this subjective judicial approach which led to the strange result in *Attwood*.

However, whichever approach is applied, it is quite clear that whether severance is available is entirely dependent on the facts of the case. A very good example of what cannot be achieved by severance is found in *Baker v Hedgecock* (1888) L.R. 39 Ch. D. 520. In that case there was an agreement by the defendant with his employer, a tailor, not to carry on "any business whatsoever" for a period of two years within a certain area. The employee set up as a tailor within the relevant area within two years of leaving his employment. It was held that the agreement was void and that effect could not be given to it by rejecting the general restraint which appeared in it and limiting the agreement for the purposes of the action to carrying on the business of a tailor.

For a more recent example of a case dealing with severance see *Business Seating (Renovations) Ltd v Broad* [1989] I.C.R. 713 the facts of which are set out at para.8.5.2 below. There Millett J., having held that the part of a non-solicitation clause which gave protection to the plaintiff was valid but that the part which sought to give protection to an associated company of the plaintiff was invalid, had then to decide whether the invalid part could be severed or whether the whole clause was invalid. He concluded that in this case there were two companies each with its own separate and distinct business and each with its own customers although many of the customers were common to both. He said that although there was a single clause there were in effect two separate covenants each taken with the plaintiff but for the protection of the respective business of each company. He decided that there was not only no difficulty grammatically in severing the two covenants but that severance left entirely unaffected the covenant which related to the customers of the plaintiff company itself. Accordingly he severed the invalid part from the valid part and granted an injunction based on the latter. See also *Rex Stewart of Jeffries Parker Ginsberg Ltd v Parker* [1988] I.R.L.R. 483 in which that part of a clause which related to "associated companies" was severed; *TFS Derivatives Ltd. v Morgan* [2005] I.R.L.R. 246, QBD, where the words "or similar to" were "blue pencilled" from a covenant not to "undertake, carry on or be employed, engaged or interested in any capacity in either any business which is competitive with or similar to a relevant business within the territory . . ." following *Sadler* and *Marshall* below and *Beckett Investment Management Group Ltd. v Glyn Hall* [2007] EWCA Civ 613 where Maurice Kay L.J., giving the principal judgment, followed *Attwood* and *Sadler* and severed more than half of an extensive definition of "relevant client" that deemed certain parties to be clients but who were not.

The question of the availability of severance was crucial in the case of *Sadler v Imperial Life Assurance Co of Canada Ltd* [1988] I.R.L.R. 388, the facts of which are set out at para.3.1.1 of this chapter. In that case the judge found that a proviso to a clause dealing with the payment of post-termination commission to an insurance agent was an indirect and unreasonable restraint of trade. The former employee, who was the plaintiff and who sued for the payment to him of commission under the first part of the clause argued that the proviso could be severed and that therefore the obligation of the defendants to pay him such sums remained. The defendants argued that the proviso could not be severed and that as it had been found to be an unreasonable restraint of trade the whole of the clause was void. The judge having reviewed the relevant authorities said that a contract which contains an unenforceable provision nevertheless remains effective after removal of the severance of that provision if the following conditions are satisfied:

(a) The unenforceable provision is capable of being removed without the necessity of adding to or modifying the wording of what remains.

(b) The remaining terms continue to be supported by adequate consideration.

(c) The removal of the unenforceable provision does not so change the character of the contract that it becomes "not the sort of contract that the parties entered into at all".

He concluded that all three conditions were satisfied in this case and gave judgment for the plaintiff. See also *Marshall v NM Financial Management Ltd* [1996] I.R.L.R. 20, Ch D [1997] I.R.L.R. 449, CA in which the approach in *Sadler* was followed but an addition of a fourth condition made at first instance viz the severance must be consistent with the public policy underlying the avoidance of the offending term.

In *D v M* [1996] I.R.L.R. 192, Laws J., having considered the main authorities on severance, concluded that in a case in which no separate and distinct covenants exist, severance could only occur if the part sought to be severed is "of trivial importance or merely technical" (Lord Moulton's words in *Mason v Provident Clothing and Supply Co Ltd* [1913] A.C. 724).

Finally, under the Treaty of Rome, if Art.81(1) applies, then only the relevant clauses are automatically void; the remainder of the contract is severable: see *La Technique Minière* [1966] E.C.R. 235. Whether, in fact, the whole contract is void is a matter for national law. See *Société de Vente de Ciments et Bétons de l'Est SA v Kerpen and Kerpen GmbH* (Case 319/82) [1985] 1 C.M.L.R. 511 (see further para.22.2.1). The same would apply to restrictions caught by the Chapter I prohibition of the Competition Act 1998. However, note that typically an exclusivity provision in a distribution contract is likely to be considered an intrinsic part of the commercial agreement, and if void under Article 81(2)/Chapter 1, it is likely not to be severable (see *Days Medical Aids v Pihsiang, Machinery Manufacturing Co Ltd and Others* [2004] EW HC44 and also *James E McCabe v Scottish Courage* [2006] EWHC 538, (QBD(comm)), where the non-compete obligation was 'part and parcel of the exclusive right and duty to purchase the beer and directly connected with the exclusivity granted'.

3.6 Assignment

There is no doubt that the benefit of a restrictive covenant can be assigned in accordance with normal contractual rules. It most frequently happens in the employment context after the first employer has sold his business. *Wessex Dairies Ltd v Smith* [1935] 2 K.B. 80 is an example of such a case, though there the plaintiffs sued as equitable assignees as the agreement to assign had not been executed. See also *Dairy Crest Ltd v Piggott* [1989] I.C.R. 92, CA and *Morris Angel & Son Ltd v Hollande* [1993] I.R.L.R. 169, CA, (in which it was held that a restrictive covenant applicable to a business forming an undertaking that transferred under the Transfer of Undertakings (Protection of Employment) Regulations 1981 continued to be enforceable by the transferee of the undertaking but in respect of the business forming the undertaking transferred rather than the transferee's wider business). This was a consequence of Reg.5(1) of the 1981 Regulations transferring all the transferors' rights, powers, duties and liabilities under or in connection with any contract of employment of a transferring employee (now Reg.4(2) of the Transfer of

Undertakings (Protection of Employment) Regulations 2006) and therefore more in the nature of a statutory novation. The plaintiffs were able to enforce the covenant. In contrast an attempt to introduce a new covenant (supported by new consideration) at the time of a transfer of a business to which the Regulations applied was ineffective and the covenant unenforceable in that a variation in terms and conditions of employment for a reason connected with a transfer is unenforceable *Credit Suisse First Boston (Europe) Ltd v Lister* [1998] I.R.L.R. 700, CA. TUPE can also give rise to problems of construction when a contract of employment with a pre-existing covenant transfers under the regulations (for example in terms of what constitutes the business which is protected). See *Morris Angel & Son Ltd v Hollande* above.

In business sales cases the assignment of the benefit of a restrictive covenant is usual upon a sale of goodwill and will be implied if not excluded: *Townsend v Jarman* [1900] 2 Ch. 698. What if there is no express covenant on a business sale and X purchases the business from Y and eventually sells it to Z? Can Y, the original vendor, then solicit or canvass customers of his old business? There is no doubt that there is an implied restraint as between Y and X and between X and Z and it would equally seem that the benefit of the implied covenant between Y and X would pass to Z upon the sale of goodwill. The benefit of the restrictive covenant attaches to the business itself and not to the owner and is therefore assignable. Finally the fact that a covenantor agrees only to sell to another who will accept a restraint is not in itself unreasonable: *Esso Petroleum Co Ltd v Harper's George (Stourport) Ltd* [1968] A.C. 269, *per* Lord Reid.

3.7 The consequences of a finding of unreasonableness

3.7.1 Under common law

It can be stated with some degree of certainty that both academic and judicial opinion is divided as to how to characterise a contract in unreasonable restraint of trade and the consequences thereof. Treitel describes such contracts as illegal and contrary to public policy and says that restraint of trade clauses are prima facie void. Anson agrees that they are illegal whilst Cheshire and Fifoot specifically claim they are void—but not illegal. They say that a restraint is "prima facie void" but "becomes binding" on proof of reasonableness. Chitty, on the other hand, says that an agreement in unreasonable restraint of trade is generally not unlawful if the parties choose to abide by it. It is however unenforceable if the parties choose not to do so. There is judicial support for the word "void": *Nordenfelt v Maxim Nordenfelt Guns and Ammunition Co* [1894] A.C. 535; *Haynes v Doman* [1899] 2 Ch. 13, *per* Lindley M.R. and *Greig v Insole* [1978] 1 W.L.R. 302. Lord Denning M.R. wavered in his view. In the *Littlewoods* case he described a restraint of trade clause as void, invalid and unenforceable. However, in *Office Overload Ltd v Gunn* [1977] F.S.R. 39 he settled for "unenforceable" and rejected "void or invalid". Indeed the trend of modern authority seems to have chosen "unenforceable" as the appropriate description. See Lord Wilberforce in *Stenhouse* and Lord Reid in *Esso*: ". . . an agreement in restraint of trade is not generally unlawful if the parties choose to abide by it: it is only unenforceable if a party chooses not to abide by it".

It is suggested that the words used are important. If a covenant in unreasonable restraint of trade is described as illegal then it will be impossible to recover any money paid under it. If the unreasonableness produces voidness that means that so far as the law is concerned the clause has never existed: it may well then be possible to claim in tort for the restitution of money or goods although no specific action can be brought on the basis of the contractual force of the clause. On the other hand to characterise a bad clause as voidable must mean that it is possible for one party to bring contractual relations to an end and sue for the return of money/goods. Finally, the description unenforceability really means that up until the time of judgment it was valid but thereafter cannot be used as a basis for an action. The consequences, as pointed out in *A. Schroeder Music Publishing Co v Macaulay* [1974] 1 W.L.R. 1308 in the Court of Appeal, are that all acts taken under the clause prior to judgment remain undisturbed but that future ones will, assuming the successful party chooses to rely on the judgment, be unenforceable.

3.7.2 The consequences of a clause being caught by the competition law prohibition

In relation to restraints of trade in commercial agreements, Art.82(2) EC and s.2(4) Competition Act 1998 provide that any agreement which violates Art.81(1) and s.2(1) respectively is void. Neither the EC Treaty nor the Competition Act specify what the consequence of such voidness is. It has however been established by the ECJ that it is possible to sever the offending clauses, leaving the remainder of the agreement enforceable (see further para.21.11 and Chapter 22—on severance under EU and UK competition law respectively).

In *Gibbs Mew plc v Gemmel* [1998] Eu. L.R. 588, the Court of Appeal concluded that an agreement which infringes Art.81(1) is not only void and unenforceable, but it is also illegal. As such a party to an illegal agreement cannot enforce it or seek to recover money. However, the ECJ on a reference from the UK Court of Appeal has subsequently stated that national law cannot impose *an absolute bar* on an action by one party to an agreement caught by Art.81 EC Treaty. Community law does not however prevent national law from denying a party who has "significant responsibility" for the restriction of competition the right to obtain damages from the other contracting party see *Crehan v Courage Ltd*, Case C-453/99 [2001] E.C.R. I-6297 (see further Chapters 21 and 22).

3.8 Consideration

In any contract there has to be consideration. So much so, in restraint of trade cases, that a restriction agreed in the form of a deed will still require consideration to be enforceable (*Mitchel v Reynolds* (1711) 1 P.Wms 181 and *Gravely v Barnard* (1874) L.R. 18 Eq.518, although in both cases, consideration was readily inferred from the surrounding circumstances). The question which has frequently arisen in restraint of trade cases is whether the court is at all concerned as to the adequacy of the particular consideration in the instant case. One view is that the court is not so concerned. Support for this is found in the judgment of Lord Parker in *Herbert Morris v Saxelby* [1916] 1 A.C. 688 where he said "the court no longer considers the adequacy of the consideration in any particular case". There is no doubt that in the nineteenth century the courts did consider the adequacy of consideration in restraint of trade cases, but more recently in *M&S Drapers v Reynolds* [1957] 1 W.L.R. 9 Hodson L.J. said:

> . . . although the position of the employee has to be considered, the court will not inquire into the adequacy of the consideration or weigh the advantages accruing to the covenantor under the contract against the disadvantages imposed on him by the restraint.

However in our view although many judgments pay lip service to Lord Parker's words they do, in fact, go on to examine the adequacy of consideration as relevant to the question of reasonableness. Authority for this view is found in Lord MacNaghten's judgment in the *Nordenfelt* case where he said "Of course the quantum of consideration may enter into the question of the reasonableness of the contract". This was specifically endorsed by Lord Pearce in *Esso* where he explained that what Lord MacNaghten meant was that the adequacy of consideration was a key to oppression and that oppression is a key to reasonableness. In *Clifford Davis Management v W.E.A. Records* [1975] 1 W.L.R. 61 Lord Denning M.R. expressly considered the adequacy of the consideration. He said that the publisher got the copyright in each song written by the defendant for one shilling. He described this as "grossly inadequate" and said that this was effectively a symptom of the basic unreasonableness of the contract. In *Foley v Classique Coaches Ltd* [1934] 2 K.B. 1, *Amoco Australia Pty Ltd v Rocca Bros Motor Engineering Co Pty Ltd* [1975] A.C. 561 and *Bridge v Deacons* [1984] A.C. 705, the adequacy of consideration was closely linked to the question of reasonableness. In *Amoco* Lord Cross said the fact that a covenantor had obtained and would continue to enjoy benefits under the agreement which he claimed to be unenforceble was *pro tanto* a reason for holding that the covenant was not in unreasonable restraint of trade. Dillon L.J. echoed this point in *Alec Lobb*. In *Turner v Commonwealth & British Minerals Ltd* [2000] I.R.L.R. 114, CA, the Court of Appeal also acknowledged that in determining the reasonableness of a restrictive covenant, it is legitimate to take into account that the employee is being paid something extra for it, although this does not relieve the employer of the necessity to justify the restraint.

Finally, there are two relevant matters frequently encountered in practice. The first concerns whether consideration exists when an employer seeks to amend an existing restrictive covenant (usually by making it less unreasonable) or when he seeks to introduce a covenant where none has existed before. In each case, so as to avoid argument later, the well advised employer will seek to make the changes at a time when salaries are being increased or a new bonus scheme is being inroduced. What however if that is not the case? If he seeks to make such changes without such an increase, what is the consideration? In *Steiner v Spray* December 1, 1993, CA, (unreported) the Court of Appeal suggested that merely continuing to provide employment would constitute sufficient consideration.

The second situation concerns the restrictive covenant introduced as part of a severance package. It is sometimes believed that these are likely to be looked at in a more indulgent way by the courts. We do not believe that to be the case, save where a defendant has taken his money and behaved quite disgracefully; in that instance human nature will seek to enforce the covenant. In *J A Mont (UK) Ltd v Mills* [1993] I.R.L.R. 172, CA, a payment of over £70,000 was made to the defendant and he was provided with various fringe benefits. In return he was required to submit to a restrictive covenant in the following terms: "This total payment is made on condition that you do not join another company in the tissue industry within one year of leaving our employment". The Court found the restriction unreasonable and, inter alia, refused to apply the reasoning in garden leave cases to a situation where a person had in fact ceased to be an employee albeit that he was being paid in his severance package at the same rate that he would have been if he had remained an employee. See also *Turner* above.

3.9 Pleading restraint of trade

In the typical case of an action by an employer against a former employee the employer will plead in his particulars of claim that by doing a certain thing the employee has breached express or implied terms of his contract. This follows the usual contractual claim for breach. There may also be a claim against third parties for inducing breach of contract and/or tortious conspiracy. However, does the defendant in his defence have to plead specifically the unreasonableness of the restraint? In all cases it is necessary that the defendant specifically pleads that a certain term in a contract is in unreasonable restraint of trade. However, if he fails to do so can he still ask the court to examine the contract in the light of the restraint of trade doctrine because of the existence of the public interest? The answer appears to be in the negative following the judgment of Diplock L.J. in *Petrofina (Great Britain) Ltd v Martin* [1966] Ch. 146.

However, the courts have frequently allowed a restraint of trade argument to be adduced at trial even though not pleaded. Judicial intervention is not unknown: see *Marion White Ltd v Francis* [1972] 1 W.L.R. 1423.

In addition to pleading that a provision is in unreasonable restraint of trade a defendant can also plead repudiation, vagueness and that in any event he has not acted in breach of the clause.

In seeking to enforce a restraint of trade in a commercial agreement, the claimant is likely to plead in his particulars of claim breach of express or implied terms of the agreement. The defendant however may well not only argue unreasonabless under common law, but is likely to argue invalidity and unenforceability under Art.81(2) EC or s.2(4) Competition Act 1998. UK courts are however unsympathetic to an Art.81(2) defence (commonly referred to as the "Euro-defence"), where one party to an agreement freely entered into subsequently tries to walk away from the agreement on the ground that it is void under competition law. The maxim "*pacta sunt servenda*" (contracts should be honoured) is particularly relevant where the undertaking's original intention had certainly not been to infringe competition law and it is merely due to "technicality of competition law that one undertaking then seeks to avoid a contractual obligation. Hence most of the beer tenancy cases of the 1990s have been unsuccessful in the use of the Euro-defence. See also *Panayiotou v Sony Music Entertainment (UK) Ltd* [1994] E.M.L.R. 229 Ch.D. (the George Michael case).

3.10 Burden of proof

3.10.1 Common law

Dealing first with the question of reasonableness as between the parties it is now accepted that the burden of proof falls on the party seeking to enforce the restraint. Typically this is an employer or the purchaser of a business. Support for this proposition is found in *Mason v Provident Clothing and Supply Co Ltd* [1913] A.C. 724, in *Herbert Morris v Saxelby*, and in *Attwood v Lamont* [1920] 3 K.B. 571. The earlier cases of *Mills v Dunham* [1891] 1 Ch. 576 and *Haynes v Doman* [1899] 2 Ch. 13 are now wrong on this point. The only more recent murmur of dissent occurred in Lord Reid's judgment in *Pharmaceutical Society of Great Britain v Dickson* [1970] A.C. 403 in which he expressed a doubt as to whether, in a case where a restraint was part of a professional code of conduct, the burden of proof regarding justification fell on the professional body. However the majority view was otherwise. It is important to note that the burden does not amount to proof of reasonableness itself, for that is a question for the judge, but to prove the facts from which reasonableness can be inferred. But judges attach little significance to the point and it really only plays a part if, as in *Dickson's* case, one side refuses to adduce any evidence of reasonableness at all.

Secondly, in cases relying on public policy the burden of proof is on the party raising it (see *Herbert Morris v Saxelby* and the *A-G of the Commonwealth of Australia v Adelaide Steamship Co* [1913] A.C. 781). Even in cases in which a declaration is sought, such as the *Schroeder* case, the burden of proof appears to be on the party arguing that the restraint was reasonable. The whole question of the burden of proof was nicely summed up in the *Esso* case by Lord Hodson where he said:

> It has been authoritatively said that the onus of establishing that an agreement is reasonable as between the parties is upon the person who puts forward the agreement, while the onus of establishing that it is contrary to the public interest, being reasonable between the parties, is on the person so alleging. . . . The reason for the distinction may be obscure, but it will seldom arise since once the agreement is before the court it is open to the scrutiny of the court in all its surrounding circumstances as a question of law.

Lord Pearce said "When the court sees its way clearly, no question of onus arises".

3.10.2 Competition law

Unlike restraint of trade, the application of competition law not only results in invalidity but also illegality. The burden of proving an infringement rests on the party, or competition authority, alleging the infringement. The party claiming the benefit of an exemption bears the burden of proving the restriction/agreement meets the relevant exemption criteria (see Art.2 Reg.1/2003).

Both the European Commission and the Office of Fair Trading in the UK can apply competition law administratively and fine the parties to any agreement that breaches Art.81(1) or s.2(1) and does not benefit from an exemption. Given that an infringement of Art.81 (and s.2(1)) carries with it a liability to penalties it has been held that the standard of "a high degree of probability should be applied" (*Shearson Lehman Hutton Inc v Watson Co Ltd*, [1989] 3 C.M.L.R. 429 at 570). This is a standard that is higher than in civil proceedings generally but lower than the requirement in a criminal case. In a case argued under both Art.81 and 82 EC regarding price fixing and predatory pricing by a shipping liner conference, the Queen's Bench Division applied the normal civil standard of proof, i.e. proof on the balance of probabilities, *Arkin v Borchard Lines Ltd*, [2000] Eu. L.R. 232, yet the Competition Appeal Tribunal in *Argos and Littlewoods v OFT*, [2004] CAT 24 stated that:

> strong and convincing evidence will be required before infringements of the Chapter I and Chapter II prohibitions can be found to be proven, even to the civil standard. Indeed, whether we are in technical terms applying a civil standard on the basis of strong and convincing evidence, or a criminal standard of beyond reasonable doubt, we think in practice the result to be the same.

Now it may be that the CAT, considering cases on appeal following the imposition of a penalty by the OFT, may be approaching the matter differently from a High Court ruling between two commercial parties. Furthermore the UK Enterprise Act 2002, has criminalised certain breaches of competition law, notably any hardcore restrictions which effectively consist of those agreements whose very object is to restrict competition such as price fixing, market share and bid rigging. As such, if an agreement contained any hardcore restrictions which are being challenged under the Enterprise Act, by the Office of Fair Trading (or the Serious Fraud Office) then the burden of proof would be a criminal one.

Part II

Business Secrets

Chapter 4

Interaction between Business Secrets Clauses and Restraint of Trade Clauses

It has long been recognised by the courts that the protection of business secrets is a legitimate ground for the imposition of restrictions on persons to whom such secrets have been disclosed. Two types of contractual provision are commonly used for the purpose of protecting business secrets. First, there are undertakings to maintain the confidentiality of business secrets and not to use them except for limited purposes. However, this type of business secrets clause suffers from the problem of detecting breach. Secondly, there are restraints upon the business in which the person receiving the business secrets may engage (i.e. not to compete in a certain way for a particular time because of the risk of use or disclosure of business secrets). The restraint of trade doctrine is relevant to both types of provision.

The effect of the restraint of trade doctrine on the first type of provision is to place limits on the type of information which may be made subject to the confidentiality provision. Apart from the restraint of trade considerations there would seem to be no reason why a contract under which one person undertakes to keep silent on a particular subject should not be enforceable in accordance with its terms for example; *A-G v Barker* [1990] 3 All E.R. 257, CA, where an injunction was granted against a former member of the royal household restraining breach of a contractual duty of confidence which was both worldwide and perpetual; *A-G v Blake* [2001] I.R.L.R. 36, in which the court recognised that the Official Secrets Act declaration including an undertaking not to divulge any official information gained in the course of employment created a life long duty of non-disclosure on the notorious spy, and in the same vein, *Attorney General v Shayler* [2006] EWHC 2285). See also *Campbell v Frisbee* [2002] EWHC 328 (Ch D) in which a confidentiality agreement signed by an individual providing services to a well known model under which she agreed not to disclose personal details about the model's personal life was enforced and *HRH Prince of Wales v Associated Newspapers Ltd.* [2006] EWCA Civ 1776. Also of interest is *Douglas v Hello! Ltd.* [2005] EWCA Civ 595 [2007] UK HL 21 where the law of confidence extended to photographs of a wedding and *Archer v Williams* [2003] EWHC 1670 where the claimant's PA disclosed information about her professional and private life in breach of confidentiality obligations in the employee's contract and her equitable duty of confidence. Both cases are interesting also for the interaction between the law of confidence and the provisions of the European Convention on Human Rights (see particularly Articles 8, Right to Respect for Privacy and Family Life, and Article 10, Freedom of Expression) incorporated into UK law by the Human Rights Act 1998.

However, where the restraint of trade doctrine applies, for example in contracts of employment, a confidentiality obligation will only be enforced if the information in question can fairly be regarded as a separate part of the employee's stock of knowledge which a man of ordinary honesty and intelligence would recognise to be the property of his employer and not his own to do what he likes with. (See *Printers and Finishers Ltd v Holloway* [1965] 1 W.L.R. 1.) This is, in practice, the same as saying that the obligation of confidentiality will not be enforced where the information concerned does not include a trade secret or its equivalent (see *Faccenda Chicken Ltd v Fowler* [1985] 1 All E.R. 724).

The effect of the doctrine on provisions of the second type has been the subject of more numerous decisions of the court. The protection of business secrets is one of the three grounds upon which a restraint of trade clause can in general be justified (the other two being the protection of customer connections and the maintenance of a stable workforce). The term "business secrets", where used in this book, is intended to cover any confidential information of value used in business. It is not used in the more restricted sense given to the term "trade secrets" in *Faccenda Chicken v Fowler* [1985] 1 All E.R. 724 which has now been effectively viewed as being too narrow by two members of the Court of Appeal in *Lansing Linde Ltd v Kerr* [1991] 1 All E.R. 418: see para.8.2.3 below. We think the approach in Lansing Linde is to be preferred. The extent to which covenants in restraint of trade can be justified on the grounds of protection of business secrets is discussed in general terms in Part I and, in relation to specific types of contracts, in Parts III to VI.

Chapter 5

The Characteristics of Confidentiality

Three elements are normally required for a case of breach of confidence to succeed. First, the information must have the necessary quality of confidence. Secondly, it must have been imparted in circumstances requiring an obligation of confidence. Thirdly, there must be an unauthorised use of that information to the detriment of the party communicating it (see *Coco v AN Clark (Engineers) Ltd* [1969] R.P.C. 41).

Whilst these three elements have been elaborated upon in subsequent cases they are a convenient starting point for consideration of the case law.

5.1 The necessary quality of confidence

In *Saltman Engineering Co v Campbell Engineering Co Ltd* [1963] 65 R.P.C. 203, Lord Greene M.R. defined the necessary quality of confidence thus: "it must not be something which is public property and public knowledge". As will be seen the courts have not applied this test literally. When determining whether information is public knowledge they have regard to the form in which it is available. If substantial work is required to collate the publicly available information into the material in which protection is sought then this will usually be sufficient to take the material out of the public domain. Lord Greene M.R. stated in *Saltman* that it is perfectly possible to have a confidential document, be it a formula, a plan, a sketch, or something of that kind, which is the result of work done by the maker on materials which may be available for the use of anybody. He explained that what makes the document confidential is the fact that the creator of the document has used his brain and thus arrived at a result which can only be produced by somebody who goes through the same process. In addition it is clear that the route by which information becomes public knowledge may be crucial to determining whether it thereby loses the necessary quality of confidence. In some cases the courts have upheld a duty of confidence even where the information is demonstrably publicly available. The question of public accessibility is only one of the issues which must be addressed in determining whether information has the necessary quality of confidence. The court will also consider whether the information is of a type which it is willing to protect at all. Both these issues are now considered in detail.

5.1.1 Inaccessibility

The question of the extent to which the information must be inaccessible to the public has arisen in widely differing situations and although it is difficult to formulate any more specific statement of principle than that of Lord Greene M.R. in *Saltman*, it is useful to consider some of the cases.

The issue of whether publication in one place meant that the information lost its quality of confidence everywhere at that time arose in *Exchange Telegraph Co Ltd v Central News Ltd* [1897] 2 Ch. 48. The plaintiffs gathered information as to the results of horse races from various courses and transmitted that information to subscribers on terms that it should be used only in the newspaper or posted only in the club, newsroom, office or other place to which it was delivered. The defendants also ran a wire service and it was found by the judge that they had been obtaining information from a subscriber to the plaintiff's service for republication by them. It was held that the defendants, who had acquired the information in the knowledge that the supply was a breach by that subscriber of his contract with the plaintiff, could be restrained by injunction from surreptitiously obtaining or copying information collected by the plaintiffs. The judge rejected the defendants' argument that the information was made publicly available at the race meeting and that they were accordingly free to publish it. By contrast, in a somewhat surprising decision in *Times Newspapers plc and HarperCollins Publishers Ltd v MGN Ltd* [1993] 6 Ent. L.R. 119, the court declined to grant an injunction to restrain publication of extracts from an unpublished book because it was shortly to be serialised by the plaintiffs.

The *Exchange Telegraph* case is perhaps an early example of what, following the dicta of Roxburgh J. in *Terrapin Ltd v Builders' Supply Co (Hayes) Ltd* [1960] R.P.C. 128, has come to be called the "springboard" doctrine. In that case he said:

> As I understand it, the essence of this branch of law, whatever the origin of it may be, is that a person who has obtained information in confidence is not allowed to use it as a springboard for activities detrimental to the person who made the confidential communication, and springboard it remains even when all the features have been published or can be ascertained by actual inspection by any members of the public.

In the *Terrapin* case the judge held that because all the details relating to the construction of a particular type of portable building could be ascertained by dismantling and measuring an example of it, the possessor of confidential drawings and other information still had a head start. Any other person would have to prepare plans, construct prototypes and conduct tests. Therefore the possessor of that information had to be placed under a special disability in the field of competition in order to ensure that he did not get an unfair start.

In *Alfa Laval Cheese Systems v Wincanton Engineering Ltd* [1990] F.S.R. 583 the court, following *Terrapin*, found that information available only by dismantling a piece of equipment put on sale might arguably remain confidential.

The duration and nature of his special disability has been the subject of comment in subsequent cases. The passage quoted above was adopted by Roskill J. in *Cranleigh Precision Engineering Ltd v Bryant* [1965] 1 W.L.R. 1293. In *Seager v Copydex Ltd* [1967] 1 W.L.R. 923 it was adopted by Lord Denning M.R. who added the following point concerning the difficulties which arise where part of the information disclosed to the defendant is only partly within the public domain:

> When the information is mixed, being partly public and partly private, then the recipient must take special care to use only the material which is in the public domain. He should go to the public source and get it: or, at any rate, not be in a better position than if he had gone to the public source.

This paragraph seems to indicate that it may be possible for a person who has received information in confidence which he could have obtained through other sources to relieve himself of the "special disability" under which he is otherwise placed by going to those sources. A further possibility which is suggested by Lord Denning's judgment is that in such circumstances it may not be a case for injunction but only for damages. However this does not fit well with the result of the *Terrapin* case where Roxburgh J. in fact granted an injunction.

In *Coco v AN Clark (Engineers) Ltd* [1969] R.P.C. 41 Megarry V.C. considered the implications of Lord Denning's judgment in *Seager* but was unable to reach any firm conclusion. He said that "the essence of the duty seems more likely to be that of not using without paying rather than of not using at all". However this was a matter which he thought might be resolved at the trial.

The point was briefly touched upon again by Lord Denning in *Potters-Ballotini Ltd v Weston-Baker* [1977] R.P.C. 202 where he said "although a man must not use such information as a springboard to get a start over others, nevertheless that springboard does not last for ever".

The Court of Appeal has more recently clarified the position. In *Roger Bullivant Ltd v Ellis* [1987] I.C.R. 464 they held that it was not right to extend the term of the injunction beyond the period for which the advantage might reasonably be expected to continue. Accordingly an injunction against the defendant fulfilling any contract with any person named on a card index which he had obtained from his former employer was discharged, the court saying it was bound to limit the period to one year at the longest.

In practice the question of the duration of the disability imposed by the springboard doctrine does not frequently arise because most cases concerning confidential information do not come to trial following the grant of an interlocutory injunction and it can therefore be assumed that either the parties settle the action or that interlocutory judgment is treated as final.

It is important that the springboard doctrine be understood in its context. What is being said is that the recipient of confidential information cannot use the information as a shortcut to side-step the work which other members of the public would have to do. Thus if the confidential information was published in full detail then the initial recipient would not have a head start. Members of the public would not need to prepare plans, construct prototypes or conduct tests. The need for the special disability would lapse. For example in *Mustad v Allcock and Dosen* [1963] 3 All E.R. 416 it was held that because the appellants had published the information which they alleged was confidential in a patent specification they were not entitled to an injunction restraining the respondents from disclosing that information. This case was followed by Cross J. in *Franchi v Franchi* [1967] R.P.C. 149 where he held that publication of the information in a Belgian patent application was sufficient to cause the plaintiff's claim to fail. Of course for the obligation of confidence to lapse the information published must be the same as the confidential information. In *Cranleigh Precision Engineering Ltd v Bryant* [1965] 1 W.L.R. 1293 Roskill J. held that the defendant, who had, whilst a director of the plaintiff company, been made aware of a patent held by a third party which affected the plaintiff's products, could not justify his failure to disclose the existence of the patent to the plaintiffs and his subsequent acquisition of the patent for himself on the ground that it was public knowledge, for what he had misused was his confidential knowledge of the relationship of the information in the patent to the plaintiff's products. It will frequently happen that information disclosed in confidence is or becomes known to a limited number of people or to a specific section of the public only. It is clearly a question of degree whether the information retains the necessary quality of confidence.

In *Ackroyds (London) Ltd v Islington Plastics Ltd* [1962] R.P.C. 97 a sub-contractor used the information supplied by the plaintiff to manufacture and sell goods on its own account to the plaintiff's customers. The plaintiffs obtained an injunction to restrain the defendants notwithstanding that the product in question (a swizzle stick embossed with the name of the ship upon which it was to be used) was available to anyone who happened to take a cruise on that ship. The defendants were presumably outside the class of people who were likely to have access to the information publicly. See also the *Exchange Telegraph* case and *Sun Printers v Westminster Press* [1982] I.R.L.R. 292. Megarry V.C., in *Thomas Marshall (Exports) v Guinle* [1979] Ch. 227, set out a test of four elements which is most helpful for determining whether the information is too widely known to retain the necessary quality of confidence.

> First, the owner must believe that the release of the information would be advantageous to his rivals or injurious to him.
>
> Secondly, the owner must believe the information is not in the public domain. (Megarry V.C. said that even if some or all of the owner's rivals

have the information as long as the owner believes it is confidential he is entitled to try to protect it.)

Thirdly, the owner's belief as to the first and second elements must be reasonable.

Fourthly, the information must be judged in the light of the usage and practices of the particular trade or industry concerned. It should be noted that this test was expressly limited by Megarry V.C. to secrets in industrial or trade settings.

The interesting question of whether publication by or caused by the confidant affects the existence of the confidence was discussed in *A-G v Guardian Newspapers Ltd (No. 2)* [1988] 3 All E.R. 545. Lord Donaldson M.R. said at p.609 that dissemination of confidential information knowingly in breach of the plaintiff's right cannot undermine the right itself: it can however affect the remedies available to the plaintiff especially regarding the appropriateness of injunctive relief. Lord Goff at p.664 reserved the question whether some limited obligation (analogous to the springboard doctrine) may continue to rest on a confidant, who, in breach of confidence, destroys the confidential nature of the information entrusted to him. In relation to third parties the matter was most sensibly dealt with by Bingham L.J. at p.625.

> A third party coming into possession of confidential information is accordingly liable to be restrained from publishing it if he knows the information to be confidential and the circumstances are such as to impose on him an obligation in good conscience not to publish. No such obligation would in my view ordinarily arise where the third party comes into possession of information which, although once confidential, has ceased to be so otherwise than through the agency of the third party.

5.1.2 Types of information

Sufficient inaccessibility is not the only requirement of the necessary quality of confidence. In addition the type of information must be considered. This book is concerned primarily with business secrets and so such issues as marital confidences and privacy are not considered even though they may occasionally have commercial value. (See for example *Margaret Duchess of Argyll v Duke of Argyll* [1967] Ch. 302, *Lennon v News Group Newspapers Ltd* [1978] F.S.R. 573, *Woodward v Hutchins* [1977] 1 W.L.R. 760, *Stephens v Avery* [1988] 2 W.L.R. 1280, *Campbell v MGN Group* [2002] EWCA Civ 1373, *Douglas & Ors v Hello! Ltd & Ors* [2003] EWHC 786 and *Lady Archer v Williams* [2003] EWHC 1670).

It is clear that information need not be complex in order to be the subject of confidentiality. In *Coco v Clark* Megarry V.C. said ". . . the mere simplicity of an idea does not prevent it being confidential. . . . Indeed, the simpler an idea, the more likely it is to need protection". See also *Under Water Welders and Repairers Ltd v Street and Longthorne* [1968] R.P.C. 498.

Conversely, mere volume or complexity of information disclosed will not be sufficient. In *Yates Circuit Foil Co v Electrofoils Ltd* [1976] F.S.R. 345 Whitford J. said "I know of no direct authority which has laid it down that a fetter can be placed upon the disclosure of a body of information of a general character if the body of information is over some particular size".

However, the *Yates* decision should not be regarded as authority for the proposition that a collection of individually non-confidential items of information cannot be the subject of confidentiality where the confidentiality lies in the fact that they are collected together. A typical example of a confidential collection of information might be a list of customers (see for example *Robb v Green* [1895] 2 Q.B. 315 and *William Summers & Co Ltd v Boyce & Kinmond & Co* (1907) 23 T.L.R. 724 and *Roger Bullivant v Ellis Ltd* [1987] I.C.R. 464 but *cf. Auto Securities Ltd v Standard Telephones and Cables Ltd* [1965] R.P.C. 92). It was suggested by Hirst J. in *Fraser v Thames Television Ltd* [1983] 2 All E.R. 101 that some degree of originality is required for confidential information to be protected. However it is clear from the context that all that he meant was that, where what is claimed to be confidential is an idea based on a well-known theme, it must have something such as a significant twist or slant which is not public knowledge. In that case the making of a television series by the defendants based on a concept communicated in confidence by the plaintiffs was held to be a breach of confidence. In *De Maudsley v Palumbo* [1996] F.S.R. 447, it was held that an idea for an all night dance club was not protected. (See also *Gilbert v Star Newspapers Co Ltd* (1894) 11 T.L.R. 4 and *Frazer v Edwards* (1905) MacG. Cop. Cas. (1905–10) 10.)

One further restriction on the type of information which may be subject to an obligation of confidentiality has been briefly mentioned above. Information acquired by an employee which becomes part of his general skills and stock of knowledge is not the subject of an obligation of confidentiality although during the term of the employment it may be a breach of the employee's duty of good faith to disclose it to third parties. Information relating to customers, prices, technology and business methods have been held to fall into this category (see the discussion of *Faccenda Chicken v Fowler* [1985] 1 All E.R. 724 in Chapter 8 and see *Printers & Finishers Ltd v Holloway* [1965] 1 W.L.R. 1, and *Stevenson Jordan & Harrison Ltd v MacDonald & Evans* (1952) 69 R.P.C. 10). The courts will normally refuse to allow claims of confidentiality in respect of the names and addresses of employees so as to prevent offers of other employment being made to them by departing staff (see *Baker v Gibbons* [1972] 1 W.L.R. 693 and *GD Searle & Co Ltd v Celltech Ltd* [1982] F.S.R. 92).

In *Ixora Trading Incorporated v Jones* [1990] F.S.R. 251 Mummery J. struck out the plaintiffs' writ and statement of claim which, inter alia, alleged breaches of express and implied duties of confidence. The plaintiffs were part of a group of companies which operated Bureaux de Change. The defendants had been employed as executives by the plaintiffs. The defendants had both received training in the plaintiffs' business, including familiarisation with the contents of two manuals. The defendants had in the course of their employment visited Paris to assess the feasibility of opening Bureaux de Change in France. As a result they produced a document called an "Initial Feasibility Study". Since the termination of the defendants' employment a company in the same group as the plaintiffs had opened a number of Bureaux de Change in Paris. The company set up by the defendants had also opened Bureaux de Change in Paris.

The plaintiffs relied on an express term set out in the letters of appointments written to the defendants as follows:

> You will not disclose any of the company's affairs or any of its subsidiary or associated companies business or trade secrets to a third party either during or after you have ceased to be an employee of the company without the express written consent of the company.

In addition, the defendants gave undertakings to the plaintiff, one of which was as follows:

> Any information which I have access to or knowledge which I acquire arising out of or in the course of my contract of service shall remain confidential and shall not be used by me to obtain any gain, benefit or advantage or profits for myself or for any member of my family or connected person.

The judge pointed out that in the statement of claim the confidential information relied on was described in a general way as a fund of technical knowledge and experience relating to a number of matters; in particular the contents of the manuals and the Initial Feasibility Study. The judge concluded that none of the documents or the contents of them satisfied the requirement of the kind of confidential information which an employer is entitled to prevent an ex-employee from using after the termination of the employer/employee relationship. Moreover he found that a concession made in the pleadings to the effect that the plaintiffs did not allege that the defendants had made use of any of the plaintiffs' trade secrets since leaving their employment was, in the light of the judgment of *Faccenda Chicken Ltd v Fowler* [1986] 1 All E.R. 617 fatal. That concession may not be now as fatal as the judge thought due to the extension of the meaning of the phrase "trade secret" found in the Court of Appeal judgments in *Lansing Linde Ltd v Kerr* [1991] 1 W.L.R. 251, CA. In *Lansing*, Staughton L.J. said, when addressing what might be defined as a trade secret:

> Mr. Poulton suggested that a trade secret is information which, if disclosed to a competitor, would be liable to cause real (or significant) harm to the owner of the secret. I would add first, that it must be information used in a trade or business, and secondly, that the owner must limit the dissemination of it or at least not encourage or permit widespread publication. That is my preferred view of the meaning of trade secret in this context. It can thus include not only secret formulae for the manufacture of products but also, in an appropriate case, the names of customers and the goods which they buy. But some may say that not all such information is a trade secret in ordinary parlance. If that view be adopted, the class of information which

can justify a restriction is wider, and extends to some confidential information which would not ordinarily be called a trade secret.

The judge in *Ixora* went on to find that not only was the information contained in the manuals and the feasibility study not a trade secret, but that the information contained in the feasibility study was too obvious and too vague and unspecific to be caught by any alleged fiduciary duty that the defendants were under. In the field of computer software the Court of Appeal came to a similar conclusion in *FSS Travel and Leisure Systems Ltd v Johnson* [1998] I.R.L.R. 382, CA. The employers' business in that case was designing and marketing computer software used in the travel industry. Some 2,800 separate programs were involved which were updated and modified regularly. Whilst a large proportion of the programming was routine, the work involved a creative aspect in the devising and achievement of solutions to problems. In the context of a restrictive covenant, it fell to be considered whether there were trade secrets justifying the enforcement of the covenant. *Per* Mummery L.J., "The evidence given on behalf of FSS Travel relates to knowledge on the part of Mr Johnson as to how to do his job and the acquisition of skill and experience by him in the doing of it; it is lacking in concrete examples and in solid relevant detail, identifying a separate and specific recognisable body of objective knowledge designated by FSS Travel as confidential or secret material. The solutions cited . . . are too vague and indefinite to constitute trade secrets protectable by a restrictive covenant."

In *Berkeley Administration Inc v McClelland* [1990] F.S.R. 505 the plaintiffs were a company related to Ixora. The fifth and sixth defendants had been employed by a group of companies of which the plaintiffs were a part in senior positions for short periods before being dismissed. After their dismissal the first and sixth defendants drafted a business plan for the purpose of raising finance to set up a Bureau de Change business in competition with the plaintiffs. Shortly afterwards they invited the seventh defendant who was employed by the plaintiffs' group to join them. After the seventh defendant had resigned from the plaintiffs the three refined the business plan and set up the fourth defendant and the fifth defendant companies. The plaintiffs alleged the first, sixth and seventh defendants in preparing their business plan had used five specific items of information derived from financial projections contained in an appendix to a business plan ("the blue book") of the plaintiffs namely:

(a) the average operating profit per Bureau de Change;

(b) the average profit of the first year of operation as a percentage of a full year's profit;

(c) the average costs per Bureau;

(d) the average number and/or transactions per Bureau;

(e) the average value of each transaction.

The plaintiffs contended that their business plan was confidential, that the items of information relied upon were sufficiently confidential to be protectable after termination of the defendants' employment and that it could be inferred that the defendants had used those items by virtue of alleged similarity between figures appearing in the respective business plans. Wright J. accepted that the blue book was described as a confidential memorandum by the plaintiffs and that confidentiality was heavily emphasised in its pages. A limited number of copies were produced, each copy was numbered and a record was kept of the persons to whom the copy was issued. It was plain that the document as a whole was intended to be kept confidential by the plaintiffs and that this fact was firmly impressed upon anyone who had anything to do with it. Although the three individual defendants had either signed or had been made aware of undertakings of confidentiality when they entered the employment of the plaintiff, counsel on behalf of the plaintiffs did not rely upon such undertakings before the judge but relied upon general implied principles of law in this area. The judge declined to find that any of the information contained in the blue book bore the stamp of confidentiality within the criteria laid down in *Faccenda Chicken*, i.e. it could not be described as a trade secret or anything approximating thereto.

This question has also been the subject of a decision by the Court of Appeal. In *Johnson and Bloy (Holdings) Ltd v Wolstenholme Rink plc* [1989] I.R.L.R. 499 the Court of Appeal granted an injunction to the plaintiffs to prevent the defendant from disclosing or using the information that two specified ingredients might be used in combination in the manufacture of a drier for a printing ink and from manufacturing or arranging for the manufacture of printing inks containing therein a drier containing the two ingredients. The defendant had argued that this information, i.e. the knowledge that the combination of the two ingredients produced an effective drier, could not be protected by an injunction since the knowledge of that combination was knowledge which the second defendant must inevitably have taken away from the plaintiffs when he left their employment and that he could not proceed to expunge that knowledge from his mind. Parker L.J. rejected that submission by pointing out that there was no evidence that the combination of the two ingredients was commonly known or used in the trade. Moreover he pointed out that there is no principle in English law which says that anything which is inevitably in somebody's head when they leave their employment is something which they are free to use. In certain cases such information may well be confidential. This was such a case.

In contrast in *Poeton Industries Ltd v Horton* [2000] I.C.R. 1208, CA, and *Cray Valley Ltd v Deltech Europe Ltd* [2003] EWHC 728 (Ch D) the Court held that the information in question was not protectable by means of the implied duty of confidentiality. *Poeton* involved electroplating and Mr Horton was the sales manager of the business. He left and established a competing business and in the process used some ideas utilised by Poeton in its process. The claims of confidentiality related to the electrolyte, the apparatus and a customer list.

The Court of Appeal considered the information came within the second of Goulding J.'s, three classes of confidential information in *Faccenda Chicken Ltd v Fowler* [1986] I.C.R. 297, i.e. information which could be protected without a covenant during employment but not thereafter. The court said that *Poeton* could have protected themselves by a covenant, but did not. The court would not be astute to identify category 3 (trade secrets) information contained within a much broader (but unwarranted) claim to confidential information. In *Cray Valley* the claimant company manufactured solvent based resins and contended the certain aspects of the process, their timing and temperatures were confidential. The Court held against the company on the basis much of it was published and second nature to employees. Many of the recipes were non-critical and easy to reverse engineer. A reasonable person of conscience would not regard the information as constituting a trade secret.

It is often said that there can be no confidence in iniquity. In general, however, the cases tend to view that the disclosure of iniquity is a just cause for breaking an obligation of confidentiality. Accordingly, these cases are examined in the context of breach of the duty of confidentiality (see 5.5.1 below).

5.2 Circumstances importing an obligation of confidence

The courts have found it difficult to determine a generally applicable test of the circumstances in which an obligation of confidence will arise. In part this difficulty may stem from the uncertain legal nature of the action for breach of confidence. In many cases the obligation has been held to arise out of an implied term of a contract between the parties. In others, where the courts have been unable to find any contract between the parties, the courts have had to rely on an equitable doctrine of confidence. However, in practice it is rare to find circumstances in which the court would be prepared to find that an obligation of confidence arises by virtue of an implied term of a contract but not by virtue of an equitable obligation (see for example *Thomas Marshall (Exporters) Ltd v Guinle* [1979] Ch. 227). However a plaintiff should always plead both the equitable and the contractual duty for the remedies available are different: see Part VII. The principles set out below for determining when an obligation of confidence will arise would therefore seem equally applicable to both equitable and implied contractual obligations.

Perhaps the most elegant formulation of principle was given in *Coco v AN Clark (Engineers) Ltd* [1968] F.S.R. 415 where it was said that if a reasonable man standing in the shoes of the recipient of the information would have realised that upon reasonable grounds the information was being given to him in confidence then this should suffice to impose upon him the equitable obligation of confidence. Although this formulation has been referred to in subsequent cases it has not been adopted as laying down an all embracing test. The courts have instead tended to consider a number of factors which point to the existence of an obligation of confidentiality. These factors can be conveniently categorised under three headings.

5.2.1 Express indications of confidentiality

Where the person disclosing information expressly states to the recipient that it is being disclosed in confidence this will usually suffice to impose an obligation of confidence (assuming the information has the necessary quality of confidence). For example in *Dunford & Elliott Ltd v Johnson & Firth Brown* [1978] F.S.R. 143 information supplied to investors under cover of a letter making express reference to its confidential nature was held to have been imparted in circumstances of confidence (although the action failed on other grounds). Similarly, where a product which contains a secret mechanism is supplied subject to a condition that the recipient should not examine the mechanism, this will establish confidence in the mechanism (see *KS Paul (Printing Instruments) Ltd v Southern Instruments (Communications) Ltd and EP Ellis (Male) (Trading as Ellis and Sons)* [1964] R.P.C. 118). However, in the absence of such conditions a purchaser of an item is not under any implied duty of confidence (see *Alfa Laval Cheese Systems Ltd v Wincanton Engineering Ltd* [1990] F.S.R. 583).

Displaying signs in premises indicating that an area is private may, in certain circumstances, be sufficient. In *Shelley Film Ltd v Rex Features Ltd* (1993) (unreported) an interim order was granted restraining publication of photographs surreptitiously taken of a film set which had been signed "No admittance—access to authorised persons only" and "Absolutely no photography". See also *Douglas and Ors v Hello! Ltd* [2001] 2 W.L.R. 992, CA [2007] UKHL 21, where exclusive rights to publish wedding photographs were known by Hello magazine to have been granted to their rival, OK magazine, and photography at the wedding except that authorised by the couple forbidden. Guests to the wedding were notified that no photography should take place and a sign placed at the entrance to the venue contained a similar message. The Court of Appeal held however that although the claimants might establish at trial that publication of photographs surreptitiously taken should not be allowed on grounds of confidentiality in view of the organised publicity the retained element of privacy was insufficient to tilt the balance against restraining publication by means of injunction. Damages would be an adequate remedy. By a majority, the House of Lords disagreed, per Lord Hoffman "the information in this case [photographs] was capable of being protected, not because it concerned the Douglas' image anymore than because it concerned their private life, but simply because it was information of commercial value over which the Douglas' had sufficient control to enable them to impose an obligation of confidentiality".

Unsolicited information gives rise to difficulties for it is not clearly established whether this may be made subject to an obligation of confidence. It is submitted that there is no good reason why an obligation of confidence should not arise if the supplier of the information clearly expresses it to be confidential. Provided the springboard doctrine is sensibly applied and injunctions granted only in the clearest of cases so that the recipient of the information is not effectively placed in a worse position than if he had not received it, the interests of both the supplier of the information and the recipient can be satisfied.

5.2.2 Mode of expression

Where no express indication of the confidentiality of the information disclosed has been given it is necessary to examine the circumstances surrounding the disclosure. This has frequently been necessary in the case of information obtained by employees in the course of their employment. The cases are discussed at para.8.2.2.

It would appear that an obligation of confidence may arise in relation to information which is overheard but it seems that this will only be the case where the recipient has used surreptitious means to put himself in a position to overhear the information. This question has achieved some notoriety in two cases concerning telephone tapping. In the first, *Malone v Commissioner of Police of the Metropolis (No. 2)* [1979] 2 All E.R. 620, which concerned the use to which recordings of telephone conversations made with the authority of the Secretary of State for the Home Office, Megarry V.C. said "it seems to me that a person who utters confidential information must accept the risk of any unknown overhearing that is inherent in the circumstances of the communication". In the second case, *Francome v Mirror Group Newspapers Ltd* [1984] 2 All E.R. 408, the Court of Appeal held that there was a serious issue to be tried on the question of whether information obtained by illegal tapping by private individuals was subject to confidentiality. It is however apparent from the judgment in that case that the Court of Appeal regarded information overheard as a result of accidents or imperfections in the telephone system as free from the obligation of confidence. *Francome* is important because the court recognised the possibility that information taken without anyone's consent, for example by espionage, might be held subject to an obligation of confidence (see *Shelley Films Ltd v Rex Features Ltd* above). In *A-G v Guardian Newspapers Ltd (No. 2)* [1988] 3 All E.R. 545 (part of the *Spycatcher* case) it was recognised that information which Peter Wright had unearthed by his own endeavours was clearly covered by an obligation of confidence even though one could not say there existed a "confider" or "confidant" in relation to that information. Whether the courts would extend this remedy to information in documents which were accidentally released as opposed to surreptitiously obtained was answered in *English and American Insurance Co Ltd v Herbert Smith* [1988] F.S.R. 232. The papers of counsel acting for the plaintiffs in a pending action in the Commercial Court were mistakenly sent to the solicitors for the other side. The papers were entitled to legal professional privilege. Those solicitors, the first defendant, realised what had happened and did not at first read the papers. However, they considered it their duty to tell their clients, the second defendants, that they had them. Their clients' instructions were to read the papers. They did so and informed their clients of what they had discovered; they then returned the papers. By notice of motion the plaintiffs claimed an interlocutory order restraining the defendants from making any use of any information derived from the privileged documents. Such an order would prevent the defendants using that information for any purpose of defending an action in the Commercial Court. The defendants, inter alia, submitted that the owner of confidential information could not restrain its use by a party to whom it had accidentally escaped and who had not himself undertaken the duty of confidentiality. Sir Nicolas Browne-Wilkinson V.C. granted an order limited to overt use of the information. He held that an injunction could be granted against a stranger who had come innocently into the possession of confidential information to which he was not entitled. See also *Derby and Co Ltd v Weldon (No. 8)* [1990] 3 All E.R. 762.

The courts have, however, been unwilling to extend the law of confidence to create a general right to privacy. In *Kaye v Robertson* [1991] F.S.R. 62 it was held that there was no right to restrain publication of a photograph of the plaintiff taken without his consent while he was ill in hospital. See also *Wainwright v Home Office* [2004] 2 A.C. 406 and *Campbell v MGN Ltd.* [2004] 2 A.C. 457. However, Sedley L.J., in *Douglas v Hello! Ltd* [2001] 2 W.L.R. 992 expressed the view that English Law will recognise and, where appropriate, protect a right of personal privacy grounded in the equitable doctrine of breach of confidence. So far as the rights of the parties under Arts 8 (the right to respect for private and family life) and 10 (the right to freedom of expression) of the European Convention on Human Rights were concerned, they were to be evaluated and weighed against each other with neither having primacy over the other. In *Douglas v Hello! Ltd.* [2005] EWCA Civ 595, Lord Phillips after reviewing the United Kingdom's convention obligations in respect of privacy said:

> We conclude that, insofar as private information is concerned, we are required to adopt, as the vehicle for performing such duties falls on the courts in relation to convention rights, the cause of action formerly described as breach of confidence. As to the nature of that duty, it seems to us that ss.2, 3, 6 and 12 of the 1998 Act all point in the same direction. The court should, insofar as it can, develop the action for breach of confidence in such manner as will give effect to both Art.8 and Art.10 rights. In considering the nature of those rights, account should be taken of the Strasbourg Jurisprudence. In particular, when considering what information should be protected as private pursuant to Art.8, it is right to have regard to the decisions of the European Courts. We cannot pretend that we find it satisfactory to be required to shoe-horn within the cause of action a breach of confidence claim for publication of unauthorised photographs of a private occasion.

On appeal to the House of Lords [2007] UKHL 21, the conflation of a possible right of privacy and breach of confidence was touched upon by Lord Hoffman and Lord Nicholls, but the appeal decided on grounds of commercial confidentiality (the Douglas' having ceased involvement in the proceedings at an earlier stage).

The law in relation to this category of cases might be regarded still developing and not yet settled.

5.2.3 Limited purpose of disclosure

There is a large body of authority in support of the proposition that information which is disclosed for a limited purpose is received under an obligation of confidence and cannot be used or disclosed otherwise than for that purpose.

5.2.3.1 Business negotiations

Information disclosed by one party to another in the course of negotiations will be subject to the obligation of confidence where information relates to the subject matter of the negotiations and has the necessary quality of confidence. Thus in *Seager v Copydex Ltd* [1967] 1 W.L.R. 923 details of an unpatented invention disclosed in the course of negotiations relating to a similar patented invention were held to have been disclosed under an obligation of confidence. Similarly in *Coco v AN Clark (Engineers) Ltd* [1969] R.P.C. 41 Megarry J. held that information concerning an engine supplied by the plaintiff in the course of negotiations was subject to an implied obligation of confidence. Megarry J. suggested that the test of an officious bystander could be helpful: if the parties, when asked by an officious bystander whether their discussions were confidential, would have responded "but obviously it is", that would establish the obligation.

Clearly there may be some negotiations where it would be unwise to assume that an obligation of confidence will arise. One example would be negotiations for settlement of litigation. Another example that came before the court concerned confidentiality in an offer made to a vendor of land. The vendor's agent disclosed the amount of an offer made by one potential purchaser to another. The offeror, who was unsuccessful in obtaining the property sued for breach of confidence. The court held on the facts that the vendor's agent was not under a duty of confidence (*Trees Ltd v Cripps* (1983) 267 E.G. 596).

5.2.3.2 Professional advisers and bankers

Information supplied by clients to their professional advisers will be received subject to an obligation of confidence. In the case of solicitors this is clearly shown in *Rakusen v Ellis, Munday & Clarke* [1912] 1 Ch. 831 where it was said "A solicitor can be restrained as a matter of absolute obligation and as a matter of general principle from disclosing any secrets which are confidentially reposed in him". The obligation of confidence is of wider ambit than legal professional privilege (see also *Re A Firm of Solicitors* [1995] F.S.R. 783). In *Weld-Blundell v Stephens* [1920] A.C. 956 it was held that an accountant owed a duty to keep a letter of instructions confidential. Bankers are under a similar duty of confidentiality to their clients (see *Tournier v National Provincial and Union Bank of England* [1924] 1 K.B. 461). Statutory regulation of the disclosure of confidential information in the banking sphere are found inter alia in ss. 347–354 Financial Services and Markets Act 2000 and the Financial Services and Markets Act 2000 (Confidential Information) (Bank of England) (Consequential Provisions) Order 2001. Under this the Bank of England is permitted in certain circumstances to disclose information provided to it.

5.2.3.3 Information supplied to enable the performance of contracts

Information having the necessary quality of confidence which is supplied by one party of a contract to another for the purpose of enabling that other to perform a contract will usually be subject to an obligation of confidence so that the recipient may only use it for the purpose of that contract.

A common situation where such an obligation of confidence is likely to arise is in subcontracting arrangements where the prime contractor supplies detailed information relating to the products which are to be built to his subcontractor. This information may only be used by the subcontractor for the purpose of performing the agreement.

A typical example of this was the subject of *Saltman Engineering Co v Campbell Engineering Co* (1963) 65 R.P.C. 203 where drawings of tools for the manufacture of leather punches were placed in the hands of subcontractors for the purpose of manufacturing the tools for one of the plaintiffs. The defendants used the drawings to manufacture tools which they sold on their own account. The court held that the defendants were guilty of a breach of confidence. (See also *Ackroyd v Gill* (1856) 5 E. & B. 808, *Tuck & Sons v Priester* (1887) L.R. 19 Q.B.D. 629 and *Prince Albert v Strange* (1849) 1 Mac. & G. 25.) *Schering Chemicals v Falkman* [1981] 2 W.L.R. 848 provides perhaps the most extreme example of the obligation of confidence arising from disclosure for a limited purpose. In that case Schering employed Falkman Ltd to give its executives instruction in how to deal with the media regarding one of its products. Falkman employed a freelance expert to assist it. Schering disclosed what it regarded as confidential information to Falkman and the expert for this purpose. It was held that the expert was bound to maintain the confidentiality of the information and was accordingly not entitled to use the information for the purpose of making a television film. This was the case notwithstanding the fact that all the information which was given to the expert had in fact been previously published. As Templeman L.J. put it:

> As between Scherings and [the expert] if [the expert] had obtained the information from sources other than Scherings, then it would of course not have been confidential in his hands, but, by agreeing to advise Scherings and by accepting information from them to enable him to advise Scherings, [the expert] placed himself under a duty, in my judgment not to make use of that information without the consent of Scherings in a manner which Scherings reasonably considered harmful to their cause.

This difficult case was discussed in *A-G v Guardian Newspapers Ltd* [1987] 3 All E.R. 316 at p.374, per Lord Oliver, and *A-G v Guardian Newspapers Ltd (No. 2)* [1988] 3 All E.R. 545 at p.625, *per* Bingham L.J. In *Prout v British Gas plc* [1992] F.S.R. 478 the defendant was held to be under a contractual and equitable duty to maintain the confidence of ideas presented by the plaintiff under an employee suggestion scheme.

Considerable difficulties of construction can arise in licence and distribution agreements where confidential information relating to the products is supplied to the licensee or distributor. In *Regina Glass Fibre v Schuller* [1972] R.P.C. 229 it was held that the licensee had the right to continue using improvement patents and know-how even after the end of the licence agreement. Conversely in *Torrington Manufacturing Co v Smith and Son (England) Ltd* [1966] R.P.C. 285 it was held that a distributor's right to use drawings of products supplied by the manufacturer was limited to the purpose and duration of the agreement. It could not use them to manufacture its own products (see also *Peter Pan Manufacturing Corp v Corsets Silhouette* [1964] 1 W.L.R. 96). What is required is an agreement which clearly addresses the point. For an example of the difficulties in proving what is confidential in such a case see *Suhner and Co AG v Transradio Ltd* [1967] R.P.C. 329.

An obligation of confidence will usually arise as between partners. Thus in the case of *Morrison v Moat* (1851) 9 Hare 241 when one partner communicated a secret recipe of the partnership to his son who subsequently sought to exploit that recipe for his own account, an injunction was granted to restrain him. A duty of confidence may also arise in joint projects or ventures. See *Strix Ltd v Otter Controls Ltd* [1995] R.P.C. 607.

5.2.3.4 Information supplied for statutory or official purposes

Confidential commercial information obtained pursuant to statutory powers can only be disclosed by the recipient to such persons and for such purposes as are envisaged by the statute conferring the powers (or pursuant to a court order). See *Hoechst UK Ltd v Chemiculture Ltd* [1993] F.S.R. 270. See also *Smith Kline & French Laboratories (Australia) Ltd and others v Secretary to the Department of Community Services and Health* [1990] F.S.R. 617, *Marcel v Commissioner of Police for the Metropolis* [1992] 2 W.L.R. 50 and *Hellewell v Chief Constable of Derbyshire* [1995] 4 All E.R. 473.

Information disclosed on discovery in legal proceedings is clearly held under an obligation of confidence and may be used only for the purpose of those proceedings. See for example *Distillers Co (Biochemicals) Ltd v Times Newspapers* [1975] Q.B. 613 and *Riddick v Thames Board Mills Ltd* [1977] Q.B. 881.

5.3 Duration of the duty

It is difficult to lay down any general rule for determining the period for which an obligation of confidence will last. Much will depend upon the circumstances of the disclosure, the nature of the information itself and even whether it is capable of being protected by an implied obligation. In the case of an employment contract, Scott J., in *Balston Ltd v Headline Filters Ltd* [1987] F.S.R. 330 at p.348, said that the implied obligation referred to in *Faccenda Chicken* of protecting trade secrets "will always be unlimited in time" and probably in area as well. The question of the duration of the duty in cases where the "springboard" doctrine applies has been discussed above. An example of the limited duration of an obligation of confidence in a "springboard" case is found in *Fisher-Karpark Industries Ltd v Nichols* [1982] F.S.R. 351 where account was taken in determining the duration of an injunction of the extent to which the information was generally available from public sources. The obligation will usually last only for as long as the information retains the necessary quality of confidence. For example in *Franchi v Franchi* [1967] R.P.C. 149 the obligation of confidence in information relating to a method of making stone tiles was held to have lapsed upon the publication by the plaintiff of the information in a patent application.

However, publication of the information will not always bring the obligation to an end. In *Schering Chemicals v Falkman* the fact that all the information which the defendant sought to use was already available in published material did not relieve the defendant of his duty. As Shaw L.J. said "It is not the law that where confidentiality exists it is terminated or eroded by adventitious publicity. Nor is the correlative duty to preserve that confidentiality".

The pragmatic approach of the courts to the question of when publication brings the obligation to an end is shown in *Speed Seal Ltd v Paddington* [1985] 1 W.L.R. 1327 where the publication of the plaintiff's secrets had been made by the defendant. Fox L.J. pointed out that the purpose of the injunction was to protect the plaintiff. If the defendant was the only person other than the plaintiff using the information (or one of a few) then the injunction would be effective to protect the plaintiff and would be granted.

The following conclusions can perhaps be drawn from the authorities. First, where the use to which the information is to be put is publication or sale of the information the courts will be less sympathetic to arguments that there can be no confidence. This is perhaps inevitable because in such cases it is not entirely illogical to argue that if the information was already publicly known why should anyone want to publish it or sell it? It is perhaps for this reason that the Court of Appeal in *Faccenda* left open the question as to whether an employee could sell the information which was comprised in the skills acquired in the course of employment which he could not be prevented from using himself. Secondly, that where information becomes publicly available through the actions of the plaintiff the courts will more readily find that the information no longer has the requisite quality of confidence than where publication is by a third party. It was in this context that Lord Denning in *Dunford and Elliott v Firth Brown* [1978] F.S.R. 143 added a gloss to the analysis of Megarry V.C. in *Coco v AN Clark (Engineers) Ltd* when he said that if the stipulation of confidence was unreasonable at the time of making it; or if it was reasonable at the beginning, but afterwards, in the course of subsequent happenings, it becomes unreasonable that it should be enforced: then the courts will decline to enforce it. In that case the plaintiff had made information relevant to evaluating a takeover bid for its shares available to 43 per cent of its shareholders. The information had also been disclosed in confidence to another shareholder who was using it for the purpose of making a bid for the plaintiff company. It was held that the widespread use of the information drove a hole in the blanket of confidence.

A further circumstance in which the obligation of confidence will come to an end is where an express provision of limited duration expires. In such a case it will be difficult to persuade a court to imply any further obligation: see the judgment of Lord Denning in *Potters-Ballottini Ltd v Weston-Baker* [1977] R.P.C. 202. Similarly the court in *Roger Bullivant Ltd v Ellis* took note of the duration of a restrictive covenant in a former employee's contract of employment in determining how long it would restrain the defendant from using an index of customers removed from his former employers. In *Systems Reliability Holdings Plc v Smith* [1990] I.R.L.R. 377 Harman J. decided that the injunction restraining a breach of confidence should expire at the same time as a restrictive covenant.

Lastly, an obligation of confidence, at least where it is only equitable, will come to an end when public policy will no longer be served by upholding it. This principle is unlikely to be of great relevance in cases for the protection of business secrets. It is best illustrated by the Crossman Diaries Case, *A-G v Jonathan Cape Ltd* [1976] Q.B. 752 where the court would not prevent the publication of diaries of cabinet discussions on grounds of confidentiality after a period of ten years.

5.4 Breach of the duty

The question of what constitutes a breach of the duty of confidentiality falls into two parts. There is the difficult issue of whether use as opposed to disclosure constitutes breach. In addition there are circumstances in which disclosure is permissible.

In general, it would appear that where an obligation of confidentiality arises, the courts will give relief, not only in respect of disclosure of the information, but also as to use of the information without the consent of the person to whom the duty of confidentiality is owed. This will be the case even where disclosure of the information is not an inevitable consequence of its use (see for example *Amber Size and Chemical Co Ltd v Menzel* [1913] 30 R.P.C. 433). In *Union Carbide Corp v Naturin* [1987] F.S.R. 538 the court had to consider a motion to strike out a claim in respect of possession of products manufactured by a third party in breach of confidence (sausage skins), but which did not themselves embody the confidential information. The court refused to strike out the claim but did not decide the position one way or the other. However the courts are often reluctant to grant injunctions against the use of information where such information could have been relatively easily acquired by the defendant through his own legitimate efforts (see *Seager v Copydex Ltd* and *Coco v AN Clark (Engineers) Ltd*). Care must be taken in the drafting of express contractual restraints to ensure that they clearly cover both use and non-disclosure. In *Thomas Marshall (Exporters) Ltd v Guinle* [1979] 1 Ch. 227 Megarry V.C. held that an express contractual restriction on disclosure did not also prohibit use of the information (the plaintiff was, in fact, granted an injunction against use on the grounds of the defendant's duty of good faith but this duty will not exist in all cases). For completeness, although a detailed examination of this lies outside the scope of this work, the EC Database Directive (96/9/EC) and the copyright and the Rights in Database Regulations 1997 SI1997/3032 may provide an alternative to proceedings on the basis of a breach of confidentiality (whether an express or an implied obligation). This will only be in the narrow circumstances where an employee has taken for his own, or for a third party, use an employer's computer database or part of it. Given the extremely wide use made of computers to store information of all kinds, it is conceivable that this might extend to include confidential technical information regarding products but also, customer contact details, details of suppliers, pricing information, etc. Some of this data would be clearly confidential, some not and some may inhabit a difficult twilight zone in this regard. If what is taken forms part of a database as defined in the Regulations (which require, inter alia, that the database must be one where "there has been substantial investment in obtaining, verifying or presenting the contents of the database") then the extraction or re-utilisation of all or a substantial part of the contents of the database may be actionable with the same remedies as for a normal breach of confidence claim but, usefully, without the necessity of having to embark on detailed consideration of the question of whether what has been taken is confidential.

5.5 Defences

5.5.1 Iniquity

In a long line of cases the courts have held that the disclosure of information relating to what was originally termed iniquity will not be restrained: see *Gartside v Outram* (1856) 26 L.J. Ch. 113, *Weld-Blundell v Stephens* [1920] A.C. 956; *Initial Services Ltd v Putterill* [1968] 1 Q.B. 396; *Fraser v Evans* [1969] 1 Q.B. 349; *Hubbard v Vosper* [1972] 1 All E.R. 1023; *Church of Scientology of California v Kaufman* [1973] R.P.C. 635; *British Steel Corporation v Granada Television Ltd* [1981] 1 All E.R. 417; and *Lion Laboratories Ltd v Evans* [1984] 2 All E.R. 417. This doctrine has its roots in the equitable nature of the duty of confidence but can now be regarded as covering both equitable and contractual obligations of confidence (see *Initial Services Ltd v Putterill*). Although originally the doctrine was thought to be restricted to cases of iniquity or wrongdoing on the part of the party seeking to enforce the obligation of confidence, it is now clear that this is not so. The test is whether the public interest in disclosure outweighs the public interest in the preservation of confidence. As Griffiths L.J. explained in *Lion Laboratories Ltd v Evans* "I believe that the so-called iniquity rule evolved because in most cases where the facts justified a publication in breach of confidence the plaintiff had behaved so disgracefully or criminally that it was judged in the public interest that his behaviour should be exposed" and, as he aptly stated, "there is a world of difference between what is in the public interest and what is of interest to the public". In *Times Newspapers plc and HarperCollins Publishers Ltd v MGN Ltd* [1993] 6 Ent. L.R. 119 the court held at first instance that publication of details extracted from Lady Thatcher's as yet unpublished memoirs at the time of the Conservative Party Conference was in the public interest and declined to grant an injunction restraining a breach of confidence.

In *Re A Company's Application* [1989] 3 W.L.R. 265 the plaintiff company carried on the business of providing financial advice and was subject to the regulatory scheme imposed by FIMBRA pursuant to the provisions of the Financial Services Act 1986. The defendant had been employed by the company as its compliance officer; it was his duty to supervise the procedures and practices of the plaintiff so as to secure fulfilment of the regulatory requirements imposed by FIMBRA. FIMBRA was entitled at its discretion from time to time to make spot checks on companies subject to its regulatory umbrella and therefore the details of the business carried out by the company might at any time have become known to it. In October 1988 the company gave the defendant one month's notice. On December 12, 1988 a telephone conversation took place between the defendant and one of the company's chief executives which the plaintiff's company interpreted as an attempt to blackmail, whereas the defendant contended that he had merely indicated his intentions to seek compensation for dismissal. The defendant also raised certain matters which in his view represented breaches of the regulatory scheme by the plaintiff or improprieties in regard to tax. The plaintiffs made an application for an interlocutory injunction to restrain the defendant from disclosing to the regulatory body or to the revenue its confidential information or documents. Scott J. concluded that if this were a case in which there was any question or threat of general disclosure by the defendant of confidential information concerning the way in which the plaintiff carried on its business or concerning any details of the affairs of any of its clients there would be no answer to the claim for an injunction; but it was not general disclosure that the defendant had in mind. He desired to disclose only to FIMBRA and the Inland Revenue. He asked himself whether an employee of a company carrying on the business of giving financial advice and of financial management to the public under the regulatory umbrella provided by FIMBRA owes a duty of confidentiality that extends to barring disclosure of information to FIMBRA. He answered that question in the negative and likewise in relation to the Inland Revenue. He granted an injunction restraining the defendant from using and/or disclosing confidential information but qualified it so that it did not apply to communications made by the defendant either to FIMBRA or the Inland Revenue in respect of the matters identified in the defence. In addition he accepted an undertaking by the defendant not to reveal other than to his legal advisers the fact that he had made communications to FIMBRA and the Inland Revenue.

In *W v Egdell* [1989] 2 W.L.R. 689 Scott J. had to consider the duty of confidentiality owed by a doctor to a patient. The plaintiff had applied to a Mental Health Tribunal to be transferred from a secure hospital. In support of the application he sought a report from the first defendant, an independent consultant psychiatrist. The first defendant's report was unfavourable to the plaintiff and it was sent by him to the plaintiff's solicitors. The plaintiff's solicitors withdrew the application to the tribunal. The first defendant learnt of this but also became aware that no copy of his report had been sent to the tribunal or was on the plaintiff's file at the hospital. The first defendant decided to supply a copy of it to the hospital and subsequently copies were sent to the Home Secretary and the Department of Health and Social Security. The plaintiff issued a writ against the defendant claiming that a breach of confidence had occurred. The judge was in no doubt that if the defendant had sold the contents of his report to a newspaper that would have been a breach of confidence. However the question in the present case was whether the duty of confidence which the defendant no doubt owed to the plaintiff extended so far as to bar disclosure of the report to the hospital or the Home Office. In order to answer that question the court had to balance the interest to be served by non-disclosure against the interest served by disclosure. Scott J. concluded that it was in the public interest for there to have been disclosure to those two bodies.

5.5.2 The Public Interest Disclosure Act 1998

The Public Interest Disclosure Act 1998 ("PIDA") (the principal provisions of which are incorporated into the Employment Rights Act 1996) came into force on July 2, 1999 and, whilst not strictly providing a defence to a claim of breach of confidence may, in circumstances where the Act applies, effectively negative an employer's ability to pursue such a breach. PIDA primarily provides protection from detriment or dismissal for "workers" in circumstances where they make a "qualifying disclosure" relating to certain categories of mal-practice. "Worker" is more broadly defined than "employee" and extends to include not just employees who have entered into or work under a contract of employment, but those who work under any other contract under which they personally perform any work or services, and also other groups such as agency workers and independent contractors. In order to enjoy protection against dismissal or other detriment in the event of making a disclosure (which may not necessarily, but in many instances will, involve a potential breach of a duty of confidentiality) the disclosure must be a "qualifying" one. That is to say one which, in the reasonable belief of the worker making it, tends to show that:

(a) a criminal offence has been committed, is being committed or is likely to be committed,

(b) the person has failed or is failing or is likely to fail to comply with any legal obligation to which he is subject,

(c) a miscarriage of justice has occurred, is occurring or is likely to occur,

(d) the health and safety of any individual has been, is being or is likely to be endangered,

(e) the environment has been, is being or is likely to be damaged, or

(f) the information relating to any of these matters has been, or is likely to be, deliberately concealed (s.43B Employment Rights Act 1996).

The worker must have a reasonable belief in the factual correctness of the matter being disclosed and disclosure must be made in good faith (see *Street v Derbyshire Unemployed Workers' Centre* [2004] I.R.L.R. 687, CA). In order for a qualifying disclosure to be protected, the disclosure must be made to the workers' employer, or if it relates to the conduct of someone other than his employer or is a matter for which a person other than his employer has a legal responsibility then to that other party; a legal adviser in the course of obtaining legal advice; in the case of Crown employees, to a Minister of the Crown; a prescribed person (see Public Interest Disclosure (Prescribed Persons) Order 1999, SI 1999/1549) and, in certain limited circumstances, a third party unconnected with the employment (effectively this can include the media). The protection available for workers making qualifying disclosures in relation to dismissals or other detriment arising from having made such a disclosure, is bolstered by s.43J of the Employment Rights Act 1996 which stipulates that any provision in an agreement (this may typically be a contract of employment) is void insofar as it purports to preclude the worker from making a protected disclosure. Of course, if the worker falls outside the protection of PIDA, he or she would still be liable to the employer, but the development of the case law (see in particular *Babula v Waltham Forest College* [2007] I.R.L.R. 346, CA) is such that the protection of the legislation is not lost where, in fact, there has been no criminal act or breach of a legal obligation and the worker's belief in this regard is wrong; it is sufficient that the worker reasonably believes that the facts and matters relied upon do amount to a criminal act or a breach of a legal obligation.

5.5.3 Freedom of Information and Data Protection legislation

Mention should also be made of the Freedom of Information Act 2000 and the Data Protection Act 1998. The former, which came into force in January 2005, provides a right to request information that is held by public bodies. Certain exceptions apply which include an exemption, qualified by the public interest test (see s.43), in relation to information where the disclosure "would, or would be likely to, prejudice the commercial interest with any party". Additionally, by virtue of s.41, there is an absolute exemption (to which the public interest test does not apply) from the right to have disclosed any information that, if it were to be disclosed, would "constitute an actionable breach of confidence". The latter provides, inter alia, for an individual to have a right of access to personal data held electronically and in certain manual filing systems relating to that person. For the purposes of the Data Protection Act (personal data) is electronic data or information in a "relevant filing system" (typically a manual system of personnel records) that (s.1(1)) relates to a living individual and the individual must be identifiable from those data (or in conjunction with other information the employer has or is likely to have at some point) and "includes any expression of opinion about the individual and any indication of the intentions of the [employer] or any other person in respect of the individual". The employee's right of access is the right to have communicated to him in an intelligible form:

(i) the information that forms the personal data held by the employer about him,

(ii) a copy of the information in a permanent form (unless this would require a disproportionate effort on the part of the employer, or it agreed otherwise) and,

(iii) any information available to the employer as to the source of that information.

A Data Subject Access request by an employee can prove very onerous in practice given the extent to which it may be necessary to search not just manual filing systems but, more importantly, electronic data bases. An employer may decline to provide a copy of information sought on grounds that it would entail a "disproportionate effort" but the Data Protection Act does not specify what this means beyond saying that it is a question of fact in each case taking into account:

(a) the cost of the provision of the information;

(b) the length of time it may take to provide the information;

(c) how difficult it is to provide the information;

(d) the resources (in terms of equipment and material) which will have to be deployed;

(e) whether the employer has a policy in relation to archive or other non-live data;

(f) the size of the employer's organisation;

(g) whether there is evidence that back-up data differs materially from data on the live system; and

(h) the effort that the data subject might have to make to physically view the records if copies are not made available.

Where the information in question has been provided by a third party (and is confidential) if such information would lead to the provision of information about another party who can be identified as the source of the information sought by the employee, an employer need not comply with the Data Subject Access request in this respect, unless the third party consents or it is reasonable in all the circumstances to dispense with this consent (s.7(4) and (5)). The factors to be taken into account in this regard are:

(a) any duty of confidentiality owed to third parties;

(b) any steps taken by the employer to seek the consent of the third party;

(c) whether the third party is capable of giving consent; and

(d) any express refusal of consent by the third party.

There are exceptions to the right of access to personal data (and therefore defences to this—see Schedule 7). An employee is not entitled to have access to any reference given by the employer (although a Data Subject Access request targeted at the recipient of a reference does not enjoy the same exception). Personal data that is processed for the purposes of "management forecasting or management planning" may not be accessed by an employee if it is likely to prejudice the conduct of the employer's business. This would typically cover data in relation to promotion, remuneration, reviews, restructuring/re-organisation programmes. If an employee is negotiating with an employer, any data in relation to those negotiations cannot be accessed by the employee if disclosure would prejudice the negotiations. There is a further exception on grounds that the documentation is privileged on the basis of legal professional privilege. Personal data required for the purpose of detectional prevention of crime is also exempt, and there is also a corporate finance exception applicable in certain circumstances where release of information would affect a company's share price. The remedies for a failure of comply with the Act are:

(a) an enforcement notice served by the Information Commissioner requiring an employer to take any remedial steps found to be necessary,

(b) and additionally a failure to comply with, inter alia, the Data Subject Access Rights can be enforced through the Courts on the part of the employee by seeking an order for disclosure and for compensation if any damage has been suffered as a consequence of a breach. Compensation for any distress may also be recoverable.

5.5.4 Miscellaneous

It will be no breach of confidentiality to disclose documents on discovery in the course of litigation even if they are held subject to a duty of confidence owed to a third party. See for example *Chantry Martin & Co v Martin* [1953] 2 Q.B. 286 and *Alfred Crompton Amusement Machines Ltd v Commissioners of Customs & Excise* [1974] A.C. 405. Similarly, disclosure under compulsion of law is not normally a breach of the duty. See *Robertson v Canadian Imperial Bank of Commerce* (1994) *The Times*, November 16, 1994. However in a proper case the court is prepared to balance the public interest in full disclosure on discovery against the public interest in honouring an obligation of confidence. Thus in *D v NSPCC* [1978] A.C. 171 the court was willing to permit the NSPCC to withhold the name of their informant and similarly in *Broadmoor Hospital v Hyde* (1994) *The Independent*, March 4, a journalist was not required to disclose a source, but in *British Steel Corporation v Granada Television Ltd* [1981] 1 All E.R. 417 the defendants were ordered to disclose the name of the plaintiff's employee who had supplied them with confidential information belonging to the plaintiff. It is interesting to note that the European Court of Human Rights ruled that a fine imposed under the Contempt of Court Act 1981 on journalist William Goodwin for failing to reveal his sources infringed Art.10 of the European Convention of Human Rights which protects freedom of expression.

Similarly an obligation of confidence may not be prayed in aid of a refusal to disclose secret information to a trustee in bankruptcy if it can be regarded as part of the bankrupt's property (see *Keene, Re* [1922] 2 Ch. 475).

5.6 The question of detriment

It has been suggested in some cases (see *e.g. Coco v AN Clark (Engineers) Ltd* [1969] R.P.C. 41) that an obligation of confidence will not be enforced unless the disclosure or use of the information results in a detriment to the plaintiff or an advantage to his competitors. See also *Meadowstone (Derbyshire) Ltd. v (1) Kirk (2) Hill* [2006] UK EAT/0529/05/ZT, where the EAT found the dismissal of two executive directors to be wrongful and unfair in circumstances where confidential, financial and commercial information prepared in the context of a management buyout proposal was disclosed by them in the course of preparing an alternative proposal. The EAT observed that it was not the interests of the company that might have been damaged by this conduct, but those of the individuals involved in the rival management buyout proposal (it was in the company's interest that the best possible price should be obtained) and, in these circumstances, the defendants were to be taken to have been authorised by the company to take the action that they did. This was so, notwithstanding that the defendant's service agreements each contained clauses prohibiting the use of disclosure of the company's confidential information. As far as any remedy in damages is concerned the presence or absence of detriment or advantage will not be of any significance as damages need to be proved (see *e.g. Universal Thermosensors Ltd v Hibben* [1992] 1 W.L.R. 840) and it is most unlikely that any action would be brought in a business secrets case unless some damage or advantage to a competitor had occurred or was thought likely to do so. However in an application for an injunction it is of great significance. The matter was discussed in *A-G v Guardian Newspapers Ltd (No. 2)* [1988] 3 All E.R. 545. Lord Keith at p.640 said, as a general rule it is in the public interest that confidences should be respected, and the encouragement of such respect may in itself constitute a sufficient ground for recognising and enforcing the obligation of confidence even where the consider can point to no specific detriment to himself. Information about a person's private and personal affairs may be of a nature which shows him up in a favourable light and would by no means expose him to criticism. The anonymous donor of a very large sum to a very worthy cause has his own reasons for wishing to remain anonymous, which are unlikely to be discreditable. He should surely be in a position to restrain disclosure in breach of confidence of his identity in connection with the donation. ". . . I would think it a sufficient detriment to consider that information given in confidence is to be disclosed to persons whom he would prefer not to know of, even though the disclosure would not be harmful to him in any positive way". Lord Griffiths at pp.649–50 concluded that "detriment or potential detriment" was necessary in order to obtain an injunction. Lord Goff at p.659 went further in saying "I would . . . wish to keep open the question whether detriment to the plaintiff is an essential ingredient of an action for breach of confidence". However, he pointed out that in most cases detriment will exist. This is certainly correct in commercial cases, although see *Jack Allen (Sales & Service) Ltd v Smith* [1999] I.R.L.R. 19, Ct Session (OH) where an express confidentiality obligation was not enforced by injunction where the former employers totally failed to identify a real loss which would result from its breach.

5.7 *Locus standi* (to whom is the duty owed)

Leaving aside the question of duties of third parties who receive confidential information which is dealt with below, the question of *locus standi* to bring a claim for breach of confidence has not often come before the courts. The leading case is *Fraser v Evans* [1969] 1 Q.B. 349. That case concerned an article which *Sunday Times* were proposing to publish. It was to be based on a report which the plaintiff had prepared for the Greek Government. The plaintiff's contract with the Greek Government placed him under an obligation of confidence but placed the Greek Government under no such obligation. It appeared that *Sunday Times* had obtained their copy of the report from an unauthorised Greek Government source. It was said by the court that the plaintiff's case must fail because any duty of confidence which might exist was owed to the Greek Government and not to the plaintiff.

It therefore seems clear that in order to found an action for breach of confidence the defendant must have obtained the information as a result of a disclosure by the plaintiff in circumstances of confidence. Presumably it is also possible to acquire *locus standi* to bring a claim by means of an assignment, subject to the usual limitations on the assignment of bare causes of action.

5.8 Third parties

Without doubt the courts will in proper circumstances restrain a breach of confidence by third parties who have come by confidential information. The nature of those circumstances is unclear.

Two clear situations can be discerned. First, if the defendant receives the information in the knowledge that it is being disclosed in breach of confidence he will be bound by an obligation of confidence (see for example *Prince Albert v Strange* (1849) 1 Mac. & G. 25, *Schering Chemicals v Falkman* [1981] 2 W.L.R. 848). Secondly, if X discloses information in confidence to Y and Y then discloses the information in confidence to Z (but does not tell Z that he has obtained the information from X) then X will be able to proceed directly against Z if Z disregards the obligation of confidence (see *Saltman Engineering Co v Campbell Engineering Co* [1963] 65 R.P.C. 203).

Greater difficulties arise where the defendant comes by the information without notice of any restrictions on its disclosure. In certain cases it might well be that the defendant's ignorance will not help him. In *Argyll Group plc v Distillers Co plc* [1986] 1 C.M.L.R. 764 the confidentiality of documents produced on discovery was in issue. Talbot J. said "those who disclose documents on discovery are entitled to the protection of the court against any use of the documents by any person into whose hands they come unless it is directly connected with the action in which they are produced". There was no suggestion that an innocent recipient should be permitted to use the documents (by the same token there was no suggestion that the recipients were innocent of the means by which the documents had been obtained).

In other cases an innocent recipient may be protected at least until he becomes aware of the confidential nature of the information. As Lord Denning said in *Fraser v Evans*:

> No person is permitted to divulge to the world information which he has received in confidence, unless he has just cause or excuse for doing so. Even if he comes by it innocently, nevertheless once he gets to know that it was originally given in confidence, he can be restrained from breaking that confidence.

However it should be recalled that even if an obligation of confidence is held to exist the grant of an injunction is in the discretion of the court. Where the defendant has innocently made a substantial investment on the basis of information innocently acquired it is most unlikely that an injunction would be granted to restrain him from making use of that information (although the fact that an injunction might drive the defendant into liquidation is not relevant if the tests in *American Cyanamid Co v Ethicon* [1975] A.C. 396 have been satisfied; *per* May L.J. in *Roger Bullivant Ltd v Ellis* [1987] I.C.R. 464). Thus, in *Seager v Copydex Ltd* [1967] 1 W.L.R. 923 no injunction was granted to prevent the defendant's use of information supplied by the plaintiff in ignorance of the duty of confidence but the plaintiff had a remedy in damages. In *A-G v Guardian Newspapers Ltd (No. 2)* [1988] 2 W.L.R. 805 at p.873, Lord Donaldson M.R. stated that, at first instance, Scott J. had come to the conclusion that the duty to maintain confidentiality was not necessarily in all circumstances the same in relation to third parties who became possessed of confidential information as it was in relation to the primary confidant. He agreed with that proposition and stated:

> The reason is that the third party recipient may be subject to some additional and conflicting duty which does not affect the primary confidant or may not be subject to some special duty which does affect that confidant. In such situations the equation is not the same in the case of the confidant and that of the third party and accordingly the result may be different.

Even though this case went to the House of Lords no disagreement with that statement of principle is found in the judgments there (see also *Lord Advocate v Scotsman Publications* [1990] 1 A.C. 812 at p.822).

5.9 Equity, law and property

There has been much academic discussion about the nature of the law of confidence. It is clear that one cannot own confidential information in the sense that one can own a car. This is because information is not the same sort of thing as a car. This is obvious when one considers that two identical copies of a blueprint clearly contain the same information, but two identical cars are not the same car. To talk of owning information is therefore misleading. All one may own are such rights as the law confers upon someone who holds confidential information.

These rights do not exist in the information itself but arise from its confidential nature and the circumstances in which persons other than the originator of the information come by it. As has been seen the courts prefer, where possible, to give these rights a contractual basis (see *Faccenda Chicken Ltd v Fowler* [1985] 1 All E.R. 729). However, where no express or implied contract exists, as for example will be the case where third parties come by confidential information, the rights are presumably equitable in nature. The judgments in *A-G v Guardian Newspapers Ltd (No. 2)* [1988] 3 All E.R. 545 made no distinction between contract or equity as a basis for the duty of confidence. It should not however be supposed that because of the equitable nature of these rights a bona fide purchaser for value will be protected. This was confirmed in *Valeo Vision SA v Flexible Lamps Ltd* [1995] R.P.C. 205 where it was held that the duty of confidence attached to a third party if their conscience was bound, not whether they were a bona fide purchaser for value. The difficulty of characterising the nature of the duty of confidence was highlighted in the Canadian case *Lac Minerals Ltd v International Corona Resources Ltd* [1990] F.S.R. 441 where two judges held that a fiduciary obligation not to use confidential information and two specifically held that no fiduciary relationship existed. Notwithstanding this the Supreme Court held, by a majority, that property acquired through the misuse of confidential information should be held on constructive trust. Although the point is undecided (but see the Australian case *Wheatley v Bell* [1984] F.S.R. 16) the nature of information would seem to conflict with the existence of any legal estate. Equity only protects the bona fide purchaser for value of a legal estate and so the rule should be of no application. It is more probable that the whole matter lies in the discretion of the court as to the grant of an injunction (or damages in lieu). In one respect, however, confidential information can be regarded as property. It is possible to transfer it from one person to another so that the recipient can exercise such rights against third parties as may arise (see for example *Keene, Re* [1922] 2 Ch. 475.

See also *Douglas & Others v Hello! Ltd. & Others* (No3) [2005] 4 All E.R. 128, CA, in which the Court of Appeal held that what was given was a licence to publish certain approved photographic images and exploit those photographs commercially for a period, and this did not carry with it the benefit to claim breach of confidence in relation to other confidential information, or the right to sue a third party for infringement of a right invested in the licensor to object to publishing of the photographs of the event in question. However, on appeal, [2007] UKHL 21, the majority of the House of Lords accepted that the publication of "spoiler" photographs of the wedding of Michael Douglas and Catherine Zeta-Jones by *Hello!* Magazine infringed *OK!* Magazine's commercially confidential information (deriving from the licence to publish authorised photographs of the Douglas' wedding) reinstating the trial Judge's award of damages. The minority view was that the rights of confidentiality did not continue once *OK!* Magazine published the photographs it was permitted to under the terms of its agreement with Mr. and Mrs. Douglas.

If this is the aim it will, by the agreement of transfer, be necessary to specify that the transferor will not further use or disclose the information himself, otherwise the transferee will simply be one further person who is aware of the information. The right of the transferee to sue, in his own name, persons who used information obtained from the transferor in breach of confidence before the date of the transfer is not clearly established (although see *Douglas* above). Any well-drafted transfer will therefore provide for the transfer of the right to sue for such breaches. In addition, it will be prudent for the transferee to join the transferor as a party to any such action.

5.10 Contractual rights

The courts adopt substantially the same rules when implying an obligation of confidence into a contract and when finding an equitable obligation of confidence. This is shown by the judgment of Lord Greene in *Saltman* where he said:

> If two parties make a contract under which one of them obtains for the purpose of the contract or in connection with it some confidential matter, even though the contract is silent on the matter of confidence the law will imply an obligation to treat that confidential matter in a confidential way as one of the implied terms of the contract; but the obligation of confidence is not limited to cases where the parties are in a contractual relationship.

This passage also shows the clear preference of the courts to rely on an implied contractual obligation (see also *Faccenda*).

5.10.1 Relationship between intellectual property rights and confidentiality

As a general rule of thumb, under competition law, restrictions relating specifically to the protection of intellectual property rights and confidential information relating to them are more likely to be seen as permissible and not necessarily caught by the prohibition of Article 81 or Chapter 1.

It is however important to remember that the actions for breach of confidence and breach of intellectual property rights are fundamentally different.

Whereas, for example, copyright protects the form in which an idea is expressed but not the idea itself, confidence can protect both the form and the idea. There is no reason why a claim for breach of confidence and infringement might not arise on the same facts (see for example *Alfa Laval Cheese Systems Ltd v Wincanton Engineering Ltd*).

On the other hand, contractually seeking to impose further restrictions (such as a non-compete or confidentiality restriction) on an inventor, going beyond that which Parliament had thought necessary in legislation relating to patent protection has to be regarded as exceptional for it to be justified as reasonable in the public interest under the restraint of trade doctrine (see *Dranez Anstalt v Hayek* [2002] All E.R. (D) 377), and we would contend similarly for it not to be in breach of competition law.

Part III

Employer and Employee

Chapter 6

The Classic Problems

6.1 Introduction

There are two categories of case to which the restraint of trade doctrine has traditionally been applied: contracts between employers/employees and business sale agreements. In Chapters 10–12 we examine the latter and in the next four chapters the former. The general law relating to restraint of trade and business secrets is analysed in the first five chapters.

The usual difficulties which arise from restraint of trade and business secrets clauses in employment contracts occur because an employee has decided to set up as, or work for, a competitor of his employer. His former employer will quite clearly not benefit from this conduct and the courts are concerned with defining how far the employer can restrict such competition. It is important to divide the analysis between the position during employment and what happens once the employee has left because, generally, the courts are much more protective of the employer's interests during employment. During employment the employee may damage or appear to damage his employer's business in the following ways:

(a) working for a competitor during his hours of employment;

(b) working for a competitor in his spare time;

(c) making preparations in order to compete with his employer after he has left;

(d) disclosing or using the employer's business secrets; or

(e) failing to disclose information which may be of use to his employer and in some instances personally profiting from its use.

Once employment has terminated the employee may still damage or appear to damage his former employer's business by:

(a) competing with his former employer;

(b) canvassing or soliciting his former employer's business connections;

(c) using or disclosing his former employer's business secrets; or

(d) enticing his former colleagues away from his former employer to his new employer or business.

This Part analyses the limits which the courts have placed on the freedom of an employee in the absence of express restrictive covenants and upon the ability of employers to restrain employees by contractual restrictions.

6.2 The attitude of the courts

The courts have developed a practice of viewing the position of an employee as particularly special and significant when dealing with restrictive covenant claims by an employer. The reasons for this approach are clear. Traditionally the contract of employment was drawn up by the employer and there was little or no negotiation as to its contents. The employee was thought to lack bargaining power. In *M&S Drapers v Reynolds* [1956] 3 All E.R. 814 Denning L.J. said:

> During the last 40 years the courts have shown a reluctance to enforce covenants of this sort. They realise that a servant has often very little choice in the matter. If he wants to get or to keep his employment, he has to sign the document which the employer puts before him and he may do so without fully appreciating what it may involve. Moreover if these covenants were given full force, they would tend to reduce his freedom to seek better conditions even by asking for a rise in wages; because if he is not allowed to get work elsewhere he is very much at the mercy of his employer. Whilst showing proper reluctance to enforce these covenants, the courts will, however, do so if they are shown to be reasonable . . .

Another reason for this special approach is that the employer does not usually pay a premium for freedom from competition from his employee. On the other hand on the sale of a business the purchaser frequently does pay such a premium and the vendor correspondingly receives a price higher than if no restraint existed (see *Herbert Morris Ltd v Saxelby* [1916] 1 A.C. 688, *per* Lord Atkinson). In order to override this objection there is no reason why an employer should not make specific financial provision which genuinely compensates the employee for the existence of the restrictive covenant although such payment will not in itself, either save the clause from rigorous analysis and, if appropriate, a finding of unreasonableness: see *D v M* [1996] I.R.L.R. 192 and *Turner v Commonwealth & British Minerals Ltd* [2000] I.R.L.R. 114, CA. Another reason for the special attitude of the courts in employment cases was given by Younger L.J. in *Attwood v Lamont* [1920] 3 K.B. 571: the employer cannot prevent the employee from using skill and knowledge once he has left, but he frequently tries to do so. His attempts must be curbed.

In more recent times and in a case which did not strictly involve an employee, Lord Diplock said that the real concern of the courts was simply to ask whether the party with the greater bargaining power had exacted an unfairly onerous benefit (*A. Schroeder Music Publishing Co v Macaulay* [1974] 3 All E.R. 616).

However, the existence of the special approach towards employees can be overstated and it is dangerous to assume its existence in every case. Although a managing director will usually be an employee the courts sensibly view him in a different light from that of a manual worker. As Denning L.J. said in the *M&S Drapers* case: "A managing director can look after himself". These words have more recently been repeated by Dillon L.J. in *Hanover Insurance Brokers Ltd v Shapiro* [1994] I.R.L.R. 82. In other words the courts are not required to be so vigilant in his case as he is presumed to have negotiated the terms of his contract. It may also be thought that when an agreement is negotiated by a trade union inequality of bargaining power as understood in the cases is not often a relevant factor. However, there is no reported case in which this point has been taken by an employer in order to argue that the special approach is not always applicable; it may be that the special approach is so entrenched in judicial thinking that even an employer who is able to demonstrate that the factual bases for the special approach do not exist in the instant case will not succeed in persuading the court to abandon it. However it must be worth trying to do so especially if a senior employee has received independent legal advice before entering the agreement and has been specifically compensated (as is common in the USA) for accepting the restraint.

The courts have in more recent times demonstrated a reaction against an absurdly over-generous approach to the construction of agreements in the employee's favour: see *Home Counties Dairies Ltd v Skilton* [1970] 1 W.L.R. 526 in which the defendant was employed by the plaintiffs as a milkman and he expressly agreed that for a period of one year after his employment terminated he would not "serve or sell milk or dairy produce" to any person who had been a customer of his employers and who had been served by him during the six months prior to his leaving. Harman L.J. noted that the clause appeared to have been carefully limited to avoid the usual pitfalls associated with an employer trying to get too much. The defendant did leave and worked as a milkman for a competitor of his former employer. At first instance, the court found that the restriction was unreasonable. It acceded to an argument that it would prevent the defendant being employed by a grocer in selling dairy products in his shop. This construction meant that the clause went beyond the protection of the goodwill of the employer's business. On appeal, the court took a much more sensible view of the clause: it allowed the appeal on the basis that the clause should be read in the context of the whole employment agreement. That agreement made it clear that the defendant was employed as a milkman and that the intention of the clause was to afford the employer protection only against the activities of an employee who worked as a milkman once his employment ended. The court was adamant in its rejection of fanciful interpretations of the clause so as to make it so wide as to be unreasonable. This case has been extensively cited and approved in for example, *Littlewoods Organisation Ltd v Harris* [1978] 1 All E.R. 1026.

In *Turner v Commonwealth & British Minerals Ltd* [2000] I.R.L.R. 114, the Court of Appeal held that if a particular construction of a covenant would lead to the view that the provision was unenforceable, an alternative view which did not lead to the same view, if legitimate, ought to be preferred (See also *TFS Derivatives Ltd. v Morgan* [2005] I.R.L.R. 246). The same case also held that where an employee was paid something additional for the covenant (here the covenant was in a severance agreement) whilst it did not relieve the employer of the need to justify the restriction, it was a legitimate factor to have regard to in considering the interests of the parties and so too the fact that the employee had received legal advice and there was equality of bargaining power which was relevant to the issue of enforcement. In *Rock Refridgeration Ltd v Jones and Seward Refridgeration Ltd* [1996] I.R.L.R. 675, CA, the court declined to hold that covenants operating on the termination of employment "howsoever occasioned" were necessarily unreasonable and unenforceable because they purported to be binding in circumstances where there was a wrongful dismissal. In *Hollis v Stocks* [2000] I.R.L.R. 712, CA, the court was prepared to "read in" the words "as a solicitor" into a covenant which had the effect of preventing a solicitor from working within 10 miles of his former employer's office for 12 months but failed to include the words "as a solicitor".

Most recently the Court of Appeal in *Beckett v Glyn Hall* [2007] EWCA Civ 613, followed Lord Denning M.R. in *Littlewoods* ("Agreements in restraint of trade, like other agreements, must be construed with reference to the object sought to be attained by them") and construed a covenant in favour of the employing parent company as including its subsidiaries (who were actually conducting the business sought to be protected, whereas the parent company was not).

The courts do not appear to exhibit as great a protective attitude towards the employee when asked to control his misuse of business secrets. The result of this dichotomy is that the employer who can rely on the right to protect his business secrets is much more likely to succeed in court than when he seeks to enforce a traditional restraint of trade clause.

Chapter 7

Implied and Express Duties during Employment

7.1 Implied duties

During employment the employee owes his employer a duty of "fidelity", alternatively called "good faith". The employment relationship is not a fiduciary relationship (unlike the case of a director) but fiduciary duties may arise out of the employment relationship (see *Nottingham University v Fishel* [2000] I.R.L.R. 471, *per* Elias J. and also paragraph 7.2.4). This general duty has been considered in many cases and is quite clearly based on what a person of ordinary honesty would consider honest/dishonest (see *Robb v Green* [1895] 2 Q.B. 315; *Printers and Finishers Ltd v Holloway* [1964] 3 All E.R. 731 and *Roger Bullivant Ltd v Ellis* [1987] I.C.R. 464 at p.475, *per* Nourse L.J.). In *AG v Blake* [1998] 2 W.L.R., 805, AC, Lord Woolf M.R. described it thus:

> The employee must act in good faith; he must not make a profit out of his trust; he must not place himself in a position where his duty and his interest may conflict; he may not act for his own benefit or the benefit of a third party without the informed consent of his employer.

In *Robb v Green* Lord Esher M.R. justified the implication of such a term:

> It is impossible . . . that a master would have put a servant into a confidential position of this kind unless he thought that the servant would be bound to use good faith towards him; or that the servant would not know . . . that the master would rely on his observance of good faith . . . .

However, as was recognised by Lord Greene M.R. in *Hivac Ltd v Park Royal Scientific Instruments Ltd* [1946] Ch. 169, "The practical difficulty in any given case is to find exactly how far that rather vague duty of fidelity extends".

The general duty of fidelity will be examined in the next five sections.

7.1.1 The employee's duty not to compete during working hours

This aspect of the duty of fidelity requires the employee not to work for any person who is or who might be in competition with his employer during the working day. In *Thomas Marshall (Exporters) Ltd v Guinle* [1978] 3 W.L.R. 116 whilst managing director of the plaintiffs and without their knowledge or consent, the defendant placed orders for the benefit of himself and his own company with the plaintiffs' suppliers. He also sold goods for his own benefit to customers of the plaintiffs. His conduct was described by Megarry V.C. as amounting to gross and repeated breaches of his implied obligation to be faithful to the plaintiffs. There could be no doubt that by competing with the plaintiffs both as regards supplies and customers he had placed himself in a position in which there was a conflict of interest and duty. Even though this case dealt with a managing director who was clearly in a fiduciary position, its principles are equally applicable to other employees (see *Sanders v Parry* [1967] 2 All E.R. 803).

This duty also prevents an employee from taking advantage of any approach which is initiated by a customer or supplier even though the employee did not seek or even encourage it, as happened in *Sanders*' case.

The degree of involvement which an employee has to demonstrate in order to fall foul of this duty need not always be very great. He may simply assist a competitor in any way which does or may have an adverse and material effect on his employer's business. As Brightman J. said in *United Sterling Corp Ltd v Felton and Mannion* [1974] R.P.C. 162:

> This contractual obligation of fidelity . . . may prevent a skilled employee from giving his assistance to a competitor despite the fact that such assistance is provided by the employee in his own time and despite the fact that no information has been disclosed to the employee in confidence.

However, it should not be thought that *any* assistance given to a competitor by the employee is necessarily a breach of his duty, for it may have been done with the employer's authority, though this will be a rare occurrence. In practice, an employer will not always rely on the implied duty of fidelity: there will often be an express clause in the employment contract which directs the employee to devote his time exclusively to the promotion of the employer's business.

Additionally an employee placed on garden leave by his employer may not be precluded from working for a competitor during such a period in the absence of a typical "exclusive services" type of provision (or perhaps an express prohibition in the garden leave provision itself) in the contract of employment as, *per* Scott V.C. at first instance in *Symbian v Christensen* [2001] I.R.L.R. 77, CA, the implied duty of good faith does not survive during a garden leave period. The Court of Appeal did not comment on this proposition, although counsel for Mr Christensen "confessed to some difficulty" in relation to justifying this part of the Judgment in his favour. The issue was rendered otiose as Christensen did have an exclusive services provision in his contract. For a more detailed review of garden leave provisions, see paragraph 23.10. These are often used in conjunction with restrictive covenants and the inter-relationship between the two different types of provision (often intended to secure a similar objective) is not without difficulty in practice.

7.1.2 The employee's duty not to compete in his spare time

As a general rule an employee cannot compete with his employer in his spare time without being in breach of his duty of fidelity. The basic question is: do the activities of the employee interfere with the employer's legitimate interests or are they likely to do so? If the answer is positive then the employer can seek redress.

In *Hivac Ltd v Park Royal Scientific Instruments Ltd* [1948] 1 Ch. 169 employees of the plaintiffs who were highly skilled in assembling hearing-aid valves had Sundays off. The defendants who manufactured similar valves and were effectively competitors of the plaintiff company offered work to the plaintiff's employees on Sundays. The employees accepted. The defendants alone were sued for inducing/procuring the employees to breach their contracts of employment. There was no evidence that the employees had misused any of the plaintiffs' business secrets. The Court of Appeal concluded that this was a case of deliberate and secret action by the employees and the defendants in circumstances in which they must have known the exact result of what they were doing and must have known it was wrong. In addition to this breach of the moral duty of fidelity, the court appears to have been concerned with the risk of confidential information being passed to competitors, because it was satisfied that the plaintiffs did own certain business secrets of which the employees had knowledge.

The court also commented that a manual worker might owe a duty which did not extend outside his hours of employment and this seems sensible. On the other hand the very nature of the work may be such as to make it quite clear that the duties of the employee to his employer cannot properly be performed if he engages in certain activities in his spare time. Each case depends on its facts. In *Hivac* the court discussed the example of a solicitor's clerk and said that in such a case it would be improper for him to work for another solicitor in his spare time. There might be a real risk of embarrassment to his full-time employers if he were asked to act for a client in his spare time who was on the other side of a case in which his main employers were engaged.

The important points which emerge from this case are that the employer will be able to rely on this part of the duty of fidelity if it can be shown that the employee works for a trade competitor in his spare time and:

(a) knows of business secrets which may be of use to the competitor; and/or

(b) occupies a position which makes it expedient to recognise the existence of his duty to work for the employer alone.

As the Master of the Rolls, Sir Thomas Bingham, said in *Lancashire Fires Ltd v SA Lyons & Co Ltd* [1997] I.R.L.R. 113:

> Indeed any employee with technical knowledge and experience can expect to have his spare time activities in the field in which his employers operate carefully scrutinised in this context.

See also *Nova Plastics Ltd v Froggatt* [1982] I.R.L.R. 146 which concerned an "odd-job" man.

7.1.3 The employee's duty not to make preparations in order to compete with his employer after he has left or to enable another to do so

The employee cannot make preparations during his employment, either during the working day or in his spare time, with a view to competing with his employer once his employment is over if such preparation has a material effect on his employer's business. Obviously, an employee is free to apply for another position even with a rival of his present employer, or to find premises in which to set up a future business so long as in doing so he is not in breach of any valid express term in his employment contract: see *GD Searle & Co Ltd v Celltech Ltd* [1982] F.S.R. 92. Certainly, the law will not imply a term which prevents him from doing so. What he cannot do without infringing the duty of fidelity is to make such preparations in his employer's time or use or disclose either the business secrets or trade connections of his employer. Only after he has left is he free, in the absence of express restraint, to make use of the latter though never the former. The difficulty in practice, as it emerges strongly from the decided cases, is to identify, in what are usually fact sensitive situations, the point at which the permissible turns into the impermissible. This is further complicated in circumstances where the individual is not only an employee owing a duty of fidelity and good faith, but also a director owing fiduciary duties and complicated still further by those cases where it might be successfully argued, in the particular circumstances of the case, that an employee also has fiduciary duties (see in particular paragraphs 7.1.6 and 7.1.7 below).

In *Thomas Marshall (Exporters) Ltd v Guinle* [1978] 3 W.L.R. 116 the defendant was not simply competing with the plaintiff during his employment but was also taking steps to prepare to compete once he had left by dealing with customers and suppliers of his employer. This was a very clear example of breach but others are less obvious. Detection is a great problem as breach is frequently only discovered after employment ends. The employer may find it difficult when he becomes aware of the fact that his former customers are now dealing with his former employee to prove that enticement did in fact take place during employment. The usual way in which this duty is breached is for the employee to mention to customers that he is leaving and either directly or indirectly suggest to them that he is available to meet their needs once he has left.

In *Robb v Green* [1895] 2 Q.B. 315 the defendant, employed by the plaintiff as the manager of his business, surreptitiously copied from the plaintiff's order book a list of names and addresses of customers with the intention of soliciting them after he had left employment and had set up a similar business on his own. Subsequently he did leave and did use the list. The Court of Appeal affirmed the existence of an implied duty not to prepare to compete and gave judgment for the plaintiffs. However, they did not deal with a suggestion made by Hawkins J. at first instance that, in some circumstances, an employee could "legitimately canvass, issue his circulars, have his place of business in readiness, hire his servants, etc" [1895] 2 Q.B. 1. He was relying on the earlier case of *Nichol v Martyn* [1799] 2 Esp. 732, but in *Wessex Dairies Ltd v Smith* [1935] 2 K.B. 80 Maugham L.J. cast doubt on both those judgments and so far as the modern law is concerned they should not be relied on to the extent that they indicate the employee can canvass or issue circulars to customers of his employer before he leaves. Nor can the employee do anything else in Hawkins J.'s list in his employer's time.

In the *Wessex Dairies* case, it was found that on the last day of his employment as a milkman the defendant, whilst on his round, informed customers that he would soon cease to be employed by the plaintiffs, that he was going to set up business on his own and could supply them with milk. The court said that he was plainly soliciting their custom at a time when he was under a duty of fidelity to his employer and awarded his former employers damages. A more recent example is *Sanders v Parry* [1967] 1 W.L.R. 753 which concerned a solicitor's practice. After joining the plaintiff as an assistant solicitor the defendant entered an agreement with T, one of the plaintiff's clients. The agreement stated that the defendant would leave the plaintiff's employment and set up on his own in premises which T would lease to him and T would transfer his custom to the defendant. When the plaintiff heard of this, he dismissed the defendant, and sought an injunction to prevent him breaching his duty of fidelity. In his defence, the defendant claimed that it was T who had approached him and that he had not initiated the agreement. Havers J. accepted this but said:

> . . . there was a duty on the defendant at all times during the subsistence of [the employment] agreement to protect his master's interests, especially to do his best to retain Mr Tully as a client of his master. . . . Now, in accepting Tully's offer, the defendant was not protecting his master's interests . . . [he] was placing himself in a position in which there was a conflict of interests between him and his principal and he was looking after his own interests to the detriment of his master's interests. He was knowingly, deliberately and secretly acting, setting out to do something which would inevitably inflict great harm on his principal.

However, the dividing line between what is and what is not permissible is often difficult to draw, as Maugham L.J. illustrated in the *Wessex Dairies* case:

> . . . although the servant is not entitled to make use of information which he has obtained in confidence in his master's service he is entitled to make use of the

> knowledge and skill which he acquired while in that service, including knowledge and skill directly obtained from the master in teaching him his business. It follows, in my opinion, that the servant may, whilst in the employment of the master, be as agreeable, attentive, and skilful as it is in his power to be to others with the ultimate view of obtaining the benefit of the customers' friendly feelings when he calls upon them if and when he sets up business for himself.

What he cannot do is anything more positive although this is subject to fact sensitive judicial nuance in some more recent cases.

In *Island Export and Finance Ltd v Umunna* [1986] B.C.L.C. 460 it was held that a director's fiduciary duty did not necessarily come to an end when he ceased to be a director. A director was precluded from diverting to himself a maturing business opportunity which his company was actively pursuing even after his resignation where the resignation was prompted or influenced by a desire to acquire that opportunity for himself (see further paragraph 7.1.7 and the Court of Appeal's review of directors' fiduciary duties in cases such as this in *Foster Bryant Surveying Ltd. v (1) Bryant and (2) Savernake Property Consultants Ltd.* [2007] EWCA Civ 200). However, on the facts of the case the plaintiff's claim failed as it had not proved:

(a) the existence of a "maturing" business opportunity;

(b) that it was actively pursuing the business either when the defendant resigned or when he subsequently obtained the contracts; or

(c) that his resignation was prompted or influenced by the wish to acquire the benefit of the contracts for himself.

It is to be noted that even in the case of a fiduciary the ambit of his duty once he has ceased to be for example, a director, is circumscribed. A difficult question is whether in the case of an employee who is not a fiduciary the same principles also apply. It is submitted that, on the whole, most employees are under no such implied duty once employment has ceased. If the employer requires protection he should have the foresight to include an express restrictive covenant in the employment contract.

This subject has been considered by the Employment Appeal Tribunal in *Laughton v Bapp Industrial Supplies Ltd* [1986] I.C.R. 634. In that case the employees, who were warehousemen employed by a company which supplied nuts and bolts, wrote to ten of their employers' suppliers informing them that they intended to start up in business on their own trading in nuts and bolts, and asking for details of their products. The employers learned of the letters and summarily dismissed the employees for gross misconduct. On their complaints of unfair dismissal an industrial tribunal found that the employers were justified in their decision that the employees were in breach of their implied duty in their contracts of employment that they should be loyal to their employers and that the dismissals were not unfair. The employees appealed and it was held, allowing the appeal, that the industrial tribunal had erred in law in holding that an intention to compete in the future with their employers expressed by the employees in letters to their employers' suppliers was in itself a breach of a duty of fidelity owed by the employees to the employers and that accordingly the dismissals had been unfair. Peter Gibson J. said, at p.638:

> An employee with experience in a particular industry who is intending to leave, whether to join a competitor as an employee or to set up in competition on his own account, commits no breach of contract in doing so unless either there is a specific term of his contract to that effect which does not fall foul of the doctrine against restraint of trade or he is intending to use the confidential information of his employer otherwise and for the benefit of his employer.

See further *Harris and Russell Ltd v Slingsby* [1973] I.R.L.R. 221. See also *Ixora Trading Inc v Jones* [1990] 1 F.S.R. 251, *per* Mummery J. at p.262. There the evidence before him merely disclosed that the defendants whilst being employed by the plaintiffs made plans or preparations for their future post termination activities. This, he said, could not be characterised as having breached the duty of good faith which amounted to no more than a principle of fair and honourable dealing.

A further illustration of how far an employee can go is found in the judgment of Falconer J. in *Balston Ltd v Headline Filters Ltd* [1993] F.S.R. 385 which is, unusually in this field, a report of a judgment after a full trial. In that case H, an employee and director of the plaintiff company, had decided to resign and on March 14, 1986 he agreed to take the lease on certain business premises. On March 17, 1986 he gave notice of termination of his employment which was to expire on July 11, 1986 in order that he would be able to exercise a share option on July 9. On April 16, 1986 it was agreed that H would resign his directorship of the plaintiff and that he need no longer attend for work or otherwise perform any duties for the plaintiff after April 18. He formally resigned his directorship on that date. On April 25, 1986 H bought the first defendant company off the shelf. On May 2, 1986 H was telephoned by a representative of one of the plaintiff's customers concerning a meeting on May 1 between representatives of the plaintiff and the customer at which the plaintiff had informed the customer of a price increase for its products and had said that the plaintiff was only prepared to continue to accept orders for such products for a limited period. During the course of the conversation H said that he was leaving the plaintiff's employ and that after July 12 he would be in a position to provide the product to the customer. On May 8 H visited the customer and it was agreed that the customer would place an order with the first defendant company for delivery from July 14, 1986 to December 1987. Following the May 2 telephone call H made active preparations for the first defendant to commence manufacture of the products on or as soon as possible after July 14. Such preparations included the purchase of equipment and the engaging of persons as employees of the first defendant, including certain employees and ex-employees of the plaintiff. H commenced manufacture of products for the customer on July 13 and showed them to him on July 14. The plaintiff brought an action alleging various breaches of H's fiduciary duty as a director, his duty of fidelity as an employee and his duty not to use or disclose the plaintiff's trade secrets after the termination of his employment. In relation to the claim for breach of fiduciary duty, the plaintiff's main contention was that H had formed the intention to set up in competition with the plaintiff whilst still a director of the plaintiff, that that intention had caused a conflict between his personal interests and that of the plaintiff, and that by failing to disclose that intention and the resulting conflict of interest, he had actually been in breach of his fiduciary duty. In relation to the claim for breach of the duty of fidelity, the plaintiff relied on a number of alleged breaches, including H's competition with the plaintiff for the custom of the customer and his enticement of fellow employees. In relation to the claim for the misuse of confidential information, the plaintiff contended that H, in producing the first defendant's range of filter tubes, had used confidential information relating to the fibre recipes used by the plaintiff to arrive at his own fibre recipes. Falconer J. held that an intention by a director of a company to set up in business in competition with the company after his directorship had ceased was not to be regarded as an interest which conflicted with his fiduciary duty to that company. Nor was the taking of any preliminary steps to investigate or forward that intention as long as there was no actual competitive activity while he remained a director. It followed that H was not in breach of fiduciary duty as a director in not disclosing to the plaintiff his intention to set up a business in competition or in taking such steps as he had to forward that intention prior to April 18, 1986. However, the judge found that from May 8, 1986 onwards H had been in active competition with the plaintiff for the custom of the customer. In so doing he was clearly in breach of his duty of good faith as an employee. He was also in breach of his duty of good faith in approaching one of the plaintiff's employees and offering employment to her with his new company. It is clear from the judgment in this case that the cut-off point in respect of what is allowable behaviour concerns whether the former employee was involved in any "actual competitive activity". If the former employee was not, then he will not be found liable. It may well be that this case went too far in its statement of principle and that in many cases where the employer is able to rely on express duties it will be distinguishable. So, in *Helmet Integrated Systems Ltd. v Tunnard* [2007] I.R.L.R. 126, CA, it was held that a "middle-ranking senior salesman" working for a company producing and selling protective equipment including a helmet for use by, inter alia, the London Fire Brigade, was not in breach of an express obligation in his contract to report on "competitor activities" (which on its terms did not extend to his own activities) or his duty of fidelity and good faith when, in the course of his employment, he began designing such a helmet. This was so, notwithstanding that the new helmet was primarily, although not exclusively, for fire fighters, and that he identified, when applying for DTI funding to further develop his project whilst still employed, a UK subsidiary of a US rival to his employers as a potential partner and his own current employer as a competitor in relation to the product he was developing. What seems to have influenced the Court at first instance and the Court of Appeal, was that he had not misused any confidential information; no other employee was involved; he had carried out his work in his own time without recourse to any of his employer's property; no agreement had been entered into before he left his employers; there was no competition before he did so, and he was a middle-ranking senior salesman and not a director or employed at a similar level. Additionally, he was not subject to any restrictive covenant. The employers claim that the employee had a fiduciary duty and that there had been a breach of it was also unsuccessful (see paragraph 7.1.6 below).

Examples of cases in which the employer succeeded are *Marshall v Industrial Systems & Control Ltd.* [1992] I.R.L.R. 294; *Adamson v B & L Cleaning Services Ltd.* [1995] I.R.L.R. 193; *Lancashire Fires Ltd. v SA Lyons & Co. Ltd.* [1997] I.R.L.R. 113, CA; *Ward Evans Financial Services Ltd. v Fox* [2002] I.R.L.R. 120, CA; *LC Services Ltd. v Brown* [2003] EWHC 3024; and *Shepherds Investments Ltd. v Walters* [2007] I.R.L.R. 110 Ch D. In *Marshall* Mr Marshall, the managing director of the respondent company, approached another company for whom the respondent distributed software with a view to taking that business away with him when he left. He also tried to induce a key employer to join him in his new business. This certainly went beyond forming the intention to compete; it provided the basis for a fair dismissal. In *Adamson*, Mr Adamson sought to tender for work currently done by his employers. This action was found to have overstepped the mark. In *Lancashire Fires* the employer was engaged in the manufacture of artificial coals and logs for use in gas fires. The licensed process used had been changed over time substantially altering the nature of the mould and enabling production of much larger quantities. The younger brother (Arthur Wright) of the owner (Jim Wright) decided to set up his own business. He obtained finance from what had been a prospective Canadian outlet for the products, acquired equipment and premises and agreed to supply the Canadian backers. Prior to his resigning, Arthur Wright spent his spare time improving the run down premises he had acquired and working on the equipment needed for his production process. He was found out, confronted and resigned. The employer claimed that there had been a breach of the duty of confidentiality (identifying the process improvements as a trade secret) and a breach of the duty of fidelity (in connection with the steps taken to set up a competing business). The Court of Appeal held that the process improvements were a trade secret and that the steps taken to set up a competing business were "well on the wrong side of the line". The fact that the employer had never drawn Arthur's attention to the fact that the process he was familiar with (having unrestricted access to the relevant area of the premises) did not matter. Possibly a higher standard of fidelity is due where the employee is exposed to confidential information. The boundary between what may be permissible preparation for the future and impermissable competition remains grey, but this case suggests that the range of actions that might be regarded as constituting competition can be quite broad in practice. In *Ward*, the Court of Appeal held that the formation of a company by two employees during the course of their employment did, despite the fact that it did not trade, breach an express "trust and confidence" agreement in that it impaired their obligation to the company to act in its best interests. *LC Services* involved the formation of a company at the time the departing employee (and director) gave three months' notice and the procuring of business for and the transfer of confidential information to that new company during the notice period. This was held to be a breach of the director's fiduciary duties and a breach of the express terms of his service agreement. Finally, in *Shepherds* the court was concerned with three former employees (two of whom were directors of companies in the claimant's group, and the third held to be a de facto director) who were found to have breached both their fiduciary duties as directors and their duty of fidelity as employees in the course of setting up a competing business. The claim against the three relevant defendants was for damages or (the advantage of being able to establish a fiduciary duty and a breach of that duty) an account of profits arising out of the various breaches of duty and contract, including, particularly, setting up a competing business, diversion of a business opportunity and misuse of confidential information. The claimant was an open-ended investment company and had two subsidiaries, one of which carried on the business of investing in US traded life policies (providing an investment opportunity in these through the purchase of interests in life policies which had been acquired by market makers from persons living in the US who wished to raise money from the policy prior to maturity on the death of the assured) and the other subsidiary carried on a similar business investing in UK traded endowment policies. In the first half of 2003, the group began to give consideration to the establishment of a "whole policy" investment fund which would purchase whole life policies rather than interest in fractionised policies, and market research was undertaken and a report written by an employee engaged for these purposes. Broadly in parallel, the defendants began discussions between themselves regarding the idea that they might establish a new investment fund which would invest in whole life policies, and the draft business plan was prepared by July 13, 2003. Thereafter, Cayman Island's attorneys were consulted about various aspects of the proposal, auditors and custodians identified and agreements relevant to the establishment of the new enterprise executed on November 28, 2003. The de facto director and one of the formally appointed directors resigned as employees (and the formally appointed director as a director), and their employment terminated on October 10, 2003. 2004 saw promotional literature for the new business being printed in January 2004, the first agreements in relation to the supply of whole life policies for the new business being entered into, the remaining appointed director resigning as an employee and as a director in May 2004, and in June 2004 the first purchase of a whole life policy for the new business. As directors and employees, their obligations were that of good faith and fidelity (*Robb v Green*) and the duty to act as a director in what he, in good faith, considers to be in the best interest of the company (*Item Software (UK) Ltd. v Fassihi*). Etherton J. considered the arguments of the claimants based on *British Midland Tool Ltd. v Midland International Tooling Ltd.* and the defendants based on *Balston Ltd. v Headline Filters Ltd.* For the claimants, they adopted the reasoning and the decision of Hart J. in *British Midland*:

> A director who wishes to engage in a competing business and not disclose his intentions to the company ought, in my judgment, to resign his office as soon as his intention has been irrevocably formed and he has launched himself in the actual taking of preparatory steps.

The defendants relied on Faulkner J's approach in *Balston*:

> In my judgment an intention by a director of a company to set up business in competition with the company after his directorship has ceased, is not to be regarded as a conflicting interest within the context of the principle having regard to the rules of public policy as to restraint of trade, nor is the taking of any preliminary steps to investigate or forward that intention so long as there is no actual competitive activity, such as, for instance, competitive tendering or actual trading, while he remains a director.

Etherton J, considered both approaches correct but to the extent there was any conflict between them, preferred the decision and reasoning of Faulkner J in *Balston*. The judge went on to say:

> In my judgment it is plain that the necessary starting point of the analysis is that it is the fiduciary duty of a director to act in good faith and in the best interests of the company (*Item Software* at paragraph [41]), that is to say, to do his best to promote its interest and to act with complete good faith towards it, and not to place himself in a position in which his own interests conflict with those of the company

(See *British Midland Tool* at paragraph [81]) and *CMS Dolphin Ltd. v Simonet* [2001] 2 B.C.L.C. 704 at paragraph [84]). It is difficult to see any legitimate basis for the "trumping" of those duties by "rules of public policy as to restraint of trade" as suggested by Faulkner J in *Balston* at para.412. There is no reference to any such principle in any of the relevant cases prior to *Balston*" (the judge mentioning in this context *Robb*; *Wessex Dairies*; *Hivac Ltd*; *Laughton* and *British Midland Tool*). Interestingly, Etherton J appeared to feel that Hart J in *British Midland Tool* "may have been too prescriptive in saying, . . . that the director must resign once he has irrevocably formed the intention to engage in the future in a competing business and, without disclosing his intentions to the company, takes any preparatory steps".

On the facts of the case, the judge held that, by August 12, 2003 when the Cayman Island attorneys were contacted, thereafter the defendants had formed an irrevocable intention to proceed with new business, and from that date onwards they did act in breach of their fiduciary duties creating a plain conflict between their personal interests and the best interests of the employing group. By that date, he also considered that each of the individual defendants was under an obligation to disclose the actual or threatened activity of the other defendants in relation to the establishment of a competing business. He distinguished *Balston* on its facts, and on the basis that the intention to compete did not appear to have been formed before the resignation of the relevant defendant in that case. There was, however, no separate and independent duty of disclosure, it was simply a breach of the normal fiduciary duty (in this he followed Arden L J in *Item Software*). In relation to the two directors who resigned first it was held (based on *CMS Dolphin v Simonet*) that, having resigned to exploit a maturing business opportunity which had been under consideration by the employing group during 2003, the two directors became constructive trustees of the resultant fruits of this breach. Two of the directors had express terms in their contracts of employment which prohibited, without the written consent of the company, their being "directly engaged, concerned or interested in or connected with any other company, business or concern". The first two directors to resign would not have been in breach of this on the basis that the judge considered the words related to a business enterprise which was actively engaged in some business activity, but the last of the directors to resign, on the chronology of events, was held to be in breach of this obligation. Although this received less attention, it broadly followed that, in light of breaches of the fiduciary duties owed, there were corresponding breaches of their duty of fidelity as employees.

7.1.4 The employee's duty not to disclose or use his employer's business secrets

What constitutes a legitimate business secret has been discussed earlier. However, given the existence of such a secret there is an implied duty that an employee will not disclose such secrets to another or use them himself. A general principle in the employment field was laid down in *Printers and Finishers Ltd v Holloway* [1964] 3 All E.R. 731 where Cross J. said that employees are prohibited from using information which "can fairly be regarded as a separate part of the employee's stock of knowledge which a man of ordinary honesty and intelligence would recognise to be the property of his old employer and not his own to do as he likes with". (See also *Bents Brewery Co Ltd v Hogan* [1945] 2 All E.R. 570.)

Unfortunately, this test has proved somewhat difficult to apply to practical situations. However it was used in *Industrial Furnaces Ltd v Reaves* [1970] R.P.C. 605. The defendant had been a director of the plaintiffs for 13 years and had been in charge of the development and sales of a certain type of heater. On leaving the plaintiffs, the defendant set up another company which sold heaters of a similar type to some of the plaintiffs' previous customers. On being sued by the plaintiffs for breach of the implied duty of confidentiality, the defendant claimed that he had made all his calculations in designing the heater from information which had been published in a readily obtainable leaflet. Graham J. found that such information was not readily available and went on to say that the information had been obtained as a result of considerable labour and expense on the part of the plaintiffs and was therefore valuable and, it followed, confidential.

A particular problem which frequently arises is a claim by an employee that even if he must have realised, in accordance with the principle laid down in the *Printers and Finishers* case, that he was under a duty to maintain a confidence, such duty was in fact overridden by the way in which his employer acted towards the information, i.e. that the employer is estopped from now relying on confidence. An example of such a case is *GB Bjorlow Ltd v Minter* [1954] 71 R.P.C. 321 in which the employer claimed that a process was secret and had been wrongfully used and disclosed by the defendant, a former employee. The plaintiff could not prove that the defendant knew it was a secret process either because of its nature or because he had been specifically told that it was and Vaisey J. pointed out that if it were really secret it was surprising that the defendant's employment had brought him into contact with it; he had been to prison in the past. He said that the defendant had never been told he was being entrusted with secrets, there was no express covenant covering business secrets and the defendant never knew that he must not talk about his work outside his employment. Vaisey J. went on to say that the employers had shown "the utmost carelessness in allowing this defendant to get knowledge of what they knew was a very valuable secret. . . . People with valuable secrets ought not to allow subordinate employees . . . to obtain knowledge of this kind, and if they choose to do it without warning them they will find it very difficult to claim interlocutory relief successfully".

Evershed M.R. said that "the plaintiffs took no steps whatever . . . to impress upon anybody that there was here any important secret which they desired to preserve". However, compare this to the decision in *Lancashire Fires* above where the court held it was not necessary to draw the employee's attention to the fact that a process to which he had unrestricted access was a trade secret. Given the employee's position in the employer he must have known that the process included aspects which could fairly be regarded as a trade secret.

Bjorlow illustrates neither that employers should refuse jobs to those who have a murky past nor that they should not entrust secrets to subordinate employees—that is impracticable—but that they should not simply rely on the implied duty of confidence; it can lead to misunderstandings and difficulties as to what is really secret. A prudent employer will always have an express contractual term protecting business secrets.

Whether the court's approach in cases such as *Bjorlow* would also be adopted even if the employee made use of or disclosed business secrets during employment has not been determined: in *Bjorlow*, the defendant made use of the information only after he had left. It is submitted that in the former case the approach would probably be modified by the basic duty of fidelity to the extent that confidentiality would be lost only if the employer could be said to have shown *wilful* disregard to the quality of the confidence, rather than having been merely negligent and this is supported by *Lancashire Fires*.

In *Faccenda Chicken Ltd v Fowler* [1985] 1 All E.R. 724; [1986] 1 All E.R. 617 Goulding J. and the Court of Appeal considered information which was not protected by an express clause and which was clearly used by employees once employment had ended. In addition, comments were made about the ambit of the implied duty of fidelity and business secrets during employment. There is a full discussion of this case at para.8.2.2.

7.1.5 The employee's duty to disclose to his employer information which may be of use to that employer (and not personally to profit from it)

If, during the course of employment, an employee receives, qua employee, information which is or may reasonably be relevant to his employer's business then he is under a duty:

(a) to disclose all relevant information received to the employer; and

(b) not to use that information for his or another's benefit unless the employer consents.

The source of the information is irrelevant. Moreover, the information need not be confidential as is shown in *Sanders v Parry* [1967] 1 W.L.R. 753 and *Swain v West (Butchers) Ltd* [1936] 1 All E.R. 224; 3 All E.R. 261; though it was in *Cranleigh Precision Engineering Ltd v Bryant* [1966] R.P.C. 81. It need only be relevant to the wellbeing of the employer's business and have become known to the employee in his capacity as an employee. It is doubtful whether information learnt by the employee at a private social event is embraced by this duty.

In *Sanders v Parry*, the defendant whilst in the plaintiff's employment as an assistant solicitor was told by another member of staff that she was dissatisfied with her employment. It seems that the other staff member had never spoken to her employer on the subject, though she had opportunity to do so. Moreover, an important client of the plaintiff told the defendant that he was dissatisfied with the plaintiff's conduct of his affairs. Instead of passing on this information, the defendant persuaded the other employee to leave and join his own business; the discontented client in the meantime had agreed with the defendant that he would use him as his legal adviser in the future. The result of the case—in which the defendant was found in breach of his duty of fidelity—was inevitable. The defendant had placed himself in a position where his duty and interest conflicted even though both the employee and client appear to have had no intention of remaining with the plaintiff. In *Swain v West (Butchers) Ltd* it was held that an employee, having learnt of detrimental behaviour of another employee, which was relevant to his employer's business, was under a duty to report that fact to his employers. Although there was an express clause in the employment contract by which the employee was under a duty "to promote, extend and develop the interests of the company" the court would clearly have reached the same conclusion on the basis of the implied duty of fidelity. Obviously, what is or may be of importance to an employer's business is a question of fact; and it was no doubt significant in *Swain* that S was the general manager, the wrongful employee was the managing director, his conduct was dishonest and it could have had a material effect on the defendant's business (labelling meat as "Empire Products" when it was not). Moreover, Greer L.J. specifically said:

> I do not decide that in every case where the relation of master and servant exists it is the duty of the servant to disclose, or to disclose upon inquiry, any discrepancies of which he knows of his fellow servants.

This caveat was echoed in *Sybron Corp v Rochem Ltd* [1983] 3 W.L.R. 713 where it was said that if an employee were required to report each and every breach of duty by fellow employees this would ruin good industrial relations. The ambit of the duty must depend on the circumstances, especially the respective positions of those involved. Moreover that case established that the duty still exists even if by reporting the conduct the reporter incriminates himself. The Court of Appeal in *Sybron* were not in a position to criticise the House of Lords' decision in *Bell v Lever Bros Ltd* [1932] A.C. 161 though they distinguished it. *Bell* says that a contract of employment is not a contract *uberrimae fidei* so as to require disclosure by the employee of his own misconduct (as opposed to that of others), either before he is taken into employment or during the course of his employment. However, see *Horcal Ltd v Gatland* [1984] I.R.L.R. 288 and *Item Software (UK) Ltd v Fassihi* [2003] I.R.L.R. 769 (upheld on appeal [2004] I.R.L.R. 928, CA). *Item* involved the sales and marketing director of Item and a relationship with a major customer which was terminated when the party could not reach agreement with the employer on a reduction in a royalty on sales made. It was replaced by an agreement with that customer entered into by a company controlled by a friend of the sales and marketing director. The employee was involved in the negotiations on behalf of his employer; during these he proposed to the customer that he establish his own company to take over the businesses and at the same time counselled his employer to take an aggressive stance with the customer in negoitations. The usual rule in *Bell v Lever Brothers* was held by the court to be subject to two exceptions which were relevant here. First the employee was involved in the negotiations and had a "super-added" duty to disclose important information in relation to these. Just as this would apply to information about a third party trying to sabotage the process, so too it applied where it was him trying to do so. Second, the employee had acted fraudulently in trying to rob the employer of the business and *Bell v Lever Brothers* was not a case involving fraud.

Cranleigh Precision Engineering Ltd v Bryant [1964] 3 All E.R. 289, is another example of the misuse of confidential information received by an employee for his employer's benefit. B was the managing director of the plaintiffs. However, he had, unknown to the plaintiffs, set up another business which was dormant until he left their employment. Whilst still employed by the plaintiffs, B was told by that company's patent agents of a foreign invention of a product similar to that of the plaintiffs. That invention had been awarded an English patent but B did not mention that fact to the plaintiffs, and after he left he acquired it. Roskill J. said that B was in breach of an implied duty in:

(a) not communicating to the plaintiffs' board the information which he received from the patent agents and in taking no steps to protect the plaintiffs against possible consequences of the existence of the patent; and

(b) using information regarding the patent for his own benefit.

Moreover, as the patent specification was not published by the plaintiffs but by another party, its publication did not cause the information to lose its quality of confidence and therefore B was not released from his duty to the plaintiffs. B was enjoined from using the patent; see also *Industrial Development Consultants v Cooley* [1972] 2 All E.R. 162.

7.1.6 Employees and fiduciary duties

Elias J. comprehensively reviewed the authorities on the extent of an employee's fiduciary duties in *Nottingham University v Fishel* [2000] I.R.L.R. 471. Typically (as previously said) the employment relationship is not fiduciary at all. *Per* Elias J:

> Its purpose is not to place the employee in a position where he is obliged to pursue his employer's interests at the expense of his own. A relationship is a contractual one and the powers imposed on the employee are conferred by the employer himself. The employee's freedom of action is regulated by the contract, the scope of his powers is determined by the terms (expressed or implied) of the contract, and as a consequence, the employer can exercise (or at least he can place himself in a position where he has the opportunity to exercise) considerable control over the employee's decision making powers. Accordingly, in determining whether a fiduciary relationship arises in the context of an employment relationship, it is necessary to identify with care the particular duties undertaken by the employee, and to ask whether, in all the circumstances, he has placed himself in a position where he must act solely in the interests of his employer.

So in practice, an employee may, in relation to part of his or her duties, become a fiduciary but not in relation to others. Moses L.J. in *Helmet Integrated Systems Ltd. v Tunnard* [2007] I.R.L.R. 126, CA, put it succinctly as follows:

> The distinguishing mark of the obligation of a fiduciary, in the context of employment, is not merely that the employee owes a duty of loyalty but of single-minded or exclusive loyalty.

In terms of the difference between the duty of fidelity owed by an employee and a possible fiduciary duty Hart J. said in *British Midland Tool Ltd. v Midland International Tooling Ltd.* [2003] EWHC 466:

> The employee's duty of fidelity to his employer, although in some respects similar in content to the director's fiduciary duty to the company and although it is itself sometimes described as a fiduciary duty (see e.g. *A-G v Cape Blake* (Jonathan Ltd., third party) [1998] Ch.439, is by no means identical. Importantly, it does not include, in the usual case, any prohibition as such on being in a position where his duty as employee and his self interest may conflict.

In practice, as this passage suggests, in the case of employees, in those instances where, as a result of the special factual circumstances, an employee may be under a fiduciary duty in relation to part or possibly all of his or her duties whilst not being a director, there will generally be a parallel duty of fidelity. The real distinction is that breach of the latter (leaving aside the possibility of an injunction) will, in appropriate circumstances, result in an award of damages, whereas the former carries with it the possibility of an account of profits (although exceptionally in *Attorney General v Blake* [2001] I.R.L.R. 36, HL, the House of Lords held that the Attorney General could recover an amount equal to the profits made by George Blake from his autobiography published in breach of his contractual undertaking to his employer not to reveal information he obtained as a consequence of his employment—this is possible, per Lord Nicholls, where the employer has "a legitimate interest in preventing the defendant's profit-making activity and, hence, in depriving him of his profit").

7.1.7 Fiduciary duties of directors

As already indicated above, it should be borne in mind, where employees are also directors, that their fiduciary duties as a director may be as relevant, if not more so, than their duties as an employee when it comes to determine the scope of their duties and responsibilities in various situations referred to above, as their fiduciary duties are arguably more onerous. See for example, *CMS Dolphin Ltd. v Simonet* [2001] 2 B.C.L.C. 704 (exploitation of maturing business opportunity of the company after resignation as a director of the company—the director became a constructive trustee of the benefits acquired where he knowingly had a conflict of interest and resign to exploit the business opportunity); *Buller Bros Ltd.* re [2003] EWCA Civ 424 (two directors of a investment company acquired property adjacent to the company's) *British Midland Tool Ltd. v Midland International Tooling Ltd.* above (four directors planned a computer business, one retired to commence the business whilst the others remained for their notice periods during which the plan for the new business was implemented, and members of the company's) workforce indirectly approached to join the new business—held a breach of the good faith obligation and the duty to act in the company's best interests); *LC Services*

Ltd. v Brown [2003] EWHC 3024 (QB) (director involved in establishing a subsidiary of a competitor whilst serving out his notice period under his service agreement and passing on customer details and confidential information to the competitor and its new subsidiary) and *Item Software* above. See also the provisions of the Companies Act 2006 which represents a major step forward in that the Act codifies duties owed by directors (including shadow directors) (see ss.170 to 177). These comprise a duty to act within powers (i.e. within the company's constitution and exercising powers only for the purposes for which they are conferred) (s.171); a duty to promote the success of the company (s.172); a duty to exercise independent judgment (s.173); a duty to exercise reasonable care, skill and diligence (s.174); a duty to avoid conflicts of interest (s.175); a duty not to accept benefits from third parties (s.176) and a duty to declare an interest in proposed transactions or arrangements (s.177).

7.2 Express duties

In some instances all of the duties which are implied by law during the currency of an employment contract will be expressly included in such a contract. However, practice differs and it invariably happens that express provision is made only regarding two areas: non-competition/canvassing and non-disclosure/use of business secrets.

7.2.1 Non-competition/canvassing clauses

It is common to find in an employment contract an express clause which restricts competition/canvassing by an employee both during and after employment. Later we deal with how far a clause can legitimately restrict competition by a former employee: legitimacy is determined by whether the restriction is reasonable. However, it is important to decide at this stage whether that part of an express clause which seeks to control competition during employment is also subject to such a test. There is authority on this point. In *Esso Petroleum Co Ltd v Harper's Garage (Stourport) Ltd* [1968] A.C. 269 Lord Reid said:

> Whenever a man agrees to do something over a period he thereby puts it wholly or partly out of his power to "exercise any trade or business he pleases" during that period. He may enter into a contract of service or may agree to give his exclusive services to another: then during the period of the contract he is not entitled to engage in other business activities. But no one has ever suggested that such contracts are in restraint of trade except in very unusual circumstances . . .

See also *Warner Bros Inc v Nelson* [1937] 1 K.B. 209; *A. Schroeder Music Publishing Co Ltd v Macaulay* [1974] 1 W.L.R. 1308 and *Clifford Davis Management Ltd v W.E.A. Records Ltd* [1975] 1 W.L.R. 61.

7.2.2 Business secrets

The particular importance of an express clause covering business secrets during employment is that it avoids some of the problems encountered in *GB Bjorlow Ltd v Minter* (1954) 71 R.P.C. 321. It creates certainty as it specifically defines what amounts to a business secret and brings its existence to the mind of the employee.

Chapter 8

Interests Protectable After Employment Ends

8.1 The end of employment

8.1.1 Introduction

The end of employment is a critical and decisive event. The practical effect of it is to reduce the law's interest in implying duties largely for the reason that public policy demands that an employee be free to work for whom he chooses. This is reflected by the fact that, in the absence of express provision, it is now quite legitimate for the employee to compete with his old employer and to canvass his customers. However, the employee is still prevented from betraying his employer's business secrets. Put briefly, once employment ends he cannot, without a specific covenant, be prevented from doing anything unless his actions contravene what is perceived to be a proprietary right of his employer: *Herbert Morris Ltd v Saxelby* [1916] 1 A.C. 688.

Therefore, once he has left, the employee is allowed to pursue his own interests. How far he can go in the absence of restrictive covenants is dealt with later. Once an employee has ceased to work for a particular employer two crucial questions arise: has the contract been terminated so that only post termination duties remain? and secondly, if it has been terminated, how did this come about? i.e. did it occur in accordance with the express or implied provisions of the contract or did it occur by the acceptance of the innocent party of a repudiatory breach by the other party?

In practice, the second question arises frequently. It is crucial; if an employer commits a repudiatory breach which the employee accepts (such as wrongful dismissal) the orthodox view is that the employee will be discharged forthwith from any duties under the contract including, of course, the terms of any restrictive covenant no matter how reasonable (see *General Billposting v Atkinson* [1909] A.C. 118), but *cf. Rock Refrigeration v Jones* [1997] I.C.R. 938 [1996] I.R.L.R. 675, CA. Obviously if an employee is justifiably dismissed a reasonable restraint will be enforceable (see *Marion White Ltd v Francis* [1972] 1 W.L.R. 1423 and *Foot DC v Eastern Counties Timber Co Ltd* [1972] I.R.L.R. 83).

However, although *General Billposting* remains good law, Phillips L.J. in *Rock Refrigeration v Jones* considered that the rule in *General Billposting* accorded neither with current legal principle nor with the requirements of business efficacy. The case involved a restrictive covenant which purported to apply on the termination of the contract "howsoever arising" or "howsoever occasioned". The question for the court was whether the covenants were unreasonable and unenforceable because they purported to apply in circumstances where the employer had wrongfully terminated the contract. The Court of Appeal held a restrictive covenant that purports to operate where the termination has been wrongful is not necessarily void from the beginning as unreasonable restraint in trade. If an otherwise reasonable covenant purported to remain enforceable where the law will inevitably strike it down that is not justification for holding that it is, on that basis, an unlawful restraint of trade. Phrases such as "whether lawfully or not" are merely writ in water and unenforceable under the *General Billposting* principle. Phillips L.J. considered that it was at least arguable that not every restrictive covenant would be discharged upon a repudiatory termination of the contract of employment. In his view negative restraints which were agreed would apply after the termination of employment should not be equated to primary obligations which are discharged when the contract of employment is terminated as a result of a repudiation. The consideration for such restraints was not the obligation to give the appropriate notice period but the granting of employment that afforded access to confidential information and goodwill. It remains to be seen whether this view gains support but, particularly where long notice periods are involved, a repudiation by an employer followed by an attempt to prevent the employee from mitigating his loss by reference to a restrictive covenant that purports to survive such an event is unattractive. In *Campbell v Frisbee* [2002] EWHC 328, Ch D Lightman J., considering the effects of repudiation on an express confidentiality obligation, indicated that if necessary to decide the effect of this he would unhesitatingly hold that the repudiation and acceptance would not prejudice rights in respect of confidential information. "There can be no conceivable justification for granting as a windfall to a wrongly dismissed employee a present of his employer's trade or other secrets or confidences." This was not however a case involving a contract of employment or a restrictive covenant. The suggestion that a provision of the type considered in *Rock* is void on the basis that it does not pass the reasonableness test in the Unfair Contract Terms Act 1977 (which could have been based on the proposition that the Act applies to contracts of employment (*Brigden v American Express Bank Limited* [2000] I.R.L.R. 94) appears to have been dealt a mortal blow by the Court of Appeal (*Keen v Commerzbank AG* [2007] I.R.L.R. 132). The employee was not, in the Court of Appeal's view, dealing with his employers "as a consumer" in contracting with it in respect of pay for work (this being a case in relation to a discretionary bonus). The employee was not dealing with his employers on its "written standard terms of business" and the business of the employer was banking, not employing its employees.

8.1.2 The termination of the contract

In most cases the first question, viz has termination occurred, is answered in the affirmative. In most cases the employee has resigned or been given notice in accordance with the contractual terms or has, he claims, been wrongfully dismissed. Where however there has been a wrongful repudiation the pre-termination contractual duties only cease once there has been acceptance of that repudiation, as discussed below. If there has been no such acceptance the court will conclude, as Megarry V.C. did in *Thomas Marshall (Exporters) Ltd v Guinle* [1978] 3 W.L.R. 116, that the contract continues to subsist with the effect that, in this case, for its remainder (circa four and a half years), the defendant was bound by its terms. His status as an employee had ended but the continuing terms of the contract of employment stayed in place. This meant, inter alia, that a provision of the contract which permitted him to solicit business once employment was over did not come into effect until the full period of the contract had elapsed.

8.1.3 Repudiatory breach of contract

If a breach of a fundamental term ("a repudiatory breach") of the contract occurs the innocent party can elect as to whether to affirm the contract or to bring it to an end by accepting the breach.

8.1.3.1 What amounts to a repudiatory breach?

Such a breach must relate to conduct by one party which amounts to a significant breach going to the root of the contract, or which shows an intention no longer to be bound by one of the essential terms of the contract (see *Western Excavating Ltd v Sharp* [1978] Q.B. 761, CA).

A good example in the restraint of trade field is *Briggs v Oates* [1991] 1 All E.R. 407 in which the plaintiff and his partner in a firm of solicitors employed the defendant as a solicitor for a period of five years. His contract of employment contained a restraint of trade clause. Following the dissolution of the partnership in August 1983 the defendant wanted to practice with other solicitors in prima facie breach of that clause. The plaintiffs sought to enforce the clause but Scott J. dismissed the action for he found that, on its true construction, the employment agreement was a contract of employment of the defendant by the two partners, that the dissolution of that partnership within the term of the employment constituted a breach of the contract of employment and brought it to an end and that accordingly the restraint of trade clause ceased thereafter to be binding upon the defendant.

8.1.3.2 The need for acceptance

It would seem now, although there were judicial murmurs of dissent; see *Boyo v London Borough of Lambeth* [1995] I.R.L.R. 50, CA, that it is necessary for the innocent party to accept the repudiation in order to bring the contracts to an end. For a considerable time, however, there was some dispute as to whether a breach of a fundamental term brought the contract to an end independent of any rights of election. This so-called "unilateral" view is supported in, inter alia: *London Transport Executive v Clarke* [1981] I.R.L.R. 166 (*per* Lord Denning); *Gunton v Richmond-on-Thames London Borough Council* [1980] I.R.L.R. 321 (*per* Shaw L.J.). The opposing and now probably decided view is that the contract is only brought to an end when it has been accepted by the innocent party. This "acceptance" view is found in such cases as *Dietmann v Brent London Borough Council* [1987] I.R.L.R. 259; *Thomas Marshall (Exports) Ltd v Guinle op. cit*. and the majority judgments in *Gunton*.

8.1.3.3 Has there been acceptance?

When confronted by a repudiatory breach the innocent party must elect whether to accept the repudiation or affirm the contract. If he decides to accept he must do so unambiguously and with sufficient dispatch. If his purported acceptance is equivocal and/or delayed he runs the risk of a court finding that his action has not been sufficient to discharge the contract. Indeed, as the examples in the cases illustrate it is sometimes difficult to decide whether acceptance has occurred or not.

In *Marriott v Oxford and District Co-Operative Society Limited (No. 2)* [1970] Q.B. 186, the employee was a supervisor. The employers informed him that they could not retain him in his position because its business was contracting. They offered him employment at reduced status and with reduced pay of £3 per week. He protested, refused to accept the offer and sought alternative employment. The employers subsequently varied their offer to a reduction of £1 per week. The employee again protested but continued to work at a reduced rate of £1. He subsequently found other employment and claimed a redundancy payment. The core question was whether Mr Marriot had lost his redundancy payment because he had stayed on for three or four weeks whilst he searched for another job. The court found that he had not lost the redundancy payment, as he had never agreed to the dictated terms, protested against them and only submitted to them because he did not want to be out of a job.

By contrast in *Cox* (*WE Toner*) *v Crook* [1981] I.R.L.R. 443 the appellant was a director of the respondent who went on business to Holland and prolonged his stay to embrace a holiday. The board of the respondent informed the appellant that this amounted to grounds warranting dismissal. Mr Crook replied in detail refuting these allegations; correspondence ensued between the parties, and eventually he resigned. He had delayed for seven months. The court stated that an innocent party must at some stage choose between affirming the contract or treating it as having been repudiated. Mere delay by itself unaccompanied by any express or implied affirmation of the contract did not constitute affirmation of the contract, but if it were prolonged it might constitute evidence of an implied affirmation. Thus if an innocent party calls on the guilty party for further performance of the contract he will normally be taken as having affirmed the contract. Moreover, if the innocent party commits acts which are only consistent with the continued existence of the contract, such acts will normally show affirmation of the contract. However, if the innocent party further performs the contract to a limited extent, but at the same time makes it clear that he is reserving his rights to accept the repudiation, or he is only continuing so as to allow the guilty party to remedy the breach, such further performance does not prejudice his right subsequently to accept the repudiation. Delay is important not in its own right but because any delay normally involves further performance of the contract by both parties. What happens during the period of delay is therefore the crucial point (see also *Bashir v Brillo Manufacturing Company* [1979] I.R.L.R. 295; *Cantor Fitzgerald International v Callaghan* [1999] I.R.L.R. 234, CA and *Cantor Fitzgerald v Bird* [2002] I.R.L.R. 867). Provided the employee makes clear his objection to what has been done, he is not to be taken to have affirmed the contract by continuing to work and draw pay for a limited period of time, even if his purpose is merely to enable him to find another job. However, in *Cox* the EAT found that, as throughout the seven-month period Mr Crook continued to work and was paid under the contract which he subsequently claimed to have been repudiated, he had not accepted any repudiation. In contrast in *Cantor Fitzgerald v Bird* the employees argued that proposed changes to the remuneration arrangements were aggressively pursued by the employer with misleading explanations (accompanied by much hard language). Salaries had also been stopped for one day and there was no real consultation about the proposed changes. A delay of two months before the relevant employees left was not such that they affirmed the contracts. McCombe J. described affirmation (having reviewed the cases) as "essentially the legal embodiment of the everyday concept of 'letting bygones be bygones' ". An employee will not be taken to have affirmed the contract until

(a) he has knowledge of the facts constituting the breach and

(b) knowledge of the legal rights to choose the alternative courses of action open to him.

In this case the employees considered their position for some time during which they indicated their discontent and were showing signs of their intention to leave the company's employment.

In *Normalec Ltd v Britton* [1983] F.S.R. 318 it was decided that by not leaving at the time a fundamental breach occurred but in giving notice in accordance with a relevant contractual term the employee had affirmed the existence of the contract rather than having made an effective acceptance of a repudiation. In *Spencer v Marchington* [1988] I.R.L.R. 392 it was held that there was no evidence that the plaintiff had accepted what she considered to be a repudiation when she was not allowed to carry out her duties during a two-month period out of a 12 month contract. By staying away from work (and in keeping and using a company car) the plaintiff was only doing what she had been asked to do: that was as indicative that she was affirming a varied contract (or waiving any breach) as that she was accepting any repudiation.

In *Reid v Camphill Engravers* [1990] I.R.L.R. 268 the EAT held that the Industrial Tribunal had erred in dismissing the employee's complaint of constructive dismissal on the ground that, notwithstanding that for more than three years prior to his resignation the employers were in material breach of contract in failing to pay him the statutory minimum rate of remuneration set out in the appropriate Wages Council Orders, the appellant had delayed in acting upon the breach. The EAT held that paying an employee a weekly sum in wages less than the required amount is a continuing breach of contract. Even if an employee does not react to an initial breach of contract, it is open to him to refer to that initial breach, where, as in the present case, the employer continues to commit further breaches. In any case the court held where an employer has a statutory obligation to make the appropriate weekly payments, it is not open to an employee to agree and affirm the contract for a lower sum in wages than that decreed by Parliament. In the present case therefore the concept of affirmation by the applicant was not relevant.

In conjunction with judicial recognition of the implied trust and confidence term in contracts of employment (see para. 8.1.4.6) the development of the "last straw principle" can further complicate identifying a repudiatory breach, the point at which it needs to be accepted and the extent to which acceptance might still validly be delayed without compromising the employee's right to accept repudiatory conduct as terminating the employment. Neill L. J. said in *Lewis v Motorworld Garages Limited* [1985] I.R.L.R. 465, CA, that "the repudiatory conduct may consist of a series of acts or incidents, some of them perhaps quite trivial, which cumulatively amount to a repudiatory breach of the implied term" of trust and confidence. The Court of Appeal in *Omilaju v London Borough of Waltham Forest* [2005] I.R.L.R. 35, held that it was not necessary in order for there to be a breach of the implied term of trust and confidence that the "final straw" event should itself be a breach of contract, it was sufficient that it was an act in a series of earlier acts which cumulatively amount to a breach of the implied term. "The only question is whether the final straw is the last in the series of acts or incidents which cumulatively amount to a repudiation of the contract by the employer. The last straw must contribute, however slightly, to the breach of the implied term of trust and confidence." Per Dyson L. J.:

> If the final straw is capable of contributing to a series of earlier acts which cumulatively amount to a breach of the implied term of trust and confidence, there is no need to examine the early history to see whether the alleged final straw does in fact have that effect. Suppose that an employer has committed a series of acts which amount to a breach of the implied term of trust and confidence, but the employee does not resign his employment. Instead, he soldiers on and affirms the contract. He cannot subsequently rely on these acts to justify a constructive dismissal unless he can point to a later act which enables him to do so. If the later act on which he seeks to rely is entirely innocuous, it is not necessary to examine the earlier conduct in order to determine that the later act does not permit the employee to invoke the final straw principle.

The final straw principle in practice means that the repudiatory breach may be less obvious and may give rise to instances where quite long periods can elapse without necessarily prejudicing the right to treat a final straw incident as a repudiation (see *Logan v Commissioners of Customs & Excise* [2004] I.R.L.R. 63, CA where an eighteenth-month period between circumstances arising where the employee might have treated the employer's conduct as repudiatory and a last straw incident was not held to be fatal to the employees' claim of constructive dismissal).

8.1.4 Common examples from the authorities of when a repudiation may have occurred

In this section we shall briefly discuss some types of duty a breach of which by the employer will usually/often be regarded as being fundamental.

8.1.4.1 Wages: the obligation to pay and reductions

In *FC Gardner Ltd v Beresford* [1978] I.R.L.R. 63, Mrs Gardner resigned and claimed constructive dismissal on the ground that whereas other employees had received pay increases she had received no increase in two years. The EAT held that although in the present case there was no express contractual term relating to pay increases, in most cases it would be reasonable to infer a term that an employer will not treat his employees arbitrarily, capriciously or inequitably in matters of remuneration. If there was evidence to support a finding that the employers were deliberately singling out the respondent for special treatment inferior to that given to everybody else and were doing so arbitrarily, capriciously and inequitably that would amount to a breach (see also *Cantor FitzGerald v Bird* above). Since *Gardner* the implied "trust and confidence" term in contracts of employment has matured to the point where irrational or peverse decisions in relation to such matters would clearly be a breach of the term (see *Clark v Nomura International plc* [2000] I.R.L.R. 766), but cp *Keen v Commerzbank AG* [2007] I.R.L.R. 132, CA where Mummery L. J. emphasised that it would require an overwhelming case to persuade the

Court to find that the level of a discretionary bonus was irrational and perverse where so much depended on the discretionary judgment of the Bank and fluctuating market conditions, making clear, in the process, the reluctance of the Courts to be drawn into adjudicating on the size of bonuses. Unlike *Clark*, where no discretionary bonus was paid, *Keen* involved a dispute about the level of the bonus paid.

In *Adams v Charles Zub Associates Ltd* [1978] I.R.L.R. 551 Mr Adams was employed as a senior consultant for the respondent management consultants. The company's reliance on income from overseas caused problems, particularly in the honouring of cheques. Mr Adams had not been paid his monthly salary on the due date. Mr Adams resigned and claimed constructive dismissal. The EAT held that failure by the employer to pay the appellant employee his monthly salary on the due date, though a breach of contract, was not so serious a breach as to justify the appellant in resigning and claiming constructive dismissal. Failure by the employer to pay an employee's salary may amount to conduct which constitutes a breach going to the root of the contract, or which shows that the employer has no intention thereafter to honour the contract and thus justifies the employee in resigning. In *Adams*, however, the appellant had been informed that the money to pay his April salary was to come from a client in Argentina and he knew that the company's income depended on the receipt of payment from foreign clients. He had been told that the problem was going to arise, he had been informed that the money was on the way and initially he had raised no objections. Further, he knew that the company was anxious to pay and would pay as soon as the money arrived. In the light of all of this, it was held that breach of a fundamental term was not made out.

In *Gillies v Richard Daniels and Co Ltd* [1979] I.R.L.R. 457 a reduction in the appellant's payment for additional duties amounting to no more than £1.50 a week (out of £60) though a unilateral change and a clear demonstration of an intention by the respondent no longer to implement a term of the contract, was not held to be material breach of contract on the employer's part sufficient to justify the appellant in resigning and claiming constructive dismissal. The important factor was the materiality and significance of the breach. Whether a unilateral reduction in additional pay or fringe benefits or indeed basic pay by the employer is of sufficient materiality as to entitle an employee to resign and claim constructive dismissal is a matter of degree (generally the employee will in any event be able to recover the amount in question by making a complaint of unlawful deduction from wages to an Employment Tribunal – s.13 Employment Rights Act 1996).

In *RF Hill Ltd v Mooney* [1981] I.R.L.R. 258 Mr Mooney was employed by the appellant as a salesman; the basis of his remuneration being a salary plus a 1 per cent commission on all sales. In February 1980 the company sought to introduce remuneration based on a 1 per cent commission only for sales exceeding a given target. Mr Mooney was dissatisfied with this scheme and resigned claiming constructive dismissal. The EAT found that the obligation of an employer to pay remuneration is one of the fundamental terms of a contract. Although a mere alteration in the contractual provisions does not necessarily amount to a fundamental breach constituting repudiation, if an employer seeks to alter the contractual obligation in a fundamental way, such attempt is a breach going to the very root of the contract and is necessarily a repudiation. The obligation on the employer is to pay the contractual wages, and he is not entitled to alter significantly the formula whereby those wages are calculated. In the present case, what the employers had sought to do was to tear up the existing contractual obligation as to the computation of the remuneration by reference to a given formula, the exact operation of which at the date at which they attempted to impose it was incapable of assessment. However, as was pointed out by the EAT in *White v Reflecting Roadstuds Ltd* [1991] I.R.L.R. 331, where an employer acts within the contract of employment the fact that his action causes a loss of income to the employee does not render the employer in breach of contract; see also *Spafax Ltd v Harrison* [1980] I.R.L.R. 443 and *High v British Railways Board* [1979] I.R.L.R. 52. In *Farrell Matthews & Weir v Hansen* [2005] I.R.L.R. 160, the EAT were concerned with an assistant solicitor who had no contractual right to receive any bonus. During the four years of her employment, she had received one, ad hoc, bonus but when one of the two equity partners had retired, the employee was offered a bonus payable by 12 monthly installments provided she did not resign her employment. The EAT upheld the Employment Tribunal's finding that the employee was entitled to treat the employer's conduct in imposing conditions on the payment of the non-contractual discretionary bonus, to the effect that she could be deprived of the balance of the bonus if her employment terminated for any reason, including redundancy, coupled with the firm's refusal to give her access to the accounts on which the decision to impose the conditions was claimed to be based (it being said the firm's finances had been taken into consideration), amounted to a fundamental breach of the implied trust and confidence term entitling her to resign and claim constructive dismissal.

8.1.4.2 Change in job functions, hours and duties

If an employer unilaterally changes an employee's job functions by either taking away or adding different duties this may amount to a fundamental breach warranting an employee in leaving and claiming constructive dismissal. In *Coleman (DA) v S&W Baldwin* [1977] I.R.L.R. 342 Mr Coleman had been employed by Covent Garden Supply Co since 1940. He progressed to the position of acting manager, with one of his main duties being the buying of the greengrocery which the firm sold. In 1976 whilst he was on holiday his buying duties were carried out by another member of staff and when he returned he was informed that this duty was to be taken away from him permanently.

He resigned and claimed constructive dismissal. The EAT held that notwithstanding that the employer had not imposed other duties on him it had unilaterally changed the whole nature of the appellant's job and in so doing had repudiated his contract of employment. The buying duties were the most interesting and prestigious and gave the appellant job satisfaction; without them his job would have been humdrum.

In *Seligman & Latzman Ltd v McHugh* [1979] I.R.L.R. 130 Mrs McHugh was employed as a ladies hairdresser at Selfridges department store. Selfridges transferred their hairdressing business to the appellants, on a concessionary basis. Mrs McHugh was re-engaged on terms which were stipulated to be no less favourable than those that applied to her employment with Selfridges. One of those terms was that Mrs McHugh worked with a junior hairdresser. The junior left and despite repeated requests by Mrs McHugh the employers failed to secure a replacement. Eventually, Mrs McHugh left. The EAT held that the respondent employee was entitled to regard herself as constructively dismissed on grounds that the appellant employers were in breach of an implied condition in her contract as a hairdresser that if she were busy she would have the assistance of juniors and that the breach was a fundamental one which went to the very root of the contract.

In *Pedersen v Camden London Borough* [1981] I.R.L.R. 173 Mr Pedersen was employed initially as a bar steward/catering assistant with a primary focus on the job of bar steward. After a decline in business in the St Pancras assembly rooms Mr Pedersen found himself working primarily as a catering assistant. The Court of Appeal in disagreeing with the EAT found that the appellant was not appointed to two linked jobs, but, as was clear from the letter of appointment, was primarily employed as a bar steward. Therefore, there was evidence that amounted to a breach of contract which was so fundamental as to entitle him to regard it as repudiation and treat himself as dismissed. See also: *Warnes v Trustees of Cheriton Oddfellows Social Club* [1993] I.R.L.R. 58, *Greenaway Harrison Ltd v Wiles* [1994] I.R.L.R. 380 and *Alcan Extrusions v Yates* [1996] I.R.L.R. 327. In *Land Securities Trillium Limited v Thornley* [2005] I.R.L.R. 765, the EAT were concerned with an architect employed under a contract of employment which included a clause to the effect "you will perform to the best of your abilities all the duties of this post and any other post you may subsequently hold and any other duties which may reasonably be required of you and will at all times obey all reasonable instructions given to you". The employee was promoted to the post of senior project leader with the duties of the position being described as being "to undertake . . . the overall design, planning and management of major projects." Her main duties were expected to be the undertaking of a "full service" project which would entail "hands-on" involvement from inception to completion. In the event the employer was not assigned any full service projects and, following a transfer of the department in which the employee worked for the BBC to LST, it was proposed to restructure the employee's department in such a way that she would be monitoring the work of external consultants rather than undertaking architectural duties herself. In the context of the re-organisation, the employee's job title was changed to that of "senior architect" and her main duties and responsibilities configured in such a way that they were "at a remove" from the hands-on architectural work that she had previously expected to undertake and, as a consequence, her job had effectively changed to that of a managerial role. The employee resigned and was held to have been constructively unfairly dismissed. The original flexibility clause in her contract of employment did not entitle the employers to change the content of her work so substantially that its nature was changed and the duties would have the effect that she would lose her skills.

In *Spencer v Marchington* [1988] I.R.L.R. 392, a restraint of trade case, one of the issues involved whether the employers had repudiated the plaintiff's contract of employment by refusing to allow her to carry out her duties in managing an employment agency until her fixed term contract expired. The High Court (perhaps surprisingly) held that asking her to stay away from work for the last two months was not sufficient to amount to a fundamental breach, even in the context of a twelve-month contract under which the employee was entitled to a share of the profits of the business.

In our view, where an employer seeks to send an employee home during the notice period, then unless express provision exists to enable this to happen, it is very likely to amount to a repudiation: see *Provident Financial Group plc v Hayward* [1989] 3 All E.R. 298, CA, *per* Dillon L.J. and *J A Mont (UK) Ltd v Mills* [1993] I.R.L.R. 172, CA at para.41 and see also *William Hill v Tucker* [1998] I.R.L.R. 313, CA.

8.1.4.3 Notice periods

A failure to give notice as laid down by the contract may and, absent grounds for summary dismissal or an express pay in lieu provision, usually will amount to a fundamental breach as may the absence of reasonable notice where none is expressed. However, that this is not invariably the case was shown in *David Lawrence Ltd v Ashton* [1991] 1 All E.R. 385. There it was accepted by the plaintiffs that the termination of the defendant's contract was in breach of contract: it was neither written nor of the agreed period of one month. What actually happened is not clear but it seems that the defendant was originally given oral notice of termination of a period just short of a month, that this was shortly followed by written confirmation which seems to have envisaged the defendant leaving at once but being paid "in lieu of notice" and that in fact he worked for only nine days of the month. Perhaps the refusal of the court to accept that there had been a wrongful repudiation is explicable by factual confusion although reliance was placed on *W Dennis & Sons Ltd v Tunnard Bros and Moore* (1911) 56 S.J. 162 for the proposition that not every dismissal without proper notice may be repudiatory.

8.1.4.4 Payment in lieu of notice

If there is no express provision for such payment then such payment may well constitute a repudiatory breach: *Dixon v Stenor Ltd* [1973] I.C.R. 157. Care should also be taken in drafting pay in lieu of notice (PILON) clauses in contracts of employment to avoid ambiguity and, with it, scope for dispute as to what is actually to be paid in satisfaction of such a clause in order to effect a lawful termination of the employment. A simple payment of "salary" (properly defined) for the notice period will usually prove satisfactory. But a less precise provision (perhaps referring to "remuneration" rather than salary where this is not a defined term) or one which purports to include the value of non-monitory benefits or discretionary bonus but without a stipulated formula for calculating these might prove ineffective in operation as a basis for lawfully terminating the contract.

8.1.4.5 Health and safety

A further duty of the employer in the workplace is the obligation to make adequate provision for health and safety for his workforce. It is a fundamental term of the contract of employment that an employer shall take reasonable care to operate a safe system of work and take reasonable care to have safe premises. Failure to provide such a system may give the employee grounds to leave and claim constructive dismissal.

In *Keys v Shoefayre Ltd* [1978] I.R.L.R. 476 the lack of adequate security precautions to protect the staff in an area where crime was rife and violent crime was well known was held by the Industrial Tribunal to amount to a breach of that term.

In *British Aircraft Corp Ltd v Austin* [1978] I.R.L.R. 332 it became necessary for the employee and her fellow employees to wear eye protectors when performing their work. Mrs Austin was initially provided with goggles which were not suitable. She complained to the manager and in November 1976 the safety officer looked into the matter. He decided to approach the management to see whether they would put special eye protectors in the goggles. Nothing was done about the matter and in May 1977 Mrs Austin decided that she had no alternative but to resign. The EAT decided that employers are under a duty to act reasonably in dealing with matters of safety or complaints of lack of safety which are drawn to their attention by employees. They are bound to investigate such complaints quickly unless they are obviously bogus or frivolous. The failure in this case to investigate promptly amounted to a fundamental breach as it put the employee in an entirely unfair dilemma; either she had to carry on with no prospect of anything being done about her complaint with, as she saw it, a risk to her health and her eyesight; or she would be obliged to give up her job with all the difficulties and uncertainties of finding another.

8.1.4.6 Trust and confidence

The trust and confidence term implied into contracts of employment received affirmation by the House of Lords in *Malik v Bank of Credit and Commerce International SA* [1997] I.R.L.R. 462. As formulated by Lord Steyn, the implied term is to the effect that:

> The employer shall not without reasonable and proper cause, conduct itself in a manner calculated and likely to destroy or seriously damage the relationship of trust and confidence between employer and employee.

However, the EAT in *Baldwin v Brighton & Hove City Council* [2007] I.R.L.R. 232, held that, whilst this test is to require the claimant to show both that the employer's conduct was likely to destroy trust and confidence and also that it was intended by the employer to do so, the test as articulated by Lord Steyn was based on, Mr. Justice Browne-Wilkinson formulation in *Woods v WM Car Services (Peterborough) Limited* [1982] I.R.L.R. 413, CA, where the word "or" was used in place of "and", and that Lord Steyn, in approving the formulation of the test in *Woods*, had no intention of altering it from a disjunctive to a conjunctive test. As a result, it is sufficient for the claimant to show conduct by the employer "which, objectively considered, is likely to seriously undermine the necessary trust and confidence in the employment relationship".

The evolution of the implied term and its practical application can be seen from earlier cases. In *Courtaulds Northern Textiles Ltd v Andrew* [1979] I.R.L.R. 84 the respondent overseer was entitled to treat a statement by the appellant company's assistant manager that "You can't do the bloody job anyway", where that was not a true expression of the manager's opinion, as conduct which justified him in resigning and claiming constructive dismissal. There was an implied term that the employers would not without reasonable and proper cause conduct themselves in a manner calculated or likely to destroy or seriously damage the relationship of confidence and trust between the parties. Further, the breach was fundamental as any conduct which is likely to destroy or seriously to damage the relationship of mutual trust and confidence between employer and employee must be something which goes to the root of the contract.

In *Post Office v Roberts* [1980] I.R.L.R. 347 the EAT decided that there did not have to be deliberate conduct or bad faith for the obligation of mutual trust and confidence to be destroyed. Whether the conduct of the other party whose behaviour is challenged amounts to a repudiation of the contract must be determined by whether it is such that its effect, judged reasonably and sensibly, is to disable the other party from properly carrying out his or her obligations. In this case the obligation was broken when the employee had been appraised as a competent worker but, without proper consideration, had been given a bad report by the senior sales superintendent. When she applied for a similar position at another office she was refused it on the basis of that report but was led to believe that it was because there were no suitable vacancies. She subsequently ascertained the real reason. The relationship had been fatally damaged by the employer's conduct in dealing with the transfer requested.

In *Dryden v Greater Glasgow Health Board* [1992] I.R.L.R. 469 Mrs Dryden was a compulsive smoker. Her job as a nursing auxiliary was such that she was not able to leave the building during the day. Prior to 1991 that posed no problems as certain designated smoking areas were set aside. However, from July 1991 after consultation a no-smoking policy was introduced. She resigned and claimed constructive dismissal. The EAT held that there was no doubt that an employer is entitled to make rules for the conduct of the employees in the place of work. It also found that there was no implied term in the contract of employment that the appellant was entitled to smoke. It said that whilst it was not difficult to envisage an implied term to the effect that the employer will not change the rules of the workplace in a way which adversely affects an employee or group of employees without reasonable notice and without consultation or, perhaps without some substantial reason, it was more difficult to recognise the existence of an implied term restricting the employer's right to change the working rules by reference to the views, or even the requirements of each particular employee. See also *Cantor Fitzgerald v Bird* [2002] I.R.L.R. 867 above where the aggressive and unreasonable promotion of new remuneration arrangements were found to breach the trust and confidence term. See also the cases referred to in 8.1.4.1 and 8.1.4.2. It has also been suggested that breach of a statutory right may also give rise to a parallel breach of the implied term of trust and confidence (*Greenhoff v Barnsley Metropolitan Borough Council* [2006] I.R.L.R. 98, EAT). This was a case where a failure to make reasonable adjustment as required by the Disability Discrimination Act 1995 over a period of time resulted in the finding that this "was almost bound to be a breach of the implied term of trust and confidence which Mr Greenhoff would be entitled to treat as being a repudiatory breach of contract, as he purported to do" (Judge Serota). However, cp *Doherty v British Midland Airways Limited* [2006] I.R.L.R. 90, EAT, where Judge McMullen QC, in the context of the claim of constructive dismissal arising from an alleged abuse of the employee's trade union rights, regarded the proposition that this was also a breach of the duty of mutual trust and confidence as "wholly misconceived" on the basis that if there were an implied contractual term covering the same issue as a statute covered, it would mean that every breach of a statutory right would be actionable as a breach of contract.

8.1.4.7 Mobility clauses

In *United Bank Ltd v Akhtar* [1989] I.R.L.R. 507 Mr Akhtar learned in accordance with the mobility clause in his contract of employment that he was to move from the Leeds branch of the bank to the Birmingham branch.

He received written notification on the Friday to leave on the following Monday. Mr Akhtar wrote to his manager stating that in view of his wife's ill health and the impending sale of his house he be given three months' postponement of the transfer. That request was turned down. On the day he was supposed to work in Birmingham he wrote another letter asking for 24 hours leave in order to sort out his affairs. He then consulted a law centre who wrote to the bank asking for two months to settle his affairs and received a response that Mr Akhtar, in accordance with clause 13 of his terms of employment, could be transferred in accordance with the exigencies of the moment. Eventually, Mr Akhtar was given 24 days' holiday leave backdated and received some holiday pay. Despairing of any concrete resolution of the problem Mr Akhtar eventually resigned and claimed constructive dismissal; his claim was upheld. The case is effectively an example of the implied trust and confidence term controlling or qualifying the operation of an express contractual provision.

This can be seen in *Prestwick Circuits Ltd v McAndrew* [1990] I.R.L.R. 191 there the Court of Session held that a mobility clause was subject to the implied term that reasonable notice of a requirement to work elsewhere must be given and that the relocation is a reasonable distance away. See also *Bass Leisure Ltd v Thomas* [1994] I.R.L.R. 104 and *Aparau v Iceland Frozen Foods plc* [1996] I.R.L.R. 119.

8.2 Implied duties

8.2.1 Competition with previous employer

The courts will not imply any duty which prevents competition with a previous employer or the canvassing of his customers: *Attwood v Lamont* [1920] 3 K.B. 571 and *Wallace Bogan & Co v Cove* [1997] I.R.L.R. 453, CA. Therefore, if an employer feels that such protection is necessary he must include express restrictions in the contract of employment. The plaintiff in *Diamond Stylus Co Ltd v Bauden Precision Diamonds Ltd* [1973] R.P.C. 675 paid the price for not having an express covenant restraining employees from soliciting customers after employment ended and was forced to argue that solicitation could only have come about because of the misuse of business secrets. Graham J. concluded that the defendants had simply remembered the names of clients, the number of whom was very small. They had not consciously memorised the names nor done anything which an honest man would consider wrong.

However, what appears to be competition/soliciting which cannot be restrained without an express clause frequently amounts to a breach of the duty of fidelity. For example, it often happens that the ability to compete/canvass arises from a breach of duty committed *during* employment. In *Wessex Dairies Ltd v Smith* [1935] 2 K.B. 80 Smith breached his duty of fidelity by canvassing his employers' customers during his last day of employment when he made his last milk round. Subsequently, as a direct result of such canvassing, they became his customers. It would be absurd if the law did not recognise the causal connection between these events despite its refusal to imply a non-competition restriction post employment. In this case it did so recognise that connection and Smith had to pay damages. Similarly, the ability to compete may arise from the use and disclosure of business secrets. Even if these are used only after employment ends the implied duty not to use or disclose may well mean that the employer can effectively prevent any competition based on breach, although the duty not to disclose or use confidential information does not necessarily translate into a general duty not to work for a trade rival (see *J A Mont (UK) Ltd v Mills* [1993] I.R.L.R. 172 at para.31).

It is therefore vital that what appears to be a non-restrictable act is examined in order to find what really lies behind the employee's ability to compete/canvass.

8.2.2 Business secrets

The implied duty to maintain confidence in the employer's business secrets continues after employment ends. The most common example of breaches of this duty are the use or disclosure of a former employer's client list or of a secret process belonging to him. See *Under Water Welders and Repairers Ltd v Street and Longthorne* [1968] R.P.C. 498.

The principal case which authoratively reviewed the implied duty of fidelity as it applies to the use of confidential information once employment has ended, is *Faccenda Chicken Ltd v Fowler* [1985] 1 All E.R. 724; [1986] 1 All E.R. 617, CA. The company claimed that Fowler, a former senior employee and eight other former employees and a new company set up by Fowler had wrongfully made use of confidential information which had been acquired during employment. The information was:

(a) the names and addresses of customers;

(b) the most convenient routes to be taken to reach the individual customers;

(c) the usual requirements of individual customers, both as to quality and quantity;

(d) the days of the week and the time of the day when deliveries were usually made to individual customers;

(e) the prices charged to individual customers.

It was argued that all of the information, as a package, was confidential and that (e) was itself secret. Goulding J. found as a fact that all parts of the sales information had been used for the purposes of the defendant's business and he divided information into three categories where it was not the subject of any express provision:

(1) Information which because of its triviality or public accessibility was not confidential at all.

The employee, either during or after employment, was free to impart it to anyone—including his employer's competitor.

(2) Information which was confidential in the sense that the employee had been told it was or because from its character it was obviously so. Goulding J. was in fact referring to the employee's skill and knowledge acquired in the course of his present employment.

During employment the employee could not use or disclose this information without breaching the duty of fidelity. However once employment had ended it could be used or disclosed by an employee in competition with his former employer. The employer could only be protected by an express stipulation. The Court of Appeal specifically disagreed with Goulding J. on the ability of the employer to prevent use of such information once employment had ended.

(3) Information which was confidential, such as details of a secret process; this type was so confidential that it could not be used by the employee at any time for the benefit of anyone but the employer.

He concluded that the information in the case came within category (2). As it had been used after employment it could only have been protected by an express term. The absence of such a term meant that there had been no breach of duty and therefore he dismissed the plaintiff's claim. The plaintiff appealed.

The Court of Appeal decided to undertake a review of the basic principles of the law in this area. Neill L.J. giving the judgment of the court said:

> (1) Where the parties are, or have been, linked by a contract of employment the obligations of the employee are to be determined by the contract between him and his employer. (No mention is made here of express terms which are defective and if in that event the court is free to imply terms, though as we suggest below, there is such power.)
>
> (2) In the absence of an express term, the obligations of the employee in respect of the use and disclosure of information are the subject of implied terms.
>
> (3) While the employee remains in the employment of the employer the obligations are included in the implied term which imposes a duty of good faith or fidelity on the employee. It is to be further noted:
>
> (a) That the extent of the duty of good faith will vary according to the nature of the contract;
> (b) That the duty of good faith will be broken if an employee makes or copies a list of the customers of the employer for use after his

employment ends or deliberately memorises such a list, even though, except in special circumstances, there is no general restriction on an ex-employee canvassing or doing business with customers of his former employer (but see *SBJ Stephenson Ltd v Mandy* [2002] I.R.L.R. 233 below).

(4) The implied term which imposes an obligation on the employee as to his conduct after the determination of the employment is more restricted in scope than that which imposes a general duty of good faith. It is clear that the obligation not to use or disclose information may cover secret processes of manufacture such as chemical formulae, or designs or special methods of construction, and other information which is of a sufficiently high degree of confidentiality as to amount to a business secret. The obligation does not extend, however, to cover all information which is given to or required by the employee while in his employment, and in particular may not cover information which is only "confidential" in the sense that an unauthorised disclosure of such information to a third party while the employment subsisted would be a clear breach of the duty of good faith. Therefore, in this context there are clearly two classes of confidential information when the employer is having to rely on the implied duty in order to protect his business secrets. The first class is of wider ambit than the second and exists only during the period of employment. The second class is apparently restricted to what the judgment calls a "business secret", e.g. a secret process. In the absence of any express provisions once employment has ended the law will only protect information within the second class. It is submitted that the only way for an employer to protect all forms of confidential information post employment is to have an express contractual provision relating to confidentiality. *Faccenda* had made the mistake of not having such an express term in their employment contracts.

(5) In order to determine whether any particular item of information falls within the implied term so as to prevent its use for disclosure by an employee after his employment has ceased, it is necessary to consider all the circumstances of the case.

The Court of Appeal was satisfied that the following matters were among those to which attention should be paid.

8.2.2.1 The nature of the employment

Employment in a capacity where "confidential" material is habitually handled may impose a high obligation of confidentiality because the employee can be expected to realise its sensitive nature to a greater extent than if he were employed in a capacity where such material reaches him only occasionally or incidentally. (This is no doubt in some way concerned with the employee's honesty.)

8.2.2.2 The nature of the information itself

Information will only be protected if it can properly be classed as a business secret, or as material which, while not properly described as a business secret, is, in all the circumstances, of such a highly confidential nature as to require the same protection as a business secret *eo nomine*. The restrictive covenant cases demonstrate that a covenant will not be upheld on the basis of the status of the information which might be disclosed by a former employee if he is not restrained, unless it can be regarded as a business secret or the equivalent of a business secret. The court appeared to disagree with Goulding J. at first instance in that it seemed to say that confidential information which cannot be described as a "business secret" (in the narrow sense of that phrase) could not be protected by an *express clause*. This difficulty in the court's approach was addressed by Scott J. in *Balston Ltd v Headline Filters Ltd* [1987] F.S.R. 330 who stated that *Faccenda* was not authority for the proposition that confidential information that could not be protected by an implied term *ipso facto* could not be protected by express agreement. Scott J. pointed out that an implied obligation may involve different considerations from an express one in that an implied obligation will be unlimited in time.

The court then went on to say that it was impossible to provide a list of matters which will qualify as business secrets or their equivalent. Secret processes of manufacture provide obvious examples, but innumerable other pieces of information are capable of being business secrets, though the secrecy of some information may only be short lived. In addition, the fact that the circulation of certain information is restricted to a limited number of individuals may throw light on the status of the information and its degree of confidentiality.

8.2.2.3 Whether the employer impressed on the employee the confidentiality of the information

Thus, though an employer cannot prevent the use or disclosure merely by telling the employee that certain information is confidential, the attitude of the employer towards the information provides evidence that may assist in determining whether or not the information can properly be regarded as a business secret. (This is obviously correct; one does not make something a business secret by simply describing it as such. It needs to have the necessary quality of confidence about it).

8.2.2.4 *Whether the relevant information can be easily isolated from other information which the employee is free to use or disclose*

This to some extent relies on the intelligence and honesty of the employee. The court said that it would not regard the separability of the information in question as being conclusive, but the fact that the alleged "confidential" information is part of a package and that the remainder of the package is not confidential is likely to throw light on whether the information in question is really a business secret. (This perhaps indicates that it was tactically unwise in this case for the plaintiffs to seek to persuade the court that the whole package of information was confidential.)

8.2.2.5 *Whether additional protection should be afforded to an employer where the former employee is not seeking to earn his living by making use of the body of skill, knowledge and experience which he has acquired in the course of his career, but is merely selling to a third party information which he acquired in confidence in the course of his former employment*

Goulding J. drew no such distinction. The distinction is an interesting and telling one. Although the Court of Appeal expressed no opinion on it, the court was clearly concerned that the employer might possibly be able to protect himself from the use of the employee's skill and knowledge post employment by means of express provision if the employee were simply to sell that knowledge as a commodity (i.e. not use it as a means to gain further employment). Presumably this could happen if the employee retired and sold the information or if he joined company X and yet sold the information to company Y. It may be a recognition by the Court that the attitude of the courts generally towards employees since 1913 has, in some cases, been over-generous. The correct answer to the question seems unclear. If one accepts, as so many cases do, that the skill and knowledge of the employee has become part of himself then it is difficult to see why any distinction should be made as postulated in the question. He should be free to use or disclose or sell his skill and knowledge after the end of employment in any way he thinks fit. However that theory has to a certain extent been undermined by the ratio of this judgment which says that during employment the employee may not disclose or use his skill and knowledge to the detriment of his employer without being in breach of his duty of fidelity. The alternative view is that the reason for the present rule regarding skill and knowledge is that without it the employee might well be prevented from earning his living in the area in which he has the greatest experience. This is clearly not in his interests and is clearly contrary to the public policy as well. If one then takes away the element of his ability to earn his living by the use of his skill and knowledge and supplants it with the notion of the employee selling that skill and knowledge as some commodity to a competitor of his former employer does that significantly change the situation? It could be said that by doing so he was simply in some way earning his living.

The court then went on to apply the law as it saw it to the facts of the case. It decided that the information about prices or as to sales information as a whole was not a business secret in this case. It did so despite the fact that Goulding J. had found that an experienced salesman quickly acquired a good idea of the prices obtained by his employer's competitors, but that such knowledge was usually only approximate and that in this field accurate information was valuable, because a difference of even one penny a pound might be important. The court accepted that in certain circumstances information about prices could be invested with a sufficient degree of confidentiality to make that information a business secret or its equivalent but in the present case it found factors which led it to the conclusion that neither the information about the prices nor the sales information as a whole had the degree of confidentiality necessary to support the plaintiff's claim. These factors were as follows:

(1) The sales information contained some material which the plaintiff conceded was not confidential if looked at in isolation. (The concessions related to the defendant's entitlement to make use of any recollection they might have of the names and addresses of the plaintiff's customers as well as the most convenient routes by which the premises of such customers could be reached. There was a muted concession made regarding the requirements of the plaintiff's customers and the times when deliveries were made to them.)

(2) The information about the prices was not clearly severable from the rest of the sales information.

(3) Neither the sales information in general, nor the information about the prices in particular, though of some value to a competitor, could reasonably be regarded as plainly secret or sensitive.

(4) The sales information, including the information about prices, was necessarily acquired by the defendants in order that they could do their work. Moreover, as Goulding J. had found, each salesman could quickly commit the whole of the sales information relating to his own area to memory.

(5) The sales information was generally known among the van drivers who were employees, as well as secretaries, at quite a junior level. This was not a case where the relevant information was restricted to senior management or to a specific category of staff.

(6) There was no evidence that the plaintiffs had ever given any express instructions that the sales information or the information about prices was to be treated as confidential.

8.2.3 Problems caused by the judgment in *Faccenda Chicken*

The judgment of the Court of Appeal in the *Faccenda* case has been perceived to cause problems. The real area of difficulty is based on whether an express clause can validly protect information which does not fall within the Court of Appeal's narrow definition of a trade secret. It is sometimes claimed that the Court of Appeal said that information that came within Goulding J.'s second category cannot be protected by an express clause and that this is the wrong approach. It is submitted that this reading is incorrect because the second category was meant to relate only to the skill and knowledge of the employee acquired during employment and the Court of Appeal's approach is consistent with authority and is correct. However, others have not read the judgment in that way. They have seen the Court of Appeal's judgment as stating that even an express clause cannot validly protect confidential information unless it is a narrow trade secret or its equivalent.

The first reported expression of dissent occurred in *Balston Ltd v Headline Filters* [1987] F.S.R. 330 where Scott J. at pp. 347 and 348 said, having quoted from the judgment of Neill L.J. in *Faccenda*:

> both counsel before me express some reservations about that passage insofar as it suggests that confidential information cannot be protected by a suitably worded restrictive covenant binding on an ex-employee unless the information can be regarded as a trade secret in the third of the categories described by Goulding J. I am bound to say that I share these reservations. I do not however think the Court of Appeal can have intended to exclude all information in Goulding J.'s second category from possible protection by a restrictive covenant.

He pointed out that trade secrets falling in to the third category would subsequently upon the judgment of the Court of Appeal be protected under an implied term of the contract and therefore an express restrictive covenant would not be needed to protect trade secrets or their equivalent. Therefore Neill L.J. must have been contemplating protection by an express restrictive covenant of confidential information in respect of which an obligation against use or disclosure after the determination of the employment could not be implied. He concluded that he declined to read the *Faccenda* case as holding that confidential information which could not be protected by an implied term *ipso facto* could not be protected by a suitably limited express covenant.

The concerns of Scott J. were echoed by Harman J. in *Systems Reliability Holdings Plc v Smith* [1990] I.R.L.R. 377 where the judge concluded (in a case where he was concerned with an express restriction on the use and disclosure of, in particular, the knowledge acquired by the defendant during his employment of the ability to modify an old computer by a small addition so as to make a new product of significant commercial value) that the controversial part of Neill L.J.'s judgment did not bind him to hold that there cannot be in an express restrictive covenant any restriction on information held by an ex-employee which is not a trade secret or something similar. He distinguished *Faccenda* on two bases; the first was that the case was clearly dealing with implied covenants and therefore any observations made by the court relating to express restrictions were clearly *obiter*. Secondly, that he was in fact dealing with a purchaser/vendor agreement and not with an employer/employee one. However whilst these two bases are distinct, it is clear from Harman J.'s judgment that even if he had been dealing with an express confidential information clause in an employment agreement he would have declined to have followed *Faccenda*.

In *Lansing Linde Ltd v Kerr* [1991] 1 All E.R. 418, CA Staughton L.J. discussed (a) the definition of trade secrets and (b) whether and if so how, trade secrets differ from confidential information. He defined trade secrets (at p. 425 a–j) as:

(a) information used in the trade or business;

(b) of which the owner limits the dissemination or at least does not encourage or permit widespread publication;

(c) and which if disclosed to a competitor would be liable to cause real or significant harm to the owner of the secret.

He said that was his preferred view of the meaning "in this context" by which he seems to have meant that it was not an exhaustive definition. He continued "it can thus include not only secret formulae for the manufacture of products but also in an appropriate case, the names of customers and the goods which they buy". He anticipated that some might say that not all such information is a trade secret in ordinary parlance but if that were correct then "the class of information which can justify the restriction is wider and extends to some confidential information which would not ordinarily be called a trade secret". His approach is a clear indication that the apparent rigours of *Faccenda* are being mitigated by judges because the definition of trade secrets given in that case has been found to be too narrow to be workable. Staughton L.J. said that in this case plans for development of new products and for the discontinuance of existing products were likely to qualify as trade secrets or as confidential information which could be protected. The evidence showed that the defendant was aware of the timing of the phasing out of old products, the timetable for the development of a prototype, the commencement of the production and of the sales of new products. Knox J. at first instance had assumed that this information was confidential as he did prices and discounts allowed to customers. The Court of Appeal accepted his assumption. Butler-Sloss L.J. said that the meaning of the words "trade secrets" had developed since *Herbert Morris v Saxelby* and was now interpreted in the wider context of "highly confidential information of a non-technical or non-scientific nature . . .".

In *J A Mont (UK) Ltd v Mills* [1993] I.R.L.R. 172 the Court of Appeal appears to have used the phrases "confidential information" and "trade secrets" interchangeably.

In *SBJ Stephenson Ltd v Mandy* [2000] I.R.L.R. 233, Bell J. considering an express confidentiality provision in the contract of employment which was expressed in wide terms restricting disclosure of "information in relation to the affairs of the company . . ." held this was valid and in doing so expressed the view;

(a) That the distinction between information deliberately learned and that innocently carried away in the employee's head cannot be definitive of what information can be legitimately protected after the employment ends. The true distinction was that drawn by Lord Shaw in *Herbert Morris* between "objective knowledge" which is the property of the employer and "subjected knowledge" which is the employee's own property. Innocently remembered information can be both.

(b) The restriction would be read by an ordinary sensible person as applying to information which could justify a restriction. "That, as Staughton L.J. said in *Lansing Linde* [1991] I.R.L.R. 80, meant information which its owner used in a trade or business; dissemination of which he limited or at least did not encourage or permit on a widespread basis; and which if disclosed to a competitor, would be liable to cause real or significant harm to the owner. The class of such information was wider than trade secrets, strictly so called, but was narrower than confidential information, generally so called. The bounds of the class can only be decided by examination of each case." See Mummery L.J. in *FSS Travel and Leisure Systems Ltd v Johnson* [1998] I.R.L.R. 382, CA, at p. 385.

See, for example, also *Corporate Express Ltd. v Day* [2004] EWHC 2943 (QB) where the contract of employment did not define what the employer's confidential information comprised but the employee's knowledge of customer requirements in relation to tenders (sealed tender bids being a feature of the business supply trade) was considered by the court to be clearly confidential and the employee would have appreciated this.

8.2.4 The employee's skill and knowledge

Although the courts are anxious to uphold the employer's right to have his business secrets protected they have ensured that the employee is not prevented from using, once he has left his employer, the general skill and knowledge which he has acquired during employment even though this may have been acquired at some cost to the employer. Frequently, a claim by an employer based on breach of confidence has failed as it has been perceived to be an attempt to prevent the employee from working in the same field by offering his skill to another employer. Even in such an early case as *Herbert Morris Ltd v Saxelby* [1916] 1 A.C. 688 the plaintiffs abandoned a claim based on an express restraint because, as Lord Atkinson said, the clause prevented the defendant using ". . . in the service of some other employer that skill and knowledge which he had acquired by the exercise of his own mental faculties on what he had seen, heard, and had experience of in . . . employment . . ." (see also *WC Leng & Co Ltd v Andrews* [1909] 1 Ch. 763 where it was held, inter alia, that the defendant was entitled to use his acquired skill and knowledge for the benefit of himself and the benefit of the public who gained the advantage of him having had such admirable instruction). The courts have said that the general skills of an employee are his property and the employer can only protect *his* property—business secrets. The matter was discussed in *Commercial Plastics Ltd v Vincent* [1965] 1 Q.B. 623 where it was said:

> It is clear from the authorities that the plaintiffs were not entitled to impose a restriction which would prevent the defendant from using in competition with the plaintiffs the skill and aptitude and general technical knowledge acquired by him in his employment by the plaintiffs. The restriction has to be justified in this case as being reasonably required for the protection of the plaintiffs' trade secrets by preventing the defendant from disclosing confidential information imparted to him by the plaintiffs in the course of his employment. . . . The defendant has no doubt gained much skill and aptitude and general technical knowledge with regard to the production of PVC calendered sheeting in general and particularly for the production of such sheeting for adhesive tape. But such things have become part of himself and he cannot be restrained from taking them away and using them.

A good example of general skill and knowledge was given by Younger L.J. in *Attwood v Lamont* [1920] 3 K.B. 571, CA. There, a former customer of the plaintiffs gave evidence that he had met the defendant in the street and mentioned to him that he had heard he had set up his own business and wanted the defendant to cut him a suit. Younger L.J. said "The appellant is a dangerous rival of the plaintiff . . . not by reason of any knowledge of the plaintiff's connection or customers possessed by the appellant, but by reason of his own skill".

Although the cases lay down the rule that a distinction between general skill and knowledge and business secrets must be maintained, it is impossible to formulate any general test. Each case turns on its own facts but once the boundary between protectable secrets and general skill and knowledge is crossed the employer cannot, even by way of express covenant, restrict the employee's ability to use those skills once employment has ended (*Faccenda Chicken Ltd v Fowler* [1985] 1 All E.R. 724).

Whilst it is clear that an employee cannot be prevented from using his general skill and knowledge once employment is over, there had been some doubt as to whether the employer could exert any control over such use during employment or whether the law would imply such control. Brightman J. in *United Sterling Corporation Ltd v Felton and Mannion* [1974] R.P.C. 162 suggested that such control would be implied. However, in *Strange (SW) Ltd v Mann* [1965] 1 All E.R. 1069 Stamp J. said that it was against public policy to allow an employer to exercise control by way of contract over an employee's skill and knowledge. It seems that he would have come to the same conclusion regarding the implication of such control. However, there is no doubt that many express terms which bind the employee to devote his time to his employment and to devote his energies to furthering his employer's business contemplate control over his skill and knowledge. Now, there is no doubt that the law will imply control over skill and knowledge during employment as being relevant to the general duty of fidelity (see *Faccenda Chicken*).

However, the fact that an employer may have evidence to support his claim does not preclude the employee from arguing that the employer has conducted himself in such a way that despite an express clause confidentiality no longer exists. For example, an employer who has allowed all his employees access to information or has entrusted it to the least skilled may find the court unsympathetic. Likewise, if visitors have been allowed to walk around his premises without restriction then the court will take this into account in its examination of the claim. This is especially so in the case of visiting competitors. If an employer does not prevent them availing themselves of the opportunity to learn business secrets how can he later seek to restrain an employee from using the same information. The existence of any secrecy which might have existed will have been destroyed by the indifference of the employer (see for example *Sun Printers Ltd v Westminster Press Ltd* [1982] I.R.L.R. 292). Mere negligence on the part of the employer may be sufficient to defeat confidence.

In practice, unless the employer can show that the employee has copied or physically removed a list of names or the details of a process then it may be very difficult to establish that the knowledge of the employee is exclusively due to confidential information. If the court is left in doubt as to whether the information might not have been acquired wholly or partly from the general experience gained by the employee then the employer will fail. A simple process may become part of his general knowledge but the more complex it is the less reasonable will be his claim that knowledge of it is part of his general skill and knowledge; the difficulties can be illustrated in *United Indigo Chemical Co Ltd v Robinson* [1931] 49 R.P.C. 178. The plaintiffs were manufacturers of a boiler disincrustant and claimed that it had been produced by a secret process. They sought to restrain the defendant, who had been employed as their works manager, from using or disclosing information obtained in their service. They alleged that the product marketed by his company could only have been made by his wrongful use of their business secrets. They claimed that he had made and taken away copies of, or had memorised extracts from, a book of secret formulae. The plaintiffs conceded that their product was not made of secret materials but secrecy arose from the way in which the materials were mixed, the temperature employed in various stages of manufacture and the method of testing the consistency of the product. The defendant denied that any secret process existed or that he had taken and used any information. Bennett J. found that the defendant had not copied any formulae from the book; that he had not been warned as to secrecy when he entered his employment and that he was able to learn the relevant processes without difficulty; indeed this was information which he could not help acquiring in the course of his work. That knowledge had become his own and he had acquired it honestly and not surreptitiously. The plaintiff's claim failed. See also *Cray Valley Ltd v Deltech Europe Ltd* [2003] EWHC 728 CLD for a similar case involving solvent based resins where the court held the information regarding the manufacturing process did not have the necessary quality of confidentiality. Much of the information was published already, non-critical to the process and easy to reverse engineer. Employees had also never been told that the manufacturing "recipes" were trade secrets or constituted confidential information and the processes were really second nature to the employees involved.

There is no doubt that dishonest or surreptitious acquisition of information is usually overwhelming evidence that information was confidential and not part of the defendant's skill and knowledge. Indeed, the courts will take a pragmatic view of the complexity of the information and the employee's ability to remember it as a test of whether it has been wrongfully used/disclosed by him. In *Herbert Morris Ltd v Saxelby* there was no doubt that the defendant knew of business secrets but the court decided that they were far too complicated and detailed for the defendant to have been able to carry them away in his head and as there was no evidence of actual copying, this part of the claim failed.

Another problem which frequently arises in practice is the claim by the employee that, after the end of his employment, he only used information which was already in his memory. This claim is then used as evidence of the fact that the information has become part of his general skill and knowledge and is not a business secret. The employee will further claim that he made no conscious effort to memorise the information. In *Printers and Finishers Ltd v Holloway* [1964] 3 All E.R. 731 Cross J. made a distinction between the two concepts of remembering something and conscious memorising:

> The mere fact that the confidential information is not embodied in a document but is carried away by the employee in his head is not . . . of itself a reason against the granting of an injunction to prevent its use or disclosure by him.

He then went on to discuss whether an employee could use his recollection of any features of the plaintiff's plant, machinery or process which they claimed were peculiar to them even though they admitted that their competitors used similar machinery. Cross J. in dismissing the claim, went on to say:

> Recalling matters of this sort is . . . quite unlike memorising a formula or list of customers or what was said (obviously in confidence) at a particular meeting.

However, in *SBJ Stephenson Ltd v Mandy* [2000] I.R.L.R. 233, Bell J. said:

> In my view, the distinction between information deliberately learned and that innocently carried in the employee's head cannot be definitive as a matter of principle of

> what information can be legitimately protected and what cannot, after the termination of employment . . . Many true and vital trade secrets in the strict sense, including such things as the ingredients of chemical compounds and other sophisticated products, must rest firmly in the minds of those who have worked with them and been interested in them, ready to recall.

If, however, it can be said that the employee had reasonable grounds for believing the information to be part of knowledge properly acquired during his employment then his defence would be likely to succeed. In the *United Sterling* case the basis for dismissing the motion was that there was no evidence that the defendant was given any special information which he ought to have regarded as a separate part of his stock of knowledge which an honest employee would have recognised as property of the employer.

8.2.5 Business methods

A further problem which frequently arises in practice is the ability of an employer to claim that information about "business methods" or "business organisation" constitutes a business secret which is protectable. The main problem with such a claim in the employment context is the difficulty of separating knowledge of business methods from the general skills etc of the employee. A claim in *Herbert Morris* regarding general business methods was defeated because of this difficulty. A similar view was taken in *WC Leng v Andrews*. For the same conclusion see *Commercial Plastics Ltd v Vincent* [1965] 1 Q.B. 623, *per* Pearson L.J. and *Littlewoods Organisation Ltd v Harris* [1978] 1 All E.R. 1026, *per* Megaw L.J. Megaw L.J. in *Littlewoods* however gave examples of what went beyond mere knowledge of the way in which the plaintiffs ran their business. These were the trends of mail order sales, the percentage and identity of the returns, the sources of manufacture, market research results, plans for mail order catalogues in the future and that Harris knew intimately the chairman of the manufacturers. See also *Greer v Sketchley Ltd* [1979] F.S.R. 197. In *Amway Corporation v Eurway International Ltd* [1974] R.P.C. 82 Brightman J. described "business methods, and paperwork" as "mere know-how". However, this case was an extreme example of disregard by the plaintiffs towards the quality of confidence (a tape recording was provided to, inter alia, the defendants, saying that the plaintiff's sales and marketing plan was available to anyone and could be copied by them: the tape gave details of the plan).

In *Under Water Welders and Repairers Ltd v Street and Longthorne* [1968] R.P.C. 498 Buckley J., on motion, said nothing adverse about a clause which sought to make "the policy" of the company a business secret.

The conclusion must be that it will be unusual, though not impossible to envisage, that business policy etc. will be protectable. Relevant factors will be the type of business, the attitude that the employer has demonstrated towards the information and the precise type of information. If blanket assertions regarding business methods can be broken down into categories then a claim of confidence may succeed. For example information about prices can, in certain circumstances, constitute a business secret: see the discussion in *Faccenda Chicken Ltd v Fowler* [1985] 1 All E.R. 724 and *Lansing Linde Ltd v Kerr* [1991] 1 All E.R. 418.

8.3 Express duties once employment has ended

By including express restrictive covenants in an employment contract an employer will seek to achieve five goals once employment is over:

(a) to prevent the ex-employee canvassing orders from the employer's customers/potential customers;

(b) to prevent the ex-employee from dealing with those customers;

(c) to prevent the ex-employee competing with his business (usually within a defined geographical area);

(d) to prevent the ex-employee from using/disclosing any legitimate business secrets;

(e) to prevent the ex-employee soliciting employees to leave the employer.

Note that (a) and (d) alone are not enough: neither would prevent an employee from serving those customers of his ex-employer who approached him. Similarly (c) alone may not be sufficient as the courts have laid down principles which effectively restrict the time for which any such covenant can run and also the geographical area it can cover. A clever employee would be able to set up business outside the restricted area and be able to serve former customers from there if (a) did not exist.

In summary, the law is that the courts will not enforce any post employment restraint on the activities of an employee unless the restraint is reasonable. What amounts to reasonableness is a question of fact and any answer approaching certainty can only be given after examining the circumstances of each case. However, what generally amounts to reasonableness can be examined by reference to three criteria although they inevitably overlap. The theoretical difference between the categories may well come down to a question of the burden of proof, though in practice a party seeking to uphold the validity of the restrictive covenant—usually the employer—has to make all the running. The three criteria are:

(a) Does the employer have an interest which merits protection?

(b) Is the restraint reasonable as between the parties?

(c) Is the restraint reasonable in the public interest?

Mrs Justice Cox in *TFS Derivatives Ltd. v Morgan* [2005] I.R.L.R. 246, expressed it slightly differently, although the second and third of her three stage consideration covers broadly the same ground:

> Firstly, the court must decide what the covenant means when properly construed. Secondly, the court will consider whether the former employers have shown on the evidence that they have legitimate business interests requiring protection in relation to the employee's employment . . . Thirdly, once the existence of legitimate protectable interest has been established, the covenant must be shown to be no wider than is reasonably necessary for the protection of those interests. Reasonable necessity is to be assessed from the perspective of reasonable persons in the position of the parties as at the date of the contract, having regard to the contractual provisions as a whole, and to the factual matrix to which the contract would then realistically have been expected to apply.

One can sum up the position as being that a restraint will be invalid if it is imposed in order to prevent competition simpliciter or the use of personal skill and knowledge of the employee.

8.4 The existence of an interest which merits protection

The employer will be required to show that the restraint protects a valid interest: see *Herbert Morris Ltd v Saxelby* [1916] 1 A.C. 688 "a proprietary right". There are generally three possible valid interests on which he may rely; special trade connections, business secrets and the maintenance of a stable workforce. He is entitled to protect all of these: see *Herbert Morris, Attwood v Lamont* [1920] 3 K.B. 571, *Alliance Paper Group plc v Prestwich* [1996] I.R.L.R. 25 and *Dawnay, Day & Co Ltd v De Braconier D'Alphen* [1997] I.R.L.R. 442, CA.

8.4.1 The employer's special trade connections

The employer is entitled only to protect his business against use of his special trade connections by others but not to protection from competition from his former employee: see the *Herbert Morris* case. Protection from pure competition is known as "a covenant in gross" and has always been rejected by the courts.

We use the phrase "trade connections" rather than "customer connections" because the interest is not limited to customers of the employer; it can in certain cases extend to potential customers and also to suppliers: see *Gledhow Autoparts Ltd v Delaney* [1965] 3 All E.R. 288 and *Thomas Marshall (Exporters) Ltd v Guinle* [1978] 3 W.L.R. 116.

In practice the employer must show two things:

(a) the existence of trade connections which are to an extent "special" to him; and

(b) that the employee is or will be in a position to take advantage of those special trade connections.

The first requirement will usually be simple to establish. The customers on a milk round are an obvious example of a special trade connection; see *Home Counties Dairies Ltd v Skilton* [1970] 1 All E.R. 1227 and *Wessex Dairies v Smith* [1935] 2 K.B. 80; so are the clients of a solicitor: see *Sanders v Parry* [1967] 1 W.L.R. 753; as is a person who uses an estate agent's services: see *Scorer v Seymour-Johns* [1966] 3 All E.R. 347. All of these examples concerned customers who had or were likely to use the employer's services on more than one occasion. This is what made them "special". However, it is not necessary for an employer to prove that the connections are exclusive to him and they need not be long established. A customer may buy from several competitors in a given field; a supplier will invariably supply to more than one business and yet, depending on the facts, the employer may be able to argue that these connections are sufficiently special. Obviously, the more widely dispersed the loyalty of customers or suppliers, the less likely the employer will be able to succeed in claiming the speciality required. If a customer is known to buy from nearly every producer in the field then it will be very difficult to establish speciality.

In order to establish whether an employee was or is in a position to take advantage of his employer's special trade connections, it is necessary to examine the quality of the contact between the employee and those connections: "the character of the work done", *per* Younger L.J. in *Attwood's* case. It is usually not sufficient for the employer to demonstrate that *some* contact has taken place. It is suggested that there must usually be a special element in the employee/connection contact which creates a reasonable risk that the employee will be able to appropriate some part of the business when he leaves because of the chance that customers would seek him out on account of his knowledge of their requirements. A milkman who serves the same customers every day and who is usually known to them personally will clearly have sufficient contact. It was said in *Scorer v Seymour-Johns* [1966] 3 All E.R. 347, *per* Salmon L.J. that the special element can be characterised as the customers relying on the employee to the extent that they regard him as the business rather than his employer: in that case the employer's business had many recurring customers (*cf. Fellowes & Son v Fisher* [1975] 2 All E.R. 829). He said:

> When the employee was in the Kingsbridge office he *was* in effect the Kingsbridge office. Every customer who came into that office dealt with him. He was in a position in which he would have every opportunity of gaining knowledge of the customers' business and influence over the customers. Moreover, he was in sole charge of a relatively new branch office. However, it is important to realise that it is not always necessary to be able to characterise an employee "as the office".

The factual question is whether sufficient quality of contact has been demonstrated. In *TFS Derivatives Ltd. v Morgan* [2005] I.R.L.R. 246, the court was concerned with an equity derivatives' broker specialising in the DAX market. In the relevant market, there are a finite number of clients using the services of the brokers, predominantly banks and other institutions. Although the brokers do not work exclusively for the clients, they nevertheless endeavour to develop strong client relationships and knowledge of the client's requirements with a view to solidifying and building on the employer's position in the market. Per Cox J:

> The nature of the job is such that it is extremely important for the brokers to build up good relations with their trader contacts within TFS's client organisations. The market in which the brokers are dealing is a specialist one, and the number of traders operating in it is relatively small. It is essential for the brokers to cement their relationships with the traders. If a solid relationship can be established, the broker will usually be able to count on that trader for repeat business. Broking . . . is a verbal business. As a result, working in the room, brokers generally tend to develop a knowledge of which clients use which brokers, how strong those relationships are and the number of trades that brokers are doing for specific clients. They know which relationships are strong and which are in difficulties, together with the reasons behind any change. Brokers may need, on occasions, to cross their products to brokers dealing on other markets. For example, a broker who regularly trades on the DAX index may need to cross-sell on the CAC where a client asks them to broker a specific trade for them.

This it was held was sufficient evidence to establish a legitimate business interest in the protection of client connections. A clear example of an employee who was not in a position to influence customers is found in *Herbert Morris v Saxelby*. The real question is whether the employee has any power over customers. See also *Stenhouse Australia Ltd v Phillips* [1974] A.C. 391 (insurance brokers), and also *Routh v Jones* [1947] 1 All E.R. 758:

> . . . the character of a general medical practice is such that one who is employed therein as a medical assistant, necessarily acquires such a special and intimate knowledge of the patients of the business that the employers . . . are entitled to protect themselves against unfair competition on the servant's part (*per* Evershed J.)

Can mere contact ever be enough? In *Gilford Motor Co Ltd v Horne* [1933] Ch. 935 Romer L.J. suggested that mere contact between an employee and a customer was sufficient. That cannot be a statement of general application although in *Horne's* case it was undoubtedly correct. Horne had been the managing director and had had the fullest opportunity of getting to know every customer. It is submitted that it is crucial to examine the position of the employee and the type and size of the business in order to discover what, if any, ability he might have had to influence customers. If mere contact were always enough then manifest injustice would be done in many cases. For example, a telephonist in a large company may have contact with a customer by answering his calls but this cannot be a reasonable basis for preventing that person from working for a trade competitor. Even employees who come into personal, face to face contact with the employer's trade connections cannot always be said to have sufficient quality of contact. For example, a receptionist at a solicitor's office will no doubt meet clients but it would be most unusual for her to be in a position to take advantage of that connection to the detriment of her employer once she has left his employment. On the other hand a sales manager who does not have direct dealings with all clients may still have some influence over where they place their business.

However the nature or quality of that contact is important. In the case of *Strange (SW) Ltd v Mann* [1965] 1 All E.R. 1069 the defendant, who was employed as the manager of bookmakers, only met customers once (if at all) as most business was done by telephone and was of a credit nature. It was immaterial to the customers who dealt with them on the telephone. Even though the defendant knew the names and addresses of all customers, the quality of contact was not of the degree required in order to establish that he was ever regarded as "being the business" or had any influence over the customers. See also *International Consulting Services (UK) Ltd v Hart* [2000] I.R.L.R. 227 which concerned a non-solicitation and non-dealing covenant that extended to those who, within 12 months of the termination of employment, were negotiating with the employing company for the supply of services. Contact with them was not enough—it had to be negotiation in the sense of discussion regarding the terms of a contract which was a real possibility. In that case it was not essential that the employee should have been engaged in the negotiations (if he had input to them or he had contact with the prospective customers). Ultimately the need (and extent) for contact will depend on the facts of the case.

What of special trade connections introduced by an employee; can he freely take these with him when he leaves? It often happens that when an employee enters new employment he legitimately brings with him trade connections of use to his new employer. When he eventually leaves that employer how far can the latter control the ex-employee's ability to deal with the clients which he brought with him. Such a problem was analysed in *M&S Drapers v Reynolds* [1956] 3 All E.R. 814 when Denning L.J. said:

> I do not . . . see why the employers should be able to forbid him to call on the people whom he already knew before he worked for them. . . . His knowledge of these people and his influence with them, was due to his own efforts—or at any rate they were nothing to do with these employers. His goodwill with those customers belonged to him and cannot reasonably be taken from him by a covenant of this kind.

Moreover, Hodson L.J. said that as well as the period of restriction, an added circumstance which has to be taken into account in assessing reasonableness was the fact that many of the customers covered by the covenant had been introduced by the defendant. The other members of the court were of a similar view. The court seems to have taken the view that these connections were effectively part of the defendant's tools of his trade.

There seems no reason why, by express provision, an employer should not be able to appropriate the goodwill which an employee brings with him.

Such is common in partnership agreements. In any event, the fact that a customer is brought to his employer when that employment starts or is subsequently introduced to him will, even if no express provision exists, usually mean that he becomes a customer of the business and part of its goodwill. The fact that a restrictive covenant may prevent him doing business with them once he has ceased to be employed will not, in most cases, render the restraint unreasonable (*Hanover Insurance Brokers Ltd v Shapiro* [1994] I.R.L.R. 82).

The final point to consider in this section is the ability of an employer to seek protection for the trade connections not only of his own company but also of other associated companies. In *Henry Leetham & Sons Ltd v Johnstone-White* [1907] 1 Ch. 322 Farwell L.J. commented:

> . . . a man whose business is a corn miller's business, and who requires to protect that, cannot, if he has also a furniture business, require the covenantee who enters into this service as an employee in the corn business to enter into covenants restricting him from entering into competition with him in the furniture business also, because it is not required for the protection of the corn business in which the man is employed, however much it may be beneficial to the individual person, the owner both of the corn business and of the furniture business.

That is a clear example where there was no real common interest between the businesses. But, it did not accord with the facts of the case before him in which all companies within a group were millers. The Court of Appeal decided however that the defendant had really only contracted with one company within the group and that regarding the area in which it did its business a countrywide restraint was unreasonable. It rejected the idea that the associated companies which together did have a countrywide business were in any way relevant. By applying a strict rule of corporate personality it decided that a restriction which benefited any person other than the contracting parties was "in gross" and therefore unenforceable. In *Stenhouse Australia Ltd v Phillips* [1974] A.C. 391 the Privy Council chose to ignore strict rules of corporate personality between different companies in a group because of the existence of a patent identity of interest. It now seems that only in those cases where there is no identity of interest will the problem of other businesses gaining the benefit of a restrictive covenant be at all important and the courts will not take account of the doctrine of incorporation or of privity of contract if such an identity exists. This is further demonstrated by the decision in *Littlewoods Organisation Ltd v Harris* [1978] 1 All E.R. 1026. See also *Business Seating* at para.8.5.2. In *Beckett Investment Management Group Ltd. v Hall* [2007] EWHC 241 (QB) a non-dealing covenant in a contract of employment between the employees and the holding company in the group was held to be unenforceable because restriction was in relation to doing business with clients for the purpose of supplying or seeking to supply advice of the type provided by the holding company, whereas, in fact, the holding company had no business and therefore no legitimate interest which would have been protected by the covenant, in contrast to the subsidiary companies. However, the Court of Appeal ([2007] EWCA Civ 612) rejected a purest approach based upon corporate identity and held that the restriction applied to the holding company's subsidiaries as well. Per Maurice Kay L.J., "[the employees] were familiar with the restructuring which was the catalyst for the new contracts and were well aware of what the respective roles in the holding company and the subsidiaries were going to be thereafter. In these circumstances, I would be reluctant to find a construction which deprives a covenant of all practical utility in circumstances where all the parties were familiar with the background and aim of the clause."

8.4.2 Business secrets

There is no doubt that business secrets are recognised as constituting an interest meriting protection. In the *Littlewoods* case in which the court upheld a twelve-month restraint allied to protectable business secrets, Lord Denning M.R. said that the information acquired by Harris was confidential:

> It has been acquired at great expense and by great expertise by Littlewoods. No servant should be at liberty to carry it off to a rival in trade and thus save him the expense and expertise of doing it himself.

The employer is entitled only to adequate protection for his business secrets: the concept of adequacy prevents the employee being restricted from using his general skills and knowledge.

The only doubt about this was raised by the Court of Appeal in *Faccenda Chicken Ltd v Fowler* [1985] 1 All E.R. 724 where the court specifically left open the question whether additional protection should be afforded to an employer where the former employee is not seeking to earn his living by making use of the body of skill, knowledge and experience which he has acquired but is merely selling the knowledge to a third party (see para.8.2.2 above).

In *Commercial Plastics Ltd v Vincent* [1965] 1 Q.B. 623 the restrictive covenant read:

> In view of the highly technical and confidential nature of this appointment you have agreed not to seek employment with any of our competitors in the PVC calendering field for at least one year after leaving our employ.

Therefore, the basic question was: what were business secrets? There were none in the general field of PVC calendering but only in the special field of PVC for adhesive tape. As the restriction sought to prevent the defendant from taking employment with a competitor in the general PVC calendering field it was held to be too wide.

8.4.3 The employer's interest in maintaining the stability of his workforce

It is common in employment contracts to see a restriction which seeks to prevent the employee from, for a certain period, soliciting or employing or working with former colleagues. Until relatively recently, apart from indirectly in *Kores Manufacturing Co Ltd v Kolok Manufacturing Co Ltd* [1957] 1 W.L.R. 1012 CA there was no firm authority on the question as to whether such clauses could be valid. Advisers were divided in their views as to whether an employer could possess an interest which merited protection by such a clause. Those who supported the existence of such an interest usually advised that the clauses should be targeted at specific staff levels and should not be applicable to all former colleagues. In *Hanover Insurance Brokers Ltd v Shapiro* [1994] I.R.L.R. 82, CA the plaintiff's cross appeal was solely concerned with this point. The court held that the employer did not have an interest in maintaining the stability of his workforce which merits protection no matter how well targeted. The basis for this view was that ". . . the employee has the right to work for the employer he wants to work for if that employer is willing to employ him" (Dillon L.J.). The employer must instead seek covenants directly from that employee. However, the weight of opinion since *Hanover* has supported the proposition that an employer does have a legitimate interest in maintaining the stability of the workforce. Shortly after *Hanover* a different division of the Court of Appeal (without referring to the case and a few days before it was reported) held that an employer does have a legitimate interest in maintaining a stable, trained workforce in what was accepted in that case to be a highly competitive business (*Ingham v ABC Contract Services* December 12, 1993 [unreported]). Shortly after Judge Levy in *Alliance Paper Group plc v Prestwich* [1996] I.R.L.R. 25, in a case involving a managing director, who was also the vendor of the business in which he was employed seeking to enforce the restriction, followed *Ingham* and held that a no-poaching covenant in the service agreement was enforceable and this, notwithstanding, that the restriction focused upon those who fell into the somewhat vague category of being employed "in a senior capacity". Then in *Dawnay, Day & Co Ltd v De Braconier D'Alphen* [1997] I.R.L.R. 442 the Court of Appeal in context of considering a no-poaching provisions in a shareholders agreement and in contracts of employment, held that an employer's interest in maintaining a stable, trained workforce is one which can be properly protected within the limits of reasonableness by means of a non-solicitation covenant although it did not follow that this would always be the case. The employer's need for protection arose because the ex-employee might seek to exploit the knowledge that he had gained of the employees' qualifications, rates of pay and so on. In that case the managers had acquired confidential information of that kind and the court considered that a one-year restriction was justified. Again the reference to "senior employee" in the covenant was held not to be uncertain and therefore the provision was enforceable. *TSC Europe (UK) Ltd v Massey* [1999]

I.R.L.R. 22 and *SBJ Stephenson Ltd v Mandy* [2000] I.R.L.R. 233 are further examples of circumstances where covenants against poaching employees were held to be enforceable. It therefore seems that, whatever the uncertainty arising from *Hanover*, with the passage of time the legitimacy of the interest of an employer as a basis for this type of covenant has been accepted and the issues for the future will be the reasonableness of a particular covenant's scope in any particular set of circumstances.

8.5 Reasonableness between the parties: canvassing/dealing and competition

The fact that an employee has agreed to be bound by a restrictive covenant does not in itself make that restriction reasonable between the parties. Instead, the courts will subject the clause to the objective test of reasonableness. But it is always prudent to remember the words of Glidewell L.J. in *Rex Stewart Jeffries Parker Ginsberg Ltd v Parker* [1988] I.R.L.R. 483: "in the end, whether a particular provision is or is not reasonable to protect the employer's legitimate interest is a matter of impression".

The topics discussed below are frequently seen as difficult and obscure; there is no doubt that most litigation is concerned with considering whether an express covenant in an employment contract is reasonable or not. There are a number of fundamental points however which should always be borne in mind:

(1) The courts invariably prefer non-canvassing/soliciting restraints to those which prevent a former employee from working for no matter how short a time in a particular field or geographical area: the classic modern approach of the courts is best expressed in *Office Angels Ltd v Rainer-Thomas* [1991] I.R.L.R. 214, CA which is the first case which should now be read on the subject.

(2) Even non-solicitation clauses can be unreasonable, particularly when such clauses prevent solicitation of the employer's customers without qualification, e.g. no contact with them or knowledge of them by the employee is referred to in the clause; see *Marley Tile Co Ltd v Johnson* [1982] I.R.L.R. 75 and *Austin Knight (UK) Ltd v Hinds* [1994] F.S.R. 52 on the one hand and *Plowman (GW and Sons Ltd) v Ash* [1964] 1 W.L.R. 568 and *Business Seating Renovations Ltd v Broad* [1989] I.C.R. 729 on the other.

(3) It is usually quite legitimate to prevent not only solicitation but also "doing business with", "dealing with" or "accepting business from" customers: see *Home Counties Dairies Ltd v Skilton* [1970] 1 W.L.R. 526; *John Michael Design v Cooke* [1987] 2 All E.R. 332 and *Office Angels Ltd v Rainer-Thomas* [1991] I.R.L.R. 214, CA.

(4) Non-competition clauses may, exceptionally, be upheld if there is a real need to protect confidential information and there is a real basis for fearing that the adherence to such duty will be difficult to police; see *Littlewoods Organisation Ltd v Harris* [1977] 1 W.L.R. 1472, CA. In some cases the similar point can be made about solicitation of customers; particularly where it may be difficult to identify recurring customers (such as in a cash business) or where the employer is likely to find that customers have a particular tendency to follow an employee to a new employer, e.g. in jobs such as hairdressing or milk deliveries. See e.g. *Steiner UK Ltd v Spray* December 6, 1993 (unreported), CA in which, perhaps surprisingly, a six month non-competition clause was upheld in the case of a very young hairdresser.

8.5.1 Non-competition clauses

When an employer seeks to uphold a non-competition clause he invariably relies on the judgments of Lord Denning M.R. and Megaw L.J. in *Littlewoods Organisation Ltd v Harris* [1977] 1 W.L.R. 1472. In a much quoted passage Lord Denning M.R. said:

> It is established that an employer can stipulate for protection against having his confidential information passed on to a rival in trade. But experience has shown that it is not satisfactory to have simply a covenant against disclosing confidential information. The reason is because it is so difficult to draw the line between information which is confidential and information which is not; and it is very difficult to prove a breach when the information is of such a character that a servant can carry it away in his head. The difficulties are such that the only practicable solution is to take a covenant from the servant by which he is not to go to work for a rival in trade.

Despite the fact that those words are based on the judgment of Cross J. in *Printers and Finishers Ltd v Holloway* [1965] 1 W.L.R. 1 and were echoed in the instant case by Megaw L.J. they are not easy to understand. Why should information which may not even be confidential or which if confidential is of an ephemeral nature give rise to an injunction which keeps the employee out of the market when if he had possessed concrete confidential information he would have not been so prevented but would have been enjoined from using/disclosing the information? The basis for this approach must lie in pragmatism for after all the employee will only be kept out of the market for, say, 12 months. Even so, the effect on him could be very great and we must always remember that the reasoning in *Littlewoods* may have been influenced subconsciously by the knowledge that Mr Harris was indemnified, not just for his costs but also for all losses, by GUS and that he was a very senior and very well-paid employee. It is submitted that the correct approach for the court is to look at the quality of the information and the past conduct of the defendant; if it concludes that the information is of significant commercial value and that he cannot be trusted to abide by his duty of confidence he should then and only then have temptation removed from his grasp by being removed himself from the market. The other situation in which a non-competition clause may be generally reasonable—where customers are difficult to identify or are notoriously likely to follow the employee to a new business—have been mentioned above.

The geographical area covered by the restrictive covenant must have a reasonable nexus with the need to protect the employer's trade connections. It is usually the case that the more extensive the area sought to be covered the less likely it is to be reasonable. It is clear that if no space limit is expressed in the covenant it will be construed to impose a worldwide ban: see *Dowden and Pook Ltd v Pook* [1904] 1 K.B. 45 and *Commercial Plastics Ltd v Vincent*, but *cf. Littlewoods Organisation Ltd v Harris* [1977] 1 W.L.R. 1472, CA and *Emmersub XXXVI Inc v Wheatley* [1998] Q.B.D., Wright J. [unreported] where a worldwide restriction was limited by the fact that it was anywhere in the world "in competition" with the party in whose favour the covenant was given which refined its scope to countries in which competition would result. See also *Thomas v Farr plc* [2007] EWCA Civ 118, where the geographical area of the non-competition covenant was defined by reference to areas in which the employer and its sister companies had conducted business, and for which the employee had been responsible, in the 12 months preceding termination (a more flexible approach with more utility than a fixed geographical area where the circumstances allow such an approach to be adopted). See also *TFS Derivatives Ltd. v Morgan* [2005] I.R.L.R. 246, where a non-competition covenant geographically limited to the "territory" which comprised England and any other country or state in which the company or any associated company was operating or planning to operate with the added proviso that a business would be operating within the territory if either any such business in which the individuals involved at any time during the relevant period was located or to be located within the territory or was conducted or to be conducted wholly or partly within the territory, was held to be valid, regard seemingly being had to the fact that the context was employment in relation to global financial markets using the most sophisticated communication technology. For other examples where non-competition covenants without territorial limits to their operation have been held to be valid see *Dyson Technology Ltd. v Strutt* [2005] ALL ER(D) 355, Ch D, and *Intercall Conferencing Services Ltd. v Steer* [2007] EWHC 519. In each case, the employers' businesses were international in nature but in both there was the limitation that the activity must be in competition which arguably indirectly limited the scope of the covenants to those geographical areas where competition took place.

In the *Nordenfelt* case a clause which included a worldwide restriction was upheld: however that was a very special case and in any event dealt with a business sale and not with employment. In *White, Tomkins and Courage v Wilson* (1907) 23 T.L.R. 469 a worldwide restriction lasting five years on a brewery manager was upheld. However, in that case there may have been protectable business secrets belonging to the plaintiffs, although the report is unclear on this. The more usual attitude to such restrictions in employment cases is set out in *Vandervell Products Ltd v McLeod* [1957] R.P.C. 185 at p. 191, *per* Lord Evershead M.R.:

> This is not a case of the sale of goodwill but of a master and servant, and it must be rare . . . to find an ex-servant restrained from exercising his trade in a competing business anywhere in the world . . .

In *Commercial Plastics* it was argued that although the restriction without these limitations or qualifications was of worldwide ambit that width was cut down by a reference to "competitors" of the plaintiffs and that such limitation made it reasonable. Pearson L.J. said in response to this: "There would have been considerable force in that argument if the evidence had supported it"; however he concluded that there was no evidence to prove that the plaintiffs needed the potentially worldwide restriction.

In *Scorer v Seymour-Johns* [1966] 1 W.L.R. 1419 Dankwerts L.J. said "in present day conditions a radius of five miles is not a great distance, particularly in a district which is mainly rural". This highlights two points: the first is that the ease of travel is relevant—a distance of five miles in the nineteenth century was effectively a much greater restriction than the same distance today. Secondly, it shows that the same distance in a town or city will usually be much more restrictive than in the country: quite simply, the potential market is much greater in the town or city and therefore the likelihood of the employer having protectable trade connections over the whole city is less likely. However, these points are subject to the facts: if an employer is a seed merchant or feed supplier a comparison between country and town may well be irrelevant.

It is generally true to say that preventing an employee from working or canvassing in a certain area is often a crude way for an employer to obtain protection for his trade connections and this crudeness has often resulted in an area covenant being held unreasonable: see *Attwood v Lamont* [1920] 3 K.B. 571. In many cases if a pure geographical restriction had been supplanted by a restriction preventing the employee from soliciting certain customers and/or dealing with them then it would have stood a greater chance of success. In *Allan Janes LLP v Johal* [2006] I.R.L.R. 599, Ch D, an assistant solicitor was subject to restrictive covenants in her employment contract which comprised a non-competition covenant with a radial restriction of six miles from the office where she was employed and for a period of one year, and a non-dealing clause for the same period prohibiting her from working for any person who had been a client of the firm in the previous 12 months. As is frequently the case, the non-competition covenant based on a radial restriction failed as the area covered included a very large number of commercial entities which were either not clients or had ceased to be clients of the firm and this was held to be too wide. Interestingly, however, although the assistant solicitor had only acted for a very small proportion of the clients of the firm, the non-dealing covenant which covered all clients of the firm was held to be enforceable on the basis that when the covenant was entered into, it was against the background of the likelihood of progression to partnership shortly thereafter. However, there are situations in which a geographical restriction is necessary, especially if the customers cannot be readily identified—thus making detection and enforcement very difficult. See *Empire Meat Co Ltd v Patrick* [1939] 2 All E.R. 85 and *Marion White Ltd v Francis* [1972] 1 W.L.R. 1423. In *Strange (SW) Ltd v Mann* [1965] 1 All E.R. 1069, Stamp J. rejected the defendant's argument that an area restriction is always inappropriate in the case of an exclusively credit business. The reason for this was that a covenant not to deal with those who were customers during employment is not always sufficient for the employer. He may legitimately want to guard against the danger of the employee joining a business rival. However, he found on the facts that although a non-solicitation covenant would have been reasonable an area covenant which included both Cheltenham and Gloucester was too wide.

Covenants which restrain an employee from competing in any area in which his employer has customers, were frequently regarded as reasonable in a number of nineteenth and early twentieth-century cases. It is submitted that such clauses as in *Office Angels Ltd v Rainer-Thomas* [1991] I.R.L.R. 214, CA, *and Allan Janes LLP v Johal, above*, are unlikely to be upheld today unless there are exceptional circumstances. An example of such a case is *Standex International Ltd v C B Blades* [1976] F.S.R. 114 in which the Court of Appeal upheld a restraint which lasted for five years and which prevented the employee from being engaged in or concerned with the business of mould engraving within Great Britain and Northern Ireland. The particular feature of this case was that the plaintiffs were the only manufacturers in the field in that area. It is submitted that market share is the key to this decision. A pure geographical restriction limited to a five-mile radius from the employer's place of business was upheld in *Scorer*, but Salmon L.J. stated that he was troubled as to whether the employer's interests might not have been adequately protected by a restraint which prevented the defendant from doing business with persons who had been customers of the employer at the office of which the defendant had been in charge. He concluded that such a covenant might be impractical because breach might be very difficult to prove. It is submitted that, in most cases a pure area covenant related to the prevention of solicitation/canvassing by a former employee will invariably be indefensible unless the employer can demonstrate that a less oppressive clause would result in great difficulties regarding the detection of breach.

In *Spencer v Marchington* [1988] I.R.L.R. 392 the defendant in a counter claim sought to enforce a clause which read:

> Upon termination of this employment you shall not for a period of two years after such termination, either alone or in partnership with any other person or persons,

> or as servant or agent or officer of any person, concern or company, carry on or in any way be engaged or concerned or interested in the business of any employment agency within a radius of 25 miles of the Banbury office and 10 miles of the Leamington office.

The judge pointed out that 25 miles from Banbury in all directions is an area of nearly 2,000 square miles. He found that the great majority of the defendant's customers were in Banbury itself or at Bicester which was under 14 miles from Banbury. The judge concluded that it was not necessary to extend the area beyond 20 miles at the most from Banbury especially as the defendant's goodwill could have been as effectively protected by a clause which would have prevented the plaintiff from dealing with the defendant's customers. He pointed out that the object of the rule of public policy against too wide an area on a former employee's future activities is not primarily to protect the employee but to keep the market open to prospective customers, to maximise the number of, in the present case, employment agencies available to them and to promote competition among them. Moreover, the employer could have adequately protected the goodwill of its business by a non-solicitation clause. See also *Office Angels Ltd v Rainer-Thomas* [1991] I.R.L.R. 214, CA. This case contains a very useful and succinct statement of a number of general principles. The plaintiffs ran a number of employment agencies including one in the City. The majority of the business was the provision of temporary workers. Most business came from clients who telephoned the relevant branch. It was not important to clients precisely where the branch was situated. The defendants worked at a particular branch. The relevant clause read:

> In the course of his or her employment by the company the employee has dealings with clients of the company and in order to safeguard the company's goodwill the employee agrees:
>
> (a) That he or she will not at any time during the six months immediately following the termination of his or her employment, whether on his or her own account or on behalf of any other person, firm or corporation, solicit custom from, deal with or supply (in connection with the trade or business of an employment agency) any person, firm or corporation who or which was a client of the company at any time during the period that the employee was employed by the company.
>
> (b) That he or she will not at any time during the six months immediately following the termination of his or her employment whether on his or her own account or on behalf of or in the course of employment by any other person, firm or corporation, engage in or undertake the trade or business of an employment agency within a radius of 3,000 metres of the branch or branches of the company at which the employee was employed for a period of not less than four weeks during the period of six months prior to the date of such termination or, in the case of branch or branches in the Greater London area, then within a radius of 1,000 metres.

At first instance (unusually, after a trial) clause (a) was found to be unreasonable on the basis that of the 6,000–7,000 clients covered by it only about 100 were known to the defendants (it seems likely the judge followed *Marley Tile Co Ltd v Johnson* [1982] I.R.L.R. 75—see para.8.5.2 below). However clause (b) was upheld. The Court of Appeal disagreed and discharged the injunction. Sir Christopher Slade giving the judgment of the Court reiterated the basic but vital proposition that any reasonable restrictive covenant must afford no more than adequate protection to the benefit of the party in whose favour it is imposed. The plaintiffs argued that clause (b) was imposed for the purpose of protecting not only its trade connection with its employer clients but also its trade connection with its pool of temporary workers. The Court rejected that point; it said that if an employer, as here, chooses specifically to state the interest which the covenant is intended to protect he cannot thereafter seek to justify it on a different basis. The plaintiff's clause had contained introductory words which made it clear that it existed to protect its trade connections with clients and that was therefore the only basis on which it could now seek to justify it. The plaintiff argued that the difficulties in policing a non-solicitation clause provided reason for the existence of clause (b). The Court rejected this. It also found that clause (b), which it construed as having the effect of preventing the defendants from setting up a business located in the area (and did not have the wider effect of preventing the defendants from seeking to recruit clients from within the area) would in fact do little to protect the plaintiff's trade connections with its clients. Those clients did business over the telephone with the plaintiff; in general it was no concern to them whether the plaintiff's office was situated inside or just outside the area. This was, however, a case in which the plaintiff's legitimate interests could have been protected by a suitably worded non-solicitation and non-dealing covenant. However in *Steiner (UK) Ltd v Spray* [1993] CA [unreported] a six month non-compete restriction to operate within three eighths of a mile of any salon where the hairdresser worked was upheld with the court being influenced by the fact that although this covered 40 salons in the centre of Norwich a non-solicitation covenant would be of little use given customers propensity to follow a popular stylist and a non-dealing covenant impracticable to police.

Another type of geographical covenant is one which seeks to restrain an employee from competing in any area in which he was active. This is generally preferable to the first example, however it may prove to be a very heavy handed way of providing protection. The existence of such a provision was the only reason why the employer failed in *Gledhow Autoparts Ltd v Delaney* [1965] 3 All E.R. 288. Take the example of a salesman who visits customers regularly in Dorset. His employer has only a small market share there. When he leaves the employer the latter may claim that his former employee should not canvass or deal with those customers, but we can see no reason why he cannot canvass others in Dorset. Obviously if that employer can demonstrate substantial and extensive goodwill in the area he will be able to rely on this type of clause though he does not need, as Dankwerts J. said in *Kerchiss v Colora Printing Inks Ltd* [1960] R.P.C. 235, to go so far as to prove sales in every part of the area in question. Indeed, in that case the defendants succeeded even though they could not show any business in one particular country at all; however, they did have clients in the remaining 15 countries covered by the clause. It must be remembered that the particular product and the nature of the customers can be crucial. In *Kerchiss*, although a wide geographical restraint was upheld, the company was not selling to the general public—if it had been the restriction would certainly have been too wide—but to printers who wanted particular types of ink.

Other problems associated with crude geographical restraints are that the size of the area and its character may have been drawn too widely as in *Mason v Provident Clothing and Supply Co Ltd* [1913] 1 K.B. 65, and also the difficulty encountered when the prohibited areas are defined by reference to the employer's places of business. In *Clarke, Sharp and Co Ltd v Solomon* (1921) 37 T.L.R. 176 the restriction sought to prevent the defendant from working in the same trade as his employers for a period of five years in an area within a five-mile radius of any railway station or port from which the employers then or at any future time during employment delivered coal. The Court of Appeal held that the restriction was clearly unreasonable: not only was there not sufficient contact between the defendant and customers to warrant protection, but the result of upholding the covenant would have been to restrict the defendant even if the plaintiffs had supplied only a single ton of coal from any station or port.

A problem can arise when dealing with branch offices. In *Scorer's* case, the branch in Dartmouth was effectively run as a separate entity from the one in Kingsbridge. The defendant worked at the latter office and had no real connection with the former. The covenant which restricted him working within ten miles of both offices was held to be too wide; fortunately for the employer the restriction was severable and that part applicable to Kingsbridge enforced.

8.5.2 Non-canvassing/solicitation of or dealing with customers

The version of this clause which is most likely to be considered to be reasonable is one which concerns a promise not to solicit any of the employer's customers with whom the employee dealt within a certain time period before employment ceased. This type of clause is the most acceptable to courts because it covers only the employer's trade connections over whom the employee may have gained any influence; it also has the merit of certainty so far as the employee is concerned (see *Gledhow's* case). The clause may be limited to actual solicitation and therefore it is not breached by an employee who is approached by a customer. In order to cover that possibility the clause should include words such as "or deal with". However, there may be objections to the use of such a wide term. The objection is that a customer should be free to buy where it best suits him: unencumbered by an agreement between others. Moreover, there may be a very good reason why the customer has decided to do business with the former employee: he may be more efficient and/or provide goods at a lower price. To deny a customer the ability to take advantage of these matters cannot be in the public interest. Also, if the employee were found to be in breach even if the customer had approached him then he would be in the embarrassing position of turning the customer away—this is of benefit to neither and there is no guarantee that the customer will go back to the former employer. Moreover, a prohibition on dealing may encourage further breaches which the employer may find difficult and costly to detect. That leads to another waste of resources. However, it has to be stated that these worries do not appear to reflect current judicial thinking and it is usually safe to rely on the wider version of this clause (although see also *T Lucas and Co Ltd v Mitchell* [1974] Ch. 129).

Can a non-solicitation clause legitimately extend beyond actual customers and seek to cover those with whom the employee came into contact in order to get business for his old employer? In theory, we see no reason why such a clause should not be reasonable. The answer will depend on the facts of each case: relevant matters will be the type of business, whether the employee knew about the precise requirements of the contact and how long ago the enquiry was made. In *Gledhow's* case both Sellers and Diplock L.J. indicated that it may be possible to have such a clause. A restraint of this type sometimes encompasses former customers of the employer (i.e. those who are no longer his customers). What interest the employer can have in this connection, apart from the chance that they may return, is unclear. However, in *Plowman's* case, after some hesitation, Harman L.J. held that a clause which did not exclude people who had ceased to be customers of the employer and therefore formed no part of the present goodwill of his business, was still valid. He did so on the basis that hope of them becoming customers again of the employer should not be abandoned. This is not very convincing. There is, though, little doubt that an argument which claims that a clause is unreasonable simply because it includes some former customers is unlikely to succeed. Indeed an injunction may be granted to cover customers who apparently have no intention of doing business in the future with the plaintiffs. In *John Michael Design plc v Cooke* [1987] 2 All E.R. 332 the facts were that towards the end of 1985 the defendants, an associate director and a senior designer employed by the plaintiffs, left to set up business on their own. Their contracts of employment with the plaintiffs contained a covenant not to canvass, solicit or accept from any client of the plaintiffs any business in competition with or similar to that of the plaintiffs for a period of two years from the termination of the contracts. In December 1986 the plaintiffs learnt that clients of theirs were proposing to place a contract with the defendants' firm and were not, in any event, going to do further business with the plaintiffs. The plaintiffs sought an injunction to restrain the defendants from acting in breach of their covenants. The judge found that the covenants were prima facie enforceable and that the plaintiffs were entitled to an interlocutory injunction pending trial in general form, but on the balance of convenience he excluded the particular contract from the scope of the injunction. The plaintiffs successfully appealed. It was held that although a covenant restraining competition by an ex-employee would always be looked at closely, if the court decided that it would be just to grant an interlocutory injunction pending trial by way of enforcement of that obligation, the plaintiff was prima facie entitled to protection in respect of all his customers who fell within the ambit of the covenant and, in granting the injunction, it was wrong in principle to try to exclude some customers or some parties on whom it would otherwise bite. The fact that a particular customer would not do any further business with a plaintiff was not per se a reason for excluding that customer from the scope of the injunction since such an eventuality was the very thing against which the covenant was designed to give protection.

Another version of this covenant is one which seeks to prevent solicitation of any of the employer's customers irrespective of whether the employee dealt with them. However, it is important to remember that an employer is *not* entitled to be protected by a covenant which restricts the employee in relation to customers over whom he had no control. The reason is because the employer is only entitled to restrictions which are necessary (i.e. without which his business might or would be endangered). This covenant may restrict the employee from dealing with those who were the employer's customers at any time in the past or future (i.e. not merely during employment). Unless it can be construed so as to refer to the period of employment and only to those customers over whom the employee had any control (which is unlikely), the clause is bad. It gives excessive protection to the employer and is embarrassing to the employee: see *GW Plowman and Son Ltd v Ash* [1964] 2 All E.R. 10. An even more limited version—restricting the employee from dealing with any of the employer's customers during the period of employment irrespective of contact—may be too wide in some cases: see *Marley Tile Co Ltd v Johnson* [1982] I.R.L.R. 75 but cp *Allan Janes LLP v Johal*, [2006] I.R.L.R. 599, above. However, in *Plowman's* case, it was upheld by the Court of Appeal. Harman L.J. dealt with an argument that the clause, which precluded canvassing of any persons who were at any time customers of the employer during the period of employment, was too wide because it was not restricted to customers with whom the employee had come into contact and did so by relying on *Gilford Motor Co Ltd v Horne* [1933] Ch. 935 in which the Court of Appeal, overruling Farwell J. at first instance, had come to the conclusion that such contact was not necessary. However, he gave no reasons for so doing and the prudent draftsman will think carefully before including this type of covenant. It can be inherently vague and potentially embarrassing to the employee as was recognised by Edmund Davies L.J. in *Plowman's* case. No doubt it will be more easily justified in a case of a manager, *e.g.* a sales manager or a director. See also *Marley Tile Co Ltd v Johnson* [1982] I.R.L.R. 75 in which *Plowman* was distinguished. Lord Denning M.R. pointed out that in *Plowman* the firm's customers were all situated around Spalding, it only employed five salesmen and it might well have been that Ash knew all of the customers. However, in the instant case the relevant customers numbered 2,500. Johnson could not have had influence over more than a small percentage of them. The clause was therefore unreasonably restrictive (see also *Spafax Ltd v Dommett* July 6, 1972 (unreported)). In *Spafax Ltd v Harrison* [1980] I.R.L.R. 442 a narrower clause was upheld. It prevented the employee, a branch manager, from soliciting any person "to whom during the period of 12 months prior to . . .termination of his employment the manager or to his knowledge any member of his staff shall have sold such goods on behalf of the company". See also *Austin Knight Ltd v Hind* [1994] F.S.R. 52 which reached a conclusion similar to that in *Marley Tile* although surprisingly the latter case was not cited to the court.

Plowman v Ash was applied by Millett J. in *Business Seating (Renovations) Ltd v Broad* [1989] I.C.R. 729. In that case the plaintiff carried on the business of repairing or renovating office furniture and commercial seating. It had an associated company with the same directors and shareholders which carried on the business of manufacturing and selling new office furniture and commercial seating. The two companies shared many customers but there were also customers of each which were not customers of the other. The defendant was employed by the plaintiff as a sales representative. Having worked for the plaintiff for just over two years he resigned and within a few days took employment with a company which supplied office furniture and fittings and had a rather wider and larger range of activities than either the plaintiff or its associated company. One per cent of the turnover of his new employer was concerned with re-upholstering and renovating office chairs and other furniture so that to a small extent it appeared to compete with the plaintiff and to a larger extent with the business of the plaintiff's associated company. The plaintiff sought an injunction to prevent the defendant from breaching clause 13 of his contract of employment. That stated:

> For a period of one year after the termination of the agreement for any cause whatsoever the employee shall not canvass, solicit or endeavour to take away from the company or any associated employer the business of any customers or clients of the company or any associated employer who have been customers or clients of the company or an associated employer during the period of one year immediately preceding the termination of the employment.

It was argued by the defendant that this clause was in unreasonable restraint of trade and therefore invalid. It was complained that the clause was not limited to customers who were known to the defendant whilst he was employed by the plaintiff or with whom he had had any contact. Moreover it was said that it included discontinued customers and was not limited to the areas within which the defendant had worked for the plaintiff. He worked only in two areas and the plaintiff's business was nationwide. Millett J. found that the principles set out by Harman L.J. in *Plowman's* case applied here and that these arguments were unsustainable. However he went on to accept the defendant's objection that the clause was unreasonable to the extent that it extended to prohibiting canvassing or soliciting customers or clients of the associated company of his employer. The judge pointed out that insofar as any customer was a customer of both companies then soliciting of his custom would be within that part of the clause which he had already held to be reasonable. He stated that he was concerned with the position of the defendant in relation to customers or clients of the associated company who were not customers or clients of the plaintiff company during the relevant period with whom the defendant had no contact and of whose existence he might have been wholly unaware. He found that the plaintiff had no connection at all with the associated company itself or any of its customers who were not customers of the plaintiff. He said that so far as the plaintiff was concerned its only interest in customers of the associated company was as potential customers of its own. He regarded it as an unwarranted extension of *Plowman* to uphold the validity of a non-solicitation covenant which prohibited solicitation of potential customers of the plaintiff notwithstanding that they are defined as existing customers of some other connected business. It is our view that if they had been potential customers of the plaintiff in the sense that they had made enquiries of the plaintiff or had responded in some positive way to canvassing by the plaintiff then the plaintiff could have legitimately protected that connection. See also *Hinton & Higgs (UK) Ltd v Murphy* [1989] I.R.L.R. 519 (Court of Session) and *International Consulting Services (UK) Ltd v Hart* [2000] I.R.L.R. 227 where a restriction extending to cover parties who were negotiating with the employer was held to be validly included in non-solicitation and non-dealing covenants. As always, however, the particular facts of each case play a major role in determining the enforceability of such covenants and in *Berry Birch & Noble Financial Planning Ltd. v Berwick* [2005] EWHC 1803, the court was concerned with the company that operated an independent financial and investment advice service and was seeking an injunction against agents that it employed. The injunction was sought to enforce a prohibition on using any confidential information for a period of five years after the termination of their relationship with the company (which was held to be too broad to be enforceable covering, inter alia, ideas relating to the business which could include information about the style of the office furniture or the venue of the company's Christmas party). However, in addition, the employer sought to enforce a non-solicitation of client's covenant which applied for a twelve-month period following the termination of the agency agreement with the individuals to all the clients within the scope of the covenant who included:

(a) those who had placed business with the company;
(b) those who had been in direct or indirect commercial negotiations with a view to placing business;
(c) those who had been visited by the agent on behalf of the company; and
(d) those that have a continuing business with the company.

Mrs Justice Cox held that the provision was too broad on the grounds that it extended to cover those who had been in negotiations with the company but who had ultimately never become a client of the company with the consequence that, in her view, there was no actual legitimate business interest to protect and, in addition, it also covered clients who were currently conducting business with the company but who had no dealings with the agents concerned. In the absence of any material contact with the clients, the agents were not in a position to damage the company's legitimate interest. The case underlines the value, where the basis for the covenant is the protection of trade connections (and notwithstanding the decisions in *Plowman* and *Business Seating*) of focusing on customers with whom the departing employee has dealt (and therefore may have influence over) where possible when drafting non-solicitation/non-dealing covenants.

8.5.3 Time

Time and area are often very closely connected. When considering whether the area is too wide the court is bound to consider the duration of the restraint. It, therefore, follows that if it is felt necessary to have a wide or pure area restraint this may only be perceived to be reasonable if the period of the restraint is short. The Court of Appeal in *Plowman's* case seems to have found in the plaintiff's favour, in spite of many misgivings because the restraint lasted for two years. There is no mean reasonable time, though Lord Denning M.R. was frequently keen on 12 months (see *Fellowes & Son v Fisher* [1975] 2 All E.R. 829; *Office Overload Ltd v Gunn* [1977] F.S.R. 39) and 12-month restrictions appear the most common in practice such that their prevalence makes periods of the length enforced in *Plowman* appear somewhat ambitious nowadays although, as always, the interplay between time and other factors relevant to determine the scope of a particular covenant (and the fact sensitivity of each case) will always be relevant.

The length of time is only reasonable if it does no more than is necessary to protect the employer. This has been characterised as the period in which it takes an employer to start a new employee at the task and for the latter to have a reasonable opportunity to demonstrate his effectiveness to customers. In short, it is not the period the employer would want (or like) but the period he demonstrably needs. In general, life-long restrictions are bad, see *Attwood v Lamont* [1920] 3 K.B. 571 and *WC Leng and Co Ltd v Andrews* [1909] 1 Ch. 763 for the courts will not allow a person who has been trained or gained some aptitude in an area to be deprived of using that ability for the rest of his life. In *Jenkins v Reid* a lifetime restriction on a medical practitioner was held unreasonable (*cf. Fitch v Dewes Fernau* [1921] 2 A.C. 158 which was surely wrong on this point). In *Wyatt v Kreglinger and Fernau* [1933] 1 K.B. 793 a similar view was taken even though the plaintiff was aged 61. This seems to have been an extreme case.

In *Stenhouse Australia Ltd v Phillips* [1974] A.C. 391 a five-year restriction on an insurance broker who had been the managing director of various companies within a group was upheld by the Privy Council and an indication was given on how to approach questions of time. Lord Wilberforce said:

> The question is not how long the employee could be expected to enjoy by virtue of his employment, a competitive edge over others seeking the client's business. It is, rather, what is a reasonable time during which the employer is entitled to protection against solicitation of clients with whom the employee had contact and influence during employment and who were not bound to the employer by contract or by stability of association. This question . . . [we] do not consider can advantageously form the subject of direct evidence. It is for the judge, after informing himself as fully as he can of the facts and circumstances relating to the employer's business, the nature of the employer's interest to be protected, and the likely effect on this if solicitation to decide whether the contractual period is reasonable or not.

In *Dairy Crest v Pigott* (1989) I.C.R. 92 the court was concerned with an application to enforce a clause which read:

> Not at any time within two years after the termination or cessation in any manner of the service hereby created, either as master or servant to canvass, solicit or serve or cause to be served with milk or dairy produce, any person, firm or company who during the employee's service with the board and within one year prior to such termination or cessation has been so supplied by the employee on behalf of the board, and at the time of such soliciting or alleged soliciting continues to reside or carry on business at any address at which milk was supplied by the employee on behalf of the board.

The defendant was a milkman. The Court of Appeal having considered the judgment of Lord Wilberforce in *Stenhouse* and applying *American Cyanamid* granted the injunction. Balcombe L.J. said that he shared some of the doubts of the judge at first instance about whether a two-year period was or was not reasonable but that he could not say that there was no issue of law here to be decided. There was therefore a serious question to be tried. The injunction was granted. In *Rex Stewart, Jeffries, Parker, Ginsberg Ltd v Parker* [1988] I.R.L.R. 483 the Court of Appeal at the interlocutory stage held that a clause which operated to restrain a managing director who had been with the plaintiffs for seven years from soliciting customers for a period of 18 months was not unreasonable. It was pointed out that he had had opportunities to develop relationships with customers.

In *Lawrence David Ltd v Ashton* [1989] I.R.L.R. 22 the Court of Appeal granted an injunction in the terms discussed below in Chapter 23 in relation to a clause which sought to restraint the defendant for a period of two years from the determination of his contract of employment from carrying on or being employed in the business of manufacturing certain products.

8.5.4 Restricted activities

If the employer seeks by contractual restraint to restrict the activities of a former employee by proscribing the types of business in which the employee may become engaged once employment is over then he can do so if he can establish a close connection between the restriction and the work done by the employee prior to leaving. Moreover, the employer can only protect himself from activities by his employee which might reasonably affect the customer connection which has been built up.

The first question which has to be answered is: what is the employer's business? This is a question of fact but it is crucial. See *Routh v Jones* [1947] 1 All E.R. 758. The defendant was prohibited from practising "in any department of medicine, surgery or midwifery". This clause was construed by both Evershed J. and the Court of Appeal to include acting as a consultant. Therefore, the plaintiffs, a partnership in general medical practice, were seeking to prevent an employee once he had left, from, inter alia, practising as a consultant within a certain area and for a certain time. The court found that as practice by the defendant as a consultant could not injure the plaintiffs' professional business, the clause was too wide in that it sought to encompass activities in which the plaintiffs did not have a legitimate interest. Moreover, the covenant went on to restrict the defendant's ability to accept any professional appointment. This was held to be reasonable during employment but was construed as being too wide post employment as it would prevent the defendant becoming a medical officer of health in which capacity he could not prejudice the plaintiff's goodwill. See also *Jenkins v Reid* [1948] 1 All E.R. 471. Moreover, it may not be enough for an employer to say "I'm a wine merchant and my ex-employee is now working as a wine merchant and so I am entitled to enforce an express restriction". It may be that the ex-employee is now working in an entirely different area of that business, such as wholesale, whereas his former employer's business is retail. The distinction between the wholesale and retail sides of a business was discussed in *Rogers v Maddocks* [1892] 3 Ch. 346.

Once the relevant scope of the employer's business has been established the next question is whether the restriction does no more than protect any existing customer connection. In *Technograph Printed Circuits Ltd v Chalwyn Ltd* [1967] R.P.C. 339 a restrictive covenant prevented the employee for a period of two years after the end of his employment from being associated with any company in the UK concerned with manufacture of "printed electrical circuits". It was found that such a restriction would prevent employees from being associated with a manufacturer of single-sided-printed circuit boards and yet it was only in relation to multi-layered printed circuit boards that the plaintiff had any interest. Therefore the restrictions went beyond what was necessary.

Some restrictions go too far in their precision and thus are judged unreasonable whilst others are struck down as being too imprecise and/or wide. An example of the first type is found in *Herbert Morris Ltd v Saxelby* [1916] 1 A.C. 688 where the defendant was bound for seven years after employment not to work in the UK or Ireland in the sale or manufacture of pulley blocks, hand overhead runways, electric overhead runways or hand overhead travelling cranes. The court found that all his experience had been in these areas; he had always worked for the plaintiffs and therefore the clause rendered him unemployable over a very wide area for a significant time. The clause was held to be unreasonable. Later cases have also insisted that if an employee is to be prevented from working in that area in which he has gained great expertise then the covenant is unlikely to be upheld. See *Commercial Plastics Ltd v Vincent* [1965] 1 Q.B. 623.

Examples of the second type are cases such as *Davies, Turner and Co v Lowen* (1891) 64 L.T. 655 in which a clause sought to prevent an employee entering any business similar to that "now or hereafter to be carried on" by the employer; or *Perls v Saalfeld* [1892] 2 Ch. 149 in which a clause preventing an employee from accepting "another situation as clerk or agent" was struck down.

That said, the difficulty of accurately describing an employer's business that a restriction is endeavouring to protect and the tendency not to update or revise covenants during the life time of the employment relationship has resulted in fairly frequent use of more general language without necessarily prejudicing the enforceability of the restriction. See for example, *Dyson Technology Ltd. v Strutt* [2005] ALL ER (D) 355, Ch D, where restriction against carrying on any business, or having any interest in a business which was similar to or competed with the employer's business for 12 months was upheld, and similarly in *TFS Derivatives Ltd. v Morgan* [2005] I.R.L.R. 246, where the prohibition was against undertaking or carrying on or being employed, engaged or interested in any capacity in any business which was competitive or similar to any business of the employing company or an associated company in which the individual had been materially involved. In practice, as both these cases demonstrate, this leads to a close analysis of what is meant by "in competition" but, like *Dyson*, *TFS* reflected a pragmatic and realistic approach on the part of the courts when it came to determining what was meant by such language, although interestingly, it was necessary in *TFS* for the words "or similar to" to be "blue pencilled" in order to save the provision as the words were not qualified by the requirement that such a business should be in competition; plainly a provision that purported to restrict the involvement in a business in competition with that of the employer would fail in ordinary circumstances if it also included a business which was similar to that of the employer (but not in competition).

8.5.5 Miscellaneous points

The following matters may also arise when the reasonableness of a clause is considered:

(a) the employee's position;

(b) the type of business;

(c) the notice period under the contract;

(d) potential customers;

(e) protecting connections with suppliers; and

(f) that a different form of restriction is more appropriate.

8.5.5.1 The employee's position

In *Kores Manufacturing Co Ltd v Kolok Manufacturing Co Ltd* [1957] 3 All E.R. 158 it was said that a restriction of five years was too long for a manual worker and for all categories of employee up to assistant works manager. Whilst a similar view will be taken in nearly all cases involving manual workers, it is unwise to assume that the latter part of this judgment will always be followed: it all depends on the facts of the case; particularly the type of business. In *M&S Drapers v Reynolds* [1956] 3 All E.R. 814, the Court of Appeal had to examine a restrictive covenant which gave the employer protection from competition/canvassing for five years after the end of employment. During that period a former employee was forbidden from soliciting any person whose name had been on the books of the company and upon whom the employee had called during a period of three years before the end of employment. The defendant had been employed as a credit draper and, as he had called on customers, had considerable personal contact and influence over them, however the court held that five years was too long for a man in the defendant's position, especially as he received only a modest wage. The point was highlighted by Hodson L.J. when he said "The managing director is not regarded in the same light as the traveller or canvasser" (i.e. the latter is not as great a threat to the employer as the former and therefore any time restriction should reflect this)—*cf. Hanover Insurance Brokers Ltd v Shapiro* [1994] D.R.L.R. 82, CA in which *M&S Drapers* was distinguished in this very point; Mr Shapiro and his fellow defendants were all senior managers or directors. It is not only employees who are protected by the vigilance of the courts regarding periods of time. In both *Schroeder* and *Clifford Davis*, contracts which were to run for ten years were struck down as unreasonable as was 21 years in *Esso Petroleum Co Ltd v Harper's Garage (Stourport) Ltd* [1968] A.C. 269.

8.5.5.2 The type of business

In *M&S Drapers* this point was crucial to Morris L.J.'s judgments:

> . . . the customers of one credit draper are likely to be canvassed by other credit drapers. In a sphere where competition is normally free, since every householder is a potential purchaser, and where successful selling must to some extent depend on

> the personal abilities of particular salesmen and also to some extent on the quality or attractiveness of the goods which the salesman's employer can offer. . . .

A five year restriction was too long.

8.5.5.3 Length of notice

In *Gledhow Autoparts Ltd v Delaney* [1965] 3 All E.R. 288, two members of the Court of Appeal commented on how length of notice can be an indication of reasonableness regarding time. Diplock L.J. pointed out that the defendant's employment could have been terminated only two weeks after it started and yet according to the clause, he would have been restrained from seeking any orders in similar goods, in any district he had operated (even though he may have called on very few customers) for a period of three years. The clause was struck down on other grounds, so this comment was *obiter* but it is submitted that it has much force. The shorter the period of notice the less important to the company the employee's services would appear to be and the more lowly his position is likely to be. Accordingly, the perceived need for protection is diminished. An alternative view, found for example in the judgment of Hodson L.J. in the *M&S Drapers*' case that the period of notice is really within the ambit of consideration, the adequacy of which is not a concern of the court, is, it is submitted, unduly restrictive and technical. The practical and better view is that there is an inextricable link between reasonableness and the adequacy of consideration.

8.5.5.4 Potential customers

Can a plaintiff claim to protect itself against solicitation etc of "potential customers"? The answer appears to be yes in principle so long as the customers are genuinely "potential". "Potential customer" must be a term of art in restraint of trade law; it cannot, for example, include the thousands of persons to whom a circular letter has been sent by the plaintiff in the hope that they might do business with him. To take the argument to its extreme it could be said that every person is a potential customer for an everyday product. However does the plaintiff have to demonstrate that a potential customer is a person who is more likely than not to place an order with him. It seems to us that this approach may go too far in the other direction. In principle the plaintiff must be able to show a real and not merely a speculative or fanciful connection with the person whom he describes as a potential customer. It is possible to debate the relevant definitions *ad nauseam* but in practice it is our view that the prudent covenantee will seek to limit the ambit of who constitutes a potential customer by reference to the connection which the covenantor has had with that person. For example, a clause in an employment contract in which the covenantor is a salesman could properly seek to restrict the salesman's activities after termination of employment in relation to potential customers by identifying them as having been persons "with whom the employee has dealt with a view to obtaining business".

8.5.5.5 Suppliers

Generally, it is unlikely that an employer can legitimately prevent canvassing or doing business with his suppliers; however if the particular goods/services are in short supply he may seek to prevent them being supplied elsewhere.

8.5.5.6 More appropriate alternative

Although comparatively rare given the modern tendency to include all the various permutations of restrictive covenant in contracts of employment (non-competition, non-dealing, non-solicitation together with provisions relating to confidentiality and garden leave) an argument regarding the reasonableness of a restriction may be bolstered by demonstrating that, on the facts of a particular case, an employer would have been better choosing a more appropriate restriction than that relied upon. A recent and somewhat novel illustration of (an ultimately unsuccessful attempt in this regard) may be found in the case of *TFS Derivatives Ltd. v Morgan* [2005] I.R.L.R. 246, QB, where it was suggested in support of a contention that a six-month non-compete provision was in unlawful restraint of trade because an alternative, garden leave, provision would be more appropriate, more effective and more reasonable.
Per Cox J.:

> Mr. Sendall submits, correctly, that there is as yet little authority on the interplay between garden leave and post-termination covenants. He invites me, therefore, to provide such guidance in this case, and to find on these facts that six months' notice on garden leave would have been a more flexible and more reasonable restriction to impose on this defendant. He contends that the court should view suspiciously non-compete clauses of the kind contained in clause 12.1(a) and should recognise the greater flexibility inherent in garden leave clauses of the kind he advocates. One of his principal submissions in support of this proposition was that employers who wish to restrict the future employability of a former employee should be prepared to pay for such restrictions. He acknowledges that employees such as this defendant, working as brokers in the financial sector, command extremely high earnings, but points out that they enjoy a lifestyle commensurate with such earnings and have higher bills to pay than most.
>
> Interesting though his invitation is, it seems to me that this is not a case in which it is appropriate to make any general observations or seek to provide general guidance in relation to the role and usefulness of garden leave clauses as opposed to non-compete clauses of the kind included in this contract.
>
> I am not persuaded that the clause Mr. Sendall suggests to be preferable would in fact be more reasonable than clause 12.1(a) as I have construed it.

> My reasons are these. Firstly, six months' notice will enforce garden leave for the whole of that period can legitimately be regarded, in my view, as more onerous for this defendant than the three months' non-compete clause in clause 12.1(a) the effect of it would be keep this defendant out of employment completely and unable, therefore, to exercise his skills as a broker in any capacity. A broker's skills in the market place were tend, it seems to me, to atrophy at least to some extent during six months' enforced leave. That would be neither reasonable inter partes nor in the public interest.
>
> Secondly, such a clause would not be appropriate in the case of an employee who is summarily dismissed from his employment, or who simply walks away without giving his contractual notice, in which case a reasonable and enforceable non-compete clause would be necessary in order to protect the employer's legitimate interest.
>
> Thirdly, a six-month enforced period of garden leave, even if in accordance with an express term of a contract, would in any event be likely to face resistance on the basis that its use amounts to a breach of the implied term of trust and confidence.
>
> Fourthly, in relation to the submission that the employer should be prepared to pay his employee to stay at home in such circumstances, it seems to me that the question whether the individual employee is being paid is relevant only to the question of whether the terms are reasonable between the parties. Notwithstanding that this is a case occurring in the employment context, for employees such as this defendant, who are highly valued and most generously rewarded, the inequality of bargaining power, which is recognised to apply in many employment relationships, simply does not exist, or, at any rate, does not exist to such a degree as to render a non-compete clause of the kind which appears in 12.1(a) unreasonable as between the parties.

The judge also considered that the choice in this particular employee's contract of a non-competition covenant rather than a non-solicitation covenant (save to the extent of employees) was not unreasonable on its facts, given the observation that non-solicitation clauses in circumstances of the case "are almost impossible to police.

8.6 Reasonableness between the parties: business secrets

8.6.1 Restricted activities

The employer must show that the three tests identified by Megarry J. in *Coco v AN Clark (Engineers) Ltd.* [1969] R.P.C. 41 are met (that is to say, in order to found a claim for breach of confidence, the relevant information must have "the necessary quality of confidence about it"; it must have been imparted in circumstances importing an obligation of confidence and there must be either an unauthorised use or a threatened unauthorised use of the information damaging to the party communicating it) and must show that he is not seeking to restrict an employee's use of his general skills, knowledge and experience. Two cases in this area bear some study. In *Commercial Plastics Ltd v Vincent* [1965] 1 Q.B. 623 the plaintiffs claimed protection for their confidential information in the field of PVC calendered sheeting. The court found that the plaintiffs had 80 per cent of the UK market in this sheeting for use as adhesive tape; this was very difficult to produce and secret processes were involved which were kept in code to which only a few employees had access. The defendant was recruited to be responsible for research and development in the plaintiff company. His contract contained an express term which stated that because of the highly technical and confidential nature of his appointment he was not to seek employment with any of the company's competitors in the PVC calendered sheeting field for a period of one year after leaving. The court found that as there was no geographical limit the restriction must have been of worldwide effect, and that by referring to "competitors" the restriction must have meant those who were competitors at the time when the defendant's employment ended. The court also found that:

(a) technical knowledge of PVC calendered sheeting had become part of the defendant himself and was therefore not protectable:

(b) although the defendant had access to secret mixing specifications and test reports he could not take them away in his head and there was no question of him having actually taken documents;

(c) the plaintiffs' schemes and business organisation methods were not confidential;

(d) however, there was some confidential information which was protectable: the defendant was not likely to remember minute details recorded in mixing specifications, but would be likely to remember in general terms the nature of problems and solutions, what experiments had been made and whether the results had been positive or not: he would be likely, when the need arose, to dredge up from his memory the particular secret which he had found appropriate to deal with the customer's requirements.

Therefore, the plaintiffs had established an interest meriting protection. However, had the plaintiffs succeeded in preventing him from working for a competitor for a year so that he would not be tempted to breach confidence? The court said that the clause was not reasonable to protect the interest of the plaintiffs. It was too wide because:

(a) it would stop the defendant from entering the employment of a competitor anywhere in the world, and yet the plaintiffs only operated in the UK;

(b) it was not limited to those who competed in the field of PVC sheeting for adhesive tape but extended to anyone who competed in any part of the PVC calendered field, and yet the business secrets only attached to the former area of manufacture;

(c) it was not limited to working in some department or activity connected with the production of sheeting for adhesive tape.

Although this decision was criticised in *Littlewoods Organisation Ltd v Harris* [1978] 1 All E.R. 1026, it is an indication of how the courts may approach this area. In *Thomas Marshall (Exports) Ltd v Guinle* [1978] 3 W.L.R. 116, the defendant was the managing director of the plaintiff company who bought and sold textiles especially from countries which had restricted exports. An express clause in his contract of employment said that he was not, during or after employment, to "disclose" any confidential information re the affairs, customer or trade secrets of the plaintiff company. Megarry V.C. decided that apart from the express term, the defendant had breached his implied duty of fidelity as an employee and his fiduciary duty as a director. He then went on to consider the business secrets clause. It was argued by the defendant that this only prevented "disclosure" of any business secrets and did not prevent him "using" the information himself. It was argued that as another clause used the phrase "use or disclose" the draftsman had intentionally left "use" out of the business secrets clause. Megarry V.C. agreed. He said he could not imply "use" in "disclose" nor add it on. On the facts of this case this conclusion was obviously right; by showing that another clause did include "use" the defendant convinced the judge that by the word "disclose" alone the draftsman had meant to exclude the implied duty regarding business secrets which would extend to use as well as disclosure. However, the judge went on to say:

> I can conceive of methods of use which would amount to making a disclosure. If any employee were to use his secret knowledge in such a way as to make it plain to others what the secret process or information was that might well amount to a disclosure. The mode and circumstances of use may be so ostentatious that they plainly constitute a disclosure.

The moral of this case from the draftsman's point of view is: be consistent. In this case activities which should have been restricted were not covered by the business secrets clause and, but for other matters, the defendant would have been free to carry on damaging his former employer's business.

It is to be borne in mind in relation to both express and implied obligations of confidentiality and their inter-relationship with, in particular, non-competition covenants, that the courts have recognised that once what may be termed as a critical mass of confidential information (be it a trade secret or something akin to this) has been found to be in the knowledge of a departing employee, the difficulty of drawing a line between information which is confidential and information which is not, making it difficult to prove a breach of an express confidentiality provision or the implied duty of confidentiality, will often provide an argument in support of granting injunctive relief, rather than the reverse (see *Littlewoods Organisation Ltd. v Harris* [1977] 1 W.L.R. 1472 (Lord Denning M R at page 1479) and *Dyson Technology Ltd. v Strutt* [2005] ALL ER (D) 355. *Per* Waller L.J. in *Turner v Commonwealth & British Minerals Ltd.* [2000] I.R.L.R. 114, CA:

> Thus to enforce the covenant at all, the company would have to establish proprietary rights in the nature of trade connection or in the nature of trade secrets. I should emphasise that because those are the matters which they are legitimately entitled to protect, it does not follow that clause 5.6 must be unreasonable because covenants restraining the use of confidential information or the canvassing of trade connections could be, and indeed in this case were, imposed. It has been recognised in many cases that, because there are serious difficulties in identifying precisely what is or what is not confidential information and who may or may not have been a customer during the period of an employee's service, a restraint against competing which is reasonable in time and space will not only be enforceable, but the most satisfactory form of restraint.

However, cp *Berry Birch & Noble Financial Planning Ltd. v Berwick* [2005] EWHC 1803 (where a confidentiality covenant was not enforced because, irrespective that there may have been confidential information the scope of the covenant, the definition of what constituted confidential information within for the purpose of the restriction was simply too broad).

8.6.2 Geographical extent

It is generally true to say that much wider areas can be legitimately covered by business secrets clauses than by competition clauses and that objections to the need for pure area covenants are irrelevant. In *Caribonum Co Ltd v Le Couch* (1913) 109 L.T. 385 and 587 a restraint which was unrestricted as to time and area was upheld as was a restraint, in *Kerchiss v Colora Printing Inks Ltd* [1960] R.P.C. 235 which covered 16 countries. Indeed, it seems that the extraordinary approach to construction of the majority in the *Littlewoods* case is excusable on the basis that they were considering a restraint of trade clause which existed in order to protect business secrets. In practice, it is very difficult for an employee to argue that the geographical area attached to a business secrets clause is too wide; even the duty implied by law does not include geographical limits. It may, however, be possible to argue that use or disclosure of business secrets in a geographical area with which the employer has no and can have no reasonably foreseeable connection is not an effective breach of the restraint but query, all the same, whether it makes it unreasonable. Of course, should the secret come to lose its quality of confidence then any restriction will be irrelevant.

8.6.3 Time

Unlike the subject of geographical area, the courts have more reason to question time periods relating to business secrets. Such secrets rarely remain confidential for ever and it would be unfortunate if former employees were the only people prevented from using the information. It is submitted that the relevant matters are:

(a) the position of the employee: the higher up he or she is the more likely a longer term will be reasonable: see *Attwood v Lamont* [1920] 3 K.B. 571; and

(b) the type of industry involved: it may well be that in the more technologically advanced industries, the reasonable period of protection may be surprisingly short. For example, computer software is an area in which the state of the art is anything but static. The greater the susceptibility of the industry to change, the greater likelihood of the need to restrict time factors in business secrets clauses.

In *Commercial Plastics Ltd v Vincent* the plaintiffs had sensibly limited a restraint of trade clause based on business secrets to one year for the reason that the industry was growing and changing so fast that this was thought to be a sufficient period. In *Under Water Welders and Repairers Ltd v Street and Longthorne* [1968] R.P.C. 498 the plaintiffs were licensees using a novel process and were the only company using it in the UK. Longthorne was prevented from competing or helping others to compete with the plaintiffs for three years insofar as such competition used "any invention, principle or idea" practised by them. This was upheld.

In *Littlewoods Organisation Ltd v Harris* [1978] 1 All E.R. 1026 the plaintiffs had sensibly limited a restraint of trade clause which was designed to protect business secrets to a period of 12 months. As the secrets related to seasonal catalogues in the mail order business, any longer period might well have made the clause unreasonable.

In *Roger Bullivant Ltd v Ellis* [1987] I.C.R. 464 the Court of Appeal limited the period for which it was prepared to grant an injunction in a case concerning confidential information within the "springboard" category to 12 months—the period of an express restrictive covenant in the context of employment.

8.7 Miscellaneous points on reasonableness

8.7.1 Professional restraints

In *Scorer v Seymour-Johns* [1966] 1 W.L.R. 1419 Sellers L.J. suggested that the existence of a professional restraint may be relevant to the question of reasonableness. Although the need for a covenant may be diminished by the existence of a professional rule of conduct, it really depends on whether the professional body in question has any effective sanction with which to enforce its rules of conduct and how quickly it can do so. The courts can act much more quickly to provide relief than any professional disciplinary body and in most cases speed is essential from the employer's point of view. In *Oswald Hickson Collier and Co v Carter-Ruck* [1984] A.C. 720, a more recent case in which the existence of a professional restraint was referred to, the court did not deal with the point at all.

8.7.2 Trade usage

If it can be shown by a defendant that a particular restriction is unusual within a certain trade then this may have some bearing on the question of reasonableness, and, more fundamentally, it may be relevant to whether the restraint of trade doctrine applies at all. In *Page One Records Ltd v Britton* [1968] 1 W.L.R. 157 Stamp J. was impressed by the fact that there was no evidence from the trade that any of the agreements were unusual or unfair. However, in *A. Schroeder Music Publishing Co Ltd v Macaulay* [1974] 1 W.L.R. 1308, the fact that an agreement was in standard form did not help the appellant company. As Lord Diplock said, standard form contracts were of two types. The first were those which set out the terms upon which mercantile transactions of common occurrence were to be carried out. The second type (an example of which was found in this case) was that resulting from superior bargaining power. The main difficulties with the trade usage argument are:

(a) actually getting evidence of what is common in the trade; and

(b) demonstrating that this particular employer has a business which is of a standard nature for the trade.

Obviously, even if there is evidence of trade usage it is still open to a plaintiff to argue that his business is so different from others that the standard approach is irrelevant. However, that argument was not possible in *WC Leng and Co Ltd v Andrews* [1909] 1 Ch. 763 and one of the reasons given by the court for finding the restriction unreasonable was the fact that it was unusual in the relevant trade.

8.7.3 Provisions which permit consent

In some employment contracts there is a provision which states that a restriction will not apply if the employer consents, which consent will not be unreasonably withheld. In *Kerchiss v Colora Printing Inks Ltd* [1960] R.P.C. 235 Dankwerts J. said that such a provision was relevant to reasonableness. In answer to defence submissions that a restrictive covenant was unreasonable he said:

> I have come to the conclusion that having regard to two things, first . . . the way in which the restriction is cut down by the provision for consent which cannot be unreasonably withheld and having regard also to another consideration, that the plaintiff is to be paid a substantial salary if he is not allowed to take up employment during the period in question and during which the restriction exists, there is something to be said for the view that this covenant . . . does not go too far.

It may well be that it was the second point which was decisive. We think it unlikely that consent alone would have been enough for it is difficult for an employee to show that his former employer is acting unreasonably in withholding consent; obviously, if there is a financial penalty for so doing the employer will think twice before refusing permission. In our experiences such salary provisions are rare and will only be applicable in special situations. As in *Kerchiss*, they will probably only be found where the employee is a director or is very senior. Therefore, despite *Kerchiss*, it is our view that most courts will treat a "consent" proviso as irrelevant in most cases. In *Chafer Ltd v Lilley* (1947) L.J.R. 231 176 L.T. 22 such a provision was described as a "device". They are frequently cosmetic and meaningless. If a clause is clearly unreasonable a consent proviso cannot redeem it and the fact of its inclusion may lead the judge to question whether the parties ever regarded the clause as reasonable. If the clause is reasonable anyway, the consent proviso is irrelevant. Moreover, in *Perls v Saalfeld* [1892] 2 Ch. 149 a consent provision militated against the narrower construction of the clause for which the plaintiffs argued and in *Technograph Printed Circuits Ltd v Chalwyn Ltd* [1967] R.P.C. 339 it did not help the plaintiffs defeat a defence of unreasonableness. In *TRP Ltd v Thorley* July 13, 1993 (unreported), CA, Hoffman L.J. made the following remarks about a clause which set out detailed consent provisions:

> There seems to be no justification in law for requiring an ex-employee (merely because he intends to compete with his former employer) to give details of his new business or employment so that the employer may judge whether it prejudices his trade secrets, connection or goodwill. In any case, the mere fact that an ex-employee is trying to take away his former employer's customers is something which in law he is perfectly entitled to do. That would inevitably be calculated to prejudice the employer's connection or goodwill and make the proviso for consent useless.

8.8 Suing third parties

Most successful restraint of trade actions against employees suffer from a major deficiency: they control the former employee's activities for a short time in the future but they fail to deal with the party which has probably gained most from the defendant's breach of contract, i.e. the new employer. For tactical and commercial reasons it may be undesirable to start an action against the new employer. The view is often taken that as the new employer or competing company may well be represented by separate lawyers from those representing the former employee an effect of suing it will be to ensure that two sets of lawyers line up in opposition to the plaintiff's claim. Moreover, as most plaintiffs are not primarily interested in pursuing a damages claim there may be little point in proceeding against another party when an injunction against the former employee will have the effect of restricting the ability of the third party to compete unfairly. Further, in this difficult area of the law a plaintiff cannot always foresee the outcome of the litigation with any degree of confidence. If he had obtained an injunction against the new employer as well as the former employee, but that is later discharged, he is likely to be met with a claim under the cross-undertaking in damages which he has given. In real terms, the new employer's claim will probably be for a larger amount than that of the former employee. That said, there may be circumstances where it is prudent to involve the actual or respective new employer at least in the pre-action correspondence. A departing employee may not have advised the new employer of the restrictions he or she is subject to (or at least not fully) and/or may have engaged in conduct prior to departure which the new employer is unaware of and would not have approved (for example, taking confidential documentation or encouraging other members of staff to leave, et.) and where, as a consequence, it may be possible to agree on appropriate arrangements and undertakings without the necessity of recourse to court.

There is also the costs consideration. If the clause is found to have been unreasonable the plaintiff will have to pay two sets of costs rather than merely one. Conversely, the importance of costs as a reason for joining the third party in the action was highlighted in *Symphony Group Plc v Hodgson* [1993] 4 All E.R. 143. The plaintiff having succeeded at the end of a trial in obtaining injunctions against a legally aided former employee sought to recover the costs of the action (which were likely to be more than £100,000) from the new employer (a non-party) under s.51(1) of the Supreme Court Act 1981. The words of that subsection were held in *Aiden Shipping Company Ltd v Interbulk Ltd* [1986] A.C. 965 to be sufficiently wide to give a court jurisdiction to order a third party to pay the costs of a successful plaintiff. At no time did the plaintiff seek to join the new employer as a party despite having learnt of its identity at an early stage and despite having intimated it was proposing to do so and the new employers' solicitors having confirmed that they had instructions to accept service of any proceedings that the plaintiffs might issue. The Court of Appeal laid down a number of general guidelines which a court should apply when faced with an application for costs against a non-party and decided on a number of grounds that such an application was not maintainable in the instant case. A main ground relied on by the court was the fact that the plaintiff had at all material times a cause of action in tort against the new employer but it had decided not to join them as party. Furthermore the plaintiff had never, prior to judgment against the employer, warned the new employer that it might seek to make it liable for costs; it was therefore deprived of an opportunity to apply to be joined as a party to the action under RSC Ord.15, r.6(2)(*b*)(i) and (ii) (now CPR 19.4).

From this case it must be concluded that if the claimant is particularly concerned about costs and if the primary defendant is legally aided careful consideration must be given to joining the new employer in the proceedings or at least to putting it on notice at an early stage that a costs claim may be made against it. However, if it is decided that he should be sued there are two causes of action which will be most commonly used: breach of confidence and inducing a breach of contract.

8.8.1 Breach of confidence

The position of third parties is discussed above at para.5.8.

8.8.2 Inducing a breach of contract

This tort is variously described as procuring, inducing or simply "facilitating" a breach of contract. The ingredients are:

(a) that a contract exists between X and Y;

(b) that Z is aware of that contract;

(c) that Z procures, induces or facilitates Y's breach of that contract.

Element (a) needs no further discussion. However, element (b) is more complex. In restraint of trade cases Z's knowledge of the existence of the contract may come from being told by Y. However X will usually not be able to prove that. What X will normally do is write to Z (having gathered that Y is joining or has joined Z as an employee) and give him notice of the relevant clause. It is clear that if Z employs Y innocently and without knowledge of the contract term (or of any breach) and then receives notice of its existence (and is warned about the breach) but continues to employ Y then he is liable for facilitating that breach: see *De Francesco v Barnum* (1890) 63 L.T. 514 in which the defendant who continued to employ the plaintiff's servants—five ballet dancers—after notice of a prior contract of service was liable for damages. In *Jones Brothers (Hunstanton) Ltd v Stevens* [1954] 3 All E.R. 677, in principle a hotel proprietor would have been liable for continuing to employ a chef after having been told of his engagement by the plaintiff as a fish frier, despite the defendant's genuine mistaken belief that he was entitled to employ the chef. In fact the plaintiff failed to establish damage because the fact that the chef was content to earn lower wages at the hotel apparently showed that the chef had no intention of going back to his fish frying job anyway.

To be liable Z need not know of the precise terms of the contract; he need only have sufficient knowledge, including knowledge of the existence of the contract, to know or be deemed to know that he is facilitating a breach (*Stratford v Lindley* [1964] 3 All E.R. 102, CA), and a defendant who deliberately shuts his eyes to the fact will be fixed with constructive knowledge (*Emerald Construction v Lowthian* [1966] 1 All E.R. 1013, CA). Contrast the defendant who suspects a breach but acts bona fide, if mistakenly, to allay those suspicions, as in *British Industrial Plastics v Ferguson* [1940] 1 All E.R. 479, HL. This case was distinguished in *Jones Bros v Stevens* where the defendant did know of the breach itself and was only ignorant of its consequences. Likewise see *Hivac v Park Royal Scientific Instruments* [1946] 1 All E.R. 350, CA, where an injunction was granted against a defendant who secretly employed the plaintiff's employees on Sundays during their spare time and realised, if not that it was legally wrong, at any rate that to do so was morally reprehensible. More recently, in *Mainstream Properties Ltd. v Young* [2007] UKHL 21, two senior employees of a property company acting in breach of their employment contracts diverted a development opportunity to a joint venture in which they were interested together with a third party whose financial assistance was essential. Whilst the third party knew they were employed by Mainstream and there was an obvious potential conflict between their duties to the company and their participation in the joint venture, the Judge at first instance found that the third party had raised this issue with the two employees and received an assurance that there was no conflict because the company had been offered the site in question but had refused it. Whilst untrue, the third party genuinely believed it and, on the facts of the case, the Judge at first instance found that the third party did not intend to procure the breach of contracts of employment or otherwise interfere with their performance as a consequence. Given the necessity for intent, the Judge's findings are upheld by the Court of Appeal and then by the House of Lords and, reaching this decision, it was observed that it was consistent with *British Industrial Plastics*.

There is no requirement that the defendant acts maliciously over and above his acting knowingly (*Jones Bros v Stevens*), and there is no need for there to exist a desire to injure the plaintiff (*Thompson v Deakin* [1952] 2 All E.R. 361, CA); motive is, broadly speaking, irrelevant.

The situation becomes more complicated when one comes across the distinction between direct and indirect interference with contractual rights, as in *Thompson v Deakin* where the defendants during an industrial dispute persuaded employees of B to refuse to deliver paper to the plaintiffs, with whom the defendants were in dispute, with the result that B were unable to perform their contract with the plaintiffs. The Court held that here there was no direct invasion of the plaintiffs' rights under the contract—the breach directly procured, if any, was the breach by B's employees of their contract with B. Liability in such cases of indirect interference (which is unlikely to be relevant to restraint of trade cases) was clearly viewed as an extension of the scope of the tort, and the Court set out the following requirements in order for liability to be established:

(a) actual knowledge of the existence of the contract with the plaintiff;

(b) an intention to bring about the breach of that contract;

(c) unequivocal persuasion, inducement or procurement with that intent;

(d) that the breach ensued as a necessary consequence.

These requirements only apply to what is sometimes called "interference with contractucal rights by blacking", and not to direct interference with the contract with the plaintiff. Most recently the House of Lords has looked again at the distinction between direct and indirect interference with contractual rights, tracing the origins of these terms back to two separate distinct torts; inducing a breach of contract (based on *Lumley v Gye* (1853) 2 El. & B.1 216, and causing loss by unlawful means (see *Allen v Flood* [1898] A.C. 1) which, in the words of Lord Hoffman in the combined appeals in *OBG Ltd. v Allan*; *Douglas v Hello! Ltd.*, and *Mainstream Properties Ltd. v Young* [2007] UKHL 21 became muddled in *GWK Ltd. v Dunlop Rubber Co. Ltd.* (1926) 42 TLR 376 and then "unified", in *DC Thomson & Co. Ltd. v Deakin*, ante. The distinction between the original *Lumley v Gye* tort and its extension in *DC Thomson & Co. Ltd. v Deakin* led to the distinction between "direct" and "indirect" interference. Lord Hoffman regarded the distinction as unsatisfactory:

> It is time for the unnatural union between the *Lumley v Gye* tort, and the tort of causing loss by unlawful means to be dissolved. To be liable for inducing breach of contract you must know that you are inducing a breach of contract. It is not enough that you know that you are procuring an act which, as a matter of law or construction of the contract, is a breach. You must actually realise that it will have this effect. Nor does it matter that you ought reasonably to have done so.

So far as the tort of causing loss by unlawful means per Lord Hoffman:

> The essence of the tort . . . appears to be (a) a wrongful interference with the actions of a third party in which the claimant has an economic interest and (b) an intention thereby to cause loss to the claimant.

In the *Lumley v Gye* tort, there must be an intention to procure a breach of contract; in the unlawful means tort, there must be an intention to cause loss.

8.8.2.1 The inducement/procurement/facilitation

Inducement or procurement in the strict sense will be impossible to prove in most restraint of trade cases. However the existence of the concept of "facilitation" does enable X to sue Z in a large number of restraint of trade cases. That facilitation alone is sufficient is established by a number of cases.

In *British Motor Trade Association v Salvadori* [1949] 1 All E.R. 208, the defendants, who were barred from being sold new cars by the plaintiffs, bought the cars instead from third parties they had put up to buy the cars from the plaintiffs, knowing that the third parties were thereby in breach of a covenant with the plaintiffs. The defendants claimed that to buy from a willing seller was not to induce a breach of contract by the seller. It was held by Roxburgh J. that:

> Lord MacNaghten (in *Quinn v Leathem* [1901] A.C. 495) preferred the word "interference" for his statement of the doctrine, and this seems to me to predicate active association of some kind with the breach, but, in my judgment, any active step taken by a defendant, having knowledge of that covenant, by which he facilitates a breach of that covenant is enough ...

and that the defendant in that case took such active steps by agreeing to buy, paying for, and taking delivery of a motor car known by him to be offered in breach of covenant.

British Motor Trade Association v Salvadori, and in particular the passage quoted above, was approved in *Rickless v United Artists Corp* [1988] Q.B. 40, CA, where Bingham L.J. said it was an authority which had never to his knowledge been doubted.

If a defendant can only be said to have facilitated a breach it may be that he can escape liability by means of the argument that the breach would have happened anyway, so that no damage has been caused (see *e.g. Jones Bros v Stevens* above).

However, there have been some copyright cases in which facilitation was *not sufficient* and the Court required there also to be a common design between the defendant and the party in breach (see *Paterson Zochonis v Merfarken Packaging* [1986] 3 All E.R. 522, CA, *CBS v Amstrad* [1988] 1 A.C. 1013, HL). Clerk and Lindsell suggest that this requirement also applies to the tort of interference with contract, and it is true that, for example, in *CBS* the Court appears to have based its decision (that there was no liability) on a distinction not between copyright and contract but between "facilitating" and "procuring". Furthermore, although it does not appear to be an express part of the judgments in *BMTA v Salvadori*, in that case too the defendants and the parties in breach did have a common design, i.e. to get round the bar against the defendants buying new cars.

However, we do not think that this would necessarily limit the application of the tort in restraint of trade cases, since arguably the scope of the common design required should be limited to what the breacher should do, rather than, say, a common design specifically that the contract be breached. This would be enough to allow for the copyright situation, where the defence being accepted by the courts is that it is up to the buyers of the goods (e.g., in the *CBS* case, buyers of Amstrad's two-deck tape recorders) to decide what to do with them, and any number of goods can be used both lawfully and unlawfully. Such an approach would also be in line with the extent of knowledge required of the defendant in the contractual cases.

8.9 Public policy

This is the final ingredient of reasonableness, but it is rarely expressed as an independent basis for assessing its existence in employment contracts nowadays. If the clause is reasonable between the parties, then it is usually assumed that it is reasonable from the public point of view. Of course, public policy does underlie the tradition of bias towards the employee especially if there is a chance that he might be unable to work at his trade because of a restriction. It is also the foundation of the distinction between the employer's protectable interests and the employee's freedom to use his acquired skill and knowledge. Evidentially, public policy can be important because its very existence may allow the judge to raise points which had not been litigated by the parties (*per* e.g. *Marion White Ltd v Francis* [1972] 1 W.L.R. 1423) although Lord Diplock said it should not: see *Petrofina (Great Britain) Ltd v Martin* [1966] Ch. 146.

In *Oswald Hickson Collier and Co v Carter-Ruck* [1984] 2 All E.R. 15 it was accepted by Lord Denning M.R. that since the relationship between a solicitor and his client is a fiduciary one it is contrary to public policy for a solicitor to be persuaded from acting for a client when that client wants him to act, especially in pending litigation. A clause in a partnership deed preventing one of the partners from acting for a client in the future was accordingly contrary to public policy because there is a fiduciary relationship between them and the client ought reasonably to be entitled to the services of such solicitor as he wishes. However, in *Bridge v Deacons* [1984] A.C. 705 the Privy Council declined to accept that proposition and in *Kerr v Morris* [1986] 3 All E.R. 217 the Court of Appeal, in a case concerning a partnership of general medical practitioners who were doing National Health Service work, did likewise. As was pointed out above (at section 2.5) it seems that public policy may well still be an important factor in some cases although in others public policy arguments are frequently the refuge of the desperate.

8.9.1 EU provisions

Article 81 of the Treaty of Rome will not apply as an individual employee is not an "undertaking" as required by Art.81: see *Sugar* (Case 40/73) [1975] E.C.R. 1663. Article 82 by its very terms is of doubtful application.

Chapter 9

Drafting Restrictions in Employment Contracts

9.1 Introduction

Set out in Appendix 5 are typical clauses in the areas of competition/canvassing and business secrets which can form the bases for restrictive covenants in employment contracts. Restrictive covenants should be considered as part of a suite of contractual terms aimed at protecting the employer and consideration should be given to the inclusion of a garden leave provision; an exclusive services obligation; a payment in lieu of notice ("PILON") term; a confidentiality provision and associated obligation to return the employer's property at the end of employment and (as appropriate) an intellectual property clause. We consider all these below.

The precise contents of each clause will depend on the industry type, the responsibilities of the employee and the aims which the employer wishes to achieve in the light of his particular business. Before those clauses are read, however, there is an important point which must be covered. The obvious need for express clauses rather than relying on duties which the courts will imply.

We have dealt with the duties implied by law in employment contracts because they complete the analysis and also because they are still frequently relied on in many situations. However, we hope that whilst what has been written about implied duties is of help to those involved in problems arising from current employment contracts, those who are concerned with drafting new agreements will include express terms. Although there are some disadvantages to these, e.g. the impossibility of anticipating what may happen, such a disadvantage also attaches to implied duties for, as explained earlier, the courts look at the reasonableness of all types of duty at the time at which the contract is entered into. Moreover, changes and amendments to the ambit of the restraint can be made effective by incorporating a clause which permits such changes etc. to be made. The advantage of an express clause is certainty. Although implied duties do cover some but not all areas protectable by express covenants, the problems which arise have an uncanny knack of falling outside the apparent scope of the implied duties thus necessitating an expensive trip to court. Moreover, from the employer's point of view, damage may have already been incurred in that the employee, unaware of the consequences of a certain course of conduct, may have done something which breaches the implied duties in the belief that the absence of express duties meant that no duty existed at all; even a swift remedy, such as an interim injunction might well be of little practical value even were it to be granted.

In *Sanders v Parry* [1967] 1 W.L.R. 753 Havers J. made a useful comment when he said:

> It may well be that the absence of a restrictive covenant gave some false confidence . . . to the defendant and encouraged him to do . . . what is alleged, in the belief that no proceedings could be taken against him by the plaintiff.

In *Printers and Finishers Ltd v Holloway* [1964] 3 All E.R. 731 Cross J. said:

> Although the law will not enforce a covenant directed against competition by an ex-employee it will enforce a covenant reasonably necessary to protect trade secrets. . . . If the managing director is right in thinking that there are features in the plaintiff's process which can fairly be regarded as trade secrets and which their employees will inevitably carry away with them in their heads, then the proper way for the plaintiffs to protect themselves would be by exacting covenants from their employees restricting their field of activity after they have left their employment not by asking the court to extend the general equitable doctrine to prevent breaking confidence beyond all reasonable bounds.

In the area of business secrets an express covenant removes the need to prove the employee's subjective consciousness of the fact that certain information is secret. The difficulty of relying on the implied duty of confidence was highlighted in *Balston Ltd v Headline Filters Ltd* [1987] F.S.R. 330 at pp.351–2. Scott J. decided that the application for an injunction before him was another example of an attempt by an employer to use the doctrine of confidential information to place fetters on the ability of ex-employees to compete. He said that employers who want to impose fetters of this sort on their employees ought to be expected to do so by express covenant (see also *Poeton Industries Ltd v Horton* [2000] I.C.R. 1208). The reasonableness of the covenant could then have applied to it the rigorous attention to which all employee covenants in restraint of trade are subject. In the absence of an express covenant, the ability of an ex-employee to compete could be restricted by means of an implied term against use or disclosure of trade secrets. However the case must be a clear one.

> An employee does not have the chance to reject an implied term. It is formulated and imposed on him subsequent to his initial entry into employment. To fetter his freedom to compete by means of an implied term can only be justified, in my view, by a very clear case. (Scott J.)

Express covenants are, of course, especially important post employment in the field of restraint of trade. Without an express covenant the employee is free to compete with his former employer at the moment his employment ends moreover there is no propsect of one being implied (see *Wallace Bogan & Co Ltd v Cove* [1997] I.R.L.R. 453 CA). He can canvass customers, accept business from them and can set up a competing business across the street. So long as he is not using business secrets to do so he is entirely free to compete.

It may happen that a draftsman is inept. He may not include in an express term all that the law would have implied. In such a situation it is quite clear that, in the absence of manifest contrary intention, the law will still imply those terms. However, he must be very careful as was shown in *Thomas Marshall (Exports) Ltd. v Guinle* [1978] I.R.L.R. 174 in which the court refused to read "disclose" as meaning "use or disclose"; the law would have implied "use" but it was decided that the contract as a whole manifested a contrary intention. What if a draftsman is so zealous in his efforts to express protection for the employer that the clause is struck down as being unreasonable: can the employer still rely on the terms implied by law? The answer appears to be yes, provided that there is no manifest contrary intention in the contract. (See *Wessex Dairies Ltd v Smith* [1935] 2 K.B. 80 and *Triplex Safety Glass Co Ltd v Scorah* [1938] Ch. 211.)

It is important to realise the need in some cases for both non-competition and business secrets clauses in employment contracts. As Dankwerts L.J. said in *Scorer v Seymour-Johns* [1966] 1 W.L.R. 1419: "It is difficult to protect . . . confidential knowledge without in some way imposing a restriction on competition" and as Lord Denning M.R. said in *Littlewoods Organisation Ltd v Harris* [1978] 1 All E.R. 1026:

> . . . experience has shown that it is not satisfactory to have simply a covenant against disclosing confidential information. The reason is because it is so difficult to draw the line between information which is confidential and information which is not; and it is very difficult to prove a breach when the information is of such a character that a servant can carry it away in his head. The difficulties are such that the only practicable solution is to take a covenant from the servant by which he is not to go to work for a rival in trade.

These words were echoed by Megaw L.J. at p.1038. This approach was clearly accepted in *Lansing Linde Ltd v Kerr* [1991] 1 All E.R. 418, CA, in *Lawrence David Ltd v Ashton* [1991] 1 All E.R. 385, CA, and in *Berry Birch & Noble Financial Planning Ltd. v Berwick* [2005] EWHC 1803. Ultimately the construction to be placed on words used in restrictive covenants in particular cases will depend upon the terms of the agreement and the normal rules of construction within the particular factual matrix. However, some of the more recent cases looking at commonly used words and phrases, are *TFS Derivatives Ltd. v Morgan* [2005] I.R.L.R. 246 ("any business" and "interested in any capacity"); *Dyson Technology Ltd. v Strutt* [2005] ALL ER (D) 355 ("business", "any business", "similar to" and "involved"); *Beckett Investment Management Group Ltd. v Hall* [2007] EWHC 241, QB ("to deal" and "client") and *Intercall Conferencing Services Ltd. v Steer* [2007] EWHC 519 (QB) ("in competition").

9.2 Introducing or amending covenants in the course of employment

Those judgments point out that there is frequently an overlap between the areas of business secrets and restraint of trade. Restraints on competition are frequently an effective means of securing protection for business secrets.

A common problem in practice is the case of the employer who has neglected to include any restraint of trade or confidential information clause in the contract with the employee but who now wishes to do so or, if has included such clauses, wishes to amend them so as to make them more effective. This is usually dealt with by inserting the relevant clauses in consideration for the payment of a higher salary. However it does happen that the employee refuses to accept any addition to his contract. This is unsatisfactory from the employer's point of view. An answer is found in the seminal case of *RS Components Ltd v Irwin* [1974] 1 All E.R. 41; [1973] I.R.L.R. 239; [1973] I.C.R. 535 (although it must be admitted that this case may have limited application). During the course of two years the appellants had received complaints from its sales force of loss of orders due to the activities of ex-employees. Apparently, on a number of occasions a salesman had left the appellants' employment after learning from experience the names and addresses of the appellants' customers within his territory, and the schedule in accordance with which calls were made on them. The salesman had then set up in business on his own account within the same territory and solicited orders from the appellants' customers. As a result of knowledge of the appellants' call schedules, the ex-employee had been able to visit a customer just before the customer was due to receive a visit from the appellants' salesman. This competition, founded on inside knowledge of the identity of the appellants' customers and call schedules, seriously prejudiced the appellants' salesman who succeeded to that particular territory and led to a loss of commission as well as reducing the appellants' profits. The appellants took advice and decided that an appropriate remedy would be to place their current sales force under a reasonable restrictive covenant. On February 1, 1973 Mr Turner, the appellants' sales director, wrote a circular letter to the respondent and to the other salesmen, enclosing a new service agreement which, it was said, would come into force on March 1. The respondent was asked to study the new agreement carefully and to return it signed by February 23. Although the letter asked for the views of the salesman, it was stated that the new terms were the only terms on which the appellants were prepared to employ any representative. It was not open to the appellants unilaterally to change the terms of the contract on which the respondent was employed. What the appellants could do at common law was to invite the respondent to sign a new contract and, if he declined, to give him the requisite period of notice to determine the existing contract, or pay him wages in lieu of notice. Having regard to his length of service the respondent was entitled, under the (then) Contracts of Employment Act 1972, to six weeks' notice. The proposed new agreement altered the pay structure of salesmen and also changed certain other conditions of their employment. It introduced for the first time a restrictive covenant in the following terms:

> If for any reason you leave our employ, you undertake that for 12 calendar months you will not solicit any firm, person or company who is or has been a customer of this Company in goods in which the Company deals within any territory covered by you as a representative for RS Components Ltd.

The introduction of this restrictive covenant was the only change in the terms and conditions of employment which had any materiality for the purposes of the present case.

On February 21 the respondent wrote to Mr Turner declining to sign the new agreement. The appellants answered the next day to the effect that if the agreement were not signed the appellants would regretfully have to give the respondent notice terminating his employment. On the following day the respondent repeated his refusal. On February 27 he called at the appellants' offices at the invitation of the chairman. The chairman discussed fully with the respondent all the variations incorporated in the new agreement and explained why the appellants considered them necessary. It was left that the respondent would think things over. In the outcome the respondent telephoned the appellants to confirm that he was not willing to accept the new agreement. At the beginning of March his employment was ended by the appellants and he was given certain financial compensation. Although the respondent was not given a period of notice determining his employment, it was accepted in court that a proper payment was made or provided for in lieu of notice.

Out of the total work force of 92 salesmen, 88 signed the new agreement. There were four dissentients of whom the respondent was one.

The respondent presented an application to an industrial tribunal. He won before the tribunal. On appeal he lost. In fact the tribunal had accepted that the covenant was fair and that the effect on the future interests of the appellants' business of the respondent's refusal to enter into the new terms of service was so substantial as to justify his dismissal. However, as a matter of construction of the phrase "some other substantial reason" (see now s.98(1)(b) of the Employment Rights Act 1996) they found for the respondent. The National Industrial Relations Court (Brightman J.) reversed the decision.

The court also commented that there might arise a situation in which it might be essential for a company embarking on a new technical process to invite existing employees to agree to some reasonable restriction on their use of the knowledge they acquire of the new technique and where it would be essential for the company to terminate, by due notice, the services of an employee who was unwilling to accept such a restriction.

What is clear both from this example and from the facts of the case is that in order to defend a claim for unfair dismissal the employer must demonstrate an objective commercial reason for varying the contract. See also *Willow Oak Developments Ltd. v Silverwood* [2006] I.R.L.R. 607, CA, in which Buxton L. J. said:

> An employee's refusal to accept covenants proposed by the employer for the protection of his legitimate interests is one that can in law form a ground for dismissal.

This was so despite the factual twist in this particular case that the restrictions the employer sought to impose were potentially unenforceable. In the event, the dismissals were held to be unfair but this was due to the manner in which the employer had tried to impose the new terms.

As to the argument that there was no consideration for the variation see para.3.8 above.

9.3 The phrase "howsoever caused" and similar phrases

Uncertainty has surrounded the effect of the inclusion of the words "howsoever caused", "for whatever reason" or variants on these when describing the termination of employment as the trigger date for the application of restrictive covenants. The argument is that the inclusion of language along these lines purporting to make a restrictive covenant applicable in circumstances where the employer may have wrongfully dismissed the employee renders any covenant which is expressed to be potentially applicable in such circumstances unenforceable, and even if the termination of the employment is in fact lawful.

The first case to raise the point was *Briggs v Oates* [1991] 1 All E.R. 407. The relevant clause stated, inter alia, "the salaried partner shall not at any time either during the continuance of this agreement or during the period of five years after it shall have determined, *for whatever reason* practice as a solicitor . . ." [emphasis added]. Scott J. said in answer to an argument from the plaintiff:

> A contract under which an employee could be immediately and wrongfully dismissed, but would nevertheless remain subject to an anti-competitive restraint seems to be grossly unreasonable. I would not be prepared to enforce the restraint in such a contract.

In that case the plaintiff had not sought to "blue pencil" the emphasised phrase although if it had done so we would have thought that would have been permitted.

The next case to consider the point was a Scottish one: *Living Design (Home Improvements) Ltd v Davidson* [1994] I.R.L.R. 69. There Lord Coulsfield had to consider a restraint which included the phrase in reference to termination "however that comes about and whether lawful or not". He decided such a phrase rendered the whole restraint unreasonable and refused to grant the injunction sought. He also refused to blue pencil the offending phrase on the basis that he doubted it was merely trivial or technical; it seemed to him to be part of the main substance and import of the clause.

In *PR Consultants Scotland Ltd v Mann* [1996] I.R.L.R. 188 Lord Caplan had to consider a restraint which stated that the defendant would not "during the period of 12 months following the termination of his employment (howsoever caused) directly or indirectly . . .". Having discussed Lord Coulsfield's judgment and conclusions reached in two other cases, Lord Caplan concluded "In my view the relevant provision 'howsoever caused' in the present case is not apt to cover unlawful termination. There are many ways in which an employment contract can be lawfully terminated". However, he continued:

> If the employer was to dismiss his employee unlawfully then by the operation of the principle of mutuality of contractual provisions the restrictive covenant would not be available to him. In the situation considered by Lord Coulsfield in the *Living Design* case the contract (for some reason) specifically provided that the covenant should cover an unlawful termination. However in the absence of such a specific provision I do not think that it can be readily inferred that the parties intended that the contract be read so as to incorporate such a provision.

In *D v M* [1996] I.R.L.R.192 the court had to consider a covenant which applied "if this appointment under this Agreement is terminated for any reason whatsoever at any time hereafter". A further clause referred to the date of termination "irrespective of the cause or manner". Laws J. found that the phrases were to be construed so as to secure "coercive rights to the employer which would survive his own contractual misconduct. I cannot think that that would be reasonable". As for severance, he rejected any suggestion

(a) that the words were capable of severance on the basis that there was more than one separate and distinct covenant and

(b) that they were of trivial importance or merely technical.

The plaintiff's application failed.

However, the Court of Appeal has now held in *Rock Refrigeration Ltd v Jones and Seward Refrigeration Ltd* [1996] I.R.L.R. 675 that *D v M*, *PR Consultants v Mann* and *Living Design (Home Improvements) v Davidson* as well as Scott J.'s obiter dictum in *Briggs v Oates* proceeded on an erroneous basis that the employee was still bound by the contractual restraint on his post-employment activities even if the employment was terminated by the wrongful act of the employer. The court said that a restrictive covenant which purports to operate even where the termination has been brought about by the employer's own breach is not necessarily void from the beginning as an unreasonable restraint of trade. Where the employer has been guilty of a repudiatory breach the principle in *General Billposting v Atkinson* [1909] A.C. 118 HL would apply: as a consequence the employee would be released from his obligations under the contract and the restrictive covenant he was subject to could not be enforced. Accordingly, the law applicable to covenants and restraint of trade was not relevant in such circumstances since it would only apply where there exists an otherwise enforceable covenant. If an otherwise reasonable covenant purports to remain binding in circumstances where the law will inevitably strike it down, there is no justification for holding that it is, on that account, in unlawful restraint of trade. A covenant including phrases such as "whether lawfully or not", is merely "writ in water" and unenforceable under the *General Bill Posting* principle. Phillips L.J. went further and questioned whether the rule accorded with current legal principle or with the requirements of business efficacy. He considered that it was at least arguable that not every restrictive covenant will be discharged upon a repudiatory termination of the contract of employment. See also *Campbell v Frisbee* [2002] EWCH 328 Ch D.

Part IV

Business Sales

Chapter 10

Introduction

10.1 Introduction

The sale of a business usually involves the purchase and sale of a number of tangible assets such as stock and intangible assets such as goodwill (i.e. the business reputation and trade connections). It is important to draw a distinction between the sale of a business and a mere sale of stock.

Only in the former case will a restriction on the vendor's power to compete with the purchaser be contemplated between the parties. Of course, there is never any guarantee that the purchaser will be able to profit from the goodwill; he may find that when he runs the business the trade connections which once existed go elsewhere and that the reputation disappears. However, once the assets of a business have been sold the law will imply a transfer of goodwill as well unless expressly excluded (*Jennings v Jennings* [1898] 1 Ch. 378) and the purchaser will not want the vendor to be able to set up next door; even if he uses a different name he will attract many of his former customers. Nor will he want the vendor to solicit the customers of his former business or use the business secrets of that business as an alternative way of competing with it. In order to protect the purchaser and restrict the vendor it is usual to have express contractual terms which circumscribe the ability of the vendor to compete. Moreover, the courts have been astute in applying the restraint of trade doctrine and the law of business secrets to make sure that the outgoing vendor does not achieve some unjust advantage because of his former association with the goodwill of the business and thereby derogate from the value of that which he has sold. If there are no express contractual terms dealing with goodwill then the courts will prevent the vendor from competing with his old business and to this end there will be imposed on the vendor the duties not to:

(a) solicit old customers;

(b) use business secrets of the old business; and

(c) represent that he is carrying on the business of the old company.

Where express provision has been made in the sale contract then the courts will consider whether such provision is reasonable in all the circumstances.

In addition the sale of a business is likely to be an agreement between "undertakings" which may raise competition issues. In particular, any non-compete clauses will need to be analysed under Art.81 of the EC Treaty (or Chapter 1 of the UK Competition Act 1998) and the doctrine of ancillary restraints. This can apply regardless of whether the business transferred is a global company, a partnership or a sole trader given that competition law applies to all manner of commercial "undertakings" or enterprises, although in the case of a sole trader the effect of the clause are less likely to have an appreciable effect on competition. Competition law would not apply to a pure employment contact, as an employee is not an undertaking (see Cases 40/73 etc. *Suiker Unie v Commission* [1975] E.C.R. 1663). While in some aspects competition law applies similar concepts as the common law restraint of trade doctrine (e.g. the ambit of activities caught, the geographic scope and the duration), the analysis and consequences can be very different. Chapters 21 and 22 deal with the substantive issues arising under UK and EU competition law, but note also some of the procedural differences in Section 23.

10.2 Distinction between employment and business sales agreements

The distinction between business sale cases and employment cases can be traced back to the speech of Lord Macnaghten in *Nordenfelt v Maxim Nordenfelt Guns and Ammunition Co* [1894] A.C. 535, 559–574 and it is well established that covenants in the latter category are more strictly scrutinised by the courts. In the case of a business sale, it is generally recognised that the interests of the public at large may require that the purchaser obtains some protection from competition from the vendor. The point was explained by Lord Watson in the *Nordenfelt* case at p.552.

> I think it is now generally conceded that it is to the advantage of the public to allow a trader who has established a lucrative business to dispose of it to a successor by whom it may efficiently be carried on. That object could not be accomplished if, upon the score of public policy, the law reserved to the seller an absolute and indefeasible right to start a rival business the day after he sold. Accordingly it has been determined judicially, that in cases where the purchaser, for his own protection, obtains an obligation restraining the seller from competing with him, within bounds which having regard to the nature of the business are reasonable and are limited in respect of space, the obligation is not obnoxious to public policy, and is therefore capable of being enforced.

However, the established categories of business sale or employment case are not rigid, nor are they exclusive, see *Bridge v Deacons* [1984] A.C. 705. It is clear that as a matter of law, covenants outside the established categories of business sale cases and employment cases *may* be upheld if the applicable legal principles are satisfied. As Evans L.J. stated in *Dawnay Day & Co Ltd v De Braconier D'Alphen* [1997] I.R.L.R. 442: "The covenant may be enforced when the covenantee has a legitimate interest, of whatever kind, to protect, and when the covenant is no wider than is necessary to protect that interest." See also *Stenhouse Ltd v Phillips* [1974] A.C. 391 and *Bridge v Deacons*.

It is sometimes difficult to draw a line between what is in substance an agreement analogous to an employment contract and one which is much closer to a business sale agreement. This problem most commonly arises when considering partnerships, especially professional partnerships and also in transactions which combine the sale of a business and the relationship of employer and employee.

Hadsley v Dayer-Smith [1914] A.C. 979 concerned an estate agent's partnership in which an article of the partnership agreement prevented competition by a former partner for a period of ten years after he ceased to be a partner. The case was dealt with by the court on the same basis as if it had been a business sale. In *Jenkins v Reid* [1948] 1 All E.R. 471, which concerned medical practitioners who were not partners, counsel for the defendant urged the court to treat the case as analogous to a sale of a business, whereas the plaintiff claimed that the matter should be treated as an employment case. Romer J. took the latter course. In *Whitehill v Bradford* [1952] Ch. 236 at first instance Dankwerts J. considered a restraint of trade clause in a medical partnership agreement, neither on the basis of it being analogous to an employment contract nor a sale of business contract. He looked at the matter from a practical point of view which was that all the parties had been legally advised about the ambit of the agreement and were professional people. In the Court of Appeal, Evershed M.R. rejected the employment approach for the reason that this was a case where the outgoing partner had sold his interest to the remaining partners.

In *Bridge v Deacons* [1984] A.C. 705 the Privy Council had to deal with a restrictive covenant which applied to a solicitors' partnership. Counsel for the appellants was so conscious of the special approach adopted in employment cases that, on behalf of the partner who had resigned and was claiming that the restrictive covenant was illegal, he urged the court to follow the US practice and view a partnership problem in the same way as an employee case. Counsel for the respondents urged the court to adopt an approach analogous to that of a business sale case. The court declined both suggestions and decided the matter on the basis of what constituted the legitimate interests of the respondents which they were entitled to protect. Their approach seems to be very close to that of Dankwerts J. in *Whitehill v Bradford*.

The reason for the enthusiasm to categorise an agreement as falling within/without a specific contract type is based on the realisation that the courts do not look at restraints associated with the business sale in the same way as in employment cases. Whereas a special rule in employment cases was borne of judicial perception of inequality of bargaining power, the opposite is generally true in sale of business cases and generally the scope and effect of covenants will be the result of negotiation between the parties (see *Emmersub XXXVI Inc v Wheatley* July 3, 1998 QBD, Wright J., [unreported] where the duration of a covenant at four years was challenged as unreasonable but the Judge placed weight on the fact that it was a negotiated compromise between three and five years). It is assumed that the parties are of equal bargaining power and that the covenantee, the vendor, is getting an enhanced price of his business by selling its goodwill: see *North Western Salt Co Ltd v Electrolytic Alkali Co Ltd* [1914] A.C. 461, *per* Viscount Haldane L.C.:

> . . . when the controversy is as to the validity of an agreement, say for service, by which someone who has little opportunity of choice has precluded himself from earning his living by the exercise of his calling after the period of service is over, the law looks jealously at the bargain; but when the question is one of the validity of a commercial agreement for regulating their trade relations, entered into between two firms or companies, the law adopts a somewhat different attitude—it still looks carefully to the interest of the public, but it regards the parties as the best judges of what is reasonable as between themselves.

And see *Blake v Blake* (1967) 111 S.J. 715 and *George Silverman Ltd v Silverman* (1969) 113 S.J. 563: a sale of shares and an associated service agreement containing a restraint was treated as analogous to a business sale. In *Silverman*, Phillimore L.J. also gave weight to the fact that the parties themselves were well able to judge where their reasonable commercial interests lay:

> These parties were well able, I have no doubt, on both sides to look after themselves in this trade, they were advised as they freely negotiated the whole of this package deal. In such circumstances it would be wrong where there is nothing to suggest that there is anything contrary to public interest to interfere with the agreement that they made.

(See also *Dawnay Day*, Evans L.J. p. 446–447, who quoted this passage).

In *Alliance Paper Group v Prestwich* [1996] I.R.L.R. 25, the Court was expressly influenced in its approach to a restrictive convenant in a service agreement by the fact that the defendant had been party to an associated share sale agreement.

There is a second distinction drawn between employment and business sales agreements which, it is submitted, is a heresy on two counts. It is contained in many judgments including that of Lord Denning M.R. in *Office Overload Ltd v Gunn* [1977] F.S.R. 39: "In master-and-servant cases, the court will not restrain a servant from competing; but in a vendor-and-purchaser case, it will restrain the vendor from competing". This notion, also taken up by Sellers L.J. in *Gledhow Autoparts Ltd v Delaney* [1965] 3 All E.R. 288 seems to be based on Lord Parker's words in *Herbert Morris Ltd v Saxelby* [1916] 1 A.C. 688 and the judgment in *Attwood v Lamont* [1920] 3 K.B. 571 of Younger L.J. These *can* support the idea that a purchaser of a business can restrain competition per se by a vendor. However, such a pronouncement cannot be taken literally as the concept of reasonableness plays a part in business sales cases—possibly not such a great part as in employment contracts—but still a significant one, and in any case Lord Parker went on to say that a restriction must be confined to an area within which competition will in all probability inure to the injury of the purchaser (i.e. there must exist an interest which merits protection from injury). Furthermore a purchaser cannot seek indefinite protection from competition as that would fall foul of Article 81/Chapter I.

In many cases covenants are entered into in transactions that combine both the sale of a business with an employment contract, whereby the purchaser of a business retains the services of the vendor as an employee after the sale. In such circumstances Evan L.J. in *Dawnay Day* (quoted above, para.10.2) rejected the submission that it was necessary to decide into which of the two categories the transaction, and therefore the covenant should be placed, so as to know whether the more stringent test of reasonableness, which is appropriate in employment cases should be applied. Evans L.J. continued:

> Both Millett J. in *Allied Dunbar (Frank Weisinger) Ltd v Weisinger* [1988] I.R.L.R. 60 and Herman J. in *Systems Reliability Holdings plc v Smith* [1990] I.R.L.R. 377 held that it was wrong and unnecessary to categorise the cases strictly in this way. The question is one on substance, not form (per Millett J. at 64), and the court has always "to try and apply the test of reasonableness to the facts and circumstances of the particular case" (per Harman J. at 382). These judgements were followed by Robert Weilher J. in the present [*Dawnay Day*] case, and in my judgement he was right to do so.

(For a more detailed discussion of *Dawnay Day*, see Chapter 8).

The Courts will therefore not look at any covenant in an employment contract in isolation, if the circumstances that lead to the employment are inter related to a business sale. It is worth considering in some detail the case of *Allied Dunbar (Frank Weisinger) Ltd v Frank Weisinger* [1988] I.R.L.R. 60. The facts were that Weisinger had for many years been a self-employed "sales associate" of Allied Dunbar Assurance plc. His income was derived from a commission based on the value of insurance policies and investments sold by him. These products included life assurance contracts, unit trusts and bonds, personal retirement policies and executive pension schemes.

He was very successful. In 1985 he earned about £194,000. He had approximately 600 clients based mainly in South Wales and the Home Counties. Almost all his business was based on personal and social connections and personal recommendation. He did almost no cold calling. New clients were obtained by recommendation from existing clients or from solicitors or accountants which, or clients of which, were among Weisinger's satisfied clients. He came to know most of his substantial clients personally and socially.

A disadvantage of being a sales associate was that it was difficult for such a person to realise any goodwill for his business connections when he retired. In order to remedy this Allied Dunbar conceived the idea of practice buyouts. In November 1985 Weisinger, then aged 50, entered into an agreement with an

Allied Dunbar company (which later became the plaintiffs). Clause 8 of the agreement stated:

> The vendor hereby undertakes that he, his servants or agents will not without the consent of the purchaser approach, canvass, solicit, entice or otherwise contact, whether directly or indirectly, any person who is at the time a client or customer of the practice for the purpose of selling or issuing life assurance or pension or annuity policies or contracts for the provision of any other financial service or commodity which competes in any way with any of the business which Allied Dunbar carries out either directly or through any of its subsidiaries, or with its sales associates or contracted independent intermediaries.

Clause 9 stated:

> The vendor hereby undertakes with the purchaser that he will not without the consent of the purchaser during the period commencing on the date hereof and ending two years after he ceases to be a consultant to the purchaser pursuant to clause 15 below, either directly or indirectly engage in or be concerned with or interested in (whether on his own account in partnership or as a director or employee, consultant, shareholder or otherwise howsoever) in any business which involves the selling (whether as principal, agent or intermediary) or issuing of life assurance or pension or annuity policies or contracts for the provision of any other financial services or commodity which competes in any way with any of the businesses which Allied Dunbar carries out either directly or through any of its subsidiaries or with the purchaser's financial management consultants or contracted independent intermediaries. This clause shall not prohibit the holding (directly or through nominees) of investments listed on the stock exchange as long as not more than 10 per cent of the issued shares or stock of any class of any one company shall be so held without the written consent of the purchaser.

Millett J. pointed out that clause 8, a non-solicitation clause, was of a kind which the court would have implied in any event. The price paid to Weisinger was for both the benefit of the restraints contained in clauses 8 and 9 and for the goodwill of his business. That goodwill comprised:

(a) his personal connections with clients including the commissions and business that could be expected to be derived from those clients in the future; and

(b) potential commission and business that could be expected to be derived in the future from other persons recommended to the plaintiffs by satisfied clients of Weisinger.

After the sale of his business Weisinger acted as a sales training consultant to Allied Dunbar. However, this arrangement proved unsuccessful and his consultancy was terminated by mutual consent after 16 months. Weisinger then wanted to work for another financial service group which mainly dealt with pensions business. His prospective employer agreed that clause 8 was valid but wished to obtain Weisinger's release from it. This was refused. It was claimed that clause 9 was unreasonable. The plaintiffs moved for an injunction. It appears that during the hearing, Weisinger, in order to persuade the plaintiffs not to rely on clause 9 or to persuade the judge that it provided unnecessary protection for them, offered to account to Allied Dunbar for any commission earned by him during the two-year period after the end of his consultancy even if clients had approached him themselves. This was giving the plaintiffs more than they were entitled to under clause 8. The plaintiffs refused this offer. They stated that adequate protection against the risk of those clients following Weisinger after the end of the two-year period could only be achieved by imposing a period of discontinuity to service them. Weisinger then made a further offer: he would refuse to have any dealings with or give any advice to former clients during the two-year period and, if so required, to refer such clients to plaintiffs. The plaintiffs refused this offer as it did not prevent Weisinger from dealing with new clients recommended to him by former clients of the practice or by accountants or solicitors. Weisinger then made a further offer: that he would refer to plaintiffs all such new clients who approached him during the two-year period. The plaintiffs refused this further offer and insisted on enforcing the strict term of clause 9. This did not merely prevent Weisinger from dealing with former clients of the practice who approached him, or with new clients introduced by them, or by professional firms but from being involved in any capacity in a business which competed with that of the plaintiffs or their parent company, Allied Dunbar. In effect, this meant in the greater part of the entire financial services sector in the UK.

The judge in stating his general approach said:

> It is well settled that, in considering the validity of covenants in restraint of trade, very different principles apply where the covenant is taken for the protection of the goodwill of a business sold by the covenantor to the covenantee from those that apply where it is taken by an employer from an employee. In the former case (though not in the latter) it may be legitimate to protect the covenantee from any competition by the covenantor, and the courts adopt a much less stringent approach to the covenant, recognising that the parties who negotiated it are the best judges of what is reasonable between them. The inclusion of such a covenant may be necessary to enable the covenantor to realise a proper price for the goodwill of his business and, by upholding the validity of the covenant, the courts may well facilitate trade rather than fetter it.

He decided that the correct approach was that applied in vendor-and-purchaser cases; the fact that the two-year period of restraint was not to begin until the termination of the consultancy agreement gave it the superfluous but deceptive appearance of being a covenant between employer and employee. The judge held clause 9 to be reasonable. It was argued that a clause which did not include a geographical restraint but which was restricted to non-dealing with existing clients or new clients introduced by them or by professional firms would have been sufficient. The judge rejected this by saying:

> The fact is that a non-dealing covenant, particularly one extending to new clients, is difficult to police and enforce, and depends to an unacceptable degree on the

> honest co-operation of the covenantor. It was conceded that such a covenant was not ideal, but it was submitted that there was no reason to doubt the defendant's honesty, and for once, in a case of this kind, I am disposed to agree. The defendant has conducted himself with unusual candour and fairness. He has been open about his intentions and generous in his offers. But in my judgment that is beside the point. The purchaser of a business who is paying £386,000 for the goodwill is entitled to protect his investment by a suitably worded covenant which does not depend for its effectiveness on the vendor's honesty and co-operation. At the very least, if he obtains the vendor's agreement to the inclusion of a covenant which avoids these dangers, it hardly lies in the vendor's mouth to argue that he should have been content with less.

In *Prontaprint plc v Landon Litho Ltd* [1987] F.S.R. 315, L was a former franchisee of P who, after the expiry of the ten-year term of a franchise agreement, had continued in business in the same premises operating the same type of service but under a new name. P sought an injunction for breach of a clause which read:

> The licensee agrees that he shall not at any time within three years of the determination of this agreement engage in or be concerned or interested directly or indirectly in the provision of the service or anything similar thereto within a radius of half a mile of the premises or within a radius of three miles from any premises in the United Kingdom at which the service or anything similar thereto is carried on by any other licensee of the licensor or by the licensor itself.

It was argued by P that although this case was neither analogous to a business sale case nor an employer/employee case, L had enjoyed the goodwill of the Prontaprint name for ten years. Whitford J. said that although this case did not concern the sale of a piece of property, the circumstances were closer to a business sale than to an employment agreement. P wanted to be able to grant franchises to interested parties and therefore wanted to ensure that he was in a position to prevent competition against franchisees whom they might appoint by persons who had been franchisees but were no longer. He granted an injunction.

In *Systems Reliability Holdings plc v Smith* [1990] I.R.L.R. 377 Harman J. had to consider a claim by the plaintiff company against Smith who had been employed by them for a number of years and had then purchased shares totalling 1.6 per cent in the company. Subsequently, however, he was dismissed on grounds of misconduct and received nearly £250,000 for his holding. The share sale agreement contained a clause which stated that for a period of 17 months he was not directly or indirectly to "carry on or be engaged or interested . . . in any business which competes with any business carried on at the date of this agreement . . . by the company or any of its subsidiaries". A further clause provided that:

> . . . none of the vendors at any time after the date of this agreement shall disclose or use for his own benefit or that of any other person any confidential information which he now possesses concerning the business or affairs or products of or services

> supplied by the company or any of the subsidiaries or of any person having dealings with the company or any of its subsidiaries.

A short time after his dismissal and of the sale of his shares in the company, S set up his own business competing with the company. Harman J., after a full trial, declined to apply the tests as to reasonableness set out in the employer/employee cases. He stated that where a purchaser buys the whole of a business from a number of vendors, some of whom have only small stakes in the goodwill and business which is being sold but who are paid a price for their shares no different from that paid to other vendors and who thereby receive a substantial sum of money, the court should apply the tests as set out in the vendor/purchaser cases. The courts will decline to apply that test solely in relation to those who were either controlling shareholders or who had major interests. Applying that test to the evidence presented to him, he granted an injunction for the remainder of the 17-month period. As the business was demonstrated to be of an international nature it was reasonable that the restriction should be worldwide. He went on to hold that the clause in the share sale agreement restricting the defendant from using or disclosing confidential information was reasonable in the interests of the parties and would be enforced. He stated that in determining the reasonableness of an express covenant deliberately imposed between a vendor and a purchaser of business, guidance could not be drawn from the limitations on implied covenants restricting the disclosure of confidential information by an ex-employee as set out by the Court of Appeal in *Faccenda Chicken Ltd v Fowler*. Where there is a covenant between a vendor and a purchaser which is plainly intended to protect the information which the purchaser hoped to get the benefit of by his purchase of the company and its know-how the reasonableness of that covenant should be judged by the tests appropriate between persons selling such a business which has the information. It is in that capacity that the vendors make the covenants, not as employees or servants of the business. On the evidence presented to him he found that it was reasonable to restrict the defendant from using or disclosing the confidential knowledge which he had in his head concerning the business or services supplied by the company but as he found that the value to the plaintiffs of that information was gradually decreasing it would be unreasonable to extend the protection of the covenant beyond the date when the competition covenants ceased to have effect (i.e. the remainder of the 17-month period).

In *TSC Europe (UK) Limited v Massey*, [1999] I.R.L.R. 22 a non-solicitation convenant was imposed on Mr Massey both in the Share Purchase Agreement whereby he sold his strategic management and consulting business relating to call centres and customer management applications, and in his contract for employment. On the question of reasonableness of the covenant in the employment contract the Judge held that it was part of the overall commercial bargain between the vendors and the employer and its shareholder which had been negotiated at arm's length and the convenants were taken for the protection of the goodwill of the business sold. The covenant, however, was held to be an unreasonable restraint of trade because first, it prohibited Mr Massey from soliciting *any employee* of the company without reference to his or her importance to the business (even though at the time of the sale of the business there were only 21 employees and with the call centre market place in its infancy it would have been extremely difficult to replace employees with people of suitable qualifications and experience). Secondly because it prohibited Mr Massey from soliciting any such employees even if their employment with the company commenced after Mr Massey had left the company. (Compare with *Alliance Paper* above where the restrictive covenant had neither of these vices.)

Chapter 11

Vendor's Ability to Compete with the Purchaser in the Absence of Express Covenants

In *Trego v Hunt* [1896] A.C. 7, Lord Herschell said "I think it must be treated as settled that whenever the goodwill of a business is sold the vendor does not, by reason only of that sale, come under restriction not to carry on any competing business". However, it is the extent to which the vendor is free to carry on trade and yet directly compete with the purchaser for the very goodwill which he has just sold which is circumscribed by the law even in the absence of express covenant. If there are no express provisions made in the contract of sale then the courts will, assuming no contrary intention is manifested by the parties, imply the following three terms or any of them.

11.1 The vendor must not solicit/canvass the customers of his old business

(See *Labouchere v Dawson* (1872) L.R. 13 Eq. 322; *Ginesi v Cooper & Co* (1880) L.R. 14 Ch. D. 596 and *Leggott v Barrett* (1880) L.R. 15 Ch. D. 306.)

The matter was further considered by the House of Lords in *Trego v Hunt*. That case concerned a partnership between Trego and Hunt in which Trego owned all the goodwill of the partnership business. It was found that Hunt had employed a clerk to copy for him the names, addresses and business of all of the firm's customers and he admitted that the list had been made so as to acquire information which could enable him, when the partnership expired, to canvass those people and to endeavour to obtain their custom for himself. Trego brought an action against Hunt and sought an injunction to restrain him from making any copy of or extract from the partnership books for any purpose other than for partnership business. This case did not directly deal with the sale of goodwill but the members of the House of Lords treated it as being equivalent to such a sale. All members of the court gave judgments in favour of implying a term that the vendor must not solicit/canvass the customers of his old business. Lord Herschell said:

> If a person who has previously been a partner of a firm sets up in business on his own account and appeals generally for custom, he only does that which any member of the public may do, and which those carrying on the same trade are already doing. It is true that those who were former customers of the firm to which he belonged may of their own accord transfer their custom to him; but this incidental advantage is unavoidable, and does not result from any act of his. He only conducts his business in precisely the same way as he would if he had never been a member of the firm to which he previously belonged. But when he specifically and directly appeals to those who were customers of the previous firm, he seeks to take advantage of the connection previously formed by his old firm, and of the knowledge of that connection which he has previously acquired, to take that which constitutes the goodwill away from the persons to whom it had been sold and to restore it to himself. It is said, indeed, that he may not represent himself as a successor of the old firm, or as carrying on a continuation of their business, but this in many cases appears to me of little importance, and of small practical advantage, if canvassing the customers of the old firm were allowed without restraint.

He went on to say that possible bases for the decision of the court were either that a man cannot derogate from his own grant or that there is an implied term in the contract of sale that prevents the same happening.

A more recent application of *Trego v Hunt* is found in *Boorne v Wickeer* [1927] 1 Ch. 667. In this case, a deed of partnership provided that on the death of a partner the surviving partner should acquire the deceased partner's share of the capital, property and assets of the partnership business, or alternatively, that the surviving partner might elect to have the whole of the assets of the partnership realised and divided. The defendant was a former employee of the partnership who had joined competitors of the partnership business and commenced to solicit the customers of that business. He had entered no covenant restraining him from soliciting the customers of the business in his capacity as an employee, but he was an executor of the dead partner and bound to give effect to the testator's contract. The plaintiff alleged that as an executor he was bound not to do anything to depreciate the goodwill of the partnership which he was selling. Tomlin J. held that the principles laid down in *Trego v Hunt* extended to the vendor's executors carrying out a contract for the sale of the goodwill of a business and ordered that the executor be restrained from soliciting customers of that business. He said that the vendor's executor:

> may or may not have actual knowledge of who the customers of the firm are, though he certainly has every opportunity of ascertaining them, but whether or not he has actual knowledge of them, it seems to me to be against common honesty that he should be free at one and the same time to complete his testator's contract and to snatch away from the purchaser the property which he is affecting to convey to him.

The rule in *Trego v Hunt* does not apply, however, to a person whose property is being sold compulsorily by the operation of the law, as in the case of a man who has been made bankrupt and whose trustee has sold his property. See *Walker v Mottram* (1881) L.R. 19 Ch. D. 355, where it was held that the bankrupt could not be prevented from soliciting customers from his former business which had been sold by his trustee in bankruptcy. The reason for this appears to be because the trustee in bankruptcy sells without the consent of the bankrupt and therefore the bankrupt cannot be described as the vendor. See also *Farey v Cooper* [1927] 2 K.B. 384 in which it was held that a debtor who had assigned his business and goodwill to a trustee for the benefit of creditors was not precluded, in the absence of express restriction, from soliciting customers of the old business even though the deed assigning that business contained a covenant by him in which he undertook to aid the trustee to realise the property assigned and the distribution of proceeds among the creditors. See further *Green and Sons (Northampton) Ltd v Morris* [1914] 1 Ch. 562.

There are two further comments to be made about the ruling in *Trego v Hunt*. The first is whether the prohibition is confined to soliciting/canvassing actual customers of the old business or whether it extends to potential customers. In our view, in the absence of any authority on the point, by applying the principle that the courts are determined to protect the goodwill of the business which has been purchased, and as potential customers must surely be included within the phrase "goodwill", they cannot be solicited by the vendor. The phrase "potential customers" means those who have made at least some contact with the business, e.g. by enquiring about products and prices but its meaning does not extend beyond that.

Secondly, it has been suggested that the restriction on canvassing/solicitation may also extend so as to prevent a vendor from dealing with customers of his former business even if they approach him. It seems that in *Ginesi v Cooper* (1880) L.R. 14 Ch. D. 596 Jessel M.R., albeit obiter, expressed a view that the rule did extend that far. The basis for his decision seems to have been that if such dealings were not prevented by the courts, it would undermine the goodwill of the business sold as much as active solicitation. However, in *Leggott v Barrett* (1890) L.R. 15 Ch. D. 306, the Court of Appeal disagreed with this view on the basis that there was no implied duty on the vendor to shut his door against a customer of his former business who came to the new business of his own free will. In *Trego v Hunt* [1896] A.C. 7, Lord MacNaghten specifically rejected Jessell M.R.'s view, as did Lord Davey. It is submitted, that their view is to be preferred. Whatever test one uses as a basis for implying the duty that the vendor should not solicit or canvass the customers of his old business, whether it is the fact that a man may not derogate from his own grant, or is based on commercial morality, or common honesty, it is quite clearly not in the public interest in the absence of express covenant that the voluntary customer should be rejected by the vendor.

11.1.1 The scope of the injunction

An injunction to prevent a vendor soliciting and/or canvassing customers of the old business can be framed simply viz:

> That the defendant, his servants or agents be restrained from personally and/or directly canvassing and/or soliciting in anyway all who, on the [day of sale], were customers of the business of the defendant formerly carried on as X at Y street in Z town and which was sold to the plaintiff on A day of B until the trial of this action or further order.

An illustration of an injunction which clearly went too far was given by Lord Davey in *Trego v Hunt*, when he referred to the earlier case of *Ginesi v Cooper*, in which case the injunction restrained the defendant from in any way endeavouring to obtain "the custom of such of the customers of the plaintiff as were customers of the old firm, or from attempting to take away any portion of the business bought by the plaintiff". It is quite clear that this form of order would prevent the defendant from issuing public advertisements, or generally carrying on business in competition with the plaintiff, whereas in fact the rule in *Trego v Hunt* quite clearly does not prevent him doing those things.

11.2 The use of business secrets by the vendor

The second example of a term which will be implied by law on the sale of a business prevents the vendor from using in his new business any business secrets which were attached to the former business and which were not specifically excluded from the sale of that business.

11.3 Representations by the vendor that he is carrying on the business sold

This duty was referred to in *Trego v Hunt*: Lord Davey said that

> the vendor may advertise himself as having been a partner in or the founder or manager of the business which he has sold, provided he does not represent the business which he is carrying on is the same business as or identical with that which he has sold.

In *David and Matthews, Re* [1899] 1 Ch. 378, Romer J. held that the name of a partnership constituted part of the goodwill and that a vendor, whilst able to carry on a similar or rival business could not carry on that business so as to lead others to the belief that he was carrying on the partnership business; the reason for this seems to have been that by doing so the vendor would be wrongly appropriating to himself part of the goodwill which he had just sold, and that he would be acting fraudulently towards his customers.

What if the vendor has the same name as that of the business he has sold? This occurred in *May v May* (1914) 31 R.P.C. 325. There it was said, obiter, that if the defendant had carried on a rival business with the same name without any attempt to pretend that the new business was the old one or in any way associated with it then no injunction would have issued. However, there was clear evidence that the defendant had intended to confuse customers by the fraudulent device of claiming an association with the old business which he had made over to his creditors. Coleridge J. said

> Prima facie every person has a right to trade in his own name, but what he has not a right to do is to pretend that he is connected with another business, and to utilise the name of that other business to palm off his own goods as the goods of that other business.

11.4 Conclusion

It is possible to sum up the implied duties of a vendor who has sold his business as follows:

(a) he can advertise generally that he has set up a new business and can compete with the old business;

(b) he can serve former customers who come to him, but he cannot solicit or canvass them;

(c) he can say that he was a partner etc. of the old business but he cannot represent that he is now carrying on the same business as the old one or in any way pretend that the new business is associated with the old one;

(d) he cannot use any of the business secrets of the old business which formed part of the goodwill which was sold.

Chapter 12

Express Covenants

It is usual to find that a business sale agreement contains express terms which govern the position of the parties post sale regarding restraint of trade and business secrets. Moreover, frequently there will be an agreement protecting business secrets during the negotiations for sale in the event of a failure to finalise the sale. These are fully considered at para.20.1 *et seq*.

The problems associated with implied terms so far as the purchaser is concerned are that they permit the vendor to act in ways which, although they do not directly allow him to derogate from his grant, may indirectly produce such a result. For example, although the vendor cannot directly solicit in person or canvass customers of the old business, he can set up a rival business and advertise its presence to everyone including his old customers. What the purchaser can achieve via express terms is considerable. He can prevent not only solicitation but any dealings with previous customers. He can prevent the vendor announcing that he was a partner or founder of the old business and, most importantly, he can prevent the vendor setting up a rival business in certain limited circumstances. Therefore, express terms are vital to protect further the purchaser's position. These terms are subject, so far as restraint of trade is concerned, to the test of reasonableness. The reason why the courts will enquire as to the reasonableness of any express terms which may restrain the vendor's trade is because of the public interest that a man who has sold his business should not be prevented from working in that area in which he is most skilled. The courts examine the goodwill of the business in question in order to decide whether a restraint is reasonable. The extent of the goodwill inevitably will circumscribe the ambit of what is reasonable. Having given value for goodwill, the purchaser will expect to be allowed to claim that any restraint attached to goodwill or reasonably referable to it is protectable. In this context, that means that it is necessary to examine whether the purchaser has an interest meriting protection and further whether the restraint is reasonable in the public interest. It is generally assumed that the restraint is reasonable as between the parties. So far as business secrets are concerned, the express terms seek to improve on the implied duty by identifying what is secret. The remainder of this section is concerned solely with examination of restraint of trade problems as the general law of business secrets applies in this area.

12.1 An interest meriting protection

As in all other areas of restraint of trade law, one cannot have a covenant not to compete per se; it must be attached to an interest meriting protection. Apart from business secrets the interest which a purchaser has which merits protection is goodwill. In *Vancouver Malt and Sake Brewing Co Ltd v Vancouver Breweries Ltd* [1934] A.C. 181, the appellants had a licence to brew a number of liquors but had only ever brewed sake. The respondents only brewed beer. There was a sale agreement between the parties in which the appellants sold to the respondents the goodwill in their brewing licence except insofar as it related to the manufacture of sake. There was a restrictive covenant in the contract by which the appellants agreed not to brew beer. The court concluded that the sale was a sham. The appellants had no goodwill to sell regarding the manufacture of beer and it was that which was purportedly restrained. The covenant was therefore a simple agreement not to compete—a covenant in gross. Lord MacMillan said:

> The receipt of a sum of money can generally be shown to be advantageous to a businessman, but his liberty to trade is not an asset which the law will permit him to barter for money except in special circumstances and within well recognised limitations.

Nowadays such an agreement could be found to amount to illegal market sharing under competion law, and the parties would be at risk of significant fines.

Protectable goodwill could appear to be only that which attaches to the business which the vendor has sold. If the purchaser attempts to protect some other goodwill (e.g. of another current business or a future one) then the clause may fail for want of a proper interest meriting protection. See *British Reinforced Concrete Engineering Co Ltd v Schelff* [1921] 2 Ch. 563. This case largely concerned the question whether, in an agreement for the sale of a business, the reasonableness of a vendor's restrictive covenant was to be judged by the extent of the circumstances of the business sold or by the extent and range of any business of the purchaser of which after transfer to him it was to form part. After reviewing the authorities, Younger L.J. concluded that a covenant which was exacted for the protection of a business with which the covenantor has never had any connection is no better than a covenant in gross. He concluded that the covenant was too wide as instead of pursuing the legitimate purpose of the protection of the business sold, it attempted to protect other businesses of the purchaser. Particular support for the views set out in this case are found in *Henry Leetham & Sons Ltd v Johnstone-White* [1907] 1 Ch. 322, though there is a contrary decision in *Smedley's Ltd v Smedley* [1921] 2

Ch. 580. In that case, the argument by the defendant that the court ought not to consider what was reasonably necessary for the protection of the three businesses already carried on by the purchasers at the time of the sale, but to confine its attention only to the business actually sold and consider whether the covenant was reasonably necessary for the protection of the goodwill of that particular business was rejected as "an entirely novel argument" by Sargant J. Until recently it has been accepted that the *Leetham* case governed. However, it is important to examine this proposition in the light of the decision of the Privy Council in *Stenhouse Australia Ltd v Phillips* [1974] A.C. 391. There, Lord Wilberforce analysed the *Leetham* case and said that it was quite clearly a case where the agreement, as interpreted by the Court of Appeal, was with one company of a group, which company had a limited business whereas the restraint was expressed in far wider terms, extending to the area covered by the operations of the group as a whole. However, the evidence in the instant case showed that the business of the Stenhouse Group was controlled and co-ordinated by Stenhouse Australia Ltd and all funds generated by each of the companies were received by the plaintiffs. The subsidiary companies were merely agencies or instrumentalities through which the plaintiff company directed its integrated business. Not only did the plaintiff company have a real interest in protecting the businesses of the subsidiaries, but the real interest in so doing was that of the plaintiff company. Lord Wilberforce went on to say that it was not necessary to resort to a concept of a group enterprise to support this conclusion. The case was, simply, that of the plaintiff's business being to some extent handled for it by subsidiary companies. It would therefore seem that it is possible for there to be a valid interest meriting protection for the benefit of a group of companies, even though the restraint of trade clause is contained in a contract with one of those companies so long as there is proof of an identity of interest between the contracting company and the rest of the group. It is submitted that the view expressed by Lord Wilberforce in *Stenhouse* takes account of the realities of modern commercial law.

12.2 Reasonableness

12.2.1 The ambit of the activities restricted

In *Goldsoll v Goldman* [1915] 1 Ch. 292, the Court of Appeal had to consider a restraint of trade clause which restricted the vendor from trading as a dealer in "real or imitation jewellery". It was found as a fact that the business sold by him dealt substantially in imitation jewellery. It was admitted that the business of the dealer in real jewellery is not the same as that of a dealer in imitation jewellery and therefore the court concluded that the provision was too wide for it was not limited to what was reasonably necessary for the protection of the covenantee's business. In the *British Reinforced Concrete* case [1921] All E.R. 202, a covenant prevented the defendant from "acting as a servant of any person concerned or interested in the business or manufacture or sale of road reinforcements in any part of the United Kingdom". This covenant was struck down for two reasons. The first was that it prevented the defendant from manufacturing road reinforcements, something which the company which he had sold to the plaintiffs had never done. Secondly, it was said to be too wide as it would prevent the defendant from working for a trust company which held shares in another road reinforcement company. Whilst the second ground may now appear somewhat fanciful, especially in the light of the authorities which deprecate such an *in terrorem* approach to construction, there can be no doubt that the first ground would still be valid today. In *Connors Brothers Ltd v Connors* [1940] 4 All E.R. 179, the Privy Council had to construe a restrictive covenant which prevented the respondent from "directly or indirectly engaging in any other sardine business". The court said that if the respondent held a small number of shares in such a competing company he might not be in breach of that clause, but if he held the controlling interest then he might. In *Ronbar Enterprises Ltd v Green* [1954] 2 All E.R. 266, the Court of Appeal had to construe the following covenant: ". . . the partner whose share is purchased shall not for five years from such date [i.e. the time of purchase] directly or indirectly carry on or be engaged or interested in any business similar to or competing with the business of the partnership". It was argued on behalf of the defendant that there had been no breach of that provision because on its true construction it did not extend to the rendering of services for a salary or wages as distinct from being engaged in business on one's own account. The Court of Appeal disagreed with this view. Jenkins L.J. said that the words were apt, particularly in view of the word "engaged", to include a case where the party, subject to the restriction, takes employment in a business of either of the kinds mentioned at a salary or wages, as well as a case in which he embarks on such a business on his own account, or in partnership. It had also been argued that if the clause did extend to prevent the defendant working as a salaried employee, then it was on that account too wide. The court also rejected this approach.

12.2.2 Geographical limits

The broad principles of how a court should approach the question of geographical limits in business sale cases were set out in *Connors Brothers Ltd v Connors* by Viscount Maugham. He pointed out that since the question of reasonableness was a matter of law for the court, in relation to the trade of a large manufacturer or merchant, it was not necessary to prove to the satisfaction of the court that the business which the covenant was designed to protect had been carried on in every part of the area mentioned in the covenant. He said:

> In the cases in which the area has been the whole of England, or a substantial part of it, such as 100 miles or 150 miles from a named town, it has never been held that

> the covenantee was under an obligation to prove that the business has been carried on within all the towns and villages within the area. In *Nordenfelt v Maxim Nordenfelt Guns and Ammunition Co* [1894] A.C. 535, no attempt was made to prove that all the governments of the world, or even of the civilised world, had ordered goods from the company, though the greater number no doubt had done so. A great deal no doubt depends on the nature of the business and the area in question.

As to the fundamental question of whether the geographical limitations set out in the restraint of trade clause are necessary to further the purchaser's legitimate business interests, the courts have given different answers depending on the different facts of each case. In *Nordenfelt v Maxim Nordenfelt Guns and Ammunition Co Ltd* [1894] A.C. 535, a worldwide limitation was upheld because of the nature of the business and the limited number of customers which it served. It was essentially a worldwide business selling armaments and guns to governments.

On the other hand, in *Goldsoll v Goldman* it was held that a restrictive covenant was unnecessarily large insofar as it was intended to cover not merely the United Kingdom and the Isle of Man, but also a number of foreign countries as well. There was no evidence that any business has ever been done outside the United Kingdom or the Isle of Man. In *Vancouver Malt and Sake Brewing Co Ltd v Vancouver Breweries Ltd* [1934] A.C. 181, a worldwide restriction was struck down as the extent of the business sold was confined to British Columbia. Finally, in *Ronbar Enterprises Ltd v Green* [1954] 2 All E.R. 266, the Court of Appeal concluded that the phrase "shall not . . . directly or indirectly carry on or be engaged or interested in any business similar to or competing with the business of the partnership" because of the words "similar to or" meant literally that if the defendant were to carry on a business similar to the business of the partnership in any part of the world, then he would be in breach of the covenant. However, the court still found for the plaintiffs as the offending words were severed.

12.2.3 Time

In *Connors Brothers Ltd v Connors*, it was said that if a restriction as to space is considered to be reasonable, it is seldom in a case where the sale of goodwill is concerned that the restriction can be held to be unreasonable because there is no limit as to time. It is submitted that this is an old fashioned view and that the issues of time and geographical scope are not always inextricably linked. An express limit as to time has in fact become much more essential with the application of competition law where indefinite clauses are often found to be an illegal restriction.

In *Pellow v Ivey* (1933) 49 T.L.R. 422 a lifetime restriction on a vendor from setting up a business similar to one sold by him was held to be unreasonable because the agreement afforded the plaintiffs more than adequate protection.

Under the common law doctrine, the position might have been different if the sale had involved business secrets as well as goodwill.

In Scotland in *Randev v Pattar* [1985] S.L.T. 270 it was doubted at the interlocutory stage whether five years was necessarily required in a covenant against competing on the sale of a hotel.

The term of an agreement, which contains a restriction must be for a definite period and cannot be subject to automatic renewals for an indefinite time, as that would be viewed as an indefinite agreement and would therefore be likely to make the clause, if not the whole agreement, void under common law, and potentially under competition law too. (See *Days Medical Aids v Pihsiang Machinery Manufacturers Co Ltd and others* [2004] EWHC 44, WBC (Comm). Discussed in Chapter 2, para.2.4.

12.3 Statutory and EU provisions

12.3.1 UK law

Previously one had to consider the Restrictive Trade Practices Act 1976 ("RTPA") and specifically whether the agreement for the sale of a business had two parties accepting restrictions. In many cases the more common restrictions in such an agreement would be exempt under the Restrictive Trade Practices (Sale and Purchase and Share Subscription Agreements) (Goods) Order 1989 (SI 1989/1081), or the corresponding Order for services. With the repeal of the RTPA by the Competition Act 1998, the RTPA only continued to be relevant for agreements existing prior to March 2000 which may be void if particulars of registrable restrictions had not been furnished to the Office of Fair Trading (see further Chapter 22 para.22.1). As of May 1, 2007 all agreements including those furnished to the OFT under the RTPA and cleared under section 21(2) RTPA are subject to the full force of competition law.

For new agreements relating to the sale of a business they will usually be considered a merger under the Enterprise Act 2002 (formerly the Fair Trading Act 1973) and excluded from the Competition Act 1998 (Sch.1 para.1(1)). To the extent that the agreement contains any standard non-compete clauses and other relevant restrictions between the vendor and the purchaser these will also normally be excluded provided that the restrictions are "directly related" to the sale and "necessary" to the implementation of the merger (see further Chapter 22 para.22.4.1). This is similar to the EU doctrine of "ancillary restraints" under the EC Merger Regulation (see further Chapter 21 para.21.14.2).

12.3.2 EU law

Under EU competition law a mere business sale, in the absence of contrary evidence, does not give rise to any restriction on competition as the purchaser simply steps into the shoes of the vendor and continues with the existing business. As such a sale agreement is not caught by Art.81(1) (see *Mecaniver* [1985] 3 C.M.L.R. 359). In that case the EC Commission also said that where a company sells its subsidiaries to another company as a going concern the commitment by the vendor not to compete with the purchaser for three years in the areas of activity of the transferred subsidiaries is a legitimate means of ensuring the vendor's obligation to transfer the full commercial value of the business which necessarily includes not only the sale of physical assets but also commercial know-how and clients. See also *Gottfried Reuter v BASF AG* [1976] 2 C.M.L.R. D44; *Nutricia* [1984] 2 C.M.L.R. 165 and *Nutricia* Case 42/84, in which the European Court of Justice said that the fact that non-competition clauses are included in an agreement for the sale of a business is not of itself sufficient to remove the clauses from the ambit of Art.81(1). Rather, it was necessary to examine what would be the state of competition if those clauses did not exist. There might then be a possibility that the vendor could force the purchaser out of the business and the European Court recognised that a non-competition clause did have the merit of ensuring that the transfer of the business had the intended effect provided the protection granted to a purchaser was limited in scope and duration to what was necessary and such clauses could contribute to the promotion of competition because they lead to an increase in the number of undertakings in the market.

EC Commission has published a *Notice on restrictions directly related and necessary to concentrations* (OJC56, 5.3.2005). This notice is an aid to the interpretation to Council Reg.139/2004 which deals with the control of mergers between companies. The 21st recital to the Regulation states that decisions clearing a merger automatically covers restrictions which are directly related and necessary to the implementation of the merger; such restrictions are called "ancillary restrictions". Under Pt III of the Notice, guidelines are set out in relation to non-competition clauses on the transfer of a business, i.e. usually a business sale. The Notice recognises that in order to take over fully the value of the assets transferred the acquirer must be able to benefit from some protection against competitive acts of the vendor in order to gain the loyalty of customers and to assimilate and exploit any know-how transferred. However it comments that such protection cannot generally be considered necessary when the transfer is limited to physical assets (such as land, buildings or machinery) or to exclusive industrial and commercial property rights (the holders of which could immediately take action against infringements by the transfer of such rights) (para.21 of the Notice). The Notice goes on to set out guidelines as to what are usually reasonable prohibitions on competition where such a prohibition is prima facie necessary to protect the purchaser. Restrictions which cannot be considered ancillary are not per se illegal. They are just not automatically covered by the Commission's decision clearing a merger. Nevertheless, they might still be justified under Art.81 of the EC Treaty or fall within the scope of a block exemption regulation. (see further Chapter 21). The following three paragraphs summarise the existing guidelines.

12.3.2.1 Duration

In most cases which involve the sale of both goodwill and know-how, a maximum period of three years is likely to be acceptable. However, where there is a sale only of goodwill a period of up to two years only will usually be reasonable. The first 1990 *Notice regarding restrictions ancillary to concentrations* (OJ 90/C203/05) used to allow a period of five years where goodwill and know-how were being acquired. No reason was given by the Commission for the reduction down to three years in the 2001 Notice (which has been reiterated in the latest Notice of March 2005). In any case these Notices are merely guidance as to current Commission practice, in particular cases the periods can be longer, for example, if it can be demonstrated that customer loyalty to the vendor will persist for more than two years, or that the economic life cycle of the products concerned is longer than three years.

12.3.2.2 Geographical area

The geographical scope of the clause must be limited to the area where the vendor had established the products or services before the sale, see for example, Commission Decision of August 4, 2000 (Comp/M. 1979—*CDC/Banco Urquijo/JV* para.18). It is, however, now also recognised that it may extend to territories where the vendor was planning to enter at the time of the sale, provided that he had already invested in preparing such entry (see paragraph 22 of the 2005 Notice).

12.3.2.3 Restricted activities

The non-competition clause must be limited to products and services which form the economic activity of the business which has been sold and can include products and services at an advanced stage of development at the time of the transaction.

The Notice also comments that the vendor may bind himself, his subsidiaries and commercial agents. However, an obligation to impose similar restrictions on others would not qualify as an "ancillary restriction". In particular, clauses which would restrict the scope for resellers or users to import or export would not be reasonable (paragraph 24).

Part V

Partnerships and Joint Ventures

Chapter 13

Partnerships

13.1 Introduction

The term partnership is used in this chapter to denote partnerships of individuals. Partnerships of companies and any restrictions imposed on them raise issues not only under UK common law (which is discussed in the following chapters), but potentially also under EU law and the statutory regime of the UK Competition Act 1998 (see further Chapters 21 and 22).

Partnerships of individuals have attributes which give rise to particular difficulties in both the law of business secrets and of restraint of trade. In practice, many disputes concerning restraints on partners will turn upon the ownership of the goodwill of the partnership. This is an issue of partnership property and a discussion of the rules governing partnership property is outside the scope of this book (for an example of the problem see *Miles v Clarke* [1953] 1 All E.R. 779). However, once the questions of partnership property have been resolved the rules of restraint of trade must be applied. As will be seen below, retiring partners may in restraint of trade cases be treated more like sellers of businesses than employees for on retirement they relinquish their share of the partnership property. Similarly, in business secrets cases they may be treated as having contributed to the partnership property the secret information and in appropriate cases be restrained from using it on their own account (see *Morrison v Moat* (1851) 9 Hare 241).

In considering possible implications of restrictions, or lack of, in a partnership agreement one has to look to both statue and common law. While many of the rules and principles have been developed by the courts, the Partnership Act 1890 provides a detailed set of provisions. More recently, and increasingly common, are limited liability partnerships (LLP's) set up under the Limited Liability Partnership Act 2000. An LLP is not strictly a partnership but a body corporate and it has "members" rather than "partners", and these members are agents for the LLP, rather than for each other. As with most Partnerships the mutual rights and duties of the LLP's member will be governed by agreement, or in the absence of agreement, by relevant regulations. Section 4(4) of the Limited Liability Partnership Act 2000 provides that a member of an LLP will not be regarded for any purpose as employed by the LLP unless, if he and the other members were partners in a partnership, he would be regarded for that purpose as an employee of the partnership. While the position has yet to be confirmed by the courts, it is assume that the enforceability of restrictions concerning members and former members of an LLP will be approached by the courts in a similar manner to that for partners in a partnership.

13.2 Implied provisions during the currency of the partnership

13.2.1 Business secrets of the partnership

The scope of the implied obligations of the partners during the currency of their partnership will depend upon the nature and purpose of the partnership. In all partnerships there is an implied obligation on each partner to act in the utmost good faith with regard to the partnership: *Green v Howell* [1910] 1 Ch. 495. This is substantially the same as the duty of fidelity owed by an employee to his employer and it will clearly place a like obligation on each partner to respect the confidence of partnership business secrets. It will also impose upon each partner an obligation to disclose to the partnership all information which he receives which is relevant to the partnership.

The Partnership Act 1890 (PA 1890) provides certain rights and duties that are to be implied into every agreement of partnership in the absence of any agreement to the contrary. Of particular relevance are the provisions of ss. 28, 29 and 30.

Section 28 requires partners to render true accounts and full information of all things affecting the partnership to any partner and his legal representatives. This section would, therefore, appear to place upon each partner a duty to disclose to his partners any information which he receives which may be of value to the partnership. Nevertheless, there will be some circumstances in which a partner may be justified in withholding information from his partners where it is in the interests of the partnership for him to do so. An example of this is found in *Rakusen v Ellis, Munday and Clarke* [1912] 1 Ch. 831. One partner in a firm of solicitors had acted for one party to an action. The other party subsequently instructed another partner who was ignorant of his partner's former involvement in the case. On an action brought to restrain him from acting the court held that, as it could rely upon the defendant not to discuss the case with his partner, there was no reason to restrain him from acting. It is clear that neither partner could have successfully brought an action against the other to require disclosure. This inability to require disclosure is clearly crucial where the increasingly large law firms may be acting for different clients, and the reason why they are able to do so despite the actual or potential conflict of interests issues is due to internal Chinese walls which are supposed to ensure information is not disclosed internally. However, in the last few years the issue of legal or commercial conflicts of interests within a partnership has become a hot topic and are best dealt with considerable care (see *Marks & Spencer plc v Freshfields*, *The Times*, June 18, 2004, where Freshfields were prevented from acting for Philip Green in his bid for M&S as they were already acting for M&S on one of its key commercial contracts. Leave to appeal was refused).

Section 29 of PA 1890 provides that every partner must account to the firm for any benefit derived by him from any transaction concerning the partnership, or from any use by him of the partnership property, name or business connection. This is perhaps just a restatement of one aspect of the duty of good faith, but it would seem to be directly applicable where one partner misuses confidential information which rightly belongs to the partnership.

By s.30 of PA 1890, it is provided that if a partner, without the consent of the other partners, carries on any business of the same nature as and competing with that of the firm, he must account for and pay over to the firm all profits made by him in that business.

13.3 Express provisions during the currency of the partnership

13.3.1 Business secrets of the partnership

Whilst the implied obligation of good faith will impose a high obligation on the partners to maintain the confidence of partnership secrets, it may well be valuable to include in the partnership agreement an express provision requiring the partners during the existence of the partnership to keep confidential the business secrets of the partnership and to use them only for the purposes of the partnership. Where particular secrets are regarded of great value, express provisions requiring formal approval or the like before any disclosure, even in the course of the partnership's business may prove useful, so long as this does not hamper the ability to do legitimate business.

13.3.2 Restrictions on engaging in other business

The implied obligation to act in good faith and the obligations imposed by PA 1890 will, as has been seen, prevent a partner from engaging in any business competitive with that of the partnership. However these implied obligations do not cover clearly the rights of partners to undertake other business not competitive with that of the partnership. The position should be covered by any well-drafted partnership deed.

The application of the restraint of trade doctrine to obligations not to engage in other businesses during the subsistence of the partnership has not been the subject of any decision of the courts. However it has been suggested, obiter, that the doctrine does not apply to obligations between partners during the subsistence of the partnership: see Lord Pearce in *Esso Petroleum Co Ltd v Harper's Garage (Stourport) Ltd* [1968] A.C. 269. However, the exemption from the doctrine was limited to restrictions which were incidental and normal to the positive commercial arrangements at which the partnership deed aims.

It would, therefore, appear that a similar rule to that applicable to contracts of employment will apply. Lord Greene M.R. said in *Hivac Ltd v Park Royal Scientific Instruments Ltd* [1946] Ch. 169:

> It would be most unfortunate if anything we said, or any other court said, should place an undue restriction on the right of a workman, particularly a manual workman, to make use of his leisure for his profit.

He was, of course, speaking in the context of the obligations to be implied into a contract of employment. But his words do seem to indicate that in a proper case the courts might intervene to prevent the enforcement of an excessive restraint. The obvious tool to use would be the doctrine of restraint of trade.

If the courts were to apply the doctrine to such a case it would be necessary for the restraint to be reasonable in the interests of the parties and in the interests of the public. The court would first assess the legitimate interests that the partners were seeking to protect. It is submitted that the courts would without doubt regard the devotion by the partners of all their efforts towards the partnership business as a legitimate aim which could reasonably be protected by a covenant restraining the partners from participating in any other business. However, where such a restraint is imposed upon a partner for some reasons not connected with the objects of the partnership, but say to protect another business in which one partner has a personal interest, then it is far less probable that the restraint will be upheld. Until an example comes before the courts the position will remain uncertain, even in the light of the principles laid down in *Stenhouse Australia Ltd v Phillips* [1974] A.C. 391.

13.4 Implied restrictions after partnership

In the absence of any contrary agreement between the members of a partnership, the only means by which a partner may retire from a partnership is upon its dissolution. In the case of a partnership at will, this may be brought about at any time by any partner giving notice of his intention so to do to all the other partners: s.26 of PA 1890. Sections 32 to 35 deal with other means by which the dissolution of a partnership may be brought about.

Upon the dissolution of a partnership, the assets of the partnership are to be applied as set out in s.44 of PA 1890. Basically, this provides that after discharging the debts of the partnership the remaining assets are distributed in the shares in which profits were distributed. The question of what restraints are imposed upon the partners upon dissolution ultimately comes down, therefore, to a question of what rights attach to the assets of the partnership which fall to be disposed of in the winding up of the partnership.

Of particular importance are the rights which attach to the goodwill of the partnership upon its winding up. It has been held that where the goodwill is sold following a dissolution, no restriction is thereby imposed on the partners preventing them from carrying on the trade in which they were formerly engaged: see the discussion of the earlier cases in *Trego v Hunt* [1896] A.C. 7. Several difficult issues are left unresolved by this case.

The first problem is the right to use the name of the old firm. This presumably is one of the assets of the firm which may be got in and, if necessary, sold upon dissolution. However, the extent of the ancillary rights which may be sold with it is more doubtful. Presumably a purchaser cannot acquire a sufficient element of the reputation in the name to enable him to bring an action for passing off against a former partner carrying on business in his own name.

Secondly, it is not clear what becomes of business secrets upon a dissolution. It is certainly arguable that all the partners should be free to use them, for to hold otherwise might prevent the partners from continuing in the trade in which the partnership was formerly engaged. This would seem to be the consequence of *Trego v Hunt*. But if the partnership has developed a valuable and secret process through the expenditure of substantial sums, it may be that this should more properly be regarded as an asset which should be sold for the benefit of all the partners. That these problems remain unresolved indicates that most persons embarking upon significant partnerships must adopt the sensible course of regulating their relationship with a written agreement.

It should not, however, be assumed that the same meaning will be given to the word goodwill where an express agreement has been made between the partners governing the ownership of the goodwill of the partnership, in the event of a retirement or dissolution. The courts will take notice of the fact that the meaning given to the word goodwill in cases where it is being sold in the winding up of a partnership due to the absence of any agreement between the partners, is not perhaps the commonly understood meaning of the word. Thus in *Trego v Hunt* and in *Leggott v Barrett* (1880) L.R. 15 Ch. D. 306, where it was expressly provided that one partner should have the goodwill, the term was construed in the same sense as it would have been in a contract for the sale of a business. Accordingly, there was an implied term that the former partner who did not keep ownership of the goodwill could be restrained by injunction from canvassing the former customers of the business, or holding himself out as carrying on business in succession to the business of the partnership. However, he would not be restrained from advertising generally even though these advertisements might reach the ears of former customers.

13.5 Express provisions after partnership

That the restraint of trade doctrine is applicable to restraints imposed on former partners is beyond doubt. Agreements between partners have some of the characteristics of employment agreements but because the partners are the owners of their business, their agreements also have some of the characteristics of agreements for the sale of businesses, at least as far as retirement and dissolution is concerned. In applying the restraint of trade doctrine it is therefore tempting to seek the closest analogous case from the field of employment or business sales and to try to apply it to the restraint in question. Indeed such an approach has been adopted in many cases: see for example *Trego v Hunt* and *Ronbar Enterprises Ltd v Green* [1954] 1 W.L.R. 815. However the Privy Council has indicated that this approach should not be adopted. In *Bridge v Deacons* they held that the proper approach is that adopted by Lord Reid in *Esso Petroleum Co Ltd v Harper's Garage (Stourport) Ltd* [1968] A.C. 269, where he said:

> I think it better to ascertain what were the legitimate interests of the appellants which they were entitled to protect and then to see whether these restraints were more than adequate for that purpose.

The interests of the covenantees (usually the remaining partners) can in general be divided into two parts: there will be the protection of their business secrets and the preservation of their goodwill.

13.5.1 Protection of business secrets

As regards the protection of business secrets, it is likely that a similar distinction between business secrets and personal skills to that drawn in employment cases will be made. For it cannot reasonably be said that a partnership has a legitimate interest in the individual skills of the partners which would justify the imposition of a restriction on a departing partner.

A partnership will, however, have an interest in its confidential information which it may legitimately protect. Since the interest of a partnership in those secrets is similar to that of an employer as regards his employees, it is probable that a partnership may protect itself in like manner to a former employer.

13.5.2 Protection of goodwill

It is in the protection of goodwill, that the difference in approach to partnership and employment contracts becomes apparent. For each of the members of a partnership has a share in the value of the goodwill of a partnership and participates by way of a share of profits in the benefits which that goodwill brings to the firm. Restraints imposed in partnership agreements have a dual function. They both protect a partner whilst he is a member of the partnership and they restrain him if he retires. In addition, they provide a means whereby an older partner may dispose of the share in the business which the partners have built up to younger men. This may be in the interests both of the public in that it ensures continuity of trade and of the parties in that it may enable the more senior partner to sell his share of goodwill to the more junior partners (either by means of a cash sum or by means of a higher share of profit during the last few years of partnership). These then are the elements of protectable interest which comprise a partnership goodwill. All these elements were taken into account by the Privy Council in *Bridge v Deacons* [1984] A.C. 705.

In *Kerr v Morris* [1986] 3 All E.R. 217 the Court of Appeal considered a restraint of trade clause in a partnership deed between general medical practitioners who worked as national health service contractors. As s.54(1) of the National Health Service Act 1977 made it unlawful to sell the goodwill of a national health service medical practice, it was argued that there was no goodwill to which any restraint could legitimately attach. Therefore, it was said the restraint was unreasonable as there did not exist an interest which merited protection. This argument was rejected. Dillon L.J. said:

> . . . goodwill, in the sense of the tendency of patients whom the doctors have treated to continue to refer to the firm for further treatment, must remain one of the most valuable assets, albeit not a saleable asset, of the partnership on which the partners' livelihood as doctors substantially depends.

This seems a sensible approach as NHS doctors are rewarded by the number of patients on their list.

The nature of the legitimate interest which may be protected by the three most common types of covenants can conveniently be considered separately. The first example is a covenant against acting for or canvassing the clients of the old firm. In the case of a sale of goodwill *simpliciter* if all that will be implied is an obligation on the seller not to canvass the customers of the business, such an obligation is in many cases inadequate. For example, in the case of solicitors canvassing for business it is in general prohibited (see Rule 1 of the Solicitors' Practice Rules). Therefore, it may be impossible to protect goodwill, except by prohibiting the outgoing partner from acting for clients of the firm. The validity of such a restraint was the subject of the Privy Council's decision in *Bridge v Deacons*. That concerned a provision placed on all retiring partners which prohibited them from acting as a solicitor in Hong Kong for a period of five years for any person who had been a client of the firm during the period of three years prior to the departure of the partner. The provision sensibly contained exceptions which permitted employment in industry or government.

The restriction was held to be reasonable. The interest of the firm which could legitimately be protected was the goodwill of the firm as a whole and they could reasonably guard against the appropriation by the retiring partner of any part of it.

The importance of this decision is that it shows that, unlike employment cases, it is not necessary to show that the retiring partner dealt with all the clients encompassed by the restriction (which happened in this case to be all clients of the firm) before his retirement or that he even knew who they were.

If the partner held a share in the goodwill of the firm as a whole, then on relinquishing that share, he could be restrained from acting for any former client for these comprised that goodwill.

It will, of course, be important to ensure that the restraint is properly for the protection of the business of the firm. Thus, if the restraint as drafted covers other businesses it will be unenforceable, unless severable: *British Reinforced Concrete Engineering Co Ltd v Schelff* [1921] 2 Ch. 563. For example, a restraint against practising as a medical practitioner will be unenforceable if what is sought to be protected is a general practice for it would prevent the covenantor from acting as a consultant: see *Routh v Jones* [1947] 1 All E.R. 758 and *Lyne-Pirkis v Jones* [1969] 1 W.L.R. 1293; *cf. Clarke v Newland* [1991] 1 All E.R. 397, CA where a covenant not to practice [*sic*] following the termination of a general practitioner partnership agreement was construed to be a restriction on practising as a general medical practitioner.

It is likely that the restriction in *Bridge v Deacons* would have been invalid had the exceptions for practice in industry and government not been included for this could not be regarded as affecting the goodwill of the business.

The second example is a covenant against trading within a defined geographical area. It has long been accepted that a restriction on trading within a defined geographical area for a specific period may be justified as necessary for the protection of goodwill. Such a restraint has an obvious advantage over a restraint on seeing customers of the old firm: it is far easier to police. The covenantees need only detect that the covenantor is carrying on business in the defined area and he can take action, if the covenant is valid. He need not prove the identity of the clients of the covenantor.

However, it must be shown that the covenant is still for the protection of goodwill. Therefore, the area must be framed carefully with regard to the nature of the business to be protected. It will be necessary to show that the protection of the goodwill of the old business reasonably required the exclusion of the covenantor from the defined area. This will require a careful examination of the scope of the business to be protected. Whilst the reasonableness of the restriction must be judged as at the date it is entered into, the parties may take into account the contemplated expansion of the business in framing the extent of the restriction: see *Putsman v Taylor* [1927] 1 K.B. 637.

Not all businesses will lend themselves to the use of area covenants to protect goodwill. If the business ranges over a wide area but has only a small share of the market in the area in which it operates, it is submitted that an area covenant would be inappropriate. Such a covenant would, whilst protecting the covenantee, deprive the covenantor of many customers who may never even have heard of the covenantee. For an example of this difficulty arising in the context of employer and employee, see *Gledhow Auto Parts Ltd v Delaney* [1965] 3 All E.R. 288. It is only in rare circumstances that a wide-ranging area covenant would be enforceable. Where vital business secrets are to be protected (see for example *Littlewoods v Harris* [1977] 1 W.L.R. 1472 and *Standex International Ltd v CB Blades* [1976] F.S.R. 114) or the covenantee has a business which is pre-eminent in the market throughout a large area (such as in *Nordenfelt v Maxim* [1894] A.C. 535), an area covenant may be reasonable.

On a smaller scale, area covenants entered into by medical practitioners prohibiting practice within a small radius (ten miles) have been held enforceable. In the case of solicitors, a five-mile radius was thought, at the interlocutory stage, not to be excessive: *Edwards v Worboys* [1984] A.C. 724.

It is, however, to be recommended that, where possible, area covenants should not be relied on as the primary means of restraint for they are blunt instruments. It is preferable to tie the restraint to the clients of the business as in *Bridge v Deacons* for this is more closely linked to the goodwill to be protected. In addition, changes in the scale of the business are automatically taken into account.

The third example is a covenant not to engage in any competing business. As has been seen earlier, an employer has no right to protect himself against competition from his former employees; he may only impose such restraints as are necessary for the protection of his customer connection and business secrets. The position of partners is different, for they are usually participants in the goodwill of their business. This goodwill includes not just its customer connection but also its reputation generally. It is therefore reasonable for the protection of that goodwill to apply a restraint upon departing members of the partnership restricting them from engaging in any competing business. The leading case on this type of provision is *Ronbar Enterprises Ltd v Green* [1954] 1 W.L.R. 815. The plaintiff and the defendant had entered into a partnership agreement for the purpose of publishing a weekly newspaper covering the sporting and entertainment business. The agreement provided that either party could terminate in the event of a breach by the other and thereupon purchase that other's share of the partnership at a valuation. In the event of such a purchase it was provided that the selling partner should not for five years from the date of dissolution of the partnership "directly or indirectly carry on or be engaged or interested in any business similar to or competing with the business of the partnership". Following a breach by the defendant, the termination and purchase provisions were applied. Soon after the defendant became involved in writing for a paper which competed with the partnership business. The covenant was attacked as being too wide to be enforceable. After finding that the words "similar to" were severable, the Court of Appeal rejected this submission. The absence of any limitation as to area was not fatal for, as Harman J. pointed out, the interest which the purchaser was entitled to be protected against in a vendor and purchaser case is competition. By contrast, in the Australian decision *Geraghty v Minter* (1979) 26 A.L.R. 141 a covenant against involvement in a "similar business" was upheld. Nevertheless, it is submitted that covenants against managing in any "similar business" should be treated with caution.

It must of course be remembered that for a restriction against competition to be enforceable the goodwill which is sought to be protected must actually exist: *Vancouver Malt and Sake Brewing Co Ltd v Vancouver Breweries Ltd* [1934] A.C. 181.

Whether *Ronbar Enterprises v Green* can be regarded as authority for the proposition that in any partnership agreement which leaves the remaining partners with the goodwill a restriction of competition by outgoing partners will be enforceable is not clear, for in this case there was a clear sale by the defendant of his share of the goodwill. In the case of agreements, such as that in *Bridge v Deacons* where no payment is made for goodwill, it is not clear whether a general restraint on competition can be justified. However in *Voaden v Voaden* (February 21, 1997 – Transcript Ch. 1997 – V – 633) the partners of a large firm of surveyors successfully applied for an interlocutory injunction restraining one of its partners (WV) from practising on his own account until his notice period had expired. Under the partnership deed WV was prohibited, while still being a partner, for a period of 12 months from engaging or having interests in any surveying business other than that of the partnership and was subject to a 12 month non-solicitation clause. Negotiations had resulted in the partners agreeing to WV's early retirement on condition he took up an offer of employment with X Co (one of the firm's clients), and adhered to the non-solicitation clause. Nevertheless shortly afterwards a number of the firm's clients began to transfer their business to a service company set up by WV and his wife, apparently as a result of approaches made prior to retirement. An injunction enforcing the restrictive covenant in the partnership deed was granted on the basis that, although X Co had employed WV's services through the new company, this did not meet the condition in the negotiated retirement agreement. In balancing the interests of the firm and an individual's right to gainful employment the judge took into account the evidence that WV would clearly be able to secure attractive employment in the interim period.

Equally, consideration was also an important factor in *Thurstan Hoskin & Partners v Jewill Hill & Bernet and others* [2002] All E.R. (D) 62. The defendant had been employed as a salaried partner by the claimant, a firm of solicitors. The deed of partnership included a restraint whereby in the event of the termination of the partnership the defendant would not canvass, solicit, or attempt to take away the business of any clients. He was then dismissed and he began proceedings claiming wrongful dismissal. In settlement of those proceedings he received a payment and the non-solicitation clause was re-enacted save that the defendant was entitled to represent four named clients of his former law firm. The defendant subsequently solicited other clients. On a claim for damages the restriction was held to be enforceable, which was confirmed on appeal although it was noted that the case was not a routine employment agreement, rather the defendant had received valuable consideration for the agreement in question (as part of this settlement) and had received legal advice.

In *Dawnay Day v D'Alphen* [1997] I.R.L.R. 285 Walker at first instance relied on the analogy of a joint venture with a partnership to allow a limited company to enforce a non-compete obligation against the other parties to the joint venture (who were individuals). Stating that "Had the relevant business been owned by the joint venturers as partners in the full sense, each partner would plainly have had a legitimate interest in restraining competition by an outgoing partner (once the business had become established with its own goodwill, as the venturers reasonably expected)" (pp.1092H–1093C). On appeal the Court considered the analogy but preferred to approach the issue in terms of whether the joint venturer had "sufficient interest" to enforce anti-competition and anti-solicitation covenants against his fellow joint venturer.

Whereas previously once a solicitor was made a partner he remained with that firm until his retirement, in recent years there has been a dramatic increase in lateral hires. Faced with this increasingly volatile market law firms have sought to protect their business by introducing or strengthening restrictions on partners leaving to work for competing law firms. These included restrictive covenants with long notice periods and gardening leave provisions to protect the firms goodwill by removing the leaving partner from continued contact with the firm's clients, thereby giving the remaining partners an opportunity to show clients the firm's ability to continue to service them without that individual partner. Gardening leave will only be enforceable if it is set down in the firm's partnership agreement as per the Court of Appeal in *William Hill Organisation v Tucker* [1998] I.R.L.R. 313. In practice however the enforcement of a gardening leave may not be in the best interests of a law firm if clients of that particular partner object to being denied access to the services of the lawyer of their choice. (See the article "Are firms being led up the garden path" by Farrell, S. in *The Lawyer* 23/08/1999).

13.5.3 Salaried v Equity Partners

The position of salaried partners, that is to say persons held out to the world as partners but in fact having no share in the profits of the firm, should be distinguished. Their position will be analysed by the court as if they were employees, for the reality of the position is that they hold no stake in the goodwill of the firm (see *Briggs v Oates* [1991] 1 All E.R. 407 and *Kao, Lee and Yip v Edwards* [1994] 1 H.K.L.R. 232). In a case in Hong Kong, *Kao, Lee and Yip v Koo Hoi Yan*, August 23, 1994, HKCA, the court distinguished between equity partners who did not enjoy the usual right to take part in the firm's management and those who did.

In *Clarke v Newland*, [1991] 1 All E.R. 397, the Court of Appeal granted an injunction when a salaried partner in a medical practice set up as a general practitioner in breach of a restrictions in the partnership agreement where he had undertaken 'not to practice' in the practice area (which was physically defined) within a period of three years in the event of the agreement being terminated. The judge at first instance had considered the covenant 'not to practice' as unreasonably wide and had refused the injunction.

13.5.4 Common aspects of reasonableness

As far as reasonableness between the parties is concerned the courts take account of the element of mutuality usually present in partnership agreements.

In *Bridge v Deacons*, the fact that the parties were solicitors who would presumably have cast their minds upon the issue of reasonableness also tended to show that the restraint was reasonable. Where the parties have taken professional advice this will be evidence as to reasonableness: *Whitehill v Bradford* [1952] Ch. 236.

The circumstances in which the restraint may come to apply may be material to considerations of reasonableness. Thus if a restraint may apply to a partner who is expelled from a partnership for no good reason and who receives no compensation, it may for that reason be held unreasonable as between the parties: see *Hensman v Traill* (1980) 124 S.J. 776 but contrast the approach in *Geraghty v Minter* where the Australian court thought this issue was irrelevant to the validity of the restraint but relevant to whether a remedy would be available in equity.

The courts generally seem to have great difficulty in assessing the reasonableness of the periods for which restraints may apply. They are most reluctant to interfere with restraints on this ground. In *Bridge v Deacons*, their Lordships considered that the justification of particular periods were hardly susceptible of proof by specific evidence. In that case, both the five-year period of the restraint, and the three-year period by reference to which the clients who the retiring partner could not act for, were defined and were held reasonable. In *Whitehill v Bradford*, a 21-year restraint on a doctor from acting within a ten-mile radius was held valid.

It should be remembered that reasonableness is to be judged at the time that the restraint is entered into (but see para.3.2). Thus, in *Bridge v Deacons* the fact that a retiring partner received no payment for goodwill had to be considered together with the fact that on entering into the partnership he did not have to make any payment for it. This was a convenient and practical arrangement.

It will, in general, be difficult to show that a restraint is contrary to the public interest as opposed to showing that it goes further than is reasonably necessary for the protection of the legitimate interest of the covenantee. The public interest in the individual's liberty to trade will have been satisfied by showing that the restraint is necessary to protect the interests of the covenantee. In *Oswald Hickson Collier and Co v Carter-Ruck* [1984] A.C. 720, it was suggested by the Court of Appeal that it might be contrary to public policy for a solicitor to bar himself from acting for any person who required his services. This was rejected by the Privy Council in *Bridge v Deacons* as being without authority and directly contrary to a considerable volume of authority including the decision of the House of Lords in *Fitch v Dewes* [1921] 2 A.C. 158. In *Hensman v Traill*, it was held by Bristow J. that a restriction on a doctor's right to practise in a partnership agreement, which might lead to a doctor being prevented from giving to patients the care which he is obliged to give them by the provisions of the National Health Service Act 1977, was contrary to public policy as mirrored by that Act. He accordingly held it unenforceable. However this decision has now been overruled by the Court of Appeal in *Kerr v Morris*

[1986] 3 W.L.R. 217 where it was held that since a doctor was free to leave the area in which he practised at any time, there could be no rule of public policy which bound him not to contract to leave. The ordinary rules of restraint of trade applied and, not withstanding the bar on sale of goodwill in a National Health partnership, the remaining partners still had an interest to protect.

It should be remembered that in many cases statutes will not be regarded as mirroring the public policy adopted by the courts in applying the restraint of trade doctrine. In *United Shoe Machinery Co of Canada v Brunet* [1909] A.C. 330, the Privy Council declined to adopt the policy of holding ties invalid evidenced by the patents legislation. Similarly, in *Regent Oil Co Ltd v JT Leavesley (Lichfield) Ltd* [1966] 1 W.L.R. 1210, the court declined to find that there was anything void or illegal at common law about an agreement containing resale price maintenance provisions in spite of the subsequent enactment of legislation prohibiting it.

When considering the question of reasonableness in relation to professional partnerships, it is useful to find out from the governing professional organisation whether it provides any guidelines to its members relating to what is generally considered reasonable in the profession. For example, the Royal College of Veterinary Surgeons in its *Guide to Professional Conduct* makes it clear that competition with a former partner or employer is not a matter for disciplinary action but for negotiation and contract. In respect of partners it recommends a maximum period of five years and points out that where a retiring partner has been paid for his goodwill, there is a much stronger case for upholding longer periods of restraint than in the case of a retiring partner who has received nothing more than undrawn profits and his share of the capital. It recommends that a restraint of trade clause between a principal and an assistant "should not in any circumstances exceed two years, the minimum might be one year . . .".

13.6 Drafting considerations

As has been seen, where no express covenants govern the obligations of partners on retirement or dissolution of the partnership, the position can become most unclear. It is, therefore, of the utmost importance that the rights of the parties are clearly specified in an express agreement. Whilst detailed drafting considerations are outside the scope of this work the following points should be covered:

(a) The partners' rights to engage in private business outside the partnership during its term should be clearly stated.

(b) The ownership of goodwill in the event of retirement, death and other dissolution of the partnership should be provided for and particular attention should be paid to rights in business secrets and to the use of the name of the firm.

(c) If retiring partners are to be subject to restrictive covenants the choice of a restriction on soliciting or dealing with clients of the firm, on carrying on business within a defined area or on carrying on a competing business must be made carefully in the light of the known or anticipated nature of the business of the partnership. It will also be important to consider the interaction of the restraints with the provisions as to ownership of goodwill.

(d) Salaried partners should be considered as employees for restraint of trade purposes and particular care should be taken in dealing with the consequences of retirement or termination of the partnership, especially in small partnerships (see e.g. *Briggs v Oates*).

13.7 Statutory and EU limitations

Old partnerships deeds may have been drafted with the Restrictive Trade Practices Act 1976 in mind (see further Chapter 22), although partnerships of individuals were rarely caught by the Act as they were considered to constitute a single person for this purpose. The RTPA has however now been repealed.

Under the Competition Act 1998 a partnership can be caught by the Chapter I prohibition, particularly if the restraints have an appreciable effect in the UK or a local area within the UK (see further Chapter 22). However s.3(d) and Sch.4 exclude from the prohibition:

(i) agreements which constitute professional rules designated by the Secretary of State;

(ii) agreements which impose obligations arising from such designated rules and

(iii) those which constitute an agreement to act in accordance with such rules (Sch.4 para.1(1)). Thus, for example, any agreement in a solicitors partnership agreement which restrains a partner from engaging in any competing business arguably falls within (ii) above to the extent that they seek to comply with the solicitors rules relating to conflict of issue and the good reputation of the profession.

It is unlikely that the very existence of a partnership will contravene Art.81(1) of the EC Treaty. Moreover, so long as post-partnership restraints on competition are reasonable and necessary, then it is unlikely that they will infringe Art.81(1). (*Reuter Gottfried v BASF AG* [1976] 2 C.M.L.R. D44.) Furthermore, some professional partnerships in the UK may not infringe Art.81(1) since they may have no effect on trade between member states will be minimal.

Chapter 14

Joint Ventures

14.1 General applicability of the doctrine

For a long time the courts had not had to consider the application of restraint of trade doctrine to joint ventures constituted by means other than partnerships, and finally addressed this by the Court of Appeal's ruling in *Dawnay, Day & Co Ltd and Another v D'Alphen and others* [1997] I.R.L.R. 442. In particular the Court of Appeal has considered the question whether a joint venturer (who is not a partner) has sufficient interest to be permitted to enforce anti-competition and anti-solicitation covenants against its fellow joint venturer, when the business is to be developed and carried on by a jointly owned company.

Evans L.J., giving the Court of Appeal's judgment, upheld the ruling of Robert Walker at first instance that the restrictive trade doctrine could apply to a party to a joint venture agreement, given that the joint venturer had made a capital contribution which had given it a clear commercial interest in safeguarding itself against competition from the managers, regardless of whether or not the interest could be classified as proprietary or quasi-proprietary.

In view of the significance of this case it is worthwhile setting out briefly the facts. In January 1992 the first three defendants who were experienced brokers of European bonds had entered into a shareholders' agreement with Dawnay Day (DD) to form a joint bond-broking venture (incorporated as Dawnay Day Securities (DDS)), with DD providing the start-up capital. By clause 9.1 of the shareholders' agreement the three managers had covenanted with DD that for a period of two years from the date of the agreement, extending to a period terminating one year after ceasing to be either an employee or a director of the company, they would not

(a) carry on or be engaged in any business competing with the business of Eurobond broking as carried on by the company,

(b) canvass or solicit in competition with the company orders or custom from any person, firm or company who had engaged the services of the company nor directly or indirectly assist any person to do so,

(c) solicit or entice away from the company any person who was for the time being a director, officer, employee or other servant of the company.

Following the incorporation of the joint venture the three managers started working for DDS and subsequently entered into service agreements with DD and DDS, which included an anti-solicitation covenant, during the agreement and for 12 months following its termination. The company's business expanded in line with the parties' expectations until four years later when the three defendants gave three months' notice to terminate their service agreements and entered into agreements with the fourth defendant to commence employment, when free to do so. DD brought proceedings to enforce the restrictive covenants. On a preliminary issue to determine whether the covenants were reasonable restraints of trade, the judge held that DD had a legitimate interest of a proprietary nature to protect, partly by reference to the concept of partnership. He found that clause 9.1(a) and (b) of the shareholders' agreement were enforceable as reasonable restraints of trade, however clause 9.1(c) was unenforceable as being unreasonably wide because it extended to solicitation of employees of all sorts, even the most junior and moreover, and it extended to employees who may have been taken on by the company (DDS) during the one-year period. It was the judge's opinion that the restriction was unreasonably wide, even in the context of a commercial arrangement and even taking account of the way in which bond-broking desks operate as teams. In relation to the non-solicitation clause in the service agreement, he held that it provided the plaintiffs with no more protection than was reasonable, rejecting the argument that it should be regarded void for uncertainty given that he felt that one could decide what amounted to a "senior" employee. To that extent the judge felt that he was bound by *Ingham v ABC Contract Services Limited*, November 12, 1993, (unreported) (see also para.8.4.3).

Counsel for the managers submitted that DD, as a shareholder and investor had no interest of a kind which has been recognised by the courts. He argued that the only reported cases where anti-competition and anti-solicitation covenants had been enforced were those where the covenant was necessary to protect the interests of a business, meaning either its goodwill or specific confidential information which it owned, and where the plaintiff (i.e. the covenantee) was the owner of the business, as distinct from being merely an investor in it. The Court of Appeal held that the circumstances in which covenants in restraint of trade may be enforced were not restricted to the established categories of vendor/purchaser (of a business) and master/servant cases, quoting the House of Lords in *Esso Petroleum Co Ltd v Harper's Garage (Stourport) Ltd* [1968] A.C. 269, and the Court of Appeal in *Office Angels Ltd v Rainer-Thomas* [1991] I.R.L.R. 214 amongst others. The established categories are not to be considered rigid nor are they exclusive. Rather, the Court of Appeal held that

> the covenant may be enforced when the covenantee has a legitimate interest, of whatever kind, to protect, and when the covenant is no wider than is necessary to protect that interest. The fact therefore that Dawnay Day was neither the purchaser of a business from the managers, nor their employer does not mean that the covenants could not be enforced.

Furthermore the Court of Appeal specifically noted that although on a literal reading it could be suggested that clause 9.1(a) of the shareholders' agreement was invalid, because both post-termination business as well as existing business was within its scope, on the evidence, there were factors (such as the extensive involvement in preparing the business plans and the nature of the client relationship which exists in the bond-brokerage business) entitled the plaintiffs to claim protection not only for those kinds of business being carried on when the managers left, but also for other kinds which were in an advanced state of preparation.

14.2 The application of EU and UK competition law in the context of joint ventures

14.2.1 Joint ventures under EU law

In determining the validity of a restraint of trade clause in a joint venture or co-operation agreement consideration must be given as to whether the clause is part of an agreement which required notification under either the EC Merger Regulation or Art.81(1). If it was notified and cleared, any restraint of trade clauses will normally have been considered at the time of notification and cleared as ancillary restrictions. (This is discussed in greater detail in para.21.14.2 (EU) and para.22.4.1 (UK)

In terms of the EC Merger Regulation this will depend on whether the joint venture is a "full function" joint venture set up on a "lasting basis". In other words whether it has been set up to operate autonomously on the market and has not been set up for a limited period (e.g. unlike consortia set up for a specific project). Next the question will be whether it has a Community dimension, i.e. whether it and any entities that control the joint venture exceed the turnover thresholds set out in the Merger Regulation (see further para.21.14). If it does not one will need to consider what national merger laws may apply to the joint venture.

If the joint venture is not full function, and therefore treated like a merger, one has to consider whether Art.81(1) (EC) or Chapter 1 (UK) applies. This will depend on whether the joint venture is between actual or potential competitors and has an effect on inter-state trade.

In terms of the application of Art.81 to joint ventures, one should carefully consider the *Commission's Notice on the applicability of Article 81 of the EC Treaty to horizontal co-operation agreements* (OJ 2001 C3/2) and such block exemption regulations as Reg.2659/2000 (on research and development agreements) or Reg.2658/2000 (on specialisation agreements). (See further Chapter 21.)

Equally where a joint venture is set up between companies operating at different levels of the production or distribution chain, it may well be that the agreement, and any non-competes may not fall within Art.81(1) or benefit from a block exemption. To determine whether this is the case one should consider the *Commission's Regulation on Vertical Agreements 2790/1999*, which is discussed in greater detail in Chapter 21.

14.2.2 Joint ventures which by their nature fall outside Article 81(1)

The EC Commission's *Notice Guidelines on Horizontal Co-operation Agreements*, sets out various forms of co-operation agreements which, in the Commission's view, are of a type that *by their nature* fall outside Art.81(1) (as distinct from those agreements which are not prohibited because they have no appreciable effect on competition). These include:

- Joint ventures between parties that are neither actual, nor potential, competitors.
- Co-operation between competing companies that cannot independently carry out the project or activity covered by the co-operation (e.g. consortia for a large construction project or co-operation on R&D which requires both parties' individual expertise).
- Co-operation concerning an activity which does not influence the relevant parameters of competition, e.g. joint ventures with the function of carrying out internal organisational tasks on behalf of parent companies (e.g. IT or payroll functions).

These three categories of co-operation could only come under Art.81(1) scrutiny if they involved firms with significant market power and are likely to cause foreclosure problems vis à vis third parties.

Many joint venture agreements will require further analysis in order to decide whether or not they fall under Art.81(1), which also includes an analysis of market-related criteria such as the market shares of the parties, the overall structure of the market and other structural factors (e.g. entry barriers).

In addition the Commission's *Guidelines on Horizontal Agreements* set out the analytical framework for the most common types of co-operative agreements, notably: R&D, production agreements (including specialisation agreements); purchasing agreements; commercialisation agreements; agreements on standards and environmental agreements.

Very briefly, with respect to joint ventures set up solely for the purpose of research and development, provided that the parents are allowed to carry on their own research and development in the same field, and that competition in the market for the resulting products is not restricted. Furthermore the co-operation must not extend to the joint *exploitation* of research results if it is to escape the application of Art.81(1). If there is an exclusivity requirement on the parties that they are only to jointly exploit the results, if this is limited to the duration of the joint venture this might be an acceptable clause under the restraint of trade doctrine, however this same clause may well be void under Art.81(1). To the extent that there is some concern that the agreement may fall within Art.81(1) one has to carefully consider whether it may benefit from the block exemption provided for research and development agreements by Reg.2659/2000, OJ 2000/L304/7.

Situations where co-operation in the form of a joint venture is, viewed objectively, the only means by which the parent companies can enter a new market, or remain in their existing market may not be caught by Art.81(1), provided that their presence will either strengthen competition or, at least, prevent it from being weakened. More likely is such an arrangement may benefit from the block exemption provided for specialisation agreements by Reg. 2658/2000, OJ 2000 L304/3.

14.2.3 Ancillary restraints in the context of joint ventures

In addition, similarly as with mergers, there may be certain ancillary agreements or restrictions which may be entered into by the joint venture and its parents as part of the overall transaction, such as restrictive or non-compete covenants, purchase and supply arrangements or intellectual property licences. To the extent that such restrictions are directly related and necessary to the implementation of the joint venture, they will be classified as ancillary restrictions and will generally be exempted for the same period as the joint venture. Restrictions which are not ancillary have to be assessed separately under Art.81 to check whether they are legally valid. This applies both to the case of full function joint ventures (i.e. joint ventures within the scope of the EC Merger Regulation) and other joint ventures.

Guidance as to the meaning of restrictions which are directly related and necessary to the implementation of a joint venture is contained in the *Commission's Notice regarding restrictions directly related and necessary to concentrations* (2005 OJ C56/24). Briefly however in order to be treated as ancillary the restrictions must be proportionate. This means that the duration, subject matter and geographical field of application of any restrictions should not exceed what the implementation of the joint venture reasonably requires.

The object and effect of these restrictions and the analysis as to whether they are ancillary takes into account whether they are being imposed on the joint venture or whether they are being imposed on the parents. In the case of joint ventures, non-compete covenants given by controlling shareholders are typically treated more liberally than similar covenants given by parties to a merger or an acquisition, where they are generally only accepted for a limited period. Indeed, insofar as a covenant provides for the permanent withdrawal of the parents from the joint ventures market(s), it will be treated as ancillary for the entire period during which the parents retain a controlling shareholding in the joint venture, but not extending beyond the lifetime of the joint venture and provided it is limited to the product and geographic markets in which the joint venture is actually active. As a general rule the EC Commission will presume that non-compete obligations between *non-controlling* parents and a joint venture are not directly related and necessary to the concentration (see *Commission Notice on restrictions directly related and necessary to concentrations*, Section IV). Similar principles apply to non-solicitation and confidentiality clauses, to the extent that their restrictive effect does not exceed that which is allowed for non-compete clauses. These clauses may moreover be considered ancillary in a large number of instances, and in the case of confidentiality provisions may exceed five years depending on the particular circumstances of the case and mindful of the parties' interests in protecting valuable business secrets.

Any extension of a non-compete covenant to areas in which the joint venture may in future decide to become active was not considered ancillary to a merger unless extensive plans and investment to extend were already in place at the time of the transaction. See *Commission Notice on restrictions directly related and necessary to concentrations*, para.22. See, for example, Case IV/JV.22 *Fujitsu/Seimens*, Commission Decision of September 30, 1999 where the restrictions went beyond what was ancillary to the merger.

An example of where the parties were required to modify the application of a non-compete clause in order to get clearance under the Art.81(3) is provided in the notification regarding *Cegetel 14*, Case IV/36.592 (no full decision was published but a notice was published pursuant to Art.19(3) of Reg.17/62, 1998 OJ C238/3). This case related to the restructuring the Cegetel which was active in the communications market in France whereby Compagnie Générale des Eaux (CGE), British Telecommunications plc, Mannesmann AG and SBC International Inc notified a set of agreements whereby they agreed on the respective contribution interests and commercial relationships in connection with Cegetel. Cegetel was to address all segments of the French telecommunications market where the incumbent telecommunications operator, France Telecom, held the dominant position. The parties' market shares were at the time of notification negligible (below one per cent). Included in the markets that Cegetel was to address exclusively was that of GSM services. However the EC Commission had already previously found that this was no longer a national market but moving towards a European market. During its investigation into the effects of the agreement the EC Commission informed the parties that the application of the non-compete clause accepted by the parents of the Cegetel in relation to the marketing and sales of GSM services appeared to be incompatible with Community competition rules. The parties were therefore required to amend their original agreements to exclude from the non-compete clause the provision by Cegetel's shareholders of GSM services to end-users located in France, and to allow Cegetel and the companies controlled by it to sell its GSM services outside France. With the modification of the non-compete clause the Commission was happy to take a favourable view of the arrangement pursuant to Art.81.

14.2.4 UK competition law

As explained in greater detail in Chapter 22, the UK competition law analysis will now follow that of the EU. Briefly, the creation of joint ventures (and any restraint of trade clauses which can be considered ancillary to its creation) are excluded from the application of the Chapter I prohibition by s.3 and Sch.1 to the Competition Act 1998.

At the time of setting up a joint venture one should consider whether a pre-merger notification to the Office of Fair Trading is required under the Enterprise Act 2002. However notification is voluntary in the UK and so it may be that the agreement was never notified. With respect to any restrictive clauses relating to the joint venture, provided that such clauses are directly related and necessary to the joint venture, they will be exempt from the application of Chapter 1, and they can be considered valid and enforceable. If any clauses restrict competition beyond this they would require an assessment of their effect on competition and whether they could be exemptible for them to be enforceable. (see *Guidelines Mergers- Substantive Assessment Guidance*, OFT 516, May 2003, Chapter II and also the EC Commission's 2005 Notice.

Part VI

Commercial Contracts

Chapter 15

Introduction

15.1 Relevance of the restraint of trade doctrine

This chapter is primarily concerned with the application of the restraint of trade doctrine to commercial contracts. Later it deals with express confidentiality agreements.

As has been seen earlier, contracts of employment and contracts for the sale of business are not the only ones to which the doctrine of restraint of trade can apply. The doctrine is potentially unlimited in its application for, being founded on public policy, the courts are clearly capable of bringing within its scope the contracts which have hitherto escaped its scrutiny. The extent of the doctrine, put at its widest, is concisely expressed by Lord Diplock in *Petrofina (Great Britain) Ltd v Martin* [1966] Ch. 146 as follows:

> A contract in restraint of trade is one in which a party (the covenantor) agrees with any other party (the covenantee) to restrict his liberty in the future to carry on trade with other persons not parties to the contract in such manner as he chooses.

However, it is clear that not all contracts which fall within this definition are in restraint of trade. For example, a contract of employment under which the employee undertakes to supply his services exclusively to his employer for the duration of the contract would not usually be said to be in restraint of trade. The difficulties of developing a test which will determine which contracts are in restraint of trade and consequently must be justified and those which are not are examined at the beginning of this book. In this chapter, the treatment given by the courts to a number of the more commonly used forms of commercial contracts is examined with a view, not so much to developing any general statement of principle (because we believe this impossible), but to show the approach of the courts and where possible to highlight some of the provisions which the courts have found particularly objectionable so that practitioners may avoid them. For this reason emphasis is placed upon more recent decisions for these reflect the current application of public policy.

15.2 Attitude of the courts

The history of the development of the doctrine of restraint of trade has been marked by a contest between two conflicting aspects of public policy. Firstly, contracts between businessmen should be upheld. Secondly, the courts should not sanction interference in liberty to trade. It is this conflict which makes the application of the restraint of trade doctrine so difficult in practice. It is not always obvious which aspect should prevail in any given case. To these two aspects of policy a third can be added, which may help to explain some of the more obscure distinctions in the field. This is the convenient administration of justice.

It would seem at first glance that no difficulties would arise if all contracts were subject to the doctrine of restraint of trade. However, the consequence of this would be that a party seeking to escape from any restrictive provision of an agreement could, however unmeritorious his case, put his opponent to proof of the reasonableness of the provision. The courts are clearly concerned that this could unnecessarily delay proceedings and add to their expense. The courts have available two weapons to deal with this difficulty. In the case of certain types of contract (for example, ties contained in leases) they may be prepared to say that the restraint of trade doctrine has no application. Thus, in *Shearson Lehman Hutten v Maclaine Watson & Co* [1989] 2 Lloyd's Rep. 570 at p.614, a restraint which did not restrict future contracts but merely affected specific contracts already in existence was held not to fall within the doctrine. Alternatively, where the court, as Lord Pearce put it in *Esso Petroleum Co Ltd v Harper's Garage (Stourport) Ltd* [1968] A.C. 269, "sees its way clearly" no question of onus arises. Thus the court can dispense with the need for the plaintiff to prove the reasonableness of the provision if there is no possibility of the provision being unreasonable.

In assessing the likely reaction of the courts to a contract in restraint of trade, it is important to remember that until now the courts have not regarded themselves as the administrators of any general economic policy. This was especially true in the consideration of the public interest as opposed to the interests of the parties. Therefore the courts listened attentively to the commercial justification of a particular period of restraint in a solus agreement. They took account of such factors as the supplier's convenient administration of contracts with his distributors and his need for a stable distribution system for his production facilities. They were not, however, unduly impressed by general economic evidence as to the effect of the solus agreement system on competition. What was of concern was the liberty to trade. A good example of this approach is provided by *Texaco Ltd v Mulberry Filling Station Ltd* [1972] 1 All E.R. 513 where Ungoed-Thomas J. said:

> For my part, I prefer to decide that the restraints relied on in this case are reasonable in the interests of the public, not on balance of existing or possible economic

advantages and disadvantages to the public, but because there is, in conditions as they are, no unreasonable limitation of liberty to trade. It seems to me to follow that much of the evidence in our case directed to general considerations of economic policy was irrelevant.

Amoco Australian Pty Ltd v Rocca Bros [1975] A.C. 561 is another example of the suspicion with which the common law courts treated economic or financial evidence: the High Court of Australia concluded that a calculation of the profitability of a filling station based on conservative estimates of the likely gallonage could not be regarded as a justification for a 15-year tie.

There is something to be said in favour of this robust approach to economic evidence. Unfortunately, while applying the common law restraint of trade the judges may have been shying away from the economic implications, the advent of a prohibition regime in UK competition law means that it will be increasingly difficult to avoid an economic analysis of the effect of restrictions, in commercial agreements where Article 81(1)/Chapter 1 is at least arguable.

Where a restraint is entered into between two actual or potential competitors (be they large corporations or sole traders) the courts are going to have to consider the *effect* of the restriction on competition in the relevant market. As the UK judges gain experience and more confidence in carrying out such economic analysis one wonders whether this approach will not also alter the approach taken under the restraint of trade doctrine, particularly as safeguarding effective competition gains prominence as a public policy objective.

Lastly, the law applicable in foreign countries is not considered relevant to the enforceability of contractual terms alleged to be in restraint of trade, see *Apple Corps Ltd v Apple Computer Inc* [1992] F.S.R. 431 at p.477, although where the restraints are to be enforced will depend on the choice of law in the contract, or the Brussels Convention, see *Besix v. Wasserreinigungsbau*, CFI, Case C-256/00 [2003] All ER (D) 280 (May).

15.3 Vertical and horizontal agreements

Whilst agreements between parties at different stages within the distribution process (e.g. between a wholesaler and a retailer) are commonly called "vertical agreements", those between different parties at the same stage (e.g. between two wholesalers) are termed "horizontal agreements".

To date the common law courts have not, in practice, adopted any markedly different test for the two types of agreement. This similarity differs from the approach of the legislature which has, on the whole, regarded horizontal agreements with greater suspicion than vertical agreements. Already the Restrictive Trade Practices Act 1976 contained exemptions for the more common types of vertical agreements. This distinction has now become more widely accepted with the EC Commission's approach in the *Vertical Agreements Regulation 2790/1999*. (see further Chapters 21 and 22).

This difference in approach is perhaps explained by the courts' emphasis on individual liberty to trade rather than the achievement of broad economic objectives. The court's only concern, in restraint of trade cases, when considering a horizontal agreement has been to ensure that the individual party's freedom to trade is not excessively restricted. The court has not been concerned with the consequences of the agreement on third parties (see for example *Mogul Steamship Co Ltd v McGregor, Gow & Co* (1889) L.R. 23 Q.B.D. 598). By contrast, parties to a horizontal agreement are more likely to fall foul of UK or EU competition law than vertical agreements because of their effect on competition in the market, and therefore on other competitors and consumers.

Chapter 16

Solus and Other Exclusive Purchasing Agreements

16.1 Introduction

Exclusive purchasing agreements are agreements under which one party to a contract agrees to purchase all his requirements for goods of a certain type from the other party alone. Two of the more common examples of this type of contract are petrol station agreements and public house ties. These have each been the subject of many decisions of the courts with many of the recent pub cases focusing on the application of Art.81 of the EC Treaty. In addition the increased use of franchises in the restaurant business and in other fields, may prove to be a fertile field for restraint of trade arguments. The European Court has already had the occasion to consider franchise agreements under the competition provisions of the EC Treaty in *Pronuptia de Paris GmbH v Pronuptia de Paris Irmgard Schillgalis* (Case 161/84) [1986] 1 C.M.L.R. 414. Also back in 1988 European Commission had issued a block exemption for franchise agreements: *Commission Regulation No 4087/88* which has now been replaced by the recent *Vertical Agreements Regulation 2790/1999* (see further Chapter 21).

Solus agreements, public house ties and franchise agreements have a number of common characteristics which are of relevance to the application of the restraint of trade doctrine. There is often a substantial difference in the size of the supplier compared to the purchaser. For example, in the case of solus agreements the supplier is often an oil company whereas the garage operator may be a small family company. However, the disparity of size need not necessarily lead to the supplier having an unfair advantage in negotiating the terms of the agreement. In the *Esso* case the evidence was that the extensive competition between rival oil companies to establish solus systems after the abolition of petrol rationing gave garage proprietors the power to negotiate with the suppliers on equal terms in many cases. Often the purchaser will be required to make a significant capital investment in making his premises conform to the suppliers' house style. The supplier may frequently assist the purchaser in making the investment by providing finance on advantageous terms. These and other factors must all be taken into account in assessing whether any agreement will, if it is in restraint of trade, satisfy the requirement of reasonableness. Under competition law an additional factor to be taken into account when assessing the effect of a restriction will be the cumulated effect on competition in the relevant market of any network of similar agreements, as well as determining whether the defense of "in pari delicto" will prevent the publican/franchisee from suing for damages for breach of competition law. (See further para.21.9).

16.2 Common restrictive provisions

The essential element of solus agreements and public house ties is an obligation placed upon the purchaser to buy its requirements for goods of a specified type, usually for sale from defined premises, only from the supplier with whom he is contracting. Franchise agreements will often include such a provision, although they will also include important restrictions relating to use of the franchisor's trademark.

The obligation on the purchaser to buy its requirements of goods of a specified type only from the supplier can be, and in practice often is, divided into two separate obligations: an obligation to purchase specified goods only from the supplier and an obligation not to sell other goods. Where the supplier is able to fulfil the purchaser's demands for all types of goods, the distinction is not of great significance. However, where the range of goods which is available from the supplier is less extensive than that which the purchaser wishes to obtain, a heavier burden of justification is likely to be placed upon the supplier.

Certain ancillary obligations often found in agreements may vary the practical effect of these basic obligations. The purchaser will often be obliged to keep his premises open for a minimum period in each week. The price at which he is obliged to purchase the goods from the supplier will often be set by the supplier. Where the supplier has entered into similar agreements with the purchaser's competitors it may, as will be seen below, be prudent to include a provision against discrimination by the supplier in favour of competitors. Consideration must also be given as to whether to allow the purchaser to seek supplies elsewhere or to terminate the agreement if the supplier's prices do not remain competitive.

16.3 Restraints falling outside the restraint of trade doctrine

As has been seen already, the precise limits to the doctrine of restraint of trade are unclear. The House of Lords in *Esso Petroleum v Harper's Garage* has given some guidance but unfortunately, due to the multiplicity of reasons given by their Lordships, no clear rule has emerged.

In *Esso*, the House of Lords were faced with the argument, which had already been rejected by the Court of Appeal only a short while before in

Petrofina v Martin, that the doctrine of restraint of trade had no application to restrictions relating only to the use to which a certain piece of land could be put. The argument was based less on any express authority but more on the fact that in many early cases relating to restrictions on particular pieces of land (including several public house ties), the issue of restraint of trade had not been considered. The House of Lords had no difficulty in rejecting this argument. They did not find it easy to explain those cases. Lord Reid was prepared to say that ordinary negative covenants preventing the use of a particular site for trading of all kinds, or of a particular kind, were not within the scope of the doctrine of restraint of trade. But, he thought, there was some difficulty if a restraint in a lease not merely prevents the doing of certain things, but also obliges the person who takes possession of the land to act in a particular way. Lord Pearce likewise accepted that covenants restraining the use of land imposed as a condition of a sale or lease were not subject to the doctrine of restraint of trade at all. But, he said, when a man fetters with a restraint land which he already occupies or owns, the fetter may come within the scrutiny of the court. Lord Morris expressed a similar view saying "In such a situation [that is, that of voluntarily taking a lease of land with a restrictive covenant] it would not seem sensible to regard the restraint of trade doctrine as having application". Lord Morris thought the same principle would apply to a sale of land.

It is difficult to know what weight to attach to these dicta for they were not strictly speaking necessary for the disposal of the case; all that was required was that the argument that restrictions on the use to be made on a particular piece of land should be held not to be automatically outside the restraint of trade doctrine. In addition, neither Lord Hodson nor Lord Wilberforce were prepared to accept that restrictions imposed on the sale or leasing of land were automatically outside the doctrine. Indeed, Lord Hodson reiterated his view that it was impossible to segregate any particular class of case so as to exclude it from the ambit of the doctrine: see *Dickson v Pharmaceutical Society of Great Britain* [1970] A.C. 403 (although he accepted that there are many cases where it is futile to raise it). A further difficulty is caused by the fact that their Lordships limited the exemption to restrictive covenants. Therefore a common provision such as an obligation to keep premises open at reasonable hours, which imposes a positive obligation regarding the trade to be conducted on the premises, would not be exempt.

The best reported example of the direct application of the dicta of Lords Reid, Morris and Pearce is found in *Cleveland Petroleum Ltd v Dartstone* [1969] 1 W.L.R. 116. There the provision in question was contained in an underlease and was in the following terms: "At all times to carry on the business of the petrol filling station at the premises and not to store handle sell or distribute on or from the premises any motor fuels other than those supplied by the lessors". Lord Denning, after referring to the speeches of Lords Reid, Morris and Pearce in *Esso*, held that when a person takes possession of premises under a lease, not having been in possession previously, and on taking possession, he enters into a restrictive covenant tying him to take all his supplies from the lessor, prima facie the tie is valid. It is not an unreasonable restraint of trade.

It seems clear that Lord Denning was aware of the difficulty created by the positive covenant to carry on the business of a petrol filling station, otherwise he would not have needed to state that the provision was not an unreasonable restraint of trade for the question of restraint of trade would have had no application at all.

In spite of the uncertainty created by the diversity of the judgments in *Esso Petroleum v Harper's*, there appears in the last decade to have been an increasing acceptance by the courts that the restraints of trade doctrine does not apply to restrictions in leases and the like where the lessee gives up no prior freedom. In *Gloucester City Council v Williams and others, The Independent*, May 9, 1990 the Court of Appeal held that the doctrine had no application to restrictions on the nature of goods which could be sold by a market stallholder imposed by the city council because at the date of the licence the stallholder had no previous right to occupy the stall or trade there. In the New Zealand Court of Appeal decision *Robinson v Golden Chips (Wholesale) Ltd* [1971] N.Z.L.R. 257 a covenant given by a purchaser of premises to the vendor to sell from those premises only chips supplied by the vendor was held, following *Cleveland v Dartstone* and *Esso v Harpers*, to fall outside the doctrine. Likewise, in the Australian High Court decision *Quadramain Pty Ltd v Sevastopol Investments Pty Ltd* (1976) 8 A.L.R. 555, the majority held that a covenant given by a purchaser or lessee of land on the acquisition of its interest in the land was not within the restraint of trade doctrine. In a more recent UK case, the High Court refused to grant a tenant an injunction and/or damages, restraining a fellow tenant from operating a gift shop despite the fact the claimant had a covenant in his lease specifically restricting such a business. The court considered the restriction a covenant to be complied with by the landlord within s.28(1) of the Landlord and Tenant (Covenants) Act 1995, and therefore could potentially be enforced against the landlord. It could not however be enforced against any other tenant in the building as they held their premises under leases which were completely separate from the claimant's lease (*Oceanic Village Ltd v United Attractions Ltd* [1999] All E.R. (D) 1398).

However, even where the provisions of a solus or like agreement are to be contained in a lease, it may be necessary to have regard to the restraint of trade doctrine in drafting the terms.

It is essential, if the exemption from the restraint of trade doctrine for disposals of interests in land is to be available, that the covenantor must not have any prior right to trade on the land in question before the transaction in question. Thus, if the owner of a site leases or sells the site to the supplier and takes a lease-back containing a tie, the fact that the tie is in a lease will not free it from the restraint of trade doctrine. This was clearly shown by the Court of Appeal decision in *Alec Lobb Garages Ltd v Total Oil (Great Britain) Ltd* [1985] 1 All E.R. 303. In that case the plaintiff, the owner of a freehold site on which it carried on business as a garage proprietor, had got into financial difficulties. In order to solve these difficulties the first plaintiff (*Alec Lobb (Garages) Ltd*) granted a long lease to the defendant in return for a premium which represented the full value of the long lease. The defendant then granted a lease for a shorter term to Mr and Mrs Lobb (the second and third plaintiffs). Mr and Mrs Lobb were the proprietors of the first plaintiff. The court held first that the choice of Mr and Mrs Lobb as lessees instead of the first plaintiff was a "palpable device" in an endeavour to evade the doctrine of restraint of trade. The court held that accordingly the second and third plaintiffs were to be identified with the first plaintiff for the purposes of applying the doctrine. The court further held that the lease and lease-back were to be treated as two essential parts of one transaction. Accordingly, the agreement constituted by the lease and lease-back was in restraint of trade. In the Australian case *Amoco Australian Pty Ltd v Rocca Bros Motor Engineering* [1975] A.C. 561, the same conclusion was reached on a similar lease and lease-back transaction.

It is clear from this case that the courts will not allow technical devices to thwart the application of the doctrine of restraint of trade founded as it is upon public policy.

As was seen earlier (at para.2.1.1) various other tests were suggested in *Esso* which could take an agreement outside the restraint of trade doctrine. Of particular relevance is Lord Wilberforce's first test. In *Esso Petroleum Co Ltd v Harper's Garage (Stourport) Ltd* [1968] A.C. 269, Lord Wilberforce was unable to accept that restraints imposed upon the disposal or leasing of land were automatically outside the doctrine. He preferred an altogether different approach. He said:

> the judges have been able to dispense with the necessity of justification under a public policy test of reasonableness in such contracts or provisions of contracts as, under contemporary conditions, may be found to have passed into the accepted and normal currency of commercial or contractual or conveyancing relations.

Lord Wilberforce was able to explain the brewery tie cases and, more generally, the cases where restraints imposed on the disposal of land had been upheld, in terms of this test. However, he indicated that the test was to be applied flexibly so that a restraint which in former times might have been acceptable could in the light of modern trading conditions become subject to scrutiny. In particular, he pointed out that if one finds a deviation from the accepted standards or some artificial use of an accepted legal technique, it is right that this should be examined in the light of public policy.

The judgment of Lord Denning in *Petrofina v Martin* [1966] Ch. 146 contains some interesting observations on the development of the law on brewery ties. He pointed out that at the time when the leading case of *Catt v Tourle* (1869) 4 Ch. App. 654 was decided, the accepted view on restraint of trade was that partial restraints (the category of restraints not covering the whole country) were good if the consideration was adequate and the restraint reasonable. The consideration was adequate because the innkeeper got his lease at a lower rent or the loan of money which he needed at a lower rate. The restraint was reasonable so long as the brewer was ready to supply good beer at a reasonable price during the continuance of the security or the loan. For this reason, Lord Denning thought, no one ever doubted the validity of the ties. This explanation whilst on all fours with that of Lord Wilberforce is at variance with the view of the majority in *Esso*. It cannot be said with absolute certainty whether a simple tie in a lease or mortgage is within the doctrine of restraint of trade.

In the case of brewery ties contained in leases there have over recent years been a spate of new cases where the legality of the restrictions have been challenged not under the restraint of trade doctrine, but rather under Art.81 of the EC Treaty (e.g. *Gibbs Mew v Gemmell* and *Crehan v Inntrepreneur Pub Co*, see further Chapter 21). This has been as a result of the growing consolidation of brewers in the United Kingdom and the potentially anti-competitive effect of the networks of tied estates. For a discussion of the market see the Monopolies and Mergers Commission Report entitled *The Supply of Beer—a report on the supply of beer for retail sale in the United Kingdom*, (1989, CM651) which led to the making of two orders concerning brewery ties under the Fair Trading Act 1973 and the 2000 *Report on the review of the Beer Orders* (see para.16.6 below).

16.4 Reasonableness

Once it has been determined that the doctrine of restraint of trade applies, the restraints must be justified.

Lord Reid in *Esso* broke the test to be applied into three elements. Firstly, it is necessary to consider whether the restraint goes further than to afford adequate protection to the party in whose favour it was granted; secondly, whether it can be justified in the interests of the party restrained, and thirdly, whether it must be held contrary to the public interest.

It is clear that as regards the second element the courts will not be quick to find that in a commercial contract a restraint is not in the interests of the party restrained. This would require the court to say that it knows the party's interest better than the party itself. An early example of this approach can be seen in *Badische Anilin und Soda Fabrik v Schott Segner & Co* [1892] 3 Ch. 447 where Chitty J. said "Although not conclusive on the subject, the opinion of mercantile men, manifested by their acts, is not to be disregarded on the question of reasonableness".

Indeed as stated by Evans in *Dawnay Day & Co v D'Alphen and others* CA [1997] I.R.L.R. 442 when considering whether two-year-non-compete and non-solicitation clauses were reasonable "in my judgment this is a matter where the court should be slow to interfere with the parties' own assessment of what a reasonable period is". The judge (at first instance) found the covenant "should be treated as part of a commercial bargain between business people of broadly equal bargaining power" and "there is ample authority that the parties are likely to have been the best judges of what was reasonable between them. No question of public interest can be said to arise".

The court will be willing to interfere on this ground in cases where there is an unconscionable conduct (see for instance *A Schroeder Music Publishing Co Ltd v Macaulay* [1974] 1 W.L.R. 1308).

Where there is no unconscionable conduct, the courts will nevertheless require proof that the restraint satisfies the first element. Generally, the third element must be raised by the defendant.

16.4.1 The interest to be protected

The courts have not given any clear guidance as to the principles to be applied in ascertaining what is a legitimate interest which may be protected. The doctrine of restraint of trade has its origins in cases concerned with two types of restraint: those imposed by masters upon their servants and those imposed upon the sales of businesses. Outside these two categories the doctrine had until recent times received little consideration. Indeed, it is clear from the nineteenth century brewery tie cases that by the time the doctrine was sufficiently well formulated to be applied to brewery ties, there had been so many decisions upholding such ties without reference to the doctrine that the court felt that they could not then subject the ties to scrutiny. This is shown by the following passage from Selwyn L.J. in *Catt v Tourle*, quoted by Lord Wilberforce in *Esso*:

> Every court of justice has had occasion to consider these brewers' covenants, and must be taken to be cognisant of the distinction between what are called free houses and brewers' public houses which are subject to this very covenant. We should be introducing a very great uncertainty into a very large and important trade if we were now to suggest any doubt as to the validity of a covenant so extremely common as this is.

The modern authorities on the nature of the interest to be protected begin with *Petrofina v Martin*. In that case Lord Denning M.R. said he thought that the early solus agreements, i.e. those entered into before most of the outlets for petrol were tied, might well have been in restraint of trade because the company which introduced them was "really seeking to protect itself from competition and nothing else". However, by the time that the agreement in that case was entered into most outlets were already subject to ties. Therefore it was important for the supplier to be able to protect his outlets from being swallowed up by his rivals. The protection by a supplier of his outlets, at least where there is a possibility that the outlets will be hard to replace, is an interest which merits protection. In the context of public houses, the existence of the tied house system and the difficulties of obtaining planning consent and appropriate liquor licences are significant barriers to entry and would seem to indicate that the preservation by a supplier of a particular public house as an outlet for his products would be an interest meriting protection. Similarly, the shortage of prime high street sites would indicate that a fast food franchisor would have good grounds for arguing that he had an interest which required protection.

Before passing on from *Petrofina*, it should be noted that whilst the court said that Petrofina might legitimately protect their outlet for petrol, they also thought that Petrofina could not impose the same degree of protection in relation to motor oils. This is somewhat curious. The reason behind the distinction was that motorists might be under the impression that it was unsatisfactory to mix Petrofina oil with their preferred brand of oil. Accordingly, motorists who wanted oil as well as petrol might pass by a garage which advertised Petrofina only. However, it is hard to understand why Petrofina should not have the same interest in securing exclusive outlets for their oil as for their petrol. One would not expect a provision in a public house tie that required the publican to purchase soft drinks and mixers as well as beer from his supplier to be unacceptable. Nevertheless, it must be of some concern in the light of *Petrofina*. Lord Reid in *Esso* doubted the reasoning in *Petrofina*; it may have been this point that he had in mind. (See also the *Supply of Beer (Tied Estate) Order 1989* discussed at para.16.6.3 below.)

Nowadays, the question of whether it is reasonable to tie certain products together (regardless of whether they are tied to beer, petrol or any other product or service) is much more likely to be scrutinised very carefully under EU and UK competition law. Generally when the tying of two distinct products is not objectively justified by the nature of the products or commercial usage, such practice may constitute an abuse within the meaning of Art.82 of the EC Treaty or Chapter II of the Competition Act 1998 (see *Tetrapak*, Case C-333/94P [1996] E.C.R. I-5987 para.37). Tying may equally be caught by Art.81 if the supplier's market share (either in terms of the tied product or the tying product) exceeds 30 per cent (see *Commission's Notice on Vertical Restraints*, section 2.7).

In *Esso*, the concept of the supplier's interest which could be legitimately protected was interpreted more widely. Lord Reid accepted that the supplier might be concerned not only with maintaining individual outlets but also with maintaining and managing his distribution system as a whole. Their Lordships held it was legitimate to take account of, not just the likely period it would take the supplier to replace the outlet following expiry of the tie, but also the number of outlets that the supplier had to manage. Esso had some 6,600 outlets and the need to avoid an excessive number of ties expiring in any year was a legitimate interest. The fact that Esso had expended large sums on the construction of refineries and accordingly needed secure outlets for the distribution of the product of those refineries, was another interest which required protection. So too the economies of distribution to be made from supplying to solus outlets were relevant interests and more generally the economies of overall planning were to be taken into account.

It is important to note that Lord Reid, at least, did not appear to think that a mortgage in respect of which the right of repayment had been deferred was an interest meriting protection. For he said

> But as [the respondents] have tendered payment, I do not think that the existence of the loan and the mortgage puts the appellants in any stronger position than if the original agreements had permitted repayment at an earlier date.

This approach is entirely logical. The supplier who provides finance to the purchaser at advantageous rates can legitimately expect to reap the corresponding advantage of a tie for so long as the purchaser takes advantage of that finance. However, once the purchaser has offered to repay that finance the supplier cannot say that his security will suffer if the tie falls away for he will no longer have any need for security.

Whilst the mortgage remains in force, however, the supplier may well have an interest to protect. He may, therefore, be able to justify the tie for so long as the loan remains outstanding provided that he does not prohibit early repayment.

Although this principle must, following *Esso*, be regarded as clearly established, it should be noted that a number of cases on the permissibility of mortgages coupled with ties in which the right of redemption has been deferred have been decided in favour of the mortgagee with no reference to the restraint of trade doctrine (see *Biggs v Hoddinott* [1898] 2 Ch. 307 and *Hill v Regent Oil Co Ltd* (1962) E.G.D. 452). If the view expressed by Lord Diplock in *Petrofina* that the court cannot raise the issue of restraint of trade of its own motion is correct, one cannot be certain that the doctrine would not have been applied in these cases had it been raised.

The approach in *Esso* should, however, be contrasted with that in *Queensland Co-operative Milling Association Ltd v Pamag Pty Ltd* (1973) 1 A.L.R. 47 D. The High Court of Australia held that a commitment by a baker to use only a particular supplier's flour which lasted so long as any sums lent to the baker by the supplier were outstanding and which prohibited complete repayment before seven years, was a reasonable covenant. The issue which had to be decided was whether a seven-year tie could be justified, leaving to one side the loan, by reference to the legitimate interests of the supplier in securing his outlets.

In *Texaco Ltd v Mulberry Filling Station Ltd* [1972] 1 All E.R. 513 it was suggested that the price stability provided by the solus system was relevant. However, as mentioned earlier, the judge preferred not to rely on the economic evidence and so it is difficult to determine whether he thought that price stability was a relevant interest.

In *Young v Evans-Jones* [2001] All E.R. (0) 120 the claimant was a pharmacist, who was a tenant under a 15-year lease of a pharmacy in the defendant doctors' purpose built medical centre. On determination of the lease the claimant was to "use his best endeavours to procure the transfer" of the licence necessary for the use of the premises as a pharmacy. The claimant argued this was an unreasonable restraint of trade because the effect of the clause was to deprive him at the determination of his tenancy of the possibility of taking the goodwill created by him to a relocation nearby. Held: dismissing the appeal, the clause was not an unreasonable restraint of trade because the defendant doctors had a legitimate interest to protect, and it was reasonable for them to want to keep a pharmacy within their medical centre.

Once the interest to be protected has been ascertained the court will then assess whether the restriction goes further than is necessary to protect that interest.

In the case of solus agreements and similar ties, the court will not look at the individual provisions of the agreement in isolation. Thus the reasonableness of a tie will depend not just upon its length but also upon the extent to which the purchaser is obliged to keep his premises open and whether the purchaser is given any protection as to the price which the supplier will charge. Whether the provisions are contained in a lease will no doubt also be extremely significant. Although, in principle, the courts will not weigh the adequacy of the consideration provided by the covenantee to the covenantor, the Australian Court, at least, has held that the quantum of the consideration may be examined as part of the circumstances of the case against which the question of reasonableness is to be decided (see *Amoco Australian Pty Ltd v Rocca Bros Motor Engineering* [1975] A.C. 561).

16.4.2 Time and other factors

The term of the tie is clearly of vital importance. In *Esso* a tie of just under five years in a petrol station solus agreement was held to be reasonable whereas a tie of 21 years was not. As was mentioned above the court took notice of the fact that Esso wished to ensure that on average no more than 20 per cent of its ties came up for renewal every year in holding the shorter tie to be reasonable. However, the court took the view that it was impossible to foresee trading conditions 20 years hence, and in the absence of any evidence to justify the tie being longer than five years were not prepared to find it reasonable.

It was, however, a material factor that Esso had not assured to Harpers Garage a supply of petrol at a reasonable price come what may. If they had done so then a longer period of restraint may have been justifiable.

In addition, their Lordships took the fact that the purchaser was obliged to carry on trading to be a restrictive element of the agreement: this could compel the purchaser to trade at a loss. This was also a factor in the decision to uphold a 15-year tie in *Amoco v Rocca Bros*.

Following *Esso Petroleum Co Ltd v Harper's Garage (Stourport) Ltd* [1968] A.C. 269 there have been two reported English cases in which there was serious consideration of the reasonableness of solus ties. Although in the first of these cases, *Texaco v Mulberry*, the judge discussed at length the economic evidence relating to the agreement in question, he did not when deciding the question of reasonableness give any real explanation as to how he reached his decision (beyond saying that he did not think that the evidence directed to general considerations of economic policy was relevant). In addition, he did not discuss the first two elements of Lord Reid's test of reasonableness separately. Accordingly, it is difficult to draw any conclusion from the judgment.

The second decision, *Alec Lobb Garages Ltd v Total Oil (Great Britain) Ltd* [1985] 1 All E.R. 303, concerned a rescue operation mounted, reluctantly, by the supplier to save an ailing garage business. The garage owner granted a 51-year lease at a premium and a peppercorn rent to the supplier. The supplier granted a lease-back to the proprietors of the owner. (As was seen above, the different identity of the garage owner and its proprietors was not considered relevant by the court.) The lease-back was for 21 years and contained a tie for the whole of that period. The lease-back gave the tenants a right to break after 7 and 14 years. The court held the tie reasonable. Amongst the factors that they took into account was the fact that it was unlikely for planning reasons that during the 21-year term the property would be used for any purpose except a filling station. The court found that it made no significant difference to the public at large whether the station sold one brand of petrol or another. Of particular importance was the right to break after seven years. Bearing in mind that the station was already subject to a tie for three to four years the court saw no real significance in the difference between a tie for five years and the term of seven years until the first break. The court did not think that the fact that upon exercising the right to break the proprietors would have to leave the site was unreasonable, for value had already been given in the premium under the lease to the supplier.

In *Amoco v Rocca Bros*, a case which like *Alec Lobb v Total* involved a sale and lease-back (although it was not a rescue operation), the Australian High Court, following *Esso v Harper's*, held a 15-year tie unreasonable. Of particular importance to the finding of unreasonableness was the obligation to purchase a specified minimum gallonage of petrol and, perhaps more importantly, the obligation to carry on the business of a petrol station throughout the term. These provisions could, if business declined, have imposed an unreasonable burden on Rocca and the long period of the lease rendered them unduly harsh.

Since these cases arose there have been numerous cases involving in particular brewery ties, some of which have not been reported. However these cases have all focused on Art.81 of the EC Treaty and the application of the Commission Reg.1984/83 (now replaced by Regulation 2790/1999) granting certain beer tie agreements a block exemption. These more recent cases do not appear to have dealt with the reasonableness of the solus ties under the common law restraint of trade doctrine (see for example *Gibbs Mew plc v Gemmell* (CA 1998), *Passmore v Morland* (1998) or *Inntrepreneur Pub v Price* (1998). See further para.16.6 and Chapter 21).

How far reasonableness might be affected by unforeseen or unlikely circumstances which might result in the tie causing hardship to the purchaser came before the Court of Appeal in *Shell UK Ltd v Lostock Garage Ltd* [1977] 1 All E.R. 481. The defendant was subject to a tie to Shell. The tie was to last for five years and was valid in the light of the circumstances foreseeable at the time it was entered into. The agreement contained no express provision to the effect that Shell would not discriminate against Lostock in the prices it would charge to its neighbours. During a spell of intense petrol price competition Shell made a support scheme available to neighbouring garages but not to Lostock. As a result Lostock had to trade at a loss. Lostock thus sought cheaper supplies elsewhere. Lord Denning, relying on some rather tenuous dicta from *Esso*, held that the principle that the reasonableness of a restraint of trade was to be assessed only in the light of the circumstances at the time the contract was entered into was fallacious. Since the effort of holding a covenant to be an unreasonable restraint of trade was merely to render it unenforceable if the court finds that a covenant has operated unfairly or unreasonably it will not enforce it. Thus Lord Denning was able to hold that for the period while Shell was supporting Lostock's competitors the restraint was unenforceable. Bridge L.J. and Ormrod L.J. found themselves unable to agree with Lord Denning's reasoning although Bridge L.J. felt able to come to the same decision as the Master of the Rolls by holding that there was an implied term in the agreement to the effect that Shell would not discriminate unfairly against Lostock.

The cases so far referred to have concerned situations where prior to the restraint being imposed the covenantor already had a right to trade on the land in question. *Cleveland Petroleum Co v Dartstone Ltd* [1969] 1 W.L.R. 116 concerned a 25-year lease of a petrol station where the original lessee had no right to trade on the land in question prior to the grant of the lease. The lease contained a tie for its entire period. The defendants took an assignment of the lease and covenanted to abide by terms of the assignment. The defendants then told the plaintiffs that they considered the tie void. The plaintiffs applied for an injunction to restrain the defendants from breaking the agreement by "storing, handling or distributing on or from Country Oak service station any motor fuels other than the plaintiffs". The Court of Appeal held that the covenant was not an unreasonable restraint of trade and that the injunction should be granted. The principle basis for the decision was, as has been mentioned before, that such a tie is prima facie valid where it is contained in a lease granted to a person not previously in possession of the land. However, if Lord Denning had been satisfied that this was sufficient to dispense with the case it is hard to explain why he categorised the tie as not being in unreasonable restraint of trade. It is possible that he thought that the existence of the positive obligation in the lease to carry on the business of a filling station could taint the simple restriction on stocking other motor fuels so as to expose it to a test of reasonableness. But it may be that this is reading too much into his words.

Another interesting point which was touched upon in *Cleveland v Dartstone* was whether the validity of a restraint in a lease as against an assignee of the lease depends upon whether the covenant would have been valid against the original lessee. In *Cleveland*, it was assumed that the original lessee did not at the time that the lease was granted have a right to trade on the premises. If this had not been the case and the restraint had accordingly been unenforceable against the original lessee the position is unclear. The answer may depend upon the circumstances of the assignment. If the incoming lessee enters into a direct covenant with the lessor to comply with the terms of the lease, it is submitted that this should cure any defects in the original lease for the new lessee has no prior right to trade on the site. But if the new lessee enters into no such covenant then, by virtue of privity of estate, the new lessee will be bound by the original covenants.

The same issue regarding the validity of a restriction under Art.81 following an assignment of a pub tie was considered in *Passmore v Morland plc* [1998] E.C.C. 461. In February 1992 Mr Passmore entered into a pub lease of 20 years with Inntrepreneur Estates (a joint venture between Grand Metropolitan and Courage). Inntrepreneur, having a significant network of tied pubs containing the same or substantially the same tie as that in Mr Passmore's lease, notified its standard form to the European Commission seeking an exemption under Art.81. Morland plc, a small regional brewer acquired a few of the latter's tied houses including that of Mr Passmore. Inntrepreneur then withdrew its notification from consideration by the Commission in October 1997. In December 1997 Mr Passmore's solicitor wrote to Morland stating that the beer tie in the Inntrepreneur lease was void *ab initio* as a result of the provisions of Art.81(1) and that it remained so, irrespective of the identity of the owner of the freehold reversion. Accordingly he maintained the tie was unenforceable by Morland, that he was free from the restrictions of the tie and he sought damages for the reduced profitability of his pub as a result of the tie. Laddie held that nullity under Art.81(2) depended on the economic conditions and that, whereas the lease may have been unenforceable as between Mr Passmore and Inntrepreneur, the change of circumstances, here the assignment to Morland, meant that the restrictions did not have any appreciable effect and consequently the obligations were enforceable. In other words as the law currently stands a clause that is void under Art.81 of the EC Treaty (and presumably as a result of s.60 this will equally apply to clauses caught by the Chapter I prohibition), can be revived and become valid again if there is a change in circumstances.

If the term of a tie is reasonable it will be reasonable to provide that the purchaser will not dispose of the business without procuring that the person to whom he disposes of it covenants with the supplier to abide by the terms of the tie. For as Lord Reid explained in *Esso*, this is the only means by which the supplier can maintain his outlet for the duration of the tie. Such a provision must, in any event, be more reasonable than requiring the purchaser to remain in occupation for the duration of the tie.

Whilst the conclusions to be drawn from the case mentioned above are directly applicable to different types of agreements they should be applied with caution in other industries. Clearly, where the person entering into the tie is entering into a lease of premises on which he had no prior right to trade, the same rule must apply. But it would be dangerous to conclude that five years would automatically be a reasonable period for a tie regardless of the product or levels of investment made by the supplier. In the case of tied pubs the ties are frequently of much longer periods. This may be reasonable on the basis that the development of a profitable trade for a new brand of beer at a particular public house may well take longer than five years, particularly in a local community and for this reason the supplier may require a longer tie.

Similarly in a franchising operation the capital investment in equipment provided by the supplier may not be recouped in five years and this may justify a longer tie.

It is not uncommon, in franchising agreements, to find some form of restriction applying after the expiry of the term of the franchise. *Prontaprint plc v Landon Litho Ltd* [1987] F.S.R. 315 was an interlocutory decision on such a restriction. An injunction was granted in respect of a restriction on the former franchises from, inter alia, engaging in the franchised services within a radius of half a mile of the franchised premises for a period of three years. *Prontaprint* was followed in *Kall-Kwik Printing (UK) Ltd v Frank Clarence Rush* [1996] F.S.R. 114, where an interlocutory injunction was granted in respect of two-year restraint in a franchise agreement without restraining the franchisee from engaging in any business competitive with the business formerly operated by the franchisee within a 10-mile radius for two years. (See also *Kall-Kwik Printers (UK) v Bell* [1994] F.S.R. 674.) Note however that in view of the limitation of a one year post-termination restriction for franchise agreements and tied estates under the European Commission's *Vertical Agreements Regulation 2790/1999*, it is believed that this shorter period will pass into the "accepted and normal currency" of commercial relations as *per* Lord Wilberforce in *Esso Petroleum*.

16.4.3 Public policy

The first two of the three elements of Lord Reid's test of reasonableness have now been examined. That leaves only the question of whether the restraint is contrary to the public interest. However, Lord Reid, in the same judgment in which he discerned these three elements, said that he thought the reason why the court will not enforce a restraint which goes further than affording adequate protection to the legitimate interest of the party in whose favour it is granted, was because too wide a restraint is contrary to the public interest. The distinction between the first and third element lies perhaps in the onus of proof. The first element is part of what has been traditionally regarded as reasonableness in the interests of the parties. The onus of proof of this generally lies on the party seeking to enforce the restriction. The third element is what has traditionally been regarded as the reasonableness in the public interest. The onus is on the party asserting unreasonableness to prove it.

In the case of solus agreements, the third element has usually been dispensed with simply by saying that the public do not much care which brand of petrol is sold at a particular filling station. It is difficult to foresee a case arising in relation to tying agreements in which the public interest would require a covenant that went no further than protecting the supplier's interests to be held unenforceable. A possible example might arise if, as part of a brewery tie, the supplier required the publican to rent gaming machines only from approved suppliers with whom the supplier had a commission arrangement. fihilst the supplier might have a legitimate interest to protect (although this is not certain) it is arguable that the arrangement might be contrary to the public interest in preventing suppliers of gaming machines access to potential customers. (See *Gibbs Mews v Gemmell* and *Greenalls Management Ltd v Canavan* [1998] Eu. L. R. 507, for a discussion as to the validity of a landlord's consent requirement regarding the installation of gaming machines in a pub under Art.81). As will be seen below, the gaming machine supplier would have no cause of action (except possibly for a declaration) in such circumstances.

16.5 Drafting

It is not sensible in a book of this nature to suggest particular forms of clause to be used as precedents in the drafting of solus and other tying agreements for each contract must be tailored to make it reasonable in the particular circumstances of the parties and the relevant industry as a whole. However, the following may serve as a useful checklist of points to be remembered when drafting tying clauses.

16.5.1 Term

In petrol station solus agreements five years' fixed term is likely to be held reasonable (see *Esso v Harper's*). It has not been decided whether a five-year rolling term (i.e. a tie terminable upon five years' notice) would be reasonable and a shorter term might be safer. Where the provisions are contained in a lease and the tenant has no prior right to occupy a tie for the duration of the lease should be reasonable but it might be wise to give the tenant a right to break, particularly where he has no guarantee as to competitive pricing (see *Alec Lobb v Total*, *Shell v Lostock*, *Amoco v Rocca Bros* (High Court of Australia) and *Cleveland v Dartstone*). Avoid ties whose terms depend upon selling specific quantities for the less benefit the purchaser receives the longer the ties will last (see *Petrofina*).

Similar rules probably apply to brewery ties, but it may well be the case that longer ties are acceptable.

It is worth noting that the European Commission's Reg.2790/1999 on vertical agreements does *not* limit the duration of a non-compete restriction to five years during the agreement, although post-compete restrictions are limited to one year. A longer post-termination restriction would not necessarily be invalid, but would need to be carefully analysed as to its effect on competition as it would not have the safe harbour provided by the block exemption. (See para.16.6.2)

16.5.2 Price

It is important that the price or means of determining the price is specified, otherwise an undertaking to supply at a reasonable price may be implied (see *Foley v Classique Coaches Ltd* [1934] 2 K.B. 1). Some means of dealing with difficulties which might arise if price competition makes the purchasers' trade unprofitable should be included, particularly in longer ties (see *Shell v Lostock* and *Amoco v Rocca Bros*).

In *Courage Ltd v Crehan (No. 1)* [1999] U.K.C.L.R. 110, CA the tenants were complaining that the supplier had sold beer to the publicans who were not subject to a beer tie at substantially lower prices than those charged to tenants who were tied.

16.5.3 Obligations to trade

If a positive obligation is to be placed on the purchaser compelling him to trade, this has two consequences. Firstly, greater attention must be paid to pricing for the purchaser may be forced to trade at a loss (see *Esso*). Secondly, an agreement in a lease which might otherwise be outside the doctrine may be subjected to scrutiny.

16.5.4 Mortgages

Including a tie in a mortgage will not automatically exclude the restraint of trade doctrine. It may be permissible to continue a tie for so long as the mortgage remains on foot, but not if the only reason for retaining the tie is that the right to redeem the mortgage has been deferred unless the duration of the tie can be shown to be reasonable independently of the mortgage.

16.5.5 Ancillary restraints

Restraints which relate to items for which the supplier cannot independently justify a tie should, if possible, not be included in the tie. (See for example the difficulties caused by including motor oil in *Petrofina v Martin* [1966] Ch. 146—*N.B.* motor oil is perhaps not a good example for it has not subsequently caused difficulty.) Tying could also fall foul of Art.81(1) or Chapter I, and could be an abuse of a dominant position if the supplier has a significant market share in either product.

16.5.6 Assignment

It should be permissible to require the purchaser to sell his business only to someone who undertakes to perform the tie. (See *Esso, Caerns Motor Services Ltd v Texaco Ltd* [1994] 1 W.L.R. 1249 and *Amoco v Rocca*.) Such an obligation may be enforced by an injunction against a third party to retransfer the business if the transfer was a device to avoid a proper tie: see *Esso Petroleum Co Ltd v Kingswood Motors (Addlestone) Ltd* [1974] 1 Q.B. 142.

16.6 EU and UK Competition Law

16.6.1 Competition Act 1998

The first thing to note is that certain agreements relating to land are excluded from the application of the Chapter I prohibition in the Competition Act 1998. That is to say agreements between undertakings which create, alter, transfer or terminate an interest in land which contain certain obligations or restrictions (see further Chapter 22 para.22.4.9). In relation to solus agreements the question will therefore be whether the restriction relates to the activity which may be carried out from the relevant land, including the types of goods or services sold (which would be excluded) or the terms on which the goods may be sold (which would need to be analysed under Chapter I).

If subject to competition law it is unlikely that the EC Regulation 2790/1999 on Vertical Agreements will apply based on the parallel exemption provided for those agreements that are local and do not have any effect on inter state trade.

16.6.2 EU law

In addition if the agreement does not have a purely local effect or is part of a network of similar agreements throughout a member state such that it may have an effect upon trade between Member States, Art.81 may apply. Of particular relevance are the provision of *Commission Regulation 2790/1999 on Vertical Agreements* and the Commission Notice *Guidelines on Vertical Restraints*, OJ 2000, C291/1. While its predecessor *Commission Regulation 1984/83* had special provisions applying to beer agreements and petrol filling stations, the new Regulation provides a general block exemption to all forms of exclusive distribution and exclusive purchasing agreements, as well as franchising agreements. However Reg.2790/1999 does make one concession to agreements relating to the sale of goods or services from premises and land either owned or leased by the supplier, and that is that the non-compete obligation is not limited to five years but may be for the same duration as the occupancy of the premises (see Art.5(a)). To benefit from the block exemption the post-termination non-compete obligation must however be limited to one year (Art.5(b)). The *Guidelines* provide further assistance on the analysis of typical franchise and exclusive supply agreements (s.2.5, para.199–213).

In the interpretation and application of the EU block exemption regulations by national courts, the English doctrine of restraint of trade can only be of very general assistance in indicating the sort of considerations that may have been envisaged.

16.6.3 The Beer Orders

Lastly one should be aware that in relation to brewery ties in the UK special rules and considerations apply due to the extensive networks of tied estates that arose following consolidation among the brewers. The former Monopolies and Mergers Commission was asked to conduct an inquiry into the supply of beer (*The Supply of Beer—a report on the supply of beer for retail sale in the United Kingdom*, Report CM 651). Following the publication of this report two orders were made by the Secretary of State under the Fair Trading Act 1973 which are of relevance to beer solus agreements. These were the Supply of Beer (Loan Ties, Licensed Premises and Wholesale Prices) Order 1989 (SI 1989/2258) and the Supply of Beer (Tied Estate) Order 1989 (SI 1989/2390), both of which were revoked in February 2003.

Article 2 of the Supply of Beer (Loan Ties, Licensed Premises and Wholesale Prices) Order 1989 provided that it was unlawful to make or carry out an agreement under, or in relation to, which a brewer, or a member of a brewery group, makes a loan or gives any other term of financial assistance to another person if it precludes "relevant purchases".

The main object of the Supply of Beer (Tied Estate) Order 1989 was to impose limits on the size of brewers' tied estate and forced national brewers to divest 11,000 pubs. However, it also provided, in Art.7, that in certain circumstances brewers must allow their tied houses to offer a guest beer and not to extend the tie to non-alcoholic drinks.

Following the Office of Fair Trading's *Report on the review of the Beer Orders* the Secretary of State decided to revoke the cap on the size of brewers' tied estates and the requirement on large brewers not to tie alcoholic drinks other than beer. Beer ties are therefore either to be analysed under Article 81 (and the Vertical Agreements Block Exemption Regulation), or post May 2004 on the same basis under Chapter 1 and a parallel exemption.

The contractual agreements between the brewer and the publican have furthermore been the subject matter of considerable litigation in the UK Courts, with several hundred cases commenced by Inntrepreneur Estates or its tied tenants (who formed an association called Group Action Ltd), with the latter seeking damages for breach of EU competition law. Most were stayed while awaiting the outcome of the test case *Crehan v Inntrepreneur*, which was referred by the Court of Appeal to the ECJ and then ultimately determined by the House of Lords. See further Chapter 21.

Chapter 17

Exclusive Distribution and Agency Agreements

17.1 Introduction

Exclusive distribution and agency agreements are amongst the most common forms of distribution arrangements found in commerce. In each case, they are used by suppliers who wish to distribute their products in particular territories but do not wish to go to the expense of setting up their own distribution network in the territory. By appointing a distributor or agent in the territory the supplier can take advantage of the distribution and marketing skills of his agent or distributor. The distributor may have local knowledge not readily available to the supplier. Furthermore, the supplier is saved the significant expense of establishing for himself the local presence.

The distinction in legal terms between a distribution agreement and an agency agreement is that under the former the supplier sells to a distributor who then resells on his own account. In the case of the latter the agent procures orders for the supplier. On each order which the supplier accepts he pays the agent a commission. For the purpose of the application of the doctrine of restraint of trade the key feature is not the distinction between distributor and agent but the exclusivity granted to the agent or distributor. Under an exclusive agreement, the supplier agrees not to give anyone else the right to sell or to procure orders from customers in the exclusive territory. Indeed, a further distinction is sometimes drawn between exclusive and sole arrangements. Under the former the supplier undertakes in addition that he will not himself sell to customers in the exclusive territory.

17.2 Typical restrictions

Three types of restriction are commonly found in exclusive agency and distribution agreements. There is the grant of exclusivity. This typically takes the form of an undertaking by the supplier not to sell the products the subject of the agreement to any other person for resale in the territory. In the case of an agency agreement, it may take the form of an undertaking not to appoint any other agent for the territory. Depending upon whether the arrangement is exclusive or sole, the supplier may himself be limited.

Next there are often undertakings by the agent or distributor not to sell, distribute or act as agent for any products which compete with the products the subject of the agreement. This restriction may last beyond the expiry of the agency or right to distribute for a period of one or two years.

Finally, there are resale price maintenance provisions. These do not arise in agency arrangements because the supplier contracts directly with the customers in the agent's territory so there is no element of resale. In distribution arrangements, the supplier may be anxious to maintain the market price of his goods and to avoid excessive discounting. As is noted later any restriction of a distributor's ability to determine his sale price, without prejudice to the possibility of the supplier imposing a *maximum* sale price or *recommending* a sale price, is considered a "hard core restriction" that will always be prohibited under competition law (see Commission Reg.2790/1999, Art.4).

It is clear that most exclusive agency and distribution agreements will be enforceable notwithstanding the restraint of trade doctrine. Indeed, there have been very few cases in which the issue of restraint of trade has ever been raised. Earlier, the tests for determining whether an agreement is subject to the restraint of trade doctrine were discussed. There is no great degree of certainty as to whether the restraint of trade doctrine will apply to exclusive distribution or agency agreements so as to render it necessary to examine their reasonableness. Lord Hodson in *Esso*, seemed to think that the doctrine applied. However, he said that he did "not anticipate a spate of litigation in which contracts of say 'sole agency' will be assailed". Presumably he thought that it was most unlikely that the court would hold such a contract unreasonable. Lord Pearce was more robust. He said:

> The doctrine does not apply to ordinary commercial contracts for the regulation and promotion of trade during the existence of the contract, provided that any prevention of work outside the contract, viewed as a whole is directed towards absorption of the parties' services and not their sterilisation. Sole agencies are a normal and necessary incident of commerce and those who desire the benefits of a sole agency must deny themselves the opportunities of other agencies.

Lord Wilberforce also indicated that contracts of sole agency would fall within the class of contracts to which the restraint of trade doctrine need not be applied.

The dicta of their Lordships would tend to suggest that all contracts of sole agency of distribution would fall outside the restraint of trade doctrine. However, the decision of the Privy Council in *AG of the Commonwealth of Australia v Adelaide Steamship Co* [1913] A.C. 781 has cast some doubt on the point. The case concerned an exclusive distribution agreement between a group of colliery proprietors and a number of shipping companies. The essence of the agreement was that the colliery proprietors undertook to supply their coal exclusively to the shipping companies and that the shipping companies undertook to purchase their requirements only from the colliery proprietors. The agreement also contained maximum (but not minimum) resale price provisions. The court held that the agreement was without doubt a contract in restraint of trade. It was not necessary for the court to decide in that case whether the contract was reasonable in the interests of the parties, for the case concerned a statutory provision which made the entry into an agreement or combination to restrain trade to the detriment of the public an offence. The court held that the agreement was not to the detriment of the public. It is not clear from the decision exactly why the agreement was held to be in restraint of trade. It may have been held so, not simply because it imposed the restrictive provisions mentioned above but because it involved the combined action of a group of colliery proprietors and a group of shipping companies which had the effect as between the members of each group of eliminating competition. The case should not, it is submitted, be regarded as authority for the proposition that ordinary contracts of sole agency are to be regarded as subject to the restraint of trade doctrine.

An example of the usual approach may be found in *Elliman Sons and Co v Carrington & Son Ltd* [1901] 2 Ch. 275. This case concerned not an exclusive arrangement but a resale price maintenance provision. The defendants were wholesalers. They agreed not to sell the plaintiffs' goods below specified prices and to bind retailers purchasing from them to do likewise. Kekewich J. held that the plaintiffs were fully at liberty to sell their goods on the terms that they did and that the doctrine of restraint of trade had no application. More typically, in *British Oxygen Co Ltd v Liquid Air Ltd* [1925] Ch. 383 and *Servais Bouchard v Princes Hall Restaurant Ltd* (1904) 20 T.L.R. 574, the issue of restraint of trade was barely considered. In *Prudential Assurance Co v Rodiques* [1982] 2 N.Z.L.R. 54, a clause providing that an insurance selling agent's entitlement to payment of commission terminated on termination of his agency (with the result that substantial repayments by the agent became due) was held not to constitute a restraint of trade.

In *Days Medical Aids v Pihsiang Machinery and others*, [2004] EWHC 44 (Comm) Langley J. had to consider the validity of a five-year exclusive distribution agreement, which had a renewal clause "for as long as permitted by law". The issue therefore revolved around whether this meant the contract was for an indefinite period and therefore void under competition law and/or unreasonable under the restraint of trade doctrine. Langley J. held that the agreement did not have an anti-competitive effect or object and was therefore not rendered void by Art.81(1) EC Treaty, and that he was precluded by the supremacy of community law from applying the common law doctrine to the extent that it would otherwise be applicable. Uniquely enough he found that while the agreement was not illegal as it was not caught by Art.81(1) but that had it been caught, it would not have benefited from an exemption as its renewal clause meant the exclusivity was for longer than five years, and therefore caught by Art.5(a) Reg.2790/1999, and equally under Art.81(3) the unlimited right of renewal was not limited to what was indispensable.

It seems, therefore, that the parties need not, when entering into sole or exclusive agency contracts containing restrictions of the type described above and no other unusual restrictions or circumstances, be concerned with the restraint of trade doctrine but rather focus on competition law. However, a note of caution must be sounded. There is a strong analogy between contracts of exclusive agency or distribution and contracts of employment. Thus, whilst restrictions placed on the agent or distributor during the term of the agreement may escape examination, restrictions applying after the end of the term are likely to require to be justified in accordance with the restraint of trade doctrine. Likewise a restriction which is not included for the purpose of directing the distributors' or agents' efforts towards the promotion of the supplier's products may require justification. Take, for example, the case of a supplier requiring the distributor, as a condition of the grant of agency for one of its products, to stop acting as agent for another supplier's products. If the other supplier's products are competitive with the products to be supplied under the agency, then all well and good. The doctrine will not apply for the restraint will be aimed at directing the agent to promoting the suppliers' products, effectively. But if the products to be dropped compete with products of the supplier which are not being made available to the agent, the doctrine may still have to be applied, for it may not be possible to show that the restraint is aimed at the absorption of the agent's services but merely at preventing competition. The size of the agent's business may be relevant. If the agent has only resources to handle only a few products at a time, the restraint may be directed to the absorption of the agent's services. Much will depend on the facts.

17.3 Reasonableness

As has been seen above it will only infrequently be necessary to justify the reasonableness of a contract of sole agency or distribution. When it is necessary to do so, it will be because of some unusual restriction which has been imposed. It is, therefore, difficult to give any general guidance as to the factor which will be taken into account in determining the reasonableness of any provision. It will be necessary to examine the position in the light of the principles set out earlier and to draw upon any analogous contracts discussed elsewhere in this book.

Unusually, in *Badische Anilin und Soda Fabrik v Schott Segner and Co* [1892] 3 Ch. 447, a restriction in an exclusive distribution agreement came before the court. The defendants had been appointed exclusive agents for the sale of the plaintiffs' products in the north of England. The agency was initially for four years but if not determined by notice it ran for successive two year periods. The defendants bound themselves after termination of the contract not to enter any like or similar business for three years. The restraint was held to be reasonable. The judge held that the restraint amounted in effect to a sale by the defendants of their interest in the goodwill of a large business built up by the capital, skill and industry of the contracting parties. The defendants had received a large remuneration and to hold the restriction void would tend to deprive persons in the position of the defendant of the advantage of making their own bargains for their remuneration. (See also *Prontaprint plc v Landon Litho Ltd* above para.16.4.2.)

In *Marshall v NM Financial Management Ltd* [1996] I.R.L.R. 20, Ch D, the Deputy Judge held that a post-termination non-compete clause on an agent was an unreasonable restraint of trade. The provision in question only paid the agent the renewal commission from business generated by him during his employment as an agent if he did not become an independent intermediary or become employed by a competitor for one year after termination of his agency agreement. The Court of Appeal subsequently considered whether the agent, who had been freed from an invalid restraint of trade clause, could still obtain the renewal commission taking into account the severance of that clause.

17.4 Competition law limitations

The provisions of EU and UK competition law must be considered (see Chapters 21 and 22). The scope of this book does not extend to a comprehensive discussion of the application of EU competition rules to exclusive agency and distribution agreements but a brief overview is provided. If the agreement is not of purely local effect and may have an effect upon trade between Member States of the European Union, Art 81(1) is likely to apply. If the agreement affects competition within the UK or a substantial part thereof—UK competition law will apply. If competition law does apply a judge will be precluded from prohibiting an agreement that is permissible under EU law unless one can show that the restraint of trade doctrine pursued a predominantly different objective—which is highly unlikely. (See Art.3(3) Reg.1/2003).

Of particular relevance is *Commission Regulation 2790/1999 on Vertical Agreements* which provides for the exemption of the more common forms of exclusive distribution agreements, provided they do not contain any so-called hard-core restrictions such as price fixing or restricting passive sales (Art.4). The Regulation basically allows vertifical agreements to benefit from a safe harbour from the application of the prohibition of Art.81(1), provided the companies' market share is below 30 per cent. The Regulation also includes certain restrictions which are not exempt, but which may under certain circumstances nonetheless be compatible with the EC competition rules. The most relevant one concerns non-compete obligations which require the distributor to resell only the brands of one supplier provided the agreement does not exceed five years (Art.5). Above the 30 per cent market share threshold, vertical agreements will not be covered by the block exemption, but they are not automatically presumed to be illegal either. They, however, require an individual assessment under Art.81(1) as to their effect as competition. Following the entry into force of Reg.1/2003 in May 2004 pre-notification and clearance from the EC Commission is no longer available and the parties, and their advisors need to satisfy themselves that the conditions for possible exemption under Art.81(3) apply.

With respect to agency agreements, the *Commission Notice Guidelines on Vertical Agreements* provides some guidance as to when they are not caught by Art.81(1) and when they are, in which case they need to be assessed under the *Vertical Agreements Regulation 2790/1999*. Broadly speaking a genuine agency agreement, where the agent does not bear any, or only insignificant, risks in relation to the contracts concluded and/or negotiated on behalf of the principal will fall outside Art.81(1) including all obligations imposed on the agent. The determining factor is the financial or commercial risk borne by the agent. This risk must be assessed on a case by case basis with regard to the economic reality rather than the legal form of the relationship (*Commission Notice* Section II.2).

Agreements for the distribution of cars and spare parts for cars have been singled out for special consideration both by the EU Commission and by UK government: *Commission Regulation 1400/2002* is a block exemption directed specifically at motor vehicle distribution and servicing agreements (OJ 2002 L203/30).

17.5 Statutory limitations

In the case of self-employed commercial agents particular regard must be had to the *EC Council Directive of 18 December 1986 on the co-ordination of the laws of member states relating to self-employed commercial agents*. This directive was implemented in the United Kingdom by the Commercial Agents (Council Directive) Regulations 1993 (SI 1993/3053) and imposes limits on the scope of post-termination restraints on agents and imposes certain requirements as to the calculation of commission owed to them.

The inquiry by the Competition Commission (*New Cars: A Report on the supply of new motor cars within the UK*, Report CM 4660 of April 10, 2000), resulted in an order expressly prohibiting the car manufacturers from discriminatory unjustifiably between fleet customers and dealers, or against dealers who sold below the recommended resale price or who imported cars from other Member States, Supply of New Cars Order 2000 (SI 2000/2088).

17.6 Drafting

It has been seen that only in unusual cases will an exclusive distribution or agency agreement be held to be in restraint of trade. Accordingly, the only guidance which may be given is that if any unusual restraint is to be included, its validity should be considered in relation to the general principles discussed at the beginning of this book. In such a case it would also be advisable clearly to separate the unusual restraints from the rest so as to ensure that, if for any reason the unusual provision is held unenforceable, the remaining provisions are not also struck down.

In any event, when drafting an exclusive distribution agreement, in all cases care should be taken to ensure one avoids the hard core restrictions that are per se illegal under competition law. Beyond that one will need to consider whether the agreement is likely to have an appreciable effect on competition. If it might, one needs to consider whether the agreement can be drafted in such a way to benefit from the safe harbour provided for by the *Vertical Agreements Regulation 2790/1999*.

With respect to agents one must consider whether any mandatory national rules apply, in particular on matters such as notice periods for termination and compensation payable following termination. In the UK regard should be had for the Commercial Agents (Council Directive) Regulations 1993, (SI 1993/3053) as amended which is based on the *EC Commercial Agents Directive* (Council Directive 86/653 on the co-ordination of the laws of Member States relating to self-employed commercial agents, OJ 1986 L382/17) and have been implemented slightly differently in the different Member States.

Chapter 18

Licences and Tying Agreements

18.1 Introduction

Patent licences have for many years been a common means by which an inventor has been able to reap the fruits of his invention without the need to involve himself in its manufacture and distribution. In the field of high technology, licences of copyright or know-how are often used to similar effect. Likewise, the owner of a valuable trademark is able to extend the availability of his products by licensing third parties to manufacture and sell goods to his specification under the trademark. Although ties have commonly been included in licences, licences are not the only agreement which contain ties; that is to say covenants to purchase goods exacted by a seller as a condition of entering into another transaction. Such obligations may for example be imposed as a condition of the sale of other goods.

In considering licenses one must almost invariably consider competition law, and in particular, the EU Technology Transfer Regulation, 772/2004, [200[4]] OJ L123/11 and its accompanying *Guidelines on the application of Article 81 of the EC Treaty to technology transfer agreements*, OJ C101.

18.2 Common restrictions

The restrictions commonly imposed upon licensees can, broadly speaking, be divided into three categories. The first category could be said to be contractual restrictions placed on an inventor going beyond what is envisaged by Parliament under the relevant intellectual property protection rights (e.g. the Patent Act). The second category contains provisions which are limits on the rights granted by the licensor. Before entering into the licence, the potential licensee could be restrained by the licensor from carrying on any of the activities prohibited by the first category of restriction through the exercise of his intellectual property rights.

The third category contains restrictions which restrain the licensee from doing things which he would otherwise have been free to do.

Restrictions falling into the second category include limits placed on the quantities of licensed products which the licensee may produce, limits on the territory in which the licensee may manufacture and sell the products, limits on the customers to whom the licensee may sell the products and limits on the field of application in which the licensee may use the licensed technology.

In the third category, one finds commitments not to be concerned with the manufacture or sale of products which compete with the licensed products, commitments to assign the benefit of any improvements to the licensed technology to the licensor, and obligations to buy products not covered by the licence from the licensor. These commitments, apart from commitments in relation to improvements, are often found in agreements other than licences.

On the basis that most licenses are entered into by "undertakings" (i.e. businesses) which can include the licensor as merely an inventor and patent holder, they are usually caught by either EU or UK competition law and are therefore subject to the provisions of the *Technology Transfer Block Exemption Regulation* which renders illegal certain restrictions. The extent to which the Regulation limits what restrictions the parties can agree will depend on whether the license agreement is one between two actual or potential competitors (see below, para.18.4).

18.3 The relevance of the restraint of trade doctrine

The first category, contractual restrictions placed on an intellectual property holder, are likely to be relatively rare in occurrence. It is however, going to be only exceptional cases "in which it could be justified as reasonable in the interest of the public to superimpose further contractual restraints on invention, going beyond what Parliament has thought necessary", see Chadwick L.J. in *Dranez Anstalt v Hayek*, [2002] All E.R. (D) 377. The facts of this case were that Dr Zamir Hayek, the inventor and original patentee of a mechanical ventilator known as the Hayek Oscillator and his company Medivent, were alleged to be subject to a non-compete restriction in favour of shareholders and investors of various companies he had formerly owned which exploited another ventilator known as the Oscillator. The disputed non-compete restriction had been entered into a side letter addressed to the Investors and had clearly been intended to be collateral to the Investment Agreement. The trial Judge had rejected the Investor's claim for an injunction to restrain further breach of the undertaking not to compete, holding that damages was the appropriate remedy. The Companies' claim for misuse of confidential information failed. As to the enforceability of the side letter, the judge held that, upon its time construction, the effect of the non-compete undertaking was to seek to impose on Dr Hayek a restriction from competing in the business of manufacturing and selling ventilators world-wide, for so long as the companies were conducting that business. The appellants, Dr Hayek and his company Medivent did not contend the judge was wrong to reach that conclusion, but argued that the Companies' business had already collapsed by the time Medivent was in a position to manufacture and sell its competing ventilator. On appeal Chadwick L.J. held that the restriction on competition was never enforceable—even during the period that the Companies were engaged in the business on the grounds of public injury.

As regards the restrictions falling into the second category, the restraint of trade doctrine would appear to have little application for the restraint, if it can properly be said to be a restraint at all, arises not as a consequence of the contract between the parties, but because of the monopoly rights granted by Parliament to the owner of the relevant intellectual property right. For the court to hold that the licensor could not limit the rights he grants, would be to place the doctrine of restraint of trade above the express provisions of statute. It is of interest that in *British Leyland Motor Corporation Ltd v Armstrong Patents Co Ltd* [1986] 2 W.L.R. 400, which concerned the use of copyright by a car manufacturer to prevent third parties from manufacturing spare parts for its cars, the House of Lords made no reference to the application of the doctrine of restraint of trade. If the doctrine were capable of being used to control the limits which a licensor could place upon a licensee, one might have expected it to have been applied in that case.

As regards restraints in the third category, there seems to be no reason in principle why the doctrine of restraint of trade should not apply. However, in practice the courts have been reluctant to apply the doctrine. In *Tungsten Electric Co Ltd v Tool Metal Manufacturing Co Ltd* [1955] 1 W.L.R. 761, the licensee was authorised under a patent to manufacture the contract material subject to a quota. If the licensee exceeded the quota, the compensation was payable to the licensor. The licensee's argument that the provision requiring payment was in restraint of trade was rejected. Nowadays such a clause would have to be considered carefully under competition law, as it might amount to a market sharing or customer allocation agreement, which would be illegal.

A more significant example of the courts' reluctance to interfere in cases involving tying restrictions was shown in *United Shoe Machinery Co of Canada v Brunet* [1909] A.C. 330. The plaintiffs had supplied machinery for the manufacture of shoes to the defendants under leases. The leases contained tying provisions which prohibited the defendants from using the machines for manufacturing shoes if any other part of the manufacturing process was carried out by machines not supplied by the plaintiffs. The court rejected the defendants' arguments that the restriction was in restraint of trade. The reasoning of the Privy Council was, as Lord Reid remarked in *Esso Petroleum v Harper's Garage* [1968] A.C. 269, not very satisfactory. The Privy Council was able to dispose of any proper consideration of the reasonableness of the restraint by saying:

> Their Lordships do not think that the case of *Nordenfelt v Maxim Nordenfelt Guns and Ammunition Co* [1894] A.C. 535 or authorities of that class can have any

> application to this case. In each of them the person restrained from trading had granted, presumably for adequate consideration, some property, privilege or right to the person who desired to impose the restraint upon him and, in order that the latter might receive, without injury to the public, that for which he had paid, the contract imposing the restraint was held to be valid only where the restraint was in itself reasonable in reference to the interests both of the contracting parties and of the public.

It is submitted that this reasoning is indeed defective for it does not take account, for example, of the many cases in which restraints on employees had been held invalid. In all likelihood a similar case nowadays would be considered under competition law as to whether it amounts to an illegal tie.

However, whilst the reasoning in *United Shoe Machinery*, such as there was, may not have been very satisfactory, the decision itself would appear to be on all fours with the dicta of their Lordships in *Esso*. The restraint imposed by the leases related only to the use of the machines which were leased by the plaintiffs. The defendants had no prior right to use the machines before the grant of the leases and accordingly, in accepting the restraint, gave up no freedom which they would otherwise have had. Similar restraints, whilst perhaps not quite so extensive in nature, are often found in modern leasing agreements for high technology equipment. These will often provide that the equipment, which might for example be a computer, should not be used in conjunction with any other equipment not approved by the lessor. It would be surprising if such a provision could be challenged on the grounds of restraint of trade, which is not to say it could not be challenged under competition law. If the logic for exempting such a restriction from the restraint of trade doctrine is indeed that the lessee gives up no freedom which he would otherwise have, then there should be no reason why a similar provision could not be imposed upon the sale of equipment. Suppose, for example, a manufacturer of computers were to sell only upon terms that the purchaser should not interconnect his equipment to that of any other manufacturer. If the reasoning of the majority in *Esso* is correct, then a purchaser should be in the same position as a lessee and the doctrine should not apply. Likewise, if a car manufacturer were to sell his cars upon terms that no spare part might be used except that of his own manufacture, the doctrine should not apply. But this would be contrary to the entire spirit of the judgment in *British Leyland v Armstrong*, referred to above, and it therefore seems probable that the court would reformulate or distinguish *Esso* and apply the doctrine. However, in *Fyffes v Chiquita Brands International Inc* [1993] F.S.R. 83, Vinelott J. held that a claim that a restriction on use of a trade mark was in restraint of trade, was not sufficiently substantial to justify interlocutory relief in the complex circumstances of the case. Among his reasons were that no freedom was being given up (based on Lord Reid's dicta in *Esso*) and also that the restraint operated wholly outside the jurisdiction of the English courts.

If the doctrine is to be applied, one has to consider whether the restriction is reasonable. The question of reasonableness as between the parties can, as has been seen above, be left to the parties in commercial contracts where there is no great inequality of bargaining power. As far as injury to the public is concerned, this will be hard to demonstrate where the restrictions are being placed by the licensor, however instead it is more likely to be competition law that fetters a licensor's discretion to impose restrictions. Under the doctrine, that leaves the question whether the restraint goes further than is necessary to protect the legitimate interests of the covenantee.

In the case of restriction in a licence against dealing in other products, the arguments discussed in relation to distribution and agency agreements will be relevant. The issue will be whether the restriction is directed towards concentrating the efforts of the licensee on the licensed products or has some other motive. As far as obligations to purchase other products from the licensor or supplier are concerned, it is arguable that these should not be held unreasonable. It is of the essence of liberty to trade that a supplier should be able to make the best use of his competitive advantages. If, therefore, he can persuade a customer to buy one product as a condition of the sale of another, so much the better (provided he does not have a dominant position in either products or he will be in breach of competition law). Due to the paucity of authority under the common law doctrine, it is difficult to predict the outcome of such a case. In any case future challenges are much more likely to concentrate on the application of competition law.

Obligations accepted by licensees to assign the benefit of any improvements to the licensor's technology to the licensor have never been considered in relation to the restraint of trade doctrine. It is submitted that such provisions would be likely to be held valid (subject to the application of competition law—see in particular Art.5(1) of the *Technology Transfer Block Exemption Regulation* 772/2004, [2004] OJ L123/11). The public is not much concerned with the identity of the owner of a particular right and so objections on the grounds of the public interest are unlikely. As between the parties, the licensor is likely to regard an agreement under which he does not receive the benefit of improvements to the technology as closer in nature to a sale of the technology than a mere licence and would accordingly be likely to require a higher licence fee. It is thus in the interests of both licensor (for it protects his rights) and licensee (for it assures a lower licence fee) that such a provision be held valid. Similar logic was used by Chitty J. in *Badische Anilin und Soda Fabrik v Schott Segner and Co* when he upheld a restraint on trading by an agent after termination of the agency when he said "to hold the restriction void would tend to deprive persons in the position of the defendant of the advantage of making their own bargains for their remuneration".

Restrictions on the use of trade marks have the potential to fall within the doctrine but there are few clear decisions. See *Hepworth Manufacturing Co Ltd v Ryott* [1920] 1 Ch. 1 discussed in Chapter 20 below. In *Apple Corp Ltd v Apple Computer Inc* [1992] R.P.C. 70 at p.79 it was held that there was a serious issue to be tried as to whether a restriction on use of a trade mark was in restraint of trade, whereas in *Fyffes plc v Chiquita Brands International Inc* [1993]

F.S.R. 83 a claim that a restriction on use of a trade mark operating wholly outside the UK was within the doctrine, was held not to be sufficiently substantial to justify interlocutory relief.

18.4 Competition law limitations

The potential application of EU or UK competition law to licences and tying agreements must be considered carefully. In terms of the application of the Competition Act 1998 ("CA"), it is our belief that the most likely issue is going to be whether the agreement benefits from a "parallel exemption". Under s.10 of the CA an agreement will be exempt in the UK from the Chapter I prohibition if it is exempt from the prohibition in Art.81(1) of the EC Treaty, either through a block exemption or an individual exemption. In other words a UK agreement is exempt from the Chapter I prohibition even if it does not affect trade between Member States, but otherwise falls within a category of agreements covered by a European block exemption (see further para.22.5.3).

Under European law a licensing agreement, whether it relates to a patent, copyright or a trade mark can infringe Arts 81(1) and 82. In *Consten and Grundig v Commission* Cases 56 and 58/64 [1966] E.C.R. 299, the European Court drew its famous distinction between the "existence" and the "exercise" of an intellectual property right. While the owner of an intellectual property right may seek to preserve the existence of his rights (e.g. preserving the brand image of goods covered by his trade mark), restrictions relating to the exercise of his intellectual property rights can affect competition.

In the *Windsuring International* case (OJ L229, 20.8.1983 p.1), the EC Commission considered the application of Art.81 to a patent licence agreement, which resulted in the finding of a breach and the imposition of fines on the owner of the intellectual property rights.

In *Sportswear SpA v Stonestyle Ltd*, [2006] All ER (D) 149 (Apr) the Court of Appeal had to consider whether a defendant was entitled to argue an agreement was in breach of Article 81 and therefore that the claimant did not have legitimate reasons to appose further dealings in the goods, within the meaning of section 12(2) of the Trade Marks Act 1994. The issue at stake was related to parallel imports and the possibility that the codes in the garment labels, which the defendant had removed, may have been imposed for the purpose of enabling the claimants to police and enforce absolute territorial exclusivity (which would be a hard core restriction in a licence under EC law). It was held that there was sufficient nexus between the anti-competition arguments alleged and the issue whether the respondents have legitimate reasons to oppose further distribution under section 12(2) Trade Marks Act, therefore the judge should not have been satisfied that the defence based on Article 81 was necessarily bound to fail.

The previous block exemption regulation which covered patent and know-how licenses (the *Technology Transfer Block Exemption Regulation 240/96*, OJ

L31, p.2) was replaced by a new one which takes a more economic approach and introduces market share thresholds (The *Technology Transfer Block Exemption Regulation* 772/2004, [2004] OJ L123/11 (hereafter the TTBE 772/2004)).

TTBE 772/2004 applies to pure patent licence agreements; pure know-how licence agreements a software copyright licence and combined patent and know-how licence agreements (so called "mixed" agreements).

Under TTBE 772/2004 patents covers:

> patents, patent applications, utility models, applications for registration of utility models, designs, topographies of semi-conductor products, supplementary protection certificates for medicinal products or other products for which such supplementary protection certificates may be obtained and plant breeders certificates.

A know-how licence agreement must concern a body of non-patented practical information resulting from experience and testing, which is: secret; substantial; and identifiable (Art.1(i)).

TTBE 772/2004 provides for exemption for agreements where the parties' combined market share does not exceed 20 per cent if they are competitors and where they are not competitors, if neither exceeds 30 per cent. Above these market shares there is no presumption that the agreements fall within Art.81(1), but the parties need to make their own careful analysis of any restrictions and the alleged benefits of the agreement. Under TTBE 772/2004 technology licence agreements may impose certain territorial restraints which, although restrictive of competition, the EC Commission considers on balance to have a pro-competitive effect and which are therefore exempt. The TTBE therefore sanctions territorial protection, on the one hand for licensees from competing exploitations or sales activities by other licensees, or by the licensor in the first licensee's territory and, on the other hand, for the licensor against competition from his licensees.

Agreements which impose an obligation on the licensee to use the licensor's trade mark or distinguish the licensed product during the term of the agreement are also exempt, provided that the licensee may also identify himself as the manufacturer of the product (Art.1(b)). This way the exploitation of a trade mark does not operate as a restraint so much as allowing both the licensor and the licensee to develop their brand image and goodwill. The TTBE 772/2004 prohibits certain clauses as hardcore restrictions, and these will vary depending on whether the agreement is one between undertakings that are competitors (Art.4(1)) or agreement between non-competitors (Art.4(2)). In addition there are certain excluded restrictions which apply regardless of who the parties are and their inclusion in any agreement would automatically mean that the block exemption would not apply. These excluded restrictions relate to any obligation on the licensee to grant an exclusive licence or assign to the licensor its own "severable improvements to or new applications of the licensed technology" or not to challenge the validity of intellectual property rights held by the licensor (Art.5(i)a–c).

The EC Commission may withdraw the benefit of the block exemption in certain limited circumstances, notably where the effect of the agreement is to prevent the licensed products from being exposed to effective competition, which may occur due to the cumulative effect of parallel networks of similar restrictive agreements. (Art.6).

Tying agreements which are most likely to be found in clauses in distribution agreements or intellectual property licenses may well offend Arts 81 and 82.

Under EU competition law, if the tying of two products is not "objectively justified by the nature of the products or commercial usage", such practice may constitute an abuse of a dominant position (under Art.82).

Article 81 may also apply to an agreement between competitors or concerted practices between competing suppliers which make the sale of one product conditional upon another distinct product. Alternatively in a vertical agreement (e.g. between a brewer and a pub landlord) tying may fall under Art.81 where it results in a single branding type of obligation for the tied product (see *Greenalls* and *Gibbs Mew*). In other words where the arrangement is based on an obligation or incentive scheme which makes the buyer (e.g. the pub landlord) purchase practically all its requirements from the supplier. In view of the potential risks of restricting inter-brand competition tying or so-called single branding is only exempt by the *Vertical Agreements Regulation 2790/1999* if the supplier's market share does not exceed 30 per cent and subject to a limitation in time of 5 years for the non-compete obligation (see *Commission's Notice on Vertical Restraints 2000* s.VI.2.7 and VI.2.1). See further Chapter 22.

Tying arrangements in licensing agreements will be exempt only if they are part of an obligation on the licensee to observe minimum quality specifications, including technical specifications for the licensed product or the obligation to procure goods or services from the licensor, insofar as these obligations are necessary for

(1) a technically proper exploitation of the licensed technology; or
(2) ensuring that the product of the licensee conforms to the minimum quality specifications that are applicable to the licensor and other licensees (see TTBE Guidelines Section 2.6).

If the tying provisions go beyond what is necessary for a technically satisfactory exploitation of the licensed technology or to ensure quality standards such clauses may be void if they result in foreclosure of the market for competing suppliers of the tied product.

See also the block exemption for research and development agreements (Reg.2658/2000) and specialisation agreements (Reg.2659/2000) and the accompanying Commission Notice *Guidelines on the applicability of Article 81 of the EC Treaty to horizontal cooperation agreements* OJ 2001 C/2.

18.5 Other statutory limitations

The provisions of s.44 of the Patents Act 1977 are of critical importance in relation to tying provisions in patent licences.

18.6 Drafting

Due to the lack of authority concerning licences and the restraint of trade doctrine, it is not possible to point to particular provisions which have been found objectionable. The advice given in relation to agency and distribution agreements may again be worth following: keep any unusual restraint separate from the more usual ones. Similarly, where provisions can be so drafted, a limitation on the extent of the licence granted is wiser than positive contractual obligations. (By all means include the same provisions as positive obligations as well).

However if the license is between "undertakings" (which can include an individual investor as licensor and a company as licensee) the EU's TTBE and its Guidelines must be considered. The first question is whether the license relates to further research and development, or to the manufacture and sale of the licensed products, in the former the *Research and Development Agreements Regulation 2658/2000* may apply, in the latter the TTBE may apply. The second question to be addressed will be whether the parties could be considered to be "actual or potential competitors" in the relevant product(s) market. This will affect which clauses are hardcore restrictions which would be illegal to include in the agreement.

Chapter 19

Cartels, Trade Associations and Co-operatives

19.1 Introduction

This section is concerned with the application of the doctrine of restraint of trade to agreements constituting cartels, co-operatives and trade associations. The inclusion of cartels in the same section as trade associations and co-operatives is not intended to imply that the normal operation of co-operatives and trade associations involves anything sinister or anti-competitive. However, on the rare occasions when the restraint of trade doctrine is of relevance to co-operatives or trade associations, it is usually because they are being operated in the manner of a cartel.

In addition because trade associations and co-operatives invariably are agreements between competitors one must ensure all activities are properly within that which is permissible under the application of EU or UK competition law, or risk very substantial fines.

19.2 Common provisions which give rise to difficulty

Three types of cases can be distinguished where restraint of trade has been an issue. Firstly, there are cases where the rules of an association have been attacked as unreasonably restricting the freedom of the members or potential members to trade as they wish. Secondly, and these cases are perhaps a subset of the first, there are the cases where the members have undertaken to supply their produce exclusively to the association and wish to escape from that undertaking. Thirdly, there are those cases where third parties have sought to proceed against the members of an association or cartel in relation to injury caused to them by the operation of the association or cartel. The boundaries between these classes of case are vague, but as little turns on the classification, this is of no great concern.

It may reasonably be stated that as a general rule, the rules of any association, co-operative or cartel are open to scrutiny under the restraint of trade doctrine (see the judgment of Lord Upjohn in *Dickson v Pharmaceutical Society of Great Britain* [1970] A.C. 403) and *Boddington v Lawton* [1994] I.C.R. 478 where the rules of the Prison Officers' Association were held to be in restraint of trade because sanctions could be imposed on members who failed to comply with strike action. There is no general rule like that put forward in the *Esso* case which might exempt them. The rules must therefore be shown to be reasonable both in the interests of the members and of the public. However, as will be seen, many of the normal consequences of a provision being in restraint of trade do not apply in relation to trade unions and employers' associations by reason of statute. There may also be specific rules applicable in particular cases. Thus restrictions on advertising imposed by the General Medical Council pursuant to s.35 of the Medical Act 1983 could not be challenged under the restraint of trade doctrine: *R. v General Medical Council, Ex p. Colman* [1990] 1 All E.R. 489 (see also *R. v LAUTRO, Ex p. Kendall* (1992) unreported transcript Marten Walsh Chever). Equally, the rules of an association can be subject to competition law—see para.19.5.1.

19.3 Reasonableness

Restraints regulating the trading activities of members of an association must be justified as being in the interests of the members individually, and as a whole, and in the interests of the public. In practice, the distinction between the interests of the members and of the public may become blurred, particularly where the association is concerned with the regulation of a large profession. Thus it will be reasonable for a professional association to impose rules which require its members to meet the highest standards of ethical conduct for it is both in the interest of the profession and the public that the public should be able to place their trust in the members of the profession (see Lord Upjohn in *Dickson v Pharmaceutical Society*). But in other fields of endeavour, such as acting, a restriction preventing persons with criminal records from entering and becoming members will be in restraint of trade (see *Faramus v Film Artistes Association* [1964] A.C. 925, where such a provision was held to be in restraint of trade but was validated by statute). In such cases, the interest of the public in the integrity of the members is not such as to justify an arbitrarily strict provision.

Where an association has acted capriciously by passing a resolution with the intent of specifically restricting the activities of a particular member, then it will prove very difficult to establish reasonableness: see *Lennon v Davenport* (1984) 56 A.L.R. 409.

Even in cases where the association may claim to represent the interests of a profession, it will be necessary to produce evidence to justify any restraint imposed upon members. Thus in *Dickson v Pharmaceutical Society* the Pharmaceutical Society passed a motion to amend the rules of professional conduct to provide that new pharmacies should only be situated in physically distinct premises and should be devoted only to a limited range of goods outside of pharmaceutical products. The respondent claimed that the motion was both ultra vires and in restraint of trade. The House of Lords found in favour of the respondent. It rejected the argument that, because the rules were not strictly speaking binding on the members except in honour, the doctrine could not apply. The Society declined to furnish evidence on the reasonableness of the restraint, preferring to rely on its argument that the matter was not justifiable (which, as has been noted, was unsuccessful). In the absence of evidence as to reasonableness, the House of Lords felt bound to decide in favour of the respondent for the motion was a manifest restraint.

The sporting world has been a field for the growth of the law of restraint of trade as applied to associations. The reason for this would seem to be that the bodies responsible for the government of the various sports cannot usually rely upon the statutory provisions which protect employers' associations and trade unions to exempt them from the consequences of the restraint of trade doctrine.

The principle which has emerged is that the bodies responsible for the management of each sport can legitimately have regard to the orderly management of the sport. Thus, in *Eastham v Newcastle United Football Club* [1964] Ch. 413, the ability of a club to transfer a player for a fee and to use that fee to acquire another player was potentially of benefit to the sport and was possibly an interest which could be protected; as the transfer system was held to be in restraint of trade on account of its combination with other rules, however, no final decision on the adequacy of this interest was made. Similarly, in *Greig v Insole* [1978] 3 All E.R. 449, Slade J. held that the International Cricket Conference, as organisers of international cricket had a legitimate interest to protect for the purpose of the restraint of trade doctrine and the Test and County Cricket Board likewise had a requisite interest. The interest was the organisation and administration of the game.

The test of reasonableness, in the light of this definition of interest is easier to apply for if the rules contain restraints which are reasonable, if the rules are more than are reasonably necessary for the protection of that interest, they will be unenforceable.

Thus, in *Eastham v Newcastle United Football Club Ltd*, the rules of the Football League and the Football Association were called into question. The plaintiff was a professional footballer with Newcastle United. He wanted to be transferred to another club but Newcastle United refused to allow him to go. They placed him on the retained list. The effect of this was that even if Eastham left Newcastle no other professional football club would employ him for to do so would be a breach of the rules of the Football Association. Eastham applied for a declaration that the rules were in restraint of trade and void. Wilberforce J. granted the declaration. The legitimate interests of the Association could not justify a restraint which effectively compelled a player to remain with one club all his playing life if the club so desired. Similar decisions have been reached in a number of Australian cases: see e.g. *Buckley v Tutty* (1971) 125 C.L.R. 353;

Adamson v Wife (1979) 27 A.L.R. 475; *Barnard v Australia Soccer Federation* (1988) 81 A.L.R. 81. See also EU law at para.19.5.1.

In *Greig v Insole* [1978] 3 All E.R. 449, the ICC and the TCCB imposed rules which effectively banned the plaintiff from first class cricket. The plaintiff had entered into an agreement with World Series Cricket to play in a number of matches. The ICC and the TCCB regarded World Series Cricket as a threat to the orderly management and finances of cricket. They accordingly responded by banning cricketers who entered into contracts with World Series Cricket from playing in test matches or first class cricket. The ban applied not only to players who entered into such contracts in the future, but also to those who had already done so. Slade J., after considering all the evidence, held that to deprive, by a form of retrospective legislation, a professional cricketer of the opportunity of making his living in a very important field of professional life was prima facie both a serious and unjust step to take. He accordingly held the rules ultra vires and in restraint of trade.

It should be noted that the courts will be slow to hold that parties whose right to work is affected by restraint of trade are not entitled to relief even if they are strictly not members of the restrictive association. Thus in *Eastham* Wilberforce J. granted a declaration, even though the plaintiff was in fact not a member of the Football Association himself. A declaration was granted in *Greig v Insole* (see also *Hughes v Western Australia Cricket Association (Inc) and others* [1969] A.L.R. 660 at p.700). Similarly, in *Nagle v Feilden* [1966] 2 Q.B. 633, the Court of Appeal held that there was an arguable case that a woman who had been refused a trainer's licence by the Jockey Club on account of her sex had power to make a declaration that the Jockey Club's practice was contrary to public policy (see also *McInnes v Onslow-Fane* [1978] 1 W.L.R. 1520). The jurisdiction is however limited to situations where the decision of the body concerned places an unreasonable restriction on the person's capacity to earn a living or he is in a direct contractual relationship with the body (see *Currie v Barton*, *The Times*, February 12, 1988, CA), although in *Hughes v WACA* it was held that the fact that the respondent had not made large sums was irrelevant if he was affected in a professional capacity (see also *Buckley v Tutty* (1971) 125 C.L.R. 353 at 325). Where the court has jurisdiction to grant a declaration the court also has jurisdiction to grant an interlocutory injunction: see *Newport Association Football Club Ltd v Football Association of Wales* (1994) 144 N.L.J. 1351. The jurisdiction should also be contrasted with the right to seek judicial review. The restraint of trade doctrine is directed at the effect of contracts or rules but does not bite directly upon the decisions of tribunals although the Australian and New Zealand courts have been willing to allow wider scope to the doctrine (see e.g. *Stininato v Auckland Boxing Association (Inc)* [1978] 1 N.Z.L.R. 1, and *Lennon v Davenport*; and *Forbes v NSW Trotling Club Ltd* (1979) 25 A.L.R. 1. The scope of judicial review has itself been extended to cover bodies whose authority does not derive from statute, statutory instrument or prerogative (see *R. v Panel on Takeovers Mergers, Ex p. DataWn plc* [1987] Q.B. 815 and *R. v Code of Practice Committee of the British Pharmaceutical Industry, Ex p.*

Professional Counselling Aids Ltd, *The Independent*, November 1, 1990 *The Times*, November 7, 1990). However, there remains a gap between the restraint of trade doctrine and judicial review through which cases may fall (see e.g. *R. v Disciplinary Committee of the Jockey Club, Ex p. Messingberd Mundy* [1993] 2 All E.R. 207; *R. v Jockey Club, Ex p. Ram Racecourses* [1993] 2 All E.R. 225; *R. v Royal Life Saving Society, Ex p. Howe* [1990] C.O.D. 440 and *R. v Disciplinary Committee of the Jockey Club, Ex p. The Aga Khan* [1993] 1 W.L.R. 909, CA).

The cases just referred to all concerned actions by individuals challenging the validity of restraints on employment. The position is no different where the restraints are challenged by an employer. For example, in *Kores Manufacturing Co v Kolok Manufacturing Co* [1957] 3 All E.R. 163 the parties, both carbon paper manufacturers, had each undertaken not to employ persons employed by the other in the previous five years. The restraint was held to be unenforceable because it applied to all categories of employees and there was no evidence to suggest that any interest which the parties might have had to protect could justify such an indiscriminate restraint. No doubt a more limited restraint could have been justified if there had been confidential information or customer connection to protect (see *Hivac v Park Royal Scientific Instruments* [1946] Ch. 169). A similar agreement between members of an employers' association was held unenforceable in *Mineral Water Bottle Exchange and Trade Protection Society v Booth* (1887) L.R. 36 Ch. D 465.

The rules of sporting associations may also be subject to the restraint of trade doctrine to the extent that they unjustifiably restrict entry by clubs. In *Stevenage Borough Football Club v Football League Ltd* (July 24, 1996) New Law Commercial Digest No. 2960712101, Carnwath J. indicated that the rule requiring ground improvements, before it was known whether a club would qualify for admission to the third division and the imposition of financial criteria not applied to existing clubs, were open to objection. However the claim was dismissed because it was brought too late.

It is not necessarily unreasonable for groups of traders to form associations and to supply all of their produce to such associations or to allocate business between them if the intention is to secure economies by improving distribution or by eliminating competition between them.

Thus in *Collins v Locke* (1879) 4 App. Cas. 674, the Privy Council held an agreement to parcel out between the various companies the business of stevedoring at a port was reasonable save in one regard: the agreement provided that in certain circumstances none of the parties was to act as stevedores. This was held to be unreasonable both in the interests of the parties (for none of them could take the benefit of this business) and in the interests of the public (for the company affected by the refusal could not get its stevedoring done). Therefore, in the absence of exceptional evidence it seems unlikely that a "blacking" contract would be enforceable.

However, where members of a trade association agree to restrict output and to fix prices under rules which last for as long as the association remains in existence, this will be unreasonable in the interests of the parties (see *Joseph Evans and Co v Heathcote* [1918] 1 K.B. 418) (and nowadays illegal under competition law). Similar reasoning was adopted in *McEllistrim v Ballymacelligott Co-op Agricultural and Dairy Society* [1919] A.C. 548. The appellant was a member of the co-operative and was as a result of a change in the rules of the society compelled to supply all his milk to the society at a price fixed by the society's committee. There were no means by which he could unilaterally withdraw from the society. The House of Lords held that the restriction was designed to do no more than protect the co-operative from competition and that, accordingly, the restraint was invalid. The inability of the appellant to withdraw from the society was again an important factor in assessing reasonableness.

English Hop Growers Ltd v Dering [1928] 2 K.B. 174 was a case where an obligation undertaken by a member to supply all his hops to the plaintiff society was held to be enforceable. There the obligation was limited to a five-year period. Scrutton L.J. said:

> In view of the fluctuating character of the yearly supply of hops, I see nothing unreasonable in hop growers combining to secure a steady and profitable process by eliminating competition amongst themselves and putting the marketing in the hands of one agent with full power to fix prices and hold up supplies, the benefit and loss being divided amongst the members.

Finally, it should be mentioned that there is authority for the proposition that "knockout agreements" between rival bidders at auctions are not in restraint of trade (see *Harrop v Thompson* [1975] 2 All E.R. 94). The position as regards dealers is regulated by statute: see the Auctions (Bidding Agreements) Act 1927.

19.4 Actions by third parties affected by cartels

Whilst there is, following *Nagle v Feilden*, the chance that an individual whose right to work is threatened by the activities of a body exercising the de facto right to control a particular trade or profession may seek redress, there seems to be no such comfort at common law for third party traders affected by combinations in restraint of trade. For, as has been mentioned earlier, an agreement in restraint of trade is not unlawful, it is merely unenforceable. (Although they may have redress under competition law where such an agreement might be illegal).

Mogul Steamship Co Ltd v McGregor, Gow and Co [1892] A.C. 25 is the classic example. The respondents, a number of shipping companies, entered into an agreement with the intent of securing as much of the Hankow and Shanghai tea-carrying trade as possible. As a result of this agreement the appellants, having sent their ships to Hankow, were unable to obtain a profitable cargo. An action ensued. The House of Lords held that the respondents had committed no wrongful act in giving effect to their agreement by joining to offer their ships at low rates. Accordingly, the appellants' claim failed. (A similar situation today would have been scrutinised very carefully under competition law, and the relevant block exemption regulation applicable to liner shipping conferences *Commission Regulation 823/2000*, OJ [2000] L100/24 (as amended) and see also *Arkin v Borchard Lines Ltd* [2003] EWHC 687.) In *Brekkes Ltd v Cattel* [1972] 1 Ch. 105, the plaintiffs were banned by the members of a market from using their own vehicles to ship fish to the market. The proceedings were based primarily on the Restrictive Trade Practices Act 1976 for the judge held, citing only *Mogul* as authority, that even if the resolution imposing the ban was in restraint of trade it would not be unlawful so as to give the plaintiffs a cause of action.

As has been seen, whilst a remedy in damages or an injunction may not be available under the restraint of trade doctrine, the courts are on occasion prepared to grant a declaration where they think it might be beneficial. However, with both injunctive relief and damages available under competition law it is far more likely that future cases will be brought under the Competition Act 1998 or Arts 81 or 82 of the EC Treaty.

19.5 EU and UK Competition Law limitations

19.5.1 EU

Under EU law there is a substantial amount of jurisprudence relating to the application of Arts 81 and 82 to trade associations. Indeed Art.81 by its very wording makes it clear that decisions of associations of undertakings (i.e. trade bodies) are prohibited if they restrict, prevent or distort competition. In practice this means that the rules of membership of a trade association can be caught as well as decisions of the trade association. Membership rules which restrict participation and thereby prevent an undertaking from operating in the relevant trade must be objectively justifiable (e.g. criteria relating to financial standing or having the necessary regulatory approvals to operate in an industry), and an applicant should be able to challenge a decision refusing him membership. (See for example the various Commission Decisions relating to the London Commodity Markets such as the *London Sugar Market*; *London Cocoa Market; London Rubber Market* and more recently the *P&I Clubs*.)

In addition some trade associations have effectively operated in such a way as to facilitate collusion of competitive behaviour between the members who were competitors. An example of a UK trade association acting as a cartel is the *Tractors Case* (Cases T-34/92 and T-35/92 [1994] ECR II 905).

In addition there have been various cases where the membership rules have been challenged under the provisions relating to the free movement of workers or the right to establishment. Having discussed in para.19.3 above the application of the restraint of trade doctrine to the transfer restrictions of football clubs a good example of the application of European law to the same issues is provided by the landmark case of *Bosman* (Case C-415/913) 1995 ECR I-4921.

Here the European Court of Justice held that Art.48 of the EC Treaty (now renumbered Art.39) which guarantees freedom of movement of workers, applied not just to acts of public authorities but also to rules of any other nature aimed at regulating gainful employment in a collective manner. Art.48 thus precluded the application of rules requiring football clubs to pay transfer fees to other clubs on the transfer of a professional footballer from one member state to another, since these unjustifiably restricted the freedom of movement of players.

In 1999 the Commission published *Preliminary Guidelines on the Application of the Competition Rules to Sport*, clarifying that the rules "inherent in sport" would not normally be caught by the prohibition in Art.81(1). In other words provided the rules are reasonable and ancillary to a legitimate objective they do not infringe Art.81(1).

Lastly, under competition law, unlike the restraint of trade doctrine, not only can the trade association, and its members, be subject to substantial fines for breach of the relevant EU or UK provision, but equally third parties can sue for damages.

19.5.2 UK

Although since March 2000 the Restrictive Trade Practices Act 1976 ("RTPA") is no longer applicable, it is worth noting that in the years prior to its abolishment there had been a spate of cases under the RTPA (sometimes in conjunction with Art.81) relating to the rules of sporting associations and whether their rules were restraints of trade contrary to the public interest.

In particular there have been various cases arising out of the fundamental changes taking place in the world of rugby football following the advent of professionalism in 1995. The Welsh Rugby Union ("WRU") was seeking to impose a regulatory discipline upon the organisation of the sport in Wales, in accordance with rules corresponding to those of the International Rugby Board ("IRB"), in particular the rules relating to tours and tournaments. The WRU demanded that the clubs wishing to join it remain members for ten years, whereas the clubs contended that five years was adequate to ensure stability. The clubs alleged that the ten-year rule was in breach of contract, in restraint of trade and in breach of Arts 81 and 82, since if they did not join the WRU they would be prevented from playing in Europe or in the Premier League. Interim relief was obtained on July 24, 1997 from Popplewell J., so that the clubs would be permitted to participate in the forthcoming rugby season (*Williams v Pugh* QBD transcript 1997—W–N. 497). The WRU notified its rules to the European Commission for either negative clearance or an exemption under Art.81(3), while the domestic proceedings were stayed (*Williams and Cardiff RFC v Welsh Rugby Union* QBD July 29, 1998, [1999] Eu. L.R. 195.)

The Restrictive Practices Court was requested by the Director General of Fair Trading to consider whether the agreements related to the establishment and rules of the Football Association Premier League Limited ("the Premier League") and to the granting by the Premier League of broadcasting rights to British Sky Broadcasting Limited ("Sky") and the British Broadcasting Corporation ("the BBC") contained relevant restrictions for the purposes of the RTPA and whether such restrictions were contrary to the public interest. Particulars of the agreements had been furnished to the Office of Fair Trading under the RTPA. The Court granted a declaration that the agreements for the supply of services were not contrary to the public interest. The presumption that a restriction would prima facie be contrary to the public interest was rebuttable if it passed the statutory "gateway" in s.19(1) and was reasonable given the balance between why it passed the threshold and any detriment it presented to the public. On the facts, public detriment would occur if the restriction was removed because of the inevitable reduction in club income from the sale of the broadcasting rights, the reduced competition between broadcasters and the inability of the league to split television revenue equally between member clubs so as to preserve the balance of competition. The arguments raised in favour of the removal of the restrictions did not outweigh the likely negative impact on the public interest.

Any case brought now would need to consider the application of the Competition Act 1998, Chapter I prohibition if their effect is purely local, and Art.81 if they affect trade between member states or a substantial part of the common market (i.e. affecting a particular trade or sport throughout the UK). The Director General has published Guidelines on the application of the Competition Act 1998 to trade associations (*Trade Associations, Professions and Self Regulatory Bodies* OFT 408, December 2004).

Since the coming into force of the Competition Act 1998, the rules and practices of the World Professional Billiard and Snooker Association ("WPBSA") relating to the sanctioning of tournaments was held to be an abuse of a dominant position resulting in a breach of ss. 2 and 18 of the Competition Act and Arts 81 and 82 EC Treaty (*Hendry v WPBSA* [2002] E.C.C. 8).

In the Chancellor of the Exchequer's March 2000 Economic and Fiscal Strategy Report, the OFT was asked to review the effect of exclusions from competition law of the rules of professions (Sch.4 of the Competition Act 1998). The review focused on three generic types of restrictions:

- rules which restrict entry to certain professions—for example disproportionately tight standards for obtaining and retaining the right to practice;
- rules on the conduct of regulated professionals such as restrictions or prohibitions on advertising or price competition—for example rules preventing professionals from including charges in adverts; and
- legal requirements which require third parties to use qualified professionals for certain transactions when other appropriately qualified people could do the job.

The professionals concerned included: the legal profession, engineers, surveyors and architects and a number of professionals whose services are mainly provided to the public sector such as teachers and health professionals (*OFT Press Release dated 26 May 2000 PN 22/00*). Following the OFT's Report *Competition in Professions* March 2001 (available on the OFT's website) various professional organisations voluntarily removed a number of restrictions that had been identified as being unjustified and anti-competitive (e.g. the Law Society has abolished the prohibition on advertising comparative fees, as well as restrictions on cold calling business clients), other restrictions are still subject to consultation and debate (e.g. the ban on multi-disciplinary practices (MDPs)) OFT Press Release PN 21/02 of April 25, 2002. Furthermore the Enterprise Act repealed the previous exemption applicable to professional rules that had been provided for in Sch.4 of the Competition Act 1998. With respect to the legal profession in November 2002 the OFT made various recommendations to the Lord Chancellor's Department in response to its consultation paper, *In the Public Interest*, July 2002.

In the *General Insurance Standards Council decision* (OFT decision January 26, 2001, available at http://www.oft.gov.uk) the OFT had to consider whether the rules of an insurance trade association were caught by Chapter 1 of the Competition Act 1998. Initially the OFT held that the rules did not appreciably restrict competition, however on appeal the Competition Appeal Tribunal disagreed, namely because of one rule which meant that intermediaries could not sell general insurance products of GISC's members unless the intermediaries were also members. Case No. 1003/2/1/01 *Institute of Independent Insurance Brokers v Director General of Fair Trading* [2001] CAT 4. The GISC dropped this rule and so the OFT was able to adopt a new decision confirming the new rules aid not infringe the Competition Act 1998.

19.6 Statutory Limitations

When considering the application of the common law rules of restraint of trade to trade associations and trade unions, the provisions of s.11 of the Trade Union and Labour Relations (Consolidation) Act 1992 are important for they effectively exempt trade unions and trade associations from the restraint of trade doctrine for many purposes (for an example of their application see *Goring v British Actors Equity Association* [1987] I.R.L.R. 122). In the absence of such legislation the rules of a trade union would be subject to the restraint of trade doctrine: see *Clark v Printing and Kindred Industries Union* (1976) 15 A.L.R. 71 and *Boddington v Lawton* [1994] I.C.R. 478.

Chapter 20

Other Agreements

20.1 Negotiation and evaluation agreements

20.1.1 Introduction

It is common for parties in the course of negotiating agreements for the licensing of technology, the sale of complex equipment, the establishment of joint ventures and many other purposes, to disclose to their opposite numbers significant confidential information regarding the products and processes to be the subject of the ultimate agreement. Likewise, information may be disclosed to the other party to enable him to evaluate the product or technology before negotiations begin. As has been seen above, it is likely that an obligation of confidence will be implied in such circumstances. However, the exact scope of the information which will be subject to the obligation and the nature of the remedy which will be available in the event of a breach are uncertain. For, as Megarry V.C. said in *Thomas Marshall (Exports) v Guinle* [1979] Ch. 227, the obligation may not be so much not to use but rather not to use without paying.

Accordingly, any party contemplating such negotiations would be well advised to ensure that before negotiations begin, the other party signs a confidentiality agreement.

20.1.2 The terms of the agreement

Generally, a confidentiality agreement should contain four provisions. Firstly, the information and the purpose for which it is to be supplied must be clearly defined. The definition of the purpose will have to be drafted afresh in every case. The definition of the information is more difficult. The first question to resolve is whether all information relating to the purpose which is disclosed is to be regarded as confidential or merely that which is marked "confidential". Generally, this will be determined by the practicalities of the situation. The advantage of the former approach is that less care need be taken in the administration of the disclosures. The advantage of the latter is that proof of the confidential disclosure may be easier should it prove necessary. The second question is whether information entering into the public domain (except as a result of a breach by the other party) should be excepted from the definition. The reason for doing this is that it is thought that it might be an unreasonable restraint of trade to include a restriction without such a proviso. As there has been no case on the point it is difficult to give positive guidance. A compromise solution is to limit the agreement to "confidential" information disclosed to the other party. The court would then have to decide whether the information had become sufficiently publicly known to bring the obligations under the agreement to an end.

The remaining provisions give rise to fewer difficulties. The other party should be obliged to keep the information confidential and to make it available only to such employees as is necessary for the purpose. This provision can vary in sophistication from a simple provision to this effect to a sophisticated procedure for approval of employees to have access and for physical access control. In many cases, it may be advisable to require a party to obtain and produce undertakings from his employees to observe the obligations of confidence. He should be obliged to use the information only for the defined purpose. Lastly, he should be obliged to return on demand the information, and all copies which have been made of it. Care should be taken when negotiating the terms of the main agreement to ensure that the information disclosed under the evaluation or negotiation agreement is adequately protected.

20.1.3 Competition law

The exchange of commercially sensitive information between companies that compete is usually in breach of Art.81, as in most cases the reason for the exchange is to facilitate a cartel. The disclosure of commercial terms or prices would indicate a price fixing cartel, while the disclosure of customer lists could be to allocate markets (see for example the *UK Tractor* cases Cases T-34/92 and T-35/92 [1994] ECR II 905). Were the EU Commission to find such information on a competitor in a company's files during a dawn raid, its suspicions would be immediately aroused. However it is clearly established practice that where companies wish to enter into a merger or joint venture they need to carry out due diligence on the operations of the relevant undertaking(s) in order to be able to negotiate the necessary representations and warranties and agree on a transaction price. The exchange of information for these limited purposes is not in breach of Art.81. However in order to avoid any possible future misconstruction as to the reasons for the exchange of the commercial information it is good practice to enter into a confidentiality agreement, and to the extent possible, limit the access of commercial people to the commercially sensitive information.

20.2 Authors and performers

20.2.1 Restraint of trade

Contracts with authors and performers have received special treatment in a number of cases which have come before the courts. In these cases, the courts have had the sometimes difficult task of reconciling the interests of promoters and publishers in protecting their sometimes sizeable investment in promoting the author and performer, and the freedom of the individual. In considering these cases two factors must be borne in mind. Firstly, each case turns on its particular facts not all of which may be entirely apparent from the judgments. Secondly, the emphasis placed upon the solemnity of contract has somewhat declined during the course of this century.

The principal factor which differentiates contracts with authors and performers from other contracts of employment is the personal reputation of the individual concerned. This reputation is in some respects analogous to the goodwill of a business. Like the goodwill of a business, it can be developed through industry and investment; unlike goodwill, it cannot be detached from the individual and disposed of separately.

Two situations in which a performer or author may enter into a restrictive agreement can be readily discerned. First, there are contracts for a short period during which the individual binds himself to work exclusively for a single promoter. Where the individual has no established reputation and the contract provides for a reasonable wage, then the contract is likely to be regarded by the court as a simple contract of employment and no unusual problems will arise (but if the restraint remains binding even if the employer gives no work to the employee and pays no wage then it will be in restraint of trade: *Young v Timmins* (1831) 1 Cr. & J. 331). Where the individual already has an established reputation, the court will in general grant an injunction to restrain a breach of the covenant and damages (see *Lumley v Wagner* (1852) 1 De G.M. & G. 604 and *Gaumont-British Picture Corporation Ltd v Alexander* [1936] 2 All E.R. 1686). It should be noted that the courts will not enforce a positive obligation to provide services. Therefore, any restraint should be phrased negatively as an obligation not to provide services to others. The court will not however grant an injunction to enforce such a covenant which would prevent the defendant from working altogether but it will be prepared to enforce the covenant to the extent required to prevent the performer from performing in breach of the covenant: see *Warner Bros Pictures Inc v Nelson* [1937] 1 K.B. 209. The decision in *Warner Bros Pictures* where a three-year injunction was granted has been criticised in recent cases. In *Warren v Mendy* [1989] I.C.R. 525, CA it was held that to grant an injunction to a manager preventing a rival manager from acting for a boxer in breach of a covenant in the boxer's management agreement would, in the circumstances, be tantamount to compelling the boxer to use the original manager. On the subject of what constitutes compulsion the court said:

> compulsion is a question to be decided on the facts of each case with a realistic regard for the probable reaction of an injunction on the psychological and material, and sometimes the physical, need of the servant to maintain [his particular] skill or talent.

Thus the fact that the boxer could have obtained work as a security guard did not diminish the element of compulsion. (See also *Nichols Advanced Vehicle Systems v De Angelis* December 21, 1979 (unreported) and *Lotus Car Ltd v Jaguar Car Ltd* July 1, 1982 (unreported).)

For a case involving an author who undertook not to write a competing text book see *Psychology Press Ltd v Flanagan* [2002] All E.R. (D) (QBD) where an injunction was granted.

The second situation in which a performer or author may enter into a restrictive agreement is that of the young artist with no established reputation seeking to break into the business. Where he enters into a long-term commitment under which he binds himself to perform exclusively for one company or to sell his works exclusively to one agent, the courts are more ready to strike down the agreement.

Some of the most striking examples of this approach concern music publishing contracts. In two separate cases contracts between agent/managers and songwriters in what was, it appears, a form common in the business, were struck down as being in restraint of trade (*Clifford Davis Management Ltd v WEA Records Ltd* [1975] 1 W.L.R. 61 and *A Schroeder Music Publishing Co Ltd v Macaulay* [1974] 1 W.L.R. 1308). In each case, the contracts were for a term of at least five years and provided for the automatic assignment of copyright of all of the artist's works to the manager. No corresponding obligation to promote the works was placed upon the management. The court held that the agreements were in restraint of trade and unenforceable. In the *Clifford Davis* case, the court set aside certain assignments of copyright which had already been made under the contract. Although the lack of bargaining power of the inexperienced artists was relevant in these cases it was not perhaps the most important factor. The principal objection in all these cases was that the artist's ability to make his livelihood was placed for a long period entirely in the hands of the other party who was under no countervailing obligation to promote the artist. In *Panayiotou v Sony Music Entertainments (UK) Ltd* (1994) 13 Tr. L.R. 532 (hereafter the "*George Michael*" case) at p.555 Parker J. noted that the only relevance of inequality of bargaining power to the application of the restraint of trade doctrine is either: to overcome the courts' normal reluctance to substitute its own (objective) view as to the interests of the parties; or, to negate an argument that the covenantor cannot complain that the terms of the contract are capable of being worked unreasonably against him since in entering into the contract he chose to repose a measure of confidence in the covenantee. *Schroeder v Macaulay* was followed in *Zang*

Tumb Tuum Records Ltd and Another v Holly Johnson [1993] E.M.L.R. 61 where certain provisions in a publishing contract made by a sister recording and publishing company with young members of a group of little business experience were held to be one-sided and unfair. The provisions singled out were the potential term (up to nine years at the option of the company), the absolute assignment of copyright and the binding up of the group exclusively to the company. Factors which were relevant to the finding included the lack of an obligation on the company to release records, the companies' freedom to terminate the agreement at 12–15 month intervals and the prohibition on the group members performing without consent. The companies' arguments that the provisions were required to compensate for the group which proved unsuccessful and to reap the benefit from early recordings did not justify such a long and one-sided term. *Zang Tumb Tuum* was itself followed in *Silvertone Records Ltd v Mountfield* [1993] E.M.L.R. 152 where recording and publishing agreements were held unenforceable in similar circumstances.

In *Watson v Prager* [1991] 1 W.L.R. 726 a three-year contract between a manager and a boxer which gave the manager an option to renew for a further three years if the boxer became champion was held to be unreasonable (although the court indicated that an option to renew for a shorter period could be reasonable). The fact that the contract was in the form required by the British Board of Boxing Control did not mean that the contract could be regarded as commonplace and outside the scope of the restraint of trade doctrine.

These cases can be contrasted with *Warner Bros v Nelson* where although the company was not bound to use the artist, they were bound to pay her an ever-increasing substantial salary. In *George Michael* at p.552 Parker J. held that the size of the consideration payable to the artist could be a positive factor tending to justify a restraint. It should be noted that restraint of trade is not the only basis upon which songwriter agreements have been attacked: in *O'Sullivan v Management Agency Ltd* [1985] Q.B. 428, CA a similar result to *Clifford Davis* was reached on the basis of undue influence. In *Elton John v Richard Leon James* [1991] F.S.R. 397 although Nicholls J. was unwilling to set aside an agreement between artist and publisher on grounds of delay, he held that the publisher occupied a fiduciary position in respect of any exploitation which it carried out, and was under a duty not to make for itself any profit not brought into account in computing royalties.

An intriguing device was used by a company of film producers before the First World War to try to retain the benefit of their efforts to promote their artists. In *Hepworth Manufacturing Co Ltd v Ryott* [1920] 1 Ch. 1 the company required the actor to work under a pseudonym and they provided in their agreement that the pseudonym would belong exclusively to them and could not be used by the actor after he left their employment. The court held the contract to be in unreasonable restraint of trade and that the actor was correspondingly free to use the pseudonym. The court was clearly swayed by two factors. Firstly, the pseudonym was of no use to the producers without the actor, therefore there was no interest to protect. Secondly, the evidence was that the actor could command only half the salary if he could not use the pseudonym. The court, therefore, held that the contract was a devise to ensure that they could retain their artists at unreasonably low wages.

Finally, even where restraint of trade considerations do not apply, the courts will only grant an injunction to enforce a covenant if the corresponding obligations of the plaintiff could be enforced by injunction. Thus in *Page One Records Ltd v Britton* [1968] 1 W.L.R. 157 a manager could not enforce a covenant to prevent a pop group using other management because his obligation to manage the group was one of trust and confidence which could not be specifically enforced by the group. This was followed in *Warren v Mendy*.

20.2.2 Competition law

It is unlikely that competition law, whether UK or EU, will be relevant in cases of performing rights of individuals as their agreements are unlikely to have an appreciable effect on competition. *George Michael* did raise the argument that his recording agreement with Sony was in breach of Art.81, but this was dismissed on the basis that the agreement did not affect trade between Member States, nor did it have an appreciable effect on trade in the field of pop records and so the requisite anti-competitive effect was not proved.

However to the extent that an agreement could have an appreciable effect on competition, the normal rules would apply, particularly those discussed in relation to intellectual property rights (see the *Technology Transfer Regulation 772/2004* and Chapter 18).

Chapter 21

European Community Provisions

21.1 Introduction to Articles 81 and 82 of the EC Treaty

This chapter considers the main principles of EU competition law which will be relevant in the context of the restraint of trade doctrine. Our purpose in doing so is to alert the reader to the relevance of EU law which until recently has frequently been ignored by the parties to a contract or dispute and by their lawyers, but this is radically changing in view of the introduction of a similar prohibitive regime in the UK and the increased awareness of EU competition law resulting from such cases as the UK beer tied-tenancy cases. Furthermore it is becoming increasingly clear that, for any agreement which has an effect on trade between Member States, the supremacy of EU competition law means that the application of the restraint of trade doctrine has been severely curtailed, if not entirely precluded. (See *Days Medical Aids v Pihsiany Machinery Manufacturing Co Ltd and others*, [2004] EWHC 44 (Comm). A more detailed discussion of competition law is to be found in such text books as Bellamy & Child's *Common Market Law of Competition*, Butterworths' *Competition Law* and Richard Whish's *Competition Law*.

Articles 81 and 82 of the EC Treaty form the starting point of any discussion (previously Arts 85 and 86 of the Treaty of Rome, which were renumbered as a result of the Maastricht Treaty). Where sales of companies and businesses are concerned the EC Merger Regulation, discussed below, may be relevant. In certain circumstances other articles of the EC Treaty, e.g. Art.39 (ex Art.48), may be relevant (see para.19.5). The text of these two key provisions is as follows:

Article 81

(1) The following shall be prohibited as incompatible with the common market: all agreements between undertakings, decisions by associations of undertakings and concerted practices which may affect trade

between Member States and which have as their object or effect the prevention, restriction or distortion of competition within the common market, and in particular those which:

(a) directly or indirectly fix purchase or selling prices or any other trading conditions;
(b) limit or control production, markets, technical development, or investment;
(c) share markets or sources of supply;
(d) apply dissimilar conditions to equivalent transactions with other trading parties, thereby placing them at a competitive disadvantage;
(e) make the conclusion of contracts subject to acceptance by the other parties of supplementary obligations which, by their nature or according to commercial usage, have no connection with the subject of such contracts.

(2) Any agreements or decisions prohibited pursuant to this Article shall be automatically void.

(3) The provisions of paragraph (1) may, however, be declared inapplicable in the case of:

- any agreement or category of agreements between undertakings;
- any decision or category of decisions by associations of undertakings;
- any concerted practice or category of concerted practices;

which contributes to improving the production or distribution of goods or to promoting technical or economic progress, while allowing consumers a fair share of the resulting benefit, and which does not:

(a) impose on the undertakings concerned restrictions which are not indispensable to the attainment of these objectives;
(b) afford such undertakings the possibility of eliminating competition in respect of a substantial part of the products in question.

Article 82

Any abuse by one or more undertakings of a dominant position within the common market or in a substantial part of it shall be prohibited as incompatible with the common market insofar as it may affect trade between Member States. Such abuse may, in particular, consist in:

(a) directly or indirectly imposing unfair purchase or selling prices or other unfair trading conditions;

(b) limiting production, markets or technical development to the prejudice of consumers;

(c) applying dissimilar conditions to equivalent transactions with other trading parties, thereby placing them at a competitive disadvantage;

(d) making the conclusion of contracts subject to acceptance by the other parties of supplementary obligations which, by their nature or according to commercial usage, have no connection with the subject of such contracts.

Article 81, which is likely to be the most relevant of the two in the context of restrictive covenants, is not as simple as it might appear. The first question is whether there is an infringement of Art.81(1). This divides into the following analysis.

21.2 Is there an agreement between undertakings?

The EC Treaty does not define "an undertaking", even though it is a key concept given that only agreements between undertakings are caught by Art.81(1). The term therefore has been the subject of numerous deliberations by both the Commission and the courts. The ECJ held in *Höfner and Elser v Macroton* (Case C-41/90 [1991] E.C.R. I–1979) that:

> the concept of an undertaking encompasses every entity engaged in an economic activity regardless of the legal status of the entity and the way in which it financed.

An undertaking is therefore most obviously a company or firm, but can also be members of the liberal professions such as customs agents, lawyers or even freelance opera singers (*Rai v Unitel* [1978] 3 C.M.L.R. 306); although there has recently been a controversial judgment by the ECJ where the regulatory rules adopted by the Dutch Bar Council for lawyers was held to fall outside Art.81(1) (*Wouters v Algemene Raad van de Nederlandse Orde van Advocaten*, Case C-309/99, [2002] E.C.R. I–577. See Whish R., *Competition Law* (5th ed) Chapter 3 for a more detailed discussion on undertakings and the *Wouters* case in particular.

Typically EU (and UK) competition law will not apply to the relationship between employer and employee because the latter is not an 'undertaking' within Article 81. In *Jean Claude Becu & Others* the ECJ held that workers (in this case dockers) are, for the duration of their employment relationship, incorporated into the undertakings that employ them and form part of the same economic unit, and do not therefore in themselves constitute 'undertakings' within the meaning of Community competition law (paragraph 26 of the Judgment, Case C-22/98 [1999] ECR I-5665).

While an employee is not an undertaking, an individual can be, and therefore an ex-employee who carries on an independent business can be an undertaking to which Article 81 can apply, see *Reuter/BASF*, EC Commission Decision 76/743, OJ [1976] L254/40. Furthermore, as competition law prohibits restrictions regarding potential competition between undertakings, it applies to both non-competition and non-solicitation clauses where a former employee (more typically a former director and/or shareholder) sets up a business in competition with his former employer.

Agreements between a principal and his agent will similarly be treated as a quasi employment relationship and Article 81(1) will not apply on the basis that a 'true' agent is not an independent undertaking, but rather a conduit through which the principal contracts directly with customers, and is therefore part of the principal's undertaking. See *Suiker Unie v Commission*, Joined Cases 40–48 etc., [1975] ECR 1663 and the Commission's *Guidelines on Vertical Restraints* [2000] OJ C291/1 which sets out the factors relevant to the assessment as to whether an agreement is a 'true' agency one.

Sports bodies such as FIFA and local football organising committees may also be treated as undertakings in their own right even if they are not for profit or do not have an economic purpose; see *Distribution of Package Tours during the 1990 World Cup* (OJ [1992] L326/31), as well as other professional trade associations.

21.3 Agreements

An agreement will usually be a contract, but because of the phrase "decisions . . . and concerted practices" the existence of a formal agreement is frequently irrelevant. Art.81 should, however, only apply to conduct by one or more undertakings which is consensual as opposed to unilateral conduct by one undertaking which, if it is by a dominant firm may be caught by Art.82. However the Commission has sought to stretch the definition of an agreement too far and has recently had a couple of decision annulled (*Bayer AG/Adatat* and *Volkswagen v Commission* (Case T-208/01 [2003] E.C.R. I upheld on appeal by the ECJ case C-74/04P)). Typically the issue as to whether an agreement exists has risen in the context of distribution systems and the extent to which there is any "agreement" between a manufacturer and local distributors regarding partitioning of national markets or maintaining resale prices.

Article 81 draws no distinction between horizontal and vertical agreements, although a clear distinction is emerging in the EC Commission's approach which views most vertical agreements, where there is no market power, as benign. This is reflected in the approach adopted in the block exemption Reg.2790/1999 relating to vertical agreements (see para.22.5.1).

21.4 Decisions

Decisions are stated to be "by associations of undertakings" and this has been held to mean that a trade association may infringe Art.81(1) by its very constitution (*ASPA* [1970] C.M.L.R. D 31).

In *Verband Der Sachversicherer* [1985] 3 C.M.L.R. 246 even a non-binding recommendation which was part of an official statement of an association's policy was held to infringe Art.81(1).

21.5 Concerted practices

The meaning of this phrase was established in two leading cases. In *ICI v Commission* (Cases 48, 49, 51–57/69 [1972] E.C.R. 619), a concerted practice was defined as being

> a form of co-ordination between undertakings which, without having reached the stage where an agreement properly so-called has been concluded, knowingly substitutes practical co-operation between them for the risks of competition.

This phrase may have led some to believe that a concerted practice was in some way a preliminary attempt at achieving an agreement which had not reached fruition. However in the *Sugar Cartel Case* (Case 40/73 [1975] E.C.R. 1663), the European Court of Justice rejected the argument that a concerted practice always required the working out of an actual plan. It stressed that each undertaking must act independently towards market conditions including, where necessary, adapting to the conduct of competitors. However, what was clearly stigmatised as a concerted practice was direct or indirect contact between undertakings intending or resulting in influence over the conduct of an actual or potential competitor or the disclosure to such a competitor of the course of conduct which they themselves had decided to adopt or contemplated adopting on the market. The evidence which the Commission is able to produce of the existence of a concerted practice is often very similar to the natural reaction of firms in an oligopolistic market to a given set of circumstances and in *Cie Asturienne v Commission* [1985] 1 C.M.L.R. 688 the court allowed an appeal against a finding of a concerted practice because the appellants were able to show good economic reasons for their conduct.

21.6 The effect on trade between Member States

The requirement is simply that there "may" be such an effect; there is no need to show that there *has* been such an effect (*Technique Minière* (Case 56/65 [1966] E.C.R. 235); nor that the effect is only prejudicial to such trade *Grundig*

(Cases 56 and 58/64 [1966] E.C.R. 299). The most important consideration in the context of this book is whether the fact that all the parties to an agreement, etc. trading solely in the UK precludes the application of Art.81. In the *Cement* decision (Case 8/72 [1972] E.C.R. 977) an agreement relating solely to the Netherlands was still held to be caught by Art.81(1).

It is necessary to examine the actual or potential effect of the agreement and if it does or is reasonably likely to affect inter-State trade to an appreciable extent then Art.81(1) will apply. In the context of modernisation of EU competition law, whereby Member States will also be applying Art.81, the Commission has issued *Guidelines on the effect on Trade Concept Contained in Articles 81 and 82* (OJ C101/2004) which contains a useful summary of the relevant case law. The EC Commission holds the view that in principle agreements are not capable of appreciably affecting trade between Member States when the following cumulative conditions are met:

(i) the aggregate market share of the parties on any relevant market within the Community aVected by the agreement does not exceed 5%; and

(ii) in the case of horizontal agreements, the aggregate annual Community turnover of the undertakings concerned in the products covered by the agreements does not exceed EUR 40 million (sales excluding tax during previous financial year). (para.52 of the EC Commission Notice).

21.7 An appreciable effect on competition

Given that an agreement etc. is within Art.81(1) it would seem logical to pass onto a consideration of the remainder of Art.81. However, this may not be necessary in two situations. The first is when there is only a minimal actual or potential effect on competition. What amounts to such an effect is partially, though not exhaustively, defined by the *Commission Notice on Agreements of Minor Importance* which do not appreciably restrict competition under Article 81(1), OJ 2001 C368/13. In this Notice the Commission sets out its views that agreements between undertakings engaged in the production or distribution of goods, or in the provision of service generally will not fall under the prohibition of Art.81(1) if the aggregate market shares held by all the parties do not exceed (a) the ten per cent threshold if it is a horizontal agreement (that is to say an agreement made between undertakings operating at the same level of production or marketing and therefore normally actual or potential competitors) or (b) the 15 per cent threshold if it is an agreement between non-competitors. However, the *Notice* does go on to stipulate that there are certain types of restrictions that are considered *always* to be a restraint of competition and caught by Art.81(1). Thus the applicability of Art.81(1) cannot be ruled out in relation to horizontal agreements, to the extent that they have as their *object* either (i) to fix prices or limit production of sales; or (ii) to share market resources of supply; and in relation to vertical agreements which have as their *object* (i) to fix resale prices; or (ii) to confer territorial protection on the participating undertakings or third undertakings, even if the aggregate market shares are well below the *de minimis* thresholds set out. The same principle applies in the UK where price fixing or market sharing agreement will always be deemed to have an appreciable effect on competition.

The second situation arises if one attempts to use a rule of reason approach towards Art. 81 rather than conceding that an agreement might be caught by Art.81(1) and concentrating on bringing it within the exemption provisions of Art.81(3). Technically the rule of reason does not exist in EU law (in contrast with the US). However in some cases the European court has accepted a rule of reason approach (i.e. not all restrictions fall within Art.81(1), see *Nungesser v Commission*, Case 258/78 [1982] E.C.R. 2015). Historicaly, one of the problems with the rule of reason approach has always been that only the EC Commission and not the national courts or authorities could grant individual exemptions under Art.81(3), which has meant that parties were supposed to notify the agreement to the EC Commission, which rarely had the resources to grant individual exemptions. However in the last few years the EC Commission has become more amenable to the suggestion that it should adopt a more "reasonable" approach to the application of Art.81(1) and it has been more willing to conclude that an agreement was not caught by Art.81(2) (see for example *DSD*, Commission Decision OJ 2001, L319/1). Ahead of the expansion of EU Member States in May 2004, the EC Commission undertook a complete review of the implementation of Art.81 and replaced the previous notification system with a raft of new regulations and guidelines aimed at a more flexible and economic approach to analysing agreements under Art.81.

Under Reg.1/2003 (which replaced Reg.17/62) not only the EC Commission, but also the national competition authorities and the national courts can apply Art.81 in its entirety, and in particular decide whether an agreement or conduct is prohibited and does not benefit from any exemption. Any analysis will be carried out on the basis of the additional block exemption regulations that have been issued, as well as the various new guidelines including the *Guidelines on the application of Article 81(3)* (OJ C101/97). Individual exemptions can now be applied for retrospectively. As a result in the majority of cases it will be down to the parties and their legal advisers to establish whether any agreement is caught by Art.81(1) and, if it is, whether it would meet the Art.81(3) criteria.

21.8 Exemptions

If an agreement is caught, or at least could be caught, by Art.81(1), the next step is to consider Art.81(3).

The most effective way of obtaining guidance as to the likelihood of an agreement falling within Art.81(3) is to examine the various block exemptions issued by the EC Commission in relation to certain classes of agreement. If the agreement falls squarely within a block exemption then it will be exempt from the voidness imposed by Art.81(2) and will be enforceable without the necessity of the parties notifying the agreement to the EC Commission requesting an individual exemption. Post-May 2004 notification is no longer possible, although where a new issue arises it will be possible to seek guidance in the form of reasoned and public "guidance letters" from DG Competition. (*Commission Notice* on informal guidance relating to novel questions concerning Articles 81 and 82 of the EC Treaty that arise in individual cases, OJ C101/78).

In 1999 the EC Commission adopted a new regulation on the application of Art.81(3) to supply and distribution agreements following a review undertaken by the Commission to streamline and adapt the rules on competition relating to vertical agreements. This *Commission Regulation 2790/1999* (OJ L 336/21, 29.12.99) replaced the previously existing three block exemptions regulations applicable to exclusive distribution, exclusive purchasing and franchising agreements (respectively Commission Regs 1983/83, 1984/83 and 4087/88) and came into force January 1, 2000. This regulation embodied a shift from the previously more formalistic regulatory approach towards a more economic approach in the assessment of vertical agreements under the EU competition laws.

By vertical agreements are meant agreements for the sale or purchase of goods or services between two or more companies operating at different levels of the production or distribution chain (Art.2). Regulation 2790/1999 therefore applies in particular to industrial supply agreements, exclusive and selective distribution agreements, franchising agreements and non-compete agreements in, for example, the beer and petrol sector. Rather than applying the straight jacket approach of the previous block exemption regulations (which provided "white lists" of the type of restrictive clauses which were allowed, "black lists" of those which were prohibited per se and "grey lists" of clauses which might be acceptable), Reg.2790/1999 adopts the approach that all vertical agreements, provided they do not include a limited number of prohibited clauses, are benign in the absence of significant market power.

Regulation 2790/1999 allows parties to an agreement whose market share is below 30 per cent to benefit from a "safe harbour" and such vertical agreements are presumed not to fall within the scope of Art.81(1). The Commission may however withdraw the benefit of the block exemption where it finds in a particular case that vertical agreements nevertheless have anti-competitive effects and in particular where access to the relevant market or competition therein is significantly restricted by the cumulative effect of parallel networks of similar vertical restraints implemented by competing suppliers or buyers (Art.8).

Where the parties to a vertical agreement have a market share exceeding 30 per cent they will not be covered by the block exemption and will require individual exemption from the EC Commission, but they will not be presumed to be illegal. Post-May 2004 they can equally be exempt by a national competition authority or court under Reg.1/2003.

Even where the parties have a combined market share of less than 30 per cent Reg.2790/1999 will not apply to two sets of restrictions. The first set concerns a limited number of so-called "hard-core restrictions". These include the imposition of resale prices and certain types of territorial and customer protection leading to the partitioning of markets (Art.4). The second set concerns certain restrictions which are not automatically exempted, but which may under certain circumstances nonetheless be compatible with the EC competition rules. The most important restriction of this kind concerns non-compete obligations. Under Art.5 of Reg.2790/1999 this covers any direct or indirect non-compete obligation contained in a vertical agreement, the duration of which is either indefinite or exceeds five years. However the five-year limitation shall not apply where the contract goods or services are sold by the buyer from premises and land owned by the supplier or leased by the supplier from third parties not connected with the buyer, provided that the duration of the non-compete obligation does not exceed the period of occupancy of the premises and land by the buyer (this limited exemption will apply to such agreements as the solus agreements or the brewery tied houses discussed in chapter 16). See *Days Medical Aids v Pihsiang Machinery Manufacturing and others* [2004] EWHC 44 (Comm) for an example of a national court's review of an exclusive distribution agreement under Reg.2790/1999, where it was held not to apply because of the way in which the duration clause operated.

Also under Art.5, Reg.2790/1999 will not apply to vertical agreements which contain any direct or indirect obligation causing the buyer, after termination of the agreement not to manufacture, purchase or sell goods or services which exceeds a period of one year after termination of the agreement. This obligation is without prejudice to the possibility of imposing a restriction which is unlimited in time on the use and disclosure of know-how which has not entered into the public domain.

Potential block exemption regulations which may be applicable are:

(1) *Regulation 2790/1999 (as amended):*

categories of vertical agreements and concerted practices OJ 1999 L336/21

(2) *Regulation 2658/2000 (as amended):*

categories of specialisation agreements OJ, 2000 L304/3.

(3) *Regulation 2659/2000 (as amended):*

categories of research and development agreements OJ, 1985 L 53/5.

(4) *Regulation 358/2003 (as amended):*

categories of insurance sector agreements, OJ 2003 L53/8.

(5) *Regulation 1017/68:*

transport by rail road and inland waterway, OJ 1968, L175/1

(6) *Regulation 1617/93 as amended:*

categories of air services and airport slot agreements (no longer in force as of 30 June 2005 following extensions).

(7) *Regulation 3652/93 (as amended):*

categories of agreements for computer reservation systems for air transport services, OJ 1993 L 333/37 (no longer in force as of 30 June 2005 following extensions).

(8) *Regulation 823/2000 (as amended):*

categories of agreements between liner shipping companies, OJ, 2000 L100/24.

(9) *Regulation 1400/2002 (as amended):*

categories of agreements in the motor vehicle sector OJ, 2002 L203/30.

(10) *Regulation 772/2004 (as corrected):*

categories of technology transfer agreements OJ 2004 L123/11.

Most of the Regulations were amended to take into account the acccession of the 10 new Member States with effect from May 7, 2004.

21.9 Individual exemptions

21.9.1 Pre May 2004

While the national courts and the EC Commission have always had concurrent powers to apply Arts 81(1) and 82, until May 2004 the EC Commission had exclusive jurisdiction in relation to Art.81(3) exemptions. If an agreement was caught by Art.81(1), but did not benefit from a block exemption, then an individual exemption could be sought by means of a notification of the agreement to the EC Commission. Following Regulation 1/2003 the national competition authorities and the national courts also have jurisdiction to grant an exemption under Art 81/3 (see further below)

Pre May 2004 frequently no decision was given or if it was, it was by way of an informal letter, a so called "comfort letters". While these comfort letters are not legally binding on the national courts, following *Gibbs Mew Plc v Gemmell* [1999] E.C.C. 97 CA the English courts must give these comfort letters great weight. The decision in *Gibbs Mew* confirms the position set out in the Commission *Notice on co-operation between national courts and the Commission* (OJ 1993 C39/6) which states that such a comfort letter is to be treated by the courts as "factual elements" (para.25).

Where the EC Commission has actually issued a formal decision that an agreement falls outside Art.81(1) or does not breach Art.82 (so called "negative clearance decision") the addressees of the decision (the notifying parties) are bound by it as well as any national court. In the context of the UK Competition Act 1998 it is worth noting that a EC Commission decision does not prevent the application of more stringent domestic competition legislation (see Case 253/78 and 1-3/79 *Procureur de la République v Giry and Guerlain* [1980] E.C.R. 2327). However Reg.1/2003 Art.3(3) only allows national law to prohibit an agreement which is allowed under EU law if the national law "predominantly" pursues a different objective than Arts 81 and 82. The UK common law restraint of trade doctrine has been held to have the same objectives as EU competition law and cannot therefore be relied on to lead to a different conclusion on the validity of an agreement (see Langley J., *Days Medical Aids Ltd v Pihsiang Machinery Manufacturing and others* [2004] EWHC 44 QBD, January 29, 2004).

A decision under Art.81(3) granting an individual exemption would bind a national court pre-May 2004 because the EC Commission had exclusive jurisdiction to grant exemptions, but equally post 2004 on the grounds of supremacy of EU law (see *Walt Wilhelm* Case 14/68 [1969] E.C.R. 1. A decision by the EC Commission under Art.81(3) can only be challenged by seeking its annulment before the European Court of Justice. An adverse decision (i.e. that an agreement falls within Art.81(1) and does not meet the requirements for an individual exemption) would also be binding on a national court (see *Iberian UK v BPB Industries plc* [1996] 2 C.M.L.R. 601.

However, the judgment of Park J., sitting in the Chancery Division, in the case of *Crehan v Inntrepreneur* (*Crehan v Inntrepreneur Pub Company and others* [2003] EWHC 1510 (Ch D)) highlights the difference between an actual Commission Decision on a particular agreement and a comfort letter or informal other expression of the Commission's views which do not bind a national judge and which he therefore feld did not preclude him from carrying out his own assessment as to the applicability of Art.81(1) and—post-May 2004—Art.81(3). This was reversed by the Court of Appeal which stated that the English court was obliged under the "duty of sincere cooperation" to give the EC Commission much greater deference to the EC Commission's earlier findings in the *Whitbread* Decision than the judge at first instance had been prepared to give. (*Crehan v Inntrepreneur*, CA, May 21, 2004). However on July 19, 2006 the House of Lords overturned the CA's award of damages, and held that English Courts (and by implication the UK competition authorities) are not bound to follow factual findings of the EC Commission reached in cases involving different parties in respect of different subject matter, even if they relate to the same market. It confirmed, however, that a court would be prohibited from making a decision that conflicted with existing or anticipated decisions of the Commission, if these decisions involve the same parties and the same subject matter, *Inntrepreneur Pub Company v Crehan* -[2006] UK HL38.

The *Crehan* litigation also involved a reference from the Court of Appeal to the ECJ on the compatibility with Community law of the English "*in pari delicto*" rule which prevents a party to an agreement which is liable to restrict competition from claiming damages as a result of such a breach from his co-contractor (Case C-453/99 [2001] E.C.R. I-6297). The ECJ ruled that where an agreement breaches Art.81(1), there is no absolute bar to a party to this agreement claiming damages from the other party. Crehan proceeded to claim such damages.

In order to decide on Crehan's claim, Park J. at the first instance had to assess whether the agreement in question indeed breached Art.81(1). There was no decision of the EC Commission regarding this particular agreement. Although the Inntrepreneur standard tenancy agreement had been originally notified to the EC Commission, the notification was subsequently withdrawn by Inntrepreneur. The EC Commission had, however, indicated informally that in its view the agreement fell within the Art.81(1) prohibition and was outside of the applicable block exemption regulation. Moreover, around the same time the EC Commission rendered three individual exemptions which also related to the UK beer market and also dealt with tried-pub arrangements (*Whitbread*, *Bass* and *Scottish & Newcastle*).

For the following reasons Park J., however, decided to carry out his own assessment of whether the agreement in question restricted competition.

On the basis of this assessment the judge came to the opposite conclusion to that of the EC Commission (both in its original indication to Inntrepreneur and its decisions). It was held that, based on the market conditions, the agreement in question could not have breached Art.81(1), this despite the fact that the EC Commission's decisions concerned the same market and similar arrangements. Also, the EC Commission had merely indicated that the agreement would fall within the scope of Art.81(1). The Court of Appeal overturned the High Court on the question of foreclosure on the basis that the judge should not have engaged in second-guessing the EC Commission and then conclude that the EC Commission was wrong. The House of Lords reversed this and stated that the court was not bound by the EC Commission's findings, but should form its own view of the issues on the basis of the evidence presented to it.

In deciding whether Art.81(3) applies so as to exempt an agreement it is necessary to examine the agreement in the light of the goals set therein (i.e. that its benefits outweigh any restriction of competition) (see para.22.1 below). However, even if an exemption is granted by the EC Commission, it can take a long while to be granted; in *Carlsberg Beers, Re* [1999] 1 C.M.L.R. 735 it took four years from notification to exemption. If notified, and the Commission took a decision granting an individual exemption, such exemption could be back-dated to the start date of an agreement (e.g. *Whitbread*, OJ

L88 31.3.1999, p.26, where the Commission backdated its agreement by nine years).

21.9.2 Post May 2004

It is in order to address these delays and reduce its workload the EC Commission de-centralised the approach to Arts 81 and 82 of the EC Treaty by granting national authorities and courts the ability to apply Art.81(3) under Reg.1/2003, which came into force in May 2004 (sometimes referred to as the *Modernisation Regulation*). One of the fundamental changes under the modernisation regime is that there is no longer such a thing as "individual exemption": an agreement will either be caught by Art.81 or not. The only valid individual exemptions that will be valid will be those that have already been granted under Reg.17/62 and that remain in force after May 1, 2004. Companies and their legal advisers will no longer be able to notify agreements to the Commission (or to a national authority to apply Art.81(3)), they will need to carry out their own self assessment of Art.81(1) and the possible application of Art.81(3). Only in exceptional circumstances will be Commission adopt a formal finding of "inapplicability" under Art.10 of Reg.1/2003, and in other cases it may provide "informal guidance". The system of block exemptions will however remain in place and if need be expanded, and so in practice most agreements will continue to be drafted in such a way as to benefit from the "safe harbour" they provide.

21.10 Article 81(2)—void and illegal?

Article 81(2) states "any agreements or decisions prohibited pursuant to this Article shall be automatically void" and the question courts have grappled with is whether they are also illegal. Restrictions contained in an agreement which are in breach of Art.81 are rendered void under Art.81(2) and are without legal effect and no consequences flow in civil law from their breach. Further, anti-competitive restrictions may not be enforced against a third party (see Case 22/71 *Beguelin Import v G.L. Import Export* [1971] E.C.R. 949 at p.962). Under English law, it would appear that restrictions caught by Article 81(1) are not merely void but also illegal (see *Gibbs Mew Plc v Gemmell*, [1999] 1 C.M.L.R. However the ECJ has since confirmed that in particular circumstances the absolute bar on an action by a co-contractor imposed by the UK common law rule of "*in pari delicto potior est conditio defendentis*" may not apply, such that one co-contractor may be able to sue for damages despite an agreement being caught by Art.81(1) (see *Courage Ltd v Crehan* [2001] E.C.R. I-6297).

Article 81(2) has both prospective and retroactive effect (see Case 48/72

Brasserie de Haecht SA v Wilkin (No. 2) [1973] E.C.R. 77 at para.27 of the judgment). Thus if an agreement falls within Art.81(1) and it was not notified then it will be void. Equally if an agreement fails to fall within a block exemption and has not been granted individual exemption then it is void. A void agreement can attract fines until the time of any notification. Notification acts as a barrier to fines regarding the agreement after notification in most cases, although the EC Commission can lift this immunity from fines.

Whether an agreement is void or not under Art.81 will depend on a comprehensive analysis of the agreement, any market power of the parties and the effect on competition of the particular agreement and its clauses. Guidance was given by the European Court of Justice in *Delimiters v Henniger Brau*, ECJ [1991] E.C.R. I-935 that, save where it is clear that the object of a provision in the context of a beer tie is anti-competitive, the court has to look at a fair amount of evidence in order to decide whether the provision in question is in fact anti-competitive or not (see Park J. in *Crehan v Inntrepreneur Pub Company*, [2003] EWHC 1510 Ch D for a detailed example of an Art.81(1) analysis by an English Judge—even if his analysis was subsequently reversed by the CA because of the Commission's findings in that particular case). The essential point in all cases of this type is that, at least save in clear cases, the question whether the effect of a particular provision is anti-competitive so as fall foul of Art.81 must be determined by reference to the provisions in question on its own. The need for an individual assessment of each agreement and clause in their overall context has been recognised in the various beer cases that have taken place (see also for example the UK Court of Appeal in *Inntrepreneur Estates v Boyes* [1993] 2 E.C.L.R. 112 and in *Gibbs Mew plc v Gemmell* [1999] 1 C.M.L.R. 1129).

In *Passmore v Morland* [1999] 3 All E.R. 1005 the Court of Appeal has held that tie provisions in a brewery tenancy agreement are capable of moving in and out of illegality, in other words that the prohibition of Art.81(1) was transient, and that it could therefore cease to be void if there was a change in circumstances.

> an agreement which is within the prohibition of Article [81(1)] at the time when it is entered into—because, in the circumstances prevailing in the relevant market at that time, it does have the effect of preventing, restricting or distorting competition—may, subsequently and as a result of a change in those circumstances, fall outside the prohibition contained in that Article, because, in the changed circumstances, it no longer has that effect. (Judgment of Chadwick L.J. [1999] 1 C.M.L.R., para.26).

Passmore was the publican of a pub under a tenancy granted by Inntrepreneur Pub Co ("IPC"). The tenancy contained a term that Passmore should purchase beer exclusively from IPC. Subsequently the reversion of the lease was acquired from IPC by Morland plc, a relatively small brewer. In a dispute between Passmore and Morland the former argued that the beer tie was unenforceable under Art.81(1). While IPC had been a significant pub company,

Morland was smaller and its agreements did not contribute to any foreclosure of the UK beer market and therefore the question for the Court of Appeal was whether the tie could cease to be unenforceable given the new effect on the market. Chadwick L.J. dealt with the argument put forward by Passmore that the principle of legal certainty should have as its consequence that the tie was and remained unenforceable. In *Shell UK Ltd v Lostock Garage* ([1977] 1 All E.R. 481, CA) the majority of the Court of Appeal had held that a restrictive covenant that was valid when it was entered into should remain valid, even if subsequent circumstances made it unreasonable or unfair to enforce it. In *Passmore* Chadwick L.J., while noting the difficulties about legal certainty felt that they should not be over-estimated. In his view what was seen in *Shell v Lostock* as a wholly novel doctrine is now enshrined in Community competition law. Agreements are prohibited when and while they are incompatible with competition in the common market and not otherwise. He did not think it would be right to give effect to what seemed to be the clear purpose and effect of Arts 81(1) and (2) because, in a different context, the Court of Appeal has held that purpose has no place in the English domestic law of restraint of trade.

In its subsequent judgment in *Courage v Crehan* (*Courage Ltd v Crehan,* C-453/99 [2001] E.C.R. I-6297) the ECJ again touched upon the effects of the nullity provided in Art.81(2).

In view of the uncertainties many parties previously considered notifying agreements requesting negative clearance and/or an individual exemption although once Reg.1/2003 comes into force in May 2004 this will no longer be an option. However it should be noted that agreements notified *do not* enjoy provisional validity merely because they have been notified to the EC Commission. This despite the considerable delay it may take for the EC Commission to reach a view as to whether Art.81 actually applies, although as stated above the parties would be protected from fines under Community law. In Case 48/72 *Brasserie de Haecht v Wilkins No. 2* [1973] E.C.R. 77 the European Court of Justice has stated:

> Whilst the principle of legal certainty requires that, in applying the prohibition of Article [81], the sometimes considerable delays by the Commission in exercising its powers should be taken into account, this cannot, however, absolve the [national] court from the obligation of deciding on the claims of interested parties who invoke the automatic nullity. In such a case it devolved on the court to judge whether there is cause to suspend proceedings in order to allow the parties to obtain the Commission's standpoint, unless it establishes either that the agreement does not have any perceptible effect on competition or trade between Member States or that there is no doubt that the agreement is incompatible with Article [81].

In practice, particularly if agreements had been notified or are about to be notified the UK courts would often stay proceedings in order to allow the EC Commission to investigate the issues more fully. Thus, for example, in *Williams & CardiV RFC v Welsh Rugby Union* High Court [1999] Eu. L.R. 195

the Judge agreed to stay proceedings while the trade association rules relating to rugby were notified to the EC Commission for review under Art.81, the trial Judge refusing to consider any arguments under the Restrictive Trade Practices Act 1976 and the restraint of trade doctrine for fear that this may lead to inconsistencies in approach between European competition law and the UK law.

21.11 Severance of restrictions

The nullity envisaged in Art.81(2) does not automatically embrace the whole agreement. Only such clauses as infringe Art.81(1) are automatically void (see for example Case 319/82 *Société de Vente de Ciment et Bétons de l'Est SA v Kerpen & Kerpen* [1985] 1 C.M.L.R. 511). A whole agreement will only become void if the offending restrictive clauses cannot be separated from the rest of the agreement. Thus in Case 56/65 *La Technique Minière v Maschinenbau Ulm GmbH* [1966] E.C.R. 235 at p.250 the European Court of Justice stated:

> The automatic nullity in question applies only to those elements of the agreement which are subject to the prohibition or to the agreement as a whole if those elements do not appear severable from the agreement itself. Consequently, all other contractual provisions which are not affected by the prohibition, since they do not involve the application of the Treaty, fall outside the Community law.

Where an agreement has been notified to the EC Commission and is found to be in breach of Art.81(1) and not found to satisfy the conditions of Art.81(3) for exemption, then the EC Commission must determine whether the restrictions are severable. This will be done by considering objectively all of the surrounding circumstances in the case, which does not include the subjective views of the parties. If the clauses are severable then the EC Commission must confine its decision to the void clauses only. In the majority of cases the parties will negotiate with the EC Commission and amend their agreement so that the offending provisions can be granted exemption.

If an agreement is being disputed before the national courts the test of severance is the question of national law and not Community law (*Ciment et Bétons v Kerpen and Kerpen* ([1983] ECR 4173). This may therefore lead to issues under the Rome Convention which determines the law that should be applied in contractual disputes. In the UK the court will first extract the offending clauses and secondly examine the residue to assess whether the contract "could be said to fail for lack of consideration or any other ground or whether the contract could be so changed in its character as not to be the sort of contract that the parties intended to enter at all" (*Chemidus Wavin v Société pour la Transformation et L'Exploitation des Résines Industrielles SA* [1978] 3 C.M.L.R. 514 at p.519, *per* Buckley L.J. Court of Appeal, In that case the Court held that the minimum royalties provision was enforceable, irrespective of whether other parts of the patent agreement might infringe Art.81(1).

Thus an agreement can fail because the consideration for the contract is contained in a void and unenforceable clause. Alternatively, the agreement can fail because, without the void clauses the parties would not have entered into the agreement at all, or the agreement would not have been materially similar to that which was originally concluded. The issue of severance has been considered by the UK courts in such cases as *Inntrepreneur Estates Ltd v Mason* [1993] 2 C.M.L.R. 293 where it was held that although a beer tie infringed the competition rules, it did not follow that a covenant to pay rent would also be unenforceable. Applying the test set out in *Chemidus Wavin* the tie could be severed leaving the rest of the agreement in force. (See also the Court of Appeal in *Inntrepreneur Estates (GL) Ltd v Boyes* [1995] E.C.C. 16 and *Trent Taverns Ltd v Sykes* [1998] Eu. L.R. 571, upheld on appeal.) In *James McCabe v Scottish Courage* QBD [2006] All ER (D) 409) an application for summary judgment the court was asked to consider whether the non-compete restriction in a supply agreement was severable if it was found to be unreasonable and void. On the basis that the non-compete obligation was part of the exclusive right and duty to purchase minimum quantities it was found not to be severable.

Recently a further consideration has been added to the analysis of whether restrictive clauses can be severed by the EC Commission. Where the restrictive clauses arise in a vertical agreement, if that agreement contains *any* of the hardcore restrictions (such as price fixing or limiting output) set out in Art.4 of the *Vertical Agreements Regulation 2790/1999*, then the benefit of the block exemption is lost for the *entire* vertical agreement (including any otherwise permissible non-compete obligations). In other words there is no severability for hardcore restrictions, although the general rule of severability set out above will continue to apply to non-compete obligation and exclusivity clauses in selective distribution systems which do not meet the conditions of Art.5 of the *Vertical Agreements Regulation 2790/1999* (*Commission's Guidelines on Vertical Restraints,* para.67).

21.12 Article 82

Many of the points made about Art.81 also apply to Art.82, though it takes a different approach to anti-competitive practices. Article 82 is concerned with the abuse of a dominant position. Note that as with Article 81, not only the EC Commission but the OFT and the national courts can apply Article 82 of the EC Treaty. There are two fundamental issues involved in its application. The first is whether the relevant undertaking has a dominant position. The existence of dominance is tested by considering the economic strength enjoyed by an undertaking in a particular product or service market and geographical area which enables it to prevent effective competition being maintained therein by affording it the power to behave to an appreciable extent independently of its competitors, customers and ultimately of its consumers. This test makes it clear that the size of the undertaking is not always relevant: the important point is its economic power in a particular market (see *Argyll Group plc v Distillers Co plc* [1986] 1 C.M.L.R. 764). As a rule of thumb however the EC Commission will consider carefully companies who have more than a 40 per cent share in the relevant market. See also the current thinking of the EC Commission as to certain types of abuses in *DG Competition Discussion Paper on the Application of Article 82 of the Treaty to exclusionary absuses,* December 2005 (to be found on the DG COMP website).

The second question is whether there has been any abuse. A non-exhaustive list of the types of behaviour that constitute abuse is given in Art.82 (see para.21.1 above). Of particular importance in the restraint of trade context is the example (a) discriminatory or unfair trading terms or prices. What amounts to an unfair trading condition is a question of fact. However, in *GEMA, Re* [1971] C.M.L.R. D 35 the EC Commission ruled that certain rules of a performing rights society amounted to unfair trading conditions. In *Michelin v Commission* (Case 322/81) [1985] 1 C.M.L.R. 282 it was decided that, although a quantity discount to customers was not an abuse, a loyalty rebate was as it tended to prevent a customer purchasing elsewhere. Finally, example (d) in Art.82 singles out tying requirements.

Where one party does have a significant market share however, exclusive agreements, or even agreements for fixed quantities, can be found to have a foreclosure effect on the market and therefore be deemed to be in breach of Article 81 and/or Article 82. Thus De Beeers purchase agreement with its most significant competitor Alrosa for fixed annual volume of rough diamonds was found to raise serious competition law concerns. As the purchase agreement pre-dated modernisation, it has been notified to the EC Commission for negative clearance/exemption. The EC Commission instead issued a Statement of Objections, and ultimately Commitments to modify (and in particular significantly reduce the volumes purchased) were entered into by De Beers. Alrosa is now appealing these commitments to the Court of First Instance on the basis inter alia that the Commitments breach the fundamental principles of freedom of contract and proportionality (Commission Press Release IP/06/205 and Memo/06/90) and Alrosa appeal Case T-170/06—*Alrosa v Commission*, OJ C212/31 of 2 September 2006).

The consequences of the existence of an abuse of a dominant position are that any contractual provision related to the abuse is void. A third party can use Art.82 as a cause of action in national courts and sue for damages/an injunction: see *Arkin v Borchard Lines Ltd* [2003] EWHC 687, Comm, for an Article 82 case before a UK court.

In relation to Art.82, where the EC Commission (or the OFT) has already investigated the matter and reached a decision finding an abuse of a dominant position and imposing a fine, it is possible for a third party who has suffered as a result of the abuse of a dominant position to sue for damages in the UK courts. In the High Court decision in *Iberian UK v BPB Industries plc*, [1996] 2 C.M.L.R. 601 the EC Commission had issued a decision in December 1988 upholding a complaint by Iberian against BPB and its subsidiary, British

Gypsum for abuse of a dominant position and imposing fines on each of them. BPB appealed, but the EC Commission's decision was upheld by the Court of First Instance and by the European Court of Justice. Iberian initiated proceedings in the English courts for damages for breach of Art.86 (now Art.82) after the EC Commission had reached its decision, but before BPB appealed to the CFI. The High Court held that where the parties have disputed an issue before the EC Commission and have had a real and reasonable opportunity to appeal from an adverse decision, they must accept the result obtained in Europe. Neither can deny the correctness of the EC Commission's conclusions before the English courts. The defendant against whom the decision is made (in this case BPB) cannot require the claimant/complainant (in this case Iberian) to prove breach of Art.82 from scratch. Though the point did not fall to be decided, the Court took the view that it would be wrong to allow the defendant a second bite of the cherry in this way against any party, whether or not they had actually been involved in the European proceedings. The Competition Act 1998, Section 47A now enshrines this position for damage claims before the Competition Appeal Tribunal.

The existence of the EC Commission or OFT Decision is therefore of major advantage to a litigant as it disposes of the need to establish breach of Arts 81 or 82 and the complainant would only have to prove that it has actually suffered loss as a result of either the existence of a restrictive agreement, cartel or the abuse of a dominant position.

21.13 EC Merger Regulation

21.13.1 Introduction

The Merger Regulation (Reg.139/2004, which replaced Reg.4064/89 on May 1, 2004) applies to mergers (defined as "concentrations" in the Regulation) having a Community dimension. A concentration has a Community dimension where the combined aggregate worldwide turnover of all the undertakings concerned is more than ECU 5,000 million and the aggregate Community-wide turnover of each of at least two of the undertakings concerned is more than ECU 250 million, unless each of the undertakings concerned achieves more than two-thirds of its aggregate Community-wide turnover within one and the same Member State. Article 1(3), which was added in 1997, has a further set of turnover thresholds introduced to catch mergers with significant turnover in more than three Member States which might otherwise have been subject to multi-jurisdictional merger filings.

Acquisitions caught by the Merger Regulation must be notified to the EC Commission prior to their implementation. The merger cannot be completed until the merger has been cleared or the relevant deadline has passed and it is deemed cleared. The Commission has one month for a preliminary look at the merger and a further four months for a detailed investigation where serious competition issues are found.

The definition of concentration set out in Art.3 of the EC Merger Regulation is broad enough to catch joint ventures which are to perform on a lasting basis all the functions of an autonomous entity (so called full function joint ventures). (See further para.14.2)

Article 21(2) provides that no Member State shall apply its national legislation on competition to any concentration that has a community dimension, subject to special exceptions provided in Arts 9 (where a case can be referred back to a Member State) and 21 (where a Member State can protect its legitimate interests).

The EC Commission appraises concentrations within the scope of the Regulation with a view to establishing whether or not they are compatible with the Common Market. A concentration which would not "significantly impede effective competition in the common market or in a substantial part of it, in particular as a result of the creation or strengthening of a dominant position", shall be declared compatible and cleared. (Article 2(2) of Reg.139/2004, referred to as the "SIEC" test which replaces the previous dominance test).

21.13.2 Ancillary restraints

The EC Commission's decision clearing a merger also covers restrictions agreed by the parties which are directly related to and are necessary to the implementation of the concentration (see Art.8(2)). Article 22 of the Regulation provides that Reg.17/62 (which gives the EC Commission power to apply Art.81 of the Treaty) does not apply to concentrations. The practical effect of this is that it is not open to a party to challenge a restriction found by the EC Commission to be directly related and necessary to the implementation of an approved concentration under Art.81 nor is it necessary (or possible) to seek exemption for such a restriction under Art.81(3).

The principles which the EC Commission applies in assessing restrictions are set out in the *Commission Notice regarding restrictions directly related and necessary to concentrations OJ 2005, C56/24*. The EC Commission accepts that restrictive covenants given by vendors of businesses will potentially meet the criteria to be regarded as "directly related" and "necessary" to the implementation of the concentration. The parties should, however, assess whether the duration, scope and geographical extent of the covenants are reasonably necessary for the legitimate protection of the business interests acquired. It should be noted that the EC Commission has exclusive competence to decide on the ancillary nature of restrictions which are normally notified to it in the context of a merger. It is now EC Commission practice to no longer comment on restrictions in its merger clearance decision, less there are specific novel or unresolved issues giving rise to genuine uncertainty. There has been a debate as to whether a national judge is competent to rule on whether restrictions are ancillary to a merger given that the EC Merger Regulation gives the EC Commission exclusive jurisdiction. (*Lagardère and Canal + SA v the European Commission*, Case T-251/00, [2002] E.C.R II-4825). However the Commission Notice 2005 on Ancillary Restraints which followed the *Lagardère* judgement claims that disputes between the parties as to whether the restrictions are ancillary to the merger and thus automatically covered by the Commission's clearance decision fall under the jurisdiction of national courts (para.2 of the *Notice*).

In the Notice the EC Commission indicates that for non-compete covenants a period of three years is recognised as appropriate where goodwill and know-how are transferred but that a period of two years will normally be the maximum where goodwill only is enclosed. This is not an immutable rule and in fact the earlier Notice of 1990 used to allow five years where goodwill and know-how were transferred. No explanation was been provided by the EC Commission when it reduced this in the 2001 Notice, and given that these Notices merely provide guidance and are not binding law, a longer period may be justified in particular cases. The geographic scope must be limited to the region in which the vendor had operated prior to the concentration and the business activity limited to the products and services of the business transferred.

The principles set out in the Notice are broadly in line with the jurisprudence developed prior to the Merger Regulation in the application of Art.81. In the Commission Decision in *Reuter/BASF* 76/743/EEC an eight-year covenant which also extended to non-commercialised research by the vendor was held to infringe Art.81(1) and was not exempted under Art.81(3), although five years would have been acceptable. In *Remia Nutricia*, Case 42/84 the ECJ dismissed an appeal against a EC Commission Decision rejecting a ten-year restriction accepted by a vendor of a sauces business. The EC Commission's view had been that a restriction of longer than four years was not permissible in the particular circumstances.

In practice since the publication of the 2001 *Ancillary Restraints Notice*, in most cases parties will draft and justify any ancillary restraints such as non-compete clauses and any exclusive supply or purchasing agreements in the light of the guidelines set out in the applicable Notice.

The EC Commission expressly indicates in its 2005 *Ancillary Restraints Notice* that the vendor may bind its subsidiaries and commercial agents but not third parties. The Notice also states that simple or exclusive licenses of patents or existing know-how may be acceptable and they may be limited to certain fields of use, to the extent that these correspond to the activities of the business transferred. However territorial limitations on manufacture reflecting the territory of the activities transferred are normally not necessary for the implementation of the merger.

Indeed in the Notice, the EC Commission states that intellectual property licences may be granted for the whole duration of the patent or similar rights, or the duration of the normal economic life of the know-how (Section B of the Notice). As such intellectual property licences are economically equivalent to a partial transfer of rights and they need not be limited in time. Territorial restrictions will be allowed in a licence of technical and commercial property rights and know-how granted by a buyer to a seller on the transfer of a business. Thus in the Commission's Decision in *Fiat Geotech/Ford New Holland* (Commission Decision of February 8, 1991, Case IV/M.009) the EC Commission was considering the granting of a trade mark licence in the context of a joint venture which fell under the Merger Regulation and its ancillary restraints doctrine. In this case the EC Commission accepted that Ford's granting of trade mark licences to Fiat for a period of up to 10 years fell outside the ambit of Art.85(1) and could be considered an ancillary restraint. This was because such licences were necessary to ensure the transfer of goodwill in the business being sold. This however can be contrasted with the EC Commission's approach under Art.81(1) where in the context of a co-operation between competitors the EC Commission grants an exemption for a limited duration and may well therefore equally limit the duration of an exclusive intellectual property licence. Thus, for example, in *Mitchell Cotts/Sofitra* (OJ 1987 L41/31) the EC Commission considered an exclusive know-how licence which had been granted to the joint venture company by one of the parent companies for an indefinite period. The EC Commission held that this arrangement was caught by the prohibition of the then applicable Art.85(1), because the licence went further than was reasonably necessary for the purposes of the joint venture. The EC Commission therefore granted an exemption for the envisaged life of the joint venture, that is to say eight years.

The 2005 Notice also deal with clauses such as service and distribution agreements, non-solicitation and confidentiality clauses (with the latter to be treated as non-compete clauses).

Chapter 22

UK Competition Law

22.1 Introduction

One of the major changes that have taken place since the publication of the first there editions of this book has been the adoption in the UK of a prohibition based regime similar to that under Arts 81 and 82 of the EC Treaty, and the repeal of the Restrictive Trade Practices Act 1976, followed by the criminalisation of certain breaches of UK competition law under the Enterprise Act 2003. Although as far back as 1989 the Conservative Government had considered replacing the Restrictive Trade Practices Act 1976 by a new prohibition of restrictive agreements based on Art.81 of the EC Treaty, at the time there was no clear consensus on the need to reform the law on monopolies and anti-competitive practices. In the event it was the labour Government that tackled the reforms. The Competition Act 1998 introduced two new prohibitions into domestic competition law:

(1) a prohibition of restrictive agreements and

(2) a prohibition of abuse of a dominant position.

In addition, it strengthened the OFT's investigative powers, introduced penalties and interim measures and other features based on EU competition law.

The general approach of the Competition Act 1998 was to replicate in the UK many elements of EU competition law, both in terms of the substantive rules, and the procedures to be followed. Furthermore, what had largely been a cumbersome administrative nature under the Restrictive Trade Practices Act, with case by case investigations by the authorities and very little litigation, this has been replaced by a system based on precedent (both EU and, as it develops, UK jurisprudence) and with much greater scope for private actions. To complicate matters, however, much of the old law relating to the investigation of monopolies (both scale and complex monopolies), as well as control over mergers was initially retained (i.e. Fair Trading Act 1973) although this too has now been changed by the Enterprise Act 2002 which came into force in June

2003. As this book is primarily concerned with the validity of restraints these latter aspects will only be dealt with to the extent that they are relevant.

The Competition Act 1998 was passed on November 9, 1998. A few provisions took effect as of the enactment date, but most have been brought into effect in stages by Statutory Instruments made by the Secretary of State. The main part of the Competition Act, that is to say the provisions relating to restrictive agreements and abuse of a dominant position, came into effect on March 1, 2000.

Lastly, as a result of the EU Modernisation of competition law, and in particular Reg.1/2003, national competition authorities and judges now have the ability (and obligation) to apply Art.81(1) and Art.81(3) to any agreement which has an effect on trade between Member States, and they are precluded from applying any national law which prohibits an agreement allowed under either Art.81(1) or 81(3)—unless the national law "predominately" pursues a different objective than Arts 81 and 82. (Article 3(3) of Reg.1/2003). In other words a national judge is precluded from applying UK competition law if EU competition law applies—and equally the common law restraint of trade. In *Days Medical Aids Ltd v Pihsiang Machinery Manufacturing and others*, [2004] EWHC 44 (Comm), Langley J. had to consider whether a clause which was allowed under Art.81(1), but did not actually meet all four conditions for Art.81(3)—could be void under the restraint of trade doctrine. He concluded that the supremacy of EU law as expressed in *Walt Wilhelm* ECJ, Case 14/68 [1969] E.C.R. 1, and as subsequently articulated by Advocate General Tesauro in the *Volkswagen* case, Case C-266/93 meant that indeed Community law precluded him from applying the restraint of trade doctrine to an exclusive distribution agreement.

22.2 The former Restrictive Trade Practices Act 1976 (the "RTPA")

The Competition Act has repealed the RTPA and introduced instead the Chapter I prohibition which concentrates on the effect of agreements rather than their form. The RTPA continued to be of some relevance for those agreements that pre-dated March 2000 which contained registrable restrictions which may be void because particulars were not furnished. Post-March 2000 all new agreements with any restrictive clauses are subject to the Competition Act 1998, and post May 1, 2007 all agreements (including those previously cleared under section 21(2) RTPA 1976) are subject to the Competition Act 1998 (SI 2004/1261).

Under the RTPA various agreements and arrangements under which parties either restricted their freedom to provide goods and services to others or supplied each other with information on their terms and prices were regulated. The RTPA did not as such prohibit them, but rather, made them subject to registration and, eventually once registered they would be brought before the Restrictive Practices Court where they had to be shown not to be contrary to the public interest. However, in reality most agreements never did reach the Restrictive Practices Court. Furthermore the RTPA had a very formalistic approach which meant that many agreements which may have been anti-competitive did not require registration in the first place.

If an agreement was caught by the RTPA the parties had an obligation to notify the agreement within three months of entering into the agreement. Whilst there were no criminal proceedings applicable in respect of a failure to register, agreements which had not been registered within the time allowed were void in respect of all restrictions accepted or information provisions included. It was also unlawful for any party to give effect to the restrictions and if they did, such breach was actionable by third parties as a breach of statutory duty.

In practice the RTPA caught numerous agreements which did not have any significant impact on competition. Section 21(2) of the RTPA, upon the Director General's representation that the restrictions accepted were not of such significance as to call for investigation by the Restrictive Practices Court, the Secretary of State could give directions discharging the Director General's from taking procedures in the Court. As a result many of the more common restraint of trade clauses found in partnership agreements and joint ventures usually received s.21(2) directions. Equally common restraint of trade clauses may have been exempt by the Restrictive Trade Practices (Sale and Purchase and Share Subscription Agreements) (Goods) Order 1989 (SI 1989/1081) and the corresponding Order for services, the Restrictive Trade Practices (Services) (Amendment) Order 1989 (SI 1989/1082) which provided a broad exemption for the restraints commonly imposed in share and business sale agreements and in share subscription agreements.

22.3 The Chapter I prohibition

22.3.1 Agreements caught by the prohibition

Set out in Chapter 1 s.2 is the prohibition of agreements which restrict or distort competition. Specifically s.2 provides:

Agreements between undertakings, decisions by associations of undertakings or concerted practices which:

(a) may affect trade within the United Kingdom, and

(b) have as their object or effect the prevention, restriction or distortion of competition within the United Kingdom

The wording of the prohibition (known as the "Chapter I prohibition") mirrors Art.81 of the EC Treaty with, broadly, the replacement of the requirement that it affects trade within the United Kingdom instead of the common market. Similarly s.2(2) of the Competition Act sets out the same list of specific types of agreements which are caught by the Chapter I prohibition as is set out in Art.81, namely agreements which:

(a) directly or indirectly fix purchase or selling prices or any other trading conditions;

(b) limit or control production, markets, technical development or investment;

(c) share markets or sources of supply;

(d) apply dissimilar conditions to equivalent transactions with other trading parties, thereby placing them at a competitive disadvantage;

(e) make the conclusion of contracts subject to acceptance by other parties of supplementary obligations which, by their nature or according to commercial usage, have no connection with the subject of such contracts.

The first thing to note is that for the purposes of the Chapter I prohibition the term agreement is wide defined and includes not only formal agreements that are in writing but also oral agreements and informal arrangements. Furthermore, unlike the definitive list set out in the RTPA ss. 6 and 11, the list of specific agreements caught by the prohibition in s.2(2) of the Competition Act is non-exhaustive and is intended merely to be illustrative of the type of agreements commonly caught. The ultimate question is whether an agreement affects trade and has either as its object or effect the prevention, restriction or distortion of competition. Section 2(4) provides that agreements which fall within the prohibition are void. However, in line with European Union law, this is to be interpreted as meaning that only those parts of the agreement which infringe the prohibition will be void (see further Chapter 21, para.21.11). To the extent that those parts are severable from the remainder of the agreement, the remainder may continue in force, subject to the provisions of any severability clause contained in the agreement itself.

22.3.2 Section 60

One of the purposes of the new Competition Act was to adopt an approach similar to that under the EC Treaty Arts 81 and 82. In order to ensure this, not only is the wording of the actual prohibitions in Chapter I and Chapter II of the Competition Act very similar to those under Arts 81 and 82 of the EC Treaty (albeit allowing for a focus on the effect on competition within the UK), the Competition Act 1998 also allows for the wholesale application of the principles of EU law and its jurisprudence through the existence of s.60. Section 60(1) of the Act declares that its purpose is to:

> ensure that so far as is possible (having regard to any relevant differences between the provisions concerned), questions arising under this Part in relation to competition within the United Kingdom are dealt with in a manner which is consistent with the treatment of corresponding questions arising in Community law in relation to competition within the Community.

Further provisions of s.60 ensure that any UK court or tribunal determining a question under the Competition Act must act with a view to ensuring that there is no inconsistency between the principles applied and the decision reached by that UK court or tribunal on the one hand, and the principles laid down by the Treaty and any relevant decisions by the European Court on the other hand. Furthermore the UK is to have regard to any relevant decisions or guidelines of the European Commission.

While the main thrust of s.60 is to ensure that there is consistency between decisions made in the UK with those made by the European institutions regarding similar questions, consistency is not however required where there is a relevant difference between the actual provisions of the Competition Act 1998 and EU competition law.

Thus, for example, account needs to be taken of the various differences which exist between the Chapter I prohibition and Art.81. For example the Competition Act 1998 specifically provides in s.2(3) that the prohibition only applies "if the agreement, decision or practice is, or is intended to be, implemented in the United Kingdom". This is, in effect, an enactment into UK domestic law of the principle set out in the *Wood Pulp* [1988] E.C.R. 5193 decision of the European Court of Justice, whereby an agreement will only be caught by Art.81(1), if it is implemented, or intended to be implemented in the European Community. Thus the Competition Act allows for a recognition of the geographic limitation to the jurisdiction of the Office of Fair Trading and the UK courts.

Equally whereas Art.81 refers to agreements affecting trade within the Common Market, but does not go on to define this, s.2(7) of the Competition Act states that the United Kingdom means, in relation to an agreement which operates or is intended to operate only in a part of the United Kingdom, that part. It also clarifies that there is no requirement that the relevant part of the United Kingdom affected be a substantial part. The Chapter I prohibition therefore applies, and is clearly intended to apply, to agreements which only operate within the UK. For example, the prohibition would therefore apply to agreements between businesses which are local such as newspapers (e.g. *Aberdeen Journals*, Case 1009/1/1/02 CAT II), bus companies (e.g. *Arriva plc and First Group plc*, Decision of the Director General of Fair Trading No. CA 98/9/2002, upheld on appeal) or otherwise limited to the UK, such as the supply of medicine to the NHS (*Napp Pharmaceuticals*, Decision of the Director General of Fair Trading No. CA 98/2/2001, upheld on appeal).

22.3.3 Agreements with a significant or appreciable effect

As a result of the application of EU law into UK law through s.60 of the Competition Act, the Chapter I prohibition only applies to agreements which have a significant or appreciable effect on competition. This is another key distinction with the former application of the RTPA which did not take into account the effect of an agreement on competition to determine whether it was registrable, although insignificant agreements were usually granted s.21(2) directions and did not require to be brought before the Restrictive Practices Court.

The Office of Fair Trading ("OFT") has indicated that it will normally regard an agreement between companies having a combined market share of less than 25 per cent of the relevant market as not having a significant effect. However, the DGFT has also made it clear that it will generally regard any agreement which fixes prices, shares markets or imposes minimum resale prices as being capable of having an appreciable effect, even where the combined market share of the parties to the agreement is below 25 per cent. The same is also considered true with regards to networks of similar agreements which have a cumulative effect on the market in question.

22.4 Excluded agreements

The wide nature of the Chapter I prohibition means that, even disregarding agreements with no appreciable effect, many agreements of a variety of types will potentially be prohibited. Having said that, certain types of agreement, notably those subject to other legislation may well be subject to the specific exclusions from the prohibitions that are listed in Schs 1 to 4 of the Competition Act 1998. Discussed below is the list of all the various exclusions that apply to the Chapter I prohibition, although in terms of the types of agreements where there may be restraint of trade provisions, these are more likely to be affected by such exclusions as those applicable to mergers and vertical agreements, although they could potentially arise in some of the other circumstances.

22.4.1 Mergers and ancillary restraints

Under Sch.1 to the Competition Act 1998, an agreement does not fall within the scope of the Chapter I prohibition to the extent that it gives rise to a merger situation within the meaning of Part IV of the Fair Trading Act 1973. That is to say to the extent that it results, or if carried out would result, in any two enterprises ceasing to be distinct enterprises for the purposes of the Fair Trading Act. Similarly, to the extent to which conduct results in a merger situation, such conduct would equally not fall within the scope of the Chapter II prohibition.

This exclusion also extends to any provision which is "directly related and necessary" to the implementation of the merger, such as vendor covenants included in a share or business sale agreement, exclusive supply agreements or licences entered into in connection with a share or business sale, or non-compete covenants between the parents to a joint venture. This is similar to the EU doctrine whereby restrictions which are directly related and necessary to the implementation of a concentration falling under the European Merger Control Regulation are assessed together with the concentration itself (see para.22.5).

Indeed the OFT's approach to ancillary restrictions should follow that of the European Commission's *Notice regarding restrictions directly related and necessary to to concentrations* as this constitutes a statement of the European Commission to which the UK authorities must have regard under s.60 of the Competition Act. The OFT has published guidelines on the types of restriction that are likely to be deemed ancillary and therefore excluded. (*OFT Guidelines: Mergers Substantive Assessment Guidance, OFT 516, May 2003* hereafter the OFT Guidelines.) Note however that these OFT Guidelines were based on the former 1990 EU Commission Notice on ancillary restrictions and not on the current 2005 Notice. As such there are significant discrepancies that exist.

As stated above Sch.1 of the Competition Act provides that a restriction must be *directly related and necessary* to the implementation of the merger if it is to benefit from the exclusion. To be considered directly related, the restriction must be connected with the merger, but ancillary or subordinate to its main object. Thus, for example, the main object of a merger agreement may be for one company to buy a particular manufacturing operation from another. In such case the added obligation of supplying certain raw materials to enable the manufacturing operation to continue following the merger would be considered directly related to the merger agreement, but subordinate to it. However it should be noted that a restriction is not automatically deemed directly related to the merger merely because it is agreed at the same time as the merger, or is expressed to be so related. If in actual fact there is little or no connection with the merger then such a restriction would not be considered ancillary.

Furthermore in order to be excluded a restriction must be necessary to the implementation of the merger. This is likely to be the case where, for example, in the absence of the restriction, the merger would not go ahead, might have less chance of succeeding if it did, or would proceed only at considerable extra cost or over a considerably longer period. In order to determine the necessity of a restriction one has to analyse its duration and geographical scope and whether they are proportionate to the overall requirements of the merger. Although the actual assessment as to whether a restriction is indeed directly related and necessary depends on the circumstances of each case. The Commission's Notice provides some general points on how the most common types of restrictions will be handled.

The exclusion relating to mergers and ancillary restrictions can however be withdrawn if the OFT gives the direction, which he may only do if, first, he considers that the agreement will, if not excluded, infringe the Chapter I prohibition and that it is not likely to grant an unconditional individual exemption and, secondly, if the agreement is not a projected agreement (Sch.1, para.4). There are four kinds of protected agreements:

(a) those which relate to a merger in connection with which the Secretary of State has announced his decision not to make a merger reference to the Competition Commission;

(b) those which relate to a merger where the Secretary of State has made such a reference, and the Competition Commission has found that the agreement would give rise to a merger situation qualifying for investigation;

(c) an agreement which relates to a merger arising through the acquisition of a controlling interest (as opposed to the acquisition of material influence or the ability to control the policy of a company);

(d) an agreement relating to a water merger which has been referred to the Competition Commission.

In addition to excluding mergers caught by the UK legislation, agreements relating to a merger and ancillary restrictions which fall within the EC Merger Regulation are also excluded as the European Commission has exclusive jurisdiction over such agreements (Sch.1, para.6(i)).

22.4.1.1 Non-competition clauses

Non-competition clauses are very common in the context of an acquisition by one company of all or part of another company. Such clauses, if properly limited in terms of their duration and geographic scope are generally accepted as being directly related and necessary if a purchaser is to receive the full benefit of any goodwill and/or know-how acquired with any tangible assets.

The terms of a particular non-competition clause must not, however, exceed what is necessary to attain that objective. The OFT will consider the duration of the clause, its geographic coverage, and the products or services affected. According to the OFT's Guidelines in general terms, a three-year period will normally be acceptable where both goodwill and know-how have been acquired, and a period of two years where only goodwill is involved. Longer periods may be acceptable depending on the individual circumstances of the agreement. Furthermore it should be noted that any restriction must relate only to the goods and services of the acquired business and to the area in which the goods and services were established under the previous owner. If they extend beyond the scope of the existing business acquired such non-compete clauses are unlikely to be considered directly related and necessary and therefore would not benefit from the exclusion. As such these non-compete clauses would then be subject to the Chapter I prohibition and be void unless they are exempt.

22.4.1.2 Licences of industrial property and know-how

Where a company acquires all or part of another company, the transaction may often include a transfer of rights to industrial or commercial property or know-how. In some instances the seller may need to retain ownership of such rights in order to be able to exploit them in the remaining part of his business. In such cases the purchaser will normally share the industrial property and know-how under licensing agreements. In this context, restrictions in exclusive or simple licences of patents, trade marks, know-how and similar rights may be accepted as necessary to the implementation of the merger, and therefore, covered by the definition of ancillary restrictions and excluded from the prohibition. These licences may be limited in terms of their field of use to the activities of the business acquired and may be granted for the entire duration of the patents, trade marks or similar rights, or the normal economic life of any know-how. However, if the licences contain restrictions that are not included within any of the above categories, they are likely to fall outside the definition of an ancillary restriction and therefore would fall within the scope of Chapter I.

22.4.1.3 Purchase and supply agreements

Where an acquired business was formerly part of an integrated group of companies and relied on other companies within its former group for raw materials, or where it represented a guaranteed outlet for the companies' products it may be necessary at the time of the merger to include a purchase and/or supply agreement between the new and former owners for a transitional period so that the businesses concerned can adapt to their new circumstances. Such agreements may be considered ancillary provided they are indeed limited to a transitional period and are not exclusive, although in very exceptional circumstances this may be acceptable.

22.4.1.4 Other types of restrictions

The three types of ancillary restrictions set out above are the most common ones. It is however possible that other restrictions may be considered ancillary provided that they are still directly related and necessary to the implementation of a merger.

22.4.2 Agreements subject to competition scrutiny under other enactments

Schedule 2 of the Competition Act 1998 excludes from the Chapter I prohibition agreements constituting bodies regulated under the Financial Services Act 1986, and certain other arrangements made by such bodies. Similarly the prohibition does not apply to agreements for the constitution of certain supervisory or qualifying bodies regulated under the Companies Act, nor to certain arrangements made by such bodies. The same applies with respect to Northern Ireland companies. In addition, the prohibition does not apply to certain arrangements relating to broadcasting which are regulated under the Broadcasting Act 1990, nor to certain arrangements made under the Environment Act 1995.

22.4.3 Planning agreements

The Chapter I prohibition does not apply to certain planning agreements (Sch.3, para.1).

22.4.4 Section 21(2) agreements

Agreements which existed prior to the starting date of the Competition Act (March 1, 2000) which imposed certain restrictions on the parties may have been furnished to the Office of Fair Trading under the RTPA. To the extent that such agreements were subject to a s.21(2) direction under the RTPA, they were excluded from the Chapter I prohibition until May 1, 2007. Post May 2007 they too will be subject to the full applicationof the Competition Act 1998 (Competition Act 1998 and Other Enactments (Amendment) Regulations 2004, SI 2004/1261).

22.4.5 Other general exclusions

Schedule 3 of the Competition Act sets out a number of general situations which are also excluded from the Chapter I prohibition. These can be summarised as follows:

(a) the prohibition does not apply to the constitution of, certain decisions and agreements made by, nor to the practices of, an EEA regulated market (in other words a regulated securities market in the EEA, outside the UK) (Sch.3, para.3).

(b) The prohibition does not apply to an undertaking entrusted with the operation of services of general economic interest, or having the character of a revenue-producing monopoly insofar as the prohibition would obstruct the performance of the particular tasks assigned to that undertaking (Sch.3, para.4). This exclusion paraphrases Art.86(2) of the EC Treaty (formerly Art.90(2). The example given of the type of business affected by this exclusion is the Post Office, which as a result of Sch.3 will be able to enter into restrictive agreements which would fall outside the prohibition provided such agreements are essential to enable it to perform its functions.

(c) A Chapter I prohibition does not apply to agreements made in order to comply with a legal requirement, that is to say a requirement imposed by or under any UK Act, by or under the Treaty of Rome or the EEA Agreement, or imposed by or under the laws in force in another Member State and having legal effect in the UK (Sch.3, para.5(1)).

(d) The Secretary of State is given the power under Sch.3 to make an Order excluding an agreement or category of agreements from the prohibition in order to avoid a conflict with an international obligation of the UK (Sch.3, para.6(1)).

(e) The Secretary of State can, by Order, exclude an agreement or category of agreements from the prohibition if he is satisfied that there are exceptional and compelling reasons of public policy why the prohibition should not so apply (Sch.3, para.7(1)). Given that ensuring that effective competition is maintained within the UK is in itself a public policy it would have to be a very compelling reason for the Secretary of State to issue such an Order.

(f) The Chapter I prohibition does not apply to an agreement that relates to a coal or steel product to the extent to which the ECSC Treaty gives the European Commission exclusive jurisdiction in relation to these products (Sch.3, para.8(1)).

(g) The Chapter I prohibition does not apply to agricultural co-operatives, subject to any adverse decision by the European Commission and furthermore the DGFT retains the power to claw-back this exclusion.

22.4.6 Professional rules

Schedule 4 of the Competition Act 1998 provides that the prohibition does not apply to the extent that an agreement constitutes a designated professional rule, imposes obligations arising from designated professional rules or constitutes an agreement to act in accordance with such rules. "Designated" professional rules means those designated by the Secretary of State and currently these would be the rules regulating the professional services such as legal, medical, dental and other professional services (see list in Part II of Sch.4). This list in the Competition Act 1998 is similar to that which used to exist in the RTPA (Sch.1). However, the effect of the Competition Act exclusion is much narrower in that it only excludes the rules themselves whereas under the RTPA any agreement relating to the scheduled professional services was outside the scope of the legislation.

In March 2000 the OFT published a consultation which was followed by an OFT Report in March 2001, *Competition in Professions*, which recommended that a number of restrictions on competition should be removed in three professions: lawyers (in particular barristers), accountants and architects. It also argued for the repeal of Sch.4 of the Competition Act. Under the Enterprise Act 2002, s.207, Sch.4 has now been repealed, with effect from April 1, 2003.

The application of the Chapter I prohibition to professional rules will now follow the same analysis as under Art.81 of the EC Treaty as to whether the rules actually amount to "an agreement between undertakings" which restrict competition (see the ECJ Judgment in *Wouters* on the Dutch bar rules, Case C-309/99 [2002] E.C.R. I–1577, see also Chapter 21, para.2)). In assessing whether any rules and decisions of professional bodies infringe Article 81/Chapter I, one should apply a proportionality test, i.e.

(i) whether the restrictions pursue a clearly articulated and legitimate public interest objective;

(ii) whether they are necessary to achieve that objective;

(iii) whether there are no less restrictive means to achieve this.

See further *OFT Guidelines on Trade Associations, Professions and Self-Regulatory Bodies*, OfT 408, December 2004.

22.4.7 Additional exclusions

Under s.3(3) the Secretary of State is granted the power to add further types of agreements to the exclusions listed in Sch.3, or amend or remove any cases, but he can only add exclusions if it appears to the Secretary of State that agreements which fall within the additional exclusion do not, in general, have an adverse effect on competition, or if they may have that effect, are best considered under Chapter II of the Act or under the Fair Trading Act 1973 as opposed to Chapter I.

22.4.8 Vertical agreements

The most significant exclusion from the Chapter I prohibition was the one initially granted to all vertical agreements. Prior to the enactment of the

Competition Act 1998 in the UK there had been a growing recognition in Europe that overall vertical agreements raised less concern than horizontal agreements, particularly when there is sufficient inter-brand competition and the parties have no market power. The UK Government therefore decided to exclude vertical agreements from the prohibition with the aim of reducing the administrative burden on businesses and the regulatory authorities by limiting the number of agreements caught by the prohibition, and avoiding the requirement for businesses to fit their agreements within the form of a block exemption. Accordingly, the Secretary of State issued an Order under s.50 which provided that the Chapter I prohibition does not apply to an agreement "to the extent that it is a vertical agreement" (*Competition Act 1998 (Land and Vertical Agreements Exclusion) Order (SI 2000/310)*), note however that vertical agreements were *not* excluded from the Chapter II prohibition. The definition of a vertical agreement set out in the Competition Act 1998 mirrors the definition set out in the new EU Vertical Agreements Block Exemption, and reads:

> An agreement between undertakings, each of which operates, for the purposes of the agreement, at a different level of the production or distribution chain, and relating to the conditions under which the parties may purchase, sell or resell certain goods or services.

However, following modernisation of competition law at EU level with the entry into force of Regulation 2003/1, the UK subsequently repeated this vertical agreement exclusion and all agreements are now dealt with in the same way of those that have an inter state effect. In other words, UK vertical agreements will be considered under Chapter 1 and will need to be assessed under ss 10(1) and (2) of the Competition Act 1998 (i.e. a parallel exemption) in conjunction with EU Regulation 2750/95 on Vertical Agreements. See further the *OFT Guidelines on Vertical Agreements*, OFT No 419 of December 2004.

22.4.9 Land agreements

Certain land agreements remain excluded from the Chapter I prohibition by the *Competition Act 1998 (Land Agreements Exclusion and Revocation) Order 2004* ("the Land Exclusion Order") SI 2004/1260. This exclusion applies to agreements between undertakings which "create, alter, transfer or terminate an interest in land (or agreements to enter into such an agreement) which contain certain obligations or restrictions". The land which is the subject of the agreement is referred to in the Order as the "relevant land".

The obligations that will be excluded from the Chapter I prohibition are those accepted by a party in his capacity as holder of an interest in the relevant land or other land and which benefit another party in his capacity as a holder of an interest in the relevant land. Such obligations would include covenants relating to the payment of rent or service charges, or which prevent alienation. The Land Exclusion Order also excludes certain restrictions which relate to the activity which may be carried out from the relevant land or other land. Such restrictions must be accepted by a party in his capacity as holder of an interest in the relevant land or other land, and must benefit another party in his capacity as holder of an interest in the relevant land or other land. Alternatively, they must be accepted by a party in his capacity as holder of an interest in other land and relate to the imposition of restrictions on the activity that may be carried out on, or from the other land which correspond to those accepted by a party to an agreement in his capacity as holder of an interest in the relevant land.

Thus, restrictions may be imposed on the types of goods or services which may be sold or offered from different premises in a shopping centre or parade of shops, but the restrictions may not relate to the terms on which the goods or services may be sold. The Land Exclusion Order provides that the OFT may withdraw the exclusion as it relates to particular land agreements (Article 6 of the Land Exclusion Order and Schedule 1 of the Competition Act 1998). See further the *OFT Guidelines on Land Agreements (No. 420 of December 2004)*.

Note that land agreements are only excluded from the application of Chapter I by the Land Exclusion Order. Article 81 EC could still apply to them, although it is unlikely that such agreements would affect trade between Member States.

22.5 Exemptions

Where an agreement is caught by the ambit of the Chapter I prohibition, in that it has an appreciable effect on competition within the UK, or any part thereof, and is not one of the excluded agreements, then it will be void unless it is exempt. Broadly speaking agreements which restrict or distort competition may still be exempt if the benefits of the agreement outweigh its negative affect on competition. The criteria for exemption are set out in s.9 of the Competition Act 1998 and mirror the criteria laid out in Art.81(3) of the EC Treaty. Thus an agreement will qualify either for an individual exemption or a block exemption if it is an agreement which:

(a) contributes to:

- (i) improving production or distribution, or
- (ii) promoting technical or economic progress, while allowing consumers a fair share of the resulting benefit; but

(b) does not

- (i) improving impose on the undertakings concerned restrictions which are not indispensable to the attainment of those objectives; or

(ii) afford the undertakings concerned the possibility of eliminating competition in respect of a substantial part of the products in question.

Although the Competition Act 1998 clearly applies to both goods and services the criteria for exemption in s.9 refers only to products and not to services. This is an anomaly that equally exists in Art.81(3), although it is clear from jurisprudence of the European Commission and the European Court of Justice that Art.81(3) is equally applicable to services.

22.5.1 Individual exemptions/ Self assessment

Where, for example, parties to an agreement for the acquisition of part of a business include a long term exclusive supply agreement which would not be considered an excluded agreement as it goes beyond what would be considered an ancillary restriction, they may nevertheless choose to enter into such an agreement. Prior to May 2004 parties could, under the then Section 13 CA 1998, notify it to the Office of Fair Trading requesting an individual exemption. Under s.4(1) of the Competition Act 1998, the OFT could grant an individual exemption if the following two conditions were fulfilled:

(a) a request for an exemption has been made by a party to the agreement; and

(b) the criteria for an exemption are met (see above).

The OFT could, after considering the effect on competition of the relevant restrictions exempt them, or alternatively it could exempt it subject to conditions or obligations. Individual exemption could be granted so as to have effect from a date earlier than that which it was granted and was normally be limited in duration . Furthermore an individual exemption could be cancelled, varied or have additional conditions or obligations attached in certain limited circumstances (see ss. 5(1) and (2)).

One of the first individual exemptions to be granted was in *LINK Interchange Network Ltd*, in relation to an agreement between various of the large high street banks to allow consumers to use each other's cash point machines. The agreement set a collective interbank payment for cash withdrawals to prevent one bank from taking a free ride on the investment of others in creating nationwide networks of cash machines (OFT Decision, October 16, 2001).

The *General Insurance Standards Council* notified their rules which included a restriction on members from entering into agreements with non-members. Initially the OFT concluded that the rules did not infringe the Chapter I prohibition (OFT Decision, January 2001), however an appeal to the CAT by various brokers, led to restriction in the rules to be held to breach Chapter I, and following an amendment the OFT adopted a second decision of no infringement (Case No. 1002/2/1/01 *Institute of Independent Insurance Brokers v Director General of Fair Trading* [2001] CAT 4, and OFT Decision November 22, 2002).

Following the EU modernisation however, the OFT also abolished the notification requirement in the UK from May 1, 2004 and parties are now required to "self assess" as to whether they meet the Section 9 CA 1998 criteria. If they do, a "legal exception" applies and the agreement is not prohibited, and no prior decision to that effect is required. It is possible to request confidential, informal advice from the OFT, and if it raises "novel or unresolved questions" the OFT may consider there is an interest in issuing an Opinion for the benefit of a wider audience, which would be published on the OFT's website. However, an Opinion will not be binding on the OFT, nor will it prejudge the assessment of the same issue by the EC Commission, the European Court or the Competition Appeals Tribunal.

22.5.2 Block exemptions

The Competition Act envisages that the OFT can recommend to the Secretary of State to make an Order specifying that certain categories of agreements which are likely to be agreements which fulfil the criteria for an exemption can be exempt (s.6(1)). Then, an agreement which falls within a category specified within such a block exemption would be exempt from the Chapter I prohibition (s.6(3)). This power to issue block exemption orders follows the practice of the European Commission of issuing block exemption regulations under Art.81(3) which apply to certain categories of agreements such as the Vertical Agreements Block Exemption Regulation, the Specialisation and R&D Block Exemption Regulations and the various industry-specific block exemptions that exist relating to for example insurance agreements, air transport agreements, rail, road and inland water agreements and many others (see further Chapter 21). In view of the existence of the various EU block exemptions and the benefit of parallel exemptions (see below) it is unlikely that there will ever be many UK block exemptions. Currently only one UK block exemption has been adopted, for public transport ticketing schemes, with effect from March 1, 2001, Competition Act 1998 (Public Transport Ticketing Schemes Block Exemption) Order 2001 (SI 2001/319), as amended by the Competition Act 1995 (Public Transport Ticketing Schemes Block Exemption) (Amendment) Order 2005 (SI 2005/3347). For a summary see *OFT Guidelines on Public Transport Ticketing Scheme Block Exemption* OFT 439 of 11/06.

22.5.3 Parallel exemptions

As a result of both the supremacy of EU law and the need for a consistent approach in accordance with s.60 the Competition Act 1998 provides that an agreement will be exempt from the Chapter I prohibition if it is exempt from the prohibition in Art.81(1) of the EC Treaty. This will apply regardless of whether the exemption is as a result of the application of an EU block exemption, an individual exemption granted by the European Commission or through the operation of the opposition procedure set out in a European block exemption regulation (s.10 of the 1998 Act). Such an exemption is referred to as a "parallel exemption". Furthermore an agreement will be exempt from the Chapter I prohibition if it does not affect trade between Member States, but would otherwise fall within a category of agreements covered by a European block exemption regulation.

A parallel exemption in the UK only applies so long as the applicable Community exemption applies. Furthermore the OFT can also attach to a parallel exemption its own conditions or obligations, or vary or remove any such conditions or obligations, or even cancel the exemption. Cancellation by the OFT raises the possibility of taking action against an agreement which is exempt under Art.81(3). Breach of a condition imposed by the DGFT has the effect of cancelling the parallel exemption and therefore it would be void under the Chapter I prohibition. This would be an automatic consequence without any assessment by the OFT.

22.5.4 Section 11 exemptions

Lastly, the Secretary of State may under the Competition Act s.11 make regulations exempting from the Chapter I prohibition agreements which are the subject of a ruling under Art.84 (formerly Art.88) of the EC Treaty, as to whether or not such agreements infringe Art.81.

22.6 The Chapter II prohibition

In addition to the Chapter I prohibition which is dealt with more extensively above, the Competition Act also introduced a new Chapter II prohibition relating to the abuse of a dominant position. Section 18(1) of the Act provides:

> Any conduct on the part of one or more undertakings which amount to the abuse of a dominant position in a market is prohibited if it may affect trade within the United Kingdom.

This prohibition (known as the Chapter II prohibition) follows the approach of Art.82 of the EC Treaty with the necessary changes so that it relates to the UK rather than the EC. Restrictive covenants imposed by an undertaking in a dominant position may fall foul of the Chaper II prohibition and would therefore be void and unenforceable. Note, however, that a party is unlikely to be dominant if its share of the relevant market is less than 40% (see *OFT Guidelines: Abuse of a Dominant Position*, OFT 402, December 2004, at

Section 4 for a discussion of the factors which are taken into account when deciding whether a company is dominant).

Commonly the types of agreements discussed in this book will require consideration under the Chapter I prohibition and therefore it is proposed not to deal extensively with the Chapter II prohibition here. However, as with the Chapter I prohibition, s.60 of the Competition Act also applies to the Chapter II prohibition and therefore, to the extent relevant the same issues which arise under Art.82 could arise under the Chapter II prohibition of the Competition Act (see further Chapter 21).

22.7 The concurrent jurisdiction of the regulators

In addition to the powers which the DGFT will be able to exercise under the Competition Act 1998 in relation to the Chapter I prohibition and the Chapter II prohibition, the Act also provides that these powers are to be exercised concurrently by the various sectional regulators. Thus to the extent that an agreement or conduct falls within the jurisdiction of a particular sectional regulator, that regulator will generally deal with the case. However, the regulator and the DGFT will consult with each other before either takes an action and in some cases the DGFT will act rather than the relevant regulator. A concurrency working group has been set up in order to ensure that there are various procedures in place in order to ensure that the DGFT and other regulators co-ordinate their activities and that efforts are made to ensure that it is the authority best placed to deal with a matter who does so, and to avoid duplication or inconsistency. Thus agreements or conduct relating to telecommunications, gas, electricity, water or sewage and railways in the UK or electricity and gas in Northern Ireland will be dealt with by the relevant sectional regulator. Where a regulator does deal with a case, he will have almost all of the powers granted to the DGFT under the Competition Act 1998, including the power to deal with notifications for guidance or a decision, granting individual exemptions, carrying out investigations, imposing interim measures and imposing penalties. (Section 54 of the Competition Act 1998 and Sch.10.)

22.8 Transitional periods

Due to the wholesale changes made to competition law in the UK by the Competition Act 1998 the Government wanted to make sure that businesses had ample time to consider the implications of the Competition Act 1998 on their agreements, particularly in the light of the fact that the Act introduces a prohibitive regime and companies for the first time in the UK could be liable to substantial fines if their agreements and practices were found to be in breach of the Competition Act 1998.

The Act itself was passed on November 9, 1998 (the "Enactment Date") and the two new prohibitions came into force 16 months later on March 1, 2000 (the "Starting Date"). Section 74(2) and Sch.13 set out what are rather complex transitional provisions which allowed for a gradual phasing out of the old law (notably the Restrictive Trade Practices Act 1976 and Resale Prices Act 1976) and a gradual phasing in of the prohibitions. Different transitional arrangements applied depend on when the agreement was entered into and whether it had already been subject to any form of scrutiny under the old law.

While transitional periods exist for many agreements under Chapter I, any behaviour which amounts to an abuse of a dominant position was subject to the Chapter II prohibition immediately it came into force on March 1, 2000.

Equally any agreements or arrangements made after the Starting Date were clearly immediately subject to the new rules and should therefore be analysed carefully as to whether they fall within either the Chapter I or Chapter II prohibition.

22.9 The Enterprise Act 2002

The Enterprise Act 2002, which came into force in June 2003 introduced two significant provisions intended to encourage compliance with competition law. Firstly, Part 6 of the Enterprise Act establishes the "cartel offence", the commission of which can result in individuals being subject to up to five years in prison and/or an unlimited fine (s.190(1)). Secondly, company directors can be disqualified for up to 15 years if they knew, or ought to have known, that their company was guilty of an infringement of EC or UK competition law (s.204).

An individual is guilty of a cartel offence if he or she dishonestly agrees with one or more other persons that undertakings (i.e. business entities) will engage in one or more of the following cartel activities: direct and indirect price-fixing (indirect price fixing would include, for example, agreements about relative price levels or price ranges, rebates and discounts); limitation of supply or production; market-sharing; or bid-rigging.

The test for dishonesty is the two-part test set out by the Court of Appeal in *R. v Ghosh* [1982] Q.B. 1053 for other criminal offences.

Any agreement which, dishonestly, sought to restrict competition by including the type of clauses listed above as cartel offences could therefore lead to criminal prosecution rather than civil litigation.

Part VII

Interim Relief

Chapter 23

Injunctions and Interim Relief

23.1 Introduction

Interim relief usually plays a major part in cases concerning restraint of trade and business secrets. In the vast majority of cases the effect of the interim hearing will be to decide the final outcome of the case. In those cases where the outcome is not determined by the result of interim proceedings they are still important as a means of providing temporary relief.

In this chapter, we consider the principles which are relevant to grant of interim relief in restraint of trade and business secrets cases.

23.2 Power to grant interim injunctions for Restraint of Trade

The Court's jurisdiction to grant injunctive relief is found at s.37 of the Supreme Court Act 1981, which provides that the High Court may grant an injunction "in all cases in which it appears to the Court to be just and convenient to do so". This also provides the basis for the award of injunctions in the County Court (by virtue of s.38 of the County Courts Act 1984).

Parts 23 and 25 of the CPR set out the practice and procedure to be followed in attaining interim relief—this is dealt with in more detail in Chapter 25.

23.3 Principles applied to the grant of interim injunctions

23.3.1 Relevance of the overriding objective

Under the overriding objection (r.1.1 of the CPR) courts must deal with cases in a way which, so far as practicable:

(a) ensures that the parties are on an equal footing;

(b) saves expense;

(c) is proportionate to the amount of money involved, the importance of the case, the complexity of the issues and the financial position of the parties;

(d) ensures that the case is dealt with expeditiously and fairly; and

(e) allots to it an appropriate share of the court's resources.

Rule 1.2 states that the court must seek to give effect to the overriding objective when it "exercises any power given to it by the rules; or interprets any rule". Although the power to grant interim injunctions lies outside the CPR, the clear intention is for the overriding objective to be applied when the court is considering the grant of a discretionary remedy such as an interim injunction.

However, in practice the principles applied by the court in deciding whether or not to grant an interim injunction are the long established criteria laid down in the case of *American Cyanamid Co v Ethicon Ltd* [1975] A.C. 396. The *American Cyanamid* principles, which are consistent with the principles contained in the overidding objective, are dealt with below.

23.4 General criteria for the grant of an interim injunction

American Cyanamid was a patent action in which an application for an interim injunction reached the House of Lords. The hearing had taken up three days at first instance, eight days in the Court of Appeal and was estimated to last 12 days in the House of Lords. It was clearly a very complex case and the House of Lords were appalled by the fact that so much court time had been taken up by an interim application. In their judgment in response to this they effectively revolutionised the law in this area. The court laid down the following criteria to test whether an interim injunction should be awarded.

23.4.1 Is there a serious question to be tried?

This means that the claimant must demonstrate that his claim is not frivolous or vexatious. Provided that the material available to the court at the hearing of the application for an interim injunction discloses that the claimant has a serious question to be tried, then the court should go on to consider whether damages is an adequate remedy and if the balance of convenience lies in favour of granting or refusing the interim relief that is sought. In cases where the grant or refusal of the injunction will effectively dispose of the action, the court may go further and consider the merits of each sides' case (see para.23.5 below), though Lord Diplock was clear in the *American Cyanamid* that the "Court is not justified in embarking on anything like a trial of the action on conflicting affidavits in order to evaluate the strength of either party's case".

However, according to Laddie J. in *Series 5 Software v Clarke* [1996] 1 All E.R. 853, in answering whether or not there is a "serious question" to be tried, the court may have regard to the relative strengths of each party's case if it is possible to form a "clear view" on the merits at the interim stage. This suggests that a claimant with a weak but arguable case may not overcome the "serious question" hurdle.

Assuming the claimant can demonstrate a serious question to be tried, the court will move on to look at the second question, namely the adequacy of damages.

23.4.2 Would damages be an adequate remedy?

The court should consider whether, if the claimant succeeds at trial, he would be adequately compensated by damages for any loss caused by the refusal to grant an interim injunction. If damages would be an adequate remedy and the defendant would be in a financial position to pay them, no interim injunction should normally be granted, however strong the claim appears to be at that stage.

A comment made by Nourse L.J. in *Warren v Mendy* [1989] 1 W.L.R. 853 at 868; [1989] I.R.L.R. 210 at 216 may assist defendants in some cases. He pointed out that in most of the decided cases it is assumed that damages will not be an adequate alternative remedy in comparison with the grant of an injunction. That was especially true of those cases which would have been tried by a jury. However as damages are now invariably assessed by a judge or master it cannot be so readily assumed that they will not be an adequate remedy. He gave an example relating to the case: it would be open to the court to refuse injunctive relief at the interim stage on an undertaking by the defendant to keep full and proper accounts of his receipts from acting in alleged breach of contract and to pay a specified proportion of them into court or into a joint account. Nourse L.J. commented:

> An arrangement such as that would achieve the twin objective of going some way to quantify the claimant's damages and preserving funds to meet any award which might later be made.

In an appropriate case a defendant might make such an offer and escape an injunction being made against him. However, it is true to say that in the vast majority of restraint of trade and business secrets cases damages are genuinely very difficult to quantify and therefore they will never be an adequate remedy. On the effectiveness of the defendant paying sums into an account pending the outcome of the trial, see also *Brupat Ltd v Sandford Marine Products Ltd* [1983] R.P.C. 61.

If, on the other hand, damages would not be an adequate remedy for that claimant, the court should then consider whether, if the injunction were granted, the defendant would be adequately compensated under the claimant's undertaking to pay damages should his defence succeed at trial. If damages in the measure recoverable under such an undertaking would be an adequate remedy and the claimant would be in a financial position to pay them, there would be no reason upon this ground to refuse an interim injunction.

Note that the existence of liquidated damages clause is a contract for services does not prevent a claimant from seeking an interim injunction where it can show a "probable higher level of the actual loss that it would suffer without an injunction" particularly where there is "no obvious disadvantage" to the defendant (*Bath and North East Somerset District Council v Mowlem plc* [2004] EWCA Civ 115).

23.4.3 Balance of convenience

Where there is doubt as to the adequacy of the respective remedies in damages, then the court will go on to consider the question of balance of convenience, see *Belfast Ropework Co Ltd v Pixdane Ltd* [1976] F.S.R. 337 in which the Court of Appeal allowed an appeal on the basis that the balance of convenience was in the claimant's favour as the defendant would not be driven out of an established business but would merely be delayed in starting it up. See also *Potters-Ballotini v Weston-Baker* [1977] R.P.C. 202 and *Series 5 Software Ltd v Clarke* [1996] 1 All E.R. 853.

According to My L.J. in *Cayne v Global Natural Resources plc* [1984] 1 All E.R. 225, the balance of convenience test can be better expressed as the "balance of the risk of doing an injustice".

A difficulty in identifying the losses that would be incurred by one party if the injunction was found at trial to have been wrongly granted is a factor that the Courts would be willing to take into account when considering the balance of convenience (see *Intercall Conferencing Services Limited v Steer* [2007] EWHC 519 where the High Court granted an interim injunction to the employer. The Court considered that if the injunction was not granted, the employer would lose customers and employees and assessing losses flowing from this would be difficult to quantify).

23.4.4 Maintaining the status quo

Where other factors appear to be evenly balanced it is a counsel of prudence to take such measures as are calculated to preserve the status quo. In a case concerning restrictive covenants on the activities of employees the relevant status quo is that which existed before breach, not at the hearing date (*Unigate Dairies Ltd v Bruce*, *The Times*, March 2, 1988).

23.4.5 Other special factors

In addition to the above, there may be many "other special factors" to be taken into consideration in the particular circumstances of individual cases. Some of these are considered below.

Finally, it is important to remember that an interim injunction does not punish the defendant for past breaches; it seeks to restrain future breaches (*Universal Thermosensors Ltd v Hibben* [1992] 1 W.L.R. 840) although unusually in *PSM International and McKechnie v Whitehouse and Willenhall Automation* [1992] I.R.L.R. 279 an injunction was granted restraining the defendant from fulfilling contracts which had been entered into at the time of the hearing.

23.5 The test to be applied where the interim application will effectively dispose of the application

Following *American Cyanamid* there were a number of cases (*NWL Ltd v Woods* [1979] 3 All E.R. 614 and *Cayne v Global Natural Resources plc* [1984] 1 All E.R. 225) in which the court decided that further special criteria should be taken into account where the grant or refusal of an interim injunction will effectively put an end to the action (for example upholding a restrictive covenant where that covenant is likely to have expired by the time of any final hearing). In *NWL Ltd v Woods*, the court recognised that *American Cyanamid* was not dealing with a case in which the grant or refusal of an injunction would have the effect of disposing of the action, and that this brought into the balance of convenience an important and additional element, namely the relative strength of each party's case. It is also a relevant consideration that *American Cyanimid* was a patent dispute between two chemical conglomerates, not a dispute between employer and (ex) employee.

The conclusion of the court in *NWL Ltd v Woods* was that although the court will wish to avoid becoming bogged down in complex, contentious issues which do not lend themselves to resolution at an interim stage, to avoid injustice in a situation where the interim decision effectively disposes of the action, the court should go on beyond the stage of considering whether the claimant has an "arguable" case and look at the merits of the claim.

The Court of Appeal added a further gloss to this potentially additional test in *Lawrence David Ltd v Ashton* [1989] I.R.L.R. 22; [1991] 1 All E.R. 385). This was an appeal from the refusal of the court at first instance to grant the defendant's employer's interim injunctions (a) against the employee disclosing confidential information acquired during the course of employment, and (b) enforcing, pending trial, a two-year contractual restriction against the employee entering into a trade similar to that carried on by the employers. The defendant was a sales director for one of the claimant's UK regions, and was given notice on the basis that he had failed to achieve the expected improvement of sales performance in his area. At trial it was accepted by the claimant that the termination of his employment was in breach of contract since he had been given neither written nor one month's notice. Whitford J. concluded that this was not a clear repudiatory breach and he doubted whether the covenant would be held at trial to be a justifiable restraint.

The Court of Appeal rejected the view that restraint of trade cases were a special category to which *American Cyanamid* did not apply, stating:

> The American Cyanamid principles governing the granting of interlocutory injunctions where either there is an unresolved dispute on the affidavit evidence before the court or a question of law to be decided, apply in cases of interlocutory injunctions in restraint of trade just as in other cases. Covenants in restraint of trade are not a special category and the legal profession should be disabused of the widely-held view that the *American Cyanamid* approach is not relevant where an interlocutory injunction is sought to enforce a contractual obligation in restraint of trade.

Applying *American Cyanamid* to this case the Court agreed with Whitford J.'s refusal to grant an injunction to protect the alleged confidential information. The court awarded the injunction for a period of about three and a half months anticipating that a trial would occur in that period. However, the court also said that no further assessment of the merits was required provided that a speedy trial could take place, and that the claimant would be able to pay any damages as a result of his cross-undertaking:

> It is only if a speedy trial is not possible and the action cannot be tried before the period of restraint has expired or has run a large part of its course, that it will be necessary to have a contest on the interlocutory application because the grant of the interlocutory injunction will effectively dispose of the action, thus bringing the case within the exception to the rule in American Cyanamid, such as was considered by the House of Lords in *NWL Ltd v Woods.*

Another way of looking at it was to consider that the longer the period of the interlocutory injunction, the more likely it is that the claimant would suffer damage which could not be compensated by the cross-undertaking as to damages and therefore it becomes necessary to consider the relative strength of each party's case.

Although the court has no express power under the CPR to order a "speedy trial" (as was previously found in RSC Order 29, Rule 5), it falls within the Court's general case management powers to list the matter "as soon as reasonably practicable" (see CPR 20.2(2) in relation to listing of Multi-Track cases), and as per the overriding objective the court must deal with matters "expeditiously". Balcombe J. also said that:

> Cases in which an employer seeks to enforce a restrictive covenant in a contract of employment are singularly appropriate for a speedy trial and the courts will be able to make time available if it is not taken up by argument at the interlocutory stage where the application of *American Cyanamid* indicates the desirability of an

> interlocutory injunction. A defendant who has entered into a contractual restraint which is sought to be enforced should seriously consider, when the matter first comes before the court, offering an appropriate undertaking until the hearing of the action.

It should normally be possible for the trial to be listed before the expiry of the covenants and for the defendant to give appropriate undertakings in the meantime, but if not the court will consider this further test.

The dictum of Balcombe L.J. was also applied in *Lansing Linde Ltd v Kerr* [1991] 1 All E.R. 418, CA, in which it was held that where trial of an action to prevent a former employee from working for a competitor in breach of a restraint of trade clause would not take place until the period of restraint would have expired, the judge when exercising his discretion to grant or refuse an interim injunction was entitled:

> to take into account the likelihood of delay in obtaining a hearing date for the trial of the action and to require the employer seeking the injunction to satisfy him not only that there was a serious issue to be tried but also that it was more likely than not that the employer would succeed at trial . . . some assessment of the merits more than merely that there was a serious issue to be tried was required.

Note that where there is only a short period left for the covenants to run, the court may simply conclude that the balance of convenience lies in the defendant's favour without considering it necessary to weigh up the merits (see, for example, *Wincanton v Cranny & another* [2000] I.R.L.R. 716 in which Sedley L.J. declined to grant an interim injunction where 9 months of the permitted twelve-month period of restraint had passed; see also *Canadian Worldwide Express Limited v Smith & another* [2005] EWHC 671 (QB)).

23.6 Special rules relating to industrial action

Where the defendant claims that he has acted in contemplation or furtherance of a trade dispute, s.221(2) of the Trade Union and Labour Relations (Consolidation) Act 1992 ("TULR(C)A") specifically provides that the Court shall, in exercising its discretion whether or not to grant an injunction, "have regard to the likelihood of that party succeeding at the trial of the action in establishing any matter which would, under sections 219-220 of the Act, afford a defence to the action."

23.7 Conclusion

In the majority of restraint of trade and breach of confidence cases, particular where the period of restraint in covenants is relatively short, there is a possibility that the interim injunction application will effectively dispose of the action. Therefore the court will consider the *American Cyanamid* principles, together with the additional merits test as laid down in *Lawrence David Ltd v Ashton*.

It is therefore advisable for the party seeking to enforce a restraint of trade or business secrets clause or duty to be armed so far as possible with witness evidence which proves that he has a strong case on the merits in addition to demonstrating that damages are not an adequate remedy for him and that the balance of convenience lies in favour of granting the injunction.

23.8 Specific performance/mandatory injunctions

Specific performance is not usually granted of employment contracts. It has long been the view of the courts that to force an employee to work for an employer smacks of slavery. Until very recently (see below) there was only one case in which a court had ordered reinstatement on common law grounds (*Hill v CA Parsons and Co Ltd* [1972] 1 Ch. 305). The statutory powers regarding reinstatement/re-engagement of an employee under ss. 113 to 117 Employment Rights Act 1996 are a concept entirely foreign to the common law.

Further, the courts will not grant an injunction if this will amount to indirect specific performance of an employment contract or if to do so will perpetuate a relationship based on mutual trust and confidence or if the applicant is seeking to enforce an unreasonable restraint of trade. It is frequently said that the special considerations only apply to the employer/employee relationship, however it is important to understand that the concept of mutual trust and confidence (see below) can encapsulate relationships much wider than those based on employment contracts (per e.g. agency).

The position, so far as employees are concerned, is reinforced by s.236 of TULR(C)A. This provides that no court shall, whether by way of an order for specific performance of an employment contract or an injunction restraining a breach or threatened breach of such a contract compel an employee to do any work or to attend at any place for the doing of any work.

However, it is still necessary to consider the common law rules and the cases. Regarding prohibiting interim injunctions there are three important primary questions.

(1) Is there an unreasonable restraint of trade? If so, then quite clearly no interim injunction will be granted.

(2) Would the interim injunction, if granted, perpetuate a relationship based on mutual trust and confidence which has ceased to exist?

(3) Would the award of an injunction amount to the indirect specific performance of a contract of personal services?

However, this area of law is very complex because it may be possible to argue when dealing with cases within (2) and (3) above that the courts should grant a negative injunction restraining the defendant from performing the type of services stipulated in the contract for anyone else but the claimant. Whether the court can, must or must not grant an injunction in these cases is a matter of debate for there are three distinct lines of authority.

The first view, which in our opinion is the correct one, is that the court simply has a discretion to grant an interim injunction if that is just and convenient in the circumstances of the particular case. We see no reason why s.37 of the Supreme Court Act 1981 should not govern in this instance. However, this discretion is subject to a well-established principle laid down by the cases: this is that the court will not grant an injunction if the effect of it is to force the defendant either to perform his contract with the claimant or to remain idle. Authority for this principle is found in *Warner Brothers Ltd v Nelson* [1937] 1 K.B. 209, *Ehrman v Bartholomew* [1898] 1 Ch. 671 and in *Page One Records Ltd v Britton* [1968] 1 W.L.R. 157. The question of idleness is one of fact: in the *Warner Brothers* case (rather surprisingly) it was found that the defendant, Bette Davis, would be able to find alternative employment even though it might not pay as well as if she had performed her contract with Warner Brothers. However, in *Page One Records*, it was found that the group in question, the Troggs, needed a manager and if the negative covenant had been enforced by injunction then they would either have had to accept the claimant as their manager or starve. In that case Stamp J. held, in what appear to be entirely separate reasons for refusing the injunction, that a court will not grant an injunction to enforce a negative covenant either:

(a) if there is no mutuality (it was on this basis he distinguished *Lumley v Wagner* (1852) 1 De G.M. & G. 604); and/or

(b) if the defendant's obligations are not only obligations of personal service but also involve trust and confidence; and/or

(c) if the totality of the obligations between the parties approximates to a joint venture or partnership.

It used to be generally accepted that there was no mutuality in contracts of personal services (i.e. there is usually no possibility of the defendant enforcing the claimant's obligations to employ by way of specific performance or injunction). However, in the light of the cases discussed below, this will depend upon the facts in each case.

The second view states that the court will never grant the type of negative injunction referred to. This approach, founded on the doctrine of "automatic determination", is supported by the Court of Appeal judgment in *Denmark Productions Ltd v Boscobel Productions* [1969] 1 Q.B. 699. The court held that even though the defendant's repudiation had not been accepted and that the claimant thus purported to keep the contract alive, the contract, being one for personal services, had been brought to an end unilaterally. The claimant could therefore only sue for damages after the date of repudiation and could not claim for an account of the defendant's earnings after that date. Furthermore, the claimant was under a duty to mitigate his damage. Further support for this doctrine can be found in *Decro-Wall International SA v Practitioners in Marketing Ltd* [1971] 1 W.L.R. 361 and in *Sanders v Ernest A Neale Ltd* [1974] I.C.R. 565, *per* Sir John Donaldson

> . . . repudiation of a contract of employment is an exception to the general rule. It terminates the contract without the necessity for acceptance by the injured party. . . .

There are dicta in other cases which also purport to follow the doctrine, see for example the dissenting judgment of Shaw L.J. in *Gunton v Richmond-upon-Thames LBC* [1981] Ch. 448. However, the doctrine has been doubted in *Thomas Marshall (Exports) Ltd v Guinle* [1979] Ch. 227 and in the majority judgments in *Gunton*. In the former case, Megarry V.C. said:

> If cases of master and servant are an exception from the rule that an unaccepted repudiation works no determination of the contract, and instead are subject to . . . the doctrine of automatic determination, the result would be that many a contract of employment would be determined forthwith upon the commission of a fundamental breach or a breach of a fundamental term, even though the commission of this breach was unknown to the innocent party, and even if he had known he would have elected to keep the contract in being.

He also went on to reject a narrower formulation of the rule which said that, in employment cases, a breach amounting to a repudiation did not forthwith determine the contract unless the party breaking the contract intended to bring it to an end. In conclusion one can say that there is some authority which supports a rule of automatic determination; however the trend in recent cases is against such a doctrine (although see *Boyo v London Borough of Lambeth* [1995] I.R.L.R. 50). The doubts about the rule, which we feel are well founded, concern the fact that it allows the defendant simply to say that the contract is at an end and to be free from the contractual restrictions which applied whilst employment or the relationship continued.

It would be anomalous if as a matter of law an employer was entitled to affirm the contract after repudiation by the employee (*Evening Standard v Henderson* [1987] I.C.R. 588) but that the employee did not enjoy the same entitlement. The unilateralist view has been challenged by a number of recent authorities (and backed up by a growing number of cases where injunctions have been granted) which indicate that in principle an employee can affirm a contract. In *Rigby v Ferodo* [1988] I.C.R. 29, HL, the employer unilaterally imposed a reduction in wages on the workforce. This variation was never accepted by them but they carried on nevertheless. Mr Rigby commenced proceedings claiming damages for breach of his contract of employment, an order for payment of a weekly wage at the rate prevailing before the reduction and a declaration. Lord Oliver made it quite clear that a repudiatory breach in a contract of employment as a matter of law is no different from any other contract. At p.34 he said:

> whatever may be the position under a contract of service where the repudiation takes the form either of a walkout by the employee or a refusal by the employer any longer to regard the employee as his servant, I know of no principle of law that any breach which the innocent party is entitled to treat as repudiatory of the other party's obligations brings the contract to an end automatically.

The third view is that the court *must* always grant an injunction to prohibit a party to a contract breaching a valid express negative covenant and has no discretion to do otherwise. The theory supporting this approach is that the injunction reflects what the parties have agreed. Authority for this view is found in the dictum of Lord Cairns L.C. in *Doherty v Allman and Dowden* (1878) 3 App. Cas. 709. Although in *Warner Brothers Pictures Inc v L Nelson* [1937] 1 K.B. 209 and more recently in *Hampstead and Suburban Properties Ltd v Diomedous* [1969] 1 Ch. 248 the judgments purported to follow and apply Lord Cairns' words it is submitted that they did not do so and that the dictim should be consigned to legal history. It would seem extraordinary if there were no discretion to grant a discretionary remedy.

The law is inconclusive and may well change further. For practical purposes the only advice we can give is that the parties should proceed on the basis that the court does have discretion to award an injunction to enforce a negative covenant except in those instances set out in the *Page One Records* case. Indeed the approach of Stamp J. has recently been applied in the Court of Appeal in preference to that of Branson J. in *Warner Brothers*.

In *Warren v Mendy* [1989] 1 W.L.R. 853; [1989] I.R.L.R. 210 the Court of Appeal upheld Pill J.'s discharge of an injunction in a case between boxing promoters. The facts were that in January 1988 the claimant, a manager and promoter licensed by the British Boxing Board of Control, entered into a written agreement in the Board's standard form to manage the professional affairs of B, a talented young boxer, for three years. By clause 2 of the agreement the claimant agreed to supervise B's training programme and to use the best endeavours to arrange suitable professional activities and secure for him proper reward. By clause 4, B agreed to be managed exclusively by the claimant for the duration of the agreement. Thereafter the claimant acted both as B's manager and promoter in respect of a number of professional contests. By June 1988 B had lost confidence in the claimant, and, asserting that the agreement was unenforceable as an unreasonable restraint of trade, began an action against him for, inter alia, an account on the ground that he held undisclosed funds as constructive trustee. At about the same time B entered into an agreement with the defendant for the introduction of commercial opportunities. The claimant obtained ex parte injunctive relief against the defendant on commencing proceedings to restraint him from inducing B to act in breach of the agreement and from acting for B in relation to his professional career. On the defendant's application to discharge the injunctions the judge found that as a boxer B's professional career was relatively short-lived involving the continuing need to exercise a specialist skill, that the boxer-manager relationship gave rise to mutual trust which B no longer felt and that the claimant was likely to seek relief not only against the defendant but against any other person attempting to supplant him. He concluded that the effect of the relief sought against the defendant would be to compel B to perform his agreement with the claimant and discharged the injunctions. On B's application he joined him as a party to the proceedings.

The Court of Appeal held

(a) that where a contract for the performance of personal services involved the continuing exercise of some special skill or talent and a high degree of mutual trust and confidence the court would not enforce negative stipulations under the contract if to do so would effectively compel performance of the positive obligations;

(b) that compulsion, being a question of fact, might be inferred where relief was sought against a third party who might be the only alternative master, or where the current master was likely to seek relief against any other alternative master; and

(c) that since the claimant's position as both manager and promoter gave rise to a potential conflict of duty and interest and since the evidence filed in B's action supported his assertion that the claimant held undisclosed funds as constructive trustee, it would be inappropriate to grant relief which tied B to any further contractual relationship with the claimant.

One exception to the general rule that specific performance will not usually be granted of an employment contract is where an injunction is granted to restrain an employer from suspending or dismissing an employee in breach of contract. The Court of Appeal in *Mezey v South West London and St George's Mental Health NHS Trust* [2007] EWCA Civ 106 upheld an interim injunction restraining the employer from suspending an employee on the basis that suspension is not a neutral act, it changes the status quo from work to no work and is capable of being a breach of contract that is capable of not being fully compensable in damages.

23.9 Re-instatement

The general rule that a court will not order re-instatement of an employee (save where statute makes provision for this) has been abrogated in some cases. See *Irani v Southampton Health Authority* [1985] I.R.L.R. 203; *Powell v Brent LBC* (1987) I.R.L.R. 466; *Hughes v Southwark LBC* [1988] I.R.L.R. 55; *Wadcock v Brent LBC* [1990] I.R.L.R. 223 and *Robb v Hammersmith & Fulham London Borough* [1991] I.R.L.R. 72. In *Wadcock v Brent LBC* the court granted an injunction restraining the council from acting on its purported determination of the employee's contract coupled with an order that he be paid his salary pending trial. The result of this case may turn on the special fact that the claimant apparently gave an undertaking to the court which went to the root of the litigation. However, it should be noted that in some cases the claimant has failed to bring his case within the limited exception to the usual rule: see for example *Alexander v STC Ltd* [1990] I.R.L.R. 55 and *Wishart v National Association of Citizens Advice Bureaux Ltd* [1990] I.R.L.R. 393.

See also *Kircher v Hillingdon* PCT [2006] EHWC 21 (QB) in which the Court granted an interim injunction, the effect of which was to prevent the employer relying upon notice of termination that would have otherwise deprived the claimant of the opportunity of taking part in the PCT' s disciplinary process.

23.10 Garden Leave

The general rule may also appear to have been disregarded in cases concerning what are called "garden leave" clauses. The first case dealing with this topic is *Evening Standard Co Ltd v Henderson* [1987] I.R.L.R. 64. Mr Henderson had been employed on the London *Evening Standard* for about 17 years. In 1979 he was appointed manager of the production room. His contract of employment provided for one year's notice on either side. It also contained a provision preventing him from working for anyone else during the currency of the contract.

During 1986 it became known that a rival publisher was planning to start another London evening newspaper that would compete with the *Evening Standard*. Mr Henderson agreed to join the staff of that proposed rival and in September he sent a letter to his employers saying that he wished to terminate his contract as from November 1986. He therefore failed to give the one year's notice that his contract required.

The company applied for an injunction to restrain Mr Henderson from working for a rival newspaper during the period of about ten months between the time the notice he had given expired and the contractual one year's notice. That application at first instance was refused notwithstanding that the company had given an undertaking that they would carry on paying Mr Henderson throughout the contractual notice period. In the course of proceedings before the Court of Appeal, the company offered to let Mr Henderson continue to perform his work if he so wished and undertook not to seek any damages against him for the period when he was not working for them. The Court of Appeal granted the injunction.

The second case was *Provident Financial Group plc v Hayward* [1989] 3 All E.R. 298. The defendant was employed by the claimants as financial director of the estate agency business they operated from offices in various towns in the north of England and the Midlands. Under his contract of service the defendant was required to perform the duties assigned to him, although the claimants were under no corresponding obligation to assign any duties to him or provide him with work. The contract further required him to devote the whole of his time to carrying out his duties under the contract and prohibited him from undertaking any other business or profession during the continuance of his employment. On July 1, 1988 the defendant tendered his resignation to the claimants and it was mutually agreed that the period of notice should be 6 months instead of the 12 months specified in the contract provided the defendant undertook not to disclose any confidential information to any person, including future employers, for a period of two years from the date of the end of employment. The defendant continued to work for the claimants until September 5, when, at their request and for the purpose of preventing him from acquiring any further confidential information, he ceased to work on their premises and was sent home while continuing to receive full pay and other benefits. On October 13 the defendant notified the claimants of his intention to start work for a supermarket chain as financial controller of their estate agency offices, which were situated in their stores throughout the country. The claimants sought an injunction to restrain the defendant from working for anyone else until the period of his notice expired (on December 31). The judge refused their application. The claimants appealed. The Court of Appeal held that since the court would not specifically enforce a contract of personal service between an employer and his employee, it would not grant an injunction in very wide terms, reproducing a term in the contract, preventing the employee from working for anyone else during the continuance of his service agreement if the effect of granting such an injunction would be to compel the employee to return to work for his previous employer. However, an express negative covenant not to work for anyone else during the term of the service contract was not a mere corollory of the positive obligation to devote his whole time to the employer's business and, accordingly, was enforceable by the court as a matter of discretion. However the court would not enforce such a term where the other business for which the employee wished to work had nothing whatever to do with the employer's business, even if the employee was offered full pay, because an employee had a concern to work and exercise his skills. In the circumstances, an injunction would not be granted because the defendant did not have any relevant confidential information of the claimants which would be of use to the rival company and there was no real prospect of serious or significant damage to the claimants from the defendant working as financial controller for the rival company for the short period which remained of his contract. The appeal was dismissed.

The case was important because unlike in the *Evening Standard* case the claimants were not even prepared to allow Hayward to spend the remainder of the notice period at work. They offered him no choice; they required him to stay at home.

From these two cases the following principles can be stated. In order to have a chance to obtain a "garden leave" type injunction the court will have to be satisfied of the following:

(a) That the employer has not accepted the employee's repudiatory breach.

(b) That the employer has not agreed to provide the employee with any particular type of work. If there is such an agreement and the employee is required to be on "garden leave" he can argue that the employer has repudiated the agreement. Difficulties may also arise in the case of directors. Clearly their contracts of employment should provide that once put on garden leave they automatically cease to be directors. The employer will invariably wish that they do not attend board meetings or have any management role whilst on garden leave; unless express provision is made to exclude them from meetings of management they may be able to claim exclusion is a repudiatory breach by the employer disentitling him from interim relief.

(c) That the employee will receive the same salary and benefits whilst on garden leave as he would have done if he had remained at work. Unless there is an express provision dealing with the point this means that he must be able to participate in any bonus scheme during the relevant period. The difficulty with an express provision which excludes any right to a bonus is that its existence may militate against the grant of an injunction.

(d) That the employer can demonstrate existing or likely detriment. In *Provident* it was said that fostering the profitability of a trade rival can constitute detriment: one obvious way in which that can exist is if the employee possesses confidential information which may be of use to his employer's competitor.

(e) That the period for which garden leave is sought is not excessive.

(f) That the employee is not engaged in an activity where to grant a garden leave injunction might deprive him of future work or if his skills might atrophy during the relevant period.

In *GFI Group Inc v Eaglestone* [1994] I.R.L.R. 119 Holland J. granted an injunction against competition during the notice period against the defendant for 13 weeks; he decided that it was not necessary to protect the claimant's goodwill for the 20 weeks provided for in the contract. As is usual in these cases the claimants undertook to the court to pay his salary and bonuses throughout the notice period and not to claim back such sums as damages for breach of contract in any subsequent proceedings. In *Euro Brokers Ltd v Rabey* [1995] I.R.L.R. 206 an injunction in similar terms was granted based on a garden leave clause for six months.

In *Credit Suisse Asset Management Ltd v Armstrong* [1996] I.R.L.R. 450 the Court of Appeal refused to overturn a decision at first instance in which injunctions had been granted to restrain post-termination non-canvassing/dealing by the defendants for a period of six months even though each defendant had already for varying time periods been sent home on garden leave. However, the court declined to grant injunctions to enforce any remaining periods of garden leave. In some cases this was as long as six months. However, the main point taken on behalf of the defendants was this: the restrictive covenants were of six months' duration, but if the court were to enforce them, given the fact that most of the defendants had been on garden leave for six months, they would be out of the marketplace for twelve months: that was too long, an exclusion for six months in total being sufficient. The court declined to order any set-off against the period of garden leave but left open the possibility that in an exceptional case where a long period of garden leave had already elapsed (such as substantially more than a year) the court might decline any further protection based on a restrictive covenant.

In *William Hill v Tucker* [1998] I.R.L.R. 313, CA, Morritt L.J. expressed the view that the Court should take care not grant an injunction to enforce garden leave which goes beyond that would be granted by a justifiable restraint of trade clause previously entered into by the employee. This case established the principle that garden leave provisions will not be enforced in the absence of express covenants. Although not directly commented upon in this case, the implication of both the *Credit Suisse* and *William Hill* cases is that it may also be prudent when drafting contracts of employment to ensure that any period of garden leave period is set off against any further protection based on restrictive covenants.

That said, the uncertainty about the inter-relationship between a garden leave provision and restrictive covenants continues. The intent of both is generally the same, i.e. to protect the business interests of the employer. As such, it is interesting to note that in *Sendo Holdings plc (in administration) v Brogan* [2005] EWHC 2040, Mrs Justice Dobbs, in the course of continuing an injunction restraining an employee from entering into competitive activity in breach of a garden leave provision, appears to have regard to public policy considerations as would be the case in relation to non-competition provisions in restraint of trade to the effect that the employer in that case needed to show that they had a legitimate interest in seeking to enforce the garden leave arrangement. Another uncertainty in terms of how the court will approach an employee acting in breach of a garden leave provision stems from *Symbian Ltd. v Christensen* [2001] I.R.L.R. 77, CA. In that case, at first instance, Scott V C considered that the implied duty of good faith did not survive during a garden leave period. The Court of Appeal did not deal with this particular observation, albeit noting that counsel for *Christensen* "confessed to some difficulty" when it came to trying to justify that part of Scott V C's judgment. The carefully drafted garden leave provision will, in light of this, include an express obligation of good faith on the part of the employee during the garden leave period. However, this still leaves open the possibility that in the circumstances of a particular case the imposition of garden leave may still constitute a breach of the implied term of trust and confidence (cp *Sendo* above where the approach adopted was more in line with that followed when considering the reasonableness of restrictive covenants). Responding to a proposition on the part of counsel for the employee in *TFS Derivatives Ltd. v Morgan* [2005] I.R.L.R. 246 to the effect that a six-month garden provision would have been a better choice on the part of the employer than a six-month non-compete provision, with the consequence that the actual choice of the latter resulted in its being in unlawful restraint of trade, Cox J. (rejecting the proposition) said:

> I am not . . . persuaded, on the evidence . . . that the point has now been reached for garden leave clauses, despite their popularity and prevalence, to negate the necessity for non-compete clauses in all cases.

The Judge then set out various reasons for this including:

> . . . a six-month enforced period of garden leave, even if in accordance with an express term of the contract, would in any event be likely to face resistance on the basis that its use amounts to a breach of the implied term of trust and confidence.

In the circumstances, it cannot be said with any confidence that the way in which the courts will approach the imposition of garden leave provisions and their enforcement by injunction is settled.

23.11 Business secrets cases

An employee is under an obligation at common law not to disclose confidential information during the employment, and after the employment to the extent that the information can be regarded as a trade secret (following the well established principles in *Faccenda Chicken Ltd v Fowler* [1985] 1 All E.R. 724; [1985] I.R.L.R. 61 affirmed [1987] Ch. 117; [1986] 1 All E.R. 617; [1986] I.R.L.R. 69, CA. In addition the employee may be subject to express restrictions in his contract of employment which may seek to expand the class of confidential information protected.

The defences on which the defendant will rely are either that the information was not in fact secret, that there has been no breach, or that the public interest militates against granting an injunction. In *Lion Laboratories Ltd v Evans* [1984] 2 All E.R. 417, the claimant failed to get an interim injunction because of the public interest factor. That case concerned the Lion Intoximeter which is used to measure alcohol levels in the breath. The claimant company learnt that two of its ex-employees were trying to contact national newspapers with copies of some of the claimant's internal correspondence. These documents were all confidential and indicated doubts as to the realiability and accuracy of the instruments. The claimant issued a writ claiming an injunction restraining the defendant from using/disclosing the information and damages for breach of confidence and/or copyright. An ex parte injunction was granted in the terms of the statement of case. The following day a national newspaper published an article stating that the claimant's products were prone to serious error but did so without breaching the precise terms of the injunction. The defendants then applied to have the ex parte injunction discharged but the judge continued it. The defendants appealed to the Court of Appeal relying on the public interest point and succeeded.

Four further points are of special importance in business secrets cases. First, an injunction to restrain a breach of secrecy will only be granted to a party who is the beneficiary of the duty of confidence: see *Fraser v Evans* [1969] 1 Q.B. 349. Secondly, it is frequently sought to draw an analogy between confidential information cases and defamation actions in which there is a rule that if the defendant asserts in his affidavit that he will plead justification or qualified privilege or fair comment as a defence, then an interim injunction will not be granted against him. There is no rule in confidential information cases concerning a plea of public interest. See *Lion Laboratories* per all members of the court who said that the defendant must specify the reasons in which the public interest in publication should defeat the public interest in maintaining confidence. See also *Francome v Mirror Group Newspapers Ltd* [1984] 1 All E.R. 408.

Thirdly, even if an injunction is refused it may be possible in some cases to argue that the defendants undertake a duty to keep an account of royalties on each item produced which sums be put into a special joint escrow account and to supply monthly production figures to the claimant. See *Coco v AN Clark Engineers Ltd* [1969] R.P.C. 41. An account of royalties was specifically refused in the case of *Attorney General v Blake* [2001] 1 A.C. 268, which the House of Lords considered to be a form of confiscation order for which they had no statutory power. The House of Lords did however hold that the Attorney General could bring a claim for account of profits, and that an injunction should remain in force in the meantime preventing Mr Blake, the notorious spy, from receiving payment of the royalties in relation to his book.

Fourthly, the courts have repeatedly stressed that the terms of an injunction preventing the use/disclosure of confidential information must be specific as to the identification of such information so as to enable the defendant to know precisely whether or not he has acted in breach: see *Lock International plc v Beswick* [1989] 1 W.L.R. 1268, *Lawrence David Ltd v Ashton* [1989] I.R.L.R. 123, *Mainmet Holdings plc v Austin* [1991] F.S.R. 538, *PSM International Plc v Whitehouse* [1992] I.R.L.R. 279 and *Universal Thermosensors Ltd v Hibben* [1992] 1 W.L.R. 840.

Finally, when considering where to grant relief which, if granted, might affect the exercise of the right of freedom of expression, section 12 (3) of the Human Rights Act 1998 imposes a threshold test which has to be satisfied before a court may grant interlocutory injunctive relief ("No such relief . . . is to be granted so as to restrain publication before trial unless the Court is satisfied that the applicant is likely to establish the publication should not be allowed").

The meaning of the word "likely" in this context was considered by the House of Lords in the case of *Cream Holdings Ltd v Banerjee* [2005] 1 A.C. 253, in which the court held that:

> given the disclosures the defendants wished to publish were clearly matters of serious public interest, the claimants' prospects of success at trial were not sufficiently likely to justify making an interim restraint order.

A claimant would ordinarily be required to show that he or she would be "more likely than not" to succeed at trial if the court was going to be persuaded to intervene to prevent the disclosure of information of public interest, but some flexibility was deemed by the court to be essential to dispense with this requirement where the facts of the particular case demanded it.

23.12 Interim Relief under Competition Law

To date, the incidence of claims for interim relief being sought in cases raising substantive competition law issues in the UK has been low. However, this can be expected to change in future following the greater emphasis being given to the private enforcement of competition rules, in the UK and Europe. See *European Commission Green Paper, Damages actions for breach of EC anti-trust rules*. COM(2005) 672, 19.12.2005; and *OFT Consultation Paper Private Actions in Competition Law: Effective redress for consumers and business* (April 2007). There is also an increasing tendency of the UK competition regulator, the Office of Fair Trading ("OFT"), to reject complaints received by it on administrative priority grounds or resourcing issues (see for example *Cityhook Ltd v Office of Fair Trading* [2007] CAT 18). Furthermore, second regulators such as The Office of Fair Communications ("Ofcom") are often slow and unsuitable forums for resolving disputes between commercial parties. In circumstances where the availability of regulatory redress is time consuming, limited and reducing, competition law disputes will of necessity increasingly come before the national courts. However, for the time being, whether applications for interim relief will be made to the OFT or to the High Court will ultimately depend upon the relative weight given by the party concerned to strategic considerations within its case; time, cost and burden and standard of proof will also be a major factor.

23.12.1 Competition legislative background

The UK rules on competition law, are contained in the Competition Act 1998 which came into force on March 1, 2000. This is discussed in greater detail in Chapter 22, although regard must also be had for EC Competition Law which is directly applicable in the UK and can be enforced by the UK Courts and the OFT (see Chapter 21).

23.12.2 Restrictive covenants and competition law

Restrictive covenants, agreed between parties or imposed by one party on another, which fall foul of the competition rules and which do not satisfy the exemption criteria in section 9 of the Competition Act 1998 and Article 81(3) EC, and do not fall within any exclusion or block exemption, are void and unenforceable. They are void and unenforceable from March 1, 2000 for the purposes of the Competition Act 1998, and effectively from the date of inception for the purposes of Articles 81 EC (given that EU Competition Law has been in force since 1957). The extent to which the offending covenant may be severed from an agreement will be determined according to the common law rules on severance; and if it is not possible to sever it then the whole agreement will be void. See most recently in *English Welsh & Scottish Railway Ltd (Claimant) v E ON UK Plc (Defendant) and Office of Rail Regulation (Intervener)*, [2007] EWHC 599. In this case the court held that it was not possible to sever the clauses that were an abuse of dominance, because, to do so would fundamentally change the whole nature of the contract that the parties had intended to enter into. (See also Chapter 3.5 on severance).

Section 2 of the Competition Act 1998 and Article 81 EC both contain the following non-exhaustive list of the types of agreements, decisions or practices which may fall foul of the competition rules if agreed to by two or more undertakings:

a. directly or indirectly fixing purchase or selling prices or any other trading conditions;

b. limiting production or controlling production, markets, technical development or investment;

c. sharing markets or sources of supply;

d. applying dissimilar conditions to equivalent transactions with other trading parties, thereby placing them at a competitive disadvantage;

e. make the conclusion of contracts subject to acceptance by the other parties of supplementtary obligations which by their nature or according to commercial usage have no connection with the subject of such contracts.

A restrictive covenant whose object or effect is the prevention, restriction or distortion of competition will most likely fall within the prohibition and will require scrutiny by the parties concerned. It will be necessary to consider whether it benefits from an exemption; either because any restrictive effects on competition are not appreciable or because it benefits from an exclusion or from a block exemption or under section 9 of the Act or Article 81(3) EC.

As the competition rules can render a restrictive covenant (and potentially the whole agreement) void, an assessment of the restriction under the competition rules will be a key consideration when deciding whether to seek interim relief. The competitive effects must be analysed in order to either enforce a restrictive covenant or to assess whether a burden imposed by a restrictive covenant may be avoided on the grounds that it is an illegal obligation and hence unenforceable by the other party. For example, in the *World Wide Fund for Nature v World Wrestling Federation*, [2002] UKCLR 388 the claimant was awarded an injunction to enforce the terms of an agreement entered into by the parties pursuant to which the defendant agreed not to use the initials WWF except in limited circumstances. The Wrestling Federation, albeit unsuccessfully, raised the invalidity of the provision under Article 81 EC in its defence (so called "Euro Defence").

Restrictive covenants which fall foul of the Chapter II/Article 82 EC prohibitions will also be void and unenforceable. Section 18 of the Act and Article 82 EC set out a non-exhaustive list of the sorts of practices which are prohibited if conducted by a dominant undertaking:

1. directly or indirectly imposing unfair purchase or selling prices or other unfair trading conditions;
2. limiting production, markets or technical developments to the prejudice of consumers;
3. applying dissimilar condtitions to equivalent transactions with other trading parties thereby placing them at a competitive disadvantage;
4. making the conclusion of contracts subject to acceptance by the other parities of supplementary obligations which by their nature or according to commercial usage have no connection with the subject of such contracts.

For a more detailed discussion on dominance and abuse of dominance see further Chapter 21.12 (EC) and Chapter 22.8 (UK).

For example, in *Jobserve Ltd v Network Multimedia Television Ltd*, [2002] UKCLR 184 the Court of Appeal upheld the grant of an interim injunction by the High Court restraining Jobserve from abusing its dominant position in its market. Both parties operated in the online market for the provision of advertising services to recruitment agencies. Jobserve sought to restrict agencies from advertising on the competing website operated by the defendant via a provision which would prevent any agency that did so from also advertising on Jobserve's site. The High Court and Court of Appeal both found that there was a serious question to be tried as to whether Jobserve was dominant, and whether it had abused that position of strength by seeking to impose such an advertising restriction. This mitigated in favour of the grant of the injunction.

In *Adidas-Salomon AG v Roger Draper & Derek Paul Draper (sued on behalf of themselves and the members of the Lawn Tennis Association) & Ors*, [2006] EWHC 318 the High Court also granted an injunction restraining the defendants from implementing dress code decisions in relation to the Grand Slam tennis tournaments including Wimbledon and the French Open. The claimant argued that a change in the dress code restrictions for the Grand Slam tournaments meant that it could no longer use its traditional three stripe logo on the clothing worn by players it sponsored; and this put it at a competitive disadvantage with the other tennis clothing manufacturers. The allegations were that the defendants had breached Article 82 and Article 81. The Court held that the claimant had a real prospect of success in relation to the claim that the defendants' decisions were incompatible with Article 81 and at trial these might be declared void. The issues under Article 82 were principally the same and the only effective remedy for the claimant at that stage was to grant an injunction. The Court made it clear that because Article 81 and 82 have direct effect they constrain what any undertakings may do. Where an allegation of breach is made there is a duty on the Court to scrutinise the activities complained of and interfere where necessary.

23.12.3 UK/Europe—which jurisdiction?

Before deciding which juridiction is which where to seek to enforce or prevent any restrictive covenant the parties must assess whether the agreement has an appreciable effect on UK trade only, inter-state trade, or trade within another Member State; and consider where the parties are domiciled.

If the agreement only has an effect on UK trade and is a UK agreement with no extra territorial effect then the application for interim relief will be made in the UK only. This can be done either by a complaint to the OFT (together with a request for interim measures to be imposed) or an action in the High Court (see Section 4.2 below for further details).

The High Court has held that it has no jurisdiction to hear a case which involved a non-UK company alleging breach of Chapter I and Chapter II CA98/Article 81 and 82 EC Treaty by non-UK defendants. *Sandisk Corporation v Koninklijke Philips Electronics NV & Ors*, [2007] EWHC 332. The question of whether the UK court had jurisdiction fell to be determined by reference to Council Regulation (EC) 44/2001 ("the Brussels Regulation"). The basic rule in the Brussels Regulation is that a defendant is to be sued in the courts of the member state where that person is domiciled (Article 2 Brussels Regulation 44/2001). There is an exemption in Article 5 of the Brussels Regulation which does allow a person domiciled in one Member State to be sued in another Member State, but only if, the court is in the place where the harmful event occurred or may have ocurred. Therefore, in order for the UK High Court to have jurisdiction the alleged practices would need to have taken place in the UK or caused damage to the claimant in the UK.

See also *Besix v Wasserreinigung Alfred Kretzschmar*, Case C-256/00 [2003] All ER D280 (May) where the CFI held that a single place of performance for the non-compete obligation had to be identified which would be the place presenting the closest connection between the dispute and the court hearing jurisdiction.

In relation to the availability of interim measures the High Court in *Sandisk* went on to note that jurisdiction to grant interim relief under Article 31 of the Brussels Regulation should be exercised by the court which is most able to have knowledge of and understand the effects of the interim measures (following Case 125/79, *Denilauler* [1980] ECR 1553). None of the defendants were UK companies and the orders sought are not available in UK courts. As a result, with both non-UK plaintiff and defendants, the High Court ruled that it did not have jurisdiction to grant the measures sought.

If the agreement has an effect only within another Member State then the local courts or national competition authority will be the appropriate forum for taking action.

If the agreement has an effect on Member State trade then a complaint could also be lodged with the European Commission (together with a request for interim measures to be applied). The Modernisation Regulation (Regulation 1/2003) gave the EC Commission power to grant interim measures, however, complainants are not supposed to request interim measures when making a complaint under Article 7(2). In practice, however, if a complainant requires interim measures, then most complainants include submissions on interim measures in their complaints and the EC Commission is obliged to consult the Advisory Committee (which includes representatives from the national Competition Authorities) before adopting interim measures Article 14(1) Regulation 1/2003. The EC Commission is entitled to grant interim measures, but only when it has acted on its own initiative. The following conditions must be met:

- there is a case of urgency;
- there is a prima facie finding of infringement; and
- there is a risk of serious and irrepairable damage to competition (not competitors or consumers). (Article 8 Regulation 1/2003).

Any interim measures adopted must be ordered for a specific period of time only and are subject to renewal (Article 24(1)(b)). Failing to comply with interim measures can result in a fine of up to 10 per cent of the turnover of the undertaking in question in the preceeding business year.

It is also possible to judicially review any failure of the EC Commission to impose interim measures. Case T-184/01 *IMS Health v Commission*, 2001 ECR II 3193.

Following receipt and investigation of a complaint the EC Commission can in addition to or as an alternative to imposing interim measures, make a finding of infringement and impose financial penalties; can find that Article 81 is not applicable; and can accept binding commitments in lieu of issuing an infringement decision.

23.12.4 Power to grant interim relief in UK

Applications for interim relief in cases involving competition law issues in the UK may be commenced by going directly to the OFT, by starting a civil action in the usual way before the High Court; or both. Each will be considered in turn. However, it is important to remember that both the OFT and the High Court have parallel jurisdiction in this area, and hence the decision regarding which route to follow will be informed by strategic considerations such as cost implications, time, burden and standard of proof and the fact that a cross-undertaking in damages need not be given by the applicant if interim measures are sought from the OFT.

23.12.4.1 Interim measures from the OFT

The prohibitions on restrictive agreements and on abusive conduct may be applied by the OFT either in response to a complaint made to it by or of its own volition. The range of enforcement powers available to it when exercising its statutory duties under the Competition Act 1998 include:

a. giving directions to the undertaking concerned to bring the infringement/abusive behaviour to an end;
b. giving interim measures directions during an investigation;
c. accepting commitments offered to it; and
d. imposing financial penalties of up to 10% of worldwide turnover.

The power to grant interim measures is contained in Section 35 of the Competition Act 1998. Interim measures may only be granted by the OFT if it has already commenced an investigation into the issues in question under section 25 of the Act (section 35(1)), and only if it considers it necessary for it to grant interim measures as a matter of urgency for the purpose of preventing serious irreparable damage to a particular person of category of person or for the purpose of protecting the public interest (section 35(2)). An investigation may have been commenced following a complaint, an application for leniency or on the OFT's own initiative. In addition, section 35(3) obliges the OFT to give written notice to the person to whom it proposes giving interim measures directions and to provide that person with the opportunity to make representations to it.

So far the OFT has been reluctant to exercise its power to grant interim measures. Its first such decision was made in response to a complaint by Spectron about the London Metal Exchange ("LME") and its decision to extend its trading hours to overnight. An interim measures direction was given preventing the LME from extending its trading times on the basis that were it to do so Spectron, the only other competitor in the relevant market, would not be able to compete and would be forced to exit the market (*OFT Directions Decision to the LME*, 27 February 2006). Significantly, Spectron later asked the OFT to withdraw its decision because of complaints which it, Spectron, had received from customers opposed to the OFT's decision. The OFT finally withdrew its decision on the basis of new information which it obtained but only after the LME appealed to the Competition Appeal Tribunal ("CAT") under section 46 of the Act asserting that the OFT erred in fact and law by imposing the interim measures (OFT Press Release 86/06 of 15 May 2006).

The CAT did not need to rule on the imposition of the interim measures.

However, the CAT's decision as regards LME's application for costs is instructive particularly as regards the quality of evidence and level of urgency required under section 35 of the Competition Act 1998 (*London Metal Exchange v OFT*, CAT Judgment of 8 September 2006). The CAT compared the power of the OFT to grant interim measures with that of the High Court to grant an injunction (See paragraph 138) and therefore compared the quality of the evidence which the OFT had relied upon with the quality of evidence required by a court in order to grant an injunction under Practice Direction—Interim Injunctions (CPR Part 25), 25 PD. As regards the degree of urgency involved, in this case the CAT emphasized that the OFT could not rely upon delays on the part of the complainant in providing it with information (see paragraph 160). The OFT must act in a timely manner.

Seeking interim measures before the OFT will require careful consideration of the quality of the evidence which can be submitted to support the application. The CAT stated that the OFT must satisfy itself of the quality of the evidence available to it for the purposes of section 35 of the Act (see paragraph 162). It added that the OFT should be circumspect about relying upon uncorroborated evidence obtained under its informal powers of investigation (see paragraph 137–142). An interim measures application should therefore be supported by cogent and persuasive evidence. In addition, a defence to such an application could usefully seek to exploit the quality of the evidence upon which the OFT is seeking to rely. However, disclosure may need to be obtained in order to do this and this is not easy, quick or even necessarily possible to achieve from the OFT. The typical problem facing complainants is information asymmetry, i.e. the person suffering from a breach of competition law may not have available to them all the evidence necessary to make a complaint and/or application for interim measures.

Unlike an application before the High Court, there is no obligation to provide a cross-undertaking in damages when securing interim measures from the OFT under section 35 of the Act.

23.12.4.2 Interim relief from the High Court

The competition rules will form the legal basis for civil claims for damages and interim relief in the High Court, see Civil Procedure Rules Part 16 and Practice Direction Claims relating to the application of Articles 81 and 82 of the EC Treaty and Chapters I and II of Part I of the Competition Act 1998 October 2005. For example, see *Hendry v The World Professional Billiards and Snooker Association Limited* [2001] Eu. L.R. 770; *Inntrepreneur Pub Company v Crehan*, [2006] U.K.H.L. 38. The cause of action for damages and for injunctive relief in competition law matters will be for breach of statatutory duty as per *Garden Cottage Foods Ltd v Milk Marketing Board* [1984] A.C. 130. Once breach of statutory duty has been established the claimant must show that it gives rise to a private law action. The claimant must show that:

- the damages suffered fall within the ambit of the statute;
- the statutory duty was breached;
- the breach caused the loss; and

The potential claimants are not only the parties to the agreement containing a restrictive covenant but also any third parties who can establish loss suffered as a result of the restriction and anti-competitive agreement. Third party Claimants could include direct purchasers, indirect purchasers, potential purchasers, competitors, and suppliers.

The normal civil burden and standard of proof must be met in order for an injunction to be granted (see Chapter 23 for further details). See for example *Claritas UK (Ltd) v The Post Office and Postal Preference Services* [2001] U.K.C.L.R. 2 where an injunction application was rejected because of a failure to establish an abuse of dominance. Any associated claim for damages should be appropriately pleaded in the same application for injunctive relief in order to avoid any future claim for damages being rejected as "an abuse of process of the court", *World Wide Fund for Nature (formerly World Wildlife Fund) and Another v World Wrestling Federation* [2007] All ER (D) 13 (Apr). The Court of Appeal held that the claim for *Wrotham Park* damages in these proceedings "abused the processes of the court" (See paragraph 74) because the trial judge in the 2001 proceedings was invited to decide on the issues in question on the basis that no such claim would be made.

The parallel jurisdiction which exists as between the High Court and the OFT to grant interim relief in cases raising competition law issues is evident in *AAH Pharmaceuticals Ltd and others v Pfizer Ltd and another* [2007] EWHC 565, March 5, 2007. The litigation in that case involved a decision by Pfizer Ltd to change its distribution arrangements such that, in the future, it would supply its prescription drugs directly to pharmacies as opposed to wholesalers. The latter complained to the OFT asserting that Pfizer's refusal to supply them with their pharmaceutical drugs was a breach of Article 82 EC and Chapter II of the Act. They also sought interim measures under Section 35, before the new distribution regime was implemented by Pfizer, to prevent implementation of the new distribution regime. As soon as the applicants became aware that the OFT would not be in a position to grant interim measures before the distribution regime was to change, the wholesalers applied to the High Court for injunctive relief by way of a mandatory injunction requiring Pfizer to continue to supply them. Whilst rejecting the application on the merits, the High Court expressed considerable discontent that the application to it had been made at such a late stage and so close to the date when the new distribution system was to become operational. That delay meant that the defendants and the court had been denied the opportunity of dealing with the application and hence greatly increasing the risk of injustice if the injunction was granted (paragraph 77). Richards J added, "[T]he fact that the Claimants chose to pursue their complaints with the OFT and to persist in doing so until the very last moment does not in my judgment provide a good ground for not bringing the matter before the court at a much earlier stage" (paragraph 77). Despite the jurisdiction of the OFT, and the sectoral regulators to deal with competitive disputes between private parties, the courts are happy to deal with them in the first instance.

However, the High court has noted that where the regulator might have policy views on the issue it might be appropriate to invite these views first (see paragraph 61 and 62 *Software Cellular Network Ltd v T-Mobile (UK) Ltd* judgment dated 17 July 2007).

It may, however, have been advisable to commence an action in the High Court and seek an interim injunction and then make a complaint to the OFT. The Court could then be asked to stay proceedings pending an OFT Decision (see *Synstar v ICL*, 2001 UKCLR 585).

The competition rules may also be used as a defence to civil claims which litigate a breach of a restrictive provision contained in an agreement between the parties. For example, in *P&S Amusements Limited v Valley House Leisure*, [2006] EWHC 1510 (Ch) the landlord brought a claim for injunctive relief to compel performance of a covenant contained in a sub-lease that required the tenant to purchase beer from a supplier designated by the landlord. The claimant also sought damages from the defendants. Both defendants argued in their defence, albeit unsuccessfully on the facts, that the beer tie covenant was contrary to the competition rules (the "Euro-defence"). The lack of appreciable effect under Chapter I/Article 81 and the absence of dominance for the purposes of Chapter II/Article 82 resulted in the Euro-defences being struck out and the injunction being granted in this case.

Pleading the invalidity of the provision being enforced under the competition rules should be included in any defence lodged from the outset. In *Bim Kemi AB v Blackburn Chemicals Ltd*, [2004] EWCA Civ 1490, where the defendant initially raised the invalidity of the agreement in question as a Euro-defence and then abandoned these arguments. The claimant sought to persuade the court that the Euro-defence should not be allowed to proceed on the basis of estoppel case law and *Henderson's Principle* (1843) 3 Hare 100,

114-5 as the agreement concerned was not manifestly illegal. The Court of Appeal rejected the claimant's position stating that, in the circumstances, it would not be unfair to allow the Euro-defence to be pleaded on the facts. Despite the fact that the Defendant was no longer arguing it, on the basis that Article 81 raises public policy considerations, not for the protection of the parties, but consumers generally, the Court has to take significance of it.

Note that the Lord Chancellor can make regulations providing for competition proceedings to be transferred from the High Court to the Competition Appeal Tribunal under section 16(4) Enterprise Act 2002. This provision has not yet been bought into force by the necessary regulations but may be invoked in the future to allow a highly specialist court to develop in the CAT.

23.12.5 Conclusion

To the extent that a restrictive covenant is an agreement between undertakings and that it has the object or effect of preventing, restricting or distorting competition within the UK or trade between Member States, it will fall foul of the competition rules. Similarly, the enforcement of a restrictive covenant could be the subject of challenge under the competition provisions relating to abuses of dominance. The principles and criteria as set out earlier in this chapter will also apply to injunction applications in cases raising competition law issues.

If a case involves an issue of competition law it influences the forum from which to seek the relief. When deciding upon which forum to approach, in order to secure interim relief, the considerations to take into account will include the extent to which the remedy sought is urgent, the likely costs which may be incurred in obtaining the interim relief and the obligation to give a cross-undertaking in damages.

Securing interim measures from the OFT pursuant to section 35 of the Competition Act 1998 is an attractive option both financially and perhaps substantively depending upon the complexity of the competition issues being raised in the interlocutory stage of the proceedings. However, this approach is not without considerable disadvantages. The OFT has displayed considerable hesitation in exercising its powers under section 35 to date, there are time constraints associated with the requirement that the OFT must already have opened an investigation in the case under section 25 of the Competition Act 1998 and it must satisfy itself that the quality of evidence upon which it intends to rely is satisfactory. Collectively these could make the interim measures option under the Competition Act 1998 of limited value if the interim relief is required immediately. Whilst injunction applications before the High Court can be considered expeditiously, the cost implications of this alternative may be prohibitive, as may be the obligation and ability to provide a cross-undertaking in damages. However, the use of the High Court for injunctive relief in competition cases is increasing and in the near future will develop a very important body of case law of the use of interim relief in competition law matters.

Chapter 24

Search Orders and other Ancillary Orders

24.1 Introduction

There is often a danger in restraint of trade and business secrets cases that important evidence may be destroyed once a party, or potential party, to litigation becomes aware of proceedings being brought against them. In such circumstances, the ability of a claimant to obtain an effective final remedy may be severely and irreparably compromised. Applications for orders for the detention, custody, preservation and/or inspection of such evidence (see below at para.24.7) are of limited use, since they must be made on notice, and thus give the defendant the opportunity to hide or destroy the property concerned. As a result, a practice has developed, particularly over the last 25 years, whereby a claimant can apply to the Court—without notice to a defendant—for an interlocutory order that requires the defendant (as it will normally be, but see para.24.6 below) to permit the claimant to enter its business premises, or even personal property, in order to search for, examine, copy and/or remove any material which might otherwise be hidden or destroyed.

Formerly, orders of this type were known as Anton Piller orders, deriving their name from *Anton Piller KG v Manufacturing Processes Limited* [1976] Ch. 55, a 1975 case in which the Court of Appeal acknowledged the courts' power to make orders of this type. However the Civil Procedure Act 1997 (the "CPA") introduced a statutory basis for the granting of Anton Piller-style orders, which, following the introduction of the Civil Procedure Rules 1998 (the "CPR") are now known as search orders.

In addition, it should be noted that the competition authorities (i.e. the EC Commission and the Office of Fair Trading) have themselves extensive powers to enter and search premises (referred to as "dawn raids") and/or request documents and information from companies and indviduals under both the Competition Act 1998, and the Enterprise Act 2002. Where the restraint of trade/breach of competition law is therefore not based on a contractual document it is often worth considering a complaint to the regulator rather than litigation.

24.2 The "Anton Piller" principles

Notwithstanding search orders' new statutory foundation, the decision to grant or refuse an application for such an order still rests on the discretion of the court, exercised in accordance with the principles originally laid down in the *Anton Piller* case and refined by subsequent case law. In deciding whether to grant a search order, the court must have regard to the following issues:

(a) Does the applicant for a search order have a strong case? In other words, can it demonstrate that it is the owner or exclusive licensee of some intellectual property right that is, or is in grave danger of, being infringed by the defendant? As part of the application for a search order, it will be necessary to show that a cause of action known to law has already arisen; a search order cannot be used to facilitate a "fishing expedition", or as some form of pre-action discovery, in order to establish whether a cause of action exists (*per* Lawton L.J. in *Hytrac Conveyors v Conveyors International* [1983] F.S.R. 63).

(b) Is the claimant likely to suffer serious damage if the search order is not granted? Will its business be harmed—for example, profits or market share lost—as a result of the defendant's unlawful activities?

(c) Does the defendant possess incriminating evidence and is there a real possibility that this evidence may be destroyed or hidden if the defendant becomes aware that proceedings have been, or are about to be, brought against it? As to the second limb of this particular requirement, it appears that the courts are willing to infer a threat to the property concerned if the defendant can be shown to have engaged in dishonest or criminal conduct in the past, or by virtue of anything that the defendant might have said or indicated to the claimant in relation to its future activities. Conversely, there are examples of cases where the fact the defendant is operating openly, or is a respectable company, has proved to be the decisive factor in refusing an application for a search order (see *Systematica Ltd v London Computer Centre Ltd* [1983] F.S.R. 313 and *Booker McConnell plc v Plascow* [1985] R.P.C. 425).

(d) Would the execution of a search order cause disproportionate harm to the defendant? It is well established that the scope of any search order must go no further than the minimum extent necessary to preserve the documents or articles that may otherwise be concealed or destroyed (*Columbia Picture Industries Inc v Robinson* [1987] Ch. 38). To this end, claimants should be wary of, and possibly decline, any offer by the judge himself to widen the ambit of the order sought if this would result in an order that might be oppressive to the defendant. The fact that the scope of the order may have been determined by the judge will not serve to preclude its discharge if it proves to be disproportionately prejudicial to the defendant (*Bank of Scotland v A Ltd* [2001] 1 W.L.R. 751).

The four principles set out above are usefully summarised in *Indicii Salus Ltd v Chandrasekeran* [2006] EWHC 521 (Ch) and [2007] EWHC 406 (Ch) as follows:

1. There must be an extremely strong prima facie case;
2. The damage potential or actual must be very serious for the applicant;
3. There must be clear evidence that the defendants had in their possession incriminating documents or things and there is a real possibility that the defendants may destroy such material before an on notice application is made; and
4. The harm likely to be caused by the execution of the search order on the respondent in his business affairs must not be out of proportion to the legitimate object of the order.

Above all, the courts are expected to exercise their discretion in relation to the grant of search orders cautiously. In this regard, the words of Browne-Wilkinson J. in *Thermax Ltd v Schott Industrial Glass Ltd* [1981] F.S.R. 289 should still be borne in mind:

> As time goes on and the granting of Anton Piller orders becomes more and more frequent, there is a tendency to forget how serious an intervention they are in the privacy and rights of defendants. One is inclined to forget the stringency of the requirements as laid down by the Court of Appeal [in the *Anton Piller* case].

Search orders facilitate access to an individual's home or place of business, giving rise to the violation of the privacy of a defendant who has had no opportunity to put his side of the case. It is not merely that the defendant may be innocent of any wrongdoing. The making of an intrusive order without notice, even against a guilty defendant, is contrary to the normal principles of justice, and should only be done when there is a paramount need to prevent the denial of justice to the claimant. The ability to apply for a discharge of a search order obtained improperly may be of little comfort or protection to a defendant since, in practice, this right can rarely be exercised prior to the execution of the order. Similarly, it may be the case that the undertaking as to costs that the claimant will have to give as a precondition of securing a search order cannot adequately compensate the defendant for the substantial reputational or other damage that it may suffer as a result of being subjected to a search of this type, or the harm to its business that may arise if a competitor (as it will invariably be) has sight of commercially sensitive information belonging to the defendant whilst conducting the search.

24.3 Human Rights implications

Indeed, the grant of search orders may raise issues under Art.8 of the European Convention on Human Rights ("ECHR") (the right to respect for private life) or under ECHR Protocol 1, Art.1 (the right to peaceful enjoyment of possessions). However, these are not freedoms that are granted in absolute terms, and in most cases, any interference is likely to be considered justified as necessary "for the protection of the rights and freedoms of others" (Art.8(2)) or as "in the public interest" (Protocol 1, Art.1). Thus, in *Niemietz v Germany* (1993) 16 E.H.R.R. 97, where it was established that the words "private life", "home" and "correspondence" in Art.8 ECHR also encompassed certain professional and business activities, a search order made by a German court in respect of a lawyer's office was permitted, provided that it satisfied the requirements of necessity and proportionality. Similarly, the grant and execution of a search order (or *Anton Piller* order, as it then was) were expressly upheld by the European Court of Human Rights in *Chappell v United Kingdom* (1990) 12 E.H.R.R. 1, albeit with notable limits on the manner of execution of such orders.

Nevertheless, as s.6 of the Human Rights Act 1998 makes it unlawful for a public authority—defined as including "a court or tribunal"—to act in a way incompatible with Convention rights, English Courts must give careful consideration to the scope and terms of any search orders that they may grant. In particular, the courts must have regard to the principles of proportionality inherent in the articles of the ECHR when deciding whether the aim of a search order can be achieved by means that are less restrictive of Convention rights.

24.4 Jurisdiction

Prior to the introduction of the CPA, there had been some debate as to the source of the power of the High Court to make Anton Piller orders. It was thought that this power was derived from either

(a) s.37 of the Supreme Court Act 1981, which provides that the High Court may by order, whether interlocutory or final, grant an injunction in all cases where it appeared to the court to be just and convenient to do so, or

(b) the inherent jurisdiction of the High Court to make interlocutory orders for securing a just and proper trial of issues between parties.

However, s.7(1) CPA now confers a specific power on the High Court to make orders "for the purpose of securing, in the case of any existing or proposed proceedings . . . the preservation of evidence which is or may be relevant". (For limits on the jurisdiction of county courts to grant relief of this type, see the County Court Remedies Regulation 1991, reg.2(a) and para.25.1.29 of the White Book). In summary, such orders may direct their recipient to permit any person described in the order to enter premises in England and Wales and, whilst on the premises to

(a) carry out a search for, or inspection of, anything described in the order,

(b) make or obtain a copy or record of anything so described,

(c) provide that person described in the order with any information described in the order, and/or

(d) allow that person to retain for safe keeping anything described in the order (s.7(3)–(5) CPA).

Rule 25.1(1)(h) CPR, in turn, provides that:

> The court may grant . . . an order (referred to as a "search order") under section 7 of the Civil Procedure Act 1997 (order requiring a party to admit another party to the premises for the purpose of preserving evidence, etc.)

It should be noted that the CPA does not expressly take away whatever powers the High Court may have previously have possessed (see *"Anton Piller orders: the new statutory scheme"* C.J.Q. Vol.17 p.272). Therefore, whilst the CPA should now be regarded as the primary source of the power in question, it appears that it is not the only one. This may be important in some circumstances, where s.7 CPA is limited in ways in which the inherent jurisdiction is not—for example, orders under s.7 cannot be made in respect of property outside England & Wales, whilst it is possible that they can if made pursuant to the court's inherent jurisdiction.

24.5 The rules governing search orders

An application for a search order is made on an application notice in accordance with Part 23 of the CPR (General Rules About Applications For Court Orders), as modified by the provisions of Part 25 of the CPR (Interim Remedies and Security For Costs) and its accompanying Practice Direction. The Practice Direction stipulates those specific requirements that an applicant for a search order must comply with; in particular, para.7 of the Practice Direction set out a number of measures—such as the need for an independent solicitor to supervise the execution of a search order (see "The Role of Supervising Solicitor" C.J.Q. Vol 18, p.103)—that, even prior to the advent of the CPR, the courts had insisted on as being necessary to protect the rights of those subjected to a search. Although an example of a search order is annexed to the Practice Direction, this is not a standard form and it will need to be tailored to the requirements of each individual case. However, if a search order materially departs from the requirements of the Practice Direction and the example of the order annexed to it, it may be set aside if the variations were not drawn to the attention of the judge that granted the original order (see *Gadget Shop Ltd v Bug.Com Ltd* [2000] All E.R. (D) 799).

24.5.1 Timing

Usually, an application for a search order will be made after the issue, but before service, of a claim form, although in urgent cases, an application may be made before the issue of proceedings (r.25.2(1) CPR). However, if an application for a search order is to be made before proceedings are commenced, the court may only grant such an order only if the matter is urgent, or it is otherwise necessary to do so in the interests of justice (r.25.2(2)(b) CPR). Further, the court may require the claimant to commence substantive proceedings within a fixed period (usually 14 to 21 days) as a condition of making the order.

24.5.2 Without notice applications

As a rule, an application for a court order must be made by filing an application notice (r.23.3(1) CPR) which must then be served on each Defendant (r.23.4(1) CPR). However, r.25.3(1) CPR provides that the court may grant an interim remedy on an application made without notice if it appears to the court that there are good reasons for not giving notice (i.e. the giving of notice would cause injustice to the applicant because of the urgency of the matter or because of the need to obtain a provisional remedy by surprise). In such circumstances, the evidence in support of the application must state the reasons why notice has not been given—thus, even though it may go without saying that notice of an application for a search order is likely to lead to the removal and/or destruction of the relevant property, this must be expressly stated.

The duties of an applicant for without notice relief were summarised by Bingham J. in *Siporex Trade SA v Comdel Commodities Limited* [1986] 2 Lloyd's Rep. 428 (subsequently approved by the Court of Appeal in *Marc Rich & Co Holdings GmbH v Krasner*, January 15, 1999, CA (unreported)). Those duties are:

- to show the utmost good faith and disclose his case fully and fairly;
- for the protection and information of the defendant, to summarise his case and evidence in support by affidavit;
- to identify the crucial points for and against the application (it is not sufficient that these be merely addressed in attachments and exhibits);

- to investigate the nature of the claim and the facts relied on before applying and to identify any likely defences; and
- to disclose all facts which reasonably could or would be taken into account by a judge in deciding to grant the application (it being no excuse for an applicant to say that he was unaware of the importance of matters he had omitted to state).

24.5.3 The duty to give full disclosure

A claimant is required to disclose fully to the court all matters relevant to the application for without notice relief, including all matters, whether of fact or of law, which are, or may be, adverse to it. In *Memory Corporation plc v Sidhu* [2000] 1 W.L.R. 1443 CA, Mummery L.J. noted that this was a "high duty" and required the applicant to make full, fair and accurate disclosure of material information to the court and to draw the court's attention to "significant factual, legal and procedural aspects of the case". The duty to give full disclosure has attracted considerable judicial comment, not least because of the tendency of defendants to seek to have search orders set aside on the basis of claimants' failure to comply with their obligations in this regard. Indeed, judges appear to be becoming increasingly critical of defendants alleging "material non-disclosure on rather slender grounds . . . [in the] hope of obtaining a discharge of injunctions in cases where there is little hope of doing so on the substantial merits of the case or on the balance of convenience" (*per* Slade L.J. in *Brink's-Mat Limited v Elcombe and others* [1988] 3 All E.R. 188).

The *Brink's-Mat* case—which actually concerned a "Mareva" injunction (now a "freezing order"), but whose principles, it is submitted, apply equally to cases concerning search orders—is one of the leading authorities both in relation to the duty of full disclosure and on the effect of non-disclosure or misrepresentation in relation to such interim remedies. As regards the extent of the duty of full disclosure, Ralph Gibson L.J. identified the following principles:

- Material facts are those which it is material for the judge to know in dealing with the application as made; materiality is to be decided by the court and not by the assessment of the applicant or his legal advisers.
- The applicant must make proper inquiries before making the application as the duty of disclosure applies not only to material facts known to the applicant but also any additional facts which would have been known to him had he made proper inquiries (see, for example the *Systematica* case, and *Jeffrey Rogers Knitwear Productions Ltd v Vinola (Knitwear) Manufacturing Co* [1985] F.S.R. 184).
- The extent of the inquiries that will be held to be proper and necessary depend on the circumstances of the case, including the order sought, the

probable effect on the defendant, the degree of legitimate urgency and the time available for making inquires.

Ralph Gibson L.J. concluded that whether a fact not disclosed was of sufficient materiality to justify or require the immediate discharge of the order, depended on the importance of the fact to the issues to be decided, and he acknowledged that not every omission would result in the automatic discharge of the injunction. The comments of Balcombe L.J. and Slade L.J. in relation to the Court's discretion in this regard are also instructive:

> The rule that an ex parte [as was] injunction will be discharged if it was obtained without full disclosure has a two-fold purpose. It will deprive the wrongdoer of an advantage improperly obtained . . . But it also serves as a deterrent to ensure that persons who make ex parte applications realise that they have this duty of disclosure and of the consequences (which may include a liability in costs) if they fail in that duty. Nevertheless, this judge-made rule must not be allowed itself to become an instrument of injustice. It is for this reason that there must be a discretion in the court to confirm the injunction, or to grant a fresh injunction in its place. [*per* Balcombe L.J.]
>
> By their very nature, ex parte applications usually necessitate the giving and taking of instructions and the preparation of drafts in some haste. Particularly in heavy commercial cases, the borderline between material facts and non-material facts may be a somewhat uncertain one. While in no way discounting the heavy duty of candour and care which falls on parties making ex parte applications, I do not think the application of the principle [of full disclosure] should be carried to extreme lengths. [*per* Slade L.J.]

Similarly, in *Crown Resources AG v Vinogradsky*, June 15, 2001 (unreported), Toulson J. stated that:

> . . . a court will not ordinarily embark on a trial within a trial to establish whether or not facts existed which are alleged to be material . . . where facts are material . . . there are degrees of relevance and it is important to preserve a due sense of proportion . . . In less serious cases, where there is no plausible ground for supposing that the matter would have made any difference or that there was any bad [faith] on the part of the applicant, to set aside "pour encourager les autres", may not only be unfair on balance between the parties, but may have the effect of encouraging "les autres" in the unwelcome sense of encouraging applications to set aside by a defendant against whom there was ample ground for the making of an injunction and who has suffered no prejudice by some failure on the part of the applicant to present its application in a way which was as complete and accurate as with hindsight it should have been.

Whilst *Crown Resources* also concerned a freezing order, it is submitted that the courts will deem it equally inappropriate for defendants to seek to set aside a search order for non-disclosure where proof of non-disclosure depends on proof of facts that are themselves in issue in the action, unless those facts are so plain that they can be readily and summarily established. In short, the courts are keen to avoid situations where applications to set aside orders become a form of preliminary trial in which the judge is asked to make findings (albeit provisionally) on issues which should be more properly reserved for the trial itself.

A good example of a case in which a search order was discharged for material non-disclosure is *Manor Electronics Ltd v Dickson* [1988] R.P.C. 618. In this case, the plaintiffs (as were) manufactured and sold electronic devices. The first four defendants were a former director and three former employees of the plaintiffs and the fifth defendant was a company for which they now worked. The plaintiffs believed the defendants had conspired to injure them by going into competition with them using their confidential information. The plaintiffs obtained ex parte orders restraining disposal of certain assets, and for delivery up and discovery. They gave the usual cross undertaking in damages but failed to disclose that their financial situation was "parlous"; no evidence of their financial worth had been offered. They also undertook to issue and serve the writ forthwith, but there was, in fact, a delay in serving it. On the basis of documents disclosed on the first order, they then sought and obtained an Anton Piller order, again failing to disclose their financial position. The order read in part "It is ordered that . . . [the plaintiffs' solicitor accompanied by a director of the plaintiffs] shall be entitled to enter the dwelling house, workshop and garage of Mr Dickson . . .". The plaintiffs' solicitor, who attended on the execution of the Anton Piller order, was the daughter of the plaintiffs' chief executive. On the return date, the plaintiffs sought an interlocutory injunction restraining use of confidential information. The defendants applied to discharge the ex parte orders.

Scott J. discharged the ex parte orders and refused injunctive relief on the following bases:

(a) The form of the Anton Piller order, in providing that the plaintiffs' representatives "be entitled to enter" the first defendants' premises, instead of requiring the first defendant to permit such entry, was defective.

(b) The plaintiffs' solicitor's failure to honour the plaintiffs' undertaking to serve the writ as soon as issued was regrettable (albeit an oversight) as it left the defendants in doubt as to the cause of action asserted against them.

(c) The requirement that a plaintiff's solicitor supervise the execution of an Anton Piller order is to ensure that there is some responsible person who can give reliable evidence of what has taken place. The evidence of a solicitor, as an officer of the court, is likely in the event of a dispute to be believed in preference to that of the defendant and it is desirable that the solicitor should have no personal connection with the plaintiff. Here, it had been unwise, though not a breach of the order, that the solicitor in attendance should have been closely related to the plaintiffs' chief executive.

(d) There had been material non-disclosure of the plaintiffs' financial difficulties, so that their cross undertaking in damages was worthless. In the absence of reference in the evidence to a plaintiffs' financial substance, the ex parte judge will assume that it is adequate to support the cross undertaking; he depends upon the plaintiff making full disclosure. If there has been such material non-disclosure, then the court's practice is to discharge the ex parte orders without going into the merits.

(e) The plaintiffs had been unable to identify the alleged confidential information with sufficient particularity for the court to distinguish between protectable "trade secrets" and the unprotectable technical expertise gained by the first four defendants which they were entitled to use.

In exercising their discretion to set aside search orders, the courts are required to bear in mind the CPR's overriding objective and the need for proportionality (*Memory Corp plc v Sidhu (No.2)* [2000] 1 W.L.R 1443, CA). They will also need consider the seriousness of the non-disclosure, the harm done to the defendant, the relative culpability of the claimant and his lawyers (see *St Merryn Meat Ltd v Hawkins* [2001] C.P. Rep. 116, Ch D for an example of where freezing and search orders were discharged because of the failure of the claimant to disclose the fact that its application had been based on false affidavits and illicitly obtained evidence), and the prejudice that the claimant would suffer if the interim injunction were lost. A comprehensive list of recent cases in which injunctions were discharged on grounds of material non-disclosure can be found at the note to Rule 25.3.5 of the CPR.

24.6 The rights of a recipient of a search order

In most cases, a search order will be sought against the party that is a defendant, or potential defendant, in relation to a particular claim. However, s.7(3) CPA provides that a search order may be directed to "any person". It is generally accepted that this reference is intended to reflect the fact that a search order may be directed at claimants *as well as* defendants (see *International Electronics Limited v Weigh Data Ltd* [1980] F.S.R. 423, for an example, under the old common law regime, of a case where it was the defendant that applied for a search order), and also to any employee or agent of a claimant or defendant who is present at the premises concerned and who has authority to give permission for entry and search (so that it is not necessary for the claimant or defendant to be present for the order to be executed).

It is submitted that the wording of the Act does not provide for orders to be made against "persons" other than the parties to a claim, such as witnesses who happen to possess relevant material or information. It must be the case that a search order can only be made against a person that has lawful authority to consent to the activities that the order requires them to permit. Thus, it is difficult to see how a third party who has, or controls, relevant property, but has no power to permit anyone else to deal with it (i.e. a solicitor who holds client papers, or the operator of a self-storage site), can be ordered to allow inspection and removal of that property.

Paragraph 7.4(4) of the Practice Direction that supplements Part 25 CPR stipulates that the supervising solicitor overseeing the execution of a search order must explain to its recipient the terms and effect of the order in "everyday language" and, in particular advise him of his right to:

(a) take legal advice and to apply to vary or discharge the order; (although, in practice, absent an obvious mistake in the order such as the wrong defendant being named, a defendant will not usually have enough time for an application of this sort before execution of the search order begins); and

(b) avail himself of

  (i) legal professional privilege; and
  (ii) the privilege against self-incrimination.

The standard order annexed to this Practice Direction allows the defendant two hours in order to seek legal advice, but he must, in the meantime, allow the supervising solicitor onto premises (so as to minimise the risk of the relevant property being interfered with whilst that advice is sought). The supervising solicitor may also extend the time that the defendant has to obtain such advice, but is required to consider the increased risk that might exist in relation to the relevant property during this period.

It is well established that search orders do not themselves provide lawful justification for the entry into premises, and search and seizure of property. The courts have no power at common law to issue "search warrants" in civil proceedings, and search orders may not be executed by force. Search orders merely direct a defendant to permit entry and, if such permission is given, then anything done within the scope of that permission is considered to be lawful; conversely, if that permission is not granted, the party serving the search order must withdraw. However, a defendant who refuses to permit a claimant to enter its premises in accordance with the terms of a search order runs the risk of being held to be in contempt of court, the penalty for which is up to two years' imprisonment. Alternatively, the court can impose a fine on the defendant or sequester its assets.

The decision to refuse to comply with the terms of an Anton Piller order should only be taken in the clearest of circumstances, for example where:

(a) the defendant has very strong grounds for saying either there were insufficient grounds to justify the grant of the order in the first place; or

(b) that the attempted execution of the order was improper; or

(c) that there was a material non-disclosure by the plaintiffs when applying for the order or

(d) that the order is itself flawed in some material respect.

There has been considerable debate about the legal position of a defendant who resists the execution of a search order only to subsequently succeed with an application to discharge it on one of the aforementioned grounds. *Dockray & Laddie* (1990) 106 L.Q.R. 601–620 argue that only in the case of injunctions granted pursuant to inter partes proceedings should the general rule, that an injunction must still be obeyed even if it should never have been granted, apply; since the recipients of search orders do not always have the opportunity to question their validity, then failure to comply with an order that is subsequently discharged ought not to be treated as contempt. However, if this is correct, it produces the rather peculiar and, it is submitted, unsatisfactory, situation whereby the operation of the court's process is made to depend on a subjective assessment and response of particular defendants and their advisers. It is submitted that the analysis to be preferred is that pursuant to which a defendant who resists a search order but successfully challenges it at a later date will still be in contempt unless the order was void *ab initio*. In all other circumstances, the fact that he obtains a discharge goes only to mitigation of penalty, but does not provide a defence.

The courts have seemingly struggled with the possible inequity that this orthodox analysis can give rise to—contrast *Wardle Fabrics Ltd v G Myristis Ltd* [1984] F.S.R. 263 and *Hallmark Cards Inc v Image Arts Ltd* [1977] F.S.R. 150 for examples of the differing approaches that the courts have historically taken in relation to this issue. In *Bhimji v Chatwani* [1991] 1 All E.R. 705 an Anton Piller order was served at 8am on the defendants. By about 11am they were in contact with their solicitors and had received advice from them. Later in the morning instructions were sent to counsel on their behalf and, that afternoon, an application to set aside or vary the order was made to the judge who had granted it. He heard the application at about 5pm and declined to set aside the order but made some variations to it. As soon as the hearing was concluded the defendants gave permission to the plaintiffs to enter their premises and the amended order was executed. The plaintiffs sought an order for the committal of the defendants for not obeying the original order. It was clear that the defendants had been advised by their solicitors that they should comply with the original order or apply immediately to have it discharged. However there were negotiations between the solicitors on both sides in order to obviate the need for an application to the court for a variation of the order so as to allow a search of the premises immediately to proceed. It was suggested by the defendants' solicitors that solicitors for both sides carry out a joint search of the premises and that the documents required by the plaintiffs' solicitors should be safeguarded by the defendants' solicitors for a short period to enable the defendants to make an application to the judge to have the order discharged or varied. That compromise was rejected by the plaintiffs' solicitors. Scott J. concluded:

(1) The order on its true construction required entry at the latest after the defendants had received advice from their solicitors. Thereafter until they complied with the amended order the defendants were in breach of the order truly construed.

(2) The exact moment at which entry was to be allowed under the order was not clear from its terms, judging the matter by the standards of the ordinary layman.

(3) The defendants' failure to allow entry over the period 11am to 6pm was deliberate and, accordingly, the requisite *mens rea* for contempt of court was present.

(4) But in the circumstances the breach was not contumacious in the ordinary meaning of the word since:

   (a) it was accompanied by advice from solicitors that suggested that it was permissible for entry to be postponed until after the application to the court;
   (b) a reasonable offer to provide protection of the documents was made at an early stage, was not withdrawn, but was not accepted by the plaintiffs;
   (c) there was no evidence to suggest that the making of the application was merely a device to postpone the search;
   (d) there was no evidence of any impropriety in respect of the documents in any of the premises to be searched that took place over the period of the delay; and
   (e) where delay in allowing execution of an Anton Piller order is under review, the court should take into account the nature of the order and the prima facie injustice that has already been done to the defendant in being subjected to an inherently oppressive order of the court made after a hearing at which he was not able to be heard and sought to be enforced before he has had an opportunity to have it set aside or varied.

The judge concluded that when a committal application is made something more than a mere technical breach of the obligation to allow entry forthwith was required (see also *Adam Phones Ltd v Goldschmidt* [1999] 4 All E.R. 486, concerning a "doorstop Piller" order—namely an order that, upon service, the defendant must hand over certain materials where it was held that a minor or trivial breach of a complex search order will not justify an application for committal for contempt where such action would amount to a disproportionate response).

Finally, it should be noted that s.7(7) CPA preserves the privilege against self-incrimination, previously established in common law (and subsequently recognised by s.14(1) of the Civil Evidence Act 1968) in relation to most cases. A person against whom a search order is made may invoke this privilege in relation to the part of an order that requires him to give discovery of documents, to answer questions, or to swear a confirmatory affidavit, if doing so would expose that defendant to the risk of prosecution for related criminal offences (see *Rank Film Distributors Ltd v Video Information Centre* [1982] A.C. 380). Note however that the privilege will not attach to certain criminal offences such as theft offences under s.31 of the Theft Act 1968, fraud offences under the Fraud Act 2006 and certain infringements of intellectual property rights (see s.72 Supreme Court Act 1981).

The issue of whether a person loses the right to assert privilege by delivering up documents or property in compliance with a search order, has been the subject of much debate and has been considered most recently in the case of *C v P* [2006] EWHC 1226 (Ch). Prior to *C v P* the position supported by the decision of the House of Lords in *Rank Film* and the Court of Appeal in *Den Norske Bank ASA v Antonatos* [1999] QB 271 was that privilege may be lost if a person places the material in respect of which it is claimed in the hands of the supervising solicitor or court appointed expert. In *C v P* the Respondent claimed privilege (prior to the search being carried out) in relation to any material which the search disclosed. Subsequently the court appointed computer expert found unlawful pornographic images on the hard drive of the Respondent's computer. Departing from *Rank Film* and *Den Norske* and distinguishing the judgment of *O Ltd v Z* [2005] EWHC 238 (Ch) in which the facts closely mirrored those of *C v P*, the judge held that the Respondent did not lose the entitlement to assert privilege simply by handing a disk to the supervising solicitor or computer expert in order to comply with the search order. However the judge held that once provided, the Respondent was not able to assert privilege in relation to items already on the disk as this constituted pre-existing or freestanding evidence which had not been created by the Respondent to the search order under compulsion. The judge went on to hold further that the right of the public to protection from the effect of criminal activity under the European Convention for the Protection of Human Rights and Fundamental Freedoms 1950, outweighed the Respondent's right to claim privilege which would otherwise operate to prevent the court from directing that the offending material be passed to the police. Whether *C v P* represents a permanent alteration to the law relating to the privilege against self-incrimination remains to be seen as an appeal is due to be heard later in 2007.

24.7 Ancillary orders

In some instances (for example, where the defendant's reputation or conduct is such that there is no reason to believe that property in its possession is likely to be hidden or destroyed), it will be inappropriate to seek as intrusive and powerful an instrument as a search order. There are, however, a number of other, similar, orders—usually, but not necessarily, made on notice (see r.25.3 CPR and *EMI v Pandit* [1975] 1 W.L.R. 302, in which Templeman J. held that the equivalent orders formerly set out in RSC Ord 29, r.2 could perhaps be sought on an ex parte basis)—that a claimant can apply for; these are now listed in r.25(1) CPR (as supplemented by the relevant Practice Direction), and include:

- an order for the detention, custody or preservation of relevant property;
- an order for the inspection of property;
- an order for the taking of a sample of relevant property;
- an order authorising a person to enter any land or building in the possession of a party to the proceedings for the purpose of carrying out any of the aforementioned orders;
- an order under s.4 of the Torts (Interference with Goods) Act 1977 to deliver up goods (that are the subject matter of proceedings for wrongful interference with goods, defined in the 1977 Act as including "conversion", which is significant since many business secret cases will be based on a claim for breach of confidence which will often involve an allegation of conversion).

It is also possible to apply for orders for:

(a) the inspection of property before the commencement of proceedings or against a non-party (r.25.5 CPR);

(b) the disclosure of documents before proceedings start (r.31.16 CPR); and

(c) the disclosure of documents against a person who is not a party to the proceedings (r.31.17 CPR).

Finally, it is worth noting again that r.25.1(3) CPR provides that the fact that a particular remedy is not listed in that list does not affect any power that the court may have to grant that remedy.

24.8 Dawn raids and other powers of the competition authorities

The Competition Act 1998 provides the Office of Fair Trading ("OFT") with extensive powers to investigate suspected anti-competitive behaviour which includes illegal restraint of trade agreements. Part I of the Competition Act 1998 provides the OFT with powers to investigate, on its own behalf (whether or not as a result of a complaint) suspected infringements of both Articles 81 and 82 of the EC Treaty and the Chaper I and II prohibitions. These powers enable the OFT to:

- require the production of specified documents or specified information (section 26);
- enter business premises without a warrant (section 27); and
- enter and search business and/or domestic premises with a warrant (section 28 and 28A).

For a more detailed explanation of the OFT's powers see *Guidelines on Powers of Investigation*, OFT 404 of 2004.

Part 2 of the Competition Act 1998 makes provision for the OFT to assist, or act on behalf of the EC Commission in connection with its investigations relating to Articles 81 and 82, in which case its powers will be slightly different.

Section 25 of the Competition Act 1998 provides that the OFT, when acting on its own behalf (as opposed to on behalf of the EC Commission or another National Competition Authority), may carry out an investigation if there are "reasonable grounds for suspecting":

- that an agreement falls within Article 81 and/or Chapter I prohibition; and/or
- that there has been an infringement of Article 82 and/or the Chapter II prohibition.

The OFT does not have to determine whether the agreement/conduct would benefit from an Article 81(3) exemption or Section 9(1) of the Competition Act 1998. A detailed explanation of the powers of the OFT is outside the remit of this book, however suffice it to say that for a party considering arguing that a restrictive covenant amounts to a breach of competition law, and particularly where it has little documentary evidence to rely on before a court, he should consider the possibility of a complaint to the OFT, and seeking to get the OFT to use its powers of investigation. The difficulty will be in persuading the OFT to take up the matter, and as such a party will need to put together any information and arguments that would help persuade the OFT there are reasonable grounds for suspecting a breach of competition law.

Given the ease, and low cost for a complainant, with which a complaint can be lodged with the OFT, the OFT are now seeking to prioritise their cases and have indicated that if it is purely a commercial dispute, where the parties have the resources to pursue such action in the courts, the OFT is going to encourage private enforcement (see OFT Press Release of 12 octobe 2006 on its *Prioritisation Criteria for Competition Caseload*). Nevertheless, depending on the type of restraint and the parties involved this will still remain an option. *Adidas-Salomon AG v Roger Draper and Derek Paul Draper & Ors,* [2006]

EWHC 318 is a good example of the type of case the OFT would be unlikely to take up and where the parties were better off seeking relief directly in the courts.

The EC Commission equally will not seek to investigate every alleged breach of EC competition law, but will consider whether the case has sufficient "Community interest" because of novel issues involved or the EC-wide aspect of the conduct/agreement (see, for example, Case T-411/05 - *Gerolf Annemans v Commission*, OJ 2006 C 36/32 - pending - where an individual is claiming that the EC Commission had erred in not conducting an investigation into alleged infringements of Articles 81 and 82 by Belgacom and Telenet).

Chapter 25

Practice and Procedure

25.1 The appropriate court

An application for an interim injunction may be made in either the County Court or the High Court following the procedures laid down in Parts 23 and 25 of the CPR (and see Chapter 23).

Section 38 of the County Courts Act 1984 provides that County Courts may grant injunctions. Aside from freezing injunctions and search orders (grant of which is restricted by the County Court Remedies Regulations 1991), injunctions may be granted in the County Court by any circuit judge or recorder. A district judge has more limited jurisdiction to grant injunctions: they normally would only be able to do so in the course of small or fast track cases (generally a claim which is valued at less than £15,000).

The High Court will generally be the most appropriate jurisdiction in which to seek an interim injunction and the remainder of this chapter focuses on the appropriate procedure in that forum.

Assuming that the case is to be started in the High Court the only question is which division is appropriate. There are some cases over which the Chancery Division has exclusive jurisdiction: see Sch.1 to the Supreme Court Act 1981. These include "copyright" cases. Many cases involving business secrets also involve questions of copyright; however it is not unusual (though not common) for copyright actions to be begun in the Queen's Bench Division. In most restraint of trade and business secrets cases the choice between the Chancery Division and the Queen's Bench Division will also be determined by the time which the court has available.

In the general Queen's Bench list, applications estimated to last more than one hour require a special appointment and are placed in the Interim Hearings List (thereby leading to a delay in the hearing of the application); in the Chancery Division the applications judge will hear cases of up to two hours in length.

Ordinarily, all hearings are now held in public (CPR r.39.2(1)), so the distinction which previously led parties to favour the Queen's Bench Division (private hearings) over Chancery (applications made in open Court) that existed before the advent of the CPR has now gone. CPR r.39.2(3) provides that a hearing (or any part of it) may be held in private in a number of circumstances, including where "publicity would defeat the object of the hearing" or where the claim "involves confidential information (including information relating to the personal financial matters) and publicity would damage that confidentiality".

There is some overlap here with Art.6(1) of the Human Rights Act 1998 which states that "everyone is entitled to a fair and public hearing within a reasonable time by an independent and impartial tribunal . . .". However, the European Court of Human Rights has generally taken the view that interim hearings are not determinative of civil rights within the meaning of the European Convention on Human Rights and therefore are not generally required to be public.

Practice Direction 39.1.4 provides the decision as to whether the hearing is to be held in public must be made by the judge conducting the hearing, having regard to any representations which may have been made to him. A request to hold the hearing in public should therefore be made in the Application Notice and any supporting evidence provided (see para.25.3 below). It is worth noting that a claim for interim relief under CPR r.25 is not listed in Practice Direction 39.1.5 as one of those claims which should automatically be listed for a hearing in private.

25.2 Notice of the application

25.2.1 Is a "without notice" application necessary?

In some cases the answer to this question is very clearly in the affirmative. Applications for search orders and freezing injunctions must be made without notice if they are to have any practical value. In others, the answer is reached by considering whether there is such urgency or secrecy about the case that delay or disclosure would materially prejudice the claimant's position. The power to grant relief without notice being given to the other party is found in CPR r.25.3.

Part 23 of the CPR, which sets out general rules relating to applications, provides that in normal circumstances a copy of any Application Notice must be served on each Respondent (CPR r.23.4(1)). An application may be made without serving notice if a Rule, Practice Direction or Court Order provides otherwise. Further guidance is found in Practice Direction 23.3 (see Appendix 4) which provides that an application may be made without serving an Application Notice in the following circumstances:

(1) where there is exceptional urgency,

(2) where the overriding objective is best furthered by doing so,

(3) by consent of all parties,

(4) with permission of the Court,

(5) where a date for the hearing has been fixed and a party does not have sufficient time to serve an Application Notice, or

(6) where a Court Order, Rule or Practice Direction permits.

CPR 25.3(1) provides that the Court may grant an interim remedy on an application made without notice if it appears to the Court that there are "good reasons" for not giving notice. In such a case the application "must state the reasons why notice has not been given" (r.25.3(3)).

It will generally be inappropriate to make an application without notice where the respondent is represented by solicitors and/or there has been pre-application correspondence between the parties or where there has been an unexplained delay on the part of the party bringing the application; "[without notice] injunctions are for cases of real urgency, where there has been a true impossibility of giving notice . . ." Megarry J. in *Bates v Lord Hailsham of St Marylebone* [1972] 1 W.L.R. 1373, 1380].

There are two important factors to consider before deciding to make an application without notice. First, the applicant must disclose fully to the court all matters relevant to the application including anything (whether of fact or of law) which may adversely effect the case. According to Lord Justice Mummery in *Memory Corporation plc v Sidhu (No.2)* [2000] 1 W.L.R. 1443, CA (in which the Court of Appeal considered the discharge of a freezing injunction on the grounds of material non-disclosure by the Applicant) this obligation is a "high duty to make full, fair and accurate disclosure of all material information to the Court" and to draw the Court's attention to "unusual features of the evidence adduced, to the applicable Law and the formalities of the procedure to be observed". Where an interim injunction is sought on this basis without complete information being available, there must be a real urgency for the injunction (see *Mayne Pharma (USA) Inc v Teva UK Ltd* [2004] EWHC 2934).

Practice Direction 25.3.3 further provides that in all applications (not just those without notice) the "evidence must set out the facts on which the Applicant relies for the claim being made against the Respondent, including all material facts of which the Court should be made aware". As well as identifying the crucial points for and against the application, the applicant must investigate the nature of the claim and the facts relied on and must identify any likely defences. The advocate at the hearing has additional responsibilities to draw the court's attention to any unusual features of the evidence and to the applicable law (both for and against the application).

If the duty for full and frank disclosure is not observed, the court may discharge the injunction and penalise the applicant as to costs (see for example *Alma Communications and another v Feedback Communications Ltd* [2004]

EWHC 1305). In deciding upon the consequences of any failure to disclose, the court will consider the consequences of any breach, the excuse or explanation offered, and the severity and duration of the prejudice, bearing in mind the overriding objective and the need for proportionality. Assuming that the normal cross-undertakings have been given (see below), the applicant may also be responsible for any damages suffered by the respondent as a result granting the interim injunction. Discharge is not however, automatic. In *Lombard North Central plc v Bradley* [2002] ALL E.R. (D) 230, although the court found that the claimant had fallen short in terms of disclosure the discharge of the injunction would have been disproportionate to the non-disclosure and the freezing order was confirmed.

The second consideration is that under CPR r.23.9(2), whether or not the application is successful, "unless the Court orders otherwise" the Application Notice together with any evidence in support be served upon the respondent. It is thought that the court might be prepared to order otherwise in circumstances where complying with this rule would require the applicant to disclose confidential information (in which case the court might still require the Application Notice itself to be disclosed but not the evidence in support).

This requirement, coupled with the obligation of full and frank disclosure (which includes the obligation to notify the Court—and therefore the other side—of possible defences to the claim) means that the applicant should think carefully before making an application without notice.

Applications for freezing injunctions or search orders will almost always be made without notice, as giving notice would invariably defeat the purpose of obtaining the injunction (see chapter 24 for a further discussion of this topic).

If the interim injunction is granted without notice, an order for an injunction will specify a "return date" for a further hearing at which the respondent would be present for the court to consider whether the interim relief should be continued until trial or further order (Practice Direction 25.5.1).

Claimants in cases concerning employees should beware that in recent years the courts have become less comfortable with granting injunctions without notice than was previously the case. This is particularly demonstrated in *TRP Ltd v Thorley* July 13, 1993 (unreported), CA, in which the court was highly critical, in a restrictive covenant case, of the decision by the claimant to apply for relief without giving notice to the respondent where there was no extreme urgency nor in which the purpose of the injunction would be frustrated by giving notice of the application and even though the defendant had solicitors on the record.

25.2.2 Applications with notice

Applications with notice must be served, together with any written evidence in support (including any witness statements and draft order which the applicant has attached to his application) on the respondent at least three days before the court is to deal with the application (CPR r.23.7), unless the Court grants the applicant permission to give short notice.

"Days" means "clear days" meaning that the day of the hearing and the day on which the application is served do not count towards the three-day period, so if given a hearing date on a Friday the application would need to be served on a Monday. If given a hearing date on a Wednesday, the application would need to be served on the previous Thursday (Saturdays and Sundays are excluded) (CPR r.2.8).

If the defendant does not attend and subsequently argues that he did not receive a copy of the Application Notice, he may apply to set it aside under CPR r.23.10. It is therefore sensible for the applicant to prepare a certificate of service under CPR r.6.10 prior to the hearing.

In practice, if the court has insufficient time to hear the matter when first listed the matter will be adjourned to a special appointment (QBD) or go over as a motion by order (Ch D) on undertakings or, where none can be agreed (and if appropriate) on terms set out in an interim order made by the court.

25.2.3 Informal notice

Practice Direction 25.4.3(3) provides that "except in cases where secrecy is essential, the Applicant should take steps to notify the Respondent informally of the application". Informal notice (previously "ex parte on notice") allows the respondent or his representatives to attend the hearing, but with insufficient time to consider the evidence in order to prepare a defence. Such applications are still considered to be heard "without notice", meaning that the duty of full and frank disclosure applies and the Court will still order a return date.

The consequence of the respondent attending can be that it is much harder for him to complain subsequently that full and frank disclosure was not given at an interim stage, and that the injunction should subsequently be set aside on the basis of non-disclosure by the applicant. This procedure is especially relevant if the defendant is a reputable individual or company.

25.3 Documentation required for interim injunctions

In order to obtain an interim injunction the applicant must have:

(a) an Application Notice (in form N244);

(b) a claim form or draft claim form;

(c) supporting evidence (normally witness statements);

(d) draft minutes of order.

25.3.1 The Application Notice

An Application Notice in form N244 setting out (i) what order the applicant is seeking; and (ii) why the applicant is seeking the order should be filed with the court unless the court dispenses with the requirement for an Application Notice under CPR r.23.3(2) (which it may do in cases of real urgency). If the applicant wishes to rely on matters set out in his Application Notice as evidence, CPR r.22 requires the Application Notice to be verified by a statement of truth.

If the Court dispenses with the need to file an Application Notice, the order for an injunction should contain an undertaking "to file and pay the appropriate fee on the same or next working day" (Practice Direction 25.5.1).

25.3.2 The claim form

Where time permits, the claimant should issue the claim form before the hearing. However, in cases of urgency this is not always possible, and CPR r.25.2(1)(a) provides that an application for interim relief may be made before the issue of the claim form. If an order for an injunction is made before the issue of the claim form the order itself will contain either an undertaking to issue and pay the appropriate fee on the same or next working day, or directions for the commencement of the claim (Practice Direction 25.5.1).

As interim applications are often obtained in situations of urgency (and often without full instructions having been taken from the client) it is common practice to issue the claim form and to withhold the particulars of claim (which the applicant must serve 14 days after service of the claim form (CPR r.7.4(2)). In *Hytrac Conveyors Ltd v Conveyors Intl Ltd* [1983] 1 W.L.R. 44 a failure on behalf of the claimant to heed the normal rules of service resulted in the claim being struck out, despite the fact that the search order had already been executed. CPR r.22 requires particulars of claim to be verified by a statement of truth, so by this stage at least the claimant's solicitors need to be in receipt of clear instructions regarding the nature of the claim.

25.3.3 Evidence

Applications for search orders and freezing injunctions must be supported by affidavit evidence (Practice Direction 25.3.1). Applications for other interim injunctions must be supported by evidence set out in either a witness statement, a Statement of Case (i.e. Claim Form or Particulars of Claim), or the Application Notice itself. If relying upon evidence contained in the Statements of Case or the Application Notice, they should be verified by a statement of truth.

Given the importance of setting out "all material factors of which the Court should be made aware", it will normally be appropriate for the evidence in support of the application to be contained in a witness statement (or affidavit).

The actual contents of the witness statement are very important because not only do they set out the facts upon which the judge will be asked to give the injunction or other interlocutory relief, they are potentially dangerous if the case goes to trial, as a witness can be cross-examined on any discrepancies between his evidence at the interlocutory stage and any information provided in his oral evidence at trial.

Since the Civil Evidence Act 1995, hearsay evidence has been generally admissible in civil proceedings, meaning that witness statements may contain statements of information or belief. A witness statement (or an affidavit) should be in the witness's own words, and should normally be taken by solicitors where they are instructed. Where this is not practicable, solicitors are under a duty to ensure that statements are taken by persons who can be relied upon to exercise the same standards as would apply if they had taken them (*Aquarius Financial Enterprises Inc v Certain Underwriters at Lloyds*, 151 UL.J.694 2001).

Where evidence is required urgently, it may be necessary for practical reasons for a party's representative to provide a witness statement/affidavit and there is generally no objection to this where the representative is attaching exhibits and commenting upon them, or where the facts are not disputed. However, it is thought that in relation to applications for a freezing injunction or search order, where the facts are contentious, or where the evidence is within the personal knowledge of the applicant himself then a statement/affidavit should be made by the party himself and not the by the representative (*Breacon Partners Ltd v Gutteridge*, December 17, 2001, unreported). The requirement to verify evidence with a statement of truth may further dissuade applicant's representatives from giving evidence on their client's behalf.

An essential tactical consideration for the applicant is that he will be required to give an undertaking to the Court "to pay any damages which the Respondents (or any other party served with or notified of the order) sustain which the Court considers the Applicant should pay" as a result of granting the interim injunction. For this reason the affidavit or statement in support of an injunction should deal with the Applicant's ability to pay damages to the respondent under the cross undertaking. Where there are doubts about the resources of the applicant, the court has discretion to order security for costs or to require an undertaking to be given from another body (such as a parent company). This may happen if the claimant is outside the jurisdiction or if there are serious doubts as to his solvency. See *Harman Pictures NV v Osborne* [1967] 1 W.L.R. 723 and *Ingham v ABC Contract Services Ltd* November 12, 1993 (unreported), CA.

Further guidance about the content and form of witness statements can be found at Practice Direction 32.17 (Affidavits are dealt with in Practice Direction 32.2).

A major problem for a claimant in a business secrets case which involves a secret process or something similar is just how far he should go in his evidence in revealing the substance of the information which is only partly known by the defendant. In *Under Water Welders and Repairers Ltd v Street and Longthorne* [1968] R.P.C. 498 the claimant sought interim injunctions against the defendants restraining them from using confidential information. The defendants claimed in their evidence that there was nothing confidential in the process, whereas the claimants, although denying this, did not specify its confidential characteristics. Buckley J. held, inter alia that although the claimant's evidence did not consent to any details as to the secrecy of the process, it was clear that they regarded it as such, whereas the defendant's evidence did not sufficiently negative the possibility of confidentiality in order to refute the claimant's prima facie claim for relief. He said that it is not to be expected that a claimant seeking to protect a secret would disclose it to the court particularly in interlocutory proceedings. This case may seem more liberal than in fact it was. There appears to have been other evidence before the court form which it could reasonably infer the process was secret. (See also *Amber Size and Chemical Co Ltd v Menzel* [1913] 2 Ch. 239.) However the claimant was not so fortunate in the case of *John Zink Co Ltd v Lloyds Bank Ltd* [1975] R.P.C. 385 where a statement of claim was struck out under the provisions of what was RSC Ord 18, r.19 (Summary Judgement) for not condescending to particulars. The court was convinced that the claimant's refusal to provide particulars was an indication that no confidentiality attached to the relevant information. See also *Diamond Stylus Co Ltd v Bauden Precision Diamonds Ltd* [1973] R.P.C. 675. No details of a process were given by the claimant in his application for an interim injunction. Graham J. refused the application and said:

> . . . each case must be judged in the light of its own particular facts and the governing principle in every case is that a Claimant must make out a prime facie case . . . It may be in some cases that a Claimant is able to do that without disclosing much in the way of detail about his particular process . . . On the other hand . . . depending on the surrounding circumstances and the state of knowledge generally in the art, he may have to go further and disclose at any rate the essential features of the process which he says have been taken.

It is submitted that this approach, which pre-dates *American Cyanamid Co v Ethicon Ltd* [1975] A.C. 396 is just as valid now even if *American Cyanamid* does apply to business secrets cases. After all the claimant has to show an arguable case and the balancing of convenience is very difficult if the details of a business secret are not revealed. Once the allegedly secret information is revealed to the other side there are ample powers to prevent its use or disclosure other than for the purposes of litigation. First, there is a the general implied duty not to use documents produced on discovery for a collateral or ulterior purpose (*Riddick v Thames Board Mills* [1977] 3 All E.R. 677). Secondly, the defendant may be required by the court to give an undertaking that only a certain number of people (usually himself, his lawyer and experts) be allowed access to the information disclosed by the claimant (*Warner-Lambert Co v Glaxo Laboratories* [1975] R.P.C. 354: see also *Sport Universal SA v Prozone Holdings Limited* [2003] All E.R. (D) 38.

The evidence in a business secrets case is of crucial importance for it must distinguish what are truly the business secrets of the claimant. In *Lock International plc v Beswick* [1989] 1 W.L.R. 1268 Hoffman J. commented:

> In cases which the Claimant alleges misuse of trade secrets or confidential information concerning a manufacturing process, a lack of particularity about the precise nature of the trade secrets is usually a symptom of an attempt to prevent the employee from making legitimate use of the knowledge and skills gained in the Claimant's service.

In *Lawrence David Ltd v Ashton* [1989] I.R.L.R. 22 Whitford J. at first instance is reported to have refused an injunction in respect of a breach of confidence claim because the affidavits failed to identify "with any real particularly any particular secret". This part of his judgement was upheld in the Court of Appeal [1991] 1 All E.R. 385. Balcombe L.J. said that it is a cardinal rule that any injunction must be cable of being framed with sufficient precision so as to enable a person injuncted to know what it is he is prevented from doing. The inability of the claimants to define with any degree of precision what they sought to call confidential information or trade secrets militated against an injunction of this nature being granted.

It is reasonably well established that the Court may admit evidence obtained by questionable (i.e. unlawful) means, although "the Court always has to decide what weight to give it" (*Memory Corp plc v Sidhu (No.1)* [2000] 1 W.L.R. 1443, CA), although any doubts about the methods used in obtaining the evidence ought to be put before the Court.

25.3.4 Draft minutes of order

Draft orders should follow the form described in Practice Direction Interlocutory Injunctions: Forms [1996] 1 W.L.R. 1551 which has not been updated since the advent of the CPR and should be modified accordingly. In cases where a freezing injunction or search order is sought, standard forms are annexed to Practice Direction 25. It is a well established principle that an order for an injunction should set out clearly what it is the defendant is prevented from doing, particularly since an injunction carries with it the possible sanction of imprisonment for breach (*Lawrence David Ltd v Ashton* [1991] 1 All E.R. 385). This is reinforced by Practice Direction 25.5.3 which states "any order for an injunction must set out clearly what the Respondent must do or not do".

As well as having enough hard copies of the draft order for the court and each respondent, the applicant should make available at the hearing on disk compatible with the Court Software (WordPerfect).

An order for an interim injunction must contain (unless the court orders otherwise) an undertaking by the applicant to the court to pay any damages which the respondent sustains which the court considers the applicant should pay (Practice Direction 25.5.1(1)).

25.4 General points

(1) Injunctions are not available as of right; whether they are granted is a matter of discretion.

(2) Parties: usually the claimant applies for an interim injunction; the defendant is not able to do so unless he has filed either an acknowledgement of service or a defence, or alternatively has the leave of the court (CPR r.25.2(2)K).

Frequently the claimant will claim not only against his former employee, but also against the new employer or another third party if there is any evidence that the latter knowingly induced the first defendant to breach his contract. In some cases, of which *Hivac* is an example, the claimant chose to sue the new employer.

25.5 Order for a speedy trial

It is not uncommon for an application to be made during interim proceedings for an order for a speedy trial in restraint of trade and business secret cases. A specific power to order a speedy trial was previously found in RSC Order 29, r.5, but it now falls within the general case management powers of the court. Rule 29.2(2) requires the court in multitrack cases to fix a trial date or period "as soon as practicable". This is consistent with the fourth principle of the overriding objective which is ensuring that the cases are dealt with "expeditiously and fairly".

An early trial was ordered in *Littlewoods Organisation Ltd v Harris* [1978] 1 All E.R. 1026 because of the urgency involved and in *Commercial Plastics Ltd v Vincent* [1965] 1 Q.B. 623 an order was made for a speedy trail and that the affidavits sworn for the purposes of the interlocutory hearing should stand as the pleadings. Discovery, in so far as it has not already sufficiently occurred, can often be limited in width and take place quickly. A claimant who secured an interim injunction "pending a speedy trial" had an obligation to work diligently towards achieving the speedy trial (*EDO Technology Ltd v Campaign to Smash EDO* [2006] EWHC 598).

Chapter 26

Damages

26.1 Introduction

The most common remedies sought at the conclusion of a trial by a successful claimant in restraint of trade and business secrets cases are an award of damages and a permanent injunction. In some cases a declaration is vital. An account of profits and an order for delivery up or destruction are also important remedies.

An award of damages is intended to compensate the claimant for loss and to attempt to put him in the position in which he would have been had the contract or duty not been breached. This approach is to be compared with that underlying an account of profits where it is the defendant's gain rather than the claimant's loss which is relevant. (See further section 27.2)

In both restraint of trade and business secrets cases damages can only provide a very approximate remedy as it is usually impossible to determine precisely what the claimant has lost and therefore what his compensation should be. However, the court will not be deterred by this obstacle and will do its best to achieve justice between the parties (*Sanders v Parry* [1967] 1 W.L.R. 753).

In certain exceptional circumstances it may be possible for a covenantee to claim for damages against a covenantor who acted in breach of a restrictive covenant, not on the basis of any financial loss by the former, but rather for the court to award an amount assessed as the sum which the court considers it would have been reasonable for the covenantor to pay and the covenantee to accept for the hypothetical release of the covenant immediately before the breach (consider the decisions in *Wrotham Park Estate Co Ltd v Parkside Homes Ltd* [1974] 2 All E.R. 321; *A-G v Blake* [2001] 1 A.C. 268, [2000] 4 All E.R. 385 and *Experience Hendrix LLC v PPX Enterprises* [2003] 1 All E.R. (Comm) 830.

Damages are equally available for breach of competition law, be it Article 81/82 EC or Chapter I/II UK, although to date few cases have gone to full trial. The key hurdle is whether one can establish the breach of competition law, given the economic analysis as to the effect of the relevant restrictions that needs to be carried out, unless the damage action is a "follow on" action off the back of an infringement decision by a competition regulator (e.g. the Office of Fair Trading or the EC Commission) under section 47A of the Competition Act 1998, which can be brought before the Competition Appeal Tribunal.

26.2 Damages for breach of a covenant in reasonable restraint of trade

If one takes the example of a former employee who has solicited a customer of his previous employer the court will assess the claimant's damages in the usual way for breach of contract. The claimant must show that the breach caused loss to him and that the particular type of loss was within the contemplation of the parties at the time of entry into the contract. Foreseeability is rarely a problem and even causation may be simple to prove. It is not open to the defendant to claim that the acts of a third party, such as a new employer who procures his breach of contract, have broken the chain of causation. The claimant is, however, in these circumstances, wise to sue both his former employee and the new employer for it may only be the latter who can afford to pay any damages or even costs. The most common causation problem from the claimant's point of view is that clients who were actually solicited may well emerge at the trial as witnesses for the defence to say that they were open to solicitation by the defendant and that they were going to take their business away from the claimant in any event. In this case the claimant will have suffered nominal damage only and although he would usually be awarded costs the basis for such an award will frequently leave him paying a considerable amount of his own costs himself. Moreover, if the defendant unsuccessfully attempted to solicit a client of the claimant although he will be in breach of contract the claimant will have suffered no loss and therefore once again will only be awarded nominal damages.

Therefore it is only in those cases where the defendant has successfully solicited the claimant's customers who, but for the approach by the defendant, were not intending to take their business elsewhere, that the claimant will be awarded more than nominal damages. The claimant will still have to persuade the court of the extent of his loss: typically he can provide evidence which shows the net worth of that client's custom. See, for example, *Sanders v Parry* [1967] 1 W.L.R. 753. There, the defendant who was found to be in breach of the implied duty of fidelity to his employer, a solicitor, was ordered to pay damages to the claimant when he entered an agreement with an important client, T, of the claimant. Havers J. awarded damages on the basis of a lost chance to do work for T and he accepted evidence of the net worth of that business over a period of 12 months. The reason he chose such a short time was because T had intended to change his solicitor anyway. See also *Robb v Green* [1895] 2 QB 1, *per* Hawkins J. These cases demonstrate how inadequate damages are as a remedy in most restraint of trade cases.

The relevant date for assessment of damages is usually the time of breach. However, this is not an invariable rule: if to choose that date would give rise to injustice then another time may be chosen (*Johnson v Agnew* [1979] 1 All E.R. 883; see also *Lunn Poly Ltd v Liverpool and Lancashire Properties Ltd* [2006] EWCA Civ 430). In the case of *Dunedin Independent Plc v Welsh* (2006) CSOH 174, the Scottish Courts provided some guidance on the approach to be adopted when assessing damages. In that case the claimant had claimed damages for the future commission it would have received but for the defendant's breach of covenant. It calculated this loss by applying Ogden Table 28. The Court considered that the use of the Ogden Tables was inappropriate as it did not take into account other potential factors such as the clients' needs to obtain pension money, problems of life such as divorce which effect investment plans and most importantly the effect of commercial competition.

26.3 Damages for breach of the duty of confidence

In many cases the cause of action lies in contract. In some cases, however, there may be no contractual relationship between the parties (see e.g. *Saltman Engineering Co Ltd v Campbell Engineering Co Ltd* (1948) 65 R.P.C. 203) or the court may choose to ignore the existence of the contract in which case the cause of action lies in the equitable doctrine of confidence. This is also especially useful when proceedings are against third parties who have induced the primary defendant to breach his contract. However, in the case of the equitable jurisdiction but for specific statutory provisions, it could be argued that the common law remedy of damages is usually inappropriate. However, s.50 of the Supreme Court Act 1981 provides:

> Where the Court of Appeal or the High Court has jurisdictions to entertain an application for an injunction or specific performance, it may award damages in addition to, or in substitution for, an injunction or specific performance.

This section substantially re-enacts s.2 of the Chancery Amendment Act 1858 (Lord Cairns' Act). The jurisdiction contemplated in s.50 exists in all business secrets cases as there will always be the ability "to entertain" such an application. It is submitted that these words mean that if injunctive relief is an option open to the plaintiff then the alternative remedy in damages may be available as well. Although *Saltman's* case and *Seager v Copydex (No. 2)* [1969] 2 All E.R. 718 were decided prior to the enactment of s.50, they appear to support such a view.

Further, it should be noted that s.50 allows an award of damages in addition to an injunction not simply in substitution. In *Cranleigh Precision Engineering Ltd v Bryant* [1966] R.P.C. 81 the court awarded both an injunction and damages.

In theory, there is an advantage to the claimant in an award of damages for breach of an equitable rather than a contractual duty. This arises from the fact that the contractual damages can only encompass past loss whereas equitable damages can take into account both past and future loss. In practice, however, the difficulty of successfully enquiring into future loss is very great and will rarely be fruitful. Damages by way of compensation for injury to feelings can be awarded (*Archer v Williams* [2003] EWHC 1670 (QBD)).

Finally, the possibility of a claim for exemplary damages should not be forgotten in business secrets cases, and restitutionary damages may be available in exceptional cases (see *AG v Blake* [2001] 1 A.C. 268, HL). See also *Douglas v Hello! Ltd* (No.3) at first instance, [2003] EWHC (Ch) 786; [2003] 3 All E.R. 996, paragraph 273 per Lindsay J.

26.3.1 Quantum in business secrets cases

Typically in business secrets cases the secrets possess commercial value. The primary defendant may either have used the secret or allowed another to use it or he may have disclosed it to another or simply disclosed it by his use. Pure disclosure without use makes damages very difficult to quantify. If the defendant has disclosed secrets to another, the claimant should however recover more than nominal damages and even if an injunction is granted against any further use it may be difficult for, say, a trade competitor, to expunge from his memory a particular formula or client list which has been passed on to him. There may arise "subconscious use" similar to the notion of "subconscious copying" recognised in the law of copyright. See *Seager v Copydex* [1967] R.P.C. 349. The claimant should be compensated for the real possibility of use by others as a result of unlawful disclosure to them. The claimant is only properly compensated however if he is awarded equitable rather than contractual damages as only then will the award take into account any future loss.

Where use is overt, then substantial damages will be awarded in line with the claimant's loss. Unlike restraint of trade cases, the court of Appeal has laid down special rules for assessing quantum for use of business secrets. In *Seager v Copydex (No. 2)* [1969] R.P.C. 250, Lord Denning M.R. said that damages in a business secrets case were to be assessed on the basis of the value of the information which the defendant company took but then said that the value of the information depended on its nature. The nature or quality of information fell into three categories each with its own quantum, viz:

(1) If there was nothing very special about the information, i.e. if it involved no particular inventive step but was the sort of information which could be obtained by employing a competent consultant then the value was to be equivalent to the consultant's fee. The reason for that is that ". . . the

defendant company, by taking the information, would only have saved themselves the time and trouble of employing a consultant".

(2) However, if the information was "something special", i.e. if it involved an inventive step or something so unusual that it could not be obtained by employing a consultant, then it has a higher value than information under (1). Quantum is to be assessed on the basis of the price which a willing buyer would pay for it and which a willing seller in the claimant's position would accept.

(3) If the confidential information is "very special indeed" then it may be proper to calculate damages as a capitalised royalty.

In any event, whichever method is appropriate the court said that once the damages are paid then the property in the business secrets vests in the defendant in the same way in which it does in cases where damages are awarded for conversion.

These categories are novel and there seems little doubt that whichever is applied will be largely determined by the effect of expert evidence. It is submitted that the approach of the court of Appeal in this case was unfortunate. First, why should the compensation under category (1) be calculated in accordance with what the defendant company had saved rather than by what the claimant could reasonably have gained by the sale of the information? The court decided in *Seager v Copydex* that an account of profits would not be awarded—only damages—and yet the basis under (1) seems inconsistent with this. Regarding bases (2) and (3) the problem is that they assume that the claimant would willingly have sold and the defendant bought. However, in this case the negotiations as to sale between the parties had completely broken down. Moreover, why should the information vest in the defendants once the damages are paid? The logical result for such vesting is that he could in some cases obtain a patent, and then sue the claimant for infringement. Indeed *Copydex* had applied for a patent regarding the product to which the confidential information attached. Gurry suggests that the defendant should have obtained no more than a non-exclusive licence to use the information but it is submitted that even this compromise is unreasonably favourable to the defendant. We can see no reason why he should get any rights at all in the information. The analogy with conversion is fallacious because that rule is in itself an exception to the normal principles of compensation and the analogy fails to take account of the radical differences between a chattel and a piece of information. Once the former is transferred there is no residual aspect which can remain with the claimant. That is not so with information, especially business secrets which may have been crucial to a claimant's business. Is he to shut down his business because of the wrongful appropriation by another of his property? In our view this judgment amounts to a rogues' charter. It allows a defendant to buy the freedom to infringe the claimant's rights. Moreover what if *Seager*, having broken off negotiations with *Copydex*, had sold the information to another party and warranted that it was free from any encumbrances? If the judgment in *Seager v Copydex (No. 2)* is applied then the other party would have grounds for a subsequent action against *Seager* for breach of warranty. Such a possibility produces a very unfair result.

In *Dowson and Mason Ltd v Potter* [1986] 1 W.L.R. 1419, *Seager* was distinguished. The claimants developed a new type of landing leg for articulated lorries. In breach of his duty of confidence as a plaintiffs' employee, the first defendant disclosed to the second defendants information consisting of the names and addresses of the suppliers of the leg's component parts and the price which the claimant had paid for them. The second defendants became the claimants' competitors as manufactures of landing legs and called a meeting of the suppliers and discussed the possibility of placing orders with them. The claimants issued a writ claiming against the defendants, inter alia, damages for the disclosure and use of the claimants' confidential information. By a consent order an inquiry was ordered into the damages sustained by the claimants. The defendants issued a summons seeking the court's determination of the proper basis for assessing the damages.

The district registrar held that the proper basis for the assessment was the claimants' loss of profits resulting from the wrongful disclosure and use of the confidential information. The judge affirmed the district registrar's order.

The Court of appeal held that since the purpose of damages was to put the claimants in the position in which they would have been if the defendants had not wrongly obtained and used their confidential information to compete with them as manufacturers of landing legs, the proper basis for the assessment of the claimants' damages was the loss of manufacturing profits. Sir Edward Eveleigh said that the particular position of the claimant in each case had to be considered. He gave examples. When dealing with someone who would have licensed the use of his confidential information, then almost invariably the measure of damages will be the price that he could have commanded for that information, and no question of loss of manufacturing profits will arise, as he was always ready to allow someone else to manufacture at a price. If the claimant was a manufacturer who would have licensed another to use his secret then he would, probably in all cases, be in the same position as the inventor who had sold it, because he would have exposed himself to competition and loss of profits for a price, the price for which he had sold the secret. If, on the other hand, he was a manufacturer who would not have licensed its use, then he would not have been exposed to competition at the time when he was exposed because of the defendant's wrongdoing.

He then went on to say that in *Seager* it was clear that S would have sold the information: he was an inventor who made his living from selling his inventions. He said the court in *Seager* was dealing with particular facts and was not laying down any principles. In this case the claimant was a manufacturer in a competing lien of business. By using the claimant's confidential information the defendant was wrongly depriving the claimant by competition of manufacturing profits.

In *Universal Thermosensors Ltd v Hibben* [1992] 1 W.L.R. 840 the claimants asserted that once it was shown that the defendants had stolen documents containing confidential information and that they had used those documents in soliciting orders, there arose a irrebuttable presumption that any business resulting from the orders derived from the wrongful use of the information and that the defendants were liable for damages accordingly. The court should not inquire at all into whether the defendants knew the name of the particular customer in any way. Sir Donald Nicholls V.C. rejected this approach. He considered the evidence against the need for the claimant to prove (a) that business was acquired as a result of the misuse of confidential information and (b) that, but for the defendants' company acquiring the orders, the claimant would have done so in whole or in part. He found that the claimant failed on almost all its claims and rejected its further claim for residual damages including damage to goodwill.

In *Douglas v Hello*, OK! Magazine claimed for loss of expected revenue and in the alternative for a notional licence fee. The High Court awarded damages on the compensatory basis because the notional licence fee was not as great. The House of Lords did not disturb this award. Paragraphs 6 to 64 of the judgement provide a useful insight into the Court's approach to assessing a notional licence fee. (See *(1) Douglas v (1) Hello!* [2003] EWHC 2629 (Ch)).

26.4 Damages for breach of Articles 81 and 82 / Chapters I and II

So far as English law is concerned Arts 81 and 82 can be used as swords as well as shields so as to permit the recovery of damages and/or an injunction. See *Garden Cottage Foods Ltd v Milk Marketing Board* [1984] A.C. 130; *An Bord Bainne Co-operative Ltd v Milk Marketing Board* [1984] 2 C.M.L.R. 584; *Bourgoin SA v MAFF* [1985] 1 C.M.L.R. 528; *Cutsforth v Mansfield Inns Ltd* [1986] 1 W.L.R. 558. This has been further supported by the Opinion of the Advocate General Van Gerven in *HJ Banks Ltd v British Coal* [1994] E.C.R. I-1209 (the Court itself not having to rule on this point as it found that the case fell under the ECSC Treaty and therefore not Arts 81 or 82 of the EC Treaty). The point was finally firmly established by *Courage v Crehan*. The European Commission itself has no power to award damages.

While it was always understood that damages would be recoverable for breaches of both Arts 81 and 82 in the UK, only a few actions in English courts have gone to a full trial, at which point the question of damages would arise. In cases where a claim for damages is made, once a defendant has received an indication that the claimant is serious about proceeding, and the interlocutory proceedings have indicated that the court regards there to be an issue which is worthy of going to full trial, most cases tend to settle.

A claim for damages under Arts 81 or 82 is made as a claim in tort for breach of statutory duty giving rise to a right to claim damages *(Garden Cottage Foods Ltd v Milk Marketing Board* [1984] A.C. 130). In *Arkin v*

Borchard Lines Ltd [2003] EWHC 687 (Comm) the court proceeded on the basis that it was common ground between the parties that a person who suffers loss by reason of breach of Arts 81 or 82 (both were being argued in this case) has a private action for damages analogous to a claim for beach of statutory duty. In common with other claims, the aim of damages would be to restore the party who suffered from the breach to the position it would have been but for the breach.

To prove a breach of statutory duty the claimant must show that:

(a) The loss suffered is within the scope of the statute. Arts 81 and 82 EC Treaty create rights and obligations which are directly effective in the national courts. The exception has always been Art.81(3) as only the European Commission could grant exemptions—however post May 2004 this provision will also be directly effective. A breach of Arts 81 or 82 is a breach of the statutory duty imposed by the European Communities Act 1972, s.2(1).

(b) The statute gives rise to a civil cause of action. Since the national courts have a duty to protect the directly effective rights of Arts 81 and 82 this condition is satisfied.

(c) There has been a breach of statutory duty. The claimant must show that the relevant agreement or conduct breaches Arts 81 or 82. This will be substantially easier if a claimant can rely on a Commission decision as proof of the breach (see *Iberian UK Ltd v BPB Industries and British Gypsum* [1996] 2 C.M.L.R. 601); and

(d) The breach caused the loss complained of. See *Crehan v Inntrepreneur Pub Company and others* [2003] EWHC 1510 (Ch D).

Whether the English courts would award exemplary damages for breach of Art.81 or 82 will turn on the facts of the case (*Rookes v Bernard* [1964] A.C. 1129). Damages for breach of Art.82 have been accepted for some time now (*Garden Cottage Foods Ltd v Milk Marketing Board* [1984] A.C. 130).

In relation to Art.81, the English courts have accepted that third parties who have suffered as a result of an agreement in breach of Art.81(1) can sue the parties to that agreement for damages (*Plessey v General Electric* [1990] E.C.C. 384, Ch D; *MTV Europe v BMG Records* [1997] Eu. L.R. 100). In other words, parties to the agreement owe a statutory duty to third parties (such as competitors and customers). The English courts rejected the claim that a statutory duty is also owed between co-contractors (Court of Appeal judgments in *Gibbs Mew v Gemmel* [1998] 1 C.M.L.R. 1129 and *Trent Taverns v Sykes* [1998] Eu. L.R. 571), on the basis that English law does not allow a party to an illegal agreement to claim damages from the other party for loss caused to him by being a party to the illegal agreement ("*in pari delicto*" rule), applying *Boissavin v Weil* [1950] A.C. 327 and *Tinsley v Milligan* [1993] All E.R. 65.

However, the Court of Appeal has recognised that the "*in pari delicto*" rule may not be compatible with the Community law principles and in the *Courage v Crehan* case referred this question to the European Court of Justice. The ECJ's ruling in *Courage v Crehan* confirms that there is a Community right to damages to compensate breaches of Arts 81 and 82. In relation to Art.81, the ECJ has confirmed that a party to an agreement which breaches Art.81(1) may rely on a breach of that Article to obtain damages from the other party. It also said that a rule of national law according to which a party to an agreement liable to restrict competition is barred from claiming damages for loss cause by performance of that contract on the sole ground that the claimant is a party to that contract is incompatible with Community law. The ECJ has, however, confirmed that Community law does not preclude a rule of national rule barring a party to an agreement liable to restrict competition from obtaining damages where it is established that that party bears *significant responsibility* for the distortion of competition. In the context of significant responsibility, the ECJ referred to the economic and legal context within which the parties found themselves, their respective bargaining power and the conduct of the parties which needs to be ascertained by national courts.

Of particular relevance would be whether one of the contracting parties found himself in a markedly weaker position (e.g. the publican Crehan against Inntrepreneur), so as to seriously compromise, or even eliminate, his freedom to negotiate the terms of the contract and his capacity to avoid the loss or reduce its extent. In the *Crehan* case the restrictive effect of the beer tie arose from the fact that it was one of many similar agreements having a cumulative effect on competition; in those circumstances Mr Crehan could not be considered to bear significant responsibility for the infringement of the competition rules. The high court to whom the Crehan case reverted held that the agreement did not in fact infringe Art.81 and so the claim for damages was dismissed. (*Crehan v Inntrepeneur Pub* [2003] EWHC 1510 (Ch D)). The case was then appealed to the Court of Appeal which held that the judge in First Instance was wrong to second guess the Commission's analysis and that he should have accepted that the agreement was in breach of Art.81(1), the House of Lords however held that as the Commission's decision in *Whitbread* related to different parties and a different agreement, albeit in the same market, the Court was *not* bound by the findings of fact but should make its own assessment (*Inntrepreneur Pub Company v Crehan* [2006] UK HL38).

As a result, companies contracting with individuals or smaller companies, particularly on their standard terms and conditions may wish to protect themselves and ensure that their counterparties have taken independent legal advice and have agreed to any restrictive clauses to try and level the playing field, at least insofar as the negotiations go, and therefore making them equally responsible for the contracts so that *in pari delicto* may apply.

Chapter 27

Other Remedies

27.1 Permanent injunctions

At the end of a trial a claimant will frequently apply for a permanent injunction. Unlike a claim for an interim injunction the request for a permanent injunction must be pleaded in the statement of claim. Unlike damages, which are available as of right, an injunction is an equitable remedy and is therefore discretionary. The power to grant a permanent injunction is nowadays found in s.37(1) Supreme Court Act 1981. However, despite the width of s.37(1) there are well established rules regarding what is "just and convenient".

27.1.1 Criteria for such an award

27.1.1.1 Damages are not an adequate remedy

The primary consideration in all cases in which an injunction is awarded is whether damages or damages alone provide an adequate remedy. In most restraint of trade and business secrets cases damages will not be an adequate remedy because of the difficulty of quantification. Even if damages are not difficult to assess, if the claimant can show that there exists a real risk of future injury then he will be awarded a permanent injunction. A permanent injunction is unlikely to be sought in a restraint of trade case unless the covenant is not limited by time or if the period in question extends beyond the date of judgment: obviously if the covenant is struck down as being an unreasonable restraint of trade then no question of a permanent injunction arises. It is more common in business secrets cases for a permanent injunction to be awarded to a successful claimant, although in highly technological areas, where knowledge changes quickly, there may be little point in seeking such an award or the award may be limited as to time.

27.1.1.2 Miscellaneous criteria

The court will also consider whether the claimant really deserves an interlocutory injunction. It will examine his conduct and especially whether he has clean hands or has delayed in bringing the action or has in some way acquiesced in what the defendant has done. The court will also examine the quality of the plaintiff's right and whether the breach is merely technical. However this is unlikely to be a consideration in most restraint of trade and business secrets cases. Further, the court will consider the defendant's behaviour. It is generally accepted that a defendant cannot buy the freedom to infringe the plaintiff's rights especially as in most business secrets cases those are rights which the plaintiff has specifically refused to sell. The final criteria which are of especial importance are the public interest and the special rules concerning employees and those in positions of mutual trust and confidence.

27.2 Account of profits

If the claimant has not suffered any or only minor loss or if he thinks that the defendant's gain is much greater than his loss, he may be tempted to sue for an account of profits. Although it is usual in the pleadings to request both damages and an account of profits it is not possible for the claimant to be given both remedies as this would leave him with double compensation. The claimant must therefore elect at the end of the day and he will choose an account of profits if he wishes to have his recompense measured by the defendant's gain rather than, as in the case of damages, his loss. Technically, an account of profits is only available if the court is exercising its equitable jurisdiction. We, therefore, advise that if an account of profits may be requested then the statement of claim, even in the case of an express contractual term, should include an allegation of breach of both contract and the equitable duty of confidence.

In *My Kinda Town Ltd v Soll* [1983] R.P.C. 15 Slade J. made some general observations about an account of profits. He said

> "the object of ordering an account in cases such as the present is to deprive the defendants of the profits which they have improperly made by wrongful acts committed in breach of the plaintiffs' rights and to transfer such profits to the [claimants]".

He went on to say that in ordering an account of profits in a passing off or breach of confidence case the court will ordinarily direct that the account be in a form wide enough to include all profits made by the defendant from his acts in breach of evidence.

A good example of when such a claim is appropriate is found in *Industrial Development Consultants Ltd v Cooley* [1972] 2 All E.R. 162. The defendant was the managing director of the claimants and on their behalf he entered into negotiations with the Eastern Gas Board to manage a large building project. However the Board made it quite clear that they disliked the claimants' organisation and for that reason would not award them the contract. Subsequently, they approached the defendant and told him that if he were independent of the claimants he would be chosen to do the work. The defendant procured a release from his employment contract on false grounds and eventually became the project manager. The claimants sued him for acting in breach of his fiduciary duty as a director. They claimed:

(a) a declaration that he was a trustee of the benefit of the contract for them;

(b) an account of profits; and

(c) alternatively damages.

They elected to pursue an account of profits. The advantage of doing so was that an award of damages would have, said Roskill J., been calculated as 10 per cent of the net value of the project to them as Eastern Gas Board would almost certainly not have awarded them the contract. The 10 per cent reflected the slight chance that they would have been chosen. Instead they received all the profits made by the defendant. However the dilemma of making such an award was recognised by the judge:

> ". . . if the [claimants] succeed they will get a profit which they probably would not have got for themselves had the defendant fulfilled his duty. If the defendant is allowed to keep that profit he will have got something which he was able to get solely by reason of his breach of fiduciary duty to the [claimants] . . .".

The problem was resolved on the basis that it was the defendant who had acted wrongly. An example where damages were chosen rather than an account of profits was *Saltman Engineering Co Ltd v Campbell Engineering Co Ltd* (1948) 65 R.P.C. 203 in which the defendants had made a loss on sales of a product which had been manufactured using the claimant's business secrets. However, an account of profits appears to be rarely used:

(1) because of the difficulty of calculation; and

(2) because of delay.

(1) The difficulty of calculation arises from the fact that the defendant is only liable to disgorge that element of the profit attributable to the wrongful use of the claimant's business secrets unless, of course, he is in a fiduciary position, in which case he may have to disgorge all. There may be other factors which contribute: each has to be given value. There are however cases in which it can be said that apportionment is not an issue: these appear to be where the

business secret is the final factor which creates the profit, i.e. it is the *sine qua non*: see *Peter Pan Manufacturing Corp v Corsets Silhouette Ltd* [1963] R.P.C. 45 in which it was held that the account of profits was literally the difference between the amount expended by the defendants and the amount received. Pennycuick J. rejected the argument that only that part of a profit attributable to the misuse of business secrets was relevant.

(2) Delay, so far as the plaintiff is concerned, arises from the fact that at the end of the trial, having waited a considerable period for judgment, the claimant will want to receive his compensation. Damages fulfil that need subject to the defendant's ability to pay. However, an account of profits can only be provided by the defendant. At the end of the trial, the defendant will be ordered to provide such an account. The defendant has little incentive, apart from the element of interest which may be awarded to the claimant, to get on with doing so. Once he has done so, there is often a dispute regarding the calculations made. There is frequently another trip to court, which is not always short, dealing with the profits disclosed. Judgment is then given and the claimant may find that at the end of the day he would have been much better off had he elected for damages. Once the election has been made however the claimant cannot change his mind.

It is submitted that only in the clearest cases where there is overwhelming evidence that there is a large and significant difference between an award of damages and an account of profits, should the claimant be advised to choose the latter course.

However an account of profits is not an automatic remedy, like damages, but, like an injunction, it is a discretionary one. The court will therefore take into account factors similar to those already outlined when an application for a permanent injunction is made. Although Heydon claims that in practice an account of profits will not be awarded unless the defendant has acted dishonestly, we see no reason to adopt this as a general rule although it is true that in *Seager* there was a specific finding that *Copydex* had not been dishonest and damages only were awarded.

27.3 The position of fiduciaries

Fiduciaries need not be employees but they frequently are. A director or possibly a highly placed employee in respect of certain duties and responsibilities (*Canadian Aero Service Ltd v O'Malley* (1973) 40 D.L.R. (3d) 371 and *Island Export and Finance Ltd v Umunna* [1986] B.C.L.C. 460) will usually be a fiduciary. The consequence of being a fiduciary is that as well as the general duty of fidelity (which will be enforced rigorously) the director must never put himself in a position in which his interest and duty conflict. Even if his employer refuses to take an advantage available to him or is unable to do so, he may have to disgorge his gains (see *Industrial Development Consultants Ltd v Cooley* [1972] 2 All E.R. 162). The basis of the remedy against him is not his employer's loss but his unjust enrichment. See also *Normalec Ltd v Britton* [1983] F.S.R. 318 which concerned an agent properly so called; *cf. Roberts v Elwells Engineers Ltd* [1972] 2 All E.R. 890.

27.4 Delivery up/destruction

Apart from the powers of the court under CPR 25.1(e) there is an equitable jurisdiction to make an order for delivery up/destruction. Such an order will only be made to perfect an injunction which has already been granted. The reasoning behind the equitable jurisdiction appears to be the removal of temptation from the defendant to break the terms of the injunction. It is usually the defendant who can choose between delivery up and destruction and if the latter course is chosen then the destruction must take place on oath. This means in practice that the defendant must swear an affidavit setting out the fact that destruction of certain articles has taken place. If the defendant has acted in a high handed or dishonest manner then the court may well decide, as it did in *Industrial Furnaces v Reaves* [1970] R.P.C. 605, that the better course is to order delivery up. Other cases in which delivery up was ordered are *Measures Bros Ltd v Measures* [1910] 2 Ch. 248; *Reid and Sigrist Ltd v Moss and Mechanism Ltd* (1932) 49 R.P.C. 461 and *Ackroyds (London) Ltd v Islington Plastics Ltd* [1962] R.P.C. 97. Delivery up means actual delivery to the claimant. The subject matter of an order for delivery up/destruction may encompass simply what the defendant has actually taken, for example, a customer list or a copy thereof but can go further and include what the defendant has made or has caused to be made using the business secrets.

27.5 Declarations

The power to grant a binding declaration is found in CPR 40.20: no action or other proceeding shall be open to objection on the ground that a merely declaratory judgment or order is sought thereby, and the court may make binding declarations whether or not any consequential relief is or could be claimed.

The declaration can be a very useful form of "remedy" in both restraint of trade and business secrets cases. It is particularly useful as a means of getting before a court in order to obtain judgment in those types of cases where either no contract as such exists, and/or if the party seeking relief is neither a member of a club whose rules are challenged etc. nor is a party to a contract. A declaration was used in both *Eastham v Newcastle United Football Club Ltd* [1964] Ch. 413 and in *Nagle v Feilden* [1966] 2 Q.B. 633. Lord Denning M.R. in *Boulting v ACTAT* [1963] 2 Q.B. 606 referred to "the power of the court . . . to make a declaration of right whenever the interest of the [claimant] is sufficient to justify it".

It is settled law that a declaration is not to be refused merely because the plaintiff cannot establish a legal cause of action apart from under CPR 40.20; "relief" in CPR 40.20 is not confined to relief in respect of a cause of action. See *Greig v Insole* [1978] 3 All E.R. 449 (in which the declaration was given to both the cricketers and WSC), *McInnes v Onslow-Fane* [1978] 1 W.L.R. 1520 and *Dickson v Pharmaceutical Society* [1970] A.C. 403.

A further use was found in *Marion White Ltd v Francis* [1972] 1 W.L.R. 1423 for the declaratory procedure. There the duration of the covenant had ended before the case could be heard in the Court of Appeal and therefore the dispute between the parties no longer effectively existed. However, the Court of Appeal allowed the applicants, the employers, to amend their grounds of appeal so as to include a claim for a declaration. This was done because the employers had an interest regarding their remaining employees who were employed under contracts containing a similar clause. Indeed, it is usual in all cases where the outcome of the instant case will inevitably be used as a basis for judging the validity of similar clauses, to claim a declaration.

A third, but rare, example of the use of a declaration occurred in *Greer v Sketchley Ltd* [1979] F.S.R. 197. There the claimant wanted to join a rival company of the defendants; he had been employed by the latter for many years. On learning of this the defendants reminded him that in their view by working for the rival he would be in breach of a restraint of trade clause in his employment contract. Mr Greer, instead of joining the rival and waiting to see what might happen, issued a writ claiming a declaration that the clause was invalid. The defendants counterclaimed for an injunction. Lord Denning M.R. applauded the claimant for his sensible approach and in the event the clause was declared to be invalid. There can be no doubt that many covenantors would be wise to follow Mr Greer's example. Although the clause was clearly unreasonable and would have been judged so even if he had simply joined the rival company there may be situations in which the sympathy of the court may be a decisive factor. Mr Greer obviously had that sympathy.

Other examples of cases in which a declaration was sought are *Kores Manufacturing Co v Kolok Manufacturing Co* [1959] Ch. 108 (because of a doubt whether there was an agreement at all); in *Esso Petroleum Co Ltd v Harper's Garage (Stourport) Ltd* [1968] A.C. 269 in which the defendants counterclaimed for a declaration; in *Industrial Development Consultants Ltd v Cooley* [1972] 2 All E.R. 192 in which a declaration was sought that Cooley was a trustee for the claimants of all contracts with the Eastern Gas Board and was therefore liable; see also *Malone v Metropolitan Police Commissioner* [1979] Ch. 344; *Schroeder v Macaulay* [1974] 1 W.L.R. 1308, and *Commercial Plastics Ltd v Vincent* [1965] 1 Q.B. 623 in which the claimants claimed an injunction restraining the defendant from taking up employment with a specific competitor and a declaration that he was not entitled to work for any competitors in the PVC calendering field.

Thomas v Farr Plc [2007] EWCA Civ 118 illustrates the danger of an unsuccessful application for a declaration. A departing director sought a declaration that the twelve-month non-compete covenant in his contract was an unreasonable restraint of trade and unenforceable. The Court of Appeal upheld the High Court's decision concluding that the clause was a reasonable limitation to impose in all the circumstances.

However, if an application for a declaration is contemplated the following points should be borne in mind:

(a) a declaration is not available as of right but is a discretionary remedy;

(b) a declaration will not be granted to answer an academic or hypothetical question. A declaration will not be granted where there is no breach and no threatened or intended breach of an agreement; see *Mellstrom v Garner* [1970] 1 W.L.R. 603;

(c) the fact that declarations have been granted on the basis of the public interest does not mean, of course, that there is the type of public element sufficient to warrant an application for the judicial review variety of declaration under CPR 54. See *Law v National Greyhound Racing Club Ltd* [1983] 3 All E.R. 300.

27.6 Contempt Proceedings

Deleting files on a home computer following an order for delivery up of that computer amounted to serious criminal contempt in the case of *LTE Scientific Limited v Thomas* [2005] EWHC 7. The court in that case was also prepared to dispense with the requirement for personal service of the order for the purposes of the committal proceedings in respect of the period during which the defendant was shown to be deliberately avoiding service.

Appendix 1

Restraint of Trade Cases: quick reference guide to some major decisions in relation to employees, partners and self-employed persons

Case	*Citation*	*Job*	*Time*	*Area/Restricted Activities*	*Valid*
Bromley v Smith	[1909] 2 K.B. 235	Baker	3 years	10 miles	Yes (after severance)
Mason v Provident Clothing and Supply Co Ltd	[1913] A.C. 724	Canvasser	3 years	25 miles	No
Caribonum Co Ltd v Le Couch	(1913) 109 L.T. 385	Manufacturer	5 years	British Empire and Europe	Yes (but old-fashioned approach)
Continental Tyre and Rubber (GB) Co Ltd v Heath	(1913) 29 T.L.R. 308	Salesman	1 year	UK, Germany, France	Yes (after severance)
Eastes v Russ	[1914] 1 Ch. 468	Laboratory Technician	Unlimited	10 miles	No
Hadsley v Dayer-Smith	[1914] A.C. 979	Estate Agent (partner)	10 years	1 mile	Yes
SV Nevanas and Co v Walker and Foreman	[1914] 1 Ch. 413	Manager	1 year	UK	No
Konski v Peet	[1915] 1 Ch. 530	Saleswoman	Unlimited	Solicitation of customers	No
Herbert Morris Ltd v Saxelby	[1916] 1 A.C. 688	Engineer	7 years	UK and Ireland	No

Case	*Citation*	*Job*	*Time*	*Area/Restricted Activities*	*Valid*
Forster and Sons Ltd v Suggett	(1918) 35 T.L.R. 87	Engineer	5 years	UK	Yes
The Great Western and Metropolitan Dairies Ltd v Gibbs	(1918) 34 T.L.R. 344	Cashier	6, 12, and 18 months	20 miles	No
Whitmore v King	(1918) 87 L.J. Ch. 647	Salesman/Clerk	5 years	East Anglia	No
Ropeways Ltd v Hoyle	(1919) 88 L.J. Ch. 446	Draughtsman	5 years	Unlimited	No
Attwood v Lamont	[1920] 3 K.B. 571	Tailor	Unlimited	10 miles	No
Clark, Sharp and Co Ltd v Solomon	(1920) 37 T.L.R. 176	Salesman	5 years	5 miles	No
Hepworth Manfacturing Co Ltd v Ryott	[1920] 1 Ch. 1	Actor	Unlimited	Worldwide	No
Bowler v Lovegrove	[1921] Ch. 642	Estate Agent Clerk	1 year	Portsmouth, Gosport	No
Fitch v Dewes	[1921] 2 A.C. 158	Solicitor's Clerk	Unlimited	7 miles	Yes
East Essex Farmers Ltd v Holder	[1926] W.N. 230	Manager	10 years	25 miles	No
Putsman v Taylor	[1927] 1 K.B. 741	Manager	5 years	Birmingham	Yes (after severance)
Express Dairy Co v Jackson	(1930) 99 L.J.K.B. 181	Milkman	2 years	Customers	No
Vincents of Reading v Fogden	(1932) 48 T.L.R. 613	Car Salesman	3 years	15 miles	No
Gilford Motor Co v Horne	[1933] Ch. 935	Managing Director	5 years	3 miles	Yes
Empire Meat Co Ltd v Patrick	[1939] 2 All E.R. 85	Butcher	5 years	5 miles	No
Chafer Ltd v Lilley	[1947] L.J.R. 231	Salesman	5 years	Great Britain	No
Routh v Jones	[1947] 1 All E.R. 758	Doctor	5 years	10 miles	No
Jenkins v Reid	[1948] 1 All E.R. 471	Doctor	Unlimited	5 miles	No
Whitehill v Bradford	[1952] 1 All E.R. 115	Doctor (partner)	21 years	10 miles	Yes

Marchon Products Ltd v Thornes	(1954) 71 R.P.C. 445	Chemist	1 year	UK	Yes
Ronbar Enterprises v Green	[1954] 1 W.L.R. 815	Publisher (partner)	5 years	any similar competiting business	Yes
M and S Drapers v Reynolds	[1956] 3 All E.R. 814	Salesman	5 years	customers	No
Vandervell Products Ltd v McLeod	[1957] R.P.C. 185	Foreman	2 years	Any competitor	No
Kerchiss v Colora Printing Inks Ltd	[1960] R.P.C. 235	Director	3 years	16 countries	Yes
Commercial Plastics Ltd v Vincent	[1964] 3 All E.R. 546	Researcher	1 year	Competitors, unlimited	No
Rayner v Pegler Agents	(1964) 189 E.G. 967	Partner in Estate	2 years	1 mile	No
GW Plowman and Sons Ltd v Ash	[1964] 2 All E.R. 10	Salesman	2 years	Customers	Yes
Gledhow Autoparts Ltd v Delaney	[1965] 3 All E.R. 288	Salesman	3 years	District worked	No
SW Strange Ltd v Mann	[1965] 1 All E.R. 1069	Manager	3 years	12 miles	No
Scorer v Seymour Johns	[1966] 3 All E.R. 347	Estate Agent	3 years	5 miles	Yes
Technograph Printed Circuits Ltd v Chalwyn Ltd	[1967] F.S.R. 307	Electronic Component Manufacturer	2 years	Unlimited	No
Under Water Welders and Repairers Ltd v Street and Longthorne	[1968] R.P.C. 498	Diver	3 years	Unlimited	Yes
Lyne-Pirkis v Jones	[1969] 3 All E.R. 738	Doctor (partner)	5 years	10 miles	No
Home Counties Dairies Ltd v Skilton	[1970] 1 All E.R. 1227	Milkman	1 year	Customers	Yes
Peyton v Mindham	[1971] 3 All E.R. 1215	Doctor (partner)	5 years	5 miles	No
Marion White Ltd v Francis	[1972] 3 All E.R. 857	Hairdresser	1 year	½ mile	Yes
T Lucas and Co Ltd v Mitchell	[1972] 2 All E.R. 1035	Salesman	1 year	Greater Manchester	No

Case	*Citation*	*Job*	*Time*	*Area/Restricted Activities*	*Valid*
Spafax (1965) Ltd v Dommett	(1972) 116 S.J. 711	Salesman	2 years	Customers	No
Financial Collection Agencies (UK) Ltd v Batey	(1973) 117 S.J. 416	Debt Collectors/ Salesmen	6 months	4 cities	No
StenhouseAustralia Ltd v Phillips	[1974] A.C. 391	Insurance Broker	5 years	Walthamstow, Chingford	No
Calvert, Hunt and Barden v Elton	(1975) 233 E.G. 391	Branch Manager Estate Agents	3 years	3 miles	Yes
Standex International Ltd v CB Blades	[1976] F.S.R. 114	Director	5 years	GB and Northern Ireland	Yes
Office Overload Ltd v Gunn	[1977] F.S.R. 39	Employment Agency	1 year	6 miles	Yes
Luck v Davenport-Smith	[1977] E.G.D. 73	Estate Agent	3 years	1 mile	No
Littlewoods Organisation Ltd v Harris	[1978] 1 All E.R. 1026	Director	1 year	Worldwide (but construed to be limited to (UK))	Yes
Richards v Levy	(1978) 122 S.J. 713	Solicitor's Clerk	3 years	London Borough of Ealing	Yes
Greer v Sketchley Ltd	[1979] F.S.R. 197	Director	1 year	UK	No
Spafax Ltd v Taylor and Harrison	[1980] I.R.L.R. 442	Salesman	2 years	Customers	Yes
Marley Tile Co Ltd v Johnson	[1982] I.R.L.R. 75		1 year	Devon, Cornwall	No
Normalec Ltd v Britton	[1983] F.S.R. 318	Agent	1 year	Yorkshire	Yes
Bridge v Deacons	[1984] A.C. 705	Solicitor (partner)	5 years	Hong Kong	Yes
John Michael Design plc v Cooke	[1987] 2 All E.R. 332	Director and designer	2 years	Non-solicitation or dealing with clients	Yes
Prontaprint plc v Landon Litho Ltd	[1987] F.S.R. 315 Ch D	Franchisee	3 years	No services within half a mile of the	Yes

				Franchise premises or within 3 miles of any premises in UK at which the service is carried on by another licensee or the licensor.	
Rex Stewart, Jeffries Parker, Ginsberg Ltd v Parker	[1988] I.R.L.R. 483	MD Advertising Agency	18 months	Non-solicitation clause re any customer who "is or has been" such of plaintiffs and associated companies	Yes but only after deleting "is or" from definition of customer and reference to associated companies
Sadler v Imperial Life Assurance Co of Canada Ltd	[1988] I.R.L.R. 388	Insurance Agent	Unlimited	Payment of commission after termination reliant on agent abiding with clause which prevented him working in same type of business	No: clause unreasonable (but severed: agent was paid)
Spencer v Marchington	[1988] I.R.L.R. 392	Manager Employment agency	2 years	25 miles Banbury/ 10 miles Leamington: not to work in similar business	No: 25 miles too far and adequate protection provided by a non-solicitation clause
Business Seating (Renovations) Ltd v Broad	[1989] I.C.R. 729	Sales Rep	1 year	Soliciting customers of plaintiff or any associated company	Yes after severance of restriction for benefit of associated company

Case	*Citation*	*Job*	*Time*	*Area/Restricted Activities*	*Valid*
Dairy Crest Ltd v Pigott	[1989] I.C.R. 92	Milkman	2 years	Non-solicitation	Yes
Hinton and Higgs (UK) Ltd v Murphy	[1989] I.R.L.R. 519	Unspecified	18 months	Not to work for any client of plaintiff group of companies	No: "previous or present" too wide; extent too wide; application to other companies in group too wide also
Briggs v Oates	[1991] 1 All E.R. 407	Employed Solicitor	5 years	5 miles: not practise nor solicit clients	No: partnership had dissolved prior to any breach
Lansing Linde Ltd v Kerr	[1991] 1 All E.R. 418	Divisional Director	12 months	Worldwide ban working in similar business	No
Lawrence David Ltd v Ashton	[1991] 1 All E.R. 385	Sales Director	2 years	Not working in UK	Yes
Office Angels Ltd v Rainer-Thomas	[1991] I.R.L.R. 214 CA	Branch Manager/ Consultant	6 months	1,000 metres from branch in City of London	No
Cantor Fitzgerald (UK) Ltd v Wallace	[1992] I.R.L.R. 215	Eurobond broker	6 months	Non-competition	No
A Ltd v B	unreported (Sachs J.)	Regional director of an insurance company	12 months	Canvas/deal with customers	Yes
Ingham v ABC Contract Services Ltd	November 12, 1993 unreported, CA	Branch manager of recruitment consultants	12 months	(a) Canvass/do business with customers (b) Solicit or entice	Yes: (a) and (b)

				any employees of plaintiff	
J A Mont (UK) Ltd v Mills	[1993] I.R.L.R. 172	Sales director	1 year	Not to work "in the tissue industry"	No
Morris Angel and Son Ltd v Hollande	[1993] 3 All E.R. 569	Group managing director	1 year	Not to seek to produceorders from or dobusiness with customers	Yes
Steiner (UK) Ltd v Spray	December 5, 1993 unreported, CA	Hairdresser	6 months	3 miles from Norwich city centre	Yes
TRP Ltd v Thorley	July 13, 1993 unreported, CA	Service manager	1 year	Any directly competitive business	No
GFI Group Inc v Eaglestone	[1994] I.R.L.R. 119	FX Options broker	20 week notice period	–	Yes. Injunction granted for 13 weeks
Hanover Insurance Brokers Ltd v Shapiro and others	[1994] I.R.L.R. 82	4 defendants: chairman, managing director, director,	12 months	Canvass: (a) customers (b) any employees of plaintiff manager	Yes: (a) No: (b)
Living Design (Home Improvement) Ltd v Davidson	[1994] I.R.L.R. 69	Promotions manager	6 months	Non-competition in Scotland and North of England	No: the words which related to termination—"however that comes about and whether lawful or not" caused all restrictions to be invalid
Austin Knight (UK) Ltd v Hinds	[1995] F.S.R. 52	Recruitment consultant	2 years	Solicitation of customers	No

Case	Citation	Job	Time	Area/Restricted Activities	Valid
Euro Brokers Ltd v Rabey	[1995] I.R.L.R. 206	Money broker	6 months	Any business, company or firm carrying on the business of money broking	Yes (6 months garden leave in lieu of notice)
Alliance Paper Group plc v Prestwich	[1996] I.R.L.R. 20	Managing director and major shareholder	12 months	(a) Seeking to procure orders from/do business with customers (b) Endeavour to entice away/employ former senior colleagues (c) Non-competition within 60 mile area	Yes: (a), (b) and (c)
D v M	[1996] I.R.L.R. 192	Managing director	3 years	Non-competition/ solicitation of customers	No
Marshall v NM Financial Management Ltd	[1996] I.R.L.R. 20	Self-employed financial agent	1 year	Non-competition	No
Credit Suisse Asset Management Ltd v Armstrong	[1996] I.R.L.R. 450	Fund managers/ marketing officer	6 months	Non-canvassing/ dealing with customers garden leave for periods between 3 and 6 months	Yes: even though all defendants had been on

Alliance Paper Group plc v Prestwich	[1996] I.R.L.R. 20	Managing Director/ overseeing sale of 75% of company	12 months	Carry on a competing business, seek orders/business from customers and suppliers anti-solicitation senior employees	Yes
Rock Refrigeration Ltd v Jones and Seward Refrigeration Ltd	[1996] I.R.L.R. 675	Industrial sales director	12 months	Do business with suppliers and customers	Yes
Voaden v Voaden	1997-V-633 Ch D	Partnership of surveyors	12 months	Non-solicitation	Yes
Dawnay, Day & Co Ltd v DE Bracionier D'Alphen	[1997] I.R.L.R. 442	Managers (brokers)	12 months	Not to compete, solicit business or members of staff	Yes
Marshall v MN Financial Management Ltd	[1997] I.R.L.R. 449	Self-employed financial services agent	12 months	Not to receive renewal commission if join a competitor	No (after severance of restraint so commission still payable)
Wallace Brogan v Cove	[1997] I.R.L.R. 453	Solicitors	12 months	Implied term to prevent canvassing or soliciting of clients	No
Rock Refrigeration Ltd v Jones & Seaward (CA)	[1997] 1 All E.R. 1	General Engineering Manager	12 months	Non-compete upon determination of employment contract "howsoever occasioned"	Yes
Dentmaster (UK) Ltd v Kent	[1997] I.R.L.R. 636	Dent repair technician	12 months	Non-solicitation not limited to employee's	Yes

Case	*Citation*	*Job*	*Time*	*Area/Restricted Activities*	*Valid*
				area of work or to contacts gained during a particular time frame	
Taylor Stuart& Co v Croft	[1998] 606 I.R.L.B 15	Salaried partner at an accountancy firm	3 years	Non-solicitation and damages for breach of covenant	No. Damage clause amounted to a penalty
Scully UK Ltd v Lee (CA)	[1998] I.R.L.R. 259	Technical sales engineer and General manager petrochemicals	(a) 12 months (b) 24 months	(a) Non-compete in UK regarding "any business" not limited to competing businesses (b) Non-solicitation of customers	No
Naish v Thorp Wright & Puxon	May 21, 1998	Veterinary surgeon Partner	8 years	Non-compete within 14 miles of practice	Valid
Emersub XXXVI Inc v Wheatley	July 3 1998 (unreported), QBD	Chairman (Vendor of Shares)	4 years	Non-solicit customers or employees be employed in connection with any group company anywhere in the world	Yes
FSS Travel and Leisure Systems Ltd v Johnson	[1998] I.R.L.R. 382	Computer programmer	1 year	Engage in competing business elsewhere in the UK	No (Existence of confidential information not established)

Credit Suisse First Boston (Europe) Ltd v Lister	[1998] I.R.L.R. 700	Head of European equities	12 months	Non-solicit clients and employees. No employment with competitor	No (Permission void on TUPE transfer)
Williams v Welsh Rugby Union	[1999] Eu.L.R. 195	Rugby player	10 years	WRU membership restrictions	Pending EU
TSC Europe (UK) Ltd v Massey	[1999] I.R.L.R. 22	Senior Vice President	1 year	Non-solicitation of employees	No. Not limited by reference or experience
William Hill Organisation Ltd v Tucker (CA)	[1999] I.C.L. 291	Spread betting	6 months	Non-solicitation employees and customers	Not allowed to impose gardening leave during notice period
Jack Allen (Sales & Services) Ltd v Smith	[1999] I.R.L.R. 19	Salesman	No time limit	Non-disclosure of confidential information	No (no evidence any loss would be caused)
			2 years	Non-solicitation of employees,customers and non-compete with customers and suppliers	
Polymasc Pharmaceutical Plc v Charles	[1999] F.S.R.711	Business Development and Licensing Director	1 year	Non-disclosure of confidential information and non-compete	Yes
Intelsec Systems v Grech-Cini	June 18, 1999 (unreported) Ch D	Director	2 years	Non-disclosure of confidential information	Yes (subject to restrictions)
Turner v Commonwealth & British Minerals Ltd	[2000] I.R.L.R. 114	Directors	12 months	Non-compete	Yes

Case	*Citation*	*Job*	*Time*	*Area/Restricted Activities*	*Valid*
SBJ Stephenson v Mandy	[2000] I.R.L.R. 233	Executive	–	Non-disclosure of confidential information	Yes
			12 months	Non-solicitation of clients of employees	
International Consulting Services (UK) Ltd v Hart	[2000] I.R.L.R. 227	Senior consultant	12 months	Non-solicit of suppliers and clients	Yes
Hollis & Co v Stocks	[2000] I.R.L.R. 712	Solicitor	12 months	Work within 10 miles of office	Yes
Wincanten Ltd v Cranny & SDM European Transport Ltd	[2000] I.R.L.R. 716	European operations manager	12 months	Non-solicitation of customers, suppliers. Non-compete in any-business within the UK	No
Computer Associates plc v Larner	[2001] All E.R. (D) 276	Manager of strategic accounts	12 months (severance agreement)	Non-compete, non-solicit	No
Lapthorne v Eurofi Ltd (CA)	[2001] All E.R. (D) 209	Self-employed financial consultant	During contract	Could not provide other services to non-clients of defendant without consent	No protection of legitimate interest
Symbian Ltd v Christensen	[2001] I.R.L.R. 77	Executive Vice President	6 months	Non-compete	Yes
Anstalt v Hayek	[2002] All E.R. (D) 377	Inventor and vendor	For as long as sold company engaged in business	Worldwide	Invalid. Additional restrictions exceeded those of a patent

Thurstan Hoskin & Partners v Jewill Hill & Bennett	[2002] All E.R. (D) 62	Solicitor (Partner)	6 months	Non-compete at stated places or within a 3 mile distance of any partnership office	Yes
Ward Evans Financial Services Ltd v Fox	[2002] I.R.L.R. 120	Financial Advisers	Unlimited	Non-disclosure of confidential business information	No
				Not to hold material interest in company during employment	Yes
BFI Optias Ltd v Blyth and Ors	[2002] All E.R. (D) 287	General Manager	15 months	Non-solicit/ customers/employees (in severance agreement)	Yes
		Business Development Director	12 months	Non-solicit (covering merged business but defendant only involved with some products, some customes and no geographical restrictions)	No
Dent Wizard (UK) Ltd v Thomas	[2002] All E.R. (D) 104	Area technician	9 months	Work for clients non-solicit of clients	Yes
Cantor Fitzgerald International v Bird	[2002] I.R.L.R. 867	Brokers	20 weeks	Non-solicit or transact business	No (against employees where the employer had breached the contract)

Case	*Citation*	*Job*	*Time*	*Area/Restricted Activities*	*Valid*
Vendo plc v Adams	[2002] N.I. 95	Franchisee vehicle cleaning service	18 months	Non-compete for 2 large areas within Northern Ireland and non-solicitation of customers	
Arbuthnot Fund Managers v Rawlings	[2003] EWCA Cir 518	Executive Director	12 months	Non-solicitation clients, suppliers and employees	Yes
Critical Path Associates Ltd v D'Angelo	[2003] All E.R. (D) 379	Carpenter and team leader		Non-disclosure of information and non-solicitation of customers (implied)	No
First Choice Recruitment v Hancock	[2003] All E.R. (D) 64	Branch Manager	6 months	Non-solicit customers	Yes
				Non-compete within 10 mile radius of office	No
LC Services Ltd v Brown	[2003] All E.R. (D) 239	Sales director	12 months	Non-solicit of any customer or any party negotiating with the company with whom the employee had dealings during the period of 12 months prior to termination	Yes
Axiom Business Computers Ltd v Frederic	[2003] G.W.D 37-1021	Technical support director	6 months	Seeking or accepting employment with	Yes

				competitor	
			18 months	Non-dealing with customers employee had been involved with	Yes
Cardinale v Seckington	[2003] All E.R. (D) 355	Hairdresser	6 months	Non-compete within ½ mile of salon	Yes
Peninsula Business Services v Sweeney	[2004] I.R.L.R. 49	Sales Executive		Commission for past sales not payable after termination of contract	Yes (not in restraint of trade)
Countrywide Assured Financial Services Ltd v Smart	[2004] EWHC 1214 (Ch D)	Mortgage consultant	3 months	Non-compete within 3 miles of any office of employer	No
			6 months	Non-solicitation of clients who were clients in the 12 months prior to termination of employment	No
LTE Scientific Ltd. v Thomas	[2004] All E.R. (D) 312	Technical Director	12 months	Autoclave and thermal equipment design without geographical limit	Yes
Corporate Express Ltd. v Day	[2004] EWHC 2943	Senior Sales Manager	6 months	Non-solicitation and non-dealing in respect of customers of the company in the last 12 months before termination of employment and 6 months non-	Yes

Case	Citation	Job	Time	Area/Restricted Activities	Valid
				competition by reference to a restriction on the employee joining named competitors	
First Global Locums Ltd. & Ors v Cosias	[2005] EWHC 1147 Q.B.	Recruitment Consultant	6 months	Non-solicitation of locums the employee or colleague had to his knowledge dealt with in the 12 months preceding the termination of employment; non-solicitation of employees and non-solicitation of clients	Yes in relation to the non-solicitation of locums and employees No in relation to solicitation of clients. (The relationship with locums provided by the company to clients was such that it was an asset they were entitled to protect, but the definition of client in relation to the non-solicitation of clients was too wide)
TFS Derivatives Ltd. v Morgan	[2005] I.R.L.R. 246	Equity Derivatives Broker	6 months	Non-compete No geographical restriction	Yes Court deleted wording "or similar" to relevant business

Dyson Technology Ltd. v Strutt	[2005] All E.R. (D) 355, (Ch D)	Design Engineer	12 months	Non-compete without geographical limit	Yes
Hydra plc v Anastasi	[2005] All E.R. (D) 276, Q.B.	Sales Executives for a Re-seller in the Data Networking, Internet Performance and Security Markets	First Defendant 12 months	Non-compete within a restricted area, non-solicitation of employees or the supply of goods and services from a supplier	No
			Second Defendant 9 months	Non-solicitation of customers and employees (in both cases in a compromise agreement concluded at the end of the employment)	No Inter alia because the new competing business acted as a distributor whereas the employer sold to end users
Berry Birch & Noble Financial Planning Ltd. v Berwick	[2005] EWHC 1803	Agent for independent financial and investment advice company	12 months	Non-solicitation of clients	No Clients too broadly defined to include those who had been in negotiations with the company but who never ultimately became a client and those with whom the agents in question had no contact

Case	*Citation*	*Job*	*Time*	*Area/Restricted Activities*	*Valid*
Allan Janes LLP v Johal	[2006] I.R.L.R. 599	Assistant Solicitor	12 months	(a) Non-compete within a radius of 6 miles from the employer's office;	No
				(b) Non-dealing covenant in relation to any client of the employer in the 12 months prior to termination of employment	Yes (The covenant was entered into at a time when it was anticipated the employee would become a partner in the firm, although she did not ultimately do so)
Thomas v Farr plc	[2007] EWCA Civ 118	Managing Director of Insurance Brokers	12 months	Non-compete in geographical areas where the employer and sister companies had conducted business	Yes
Beckett Investment Management Group Ltd. and v Hall	[2007] EWCA 613	Independent Financial Advisers	12 months	Non-dealing Covenant in relation to any client of the employer in the 12 months prior to the termination of employment with	Yes The covenant was only in favour of the employing parent holding company which had no relevant business/

				whom the employee dealt during this period.	clients but its business held by CA to extend to and include subsidiaries clients as well.
Intercall Conferencing Services Ltd. v Steer	[2007] All E.R. (D) 273	Head of Training and Personnel Development	6 months	Non-competition without geographical limitation	Yes
Extec Screens & Crushers Ltd. v Rice	[2007] EWHC 1043	After Sales Manager	8 months	Non-competition within stipulated geographical area	Yes In addition to a three month-“garden leave”.

Appendix 2

Business Secrets Cases: quick reference guide

Case	*Citation*	*Information*	*Relationship*	*Remedy*
Prince Albert v Strange	(1849) 1 Mac. & G. 25	catalogue of etchings	third party	injunction
Morison v Moat	(1851) 9 Hare 492	secret formula	third party (partner's son)	injunction
Gartside v Outram	(1856) 2 L.J. Ch. 113	knowledge of fraud	employee	refused
Tuck and Sons v Priester	(1887) 19 Q.B.D. 629	drawings	contractor	injunction and damages
Gilbert v Star Newspapers Co Ltd	(1894) 11 T.L.R. 4	plot of a play	third party (former employer)	injunction
Robb v Green	[1895] 2 Q.B. 1	customer list	employee	damages and injunction
Exchange Telegraph Co Ltd v Central News Ltd	[1897] 2 Ch. 48	newswire	subscriber and third party	injunction
Williams Summers and Co Ltd v Boyce and Kinmon and Co	(1907) 23 T.L.R. 724	list of customers and business terms	employee and third party	injunction delivery up and damages
Rakusen v Ellis, Munday and Clarke	[1912] 1 Ch. 831	partner's knowledge	solicitor's client	refused
Amber Size and Chemical Co v Menzel	(1913) 30 R.P.C. 433	secret process	employee	injunction
Weld-Blundell v Stephens	[1920] A.C. 956	instructions to investigating accountants	accountant	damages

Case	*Citation*	*Information*	*Relationship*	*Remedy*
Keene, Re	[1922] 2 Ch. 475	formulae	trustee in bankruptcy	disclosure
Tournier v National Provincial and Union Bank of England	[1924] 1 K.B. 461	bank account	customer of bank	new trial ordered
Reid and Sigrist Ltd v Moss and Mechanism Ltd	(1932) 49 R.P.C. 461	engineering	employee	injunction delivery up declaration
E Worsley and Co Ltd v Cooper	[1939] 1 All E.R. 290	prices and product types	employee	refused (as regards secrets)
Hivac Ltd v Park Royal Scientific Instruments Ltd	[1946] Ch. 169	manufacturing techniques	competitor	injunction
Saltman Engineering Co Ltd v Campbell Engineering Co Ltd	(1948) 65 R.P.C. 203	engineering drawings	sub-contractor	delivery up and damages
Stevenson Jordan and Harrison Ltd v MacDonald and Evans	(1952) 69 R.P.C. 10	business procedures	employee	refused
GB Bjorlow Ltd v Minter	(1954) 71 R.P.C. 321	process	employee	refused
Nichrotherm Electrical Co Ltd v Percy	[1957] R.P.C. 207	engineering drawings etc.	disclosure for limited purpose	damages
Ackroyds (London) Ltd v Islington Plastics Ltd	[1962] R.P.C. 97	tool design	sub-contractor	injunction and damages
Mustad v Allcock and Dosen	[1963] 3 All E.R. 416	engineering	employee	refused
Peter Pan Manufacturing Corp v Corsets Silhouette	[1963] 3 All E.R. 402	manufacturing	licensee	injunction and account of profits
KS Paul Ltd v Southern Instruments Ltd	[1964] R.P.C. 118	black box	lessee and third party	injunction
Printers and Finishers Ltd v Holloway	[1965] 1 W.L.R. 1	printing process	employee and visitor	visitor injuncted but not employee
Cranleigh Precision Engineering Ltd v Bryant	[1965] 1 W.L.R. 1293	engineering	director	injunction

Auto Securities Ltd v Standard Telephones & Cables Ltd	[1965] R.P.C. 92	technical information customer lists	unclear	refused
Torrington Manufacturing Co v Smith and Son (England) Ltd	[1966] R.P.C. 285	engineering	licensee	–
Terrapin Ltd v Builders' Supply Co (Hayes) Ltd	[1967] R.P.C. 375	engineering	employee	injunction
Seager v Copydex Ltd	[1967] 1 W.L.R. 923	engineering drawings and explanations	negotiations	inquiry as to damages
Franchi v Franchi	[1967] R.P.C.149	manufacturing process	employee	refused
Margaret Duchess Argyll v Duke Argyll	[1967] 1 Ch. 302	marital confidence	spouse	injunction
Suhner and Co AGv Transradio Ltd	[1967] R.P.C. 329	engineering drawings	distributor	refused
Under Water Welders and Repairers Ltd v Street and Longthorne	[1968] R.P.C. 498	hull cleaning process	employees	injunction
Initial Services v Putterill	[1968] 1 Q.B. 396	misconduct	employee	refused
Coco v ANClark (Engineering) Ltd	[1969] R.P.C. 41	engineering drawings etc.	negotiations	refused
Fraser v Evans	[1969] 1 Q.B. 349	report for government	consultant	refused
Industrial Furnaces Ltd v Reaves	[1970] R.P.C. 605	engineering	employee	injunction damages delivery up
Baker v Gibbons	[1972] 1 W.L.R. 693	agent's names	director	refused
Regina Glass Fibre v Werner Schuller	[1972] R.P.C. 299	process	licensee	refused
Hubbard v Vosper	[1972] 1 All E.R. 1023	religious sect	sect member	refused
Church of Scientology v Kaufman	[1973] R.P.C. 635	religious sect	student	refused
United Stirling Corp Ltd v Felton and Mannion	[1974] R.P.C. 162	manufacturing process	employee	refused
Aveley/Cybervox Ltd v Boman and Sign Electronics Ltd	[1975] F.S.R. 139	product design	employee	refused
Yates Circuit Foil Co v Electrofoils Ltd	[1976] F.S.R. 345	chemical processes	employees	refused (undertakings given)

Case	Citation	Information	Relationship	Remedy
A-G v Jonathan Cape Ltd	[1976] Q.B. 752	cabinet meetings	publisher of minister's diaries	refused
Potters-Ballotini Ltd v Weston-Baker	[1977] R.P.C. 202	manufacturing process	employees	refused
Woodward v Hutchins	[1977] 1 W.L.R. 760	private lives	press agent	refused
Riddick v Thames Board Mills Ltd	[1977] Q.B. 881	evidence of defamation	discovery	appeal against use allowed
Lennon v News Group Newspapers Ltd	[1978] F.S.R. 573	marital confidences	spouse/third party	refused
Dunford and Elliott Ltd v Johnson and Firth Brown	[1978] F.S.R. 143	report of company's finances	prospective underwriter	refused
Franklin v Giddings	[1978] Qd. R. 72	budwood	spouse and third party	delivery up
Thomas Marshall (Exports) Ltd v Guinle	[1979] 1 Ch. 227	supplier and customer names	managing director	injunction
Malone v Metropolitan Police Commissioner	[1979] 1 Ch. 346	telephone tapping	–	refused
Schering Chemicals Ltd v Falkman Ltd	[1981] 2 All E.R. 321	reaction to drug	public relations consultant	injunction
British Steel Corporation v Granada Television Ltd	[1981] 1 All E.R. 417	name of informant	third party	discovery
GD Searle and Co Ltd v Celltech Ltd	[1982] F.S.R. 98	staff names etc.	employee	refused
Sun Printers Ltd v Westminster Press Ltd	[1982] I.R.L.R. 292	company report	third party	refused
Home Office v Harman	[1982] 1 All E.R. 532	document disclosed in court	counsel	contempt

Fisher-Karpark Industries Ltd v Nichols	[1982] F.S.R. 351	not clear from report	employee/director	injunction
Fraser v Thames Television	[1983] 2 All E.R. 101	concept for TV series	negotiations	damages
Trees Ltd v Cripps	(1983) 267 E.G. 596	value of bid	bidder	refused
Francome v Mirror Group Newspapers Ltd	[1984] 2 All E.R. 408	telephone tapping	third party	injunction
Lion Laboratories Ltd v Evans	[1984] 2 All E.R. 417	report on intoximeter	employee negotiations	refused injunction
Wheatley v Bell	[1984] F.S.R. 17	advertising method	–	–
House of Spring Gardens v Point Blank	[1985] F.S.R. 327	design for armoured vest	licensee	damages
Speed Seal Ltd v Paddington	[1985] W.L.R. 1327	engineering designs	employee	appeal allowed
Roger Bullivant Ltd v Ellis	[1987] I.C.R. 464	customer index	employee	injunction
Faccenda Chicken v Fowler	[1986] 1 All E.R. 617	customers and prices	employee	refused
Dowson and Mason Ltd v Potter	[1986] 1 W.L.R. 1419	names and addresses of suppliers and prices paid to them	employee	claim admitted: case reported on quantum
Balston Ltd v Headline Filters Ltd	[1987] F.S.R. 330	blends of micro-fibres, tests of identity of chemicals used in manufacturing process	employee and director	refused (partial undertakings given)
Johnson & Bloy Holdings Ltd v Wolstenholme Rink plc	[1989] I.R.L.R. 499	knowledge of commercial use of the combination of 2 products	employee	injunction granted on appeal not to use/disclose/ manufacture
A Company, Re	[1989] 3 W.L.R. 265	information about a company's tax and management	employee	injunction (subject to exceptions in the case of disclosure to FIMBRA and Inland Revenue)

Case	*Citation*	*Information*	*Relationship*	*Remedy*
W v Egdell	[1989] 2 W.L.R. 689	psychiatrist's report	doctor/patient	action dismissed on basis that disclosure to limited recipients in public interest
Ixora Trading Inc v Jones	[1990] 1 F.S.R. 251	general technical knowledge of bureau de change business and of 2 manuals and a feasibility study	employee	claim struck out
Berkeley Admin Inc v McCleland	[1990] F.S.R. 505	details of a business plan	employee	claim dismissed
Systems Reliability Holdings plc v Smith	[1990] I.R.L.R. 377	ability to modify computers and information about customers of plaintiff and its subsidiaries	employee and shareholder	injunction and enquiry as to damages
Lansing Linde Ltd v Kerr	[1991] 1 All E.R. 418	plans for development of new products	divisional director	undertakings
Alfa Laval Cheese Systems Ltd v Wincanton Engineering Ltd	[1990] F.S.R. 583	design for cheese former	sub-contractor	injunction
Kaye v Robertson	[1991] F.S.R. 62	photographs of injured plaintiff	investigative photographer	refused
Prout v British Gas plc, Patent County Court	[1992] F.S.R. 478	invention disclosed under employee suggestion scheme	employer	damages
Hoechst UK Ltd v Chemiculture Ltd, Chancery Division	[1993] F.S.R. 270	information obtained under statutory power	third party	refused to discharge Anton Piller
Shelley Films Ltd v Rex Features Ltd	December 10, 1993, Ch D, unreported	film set	investigative photographer	injunction

De Maudsley v Palumbo and others, Chancery Division 19 December 1995	*The Times*, December 19, 1995	idea for an all night dance club	business associates	refused
Firm of Solicitors, A, Re (Ch D)	[1995] F.S.R. 783	client information	solicitor	injunction refused; undertakings accepted
Strix Ltd v Otter Controls Ltd, Patent Court	[1995] R.P.C. 607	design for kettle switch	joint developers	duty found to exist
Valeo Vision SA. v Flexible Lamps Ltd, Patent Court	[1995] R.P.C. 205	rear lamp cluster designs	third party	refused
Polymasc Pharmaceuticals plc v Charles	[1999] F.R.S. 711	biochemistry technology	former business development and licensing director	granted
AT Poeton (Gloucester Plating) Ltd v Horton	[2002] All E.R. (D) 748	Information about electrolyte and apparatus for plating	sales engineer	refused
Gerrard Ltd v Read and another	[2001] All E.R. (D) 355	customer list	former employee	granted
Worldwide Fund for Nature v World Wrestling Federation	[2002] U.K.C.L.R. 388	Restriction on use of the WWF initials	contractual party	injunction granted
Jobserve Ltd v Network Multimedia Television Ltd	[2002] U.K.C.L.R.184	Online advertising services to recruitment agencies	customers	injunction refused
Cray Valley Ltd v Deltech Europe Ltd	[2003] EWHC 728 (Ch D)	Resin recipes and breach of copyright	employees	claim in respect of confidential information refused. breach of copyright found.
LC Services v Brown	[2003] EWHC 3024	Customer details and technical maintenance procedures	director and employee	injunction granted; damages

Case	*Citation*	*Information*	*Relationship*	*Remedy*
Fibrenetix Storage Ltd v Davis	[2004] EWHC 1359 (QBD)	Pricing and sales information	sales manager	refused
Berry Birch & Noble Financial Planning Ltd v Berwick	[2005] EWHC 1803	Express prohibition in relation to any information relating to the employer including, without limitation, business methods, finances, ideas, strategies, concepts, methodologies, processes, formulae, source codes and software programmes, details of suppliers and clients	agents for a company engagedin independent financial investment advice	refused The confidential information was too broadly identified
Meadowstone (Derbyshire) Ltd v (1) Kirk (2) Hill	UK EAT/0529/05/0303, March 3, 2006	Financial and commercial information provided to a third party potentially interested in financing and management buyout of the company	directors/employees	none The two directors brought successful unfair and wrongful dismissal claims but, in the context, the EAT also considered there was no breach of duties of confidentiality as it was in the interest of the employing company that the

				best price should be obtained for the business; at the time another management buyout proposal by other directors was extant refused
Shepherds Investments Ltd v Walters	[2006] All E.R. (D) 213	Information regarding proposed investment in lighter policies traded before maturity	details of independent financial advisers with whom the company conducted business	Insufficient evidence of confidentiality

Appendix 3

Practice direction—interim injunctions

This Practice Direction Supplements CPR Part 25

Contents of This Practice Direction

Jurisdiction

A3.1 1.1 High Court Judges and any other Judge duly authorised may grant "search orders"[1] and "freezing injunctions"[2].

1.2 In a case in the High Court, Masters and district judges have the power to grant injunctions:

(1) by consent,
(2) in connection with charging orders and appointments of receivers,
(3) in aid of execution of judgments.

1.3 In any other case any judge who has jurisdiction to conduct the trial of the action has the power to grant an injunction in that action.

1.4 A Master or district judge has the power to vary or discharge an injunction granted by any Judge with the consent of all the parties.

Making an application

A3.2 2.1 The application notice must state:

(1) the order sought, and
(2) the date, time and place of the hearing.

2.2 The application notice and evidence in support must be served as soon as practicable after issue and in any event not less than 3 days before the court is due to hear the application[3].

2.3 Where the court is to serve, sufficient copies of the application notice and evidence in support for the court and for each respondent should be filed for issue and service.

2.4 Whenever possible a draft of the order sought should be filed with the application notice and a disk containing the draft should also be available to the court in a format compatible with the word processing software used by the court. This will enable the court officer to arrange for any amendments to be incorporated and for the speedy preparation and sealing of the order.

Evidence

A3.3 3.1 Applications for search orders and freezing injunctions must be supported by affidavit evidence.

3.2 Applications for other interim injunctions must be supported by evidence set out in either:

---

1 Rule 25.1(1)(h).
2 Rule 25.1(1)(f).
3 Rule 23.7(1) and (2) and see rule 23.7(4) (short service).

(1) a witness statement, or
(2) a statement of case provided that it is verified by a statement of truth,[4] or
(3) the application provided that it is verified by a statement of truth,
unless the court, an Act, a rule or a practice direction requires evidence by affidavit.

3.3 The evidence must set out the facts on which the applicant relies for the claim being made against the respondent, including all material facts of which the court should be made aware.

3.4 Where an application is made without notice to the respondent, the evidence must also set out why notice was not given.

(See Part 32 and the practice direction that supplements it for information about evidence.)

Urgent applications and applications without notice

4.1 These fall into two categories: **A3.4**

(1) applications where a claim form has already been issued, and
(2) applications where a claim form has not yet been issued,

and, in both cases, where notice of the application has not been given to the respondent.

4.2 These applications are normally dealt with at a court hearing but cases of extreme urgency may be dealt with by telephone.

4.3 Applications dealt with at a court hearing after issue of a claim form:

(1) the application notice, evidence in support and a draft order (as in 2.4 above) should be filed with the court two hours before the hearing wherever possible,
(2) if an application is made before the application notice has been issued, a draft order (as in 2.4 above) should be provided at the hearing, and the application notice and evidence in support must be filed with the court on the same or next working day or as ordered by the court, and
(3) except in cases where secrecy is essential, the applicant should take steps to notify the respondent informally of the application.

4.4 Applications made before the issue of a claim form:

(1) in addition to the provisions set out at 4.3 above, unless the court orders otherwise, either the applicant must undertake to the

[4] See Part 22.

court to issue a claim form immediately or the court will give directions for the commencement of the claim[5],

(2) where possible the claim form should be served with the order for the injunction,

(3) an order made before the issue of a claim form should state in the title after the names of the applicant and respondent "the Claimant and Defendant in an Intended Action".

4.5 Applications made by telephone:

(1) where it is not possible to arrange a hearing, application can be made between 10.00 a.m. and 5.00 p.m. weekdays by telephoning the Royal Courts of Justice on 020 7947 6000 and asking to be put in contact with a High Court Judge of the appropriate Division available to deal with an emergency application in a High Court matter. The appropriate district registry may also be contacted by telephone. In county court proceedings, the appropriate county court should be contacted,

(2) where an application is made outside those hours the applicant should either—

(a) telephone the Royal Courts of Justice on 020 7947 6000 where he will be put in contact with the clerk to the appropriate duty judge in the High Court (or the appropriate area Circuit Judge where known), or

(b) the Urgent Court Business Officer of the appropriate Circuit who will contact the local duty judge,

(3) where the facility is available it is likely that the judge will require a draft order to be faxed to him,

(4) the application notice and evidence in support must be filed with the court on the same or next working day or as ordered, together with two copies of the order for sealing,

(5) injunctions will be heard by telephone only where the applicant is acting by counsel or solicitors.

Orders for injunctions

A3.5 5.1 Any order for an injunction, unless the court orders otherwise, must contain:

(1) an undertaking by the applicant to the court to pay any damages which the respondent sustains which the court considers the applicant should pay.

---

[5] Rule 25.2(3).

(2) if made without notice to any other party, an undertaking by the applicant to the court to serve on the respondent the application notice, evidence in support and any order made as soon as practicable,
(3) if made without notice to any other party, a return date for a further hearing at which the other party can be present,
(4) if made before filing the application notice, an undertaking to file and pay the appropriate fee on the same or next working day, and
(5) if made before issue of a claim form—
   (a) an undertaking to issue and pay the appropriate fee on the same or next working day, or
   (b) directions for the commencement of the claim.

5.1A When the court makes an order for an injunction, it should consider whether to require an undertaking by the applicant to pay any damages sustained by a person other than the respondent, including another party to the proceedings or any other person who may suffer loss as a consequence of the order.

5.2 An order for an injunction made in the presence of all parties to be bound by it or made at a hearing of which they have had notice, may state that it is effective until trial or further order.

5.3 Any order for an injunction must set out clearly what the respondent must do or not do.

FREEZING INJUNCTIONS

Orders to restrain disposal of assets worldwide and within England and Wales

6.1 An example of a Freezing Injunction is annexed to this practice direction. **A3.6**

6.2 This example may be modified as appropriate in any particular case. In particular, the court may, if it considers it appropriate, require the applicant's solicitors, as well as the applicant, to give undertakings.

SEARCH ORDERS

7.1 The following provisions apply to search orders in addition to those listed above. **A3.7**

The Supervising Solicitor

7.2 The Supervising Solicitor must be experienced in the operation of search orders. A Supervising Solicitor may be contacted either through the Law Society or, for the London area, through the London Solicitors Litigation Association.

7.3 Evidence:

(1) the affidavit must state the name, firm and its address, and experience of the Supervising Solicitor, also the address of the premises and whether it is a private or business address, and
(2) the affidavit must disclose very fully the reason the order is sought, including the probability that relevant material would disappear if the order were not made.

7.4 Service:

(1) the order must be served personally by the Supervising Solicitor, unless the court otherwise orders, and must be accompanied by the evidence in support and any documents capable of being copied,
(2) confidential exhibits need not be served but they must be made available for inspection by the respondent in the presence of the applicant's solicitors while the order is carried out and afterwards be retained by the respondent's solicitors on their undertaking not to permit the respondent—

    (a) to see them or copies of them except in their presence, and
    (b) to make or take away any note or record of them,

(3) the Supervising Solicitor may be accompanied only by the persons mentioned in the order,
(4) the Supervising Solicitor must explain the terms and effect of the order to the respondent in everyday language and advise him—

    (a) of his right to take legal advice and to apply to vary or discharge the order; and
    (b) that he may be entitled to avail himself of—
        (i) legal professional privilege; and
        (ii) the privilege against self-incrimination.

(5) where the Supervising Solicitor is a man and the respondent is likely to be an unaccompanied woman, at least one other person named in the order must be a woman and must accompany the Supervising Solicitor, and
(6) the order may only be served between 9.30 a.m. and 5.30 p.m. Monday to Friday unless the court otherwise orders.

7.5 Search and custody of materials:

(1) no material shall be removed unless clearly covered by the terms of the order,
(2) the premises must not be searched and no items shall be removed from them except in the presence of the respondent or a person who appears to be a responsible employee of the respondent,

(3) where copies of documents are sought, the documents should be retained for no more than 2 days before return to the owner,
(4) where material in dispute is removed pending trial, the applicant's solicitors should place it in the custody of the respondent's solicitors on their undertaking to retain it in safekeeping and to produce it to the court when required,
(5) in appropriate cases the applicant should insure the material retained in the respondent's solicitors' custody,
(6) the Supervising Solicitor must make a list of all material removed from the premises and supply a copy of the list to the respondent,
(7) no material shall be removed from the premises until the respondent has had reasonable time to check the list,
(8) if any of the listed items exists only in computer readable form, the respondent must immediately give the applicant's solicitors effective access to the computers, with all necessary passwords, to enable them to be searched, and cause the listed items to be printed out,
(9) the applicant must take all reasonable steps to ensure that no damage is done to any computer or data,
(10) the applicant and his representatives may not themselves search the respondent's computers unless they have sufficient expertise to do so without damaging the respondent's system,
(11) the Supervising Solicitor shall provide a report on the carrying out of the order to the applicant's solicitors,
(12) as soon as the report is received the applicant's solicitors shall—

   (a) serve a copy of it on the respondent, and
   (b) file a copy of it with the court, and

(13) where the Supervising Solicitor is satisfied that full compliance with paragraph 7.5(7) and (8) above is impracticable, he may permit the search to proceed and items to be removed without compliance with the impracticable requirements.

General

8.1 The Supervising Solicitor must not be an employee or member of the applicant's firm of solicitors. **A3.8**

8.2 If the court orders that the order need not be served by the Supervising Solicitor, the reason for so ordering must be set out in the order.

8.3 The search order must not be carried out at the same time as a police search warrant.

8.4 There is no privilege against self incrimination in:

(1) Intellectual Property cases in respect of a "related offence" or for the recovery of a "related penalty" as defined in section 72 Supreme Court Act 1981;

(2) proceedings for the recovery or administration of any property, for the execution of a trust or for an account of any property or dealings with property, in relation to—

(a) an offence under the Theft Act 1968 (see section 31 of the Theft Act 1968[6]); or

(b) an offence under the Fraud Act 2006 (see section 13 of the Fraud Act 2006[7]) or a related offence within the meaning given by section 13(4) of that Act—that is, conspiracy to defraud or any other offence involving any form of fraudulent conduct or purpose; or

(3) proceedings in which a court is hearing an application for an order under Part IV or Part V of the Children Act 1989 (see section 98 Children Act 1989).

However, the privilege may still be claimed in relation to material or information required to be disclosed by an order, as regards potential criminal proceedings outside those statutory provisions.

8.5 Applications in intellectual property cases should be made in the Chancery Division.

8.6 An example of a Search Order is annexed to this Practice Direction. This example may be modified as appropriate in any particular case.

DELIVERY-UP ORDERS

A3.9 9.1 The following provisions apply to orders, other than search orders, for delivery up or preservation of evidence or property where it is likely that such an order will be executed at the premises of the respondent or a third party.

9.2 In such cases the court shall consider whether to include in the order for the benefit or protection of the parties similar provisions to those specified above in relation to injunctions and search orders.

INJUNCTIONS AGAINST THIRD PARTIES

A3.10 10.1 The following provisions apply to orders which will affect a person other than the applicant or respondent, who:

(1) did not attend the hearing at which the order was made; and

(2) is served with the order.

[6] 1968 c. 60.

[7] 2006 c. 35.

10.2 Where such a person served with the order requests—

(1) a copy of any materials read by the judge, including material prepared after the hearing at the direction of the judge or in compliance with the order; or
(2) a note of the hearing,

the applicant, or his legal representative, must comply promptly with the request, unless the court orders otherwise.

ANNEX

FREEZING INJUNCTION IN THE HIGH COURT OF JUSTICE **A3.11**
[ ] DIVISION

Before The Honourable Mr Justice [ ]
Claim No.
Dated

Applicant

Seal

Respondent

Name, address and reference of Respondent

PENAL NOTICE

IF YOU [ ][8] DISOBEY THIS ORDER YOU MAY BE HELD IN CONTEMPT OF COURT AND MAY BE IMPRISONED, FINED OR HAVE YOUR ASSETS SEIZED.

ANY OTHER PERSON WHO KNOWS OF THIS ORDER AND DOES ANYTHING WHICH HELPS OR PERMITS THE RESPONDENT TO BREACH THE TERMS OF THIS ORDER MAY ALSO BE HELD TO BE IN CONTEMPT OF COURT AND MAY BE IMPRISONED, FINED OR HAVE THEIR ASSETS SEIZED.

THIS ORDER

1. This is a Freezing Injunction made against [ ] ("the Respondent") on [ ] by Mr Justice [ ] on the application of [ ] ("the Applicant"). **A3.12**

[8] Insert name of Respondent.

The Judge read the Affidavits listed in Schedule A and accepted the undertakings set out in Schedule B at the end of this Order.

2. This order was made at a hearing without notice to the Respondent. The Respondent has a right to apply to the court to vary or discharge the order—see paragraph 13 below.

3. There will be a further hearing in respect of this order on [ ] ("the return date").

4. If there is more than one Respondent—

   (a) unless otherwise stated, references in this order to "the Respondent" mean both or all of them; and
   (b) this order is effective against any Respondent on whom it is served or who is given notice of it.

FREEZING INJUNCTION

A3.13 [For injunction limited to assets in England and Wales]

5. Until the return date or further order of the court, the Respondent must not remove from England and Wales or in any way dispose of, deal with or diminish the value of any of his assets which are in England and Wales up to the value of £ .

[For worldwide injunction]

5. Until the return date or further order of the court, the Respondent must not—

   (1) remove from England and Wales any of his assets which are in England and Wales up to the value of £ ; or
   (2) in any way dispose of, deal with or diminish the value of any of his assets whether they are in or outside England and Wales up to the same value.

[For either form of injunction]

6. Paragraph 5 applies to all the Respondent's assets whether or not they are in his own name and whether they are solely or jointly owned. For the purpose of this order the Respondent's assets include any asset which he has the power, directly or indirectly, to dispose of or deal with as if it were his own. The Respondent is to be regarded as having such power if a third party holds or controls the asset in accordance with his direct or indirect instructions.

7. This prohibition includes the following assets in particular—

   (a) the property known as [title/address] or the net sale money after payment of any mortgages if it has been sold;

(b) the property and assets of the Respondent's business [known as [name]] [carried on at [address]] or the sale money if any of them have been sold; and

(c) any money standing to the credit of any bank account including the amount of any cheque drawn on such account which has not been cleared.

[For injunction limited to assets in England and Wales]

8. If the total value free of charges or other securities ("unencumbered value") of the Respondent's assets in England and Wales exceeds £ , the Respondent may remove any of those assets from England and Wales or may dispose of or deal with them so long as the total unencumbered value of his assets still in England and Wales remains above £ .

[For worldwide injunction]

8.(1) If the total value free of charges or other securities ("unencumbered value") of the Respondent's assets in England and Wales exceeds £ , the Respondent may remove any of those assets from England and Wales or may dispose of or deal with them so long as the total unencumbered value of the Respondent's assets still in England and Wales remains above £ .

(2) If the total unencumbered value of the Respondent's assets in England and Wales does not exceed £ , the Respondent must not remove any of those assets from England and Wales and must not dispose of or deal with any of them. If the Respondent has other assets outside England and Wales, he may dispose of or deal with those assets outside England and Wales so long as the total unencumbered value of all his assets whether in or outside England and Wales remains above £ .

PROVISION OF INFORMATION

9.(1) Unless paragraph (2) applies, the Respondent must [immediately] [within hours of service of this order] and to the best of his ability inform the Applicant's solicitors of all his assets [in England and Wales] [worldwide] [exceeding £ in value] whether in his own name or not and whether solely or jointly owned, giving the value, location and details of all such assets. **A3.14**

(2) If the provision of any of this information is likely to incriminate the Respondent, he may be entitled to refuse to provide it, but is recommended to take legal advice before refusing to provide the information. Wrongful refusal to provide the information is contempt of court and may render the Respondent liable to be imprisoned, fined or have his assets seized.

10. Within [ ] working days after being served with this order, the Respondent must swear and serve on the Applicant's solicitors an affidavit setting out the above information.

EXCEPTIONS TO THIS ORDER

A3.15 11.(1) This order does not prohibit the Respondent from spending £ a week towards his ordinary living expenses and also £ [*or* a reasonable sum] on legal advice and representation. [But before spending any money the Respondent must tell the Applicant's legal representatives where the money is to come from.]

[(2) This order does not prohibit the Respondent from dealing with or disposing of any of his assets in the ordinary and proper course of business.]

(3) The Respondent may agree with the Applicant's legal representatives that the above spending limits should be increased or that this order should be varied in any other respect, but any agreement must be in writing.

(4) The order will cease to have effect if the Respondent—

(a) provides security by paying the sum of £ into court, to be held to the order of the court; or

(b) makes provision for security in that sum by another method agreed with the Applicant's legal representatives.

COSTS

A3.16 12. The costs of this application are reserved to the judge hearing the application on the return date.

VARIATION OR DISCHARGE OF THIS ORDER

A3.17 13. Anyone served with or notified of this order may apply to the court at any time to vary or discharge this order (or so much of it as affects that person), but they must first inform the Applicant's solicitors. If any evidence is to be relied upon in support of the application, the substance of it must be communicated in writing to the Applicant's solicitors in advance.

INTERPRETATION OF THIS ORDER

A3.18 14. A Respondent who is an individual who is ordered not to do something must not do it himself or in any other way. He must not do it through others acting on his behalf or on his instructions or with his encouragement.

15. A Respondent which is not an individual which is ordered not to do something must not do it itself or by its directors, officers, partners, employees or agents or in any other way.

PARTIES OTHER THAN THE APPLICANT AND RESPONDENT

16. **Effect of this order** A3.19

It is a contempt of court for any person notified of this order knowingly to assist in or permit a breach of this order. Any person doing so may be imprisoned, fined or have their assets seized.

17. **Set off by banks**

This injunction does not prevent any bank from exercising any right of set off it may have in respect of any facility which it gave to the respondent before it was notified of this order.

18. **Withdrawals by the Respondent**

No bank need enquire as to the application or proposed application of any money withdrawn by the Respondent if the withdrawal appears to be permitted by this order.

[For worldwide injunction]

19. **Persons outside England and Wales**
   (1) Except as provided in paragraph (2) below, the terms of this order do not affect or concern anyone outside the jurisdiction of this court.
   (2) The terms of this order will affect the following persons in a country or state outside the jurisdiction of this court—

      (a) the Respondent or his officer or agent appointed by power of attorney;
      (b) any person who—
         (i) is subject to the jurisdiction of this court;
         (ii) has been given written notice of this order at his residence or place of business within the jurisdiction of this court; and
         (iii) is able to prevent acts or omissions outside the jurisdiction of this court which constitute or assist in a breach of the terms of this order; and
      (c) any other person, only to the extent that this order is declared enforceable by or is enforced by a court in that country or state.

[For worldwide injunction]

20. **Assets located outside England and Wales**

Nothing in this order shall, in respect of assets located outside England and Wales, prevent any third party from complying with—

(1) what it reasonably believes to be its obligations, contractual or otherwise, under the laws and obligations of the country or state in which those assets are situated or under the proper law of any contract between itself and the Respondent; and

(2) any orders of the courts of that country or state, provided that reasonable notice of any application for such an order is given to the Applicant's solicitors.

COMMUNICATIONS WITH THE COURT

A3.20 All communications to the court about this order should be sent to—

[Insert the address and telephone number of the appropriate Court Office]

If the order is made at the Royal Courts of Justice, communications should be addressed as follows—

Where the order is made in the Chancery Division

Room TM 505, Royal Courts of Justice, Strand, London WC2A 2LL quoting the case number. The telephone number is 0207 947 6754.

Where the order is made in the Queen's Bench Division

Room WG08, Royal Courts of Justice, Strand, London WC2A 2LL quoting the case number. The telephone number is 020 7947 6010.

Where the order is made in the Commercial Court

Room EB09, Royal Courts of Justice, Strand, London WC2A 2LL quoting the case number. The telephone number is 0207 947 6826.

The offices are open between 10 a.m. and 4.30 p.m. Monday to Friday.

SCHEDULE A

AFFIDAVITS

A3.21 The Applicant relied on the following affidavits—

[name] [number of affidavit] [date sworn] [filed on behalf of]

(1)

(2)

SCHEDULE B

UNDERTAKINGS GIVEN TO THE COURT BY THE APPLICANT

(1) If the court later finds that this order has caused loss to the Respondent, and decides that the Respondent should be compensated for that loss, the Applicant will comply with any order the court may make. **A3.22**

[(2) The Applicant will—

(a) on or before [*date*] cause a written guarantee in the sum of £ to be issued from a bank with a place of business within England or Wales, in respect of any order the court may make pursuant to paragraph (1) above; and

(b) immediately upon issue of the guarantee, cause a copy of it to be served on the Respondent.]

(3) As soon as practicable the Applicant will issue and serve a claim form [in the form of the draft produced to the court] [claiming the appropriate relief].

(4) The Applicant will [swear and file an affidavit] [cause an affidavit to be sworn and filed] [substantially in the terms of the draft affidavit produced to the court] [confirming the substance of what was said to the court by the Applicant's counsel/solicitors].

(5) The Applicant will serve upon the Respondent [together with this order] [as soon as practicable]—

(i) copies of the affidavits and exhibits containing the evidence relied upon by the Applicant, and any other documents provided to the court on the making of the application;

(ii) the claim form; and

(iii) an application notice for continuation of the order.

[(6) Anyone notified of this order will be given a copy of it by the Applicant's legal representatives.]

(7) The Applicant will pay the reasonable costs of anyone other than the Respondent which have been incurred as a result of this order including the costs of finding out whether that person holds any of the Respondent's assets and if the court later finds that this order has caused such person loss, and decides that such person should be compensated for that loss, the Applicant will comply with any order the court may make.

(8) If this order ceases to have effect (for example, if the Respondent provides security or the Applicant does not provide a bank guarantee as provided for above) the Applicant will immediately take all reasonable steps to inform in writing anyone to whom he has given notice of this order, or who he has reasonable grounds for supposing may act upon this order, that it has ceased to have effect.

[(9) The Applicant will not without the permission of the court use any information obtained as a result of this order for the purpose of any civil or criminal proceedings, either in England and Wales or in any other jurisdiction, other than this claim.]

[(10) The Applicant will not without the permission of the court seek to enforce this order in any country outside England and Wales [or seek an order of a similar nature including orders conferring a charge or other security against the Respondent or the Respondent's assets].]

NAME AND ADDRESS OF APPLICANT'S LEGAL REPRESENTATIVES

A3.23 The Applicant's legal representatives are—

[Name, address, reference, fax and telephone numbers both in and out of office hours and e-mail]

SEARCH ORDER

IN THE HIGH COURT OF JUSTICE
[ ] DIVISION

Before The Honourable Mr Justice [ ]

Claim No.
Dated

Applicant

Seal

Respondent

Name, address and reference of Respondent

PENAL NOTICE

IF YOU [ ][9] DISOBEY THIS ORDER YOU MAY BE HELD IN CONTEMPT OF COURT AND MAY BE IMPRISONED, FINED OR HAVE YOUR ASSETS SEIZED.

ANY OTHER PERSON WHO KNOWS OF THIS ORDER AND DOES ANYTHING WHICH HELPS OR PERMITS THE RESPONDENT TO BREACH THE TERMS OF THIS ORDER MAY ALSO BE HELD TO BE IN CONTEMPT OF COURT AND MAY BE IMPRISONED, FINED OR HAVE THEIR ASSETS SEIZED.

[9] Insert name of Respondent.

THIS ORDER

1. This is a Search Order made against [ ] ("the Respondent") on [ ] by Mr Justice [ ] on the application of [ ] ("the Applicant"). The Judge read the Affidavits listed in Schedule F and accepted the undertakings set out in Schedules C, D and E at the end of this order. **A3.24**

2. This order was made at a hearing without notice to the Respondent. The Respondent has a right to apply to the court to vary or discharge the order—see paragraph 27 below.

3. There will be a further hearing in respect of this order on [ ] ("the return date").

4. If there is more than one Respondent—

   (a) unless otherwise stated, references in this order to "the Respondent" mean both or all of them; and
   (b) this order is effective against any Respondent on whom it is served or who is given notice of it.

5. This order must be complied with by—

   (a) the Respondent;
   (b) any director, officer, partner or responsible employee of the Respondent; and
   (c) if the Respondent is an individual, any other person having responsible control of the premises to be searched.

THE SEARCH

6. The Respondent must permit the following persons[10]— **A3.25**

   (a) [ ] ("the Supervising Solicitor");
   (b) [ ], a solicitor in the firm of [ ], the Applicant's solicitors; and
   (c) up to [ ] other persons[11] being [*their identity or capacity*] accompanying them, (together "the search party"), to enter the premises mentioned in Schedule A to this order and any other premises of the Respondent disclosed under paragraph 18 below and any vehicles under the Respondent's control on or around the premises ("the premises") so that they can search for, inspect, photograph or photocopy, and deliver into the safekeeping of the Applicant's solicitors all the documents and articles which are listed in Schedule B to this order ("the listed items").

---

10 Where the premises are likely to be occupied by an unaccompanied woman and the Supervising Solicitor is a man, at least one of the persons accompanying him should be a woman.

11 None of these persons should be people who could gain personally or commercially from anything they might read or see on the premises, unless their presence is essential.

7. Having permitted the search party to enter the premises, the Respondent must allow the search party to remain on the premises until the search is complete. In the event that it becomes necessary for any of those persons to leave the premises before the search is complete, the Respondent must allow them to re-enter the premises immediately upon their seeking re-entry on the same or the following day in order to complete the search.

RESTRICTIONS ON SEARCH

A3.26

8. This order may not be carried out at the same time as a police search warrant.

9. Before the Respondent allows anybody onto the premises to carry out this order, he is entitled to have the Supervising Solicitor explain to him what it means in everyday language.

10. The Respondent is entitled to seek legal advice and to ask the court to vary or discharge this order. Whilst doing so, he may ask the Supervising Solicitor to delay starting the search for up to 2 hours or such other longer period as the Supervising Solicitor may permit. However, the Respondent must—

    (a) comply with the terms of paragraph 27 below;
    (b) not disturb or remove any listed items; and
    (c) permit the Supervising Solicitor to enter, but not start to search.

11.(1) Before permitting entry to the premises by any person other than the Supervising Solicitor, the Respondent may, for a short time (not to exceed two hours, unless the Supervising Solicitor agrees to a longer period)—

    (a) gather together any documents he believes may be incriminating or privileged; and
    (b) hand them to the Supervising Solicitor for him to assess whether they are incriminating or privileged as claimed.

(2) If the Supervising Solicitor decides that the Respondent is entitled to withhold production of any of the documents on the ground that they are privileged or incriminating, he will exclude them from the search, record them in a list for inclusion in his report and return them to the Respondent.

(3) If the Supervising Solicitor believes that the Respondent may be entitled to withhold production of the whole or any part of a document on the ground that it or part of it may be privileged or incriminating, or if the Respondent claims to be entitled to withhold production on those

grounds, the Supervising Solicitor will exclude it from the search and retain it in his possession pending further order of the court.

12. If the Respondent wishes to take legal advice and gather documents as permitted, he must first inform the Supervising Solicitor and keep him informed of the steps being taken.

13. No item may be removed from the premises until a list of the items to be removed has been prepared, and a copy of the list has been supplied to the Respondent, and he has been given a reasonable opportunity to check the list.

14. The premises must not be searched, and items must not be removed from them, except in the presence of the Respondent.

15. If the Supervising Solicitor is satisfied that full compliance with paragraphs 13 or 14 is not practicable, he may permit the search to proceed and items to be removed without fully complying with them.

DELIVERY UP OF ARTICLES/DOCUMENTS

16. The Respondent must immediately hand over to the Applicant's solicitors any of the listed items, which are in his possession or under his control, save for any computer or hard disk integral to any computer. Any items the subject of a dispute as to whether they are listed items must immediately be handed over to the Supervising Solicitor for safe keeping pending resolution of the dispute or further order of the court. **A3.27**

17. The Respondent must immediately give the search party effective access to the computers on the premises, with all necessary passwords, to enable the computers to be searched. If they contain any listed items the Respondent must cause the listed items to be displayed so that they can be read and copied[12]. The Respondent must provide the Applicant's Solicitors with copies of all listed items contained in the computers. All reasonable steps shall be taken by the Applicant and the Applicant's solicitors to ensure that no damage is done to any computer or data. The Applicant and his representatives may not themselves search the Respondent's computers unless they have sufficient expertise to do so without damaging the Respondent's system.

PROVISION OF INFORMATION

18. The Respondent must immediately inform the Applicant's Solicitors (in the presence of the Supervising Solicitor) so far as he is aware— **A3.28**

[12] If it is envisaged that the Respondent's computers are to be imaged (i.e. the hard drives are to be copied wholesale, thereby reproducing listed items and other items indiscriminately), special provision needs to be made and independent computer specialists need to be appointed, who should be required to give undertakings to the court.

(a) where all the listed items are;
(b) the name and address of everyone who has supplied him, or offered to supply him, with listed items;
(c) the name and address of everyone to whom he has supplied, or offered to supply, listed items; and
(d) full details of the dates and quantities of every such supply and offer.

19. Within [ ] working days after being served with this order the Respondent must swear and serve an affidavit setting out the above information[13].

PROHIBITED ACTS

A3.29 20. Except for the purpose of obtaining legal advice, the Respondent must not directly or indirectly inform anyone of these proceedings or of the contents of this order, or warn anyone that proceedings have been or may be brought against him by the Applicant until 4.30 p.m. on the return date or further order of the court.

21. Until 4.30 p.m. on the return date the Respondent must not destroy, tamper with, cancel or part with possession, power, custody or control of the listed items otherwise than in accordance with the terms of this order.

22. [Insert any negative injunctions.]

23. [Insert any further order].

COSTS

A3.30 24. The costs of this application are reserved to the judge hearing the application on the return date.

RESTRICTIONS ON SERVICE

A3.31 25. This order may only be served between [ ] a.m./p.m. and [ ] a.m./p.m. [and on a weekday][14].

26. This order must be served by the Supervising Solicitor, and paragraph 6 of the order must be carried out in his presence and under his supervision.

---

[13] The period should ordinarily be longer than the period in paragraph (2) of Schedule D, if any of the information is likely to be included in listed items taken away of which the Respondent does not have copies.

[14] Normally, the order should be served in the morning (not before 9.30 a.m.) and on a weekday to enable the Respondent more readily to obtain legal advice.

VARIATION AND DISCHARGE OF THIS ORDER

27. Anyone served with or notified of this order may apply to the court at any time to vary or discharge this order (or so much of it as affects that person), but they must first inform the Applicant's solicitors. If any evidence is to be relied upon in support of the application, the substance of it must be communicated in writing to the Applicant's solicitors in advance. **A3.32**

INTERPRETATION OF THIS ORDER

28. Any requirement that something shall be done to or in the presence of the Respondent means— **A3.33**

    (a) if there is more than one Respondent, to or in the presence of any one of them; and
    (b) if a Respondent is not an individual, to or in the presence of a director, officer, partner or responsible employee.

29. A Respondent who is an individual who is ordered not to do something must not do it himself or in any other way. He must not do it through others acting on his behalf or on his instructions or with his encouragement.

30. A Respondent which is not an individual which is ordered not to do something must not do it itself or by its directors, officers, partners, employees or agents or in any other way.

COMMUNICATIONS WITH THE COURT **A3.34**

All communications to the court about this order should be sent to—

[Insert the address and telephone number of the appropriate Court Office]

If the order is made at the Royal Courts of Justice, communications should be addressed as follows—

Where the order is made in the Chancery Division

Room TM 505, Royal Courts of Justice, Strand, London WC2A 2LL quoting the case number. The telephone number is 0207 947 6754.

Where the order is made in the Queen's Bench Division

Room WG08, Royal Courts of Justice, Strand, London WC2A 2LL quoting the case number. The telephone number is 020 7947 6010.

Where the order is made in the Commercial Court

Room EB09, Royal Courts of Justice, Strand, London WC2A 2LL quoting the case number. The telephone number is 0207 947 6826.

The offices are open between 10 a.m. and 4.30 p.m. Monday to Friday.

SCHEDULE A

A3.35 THE PREMISES

SCHEDULE B

A3.36 THE LISTED ITEMS

SCHEDULE C

A3.37 UNDERTAKINGS GIVEN TO THE COURT BY THE APPLICANT

(1) If the court later finds that this order or carrying it out has caused loss to the Respondent, and decides that the Respondent should be compensated for that loss, the Applicant will comply with any order the court may make. Further if the carrying out of this order has been in breach of the terms of this order or otherwise in a manner inconsistent with the Applicant's solicitors' duties as officers of the court, the Applicant will comply with any order for damages the court may make.

[(2) As soon as practicable the Applicant will issue a claim form [in the form of the draft produced to the court] [claiming the appropriate relief].]

(3) The Applicant will [swear and file an affidavit] [cause an affidavit to be sworn and filed] [substantially in the terms of the draft affidavit produced to the court] [confirming the substance of what was said to the court by the Applicant's counsel/solicitors].

(4) The Applicant will not, without the permission of the court, use any information or documents obtained as a result of carrying out this order nor inform anyone else of these proceedings except for the purposes of these proceedings (including adding further Respondents) or commencing civil proceedings in relation to the same or related subject matter to these proceedings until after the return date.

[(5) The Applicant will maintain pending further order the sum of £[ ] in an account controlled by the Applicant's solicitors.]

[(6) The Applicant will insure the items removed from the premises.]

SCHEDULE D

A3.38 UNDERTAKINGS GIVEN BY THE APPLICANT'S SOLICITORS

(1) The Applicant's solicitors will provide to the Supervising Solicitor for service on the Respondent—

(i) a service copy of this order;
(ii) the claim form (with defendant's response pack) or, if not issued, the draft produced to the court;
(iii) an application for hearing on the return date;
(iv) copies of the affidavits [*or draft aYdavits*] and exhibits capable of being copied containing the evidence relied upon by the applicant;
(v) a note of any allegation of fact made orally to the court where such allegation is not contained in the affidavits or draft affidavits read by the judge; and
(vi) a copy of the skeleton argument produced to the court by the Applicant's [counsel/solicitors].

(2) The Applicants' solicitors will answer at once to the best of their ability any question whether a particular item is a listed item.

(3) Subject as provided below the Applicant's solicitors will retain in their own safe keeping all items obtained as a result of this order until the court directs otherwise.

(4) The Applicant's solicitors will return the originals of all documents obtained as a result of this order (except original documents which belong to the Applicant) as soon as possible and in any event within [two] working days of their removal.

SCHEDULE E

UNDERTAKINGS GIVEN BY THE SUPERVISING SOLICITOR **A3.39**

(1) The Supervising Solicitor will use his best endeavours to serve this order upon the Respondent and at the same time to serve upon the Respondent the other documents required to be served and referred to in paragraph (1) of Schedule D.

(2) The Supervising Solicitor will offer to explain to the person served with the order its meaning and effect fairly and in everyday language, and to inform him of his right to take legal advice (including an explanation that the Respondent may be entitled to avail himself of the privilege against self-incrimination and legal professional privilege) and to apply to vary or discharge this order as mentioned in paragraph 27 above.

(3) The Supervising Solicitor will retain in the safe keeping of his firm all items retained by him as a result of this order until the court directs otherwise.

(4) Unless and until the court otherwise orders, or unless otherwise necessary to comply with any duty to the court pursuant to this order, the Supervising Solicitor shall not disclose to any person any information relating to those items, and shall keep the existence of such items confidential.

(5) Within [48] hours of completion of the search the Supervising Solicitor will make and provide to the Applicant's solicitors, the Respondent or his solicitors and to the judge who made this order (for the purposes of the court file) a written report on the carrying out of the order.

SCHEDULE F

A3.40 AFFIDAVITS

The Applicant relied on the following affidavits—

[name] [number of affidavit] [date sworn] [filed on behalf of]

(1)

(2)

NAME AND ADDRESS OF APPLICANT'S SOLICITORS

A3.41 The Applicant's solicitors are—

[Name, address, reference, fax and telephone numbers both in and out of office hours.]

Appendix 4

Practice direction—applications

This practice direction supplements CPR Part 23

Contents of this Practice Direction

REFERENCE TO A JUDGE

A4.1 1 A Master or district judge may refer to a judge any matter which he thinks should properly be decided by a judge, and the judge may either dispose of the matter or refer it back to the Master or district judge.

APPLICATION NOTICES

A4.2 2.1 An application notice must, in addition to the matters set out in rule 23.6, be signed and include:

(1) the title of the claim,
(2) the reference number of the claim,
(3) the full name of the applicant,
(4) where the applicant is not already a party, his address for service, including a postcode. Postcode information may be obtained from www.royalmail.com or the Royal Mail Address Management Guide, and
(5) either a request for a hearing or a request that the application be dealt with without a hearing.

(Practice Form N244 may be used.)

2.2 On receipt of an application notice containing a request for a hearing the court will notify the applicant of the time and date for the hearing of the application.

2.3 On receipt of an application notice containing a request that the application be dealt with without a hearing, the application notice will be sent to a Master or district judge so that he may decide whether the application is suitable for consideration without a hearing.

2.4 Where the Master or district judge agrees that the application is suitable for consideration without a hearing, the court will so inform the applicant and the respondent and may give directions for the filing of evidence. (Rules 23.9 and 23.10 enable a party to apply for an order made without a hearing to be set aside or varied.)

2.5 Where the Master or district judge does not agree that the application is suitable for consideration without a hearing, the court will notify the applicant and the respondent of the time, date and place for the hearing of the application and may at the same time give directions as to the filing of evidence.

2.6 If the application is intended to be made to a judge, the application notice should so state. In that case, paragraphs 2.3, 2.4 and 2.5 will apply as though references to the Master or district judge were references to a judge.

2.7 Every application should be made as soon as it becomes apparent that it is necessary or desirable to make it.

2.8 Applications should wherever possible be made so that they can be considered at any other hearing for which a date has already been fixed or for which a date is about to be fixed. This is particularly so in relation to case management conferences, allocation and listing hearings and pre-trial reviews fixed by the court.

2.9 The parties must anticipate that at any hearing the court may wish to review the conduct of the case as a whole and give any necessary case management directions. They should be ready to assist the court in doing so and to answer questions the court may ask for this purpose.

2.10 Where a date for a hearing has been fixed and a party wishes to make an application at that hearing but he does not have sufficient time to serve an application notice he should inform the other party and the court (if possible in writing) as soon as he can of the nature of the application and the reason for it. He should then make the application orally at the hearing.

APPLICATIONS WITHOUT SERVICE OF APPLICATION NOTICE

3 An application may be made without serving an application notice only: **A4.3**

(1) where there is exceptional urgency,
(2) where the overriding objective is best furthered by doing so,
(3) by consent of all parties,
(4) with the permission of the court,
(5) where paragraph 2.10 above applies, or
(6) where a court order, rule or practice direction permits.

GIVING NOTICE OF AN APPLICATION

4.1 Unless the court otherwise directs or paragraph 3 of this practice direction applies the application notice must be served as soon as practicable after it has been issued and, if there is to be a hearing, at least 3 clear days before the hearing date (rule 23.7(1)(b)). **A4.4**

4.2 Where an application notice should be served but there is not sufficient time to do so, informal notification of the application should be given unless the circumstances of the application require secrecy.

PRE-ACTION APPLICATIONS

5 All applications made before a claim is commenced should be made under Part 23 of the Civil Procedure Rules. Attention is drawn in particular to rule 23.2(4). **A4.5**

TELEPHONE HEARINGS

Interpretation

A4.6 6.1 In this paragraph—

(a) "designated legal representative" means the applicant's legal representative (if any), or the legal representative of such other party as the court directs to arrange the telephone hearing; and
(b) "telephone conference enabled court" means—

(i) a district registry of the High Court; or
(ii) a county court,
in which telephone conferencing facilities are available.

When a hearing is to be conducted by telephone

6.2 Subject to paragraph 6.3, at a telephone conference enabled court the following hearings will be conducted by telephone unless the court otherwise orders—

(a) allocation hearings;
(b) listing hearings; and
(c) interim applications, case management conferences and pre-trial reviews with a time estimate of less than one hour.

6.3 Paragraph 6.2 does not apply where—

(a) the hearing is of an application made without notice to the other party;
(b) all the parties are unrepresented; or
(c) more than four parties wish to make representations at the hearing (for this purpose where two or more parties are represented by the same person, they are to be treated as one party).

6.4 A request for a direction that a hearing under paragraph 6.2 should not be conducted by telephone—

(a) must be made at least 7 days before the hearing or such shorter time as the court may permit; and
(b) may be made by letter,
and the court shall determine such request without requiring the attendance of the parties.

6.5 The court may order that an application, or part of an application, to which paragraph 6.2 does not apply be dealt with by a telephone hearing. The court may make such order—

(a) of its own initiative; or
(b) at the request of the parties.

6.6 The applicant should indicate on his application notice if he seeks a court order under paragraph 6.5. Where he has not done so but nevertheless wishes to seek an order, the request should be made as early as possible.

6.7 An order under paragraph 6.5 will not normally be made unless every party entitled to be given notice of the application and to be heard at the hearing has consented to the order.

6.8 If the court makes an order under paragraph 6.5 it will give any directions necessary for the telephone hearing.

Conduct of the telephone hearing

6.9 No party, or representative of a party, to an application being heard by telephone may attend the judge in person while the application is being heard unless every other party to the application has agreed that he may do so.

6.10 If an application is to be heard by telephone the following directions will apply, subject to any direction to the contrary—

(1) The designated legal representative is responsible for arranging the telephone conference for precisely the time fixed by the court. The telecommunications provider used must be one on the approved panel of service providers (see Her Majesty's Courts Service website at www.hmcourts-service.gov.uk).

(2) The designated legal representative must tell the operator the telephone numbers of all those participating in the conference call and the sequence in which they are to be called.

(3) It is the responsibility of the designated legal representative to ascertain from all the other parties whether they have instructed counsel and, if so, the identity of counsel, and whether the legal representative and counsel will be on the same or different telephone numbers.

(4) The sequence in which they are to be called will be—

(a) the designated legal representative and (if on a different number) his counsel;

(b) the legal representative (and counsel) for all other parties; and

(c) the judge.

(5) Each speaker is to remain on the line after being called by the operator setting up the conference call. The call shall be connected at least ten minutes before the time fixed for the hearing.

(6) When the judge has been connected the designated legal representative (or his counsel) will introduce the parties in the usual way.

(7) If the use of a "speakerphone" by any party causes the judge or any other party any difficulty in hearing what is said the judge may require that party to use a hand held telephone.

(8) The telephone charges debited to the account of the party initiating the conference call will be treated as part of the costs of the application.

Documents

6.11 The designated legal representative must file and serve a case summary and draft order no later than 4pm on the last working day before the hearing—

(a) if the claim has been allocated to the multi-track; and
(b) in any other case, if the court so directs.

6.12 Where a party seeks to rely on any other document at the hearing, he must file and serve the document no later than 4 p.m. on the last working day before the hearing.

VIDEO CONFERENCING

A4.7 7 Where the parties to a matter wish to use video conferencing facilities, and those facilities are available in the relevant court, they should apply to the Master or district judge for directions.

(Paragraph 29 and Annex 3 of Practice Direction 32 provide guidance on the use of video conferencing in the civil courts)

NOTE OF PROCEEDINGS

A4.8 8 The procedural judge should keep, either by way of a note or a tape recording, brief details of all proceedings before him, including the dates of the proceedings and a short statement of the decision taken at each hearing.

EVIDENCE

A4.9 9.1 The requirement for evidence in certain types of applications is set out in some of the rules and practice directions. Where there is no specific requirement to provide evidence it should be borne in mind that, as a practical matter, the court will often need to be satisfied by evidence of the facts that are relied on in support of or for opposing the application.

9.2 The court may give directions for the filing of evidence in support of or opposing a particular application. The court may also give directions for the filing of evidence in relation to any hearing that it fixes on its own initiative. The directions may specify the form that evidence is to take and when it is to be served.

9.3 Where it is intended to rely on evidence which is not contained in the application itself, the evidence, if it has not already been served, should be served with the application.

9.4 Where a respondent to an application wishes to rely on evidence which has not yet been served he should serve it as soon as possible and in any event in accordance with any directions the court may have given.

9.5 If it is necessary for the applicant to serve any evidence in reply it should be served as soon as possible and in any event in accordance with any directions the court may have given.

9.6 Evidence must be filed with the court as well as served on the parties. Exhibits should not be filed unless the court otherwise directs.

9.7 The contents of an application notice may be used as evidence (otherwise than at trial) provided the contents have been verified by a statement of truth[1].

CONSENT ORDERS

10.1 Rule 40.6 sets out the circumstances where an agreed judgment or order may be entered and sealed. **A4.10**

10.2 Where all parties affected by an order have written to the court consenting to the making of the order a draft of which has been filed with the court, the court will treat the draft as having been signed in accordance with rule 40.6(7).

10.3 Where a consent order must be made by a judge (i.e. rule 40.6(2) does not apply) the order must be drawn so that the judge's name and judicial title can be inserted.

10.4 The parties to an application for a consent order must ensure that they provide the court with any material it needs to be satisfied that it is appropriate to make the order. Subject to any rule or practice direction a letter will generally be acceptable for this purpose.

10.5 Where a judgment or order has been agreed in respect of an application or claim where a hearing date has been fixed, the parties must inform the court immediately. (Note that parties are reminded that under rules 28.4 and 29.5 the case management timetable cannot be varied by written agreement of the parties.)

OTHER APPLICATIONS CONSIDERED WITHOUT A HEARING

11.1 Where rule 23.8(b) applies the parties should so inform the court in writing and each should confirm that all evidence and other material on which he relies has been disclosed to the other parties to the application. **A4.11**

[1] See Part 22.

11.2 Where rule 23.8(c) applies the court will treat the application as if it were proposing to make an order on its own initiative.

Applications to stay claim where related criminal proceedings

A4.12 11A.1 An application for the stay of civil proceedings pending the determination of related criminal proceedings may be made by any party to the civil proceedings or by the prosecutor or any defendant in the criminal proceedings.

11A.2 Every party to the civil proceedings must, unless he is the applicant, be made a respondent to the application.

11A.3 The evidence in support of the application must contain an estimate of the expected duration of the stay and must identify the respects in which the continuance of the civil proceedings may prejudice the criminal trial.

11A.4 In order to make an application under paragraph 11A.1, it is not necessary for the prosecutor or defendant in the criminal proceedings to be joined as a party to the civil proceedings.

MISCELLANEOUS

A4.13 12.1 Except in the most simple application the applicant should bring to any hearing a draft of the order sought. If the case is proceeding in the Royal Courts of Justice and the order is unusually long or complex it should also be supplied on disk for use by the court office.

12.2 Where rule 23.11 applies, the power to re-list the application in rule 23.11(2) is in addition to any other powers of the court with regard to the order (for example to set aside, vary, discharge or suspend the order).

COSTS

A4.14 13.1 Attention is drawn to the costs practice direction and, in particular, to the court's power to make a summary assessment of costs.

13.2 Attention is also drawn to rule 44.13(i) which provides that if an order makes no mention of costs, none are payable in respect of the proceedings to which it relates.

Appendix 5—Precedents

A. Commercial Agreements

PRECEDENTS AND DRAFTING NOTES

1. NON-COMPETE UNDERTAKINGS BY SELLER

[A. Protecting business know-how and goodwill]

1.1 The Seller undertakes to the Buyer, for itself and as agent and trustee[1] for [the Company/each Group Company], that it will not do any of the following things: **A5.1**

1.1.1 for a period of [X] years[2] starting on the date of this Agreement,[3] either alone or jointly with, through or as adviser to, or agent of, or manager for, any person directly or indirectly carry on or be engaged, concerned or interested in or assist a business which competes,[4] directly or indirectly, with a business[5] of [the Company/a Group Company] as carried on at the date of this Agreement [or at any time in the twelve months prior to that

[1] The clause is drafted on the basis that the target Company is not a party to the Sale Agreement and that the Buyer takes the benefit of the non-compete undertakings. The Buyer can therefore enforce the non-compete undertakings on behalf of itself, but also on behalf of the Company or any Group Company (in case the level of damages recoverable would otherwise be less). This agency and trustee arrangement must be terminated by the Buyer before the Company or Group Company is sold to a third party to avoid being compelled to enforce an action against the Seller in respect of a breach once the third party sale has been completed. This agency and trustee arrangement is used as an alternative to granting rights to the Company/each Group Company pursuant to Contract (Rights of Third Parties) Act 1999.

[2] The restriction must apply for a reasonable period only. (See Chapter 12.)

[3] A buyer is entitled to protect the goodwill of the Company it acquires; hence it should be from the date the purchase takes place. Restrictions which are triggered at a later date may be unenforceable, subject to special circumstances and further considerations, (e.g. deferred consideration or earn-out).

[4] Alternatively the clause can be drafted with reference to a Competing Business and then define what the parties consider to be a Competing Business.

[5] The restriction must be limited to the business being sold and not include the Buyer's business. (See Chapter 12.)

date] in a territory[6] in which that business is or was carried on at any such date [or time];

Note It is possible to include as part of the non-compete provisions an obligation for any Seller's Group Company to offer to sell to the Buyer any business acquired after completion, where the Competing Business only represents a small part of the Seller's new target company. It could be agreed that such a competing business is offered to the Buyer at a fair market value and on fair and reasonable terms. However note that following the CA in iSoft Group plc v Misys Holdings Ltd and Misys plc [28.02.03] this type of clause is likely to be very difficult to enforce on the basis that it is an unenforceable agreement to negotiate. In the judgment it was suggested that the chances of such a clause being held to be enforceable by a court would be improved by including in the drafting some suitable machinery for settling disputes as to the terms of the acquisition (or some objective criteria for a court to use).

[B. Protecting goodwill expressly]

A5.2 1.1.2 for a period of [X] years starting on the date of this Agreement, do or say anything which is harmful to [the Company's/a Group Company's] goodwill (as subsisting at the date of this Agreement) or which may lead a person who has dealt with [the Company/a Group Company] at any time during the [twelve months] prior to the date of this Agreement to cease to deal with [the Company/a Group Company] on substantially equivalent terms to those previously offered or at all;

[Note: Part of the target Company's Goodwill will be tied up in the Company's trading name and any brand names of its products. Provisions relating to trademarks will also need to be included in the Agreement.]

1.1.3 no Seller shall at any time after the date of this Agreement use in any manner in the course of any business, or (so far as within its power) permit or encourage to be used other than by the Company, the names [XYZ], or any other trade or business name or any mark, sign or logo used by the Company or any confusing similar name, mark, sign or logo, or present itself or permit itself to be presented as in any way connected with the Company or interested in the shares.

[6] The area in which the restriction is to operate should not be too wide. If there is any doubt where the company actually operates, make the geographical extent of the prohibition clear by defining Territory. (See Chapter 12.)

[C. Protecting customer relationships]

1.1.4 for a period of [X] years starting on the date of this Agreement, on its own account or in conjunction with or on behalf of any other person in respect of the products or services of a business of [the Company/a Group Company] either seek to obtain orders from, or do business with, or encourage directly or indirectly another person to obtain orders from or do business with, a person who has been a customer of that business at any time during the [twelve months] prior to the date of this Agreement for the products or services of that business in its territory of operation; **A5.3**

[D. Protecting supplier relationships]

1.1.5 for a period of [X] years starting on the date of this Agreement, seek to contract with or engage (in such a way as to affect adversely a business of [the Company/a Group Company] as carried on at the date of this Agreement) a person who has been contracted with or engaged to manufacture, assemble, supply or deliver goods or services to that business at any time during the [twelve months] prior to the date of this Agreement; [or] **A5.4**

[E. Non-applicability of non-compete clause to share investments]

1.2 Nothing contained in clause 1.1 shall preclude or restrict the [Seller or any Seller's Group Company/Seller's Group Undertaking] from holding not more than [three] per cent[7] of the issued share capital of any company whose shares are listed on a recognised stock exchange. **A5.5**

Note: Under EU and UK competition law ancillary restrictions to a merger must be "directly related and necessary". Clauses which limit a Seller from holding shares in a competitor for investment purposes without granting him management function or a material influence over the company is not considered to be ancillary and therefore they could be open to challenge under Article 81(1) EC. See paras 21.14.2 [EU] and 22.4.1 [UK]. See also under common law Connors Brothers Ltd v Connors [1940] 4 All E.R. 179, para.12.2.1.

1.3 The Seller undertakes to the Buyer, for itself and as agent and trustee for [the Company/each Group Company], that it will not do any of the following things:

[7] Companies Act 1985, s 199 sets the minimum disclosable interest at 3% which is why it is often taken as the starting point for negotiations. 3%–5% is what is usually included for share investments, certainly below 10% which is the threshold at which a company could be deemed to have acquired "material influence" by the OFT under the Enterprise Act 2003.

[F. Non-solicitation of employees]

A5.6 1.3.1 for a period of [X] years starting on the date of this Agreement directly or indirectly solicit or contact with a view to his engagement or employment by another person, a director, officer or manager of [the Company/a Group Company] or a person who was a director, officer or manager of [the Company/a Group Company] at any time during the [twelve months] prior to the date of this Agreement, in either case where the person in question either has Confidential Information [or Knowhow] or would be in a position to exploit [the Company's/a Group Company's] trade connections; [or]

[G. Non-engagement of former employees]

A5.7 1.3.2 for a period of [X] years starting on the date of this Agreement, engage or employ a director, officer or manager of [the Company/a Group Company] or a person who was a director, officer or manager of [the Company/a Group Company] at any time during the [twelve months] prior to the date of this Agreement, in either case where the person in question either has Confidential Information [or knowhow] or would be in a position to exploit [the Company's/a Group Company's] trade connections; [or]

Note: *This clause needs to be limited to senior employees who would actually have or can be assumed to have confidential knowledge about the business. The enforceability of these clauses may be strengthened by identifying the relevant employees by name.*

[H. Confidential information]

A5.8 1.4 The Seller undertakes to the Buyer, for itself and as agent and trustee for [the Company/each Group Company], that before and after Completion the Seller shall:

1.4.1 not use or disclose to any person Confidential Information it has or acquires;

1.4.2 make every effort to prevent the use or disclosure of Confidential Information; and

1.4.3 ensure that each Seller's Group Undertaking complies with clauses 1.4.1 and 1.4.2

1.5 Clause 1.4 does not apply to disclosure of Confidential Information:

1.5.1 to a director, officer or employee of the Buyer or of [the Company/a Group Company] whose function requires him to have the Confidential Information;

1.5.2 required to be disclosed by law, by a rule of a listing authority by which the Seller's shares are listed, a stock exchange on which the Seller's shares are listed or traded or by a governmental authority or other authority with relevant powers to which the Seller is subject or submits, whether or not the requirement has the force of law provided that the disclosure shall [so far as is practicable] be made after consultation with the Buyer and after taking into account the Buyer's [reasonable] requirements as to its timing, content and manner of making or despatch; or

1.5.3 to a professional adviser for the purpose of advising the Seller in connection with the transactions contemplated by this Agreement provided that such disclosure is essential for these purposes and is on the basis that clause [ ] applies to the disclosure to the adviser.

Note 1: Confidential Information will need to be defined taking into account the business being sold and include trade secrets. It should exclude any information which is public by consent of the Buyer.

Note 2: Where the Company is an integral member of the Seller's Group before the transaction, the Seller may argue for mutual confidentiality undertakings (i.e. that the Buyer should also provide such undertakings) on the basis that it is essential to protect the integrity of the Group's Confidential Information which comes into the Buyer's possession about the Seller's retained group.

1.6 The Seller shall ensure that each [Seller's Group Company/Seller's Group Undertaking] complies with clauses 1.1, 1.2, 1.3 and 1.4.[8]

[I. Severability]

1.7 Each undertaking in clause [1.1] [1.2, 1.3 and 1.4] constitutes an entirely independent undertaking and if one or more of the undertakings is held to be against the public interest or unlawful or in any way an unreasonable restraint of trade the remaining undertaking shall continue to bind the Seller [or the parties].[9] **A5.9**

Alternatively:

1.8 The invalidity, illegality or unenforceability of a provision of this Agreement does not affect or impair the continuation in force of the remainder of this Agreement.

Note: Always bear in mind that a severability provision of this nature can be very dangerous because of the uncertainty as to the potential

[8] Consider whether a parent company of the Seller should be asked to enter into non-compete undertakings for itself and its other subsidiaries directly with the Buyer.

[9] Where the court applies the "blue pencil test" it can delete those aspects of the provision which are void, leaving the remainder in place, provided what remains of the wording after deletion of the unenforceable language stands on its own (see para.3.5).

provisions which may be found to be invalid. Such a provision risks imposing on one or other of the parties an obligation to continue to observe an agreement in circumstances where its rights under it may have been severely diminished or the agreement has otherwise fundamentally changed.

An alternative to a severance clause is to include a clause which provides for re-drafting:

1.9 If a provision of this Agreement becomes invalid, illegal or unenforceable the parties shall negotiate in good faith to agree on a mutually satisfactory provision to be substituted for that provision which as nearly as possible gives effects to their intentions as expressed in this Agreement. This Agreement terminates automatically if the parties fail to agree on a substitute provision within [ ] of the start of negotiations. During negotiations each party's obligations under this Agreement are suspended.

Note: An alternative to a severance clause is an agreement for the parties to replace the unenforceable provision with one that is enforceable. However it should be noted that a provision of this nature will be of little legal effect since it is essentially an agreement to negotiate.

1.10 Each of the Buyer and the Seller confirms that it has received independent legal advice relating to all the matters provided for in this Agreement, including the provisions of this clause. The parties agree that they consider that the restrictions contained in this clause are no greater than is reasonable and necessary for the protection of the interests of the Buyer Group and the Seller Group but if any such restriction is found by any court of competent jurisdiction to go beyond what is reasonable in all circumstances but would be adjudged reasonable if deleted in part or reduced or limited in a particular manner, such restriction shall apply with such deletion or modification as may be necessary to render it valid and enforceable.

Note: Making it clear the parties have received legal advice may go some way to encouraging the Courts to uphold what the parties considered commercially necessary and reasonable. It may also assist a defendant in arguing the in pari delicto rule.[10]

[10] Chapter 21, para.21.10 on *Courage Ltd v Crehan* and the *in pari delicto rule*.

B. Employment Contracts

1. **Whole time and attention**

   The employee shall unless prevented by sickness, injury or other incapacity during the term of his/her employment devote the whole of his/her time attention and abilities exclusively to the business and affairs of the employer [and any Associated Company] for which he/she is required to perform duties. **A5.10**

Note: The main purpose of this type of clause is to clarify the duty of the employee with regard to his or her spare time although it is clearly strengthens the employee's obligations during his or her hours of employment. See Symbian Ltd v Christensen [2001] IRLR 77. In circumstances where garden leave is imposed it also prevents the employee from working for a third party whilst on garden leave. It is usually coupled with a clause such as that set out below governing competition during employment.

2. **Duty of the employee not to compete during employment**

   The employee shall not during the continuance of his/her employment (including any period of suspension or exclusion in accordance with clause [specify garden leave provision]) without the prior written consent of the employer directly or indirectly carry or being engaged concerned or interested in any other business trade or occupation which is similar to or in competition with the business of the employer [or any Associated Company] otherwise than as a holder directly or through nominees of not more than [1] percent in aggregate of any class of shares debentures or other securities in issues from time to time of any company which are for the time being quoted or dealt in on any recognised investment exchange (as defined by section 285 of the Financial Services and Markets Act 2000). **A5.11**

Note: Whilst this clause will usually be justifiable because it covers the same ground as the employee's duty of fidelity, care should be taken if the employee is a part-time worker because it could then amount to a restraint of trade. It is important to draft such a provision to include associated companies or employers (with a definition) if the employee may be transferred, seconded or otherwise required to undertake duties for other companies or employers in the same group. The carve out in relation to shareholdings is common in contracts for more senior grades of employee where other restrictions in the contract might restrict the employee's right to hold private investments.

3. **Confidentiality during and after employment**

A5.12 (A) The employee shall not at any time (either during or after the termination of the employment) disclose or communicate to any person, firm or company or use for his/her own benefit or the benefit of any person, firm or company any confidential information concerning the business dealings affairs or conduct of the employer [or any Associated Company] its staff or business partners or any similar confidential matters which may come to his/her knowledge in the course of the employment and shall during the continuance of the employment use his/her best endeavours to prevent the unauthorised publication or misuse of any confidential information.

(B) The restrictions in clause (A) shall not apply to any:

1. disclosure or use arising in the proper performance of the employee's duties;
2. disclosure or use previously authorised in writing by the employer;
3. information already in the public domain provided that the employee is not in a position to use that information more readily than others who have not worked for the employer [or any Associated Company].

(C) For the avoidance of doubt and without prejudice to the generality of clause (A) the following is a non-exhaustive list of matters which in relation to the employer [and its Associated Companies] are considered confidential and must be treated as such by the employee:

1. any trade secrets of the employer [or any Associated Company];
2. any information in respect of which the employer [or any Associated Company] is bound by an obligation of confidence to any third party;
3. unpublished and price sensitive information relating to securities listed on any recognised stock exchange;
4. the movements and whereabouts of all personnel or private matters concerning employees and directors;
5. marketing strategies and plans;
6. customer lists and details of contacts with or requirements of customers;

7. pricing strategies;
8. discount rates and sales figures;
9. details of suppliers and rates of charge;
10. information which has been supplied in confidence by clients, customers of suppliers;
11. any other information treated as confidential by the employer on a day-to-day basis including computer software data and pass words;
12. information and details of and concerning the engagement employment and termination of employment of the employers personnel;
13. information concerning any litigation proposed in progress or settled;
14. any invention, technical data, know-how or other manufacturing or trade secrets of the employer [or any Associated Company] and [its] [their] clients or customers; and
15. any other information made available to the employee which is identified to him/her as being of a confidential nature.

Note: Although this is not necessary, the above confidentiality provision does have, by way of an example, an indicative but non-exhaustive list of what constitutes confidential information and it may be prudent to incorporate such a non-exhaustive list, tailored to the business secrets of the particular employer, in appropriate cases. This is also best supported and supplemented by a proper system of classifying distributing and safeguarding information generated in the course of the employer conducting its business (e.g. marking documents appropriately, confining circulation to appropriate personnel etc.).

4. **Garden leave**

(A) The employer may notwithstanding any other provision of this Agreement direct that the employee perform no duties and/or that the employee does not enter all or any premises of the employer [or any Associated Company] for any period not exceeding [number] months [at any time after either party gives notice of termination of the employment pursuant to any provision of this Agreement] provided that throughout any such period the employee's salary and other contractual benefits continue to be paid or provided by the employer [and provided further that at any time during such period the employee shall at the request of the employer immediately resign without claim for compensation from office as a director of the employer [and any Associated Company] and from any other office held by him/her in the **A5.13** employer [or any Associated Company] and in the event of his/her failure to do so the employer is hereby irrevocably authorised to appoint some person in his/her name and on his/her behalf to sign and deliver such resignations to the employer]. The employer reserves the right to require the employee to take any holiday entitlement to which he/she may be entitled during any period that the employee is directed to perform no duties and/or is directed not to enter all or any premises of the employer [or any Associated Company] pursuant to this Clause.

(B) During any period of suspension or exclusion, the employee must continue to comply without exception with all his/her express and implied obligations under this Agreement including, without limitation, his/her duty of fidelity and good faith.

Note: *The above is tailored for use in relation to a more senior employee but can be adapted for use in relation to any level of employee. Where the employee is entitled to a long notice period consideration should be given to providing for a reduced period of time which may be required to be spent on garden leave to minimise the risk that, although the employer is relying on express provision, the court applying the same requirements to this type of provision as to restrictive covenants may hold the period to be unreasonable. See William Hill Organisation Ltd v Tucker [1998] IRLR 313. It is also prudent to provide for a set off between any period of time spent on garden leave and the duration of any restrictive covenants. See Credit Suisse First Boston v Padiachy [1998] IRLR 504. Care should also be exercised in using a garden leave provision in circumstances where neither party has given notice. The exercise of the right will arguably be tempered and controlled by the implied "trust and confidence" term in all contacts of employment see TFS Derivatives Ltd. v Morgan [2005] I.R.L.R 246, and if the employer has no good business reason for invoking the provision, this may constitute a breach of the implied term entitling the employee to resign and claim constructive dismissal (freeing him in the process from any restrictive covenants). If an employee is remunerated in part by a bonus or commission the provision should be drafted such that the employee remains entitled to continue to receive such payments so that garden leave does not result in financial detriment and, again, the risk of constructive dismissal. See further the discussion on garden leave provisions in chapter 23, paragraph 23.10.*

5. **Intellectual and other property**

A5.14 (A) If at any time in the course of the employment the employee makes or discovers or participates in the making of discovery of any Intellectual Property relating to or capable of being used in the business of the employer [or any Associated Company] (subject to the relevant provisions of the Patents Act 1977, the Registered Designs Act 1949 and the Copyright Designs and Patents Act 1988) the employee shall immediately disclose full details of such Intellectual Property to the employer and at the request and expense of the employer shall do all things which may be necessary or desirable for obtaining appropriate forms of protection for the Intellectual Property in such parts of the world as may be specified by the employer and vesting all rights in the same in the employer [or any Associated Company] or a company nominated by the employer.

(B) The employee hereby irrevocably appoints the employer to be his/her agent in his/her name and on his/her behalf to sign any instrument, execute or do any act and generally use his/her name for the purpose of giving to the employer or its nominee the full benefit of the provisions of this clause and in favour of any third party a certificate in writing signed by any director or the secretary of the employer that any instrument or act falls within the authority conferred by this clause shall be conclusive evidence that such is the case.

(C) The employee hereby waives all of his/her moral rights (as defined in the Copyright Designs and Patents Act 1988) in respect of any acts of the employer or any acts of third parties done with the employer's authority in relation to any Intellectual Property which is the property of the employer by virtue of clause (A).

(D) All rights and obligations under this clause in respect of Intellectual Property made or discovered by the employee during the employment shall continue in full force and effect after the termination of his/her employment and shall be binding upon the employee's personal representatives.

(E) The employee acknowledges that any and all Intellectual Property created by the employee during the course of his/her employment shall vest in and be owned by and constitute the property of the employer and to the extent that they do not automatically so vest in part consideration of the monies received by the employee pursuant to this agreement the employee hereby assigns and transfers with full title guaranteed such Intellectual Property.

(F) "Intellectual Property" for the purpose of clauses (A) to (E) means letters patent, trademarks, service marks, designs, copyrights, database rights, utility models, design rights, applications for registration of any of the foregoing and the right to apply for them in any part of the world, inventions, drawings, computer programs, confidential information, know-how and rights of like nature arising or subsisting anywhere in the world in relation to all the foregoing whether registered or unregistered.

Note: Although strictly speaking falling somewhat outside the main scope of this book, a provision along the lines of the above can be seen as an appropriate adjunct to others that are intended to protect the employer's business secrets.

6. **Miscellaneous provisions relevant to the termination of employment**

A5.15 (A) The employee shall not at any time after the termination of his/her employment make any untrue or misleading oral or written statement concerning the business and affairs of the employer [or any Associated Company] nor represent himself/herself or permit himself/herself to be held out as being in any way connected with or interested in the business of the employer [or any Associated Company] (except as a former employee for the purpose of communicating with prospective employers or complying with any statutory requirements); and

(B) Shall not at [at any time] [for a period of [number] years] following the termination of employment use the name(s) [Name(s)] or any name capable of confusion therewith (whether by using such names individually or in combination as part of a corporate name or otherwise) [anywhere within [area]] in connection with the carrying on of any business which is similar to or in competition of the business of the employer [or any Associated Company] with which the employee was materially involved in the 12 months prior to the termination of his/her employment;

(C) Upon the termination of his/her employment (or at any other time required by the employer) the employee shall surrender to the employer (or if so directed erase permanently) all property comprising without limitation all documents and other things (in whatever form of media including notes, memoranda, correspondence, drawings, sketches, plans, designs and any other material upon which data or information is recorded or stored) relating to the business or affairs of the employer [and any Associated Companies] or any of its or their suppliers, agents, distributors, customers or others which shall have been acquired, received or made by the employee during the course of his/her employment, together with all copies to someone duly authorised on their behalf by the employer.

(D) The employer reserves the right in its absolute discretion to terminate the employee's employment hereunder at any time with immediate effect on payment of money in lieu of notice. Money in lieu of notice for this purpose shall mean [DEFINE e.g. a sum equal to the base salary the employee would be entitled to receive during any period of or unexpired period of notice to which he/she is entitled under this agreement].

Note: *Clauses (A) and (B) are essentially optional provisions which may or may not be appropriate for incorporation in a particular contract of employment, but clause (C) (or an appropriately modified version of this) (return of employer's property) is a very important reminder to the employee and prompt to the employer to secure the return of property which may well include material including business secrets at the end of the employment (although the provision also allows for this to be required at an earlier stage—e.g. if an employee is sent on garden leave). (D) is a pay in lieu of notice ("PILON") provision which allows the employer to lawfully terminate the employment contract immediately without prejudicing the enforceability of any restrictive covenants in the agreement.*

7. **Post termination covenants**

Definitions **A5.16**

(A).For the purpose of this clause A:

"the Business"[1] means any business carried on by the employer [and any Associated Company] at the date of termination of the employment hereunder and with which the employee has been concerned to a material extent in the [number] months immediately preceding such termination;

[Reference to "Associated Company" shall only be reference to any Associated Company in respect of which the employee has carried out material duties in the period of [number] months prior to the date of termination of the employment;]

"Confidential Information"[2] shall mean information referred to in clause [specify];

"Restricted Person"[3] shall mean any person which or who has at any time during the period of [number] months immediately preceding the

[1] It is important that the business in which the employee works is the focus for post termination restrictive covenants when it comes to post termination competition (see *Scully v Lee* [1998] IRLR 259, CA).

[2] This particular provision cross-refers and identifies what is defined as Confidential Information. If the protection of such information is the basis for the covenant (or one of the bases) it is helpful to be able identify in the body of the contract of employment what the employer regards as confidential (although describing information as such does not make it so) (see *FSS Travel and Leisure Systems Ltd v Johnson* [1998] IRLR 382, CA).

[3] As regards Restricted Persons, the thrust of the case law suggests that it would be prudent at least from a trade connections perspective, for customers, etc., to be defined by reference to

date of termination, done business [or has been in negotiation to do business] with the employer [or any Associated Company] as customer or client [or distributor or consultant] and with whom or which the employee shall have had [personal] dealings, contact with or responsibility for during the course of the employment;

"Key Employee"[4] shall mean any person who at the date of termination of the employee's employment is employed or engaged by the employer [or any Associated Company] with whom the employee has had material contact during the course of his/her employment [during the [number] months/years prior to the termination of employment] and (a) is employed or engaged in the capacity of [specify] and/or (b) is in possession of Confidential Information belonging to the employer and/or (c) is directly managed by or reports to the employee (in each case whether or not such person would commit a breach of contract by so doing).

Note: The definitions of the Business, the Restricted Person and Key Employee are important to consider given that the intention behind them in this form of covenant is to keep its scope within reasonable bounds.

8. **Basis for covenants**

A5.17 (A).1[The employee acknowledges that during the course of the employment with the employer, he/she will receive and have access to Confidential Information of the employer [and its Associated Companies] and/or that he/she will have influence over in connection with customers, clients and employees of the employer [and its Associated Companies] with which the employee comes into contact during the employment, and accordingly he/she is willing to enter into the covenants described in [specify] in order to provide the employer [and its Associated Companies] with reasonable protection for their interest].

Footnote 3 (continued)
those whom the employee has been connected with directly or indirectly, although there may be instances where, if the principal basis for the covenant is to protect confidential information, a wider definition of a Restricted Person may be appropriate.

4 Whilst the absence of temporal limits in terms of the employee's connection with a Key Employee is not essential (see *Dentmaster (UK) Ltd v Kent* [1997] IRLR 636), it may be helpful to the enforceability of the covenant to incorporate a reference period which might be reasonable in the context of a particular case (see also *Office Angels Ltd v Rainer-Thomas* [1991] IRLR 214). Also in relation to Key Employees it is clear from the cases (see *Alliance Paper Group plc v Preswitch* [1992] IRLR 25, ChD and *Dawnay, Day & Co Ltd v De Braconier D'Alpahen* [1997] IRLR 442, CA) that whilst both these cases involved somewhat generic descriptions ("senior employee" and employee employed in a "senior capacity") a more focused identification of the class of employee to be covered is important.

Note: Traditionally this type of recital is generally included in conjunction with restrictive covenants although this is neither essential to the enforceability of the covenants (the employer will have to establish to the court's satisfaction that it does have legitimate interests to protect irrespective of the inclusion of this type of provision) not likely to influence the court (see Hinton & Higgs v Murphy and Valentine [1989] IRLR 519 Ct Sess (OH)).

9. **Non-dealing and non-solicitation of customers/employees**

(A).2 The employee covenants with the employer that he/she will not in connection with the carrying on with any business in competition with the Business for the period of [number] months after the termination of his/her employment without the prior written consent of the employer either alone or jointly with or on behalf of any person, firm or company, directly or indirectly: **A5.18**

(i) [Do business with a Restricted Person] OR [Canvass, solicit or approach or cause to be canvassed or solicited or approached for orders in respect of any services provided and/or any goods sold by the employer [or any Associated Company] any Restricted Person];

(ii) Solicit or entice away or endeavour to solicit or entice away from the employer [or any Associated Company] any Key Employee.

Note: Clause (A).2(i) is alternatively a non-dealing covenant or a non-solicitation covenant (in relation to customers, etc.) although they could both be included as separate covenants and Clause (A).2(ii) is a non-enticement covenant in respect of Key Employees. A non-dealing covenant may have advantages in practice over a non-competition covenant (see below) given the difficulties of enforcement which inevitably arise in trying to define the geographical area of such a covenant reasonably. Such a covenant may also assist in circumstances where (as will often be the case) it may be difficult to prove solicitation.

10. **Non-solicitation of suppliers** **A5.19**

(A).3 [The employee covenants with the company that he/she will not for a period of [number] months after the termination of his/her employment either alone or jointly with any other person directly or indirectly induce or attempt to induce any supplier of the employer [or any Associated Company] with whom the employee had personal dealings, contact with or responsibility for during the course of employment to cease to supply or to restrict or vary the terms of supply to the employer [or any Associated Company] or otherwise interfere with the relationship between such a supplier and the employer [or any Associated Company].

Note: A covenant directed towards the possible interference of suppliers may be relevant in certain instances.

11. **Non-competition**

A5.20 (A).4 [The employee covenants with the employer that he/she will not for a period of [number] months after the termination of his/her employment without the prior written consent of the employer either alone or jointly with or on behalf of any person, firm or company, directly or indirectly carry on or set up or be employed or engaged by or otherwise assist in or be interested in any capacity (save as a shareholder of not more than [specify%] in aggregate of any class of shares, debentures or other securities of any company which are quoted on or dealt with any recognised investment exchange) in a business anywhere within [Area] which is in competition with the Business].

Note: In practice, non-competition covenants generally prove to be the most difficult to enforce given that the geographical areas are hard to get right and, over the period of employment may well become out of date aside from being inappropriate at the outset. (See Office Angels Ltd v Rainer Thomas [1991] IRLR 214, CA). Generally it may be advisable to consider the alternative of non-dealing covenant (see above). There may be circumstances where an apparently worldwide restraint on competition (which would generally be fatal to enforceability in all but a handful of cases) will be self limiting by the covenant focusing upon competition with the employer so that geographical areas where there is no such competition would not be deemed to be covered by the covenant (see Emersub XXXVI Inc v Wheatley [1998] 3 July, Wright J.) Whether this would prove to be the salvation of a particular restriction in any case will depend upon the facts and it would be prudent not to draft on the basis that it would. Recent examples of covenants of this type being upheld include TFS Derivatives Ltd. v Morgan [2005] I.R.L.R. 246 and Dyson Technology Ltd. v Strutt [2005] All E.R. (D) 355.

12. **Garden leave set-off**

A5.21 (A).5 The periods during which clauses [(A).2(i) and (ii)], [(A).3] and [(A).4] are expressed to operate shall each be reduced by such period as the employee shall have complied during his/her notice period with a direction to perform no duties and/or not enter all or any premises of the employer [or any Associated Company] pursuant to clause [specify garden leave provision].

Note: For the reasons explained in the text, it is prudent to have a set-off between any period spent on garden leave where such a provision is incorporated into the employment contract and used and the period of any restraint given the test as to the reasonableness of both types of provision will, in practice, be the same (see William Hill Organisation Ltd v Tucker [1998] IRLR 313).

13. **Further covenants**

(A).6 [The employee agrees that he/she will at the cost of the employer enter into a direct agreement or undertaking with any Associated Company whereby he/she will accept restrictions and provisions corresponding to the restrictions and provisions in clauses [(A).2(i) and (ii)], [(A).3] and [(A).4] above (or such of them as may be appropriate in the circumstances) in relation to such activities and such area for such a period not exceeding [number] months as such Associated Company may reasonably require for the protection of its legitimate business interest.] **A5.22**

Note: This is not an unusual provision to find in conjunction with restrictive covenants but unless it is restricted to an obligation to enter into an identical covenant (which may be inappropriate) it runs the high risk of constituting "an agreement to agree" and being contractually unenforceable.

14. **Severance**

(A).7 The covenants contained in clauses (A).2(i) and (ii), (A).3 and (A).4 are intended to be separate and severable and enforceable as such. **A5.23**

Note: Again, this is a fairly usual provision included in conjunction with restrictive covenants but arguably does not assist being otiose if the particular provisions are, on their proper construction, clearly severable and not necessarily likely to influence the court where they are not. (See Hinton & Higgs (UK) Ltd v Murphy and Valentine ante). The covenants above do not include a "blue pencil" clause (being an invitation to the court to substitute lesser restrictions or otherwise vary the covenants should they be unenforceable as drafted) since it is clear from the authorities that the courts will not be influenced by the existence of such a provision and will apply the rule only where it is appropriate. (See Living Design (Home Improvement) Ltd v Davidson [1994] IRLR 69).

Appendix 6—Checklists

Restraint of Trade

(A) Comparison between the Restraint of Trade Doctrine and Competition Law

Restraint of Trade Doctrine	v	**Competition Law**
Agreements between any parties		Only between "undertakings"
Must protect a legitimate interest		Must not be a hardcore restriction—consider whether the object is to prevent competition
Focus on the drafting and intention of the parties		Effect of the restriction in the relevant market(s)
Reasonableness of scope, geography and duration	–	Scope, geography and duration relevant to the analysis of the effect on competition
	–	Must have an "appreciable effect" on EC or UK market
Case by case approach		Various Regulations and Guidelines, but ultimately the effect on competition of that agreement
Legality at time of entering into contract		Assess at date of analysis—transient voidness
May be severable		May be severable if not hardcore
valid restraint—injunctions/ Damages		valid restriction—injunctions/ damages for breach
		illegal restriction—possible for third parties to get damages

Restraint of Trade Doctrine	v	**Competition Law**
		Complaint to Competition Authority—and fines
Enforceable in the national courts and through arbitration		National courts, arbitration and by competition authorities

(B) Checklist for the Assessment of Business Restrictive Covenants

1. Has the restriction been entered into **between two "undertakings"**, i.e. one of them is not an employee? It should be in an agreement between two separate undertakings that are not part of a "single economic entity". (Note: an undertaking can be a sole trader, a partnership, an Ltd or a Plc). See section 21.2.
2. Is there an **agreement** (see section 21.2)—i.e. is there a restrictive covenant in a commercial agreement or a verbal understanding regarding a restriction?
3. Is it a **restrictive** agreement—i.e. does it have either the **object** or **effect** of preventing, restricting or distorting competition?

   Excludes land agreements.
4. Does the agreement have an effect on **inter-state trade** (EC competition law) or does it have an effect on competition in the **UK** or a substantial part thereof (UK competition law)? See section 21.6.
5. Does it have an **appreciable effect** on competition?

   5.1 If it is a hard core restriction (price fixing, market sharing, limiting production) market shares are irrelevant and the agreement is deemed to have an appreciable effect on competition;
   5.2 if no hard care restriction, check if the agreement falls within the category of agreements of "minor importance" (see sections 21.7 and 22.3.3);
   5.3 if the agreement is subject to competition law, Reg 1/2003 precludes the application of the restraint of trade doctrine from prohibiting an agreement acceptable under Article 81 *unless* the doctrine can be argued to be pursuing an objective different from that of protection competition;
   5.4 if it has no appreciable effect on competition it may be legal under competition law, but could still amount to an unreasonable restraint of trade under the common law. See further paragraph 9 below.

6. Assuming it does have an appreciable effect on competition, does it fall within one of the available **Block Exemption Regulations**?
   6.1 The agreement must not contain any of the prohibited restrictions set out in the relevant regulation;
   6.2 the parties' market share should fall within the relevant safe harbour provided by the Regulation. See section 21.8

7. If an agreement does not fall within a safe harbour provided by one of the Block Exemption Regulations, it is necessary to examine whether it fulfils the cumulative conditions for **individual exemption** under Article 81(3)/section 9. In other words the agreement must:

   7.1 contribute to improving production or distribution or to promoting technical or economic progress;
   7.2 allow consumers a fair share of these benefits;
   7.3 not impose on the undertakings concerned vertical restraints which are not indispensable to the attainment of these benefits;
   7.4 not afford such undertakings the possibility of eliminating competition in respect of a substantial part of the products in question.

   See section 21.9 and Section 22.5.

8. In assessing the **effect on competition** of an agreement and its restrictions, the following factors are going to be relevant to the analysis:

   8.1 the relevant product and geographic market(s);
   8.2 market position of the parties (in a vertical agreement this may be on the supply market as well as on the purchasing market);
   8.3 market position of competitors;
   8.4 entry barriers;
   8.5 maturity of the market;
   8.6 level of trade (e.g. manufacturer/wholesale/retail);
   8.7 nature of the product(s) or service(s) covered by the agreement (e.g. homogenous/ innovative);
   8.8 other factors, for example, the cumulative effect of similar agreements, the balance of the relationship between the parties, the regulatory environment and existence of behaviour that may indicate or facilitate anti-competitive collusion.

9. **Status** of the Agreement

   9.1 If the agreement pre-dates May 1, 2004 was it notified to the EC or OFT and:

      9.1.1 is there a decision on its legality?
      9.1.2 is there a comfort letter?

   9.2 If restriction/agreement not exempt by Block Exemption or Article 81(3)/Section 9, is the restriction severable?

9.2.1 EC law provides hard core restrictions are not severable.
9.2.2 Otherwise subject to UK law. See section 21.11

10. If the agreement is not caught by EC/UK competition law, the **common law restraint of trade** will still apply, in which case one needs to consider:

    10.1 is the restriction protecting a legitimate interest?

    10.1.1 consider what type of commercial agreement it is: sale of a business, JV, partnerships, vertical agreements etc.

    10.2 are the products or services covered by the restriction reasonable?
    10.3 is the geographic scope reasonable?
    10.4 is the duration reasonable?
    10.5 the reasonableness of the restriction to be judged at the time the parties entered into the agreement, and not as under competition law at the time the effect of the restriction is being analysed.
    10.6 If illegal can the restriction be severe? See section 21.11.

(C) Practical considerations relevant to the incorporation of restrictive covenants in employment contracts

Protectable interests?

(1) Of fundamental importance when considering incorporation of restrictive covenants into a contract of employment (whether at the inception of the contract or subsequently—and indeed whether to modify these in the course of employment) is the giving careful thought to what the employer is seeking to protect. The legitimate interest capable of protection are the employers' special trade connections, business secrets and (in relation to the non-solicitation of the workforce) the maintenance of a stable workforce (**see paragraph 8.4**). On close analysis, it may be that none of these legitimate interests are present (in which event the best drafted covenants will not prevent an employee leaving and utilising his or her skill or knowledge subsequently) and it may be that some or all are present in which event, attention should turn to the type, scope and duration of the covenants.

Individually tailored

(2) Restrictive covenants should, wherever practicable, be designed with the particular individual in mind. The utilisation of a standard form of covenant carries with it the risk that it may be inappropriate in scope and/or duration in the case of certain individuals to which such restrictions are sought to be applied and, worse still, if a standard form of covenant is employed indiscriminately across a large sector of the workforce including

junior personnel, that risk is increased very considerably as it may be taken as an indication that no real thought has be given to what is necessary and reasonable to protect the employers legitimate interests.

Keep covenants up to date

(3) Restrictive covenants should be reviewed periodically; not just when an individual employee changes their role and/or is promoted. When it comes to their reasonableness, covenants will be judged by the Courts by reference to the circumstances prevailing at the time they were entered into. Businesses change, roles and job functions evolve and, in a fast moving commercial world, an employer with legitimate interests to protect needs to ensure that the terms of employment similarly change to meet new circumstances. The inclusion of a unilateral right to amend restrictive covenants will not necessarily provide the answer when it comes to amending the scope and extent of restrictive covenants during the course of employment to meet changed circumstances because of the risk of a breach of the implied trust and confidence term when material changes are sought to be made but, equally, the Courts have recognised that, properly handled, a refusal on the part of an employee to enter into restrictive covenants or to agree revisions to the scope and extent of existing covenants will be potentially fair (**see paragraph 9.2**).

Types of restrictive covenant

(4) So far as the type of covenant or covenants to be employed are concerned, the traditional suite of covenants will normally comprise a non-competition restriction, a non-solicitation/non-dealing covenant (in relation to customers and suppliers) and a non-solicitation covenant in respect of the workforce. (**See paragraph 8.5**).

The non-competition covenant

(5) When it comes to a non-competition covenant, an employer should consider various factors. First, this type of covenant tends (although each case will depend upon its own facts) to be the most difficult to enforce in practice (**see paragraph 8.5.1**). Second, what is the business to be protected (it must be capable of identification, it must be one that the employee works in or has a connection with/confidential information about) and what will constitute "competition". Third, the geographical and temporal scope of such covenants should also be carefully considered.

Territory

(6) Modern case law suggests that radial non-compete covenants stand a high risk of being unenforceable because of their arbitrary nature and propensity to cover potential customers and clients over which the

employer's business can have no legitimate claim. The territory covered by a non-competition covenant is best linked to the areas in which the employer does business at the time the employment terminates and to competition with that business (ensuring that it is a business or part of a business in which the departing employee has worked, has connection with/confidential information about). (**See paragraph 8.5.1**).

The Business to be protected

(7) Often, a detailed description of the business for the purposes of a non-competition covenant can prove problematic either through the utilisation of too generic a description, one which is too specific or one which has become out of date with the passage of time. In cases of difficulty, depending upon the facts, it may be better to limit the description of the business and provide that the restraint is against competing with the employer's business (in which the employee works or has a connection with/confidential information about) as constituted at the time the employment terminates (**see paragraph 8.5.4**).

Period

(8) The period of a restriction should be no more than is absolutely necessary for the protection of the employer's legitimate interest. As a general observation, it is fairly unusual in the employment context to see covenants longer than 12 months enforced, and it may be observed that there is a modern trend to shorter periods, particularly in certain areas of business (e.g. the financial sector). At the end of the day, the key is to determine what is essentially the minimum *necessary* to protect the employer's legitimate interests, not what the employer would *like*. (**See paragraph 8.5.3**).

Non-dealing/non-solicitation covenants

(9) Although in practice more likely to be enforced subject to considerations of reasonableness and the requirement that there should be a legitimate interest being protected by such provisions, non-dealing/non-solicitation restrictions can suffer from the major handicap of policing them in practice. Evidence of breach may be hard to obtain. On balance, a non-dealing covenant is to be preferred to a non-solicitation covenant (the latter involving, as it does, an examination of what amounts to solicitation in a particular case) but, in practice, it is generally appropriate to include both provisions in relevant circumstances (whilst ensuring that they are severable). (**See paragraph 8.5.2**).

Focus of non-dealing/non-solicitation covenants

(10) Again, a conservative approach is best with such covenants focusing not only on existing customers or clients during a recent period of time

prior to the termination of the relevant employment (12 months is not unusual) but also (where the legitimate interest sought to be protected is trade connections) those customers or clients with whom the departing employee has actually dealt (and therefore have commercial knowledge about and/or potential influence over). Including in this category prospective customers or clients with whom the employer (and ideally the employee) has been in negotiation to secure business can prove problematic if this would include prospective customers and clients who have ceased to be in negotiation with the employer and so attention should be paid to the language used having regard to the pattern of business of the employer to ensure, so far as possible, that the relevant provision does not extend to cover a class of potential customers or clients in respect of which there would be no reasonable likelihood of their becoming customers or clients in the short term. (**See paragraph 8.5.2**). The comments above in relation to non-competition covenants so far as duration of restriction are equally applicable to this type of covenant.

Non-solicitation of employees

(11) So far as the non-solicitation of members of the workforce is concerned, it is only relatively recently that the Courts have decided that such provisions are, prima facie, enforceable on the basis that an employer has a legitimate interest to protect its workforce. However, such provisions will not be enforceable (with the possible exception of small businesses) if they cover the entirety of the workforce or, more specifically, fail to focus on the class of employee in respect of which the departing individual has connection with (and possible influence over) and/or may have confidential information about (for example, terms and conditions of employment including remuneration arrangements) the misuse of which could facilitate the recruitment of that employee by the departing employee or a third party being assisted by the relevant employee. (**See paragraph 8.4.3**).

Garden leave provisions

(12) No consideration of the design of restrictive covenants for inclusion in a contract of employment should now take place without also giving thought to the incorporation of a "garden leave" provision in the relevant contract of employment (**see paragraph 23.10**). The inter-relationship between garden leave provisions and restrictive covenants is not settled, and so it may be prudent to incorporate a set-off between time spent on garden leave and the period chosen for all or any of the restraints referred to above. It seems reasonably clear from the decided cases that there must be a justification for imposing a period of garden leave (which will generally have its roots in the same considerations as those applying to restrictive covenants) but, if the notice period is long, there is an increased risk that the imposition of a long period of garden leave will breach the

implied trust and confidence term in the contract of employment, and uncertainty still surrounds the question of whether, during the period of garden leave, the employee owes a duty of fidelity and good faith. The inclusion of a prohibition against working for any other party (including self employment) and an obligation to comply with the express and implied terms of the contract (including the duty of fidelity and good faith) is therefore advisable. As a rough rule of thumb it is probably, in the present circumstances, advisable that a combined period of garden leave and non-compete restriction does not exceed what might be considered a reasonable duration for non-competition and non-solicitation/dealing covenants.

(D) Practical considerations when recruiting employees who may be subject to restrictions

(1) From the perspective of the potential employer of one or more employees who may be subject to restrictive covenants and other contractual obligations that may impede their employment (notice and garden leave provisions, confidential information obligations) a prospective employer is well advised to undertake some due diligence.

(2) First, the prospective employer will naturally need to know the employee's notice obligations to the existing employer. Second, It will also need to know whether there is any garden leave provision. Lastly, the new employer will need to have information regarding the nature of any restrictive covenants in the contract and any express confidentiality obligations.

(3) Although such knowledge can make it easier for an existing employer to later argue that there has been an inducement of their employee to breach his or her contract (it having been established that knowledge and intent in this regard are necessary—**see paragraph 8.8.2**) it may be anticipated that the new employer will be put on notice of any restrictions as soon as the employee's plans to join a new employer become known.

(4) The prospective employer should make it clear to the person or persons being recruited that the offer of employment is subject to and conditional upon the employee complying fully with his or her contractual obligations to their existing employer.

(5) Given the difficulties that can arise when it comes to the enforceability of garden leave and restrictive covenants, it will generally be appropriate for the prospective employer to suggest that the prospective employee obtains separate legal advice on their obligations in terms of disengaging from their existing employee and in relation to their ability to com-

mence working without restriction for the new employer if there is a risk of litigation. This may sometimes lead to a request on the part of the prospective employee for indemnification in relation to legal costs and/or damages. Generally, the prospective employer may wish to decline such a request on the basis that providing such an indemnity will create a discoverable document in any subsequent proceedings (with the implication that the parties were in doubt as to the enforceability of the relevant restrictions) but, if an indemnity is provided, it will generally be appropriate to limit this to legal costs (and then in circumstances where an employee is not found to be in breach of any of his or her contractual obligations to the existing employer and, if it does extend to damages, that the indemnity would be similarly circumscribed or limited to damages arising from inadvertent or accidental breach of obligations owed to the former employer).

(6) The recruitment risk does not, however, cease if there are no restrictive covenants and/or no express confidentiality provision. The prospective employer should use its best endeavours to ensure that, as far as practicable, the prospective employee does not, in the course of working out notice with the previous employer (or spending this on garden leave), act in breach of express or implied obligations in the contract of employment. Generally (although this is not an entirely settled issue in relation to periods spent on garden leave) it may be a breach of the employee's duty of fidelity and good faith if they start assisting their new employer before starting employment (**see paragraph 7.1.2** dealing with the duties of employees during employment). Where employees are also directors, they will owe fiduciary duties (**see paragraph 7.2.3**) and in some circumstances, even employees will owe such duties (**see paragraph 7.1.6**). As a consequence, a prospective employer should make it clear that such obligations are to be complied with by the prospective new employee (again, this may be best done in the letter offering employment) and should do nothing to encourage an employee to pass information onto the new employer or in any way assist the new employer during any notice period. The new contract or offer of employment should also contain an express representation on the part of the employee that he or she is not subject to any restrictions preventing their taking up the employment.

(7) The risk of the breach of the duty of fidelity and good faith owed by employees and fiduciary duties owed by directors (and occasionally by employees) is likely to be compounded in circumstances where the employer is recruiting more than one employee from the same employer at the same time. There is a high risk that, in the course of recruiting "teams" of employees, one or more of these may adopt the role of "recruiting sergeant" for the recruitment of others whether encouraged to do so by the prospective employer or as a consequence

of naturally assuming such a role. Such action may quickly lead to a breach of the relevant "recruiting sergeant's" duties of fidelity and good faith and, if a director, fiduciary duties as well. A prospective employer should, as far as practical, seek to avoid this happening by arranging that any recruitment is on the basis that this is negotiated directly with each prospective employee, and it is made clear to those being recruited, that the prospective employer does not want collaboration or liaison between the prospective recruits and/or any information regarding other potential recruits and the individuals concerned should not, in particular, approach colleagues to encourage them to leave their employment. In the real world, this may be difficult, since many "team" recruitments begin with an approach to or from a prospective employee who is likely to have knowledge of, and influence over, other individuals who would probably not change employer without that particular employee and very often, in circumstances where the particular employee would not move without some or all of his or her team. All that a prudent prospective employer can do in these circumstances is to make it clear to the individual who makes the approach to the prospective employer or to whom an approach is made by the prospective employer, that they must not act as a "recruiting sergeant", that the prospective employer does not wish to have any confidential information concerning the employee's existing employer's business or other members of staff, and that any offers of employment to other employees must be handled directly by the prospective employer and negotiated directly with the prospective employee in each case. Offers of employment conditioned upon observance of the prospective employees' contractual obligations to their existing employer may then assist if it later emerges that one or more of the prospective employees has conducted themselves in a way which breaches their obligations (unbeknown to the prospective employer) (**see paragraph 8.8.2**) regarding the necessity for knowledge of relevant contractual provisions and an intention to induce a breach of these when it comes to an action in tort on grounds of inducing breach of contract).

(8) The prospective employer should also try, so far as possible, to ensure that the prospective employee does not, during any period of notice, engage in any conduct intended to induce customers or clients to follow them to their new employer. If they are advising customers or clients that they are leaving they should be told to refrain from saying where they are going unless their existing employer has agreed otherwise.

(E) Practical considerations in relation to an express confidentiality provision

(1) It is clear (**see paragraph 7.2.2**) that there will be value in including an express confidentiality provision in an employee's contract of employment to protect (for a reasonable period of time) the confidentiality of that category of information which may properly be regarded as confidential, but which might not clearly fall into the traditional category of "trade secrets". In short, information which, if disclosed to a competitor, would be liable to cause real or significant harm to the employer.

(2) The framing of such a provision needs careful thought. Describing information as "confidential" does not make it so, and it is not infrequently the case that an employer will be tempted to be over ambitious in describing, for the purpose of an express provision, what is confidential and therefore sought to be protected by that provision (something that can happen in particular when it comes to business methods) (**see paragraph 8.2.5**). This may render the provision of no practical utility. What is required, is an objective and critical review of the employer's information that a particular employee is likely to be exposed to and a realistic assessment of what may be regarded as truly confidential, and the drafting of a provision which covers only that information.

(3) An additional advantage of trying to identify what the employer regards as confidential (although this should still be in non-exhaustive terms) in an express confidentiality provision, is that this explicitly draws the employee's attention to what the employer does regard as confidential and not part of the employee's general knowledge and skill that is transferable between different employers. However, an express confidentiality provision should not be seen in isolation. Irrespective of how the confidential information sought to be protected is identified in the express confidentiality provision (and indeed in many instances there is a limited description); an employer's culture, ethos and practice should, so far as possible, be such that when it comes to providing evidence to the Court in support of a contention that particular categories of information are confidential and are legitimately protected by an express provision, the evidence of this is readily available. So, for example, sensitive and confidential information should be so described in a documentation containing it; an employer should ensure limited circulation on a "need to know" basis of key confidential information, and access to such information should be subject to appropriate security arrangements where the information is in documentary form or electronic data etc.

(4) At the time an employee leaves employment, he or she should be reminded of the express duty of confidentiality and the way in which the employee expects this to be complied with and should be asked to provide an (ideally written) assurance or undertaking that he or she leaves without any property belonging to the company including documents and electronic data (and copies thereof) which might contain confidential information relating to the employer's business and finances and understands the duty of confidentiality that continues after the employment ends. If this proves impractical for any reason and/or the employee's conduct suggests that the confidentiality obligations may not be honoured, the employer should write to the employee (and consider writing to the new employer, if known) drawing attention to the employee's obligations.

Index

[all references are to paragraph number]

THE COMPANION CD-ROM

Instructions for Use

Introduction

These notes are provided for guidance only. They should be read and interpreted in the context of your own computer system and operational procedures. It is assumed that you have a basic knowledge of WINDOWS. However, if there is any problem please contact our help line on 0845 8509355 who will be happy to help you.

CD Format and Contents

To run this CD you need at least:

- IBM compatible PC with Pentium processor
- 8mb RAM
- CD-ROM drive
- Microsoft Windows 98

The CD contains data files of Appendix material. It does not contain software or commentary.

Installation

The following instructions make the assumption that you will copy the data files to a single directory on your hard disk (e.g. C:\Restrictive Covenants).

Open your **CD ROM drive**, select and double click on **setup.exe** and follow the instructions. The files will be unzipped to your **C drive** and you will be able to open them up from the new **C:\Restrictive Covenants** folder there.

LICENCE AGREEMENT

Definitions

1. The following terms will have the following meanings: "The PUBLISHERS" means Sweet & Maxwell of 100 Avenue Road, London NW3 3PF (which expression shall, where the context admits, include the PUBLISHERS' assigns or successors in business as the case may be) of the other part on behalf of Thomson Books Limited of Cheriton House, North Way, Andover SP10 5BE.
"The LICENSEE" means the purchaser of the title containing the Licensed Material.
"Licensed Material" means the data included on the disk;
"Licence" means a single user licence;
"Computer" means an IBM-PC compatible computer.

Grant of Licence; Back up copies

2. (1) The PUBLISHERS hereby grant to the LICENSEE, a non-exclusive, non-transferable licence to use the Licensed Material in accordance with these terms and conditions.

(2) The LICENSEE may install the Licensed Material for use on one computer only at any one time.

(3) The LICENSEE may make one back-up copy of the Licensed Material only, to be kept in the LICENSEE's control and possession.

Proprietary Rights

3. (1) All rights not expressly granted herein are reserved.

(2) The Licensed Material is not sold to the LICENSEE who shall not acquire any right, title or interest in the Licensed Material or in the media upon which the Licensed Material is supplied.

(3) The LICENSEE shall not erase, remove, deface or cover any trademark, copyright notice, guarantee or other statement on any media containing the Licensed Material.

(4) The LICENSEE shall only use the Licensed Material in the normal course of its business and shall not use the Licensed Material for the purpose of operating a bureau or similar service or any online service whatsoever.

(5) Permission is hereby granted to LICENSEES who are members of the legal profession (which expression does not include individuals or organisations engaged in the supply of services to the legal profession) to reproduce, transmit and store small quantities of text for the purpose of enabling them to provide legal advice to or to draft documents or conduct proceedings on behalf of their clients.

(6) The LICENSEE shall not sublicense the Licensed Material to others and this Licence Agreement may not be transferred, sublicensed, assigned or otherwise disposed of in whole or in part.

(7) The LICENSEE shall inform the PUBLISHERS on becoming aware of any unauthorised use of the Licensed Material.

Warranties

4. (1) The PUBLISHERS warrant that they have obtained all necessary rights to grant this licence.

(2) Whilst reasonable care is taken to ensure the accuracy and completeness of the Licensed Material supplied, the PUBLISHERS make no representations or warranties, express or implied, that the Licensed Material is free from errors or omissions.

(3) The Licensed Material is supplied to the LICENSEE on an "as is" basis and has not been supplied to meet the LICENSEE'S individual requirements. It is the sole responsibility of the LICENSEE to satisfy itself prior to entering this Licence Agreement that the Licensed Material will meet the LICENSEE's requirements and be compatible with the LICENSEE's hardware/software configuration. No failure of any part of the Licensed Material to be suitable for the LICENSEE's requirements will give rise to any claim against the PUBLISHERS.

(4) In the event of any material inherent defects in the physical media on which the licensed material may be supplied, other than caused by accident abuse or misuse by the LICENSEE, the PUBLISHERS will replace the defective original media free of charge provided it is returned to the place of purchase within 90 days of the purchase date. The PUBLISHERS' ensure liability and the LICENSEE's exclusive remedy shall be the replacement of such defective media.

(5) Whilst all reasonable care has been taken to exclude computer viruses, no warranty is made that the Licensed Material is virus free. The LICENSEE shall be responsible to ensure that no virus is introduced to any computer or network and shall not hold the PUBLISHERS responsible.

(6) The warranties set out herein are exclusive of and in lieu of all other conditions and warranties, either express or implied, statutory or otherwise.

(7) All other conditions and warranties, either express or implied, statutory or otherwise, which relate in the condition and fitness for any purpose of the Licensed Material are hereby excluded and the PUBLISHERS' shall not be liable in contract or in tort for any loss of any kind suffered by reason of any defect in the Licensed Material (whether or not caused by the negligence of the PUBLISHERS).

Limitation of Liability and Indemnity

5. (1) The LICENSEE shall accept sole responsibility for and the PUBLISHERS shall not be liable for the use of the Licensed Material by the LICENSEE, its agents and employees and the LICENSEE shall hold the PUBLISHERS harmless and fully indemnified against any claims, costs, damages, loss and liabilities arising out of any such use.

(2) The PUBLISHERS shall not be liable for any indirect or consequential loss suffered by the LICENSEE (including without limitation loss of profits, goodwill or data) in connection with the Licensed Material howsoever arising.

(3) The PUBLISHERS will have no liability whatsoever for any liability of the LICENSEE or any third party which might arise.

(4)The LICENSEE hereby agrees that

(a) the LICENSEE is best placed to foresee and evaluate any loss that might be suffered in connection with this Licence Agreement;

(b) that the cost of supply of the Licensed Material has been calculated on the basis of the limitations and exclusions contained herein; and

(c) the LICENSEE will effect such insurance as is suitable having regard to the LICENSEE's circumstances.

(5) The aggregate maximum liability of the PUBLISHERS in respect of any direct loss or any other loss (to the extent that such loss is not excluded by this Licence Agreement or otherwise) whether such a claim arises in contract or tort shall not exceed a sum equal to that paid as the price for the title containing the Licensed Material.

Termination

6. (1) In the event of any breach of this Agreement including any violation of any copyright in the Licensed Material, whether held by the PUBLISHERS or others in the Licensed Material, the Licence Agreement shall automatically terminate immediately, without notice and without prejudice to any claim which the PUBLISHERS may have either for moneys due and/or damages and/or otherwise.

(2) Clauses 3 to S shall survive the termination for whatsoever reason of this Licence Agreement. (3) In the event of termination of this Licence Agreement the LICENSEE will remove the Licensed Material.

Miscellaneous

7. (1) Any delay or forbearance by the PUBLISHERS in enforcing any provisions of this Licence Agreement shall not be construed as a waiver of such provision or an agreement thereafter not to enforce the said provision.

(2) This Licence Agreement shall be governed by the laws of England and Wales, If any difference shall arise between the Parties touching the meaning of this Licence Agreement or the rights and liabilities of the parties thereto, the same shall be referred to arbitration in accordance with the provisions of the Arbitration Act 1996, or any amending or substituting statute for the time being in force.

Disclaimer

The precedents and commentary contained in this publication are not tailored to any particular factual situation. Precedents in this publication may be used as a guide for preparation of documentation, which may be provided to clients, but distribution to third parties is otherwise prohibited. Precedents are provided 'as is' without warranty of any kind, express or implied, including but not limited to fitness for a particular purpose. The publishers and the author do not accept any responsibility for any loss of whatsoever kind including loss of revenue business, anticipated savings or profits, loss of goodwill or data or for any indirect or consequential loss whatsoever to any person using the precedents, or acting or refraining from action as a result of the material in this publication.